OLD TIP VS. THE SLY FOX

American Presidential Elections

MICHAEL NELSON

JOHN M. MCCARDELL, JR.

OLD TIP VS. THE SLY FOX

THE 1840 ELECTION AND THE MAKING OF A PARTISAN NATION

RICHARD J. ELLIS

UNIVERSITY PRESS OF KANSAS

Published by the University Press of Kansas (Lawrence, Kansas 66045), which was organized by the Kansas Board of Regents and is operated and funded by Emporia State University, Fort Hays State University, Kansas State University, Pittsburg State University, the University of Kansas, and Wichita State University.

Library of Congress Cataloging-in-Publication Data

Names: Ellis, Richard (Richard J.), author.

Title: Old Tip vs. The Sly Fox : The 1840 Election and the Making of a Partisan Nation / Richard J. Ellis, Willamette University.

Other titles: 1840 election and the making of a partisan nation

Description: Lawrence : University Press of Kansas, [2020] | Series: American presidential elections | Includes bibliographical references and index.

Identifiers: LCCN 2019045364

  ISBN 9780700629459 (cloth)

  ISBN 9780700629466 (epub)

Subjects: LCSH: Presidents—United States—Election—1840. | Harrison, William Henry, 1773–1841. | Tyler, John, 1790–1862. | Political parties—United States—History—19th century. | Political culture—United States—History—19th century. | United States—Politics and government—1837–1845.

Classification: LCC E390 .E55 2020 | DDC 324.973/09034—dc23

LC record available at https://lccn.loc.gov/2019045364.

British Library Cataloguing-in-Publication Data is available.

Printed in the United States of America

10 9 8 7 6 5 4 3 2 1

The paper used in this publication is recycled and contains 30 percent postconsumer waste. It is acid free and meets the minimum requirements of the American National Standard for Permanence of Paper for Printed Library Materials Z39.48-1992.

For Fred, for everything

THE FOX CHACE.

The Fox Chace. *A drawing from August 1840 by Edward Williams Clay, a prolific anti–Van Buren cartoonist, who made his name in the late 1820s with racist portrayals of blacks in the print series* Life in Philadelphia. *This image reflects the Whigs' confidence that the Sly Fox, as Van Buren was known, would be beaten in November. Van Buren, portrayed as a fox, is chased toward the White House steps by a pack of "cider barrel hounds" with Whig senators Daniel Webster and Henry Clay (far right) cast as the whippers-in helping to keep the hounds close on Van Buren's trail. Waiting at the steps, pitchfork in hand, is Old Tip, William Henry Harrison, who says, "Oh ho! you are making for the White house my boy! but it's no longer a cover for you, I'm put here to keep you out of it!" Van Buren, burdened with a dead bird (an albatross, perhaps) around his neck symbolizing the recently enacted Independent Treasury, is trying to "get to cover as soon as possible" but recognizes that his "race is nearly run" and curses the "D—n . . . cider barrel hounds" pursuing him. The barrels are labeled "Better Times," "Reform 1841," "Hard Cider 1841," and "Tip's Dog." Clay calls out to Harrison, "Look out General or he'll get into his hole!" and Webster assures us that "He is nearly run out! he will not go another turn! see how his tail droops!" (Courtesy of the Library of Congress)*

CONTENTS

Analogies are by definition not exact; they are, however, illustrative. And so consider a presidential election during which

An incumbent president, who had served as vice president under a popular if controversial two-term predecessor, seeks a second term.

The nation's economy goes into decline.

An obscure opponent wrests his party's nomination from a more prominent national figure.

New campaign techniques mobilize the party faithful.

Voter turnout spikes.

A third-party movement expresses dissatisfaction with the two main candidates.

The challenger, emphasizing the single issue of the economy, defeats the incumbent by a substantial margin.

This scenario will likely sound familiar. But the election in question is not 1992 (though it could be) but rather the far less well-known, yet far more consequential, election of 1840. In the pages that follow, Richard Ellis tells this fascinating, colorful, portentous story.

The conventional view of this election has long been the triumph of an old war hero, William Henry Harrison, nominated by his party without a platform, his candidacy advanced by new campaign methods: "Log Cabin and Hard Cider," "Tippecanoe and Tyler Too," torchlight parades. His opponent, Martin Van Buren ("Van Is a Used-up Man"), caricatured as a member of the Eastern establishment, according to this view never stood a chance.

Ellis's account challenges the conventional interpretation, adds richness of narrative and layers of insight, and gives this election new and compelling meaning. The campaign addressed serious issues and turned, ultimately, on the state of the economy. Moreover, not until 1840 did voter turnout demonstrate that presidential contests exceeded state contests in importance. Not until 1840 was there a genuinely competitive nominating convention. Not until 1840 did both candidates participate vigorously in the campaign. Not until 1840 did political antislavery appear on the national agenda.

This account devotes considerable attention to the Whig Party, and not simply because its candidate prevailed. The process leading to Harrison's nomination revealed fissures in both the party and the body politic that would eventually become chasms. Sectional interests shaped the convention contest, and the emergence of an antislavery party posed additional risks. The preferred candidate of slaveholding Southern Whigs, Henry Clay, might have allowed his disappointment to doom Harrison's chances. Magnanimous, and invoking the national interest, Clay set personal bitterness aside, campaigned hard for Harrison, and kept his party—and his country—intact, for neither the first time nor the last.

The American Presidential Elections Series seeks to invest seemingly well-known stories and characters with new meaning informed by research and made compelling by lucid and lapidary prose. Richard Ellis's story of the 1840 election exceeds this high standard and becomes the study against which all future accounts will be measured.

They say history is written by the winners. Sometimes, however, our historical memories are colored as much by the sour grapes of the losers. Take the presidential election of 1840, so often cast as a cautionary tale of how easy it is to hoodwink the credulous American voter with slick packaging of candidates and crude emotional appeals. It is a colorful story of log cabins and cider barrels, sly songs and catchy slogans, including the memorable rallying cry "Tippecanoe and Tyler too."

It makes a good story, one that Democrats often told in the wake of President Martin Van Buren's defeat to the Whig nominee William Henry Harrison, an elderly military officer of allegedly scant political experience. The Democrats, to be fair, had much to be bitter about. The Whigs presented Harrison as a robust frontiersman living in a log cabin when in fact he was born with the proverbial silver spoon in his mouth on a three-thousand-acre Virginia plantation. The son of a signer of the Declaration of Independence, "Old Tip" resided not in a small rustic cabin but in a cavernous house on a large estate overlooking the Ohio River. Meanwhile, the Whigs caricatured poor Van Buren, the son of a tavern owner with little formal education (Harrison had studied classics at Hampden-Sydney College), as an effete, out-of-touch aristocrat living in the lap of luxury. Democrats could be excused for thinking that a gullible electorate had been duped by the Whigs' propaganda machine.

There is another way to look at the 1840 election, however: as a story less of deluded voters than of rational ones. Yes, the Whig Party's rhetoric was deceptive—but the same could be said of the Democratic Party's portrayal of Harrison as a decrepit imbecile. Indeed, misleading rhetoric is a hallmark of almost every presidential campaign. We are all generally too quick to attribute victory to the cleverness of the winning campaign and defeat to the missteps of the losing campaign. Political scientists who study presidential elections have found that the results are often determined less by campaign rhetoric than by underlying economic conditions. Incumbents get credit when the economy soars and blame when the economy sours—and the longer the party is in office, the more difficult it is for the incumbent to avoid blame for a failing economy. From this perspective, Van Buren's failure to win reelection looks like a casualty less of clever marketing than of a dismal economy and twelve years of Democratic control of the White House.[1] A great irony of the 1840 election, then, is that a campaign remembered most for its slogans and songs is the nation's first presidential election of which it might be said, in the words made famous by Bill Clinton's successful 1992 campaign, "It's the economy, stupid."[2]

The 1840 election was not just any campaign, however. It generated unprecedented popular interest and involvement in a presidential contest. An astounding 80 percent of adult white males cast a ballot in the 1840 presidential contest. Prior to that, no more than 58 percent of the adult white male population had voted in a presidential election. Despite the growing competitiveness of presidential elections at the state level between 1828 and 1836, voter turnout in presidential elections at the national level had barely budged, hovering between 56.5 and 57.6 percent in each of those three contests. Not even the 1832 election, which featured a dramatic face-off between two of the nation's most charismatic politicians, Andrew Jackson and Henry Clay, could induce more voters to go to the polls. Neither competitiveness nor the candidates, moreover, can adequately explain the huge jump in turnout between 1836 and 1840 since the two contests featured the same two main candidates and the 1836 election was, if anything, slightly closer than the 1840 election.[3] Even if the colorful log-cabin campaign did not determine the outcome, surely it must explain the record voter turnout.

The unprecedented turnout in 1840 looks much less extraordinary, however, if one peers beneath the presidential level.[4] Although 900,000 more people voted in the 1840 presidential election than in the 1836 presidential election, relatively few of these "new" voters were first-time voters. At least two-thirds of the turnout rate increase had already been achieved in the scores of congressional and state elections held between 1837 and 1839, before Harrison was chosen as the Whig Party's nominee and before the commencement of the storied log-cabin campaign. Understanding the 1840 election thus requires close attention not only to the presidential campaign of 1840 but to the many state and congressional elections that took place between March 1837 and October 1840, which the reader will find detailed in chapters 2, 5, and 9.

Close attention to these nonpresidential elections is important not only in getting the turnout story right but in understanding the evolving dynamics of the 1840 presidential election. In 1840, not all politics was local. National presidential politics, one contemporary observed, "control to a great extent, the politics of the states, the counties, the cities, and the towns, insomuch that State and local elections are made to turn chiefly on the presidential question."[5] Leading party politicians regularly looked to congressional, state, and sometimes local (especially New York City) election results for signs of the political strength of the president and his challengers. The never-ending string of elections between March and November, in odd as much as in even-numbered years, provided a sort of surrogate public opinion polling—not always reliable but nonetheless an important source of information about voters that could lead candidates to adjust their campaign strategies and appeals.

Focusing solely on the 1840 presidential campaign at the expense of the preceding state and congressional elections not only exaggerates the effects of the log-cabin campaign on turnout in the 1840 contest but also, ironically, obscures the extent to which the 1840 election transformed the place of presidential elections in American politics. The 1840 election not only initiated the high presidential turnout that endured until the end of the nineteenth century but also created the pattern that has endured to the present day in which turnout in presidential elections exceeds turnout in congressional and state elections. From George Washington through Andrew Jackson, more people typically came out to vote for their governor and member of Congress than voted for president, whereas after the log-cabin campaign of 1840, the presidential contest would consistently attract more voters than state and congressional campaigns. A second irony of the 1840 election, then, is that the Whig Party, famously founded in opposition to Jackson's exercise of executive power, organized a campaign that helped to make the presidential contest the nation's most engrossing political spectacle.[6]

During the 1840 campaign, Harrison and the Whigs pledged to return the presidency to its proper constitutional sphere, a quixotic experiment that ended almost before it began. A month after celebrating Harrison's inauguration, the nation mourned the old man's death, and his place was taken by Vice President John Tyler, a lifelong Democrat whose vision of the presidency was more Jacksonian than Whig. Tyler's elevation to the presidency is the tragic epilogue to the log-cabin campaign but also an invitation to ponder one of the 1840 election's greatest puzzles: if the Whigs were always odds-on favorites to win in 1840—and if voters' judgments were more a rejection of the incumbent and his party than an embrace of the challenger—then why did the Whigs nominate for president an aged general of uncertain health and for vice president a states-rights Democrat who shared little in the way of policy preferences with the mainstream of the Whig Party? Rarely has a major political party made a more ill-fated choice.

Arguably, the most compelling and consequential drama of the 1840 election lies not in the log-cabin campaign between Van Buren and Harrison but in the intense jockeying for the Whig nomination that culminated in the selection of Harrison and Tyler at the Whig Party's first-ever national nominating convention. Unlike Van Buren's defeat, the Whigs' fateful choice in Harrisburg in December 1839 was far from inevitable or even predictable. Many in the country were convinced that the nominee would be Senator Henry Clay, the party's acknowledged leader in Congress. Clay, who lost to President Andrew Jackson in 1832, had not wanted the party's nomination in 1836 because he judged that Van Buren could not be beaten. But with the economy tanking, Clay saw his opportunity: he badly wanted the nomination this time. Why and how the party's political titan lost out to a political also-ran is a tale that deserves pride of place in a narrative of the 1840 election, which is why a large portion of this book (chapters 3 through 6) is devoted to the contest for the Whig nomination.

Understanding the outcome of this contest requires us to focus not so much on the state of the economy as on the strength of antislavery sentiment. Economic fluctuations between 1837 and 1839 did shape Whig deliberations: essentially, the worse the economy the more appealing Clay's candidacy to Whig politicos, and the better the economy, the more Harrison—who had more cross-party appeal—seemed the safer bet. Slavery, though, was a decisive factor in making Harrison rather than Clay the Whig nominee. Slavery mattered in making Harrison the ninth president of the United States because Whig politicians—especially in New York—worried that nominating Clay would cost them antislavery voters and lose them the state. Ironically, it was the loser Clay, not the winner Harrison, who was most responsible for making slavery the decisive factor in the nomination contest.

With our lens fixed on the Whig Party, carefully tracing the internal debate and strategizing within the party in the years leading up to 1840 helps to counteract two common if not entirely consistent views of the 1840 election. The first is that the 1840 campaign is the moment when Whigs suddenly cast aside their misgivings about democracy and "[stole] the Democrats' playbook." As historian Robert Gray Gunderson put it in his classic 1957 account *The Log-Cabin Campaign*, the 1840 election "heralded the arrival of the common man in Whig politics and . . . a new departure for sedate and aristocratic Whigs who heretofore had preferred attempts to limit the suffrage rather than to degrade themselves by taking their case to the rabble."[7] The second is that Whig party bosses cynically manufactured a "carnival campaign" (the title of Ronald Shafer's 2016 book on the 1840 election) of blither and bunkum, devoid of serious engagement with issues and governance.[8] Neither of these stereotypes is entirely without foundation, but neither does justice to the Whig Party or the 1840 election.

The first misleads by slighting the ways in which the Whigs' 1840 campaign was rooted in its own authentically populist and egalitarian (as well as evangelical) history. Many of the most influential Whig leaders, particularly in the crucial states of New York and Pennsylvania, emerged from the cauldron of the Anti-Masonic Movement, which was profoundly suspicious of established elites.[9] (Anti-Masonry originated in the latter part of the 1820s—before President Jackson's election—in response to the failure of New York's political elites, including Van Buren, to respond adequately to the abduction and presumable murder of William Morgan, who had been determined to publicize the well-guarded secrets of Freemasonry.) Moreover, it was the Anti-Masons, not the Jacksonians, who pioneered the use of popular, rather than legislative, nominating conventions for candidates. The idea of the Whigs as mere copycats also slights some of the unprecedented aspects of the 1840 campaign. William Miles's survey of presidential campaign newspapers, for instance, found almost 100 Whig campaign newspapers in 1840, which was not only far more than the Democrats' sixty campaign newspapers that year but four times the number of campaign newspapers that both parties *combined* circulated in the 1836 presidential contest. In both elections, moreover, about 60 percent of the campaign newspapers were published by the Whigs.[10] In crucial respects, it was the Whigs' playbook in 1840, only bigger and better than before.

Even more problematic is the caricature of the 1840 campaign as all froth and no substance. The Whigs certainly had their share of "cynical bosses and pious rationalizations,"[11] but their deliberations were also informed by deeply held moral commitments as well as profound anxieties about the political system.[12] Many Whigs sincerely felt that the future of the republic was at stake. Lose in 1840, they believed, and they might literally lose the republic and be compelled, as Clay warned, to resort to "resistance by force."[13] If many Whigs believed in 1840 that the country and the presidency were at a genuine crossroads, it behooves us to grapple with why they believed that.

The campaign's rhyming ditties and entertaining hoopla should not obscure the fact that Harrison and Van Buren, as we will see in chapter 8, did more to communicate their views to the American people than any previous pair of presidential nominees. Defying his reputation for "noncommittalism," President Van Buren penned numerous public letters in the summer and fall of 1840 that explained in detail his policy positions—something no previous White House incumbent had dared to do during a campaign. And Harrison, unfairly ridiculed as "General Mum," was far more loquacious than any previous presidential candidate. Indeed, his many speeches in the summer and fall of 1840 shattered the norm against electioneering by presidential candidates that had endured since the founding of the republic. Nor were Harrison's speeches simply a string of empty evasions and "irrelevancies about cabins and Indian fighting."[14] He talked public policy and advanced a pointed critique of hyperpartisan politics and president-centric governance. The ubiquitous log cabins notwithstanding, the 1840 campaign was a contest between two profoundly different visions of policy and governance, including fundamental questions about the place of the presidency and Congress in the US political system.

The "carnival campaign" caricature also fails to leave a place for the emergence in 1840 of the Liberty Party—the first independent antislavery party in American history.[15] Admittedly, the fledgling party was poorly organized, and its presidential nominee, James Birney, campaigned almost not at all; indeed, he was out of the country for virtually the entire campaign. In November, the party polled fewer than 7,000 votes of the more than 2.4 million votes cast, and in only one state (Massachusetts) did it gain more than 1 percent of the vote. But while the party's electoral impact in 1840 was minimal, its portentous challenge to the two-party system reverberated through American politics. For those who joined the Liberty Party, this was no "rollicking" campaign but a deadly serious effort to save the republic. Adherents of the Liberty Party worried not about the ruinous consequences of a fourth consecutive Democratic victory, as Clay did, but instead about the mortal threat posed by two parties in the grip of the "Slave Power." They hoped to wean antislavery Whigs and Democrats from their "party ties" by making slavery the "grand question of national politics"[16]—thereby undoing the work of Van Buren, for whom cross-sectional political parties were a vital mechanism for knitting together a nation that he feared would otherwise be torn in two. For Birney, as for Van Buren, Harrison, and Clay, this was no carnival campaign but a contest of the utmost seriousness.

The 1840 election would be better remembered not for the Whig Party's log cabins and cider barrels but for its historic nominating convention. It is well known that the Whigs refused to hold a national nominating convention in 1836, instead running different presidential candidates in different regions. It is less often appreciated, though, that in 1840 the Whigs became the first major political party to select—rather than merely anoint—its presidential nominee at a national nominating convention. When the Whig delegates descended on Harrisburg in December 1839, nobody knew who would be selected to be the party's presidential nominee. The convention's selection of Harrison was thus a new chapter in the making of a partisan nation.

The Whig convention is particularly remarkable in view of how profoundly divided the delegates were by slavery and sectionalism. Not a single slave state at the convention backed Harrison in the final vote—and only one free state backed Clay. Yet after the choice was made, the party closed ranks behind its nominee. That party unity was owing to the work of the convention's delegates but also to the reaction of Henry Clay, a strangely unsung hero of the Whigs' triumph in 1840. Even with the advantageous economy, Harrison could not have beaten Van Buren without a united Whig Party, and that in turn depended, above all else, on how Clay responded to his defeat. Contrary to the colorful, oft-told tales of Clay's supposedly ill-tempered response to Harrison's nomination, the important story is the way in which Clay—the first presidential convention loser in American history—quickly set aside his personal disappointment and worked to ensure that the party entered the campaign united behind the Whig ticket. Clay's postconvention words and deeds were formative acts in the making of the Whig victory and the nineteenth-century partisan nation.[17]

The formative work in my thinking about the Whig Party and the 1840 election is Michael Holt's opus, *The Rise and Fall of the American Whig Party: Jacksonian Politics and the Onset of the Civil War* (1999). As any reader of Holt's work will recognize, my focus on the economy in understanding the 1840 election follows a path that he charted several decades ago, as does my attention to the importance of the many congressional and state elections held between the 1836 and 1840 presidential elections.

I owe a special debt to the generosity of Mark Cheathem, project director and coeditor of the papers of Martin Van Buren. When I was unable to decipher the handwriting of Van Buren and his correspondents, Mark rode to my rescue. He also read a draft of the book, and his discerning eye saved me from many a mistake and prompted me to make many an improvement. In addition, he deserves credit for the title, *Old Tip vs. The Sly Fox*.

My work was also helped immeasurably by an array of fine librarians and archivists, starting with Liz Butterfield at Willamette University, who helped me to obtain countless secondary and primary sources. Also deserving of my fulsome thanks are Mickey DeVise at the Cincinnati History

Library and Archives, Shelby Beatty at the Ohio History Connection, and Melinda Wallington at the University of Rochester's Rush Rhees Library. My thanks also go to several Willamette students and one alum who helped me to gather primary materials, especially Andrew Wakelee, Paige Spradlin, and Rob Sumner. Another Willamette student, Kaitlyn Wells, also helped me to whip the final version into shape. I also am grateful to Willamette University for a sabbatical without which this book would not have been finished and to the Mark O. Hatfield chair, which has generously supported my scholarly work for the past two decades.

Over the past quarter century, I have had numerous occasions to thank the staff at the University Press of Kansas for their help in bringing a book to fruition. This time my heartfelt thanks go to production editors Kelly Chrisman Jacques and Jane Raese and to copy editor Connie Oehring. I am particularly grateful for the good judgment and wise counsel of acquisitions editor David Congdon and the two series editors, John McCardell and Michael Nelson. I also have Mike to thank not only for inviting me to write the book but also for giving the manuscript a careful early read that improved it in countless ways, both substantively and stylistically.

Although this is my sixth book with the University Press of Kansas (UPK), it is the first that I embarked on without the guidance and encouragement of the press's longtime director Fred Woodward. When I was barely out of graduate school, Fred for some reason showed interest in me and my barely passable dissertation and gently initiated me into the mysteries of becoming an author. For the next two decades, Fred was an unfailingly generous mentor and friend, a constant source of new ideas and projects, and a sympathetic but always savvy sounding board for my own ideas. I count myself incredibly lucky that all those years ago, Fred drew me into the blessed UPK orbit, and so I dedicate this book to him in gratitude for all the many kindnesses he showed me and for the countless other scholars he made into authors.

1

THE AGE OF VAN BUREN

Except in excruciatingly close presidential elections (think the 2000 election), Americans today are accustomed to finding out the winner on election day, or perhaps the next morning. Election day is full of suspense, but typically by the following day the contest has been called and the concession speech given. In Martin Van Buren's day, things were very different. There was no election night or uniform election day. Different states chose different dates to select the president.[1] In 1836, the presidential contest began in Pennsylvania and Ohio, where voters went to the polls on Friday, November 4. Most states voted during the second week of November, but four states, including Massachusetts and New Jersey, waited until the third week of November to begin voting.[2] One state, South Carolina, had no popular election at all, instead leaving the decision to the state legislature, which did not make its selection until December. Adding to the drawn-out suspense, news of the results in the Deep South, Southwest, and Northwest could take weeks to reach the nation's capital.

In 1836, fragmentary returns from Pennsylvania first reached Van Buren in Albany on Monday, November 7, the first of three days on which New Yorkers went to the polls. Both sides were quick to claim victory. On Wednesday November 9, the leading organ of New York's Whig Party, the *Albany Evening Journal*, assured its readers that it had received confirmation that William Henry Harrison had triumphed in Pennsylvania by at least 2,500 votes.[3] Meanwhile, on the same day, the Democratic *Albany Argus* declared confidently that the returns showed "beyond all doubt" that Van Buren had won Pennsylvania by as many as 15,000 votes.[4]

Separating voting fact from partisan fiction was no easy matter in an age when almost every newspaper was zealously partisan. Perhaps the closest thing to a nonpartisan press in the 1830s was the Baltimore-based *Niles' Weekly Register*, but even its editor, Hezekiah Niles, had difficulty ascertaining the truth. On November 12, five days after Maryland's election day, a frustrated Niles admitted that he could not "make out anything like a correct account of the elections" in view of "the numerous contradictory statements before us." The problem, he noted, was that "the returns partake so much of the wishes or fears of the parties making them that it is impossible to arrive at the truth."[5] More than wishful thinking was at stake. Partisan editors had a strong incentive to highlight the good news and downplay bad news to motivate their party's voters in states such as Massachusetts and New Jersey where the polls had not yet opened.

On the afternoon of Monday, November 14, ten days after the first votes were cast, Van Buren set off for Washington, still not knowing whether he had been elected the next president of the United States. He had yet to receive reports of returns from any state south of Virginia or west of Ohio. The vice president did know that he had almost certainly lost Delaware, Maryland, Vermont, and, most disappointingly, Ohio, a state with 21 electoral votes that had twice gone for Andrew Jackson. But the positive news far outweighed the disappointing. Even the vice president's opponents now conceded that Van Buren had secured Pennsylvania's 30 electoral votes,[6] albeit by a margin far narrower than the Democrats originally expected. He also departed for the nation's capital secure in the knowledge that he had won New York.[7] Together, those two states gave him 72 electoral votes, almost half the total number he needed to win. He was confident, too, that he had won Connecticut, New Hampshire, and Maine, which would give him another 25 electoral votes.[8] Most encouraging of all, the *Argus* that morning reported "highly favorable" news from Virginia suggesting that Van Buren would also prevail there—although that same evening the *Evening Journal* carried a conflicting report based on returns from about half the state's counties that showed that "beyond all question Virginia is safe for Harrison."[9]

By the time Van Buren reached the nation's capital at the end of the week, he still did not know for certain whether he was the president-elect, although by then even the opposition agreed that Van Buren had captured Virginia's 23 electoral votes, giving him a total of 120 electoral votes, only

Martin Van Buren. This lithograph by Philip Haas, based on a painting of the proud new president by Henry Inman, was published in Washington, DC, in September 1837. (Courtesy of the Library of Congress)

26 shy of the 146 he needed to secure a majority in the electoral college.[10] While conceding Van Buren's victory in Virginia, the *Albany Evening Journal* insisted on Friday the 18th that the result of the election was "still doubtful" and that there was "yet ground of hope." By the end of the weekend, the Whigs counted Massachusetts and New Jersey in their column, and preliminary returns suggested that they were poised to claim victory in Georgia, Indiana, and Kentucky, which would give them nine states and 98 electoral votes.[11]

The problem for the Whigs was that results trickling in at the same time from North Carolina pointed to a Van Buren victory.[12] However, the Whigs were not yet ready to throw in the towel. On Monday the 21st, the *Albany Evening Journal* conceded Rhode Island's 4 electoral votes to Van Buren but still held out hope of victory in North Carolina. By now, though, this hope was a fantasy. The following day, the vice president received confirmation that he had won a "very respectable" majority in North Carolina.[13] Thurlow Weed's *Evening Journal* sent up the white flag on the 23rd, acknowledging that Van Buren had carried North Carolina, putting him only 7 electoral votes shy of becoming the next president of the United States. Given that several of the outstanding states, notably Arkansas and Missouri, were all but guaranteed to go for Van Buren, the *Journal* declared that "there can scarcely be a doubt" that Van Buren had been elected president of the United States. Nearly three weeks after the first votes were cast in Pennsylvania and Ohio, the 1836 presidential contest was finally settled.[14]

THE WHIGS' RECKONING WITH DEFEAT

When the counting was at last done, Van Buren had won by a respectable margin (see Table 1.1), carrying 14 of 25 states (15 of 26 if one counts Michigan, which officially became a state at the end of January 1837) and winning 57 percent of the electoral vote.[15] The victory was all the more impressive because the Whigs had run not one but three candidates: Senator Daniel Webster in his home state of Massachusetts, Tennessee Senator Hugh Lawson White in nine states in the South and Southwest, and General William Henry Harrison everywhere else (South Carolina's legislature, at the direction of John Calhoun, had awarded its electoral votes—in protest against both White and Van Buren—to North Carolina Whig Willie P. Mangum[16]). This three-headed candidacy, although born of profound divisions within the fledgling Whig Party, morphed into a strategy of sorts to deny Van Buren an electoral college majority and force the election into the House of Representatives, where the Whigs hoped Van Buren could be defeated and either White or Harrison be selected instead.[17]

The strategy nearly worked. Had Van Buren lost Pennsylvania, a state he carried by only about 4,000 of the nearly 180,000 votes cast (see Appendix A, Table 1 for popular vote totals by state), the election of 1836 would have become the third in the nation's short history (the others were in 1800 and 1824) to require the House of Representatives to choose the president of the United States. But Van Buren did not lose Pennsylvania. In many ways, the party of Andrew Jackson looked stronger than ever.

Table 1.1 Electoral Vote Count in 1836

Van Buren	EV	Harrison	EV	White	EV	Webster	EV	Mangum	EV
New York	42	Ohio	21	Tennessee	15	Massachusetts	14	South Carolina	11
Pennsylvania	30	Kentucky	15	Georgia	11				
Virginia	23	Maryland	10						
North Carolina	15	Indiana	9						
Maine	10	New Jersey	8						
Connecticut	8	Vermont	7						
Alabama	7	Delaware	3						
New Hampshire	7								
Illinois	5								
Louisiana	5								
Mississippi	4								
Missouri	4								
Rhode Island	4								
Arkansas	3								
Michigan	3								
Total	170		73		26		14		11

After all, a Northern politician pilloried by opponents for being antislavery had thrashed a Tennessee slaveholder and ardent defender of states' rights who had been one of President Jackson's staunchest defenders in the Senate. Hugh White "considered himself and was presented to Southern voters as a true Jacksonian,"[18] yet Van Buren beat him in Alabama, Arkansas, Louisiana, Mississippi, Missouri, and, most important, North Carolina and Virginia; only in White's home state of Tennessee and in Georgia did the Whig candidate prevail. If a stalwart Southerner such as White could not beat a suspect Northern politician like Van Buren,[19] then what chance did the Whigs have in the South? And without the South, how could the Whigs hope to recapture the presidency?

General Harrison fared better, carrying almost half of the states in which he appeared on the ballot. But Old Tippecanoe, like Jackson, was a war hero and an Indian fighter. Van Buren, in contrast, was a mere politician with not a whiff of the heroic about him. The Whigs hated Jackson. Indeed, their party was formed in the crucible of opposition to King Andrew's alleged usurpations. But they could explain away losing to a popular and charismatic war hero. This time, though, they were the ones with the war hero. And their opponents were the ones saddled with the baggage of a "wily politician," well known for temporizing and juggling intraparty conflicts.[20] The year before the election, the Whigs were "salivating at the prospect of campaigning against" the Little Magician.[21] Yet still they lost. If they couldn't beat a career politician, whom could they beat? And if they couldn't win with a popular war hero, how would they win?

It was not as if the Whigs held back in their attacks on Van Buren. He was assailed at every turn as a corrupt and unprincipled New York politician whose sole ambition was to feather his nest and secure office for himself and his "sly-faced, cringing" underlings.[22] Unlike Harrison, a firm man of the people, Van Buren was said to be supported only by office holders and office seekers.[23] He was portrayed as a "crawling reptile" whose only qualification for the presidency was that he had slithered and wormed his way into Jackson's confidence.[24] Jackson may have been a noble lion, but Van Buren would always be the Sly Fox or, worse, as John Calhoun cast him, a weasel.[25]

The Whigs hammered away incessantly at the theme of Van Buren as a slippery and untrustworthy politician who failed to measure up to the presidential office. They also suggested that this tavern keeper's son had become an effete "dandy," more at home in a feminized, aristocratic world than in a manly democratic one. According to a widely circulated campaign biography, supposedly penned by Davy Crockett, Van Buren was no longer content "to eat and to drink and to associate with plain men." Instead he now surrounded himself with English servants, bedecked in fancy livery. As for his own dress, he "laced up in corsets, such as women in a town wear." But for his red-and-gray whiskers, Crockett wrote, "it would be difficult to say, from his personal appearance, whether he was man or woman."[26] Yet these attacks, "so extravagant in their abuse," came to naught.[27] Although "only a politician,"[28] Van Buren prevailed.

More discouraging still, the Whigs lost despite throwing over the leaders most identified with their party's favored policy positions: a national bank, high protective tariffs, and federal funding for internal improvements, the policy trinity that defined Senator Henry Clay's so-called American System. In 1832, Clay had been the standard-bearer of the National Republican Party (the precursor to the Whig Party) and was crushed by Jackson, garnering less than one-quarter of Jackson's electoral vote total. In the fall of 1834, Thurlow Weed, a former Anti-Mason and the Whig Party's sharpest political mind, had warned that the "game is up" if the party nominated "Clay, Webster, or Calhoun, or indeed any man identified with the war against Jackson and in favor of the Bank."[29] The Whigs followed Weed's advice by selecting a senator (Hugh White) who had been at Jackson's side in the fight against the national bank and a general (Harrison) whose policy commitments were as ill-defined as General Jackson's in 1828. Neither nominee had been a National Republican, yet Van Buren had dispatched them both.

Of the Whigs' nationally recognized leaders, only "the Godlike Daniel" appeared on the general election ballot, but solely in his home state of Massachusetts. Although Webster carried Massachusetts, Van Buren fared far better in the Bay State than Jackson had in 1832, when he ran against the Kentuckian Clay. Whereas Jackson received only 20 percent of the vote in 1832, Van Buren more than doubled that total, gaining 45 percent of the vote. Indeed, Van Buren fared well across New England, winning Connecticut and Rhode Island, states Jackson had lost badly in 1832, as well as New Hampshire, which Van Buren won with a staggering 75 percent of the vote, a massive improvement on Jackson's 57 percent vote share in 1832. If the Whigs could not count on New England, the bastion of Federalism and National Republicanism, on what region could they count?

Part of the rationale for fielding different presidential candidates in different regions of the country was to boost Whig prospects in state races, but that approach did not work out for the Whigs either.[30] Whig candidates fared poorly in both state and congressional elections during 1835 and 1836. Jacksonians won 63 percent of the House seats in the thirteen states that held congressional elections during 1835 and 59 percent in the fourteen states that held House elections during 1836.[31] At the state legislative level, Whigs fared even worse, securing a majority of seats in only seven states (Alabama, Delaware, Indiana, Kentucky, Maryland, Massachusetts, and Vermont).[32] In 1835, a coalition of Whigs and Anti-Masons in Pennsylvania capitalized on a rift among pro-Jackson forces to win more than two-thirds of the lower house seats, but the following October, the Jacksonians regrouped and won a whopping 72 percent of the seats.[33] Since state legislatures selected US senators in the nineteenth century (direct popular election of US senators did not begin until the Seventeenth Amendment passed in 1913), Jacksonians used their dominance at the state legislative level to ensure that they had a commanding edge in the Senate. At the opening of Van Buren's presidency (the Twenty-Fifth Congress), Jacksonians held two-thirds of the seats in the US Senate.

In many ways, the Whigs in 1835–1836 hardly seemed to qualify as a national political party. They had not so much collectively chosen to nominate multiple presidential candidates as they had failed to nominate any candidate, instead leaving it up to each state party to choose. Judging that no candidate or platform could unite Jackson's many opponents—a conglomeration of Anti-Masons, National Republicans, Nullifiers, and disaffected erstwhile Jacksonians—the party did not even try to hold a national nominating convention. As Michael Holt points out, "to call all who opposed the Jackson administration before 1836 'Whigs' or to speak of a 'Whig party' in the mid-1830s is more a literary convenience than an accurate description of fact." Many of those whom historians label Whigs did not think of themselves that way and "had not yet formed any institutional loyalties to the new Whig Party."[34] If this was true of political elites, it was even more true of ordinary voters.

Many Whigs continued to express profound reservations about the idea of disciplined political parties. Whigs boasted of being "too independent to wear the collar of party discipline"[35] and scorned those who allowed themselves to be "hand-cuffed with the manacles of party"[36] or bound by the "shackles of party."[37] One reason Whigs did not hold a national nominating convention in 1836 was that many in their ranks expressed misgivings about any national party dictating the presidential and vice-presidential nominees. The Whigs vowed that unlike the Democrats, they would not worship "at the shrine of mere party idolatry"[38] and warned that if Van

Buren won, "the necks of the American people" would be "forever subjected to the yoke of a system of party discipline subversive of personal independence."[39] Having presented the election as a momentous choice by the American people between submitting to the "tyranny of party" or becoming "masters of their own suffrage,"[40] Whig leaders now faced their own choice: whether to emulate Jacksonian methods and embrace a party system or continue to hope that they could win without party discipline and organization.

In many ways, the Whigs' attacks on the bonds of party merely made a virtue of necessity. If the other party has more loyalists, then victory requires persuading some of those in the majority to set aside their party loyalties in favor of other loyalties. This strategy was especially important in the South, where Jackson had run up huge majorities in 1828 and 1832. In 1832, Jackson received 100 percent of the vote in Alabama, Georgia, Mississippi, and Missouri, 95 percent in Tennessee, 85 percent in North Carolina, 75 percent in Virginia, and over 60 percent in Louisiana. Only by persuading voters to disregard their loyalty to President Jackson and his party (and instead embrace their identity as Southerners and slaveholders) did Whigs stand a chance in these states. Indeed, with White as the Whig nominee in each of these states, the party dramatically improved its showing, winning majorities in two states (Georgia and Tennessee) and coming close to victory in three others (Louisiana, Mississippi, and North Carolina). Whereas Clay in 1832 received, on average, about one in ten votes cast in these eight Southern states, White averaged almost 48 percent of the vote in the same eight states only four years later. The unanswered question was whether all those White voters could begin to think of themselves as Whigs and then, on the basis of that partisan identification, vote for a presidential candidate who hailed from outside the South. The future of the Whig Party hinged on the answer to that question.

The competitiveness of the races in the South was encouraging for the Whigs, as was the surprisingly close contest in Pennsylvania and the narrow victories in several Northern states that Jackson had carried, especially the unexpected Whig victory in New Jersey (unexpected because Jacksonians had won more than 60 percent of legislative seats in the state elections held only a month earlier)[41] and the crucial win in fast-growing Ohio, which already possessed the fourth-highest number of electoral votes and after the next census would eclipse Virginia for the third spot. Whigs could also take solace from having limited Van Buren to 57 percent of the electoral college vote, which was well below Jackson's 77 percent in 1832 and 68 percent in 1828. But a loss was still a loss, and a third one running at that. And in politics, where there is a loss, blame is never far behind.

Some in the Whig Party preached an American jeremiad. They blamed their defeat on the public's loss of virtue. They lamented that a once proud nation that had always selected its best men for the presidency had now settled on a small man of much cunning but no great talent.[42] In pondering the Whig defeat in Virginia, for instance, the *Louisville Daily Journal* wondered how a state that had given "birth to a Washington, a Jefferson, and a Madison" could have "thrown herself into the meshes of a New York juggler and suffered her giant limbs to be bound down by his pigmy cords." The answer was plain: "the mass are corrupted," the people now in a "fallen and degenerate state."[43] Nothing shakes faith in the people like defeat at the polls.

Most Whigs, though, responded not with nostalgia but frustration at what they saw as the "inexcusable apathy" of their supporters.[44] They felt the narrow loss in North Carolina particularly keenly. In the gubernatorial contest in August, more than two-thirds of the white male voting-age population turned out, and the Whigs prevailed. In November, turnout sank to 53 percent. The Whig vote total dropped by more than 10,000, while the Democratic total was reduced by only 3,000, enabling the Democrats to turn a 4,000-vote loss in August into a 3,000-vote victory in November.[45] The editors of the *Raleigh Register* could not contain their disappointment with the Whigs' "reprehensible neglect" of their civic duty: "The only political privilege almost left to the people is the Elective franchise; and even this, it seems, they have not the spirit to exercise."[46]

So why did Whigs stay home and allow "apathy [to take] the place of vigilance,"[47] while Democrats turned out in such large numbers? That question bedeviled Whig leaders, who were loath to credit Democrats with a civic virtue that Whigs lacked. Some explained away Democratic turnout by noting that Democratic voters were spurred by "inducements of personal interest," specifically the desire to gain or hold on to office.[48] That was hardly the sort of disinterested virtue that the Whigs hoped to see in their own voters. William Henry Harrison thought the problem boiled down to belief, or lack thereof. The Whigs, he explained, suffered from a "want of confidence." Unable to believe they could triumph over "the influence of Genl. Jackson and the application of the spoils" system, Whig voters had stayed home despite having "victory in their power."[49]

Despite their oft-expressed disdain for Jacksonians being "drilled, disciplined, like the foot soldiers of a marching regiment,"[50] many Whigs could not help but envy "the turn-out spirit" of their opponents. "Like a trained band," the *Greensboro Patriot* marveled, the Van Buren forces made sure that "at the sound of the drum every man was at his post and did his duty." Even "those who were seriously indisposed, fit subjects for physicians, were tumbled into vehicles and sent to the ballot box."[51] Here was recognition that the Whig failure might be less about a loss of individual virtue than a lack of organizational capacity, that voter turnout was as much a party responsibility as an individual one. One thing was certain: Van Buren's victory gave the Whigs four more years of "misrule and mal-administration" to reflect on why they had lost and how they could win in 1840.[52]

VAN BUREN'S PATH TO THE PRESIDENCY

While Whigs tried to figure out where things had gone wrong, Democrats responded the way winners usually do: with much boasting, a little gloating, and extravagant praise for the wisdom and sagacity of the American people. Democrats felt certain that the people had endorsed the party's principles and policies. During the campaign, after all, Democrats had stressed that they were contending for "principles, not men," especially in the South, where Hugh White was Van Buren's opponent.[53] In voting for Van Buren, Democrats insisted, the people had embraced Jacksonian principles of limited government and strict constitutional construction and rejected, yet again, the agenda of those who always "wished to enlarge the powers of the General Government."[54] The people had spoken, and in those words the Democrats divined support for President Jackson's war against the national bank and its "thirty-five millions of money"[55] as well as an emphatic stamp of approval for the administration's opposition to protective tariffs and wasteful federal spending on internal improvements. Perhaps most important, in the eyes of many Democrats, the good sense of the people had foiled the Whig plot to divide the country by region and to throw the election into the House of Representatives. The election was thus a triumph not only for the Democratic Party but for American democracy.

For Andrew Jackson, the election of 1836 was sweet vindication despite the bitter pill of Van Buren's defeat in Jackson's home state of Tennessee. The pickup of seats in the Senate meant that Jackson could look forward to the expungement of the censure that Henry Clay and his Senate allies had voted in March 1834 in response to Jackson ordering the removal of government deposits from the national bank. Opposition to King Andrew's "executive usurpation" was the core tenet around which the Whig Party organized; the party's name itself was adopted to signal an ideological affinity with the eighteenth-century English Whigs' struggle for liberty against the tyranny of King George III.[56] In Jackson's mind, the Whig Party label and antiexecutive rhetoric were ploys to disguise his opponents' elitism. Van Buren's victory meant that the people had seen through that disguise.

Van Buren's victory was very much Jackson's victory. It was Jackson who pushed John Calhoun out of the vice presidency in 1832 and elevated Van Buren in his place. It was Jackson who secured Van Buren's unanimous nomination at the Democratic national nominating convention held in Baltimore in 1835, just as it was Jackson who engineered Van Buren's selection as the vice-presidential nominee at the Democrats' first ever national convention in 1832. The Whigs made Jackson's "high-handed attempt to control the free choice of the people in the election of their rulers" a central theme of the 1836 presidential campaign. Foisting Van Buren on the American people, according to the Whigs, was Jackson's most shameful usurpation of all and threatened to subvert the republic and extinguish liberty.[57] That the American people did not heed these warnings and instead chose the Old Hero's handpicked successor only cemented Jackson's faith in the "good sense and practical judgment of the people."[58]

Jackson's backing was essential to Van Buren's nomination and election, but the result also owed much to Van Buren's theory and practice of party politics. Jackson was catapulted to political fame by his heroics in the War of 1812, particularly his defense of New Orleans against a numerically far superior British military force, a battle that brought a largely disastrous war to a passably successful close.[59] While Jackson was becoming the nationally renowned Hero of New Orleans, Van Buren was learning his trade in the labyrinthine politics of New York. Elected as a state senator in 1812 at the age of twenty-nine, he became the second-youngest person to serve in that body, a remarkable feat for one of little formal education, modest means, and "an undistinguished family."[60] That a person with no college education, no military career, and no family wealth or connections became the eighth president of the United States is still more remarkable. It had never happened before and would not happen again until 1860, when Abraham Lincoln was elected president.[61] Unlike Lincoln, though, Van Buren was a dreadful writer—his prose "tangled, wordy, ornate, and confusing," in the unsparing judgment of one biographer.[62]

Van Buren was always acutely conscious that his rivals were generally "better-educated men" who often came from well-connected families.[63] The man he displaced as vice president in 1832, John Calhoun, was a Yale valedictorian who married into one of Charleston's most prominent and politically powerful families. Each of his opponents in 1836 were his social betters, most notably William Henry Harrison, who could boast the finest aristocratic Virginian stock on both sides of his family and whose father was not only one of Virginia's largest landholders but had been its fourth governor, not to mention a signer of the Declaration of Independence. Hugh White was not of Harrison's social class, but his father was the founder of Knoxville, had been a delegate (along with Andrew Jackson) at the state's constitutional convention, and became a brigadier general after Tennessee was granted statehood in 1796. Daniel Webster's parents' farm was modest, but his education was first-rate: he attended Phillips Exeter Academy before graduating Phi Beta Kappa from Dartmouth College. Willie Mangum, who received South Carolina's 11 electoral votes, was born on a 2,500-acre plantation and graduated from the University of North Carolina.[64] In contrast, Van Buren was the son of a tavern keeper who was "firmly entrenched in the lower middle portion of a rigidly demarcated social scale"; his education at a village school stopped at age thirteen.[65]

Growing up in New York's Hudson Valley in the late eighteenth century, Van Buren knew all about the importance of inherited wealth and family connections in politics. A small coterie of powerful aristocratic families knotted together by marriage and economic interest dominated the politics of Columbia County as well as the state of New York. For a boy of modest prospects, getting ahead meant finding a benefactor, and that was what young Van Buren did, becoming an apprentice at age thirteen in the law office of Francis Silvester, whose father was Kinderhook's most prominent Federalist politician and whose mother was a Van Schaack, one of the wealthiest and most influential Federalist families in the county. The teen-aged legal apprentice would sweep the office, build a fire in the morning, and ape his master's dress, but he drew the line at adopting his patron's Federalist politics. Deference to one's betters was tightly woven into the social fabric of the Kinderhook of Van Buren's youth, but the decade's fierce ideological struggle between Federalists and Jeffersonian Republicans (Van Buren's apprenticeship began in the year of John Adams's election as president and ended the year that Thomas Jefferson became president) helped to disrupt traditional patterns of political authority in Kinderhook.[66]

Despite the "repeated remonstrances and solicitations" of the Silvesters and Van Schaacks, Van Buren stuck resolutely to the Jeffersonian politics of his father, whose tavern was both a polling place and a meeting place for Republicans. Adams's defeat in the bitterly contested presidential election of 1800, followed a few months later by the defeat of the Federalists'

New York gubernatorial candidate, Stephen Van Rensselaer (who owned three-quarters of a million acres spanning three counties in the Hudson Valley, including Columbia County), only increased the tension and "embarrassment" Van Buren felt in remaining an ardent Republican in a staunchly Federalist law office. Fortunately for Van Buren, his considerable talents and energy attracted the attention of a well-heeled and well-connected Kinderhook benefactor of the Republican persuasion, John Van Ness, who found a place for Van Buren in the New York City law office of his brother William Van Ness, a close friend of Aaron Burr—so close that he served as Burr's second in his duel with Alexander Hamilton in 1804.[67]

In his autobiography, written long after his presidency, Van Buren boasted that he had risen from his lowly station "without the aid of powerful family connexions."[68] But when the twenty-year-old Van Buren passed the bar in 1803, he had the benevolence of Kinderhook's best families to thank. Despite owing (or perhaps because he owed) his rise in the legal profession to the most well-connected Kinderhook families, Van Buren rejected the older politics defined by the "alliances and counter alliances" of the state's great families.[69] As a fifteen-year-old, in 1798, he had refused to participate in celebrating the reelection of his master's father to the New York state senate. And when it came time, in 1804, for Van Buren to vote for the first time, he cast his gubernatorial ballot not for his new benefactor's intimate friend Aaron Burr but for Morgan Lewis, the choice of the Republican legislative caucus. Van Buren's vote for Lewis came despite intense pressure from the Van Ness brothers, especially John, who permanently severed his relations with Van Buren over the vote. So intense were the feelings roused by Van Buren's perceived betrayal of his patrons that when Van Buren appeared at his local polling station in Kinderhook, he was confronted by two imposing grandees, locked arm in arm, who challenged the whippersnapper's right to vote because they said he lacked the requisite property qualification. One was the Van Ness father, whom Van Buren recalled as "very severe," and the other was Peter Van Schaack, the imperious uncle of Van Buren's former master. The former was a distinguished judge, the latter a Columbia-educated lawyer. Van Buren refused to be intimidated and was ultimately permitted to vote, but only after being forced by election officials to take an oath affirming that he met the property requirements, an "indignity" that Van Buren still keenly remembered at the end of his life—though purchasing the Van Ness estate during his presidency no doubt helped salve his wounded pride.[70]

As Van Buren looked back on his political rise, he expressed pride that "from my boyhood I had been a zealous partisan, supporting with all my power the administrations of Jefferson and Madison."[71] There is no doubting Van Buren's Republican zeal, but New York's dizzying factional feuds and ever-shifting family alliances muddied the clear partisan waters that Van Buren sought. With the decline of the Federalist Party as a national force, it became difficult to identify the true Republicans. In 1804, Van Buren decided that being a Republican meant opposing the Republican Aaron Burr, who was still Jefferson's vice president and faced fierce opposition from New York's leading Federalist, Alexander Hamilton, whose criticisms of Burr in the gubernatorial election led to the duel that killed Hamilton. Van Buren instead supported the Republican Morgan Lewis, a close ally of the powerful Livingston family, owners of a quarter of a million acres in Columbia County. Three years later, in 1807, following a rift between the Livingstons and the Clintons (George Clinton, then Jefferson's vice president after having served as New York's governor for twenty-one of the state's first twenty-seven years, and his nephew DeWitt Clinton, serving his first term as the mayor of New York City), voting Republican meant opposing Lewis's reelection and instead backing the Clintons' preferred candidate, Daniel Tompkins.

The difficulty of being a loyal Republican in New York was brought into sharp relief for Van Buren from the first awkward moments of his life as an elected official. In 1812, the backing of DeWitt Clinton, who was both New York's lieutenant governor and New York City's mayor, made it possible for Van Buren to narrowly unseat a young and hugely wealthy member of the Livingston clan. The problem for Van Buren was that when Vice President George Clinton died in April of that year, DeWitt Clinton set his eyes on the presidency, insisting that New York had played second fiddle to Virginia for long enough.[72] Clinton pressed his talented young protégé to ensure that the New York state legislature cast its electoral votes for him rather than President James Madison (not until 1828 would New York switch to the popular election of electors). Van Buren had to choose between the Republican president he had vigorously supported for four years and the Republican state leader to whom he owed his election.[73]

At first, Van Buren wavered. He was appalled by Clinton's wooing of dissident Federalists, so reminiscent of Burr's own scheming. Moreover, Clinton was Van Buren's antithesis. Whereas Van Buren was accommodating, eager to please, and easy to get along with, Clinton was haughty and imperious. Educated at Princeton and Columbia, DeWitt Clinton was wealthy, well-connected, and cultured. In short, he was "one of the greatest of the old-style aristocratic factional leaders."[74] Unlike Van Buren, Clinton had little interest in party loyalty; he thrived instead in the world of individual leadership, personal allegiances, and shifting alliances of groups and families.

Ultimately, Van Buren chose to remain loyal to Clinton and played a pivotal role in steering the state's 29 electoral votes toward his political patron. Despite winning New York, however, Clinton failed to defeat President Madison, leaving the vulnerable freshman senator scrambling to shore up his standing in the party, including with Governor Tompkins, who had by then fallen out with his erstwhile ally Clinton. Despite Clinton's challenging of the incumbent president, flirting with the antiwar Federalists, and breaking with the state's governor, his political fortunes inside New York did not materially suffer. Indeed, in 1817, with Tompkins having resigned to become James Monroe's vice president, Clinton would be elected governor, a position he retained (except for two years) until his death in 1828.

After 1812, Van Buren distanced himself from Clinton, and for most of the next fifteen years, the two men were fierce rivals.[75] The embarrassment of 1812 helped to crystallize Van Buren's growing awareness that his political ambitions and the nation's welfare required a new politics, one that rejected the factional maneuvering of dignitaries in favor of cohesive and disciplined political parties.[76] Only then would politics cease to be the plaything of the rich and famous, the well-born and the well-connected. Only then would men such as Van Buren be able to defeat the DeWitt Clintons of the world. Dependence on impersonal political parties would give Van Buren independence from the caprice of patrician benefactors. Unswerving loyalty to the party could also blunt the volatile and disruptive force of personal charisma, rewarding instead a new type of party manager and politician.[77] Such a politics, Van Buren believed, would be both more democratic and more principled—and was the only way to combat what he saw as the insidious and ever-present threat of Federalism.[78]

As a state senator (1813–1820) and attorney general (1815–1819) and then as a US senator (1821–1828), Van Buren put this party-centered vision into practice. He became the acknowledged leader of a powerful anti-Clinton political machine that would be dubbed (by its enemies) the "Albany Regency." Party discipline and organization were its watchwords. Policy and strategy were hammered out at the top by a relatively small cadre of party leaders (the likes of Benjamin Butler, Churchill Cambreleng, Azariah

Flagg, William Marcy, and Silas Wright), affirmed in the party's legislative caucus, and then transmitted across the state by the party press, which took its cues from the Regency's mouthpiece, the *Albany Argus*.[79] The caucus was king. All party officials, from state legislators to local justices of the peace, whatever their own personal feelings or interests, were bound by the decisions of the caucus. The Regency was unapologetic about the use of patronage to hold the party together; "to the victor belong the spoils of the enemy," Marcy would famously declare on the floor of the US Senate in defending President Jackson's nomination of Van Buren to be minister to the United Kingdom.

While others celebrated the breakdown of political parties and the arrival of the so-called Era of Good Feelings during the presidency of James Monroe, who was reelected without opposition in 1820, Van Buren saw the development as a disaster for the republic. "In the place of two great parties arrayed against each other in a fair and open contest for the establishment of principles in the administration of Government," Van Buren later wrote, "the country was overrun with personal factions."[80] Because all claimed the Republican label, Federalist principles seeped undetected into politics and governance, and voters were unable to distinguish friend from foe. Without the moderating and unifying influence of parties, politics dissolved into petty squabbles over interests, individual struggles for power, and, most dangerous of all, "local jealousies" and sectional antipathies that endangered the "bond of national union."[81]

After his arrival in Washington in 1821, Van Buren set out to do for the country what he had done for the state of New York, namely, build a disciplined, organized political party that would make politics a contest of party principles rather than personal loyalties and antipathies. This task took on special urgency for Van Buren at the national level, where "resuscitation of the old democratic party"[82] meant not only combating Hamiltonian Federalism but preserving the Union by joining, as he believed Jefferson had, "the planters of the South and the plain Republicans of the North."[83] The key to Van Buren's vision was to forge an unbreakable alliance between New York and Virginia. Van Buren wagered that the party that controlled those two states would control the country—a wager that paid off handsomely for him in 1836.

For Van Buren, the 1824 election perfectly illustrated why political parties were needed. During Monroe's second term, the Republican Party had "shattered into fragments,"[84] with five prominent Republicans vying to succeed Monroe: Secretary of State John Quincy Adams, Treasury Secretary

William Crawford, Secretary of War John Calhoun, Speaker of the House Henry Clay, and General (and Senator) Andrew Jackson. Van Buren looked to the Republican congressional nominating caucus—which had selected Jefferson, Madison, and Monroe—to unify the party around a single candidate. But although Van Buren managed to engineer the nomination of his preferred candidate (Crawford), the nomination was worthless because the congressional supporters of the other candidates boycotted "King Caucus," and the candidates themselves refused to be bound by a selection process they denounced as undemocratic and elitist. With multiple candidates in the field, the vote was fragmented, and no candidate came close to winning a majority in the electoral college (Andrew Jackson did best, receiving 38 percent of the electoral vote). The contest was thrown into the House of Representatives, which chose Adams after Clay's supporters switched their support to him.

Van Buren was no fan of Andrew Jackson, but he regarded Adams's election as a national calamity. Decided not by the people but by a political bargain in the House of Representatives, Adams's election cemented Van Buren's view that the absence of organized political parties enabled a stealth politics in which closet Federalists could bamboozle and divide the electorate and gain power that they would never achieve in a clear two-party contest. If the election confirmed Van Buren's conviction of the need for a strong party organization that could unite Jeffersonian Republicans committed to states' rights and strict construction of the Constitution, it also required Van Buren to rethink some of his other commitments. Not only had the Little Magician backed the losing candidate—a candidate whose health had been wrecked by a paralytic stroke, who had finished a distant third in the electoral vote, and who had received more than 20 percent of the popular vote in only two states (Virginia and North Carolina)—but he emerged from the election saddled with the reputation of being a leading advocate of the discredited King Caucus. If the old Democratic Party were to be resuscitated, it would have to be in some other way than via the congressional caucus. And it would need to find some other leader than the broken-down Crawford.

Van Buren had shown no inclination to support Jackson during the 1824 campaign. He had many of the same concerns about Jackson that he had about Adams. He worried that Jackson, like Adams, would adhere to President Monroe's misguided "amalgamating policy" that aimed to erase the distinctions between Federalists and Republicans and that he would dispense patronage without regard to political principles.[85] Van Buren also suspected that Jackson, again like Adams, was more a nationalist than a states' rights Republican—and indeed, during his brief tenure in the Senate, Jackson had shown himself much more supportive of federally sponsored internal improvements and tariff protection than Van Buren.[86] Moreover, Jackson, a popular war hero, posed a threat to the organizational politics that Van Buren was trying to build, a politics based on party principles, not charismatic individuals.

But after a disastrous election that left him "as completely broken down a politician as my bitterest enemies could desire," Van Buren began to view Jackson's "personal popularity" and his image as a Washington outsider less as a threat than as an opportunity for party building.[87] Van Buren's efforts to revive the old Jeffersonian party around Crawford and the congressional nominating caucus were swept aside by strong-running populist currents. At the state level, too, Van Buren paid insufficient heed to these populist currents when, in the effort to secure New York's electoral votes for Crawford, he opposed legislation that would have allowed the people rather than the legislature to select New York's presidential electors, an unpopular position that led to the Regency's crushing defeat at the polls and to his nemesis DeWitt Clinton making a triumphant return to the governor's office.[88] Supporting Jackson for president in 1828 would enable Van Buren to flip the script. Instead of having to defend an insiders' candidate reliant on King Caucus and the legislative selection of electors, Van Buren would be backing the candidate who had won a plurality of the popular vote but been denied the presidency by an allegedly "Corrupt Bargain" between Adams and Clay.[89] Populism could be placed in the service of party building.

But even after Van Buren committed to backing Jackson, he remained insistent that the campaign not be reduced to a personality contest. Instead, he urged Jackson and his allies to "put his election on old Party grounds."[90] He also lobbied strongly for a national convention to nominate Jackson; he was even willing to entertain the idea of a congressional caucus, although he conceded that a general convention would be "more in unison with the spirit of the times," particularly in the crucial states of Pennsylvania and New York. A convention, he told Ritchie, would ensure that the opposition to Adams would not be split among different candidates. It would clearly "draw anew the old Party lines" in a way that reliance on state-level nominating conventions alone would not. It would transform the contest from a dangerously divisive sectional battle "between a northern and Southern man" into a noble conflict of "party principle" that transcended geography. Moreover, the act of having a convention would stimulate party feelings and thereby contribute to "the revival of old party distinctions." Finally, the convention "could not fail" to affect the nominee himself. It would remind Jackson that he owed his election not to his military exploits alone but to "a combined and concerted effort of a political party, holding in the main, to certain tenets & opposed to certain prevailing principles."[91]

Van Buren failed in his efforts to call a national convention, in large part because many Jackson supporters worried that the convention would fail to reach an agreement on who should be vice president. But even without a national nominating convention, the anti-Adams forces had little difficulty uniting around the popular Jackson. While Jackson was largely content to keep his persona politically ambiguous, President Adams's ambitious proposal to use federal power to improve the country—he called for the federal government to build not only roads and canals but also a national university and an astronomical observatory—and his daring of Congress not to be "palsied by the will of our constituents" provided the spur to revive the old party lines that Van Buren desired.[92]

Van Buren was slow to get on the Jackson bandwagon—much slower than his rival DeWitt Clinton, who had declared his support for Jackson as far back as the spring of 1824—but once aboard, he assumed a leading role in lining up support for Jackson. By the spring of 1827, Van Buren had become, at least in the eyes of President Adams, "the great electioneering manager for General Jackson." Indeed, Van Buren spent that spring traveling through the Carolinas, Georgia, and Virginia in an effort to swing Crawford and his Old Republican supporters behind a Jackson-Calhoun ticket.[93] But while Van Buren went all in for Jackson, the Old Hero remained wary of Van Buren, in part because of the latter's "reputed cunning" and in part because Jackson felt a loyalty to Clinton, who had been among the first prominent figures in the North to back the general.[94] Fate intervened, though, and granted Van Buren a massive political gift: the unexpected death of the fifty-nine-year-old Clinton. At a stroke, the way was cleared for Van Buren to become the undisputed leader of New York's Republicans and Jackson's indispensable ally in the Empire State.

Van Buren had never run for statewide office (state attorney general was an appointed post, and US senators were chosen by the state legislature), but he now seized the chance to run for governor. The opportunity was fortuitous, but there was nothing lucky about the result. Van Buren had spent the past fifteen years creating a party apparatus that could elevate a "mere" party politician to the state's highest office. The opposition carped that Van Buren had substituted "combination, management and party discipline" for "open and fearless appeals to public sentiment."[95] To Van Buren, that was exactly the point: elections should not be about "man-worshipping" but about parties.[96] Van Buren made sure that the *Albany Argus* conducted the campaign on "the old party grounds" of Jeffersonian republicanism versus "the 1798 brand of aristocrats."[97] The *Argus* and Van Buren's surrogates worked tirelessly to nationalize the election, tying his opponent Smith Thompson to the Adams administration and emphasizing the unbreakable bond between Jackson and Van Buren ("Let the Cry Be Jackson, Van Buren & Liberty," blared the *Argus*).[98] In the end, the son of the tavern keeper handily bested the well-born (Thompson's father was a wealthy speculator), well-married (his wife was a Livingston), and Princeton-educated Supreme Court justice.

Van Buren also helped Jackson carry New York, a particularly impressive feat considering how anemic Jackson's popular support in the state and how robust the support for Adams had been four years earlier.[99] When the state assembly had met to choose presidential electors in 1824, not one of the 125 legislators cast a vote for Jackson, and a clear plurality—despite Van Buren's best efforts on behalf of Crawford—voted for Adams.[100] In 1828, the Jackson campaign faced an uphill battle in New York, not least because many in the state, including some close associates of Van Buren, were nonplussed at the idea of electing yet another Southern slave owner as president.[101] Worse, the Jackson-Calhoun ticket would, for the first time in the nation's history, make both the president and the vice president South- erners. Prior to 1828, every Southern (read Virginian) president had as their vice president either a New Yorker (Aaron Burr, George Clinton, and Daniel Tompkins, vice presidents under Jefferson, Madison, and Monroe, respectively) or a Massachusetts man (John Adams and Elbridge Gerry, vice presidents under Washington and Madison, respectively), and both North- ern presidents had Southerners as vice presidents (Jefferson and Calhoun had been vice presidents under John Adams and John Quincy Adams, respectively).

That a presidential ticket featuring two Southern slaveholders could win in New York, albeit narrowly, was a tribute to Van Buren's success in making the election not about geography but about party. Jackson's mili- tary record undoubtedly helped his candidacy, but what mattered most in New York was party and opposition to the Adams administration. The vote totals for Jackson, the so-called "idol of the people,"[102] were virtually iden- tical to those for the party politician Van Buren. General Jackson ran well where Van Buren ran well, as in New York City, and Jackson lost where

Van Buren lost, in western New York and the northern parts of the Hudson Valley, where what Van Buren called the "old Federalist manor influence" remained strong.[103]

Jackson's election in 1828 did not hinge on New York. His large victory in the electoral college (a 95-vote margin) was more than enough to compensate for a loss in New York. In any event, the state's decision to use the district system rather than winner-take-all to apportion electors ensured that New York's influence on the outcome would be far less than one would expect from a state with nearly one-seventh of the nation's electoral votes (not surprisingly, 1828 was the first and only time New York used the district system). But while New York was not pivotal in the 1828 contest, Jackson's victorious coalition represented the fruition of Van Buren's vision of a revival of the Jeffersonian alliance between "the planters of the South and the plain Republicans of the north." It was no accident that Jackson's most important strides forward in 1828 were in the two states that Van Buren had marked as the keystone of the revival of the old Democratic Party: New York and Virginia. In 1824, Jackson had received less than 20 percent of the popular vote in Virginia, by far his worst showing outside New England. Even Adams had done better than Jackson in Virginia, and the winner, Crawford, had outpaced Jackson there by a nearly 3–1 margin. In 1828, with the Richmond Junto behind him, Jackson carried Virginia easily, beating Adams by a better than 2–1 count.

Jackson may have been able to win the presidency without New York, but he had seen enough of Van Buren's "intelligence and sound judgment" to offer him the most prestigious position in the cabinet: secretary of state. The office was also a stepping-stone to the presidency; each of the previous four presidents had held that post, and the last three had been sitting secretaries of state at the time they were elected president.[104] Less than two months into his governorship, Van Buren agreed to join Jackson's cabinet. Over the next eight years, first as secretary of state and then as vice president, Van Buren became one of Jackson's most trusted advisers. Together they made a formidable political team, with Van Buren's skill at party management and conciliation complementing the president's instinct for the dramatic if divisive stroke. Van Buren used his persuasive skills to prod Jackson toward an acceptance of political parties and an embrace of the Jeffersonian principles of states' rights and strict construction of the Constitution.[105] Jackson, in turn, put down the bold markers—none bolder than his war on the national bank in 1832—that helped to draw the sharp party lines that the cautious and pragmatic Van Buren wanted in theory but sometimes held back from in practice. Once Jackson had committed his administration to a policy, there was none better than Van Buren at ensuring that the party fell in line behind the president.[106] Between the two of them, they helped to create what historians have dubbed the "second party system" (Jacksonians versus Whigs) but what Van Buren would always think of as a revival of the first party system, which had pitted Jeffersonian Republicans against Hamiltonian Federalists.

THE SECOND PARTY SYSTEM CIRCA 1836

Although Van Buren believed that he and Jackson were recreating the old politics of Jeffersonians versus Federalists, the political party system that emerged in the 1830s differed substantially from the so-called first party system of the late eighteenth and early nineteenth centuries. There was plenty of partisan enmity between Jeffersonians and Federalists, but powerful antiparty sentiments, even among the strongest partisans, as well as a deferential political culture meant that the first three decades of the republic are better characterized, as political scientist Walter Dean Burnham puts it, as an "experimental system, . . . a bridge between a pre-party phase in American political development and the recognizably modern parties" that emerged in the second "democratizing" party system.[107]

The gulf between the two party systems can be measured in many ways, perhaps none better than voter turnout in presidential elections. By 1836, every state but South Carolina selected presidential electors by popular vote, and about 57 percent of the white male voting-age population cast a ballot in that presidential election. In contrast, in 1800, less than one-third of the states allowed the people to cast ballots in the presidential election. Somewhere around seventy thousand Americans were fortunate enough to cast a ballot in the contest between the Federalist John Adams and the Republican Thomas Jefferson, which means that nearly one million adult white males did not vote in that closely contested election. Van Buren himself did not have the opportunity to vote for president until 1812, when he became a member of the state legislature of New York, which did not allow for the popular vote of presidential electors until 1828.

Admittedly, there was far greater popular participation in the first decades of the nineteenth century below the presidential level.[108] Indeed, one of the hallmarks of Jeffersonian politics was that voter turnout was almost always higher in state races than at the presidential level. In Pennsylvania in 1804, for instance, only about 17 percent of adult white males turned out to vote to reelect Jefferson, but in the gubernatorial contest the following year, voter turnout approached 58 percent. In 1808, in the presidential contest between Republican James Madison and Federalist Charles Pinckney, closer to one in three eligible Pennsylvanians turned out to vote, but that was still less than half the number of Pennsylvanians (72 percent) who showed up to vote in the gubernatorial contest held that same year, just one month earlier. Much of that difference stemmed from the relative lack of competitiveness of presidential elections at the state level. In 1804, for instance, President Jefferson won Pennsylvania with nearly 95 percent of the vote, whereas in the 1805 gubernatorial contest, the winner secured less than 53 percent of the vote.[109]

Although turnout data below the presidential level during the Jefferson and Madison presidencies undercut the popular characterization of Jackson's victory in 1828 as a "mighty democratic uprising,"[110] the 1828 presidential election between Adams and Jackson was nonetheless a watershed moment in the history of American *presidential* elections. More Americans voted in the contest between Jackson and Adams (over 1.1 million) than had voted in all the presidential elections between 1789 and 1820 *combined*. Moreover, the number of people who turned out to vote for president in 1828 was four times the number who had voted for president four years earlier. The turnout rate (which accounts for population increases as well as the four states—New York among them—that left the choice of president to the state legislature in 1824 but not in 1828) more than doubled, from about 27 percent to nearly 58 percent of adult white males. When historians refer to the Age of Jackson, this is the sort of explosion of popular involvement that they have in mind.

But the second party system—if it can be called that—was not born fully formed out of the 1828 election or even Jackson's presidency. So long as Jackson was on the ballot, the cast of presidential elections remained decidedly sectional. In the South Atlantic, Southwest, and New England, the presidential contest remained largely noncompetitive, with Jackson winning by huge margins in the South and losing by nearly as large margins in New England.[111] In 1828, the average vote differential between Adams and Jackson within a state was 36 percentage points. Jackson fared much better in the Northeast in 1832, but the South remained as uncompetitive as ever. In some Southern states, Jackson received virtually 100 percent of the vote.[112] Moreover, turnout rates in the South in presidential elections lagged far behind those in the rest of the country. Only 30 percent of adult white males in the South voted in the Jackson-Clay contest in 1832, whereas outside the South, turnout was more than twice as high (64 percent).[113]

In some ways, the 1836 presidential election looked a lot like the elections of 1832 and 1828. Turnout rates nationwide remained similar across the three presidential elections, and state and congressional elections remained higher-turnout affairs than presidential elections. But in other respects, the 1836 election, lamentably still "the least studied of all our presidential elections,"[114] was a key turning point, particularly in the South. As Gerald Pomper has shown, there was little correlation between the Democratic share of the state vote in the 1836 presidential contest and the Democratic share of the state vote in either 1828 or 1832,[115] largely because of the dramatic decline in the Democratic vote share in the South. In 1836, for the first time in the Jacksonian period, the presidential contest was every bit as close in the South as in the rest of the country,[116] and as a result the average differential in vote share nationwide dropped to 11 percentage points.[117] Greater electoral competition in Southern states contributed to a substantial closing of the gap between presidential turnout rates in the South (49 percent) and the rest of the country (58.5 percent).[118]

The 1836 election was a moment of transition between what William Shade describes as the first phase of the second party system (1824–1832) and the second, more stable phase of institutionalized partisan combat that followed (1840–1852). Only after Jackson ceded the political stage did politics in every region of the country become dominated by the organizing imperatives of political parties and take on many of the attributes—including record-high turnout rates in presidential elections—that we typically associate not only with the antebellum second party system of Whigs versus Democrats but with the "party period" that historian Joel Silbey dates roughly from 1838 to 1893. Van Buren's two presidential campaigns and his one term as president played a pivotal role in transforming "a politics largely rooted in elite-dominated factions" into "a populist-oriented, institutionally organized political nation dominated by a system of two party politics 'unique in its power and in its depth of social penetration.'"[119] By the close of 1836, the nation had entered what can fittingly be described as "the Age of Van Buren."[120]

2

THE POLITICS OF BOOM AND BUST

March 4, 1837, was a day of great personal triumph for Martin Van Buren, a historic day on which a tavern keeper's son took the oath of an office that had hitherto been monopolized by founding fathers and war heroes, well-bred aristocrats and wealthy slaveholders. The nation's first president, George Washington, had been all four. Van Buren, in contrast, was none of these, yet here he was, almost exactly fifty years after the convening of the Constitutional Convention, being sworn in as the eighth president of the United States and delivering his inaugural address on the Capitol's East Portico.

The speech was long, more than three times the length of either of the two inaugural addresses of his predecessor, Andrew Jackson. In a voice so low that it was virtually inaudible to the twenty thousand people who had gathered to witness the ritualized transfer of power, Van Buren sounded a triumphal tone. Americans, Van Buren reported, "present an aggregate of human prosperity surely not elsewhere to be found." Surveying the state of the nation after eight years of Democratic control of the presidency, he proudly pronounced it "prosperity perfectly secured."[1]

All eyes at that moment were on the new president. However, the events that would define Van Buren's presidency occurred not in plain view of the East Portico's stately Corinthian columns but behind closed doors in the financial hubs of New York, New Orleans, and London. Van Buren's barely audible words ultimately mattered far less to the fate of the country—and the president—than the "mysterious whispers" on Wall Street, Canal Street, and Lombard Street. The new president's speech was widely reprinted but not long remembered. In contrast, the murmurs and rumors emanating from these financial centers gradually reverberated through every corner of the country, sounding a panic that would ultimately paralyze the US economy and wreck Van Buren's presidency.[2]

THE END OF BOOM TIMES

In accounting for Jackson's popularity as well as his reelection in 1832, historians have understandably focused on the dramatic Bank War, his fame as the Hero of New Orleans, and his status as a populist symbol of a rising democracy. Too little attention, however, has been paid to how much Jackson benefited from a rapidly growing economy. Gross domestic product (GDP) increased by an estimated 50 percent during his eight years as president, a growth rate of over 6 percent a year, or about twice the annual GDP growth rate in the US between 1947 and 2018.[3] That booming economy also boosted Van Buren's electoral fortunes in November 1836. Indeed, the two years leading up to Van Buren's election saw particularly strong economic growth, fueled by a large jump in cotton prices.

The US economy in the 1830s was highly dependent on the production of raw materials such as timber and cotton—and on rising prices for those goods, which in turn rested on robust foreign demand. High prices together with abundant harvests—as in 1836—meant flush times for the nation's farmers and planters. Rising prices also meant that the merchants and traders who bought raw materials could sell them at tremendous profits. Rising prices were also at the heart of the land boom of the mid-1830s. Farmers and planters bought up more land to grow more crops, and speculators rushed to buy cheap land, confident that they could soon sell it for more. The Jackson administration, intent on extinguishing the national debt, contributed to the land frenzy by selling off government land at an unprecedented rate. The nation's debt load as a share of GDP dropped to zero as public receipts from land sales exploded from about $1.5 million in Jackson's first year to $25 million in his final year. Banks, foreign and domestic, were the essential lubricant, freely (critics said recklessly) lending money to merchants, land speculators, and planters, confident that rising prices would ensure that debts could be repaid.[4]

In the boom times of the mid-1830s, borrowing, buying, and selling seemed a surefire recipe for profiting. In Michigan, reported one investor in 1836, "no one is known ever to have lost anything by a purchase and sale of real estate." Indeed, "everyone with whom [he] converse[d] talks of 100 percent as the lowest return on an investment." Another reported that lots in one Western town were selling "for prices that made those who bought or sold them, feel like a Vanderbilt. Everyone was sure his fortune was made."[5] But while Americans celebrated the bustle of business and the flush of prosperity, there were growing concerns in the spring and early summer of 1836 that this irrational exuberance was not sustainable and that the bubble would burst.[6] Indeed, President Jackson had become sufficiently alarmed by the land boom that in July of his last year in office, he issued an executive order—known as the Specie Circular—designed to check surging land prices by requiring that all federal lands be bought with "hard" currency, that is, gold and silver coins, rather than what was called "paper money," that is, banknotes and checks, which were not legal tender.[7]

Like other "hard-money" evangelists, Jackson worried not only that the proliferation of paper money would lead to economic ruin but that it would corrupt the American people and undermine the republic. Jackson made the perils of the "paper-money system" a centerpiece of his "Farewell Address," which was circulated to the nation on the day that Van Buren took the oath of office. Jackson warned his countrymen that since paper money had no "intrinsic value" and rested entirely on "public confidence," the system was "liable to great and sudden fluctuations" that would inevitably produce "ruinous contraction," bankruptcies, and widespread misery. Moreover, by encouraging people "to amass wealth without labor," paper money undermined the "sober pursuits of honest industry" upon which republican virtue rested. Finally, Jackson warned that by concentrating tremendous economic power in the hands of bank directors, paper money helped to give a powerful few—"the moneyed power"—inordinate influence in the political process.[8]

Neither Jackson's nostalgic call "to restore the constitutional currency of gold and silver" nor Van Buren's ill-timed praise for "prosperity properly secured" offered a reliable road map for the economic challenges facing the country. For starters, both glossed over the transatlantic dimensions of the financial problems facing the United States. The booming US economy of the mid-1830s, including the financing of an array of ambitious state railroad and canal projects, had been fueled by British investment and lending. American foreign indebtedness doubled between 1833 and 1836.[9] Money was easy to get in the mid-1830s largely because British banks continued to pump specie into the lucrative US market. London, as one writer observed, was "the centre of the credit system of the whole commercial world." The problem for the United States was that "the sun of that system," the Bank of England, concerned about its own declining specie, began hiking interest rates and tightening credit in the summer of 1836. The impact was immediately felt in New York, where interest rates on short-term commercial loans doubled between the summer of 1836 and election day.[10] The effects of the Bank of England's actions were also felt acutely in the United States because the increased difficulty and cost of borrowing in England meant that British textile firms began to buy less American cotton—and less demand meant lower cotton prices. Rising cotton prices had been the principal engine of American prosperity in Jackson's second term. During the last five years of Jackson's presidency, the value of cotton exports increased nearly threefold so that by the time Jackson left office, about one of every two dollars earned by American exports came from the sale of cotton to England.[11] The downward pressure on cotton prices was compounded by cotton imports from India nearly doubling between 1834 and 1836, reaching almost 20 percent of British cotton imports by Jackson's final year.[12] Overproduction in the US—fueled by those same high prices that had increased cotton production in India—also contributed to holding down cotton prices.

At the time of Van Buren's election in November 1836, the price of cotton in New Orleans stood at fifteen cents a pound, which was where it had been, with some minor fluctuations, for the past two years. However, by the time Jackson circulated his fond farewell and Van Buren delivered his upbeat inaugural address, the price of cotton was already dropping. Reports of declining cotton prices in Liverpool first reached New Orleans in the second week of February, and by April, cotton would be selling in New Orleans for an average of about eleven and a half cents a pound, a level not seen since the summer of 1834.[13] Declining cotton prices put tremendous pressure on the New Orleans traders who bought and sold cotton. Indeed, at the precise moment that Van Buren delivered his inaugural message beneath a bright Washington sky, a thousand miles to the south, in New Orleans, where the rain was unrelenting, Edmond Forstall, president of the Citizens' Bank of Louisiana (and powerful chairman of the state assembly's finance committee), informed his board of directors of an unprecedented meeting of the city's sixteen bank presidents to be held the following morning—a Sunday, no less—to consider "the state of affairs" of the mercantile firm of Hermann, Briggs & Co., which bought and sold cotton.[14]

The meeting could not wait until Monday because Hermann, Briggs was a vital cog in the city's and the nation's cotton export industry. With railroads still in their infancy, the Mississippi River was America's most lucrative trade route, with New Orleans as its lynchpin. The booming cotton trade helped to make New Orleans the fastest-growing city in the country. During the 1830s, New Orleans more than doubled in size, surpassing both Philadelphia and Boston in population and lagging behind only New York City. But while New York City could boast three times more people (300,000 to 100,000), New Orleans by the time of Van Buren's inauguration could lay claim to being "the nation's leading export city based on the value of its produce." One measure of the stupendous increase in the wealth of New Orleans during Jackson's presidency was that whereas in 1831 New Orleans had been home to only four banks, by 1837 there were four times that many, with a total capital worth $46 million, more than five times the amount held by New Orleans banks in 1831.[15]

The sixteen New Orleans bank presidents who huddled in secret the day after Van Buren's inaugural address listened to the senior partners at Hermann, Briggs lay out the sad tale of the firm's mounting debts—which were anywhere "between 6 and 20 percent of the banking capital of the state of Louisiana." The volatility of cotton prices and uncertainty about credit markets in London and New York made the banks hesitant to extend more money to Hermann, Briggs, knowing that a host of other struggling cotton traders in Louisiana and Mississippi were queuing up for loan relief. Yet without the banks' help, Hermann, Briggs would be unable to pay its creditors, a failure that could have grievous consequences for the tightly integrated network of lenders and borrowers. Hermann, Briggs's most important creditor—to the tune of about $2 million (well over $50 million in 2020 dollars)—was the New York City brokerage firm J. L. & Joseph, which received a confidential communique informing it of Hermann, Briggs's insolvency on March 16 (the express-mail letter from New Orleans took eight days to reach New York). The next morning, the Josephs—who were themselves deeply in debt to the Rothschilds' London bank, which had already cut off further credit to the Josephs and was demanding hefty repayments—announced that Hermann, Briggs's failure had compelled them to stop payment to all their creditors. The announcement, writes historian Jessica Lepler, "sent a pulse of shock, fear, and gossip" throughout New York City. It also broadcast to every person in the city the collapse of "the House of Hermann," information that had been kept "in mist and secrecy" by Hermann, Briggs and the bank officials of New Orleans.[16]

Over the next month, newspaper readers in every part of the country would read worrying reports—often vague, sometimes conflicting, and rarely entirely accurate—of the Hermann, Briggs and Joseph failures. Before the end of March, the news had reached former president Andrew Jackson, now back at his Tennessee home, the Hermitage. In a letter penned on March 30, Jackson informed Van Buren of reports he was hearing of the failure of "a large House in New Orleans . . . some say for six, others for ten millions." Jackson was no professional economist, but he understood the danger that a failure of that magnitude posed to the nation's economy and Van Buren's presidency. He urged Van Buren to direct the treasury secretary to closely examine the specie reserves of the "deposit banks"—those banks that had been selected to hold US Treasury funds. Jackson feared that he would "find in many but little specie" and consequently, if people lost confidence in the monetary system and demanded that their banknotes—paper money—be exchanged for cash, the banks would have no choice but to refuse payment. The result, Jackson warned, would be an economic panic that would "shake your administration to its center."[17]

Jackson's warning was prescient, although his policies had done little to mitigate the problem. Indeed, the Specie Circular, by increasing the demand for gold and silver coins in the West and Southwest, had arguably aggravated the problem. During the last six months of his presidency, specie reserves in the deposit banks in New York City dropped from more than $7 million to well under $3 million, while specie during this period "accumulated rapidly" in states such as Michigan, Indiana, Mississippi, and Louisiana, where "public land sales maintained a brisk pace" despite Jackson's order—but where buyers were now required to pay for the land in gold and silver coins. Economist Peter Rousseau estimates that in the nine months following Jackson's Specie Circular as much as $8 million in specie was needed to purchase public lands. In his letter to Van Buren, Jackson expressed concern about the "safety of the deposit Banks of the west [and] the south," but the far more pressing problem was specie draining out of the largest banks in the nation's financial capital, New York City.[18]

The dramatic decline in the specie held by New York City's banks had another, more complex domestic cause. The month before Jackson issued the Specie Circular, he had signed into law the Deposit Act of 1836. Sometimes called the Distribution Act, the legislation provided that the federal surplus that had accrued during the boom times of Jackson's second term, largely through land sales and tariffs, should be equitably distributed among the states. Because the law also required that each state have at least one deposit bank and set limits on the percentage that any one bank could hold in government deposits, Treasury Secretary Levi Woodbury designated forty-five new deposit banks (from among the more than seven hundred banks that existed across the country), more than doubling the number of deposit banks that existed at the time the law was passed. The rub was that New York City's banks held federal deposits that were "far beyond the state's proportion of the national population," and so, to equalize deposits across states, Woodbury initiated a series of supplemental interstate transfers that would result in New York City banks losing more than $5 million in government deposits between August 1, 1836, and March 1, 1837.[19]

The precariously low levels of specie in New York City's banks were no secret when Van Buren took office. Indeed, on the day that Van Buren was inaugurated, the New York Herald reported that the "stock of specie now on hand is extremely low—probably not over $2,500,000 for the whole" of New York City. Adding to the financial community's anxiety was a fear that Britain would call in its debts.[20] Mounting concerns about inadequate specie reserves in New York's banks had been one of the reasons that in the final days of Jackson's presidency both houses of Congress had voted overwhelmingly (41–4 in the Senate and 143–59 in the House) to repeal the Specie Circular. An unyielding Jackson pocket vetoed the measure and urged his successor to hold firm and resist calls to rescind the order. "Check the paper mania and its corrupting consequences," Jackson promised Van Buren, "and the republic is safe, and your administration must end in triumph."[21]

While Van Buren was under intense pressure from Jackson and other hard-money Democrats to sustain the circular, he also came under growing pressure from bankers and merchants to repeal it. Politically, though, Van Buren had little choice but to side with Jackson. Repealing the circular would have split the party that he had spent his adult life building, the support of which was essential to the success of his presidency. Moreover, it is unlikely that rescinding the circular—or any other action that President Van Buren might have taken—would have averted the coming economic panic. Van Buren had no control over sliding cotton prices (which were rooted in overproduction at home and declining demand abroad), nor could he prevent the land bubble from bursting or loosen US credit markets, let alone those in London upon which the American economy so heavily depended. The fundamental problem was that lending and borrowing money, which the year before had seemed an easy way to make money, now seemed hazardous, even foolish. The monetary and commercial system rested on confidence, but there was little or nothing Van Buren could say that would stop people from worrying that their bills of exchange would soon be worthless, or at least worth less tomorrow than they were today. As confidence in banknotes eroded, and "merchants, farmers, and bankers alike all called upon each other for specie in settling debts," the prospect of a panic-induced bank run as well as the suspension of specie payments became ever more likely.[22]

THE BLAME GAME

The rumor started on Thursday morning, May 4, exactly two months to the day since Van Buren was inaugurated. The president of the Mechanics' Bank in New York City was found dead the morning after he had resigned following public reports of mismanagement. It must have been suicide, people (wrongly) assumed. Could it have been because the bank was insolvent? Not willing to wait and find out, many of the bank's noteholders and small depositors rushed to the bank to demand specie. The Mechanics' Bank stayed open all day, past closing hours, and paid out specie to every person who demanded it. Philip Hone, a former mayor of the city and an uncommon snob, recorded his disapproval of the panicked mob, "the hungry harpeys [who] gorged with specie to the contentment of their savage appetites."[23]

Although the Mechanics' Bank had withstood the run, it had not relieved the sense of panic in the city; instead, the panic spread to other banks and "seized all classes."[24] On Monday and Tuesday of the following week, an estimated $1.3 million in specie was withdrawn from banks across New York City.[25] At that pace, in two more days, every bank vault in the city would be bare. On Wednesday morning, May 10, to protect their remaining specie, every bank in the city suspended payment. The panic radiated out from New York. The morning after news of the run on the Mechanics' Bank reached New Orleans, the city's sixteen bank directors agreed to suspend payments. Over the next several weeks, every bank in the country followed New York's lead and suspended specie payments.[26]

By suspending specie payments, the banks put an end to the financial panic but brought the economy to a near standstill. As Hone observed after the general suspension in New York City, "All is still as death; no business is transacted; no bargains made; no negotiations made."[27] With banks unwilling to release specie and individuals hoarding it, the money supply contracted and prices plummeted. Planters had to sell their crops for reduced prices, and tanking land prices prevented farmers from covering their debts by selling land. Manufacturers halted production because they could not sell for a profit and were unable to secure loans that could cover their losses. States abandoned ambitious canal and railroad projects because they were unable to secure loans or investors to finance the projects.[28] Areas that only a short time before had been infused with exuberant entrepreneurial energy now felt themselves, in the words of one erstwhile optimist, "suffering the horrors of the rack."[29] The boom times were over. The question was who or what was to blame for this sudden reversal of fortune.[30]

The Whigs were sure they knew the answer. The "wretched condition" of the country was the fault of Andrew Jackson's policies—and of Van Buren's refusal to abandon or at least modify those policies.[31] Many Whigs traced both the land boom and the bust to what they still regarded as Jackson's original sin: his veto of the national bank—which many Whigs believed would have served as a stabilizing force and a lender of last resort to shore up public confidence in the banking system.[32] Even more disastrous in precipitating the panic, the Whigs insisted, was Jackson's ill-informed and wrong-headed Specie Circular and the hard-money theory that justified it. Whigs seized on the economic collapse as a vindication of what they had been saying for years: Jackson and the antibank Democratic ideologues could not be trusted as stewards of the national economy. The simple truth, as the Whigs presented it, was that a thriving democratic capitalism required the paper money that Jackson and his allies seemed intent on eradicating. The problem, Henry Clay wrote, was that the US had "a hard-money Government and a paper money people."[33]

Playing the blame game was more difficult for Van Buren and the Democrats. Although Van Buren inherited an economic mess that he bore little responsibility for creating, deflecting blame onto his predecessor was never a viable option. After all, Van Buren was Jackson's handpicked successor, his trusted political lieutenant, party builder, and vice president. In accepting the Democratic nomination for president, Van Buren had advertised his fealty to Jackson, pledging "to tread generally in the footsteps of President Jackson."[34] Their closeness had even been on display at the inauguration, when Van Buren and Jackson became the first president and president-elect to ride together to the Capitol. Repudiation of Jackson and his policies was impossible. Moreover, thanks to Jackson's "glorious triumph" over the national bank, Van Buren no longer had that "mammoth of corruption and power" to blame for the nation's problems.[35] Finally, since Jackson and his allies had repeatedly claimed that the administration's policies, especially slaying the Monster Bank, were responsible for the nation's astonishing prosperity,[36] it was difficult to claim that those same policies now had no part in producing the economic calamity.

Unlike the Whigs, Democrats did not offer a single, unified narrative. Instead, they tended to peddle several different, albeit connected narratives of blame and blame avoidance. The first narrative downplayed the scope of the crisis. Things were not as bad as they seemed. "Although money is . . . scarce," one Michigan Democrat offered reassuringly, "nobody has failed here and all wear cheerful faces."[37] The sense of crisis, many Democrats insisted throughout the spring, was being drummed up by "panic makers" who for partisan reasons hoped to embarrass the Van Buren government and bring back the national bank.[38] There is no question that Whigs seized on the crisis for partisan advantage. Some seemed almost gleeful that at last Jackson would be "as bitterly cursed as he has been blindly worshipped."[39] But downplaying or minimizing the economic crisis was a risky play, as Democrats left themselves vulnerable to charges that they were unaware of or insensitive to the people's suffering, which was why Van Buren, after initially rejecting the idea of a special session of Congress, reversed course on May 15 and called Congress into special session in September (normally the new Congress would not convene until December, more than a year after the presidential election).[40]

A closely related Democratic tactic was to portray the economic downturn as a normal part of the business cycle in a capitalist economy. Business failures were part of the natural economic order. The "difficulties and distresses of the time" were real and regrettable, but they were also unavoidable. Left to its own devices, the economy would soon correct itself, as it always did, and there was little the federal government could do to hasten the turnaround. Indeed, government intervention would only make things worse. This was the approach largely taken by Van Buren in his message to open the special legislative session in September. "Relieving mercantile embarrassments or interfering with the ordinary operations of foreign or domestic commerce," he told Congress, was "not within the constitutional province of the General Government."[41]

A third, more potent Democratic line of attack was to blame the crash on the bankers, merchants, and speculators whose unprincipled greed had again endangered the well-being of ordinary people. This was Jackson's instinct from the outset. The Monster Bank may have been slain, but Jackson insisted that the "moneyed power" still exerted its malign influence. Jackson fumed that the nation's bankers had suspended payments in order to "degrade, embarrass, and ruin" their country, make "large profits" out of the misfortunes of others, and gratify the powerful Philadelphia banker Nicholas Biddle, who upon the demise of the national bank in 1836 had become president of the US Bank of Pennsylvania, which retained all the shareholders (except the federal government) and assets of the old national bank.[42] The Panic of 1837, far from being an indictment of the govern-ment's policy, was a vindication of Jackson's insistence that the paper sys-tem needed to be done away with. Only by defeating the nefarious "aristoc-racy of the few" could the "democracy of numbers" finally triumph and the government ensure enduring prosperity for "the great working class" based on a virtuous economy of hard work and hard money.[43]

Demonizing banks and the moneyed elite had always seemed to work for Jackson, so it was little surprise that he and his allies, including Van Buren, again employed that rhetorical strategy after the banks suspended specie payments. Certainly, it seemed preferable to preaching patience or minimizing the crisis. But no amount or type of rhetoric could erase the in-escapable political fact that the Democratic Party was the incumbent party and had controlled the presidency as well as the House of Representatives for the previous eight years. Over the next year, voters in every state would have the opportunity to assign responsibility for the economic crisis. The results would show the power of economic events to trump partisan rheto-ric, image making, and position taking.

IN THE LAND OF PERPETUAL ELECTIONS

The United States in the first half of the nineteenth century was a land of perpetual elections. At the time of the 1836 election, half the states held their congressional elections in odd-numbered years. As Table 2.1 shows, congressional elections were scattered over many different dates from early spring to late fall (not until 1872 did Congress require that all congressional elections be held on the same day in November of even-numbered years).[44] In addition, gubernatorial elections happened with much greater frequency than they do now. Today, only two states (New Hampshire and Vermont, which hold gubernatorial elections every two years) have governors elected to less than four-year terms, whereas in 1836 fewer than one-quarter of the twenty-two states with popularly elected governors had four-year terms. Six New England states (Connecticut, Maine, Massachusetts, New Hampshire, Rhode Island, and Vermont) elected their governors annually, and more than two-thirds of the states held annual state legislative elections.

SPRING 1837

The first statewide elections of 1837 were held in New Hampshire only ten days after Van Buren's inauguration. New Hampshire was a Demo-cratic stronghold, but in 1835 the Whig congressional candidates had man-aged to secure about 37 percent of the votes (the state elected its five mem-

Table 2.1 Regularly Scheduled Congressional Elections for Seats in the Twenty-Fifth Congress (1837–1839)

1836		1837	
State	Date of Election	State	Date of Election
Louisiana	July 4–6	New Hampshire	March 14
Illinois	August 1	Connecticut	April 3
Missouri	August 1	Virginia	April 27
Vermont	September 6	Maryland	July 26
Maine	September 13	Tennessee	August 3
Georgia	October 3	Alabama	August 7
South Carolina	October 10–11	Indiana	August 7
Ohio	October 11	Kentucky	August 7
Pennsylvania	October 11	North Carolina	August 11
New York	November 7–9	Michigan	August 21–22
Delaware	November 8	Rhode Island	August 29
Massachusetts	November 14	Arkansas	October 2
New Jersey	November 15–16	Mississippi	November 6–7*

*After President Van Buren called for a special session in September, Mississippi moved its regularly scheduled November election forward to July 17–18, 1837.

bers of Congress in one at-large district). This time, though, the Democrats swamped their demoralized opponents, garnering more than 95 percent of the congressional vote, while the incumbent Democratic governor racked up 92 percent of the vote. In the wake of Van Buren's election, the Whig Party in New Hampshire seemed hardly organized enough to warrant the name "party."[45]

The returns were perhaps even more disappointing for the Whigs in nearby Connecticut, which held statewide and congressional elections on April 3. Unlike New Hampshire, which had gone overwhelmingly for Van Buren in 1836, Connecticut was among the most competitive states in the nation—Van Buren had prevailed there over William Henry Harrison by only a single percentage point in 1836. Although the Whigs' gubernatorial candidate, William Ellsworth, received almost 3,000 more votes than Harrison had polled in November, the incumbent Democratic governor exceeded Van Buren's total by almost 5,000 votes, resulting in a 5-point loss for Ellsworth, who failed to carry any of the state's eight counties. The Whigs also lost the other statewide offices of lieutenant governor, secretary, treasurer, and controller to the "Van Buren ticket."[46] To cap off the disappointing day, the Whigs were also shut out in each of the state's six congressional seats, a remarkable feat of futility considering that the six Whig candidates averaged nearly 48 percent of the vote.[47]

Two days after Connecticut voted, Rhode Island's voters went to the polls to select their governor (their congressional elections would be held later in the summer). The outcome was every bit as dispiriting for the Whigs as it had been in Connecticut and New Hampshire—maybe more so because the Whigs did not even bother to put up a candidate despite their gubernatorial candidate having polled a respectable 42 percent the previous year and 49 percent the year before that. Turnout plummeted as "disheartened" Whig voters stayed home, allowing the Democratic incumbent governor to roll to an easy victory over a candidate put up by the short-lived Constitutional Party. The lack of organized Whig opposition meant that Democrats' only real worry during the campaign was complacency—and they worked to motivate the party faithful with hopes of extinguishing the Whig Party altogether. As one Democratic newspaper expressed it on the eve of the election, "Suffer not an expiring faction to catch even at straws—and if it be now too weak or too contemptible to show its head, teach this faction, that it has nothing to expect from the future."[48]

The only other state to hold statewide elections in the spring was Virginia, where voters went to the polls on April 27. Here again, the results were demoralizing for the Whigs. The Democrats picked up eight seats in the state assembly, boosting their majority from 58 percent to 64 percent,[49] and won fifteen of the state's twenty-one US House seats. Although that was one House seat fewer than they had won in 1835,[50] a closer look at the results shows how badly Whig organization and support had eroded in Virginia. In 1835, although on the losing end of three-quarters of the House races, the Whigs nonetheless won 44 percent of the votes cast and ran competitive races in a great majority of House districts.[51] In 1837, in contrast, the Whigs secured only one-third of the vote and failed even to put up a challenger in seven of the twenty-one districts (in 1835, by contrast, there was only one district in which the Whigs did not field a candidate). Moreover, aside from a handful of House districts, largely in the western part of the state, interest in the 1837 election was tepid. Whereas almost 60,000 Virginians had voted in the hotly contested congressional races of 1835—and 54,000 in the recently concluded 1836 presidential election—fewer than 35,000 turned out to vote in 1837. The number of votes cast for Whig House candidates plummeted by more than half, from roughly 23,000 votes in 1835 (and 1836) to a mere 11,500 votes in 1837. So anemic was the Virginia Whig Party's performance that some worried about its survival.[52]

In sum, in each of the states to hold statewide elections in the period between Van Buren's inauguration and the bank suspensions, the results went against the Whigs. In two of those states (Rhode Island and New Hampshire), the Whig Party barely put up any organized resistance at all; in a third (Virginia), the party's organization and electoral support slipped precipitously; and in the fourth (Connecticut), the results, while more competitive, were widely seen as a setback for the Whigs—so much so that Henry Clay despaired that Connecticut's citizens "appear to prefer darkness" rather than to "open their eyes."[53] Certainly in none of these states was there any evidence of the Whig Party gaining strength or of a softening of Democratic support. Whatever economic anxieties were being felt in the country in the early spring were not being expressed through the ballot box.

However, even before the banks' suspension of specie—and the resulting economic collapse—there were signs of political trouble for the Democrats in New York City's mayoral election, which was held in the second week of April. In February, the city had been convulsed by a short-lived riot over soaring bread prices, a reminder that rising prices did not lift all boats. The protest, which resulted in the destruction of many hundreds of barrels of flour and a thousand bushels of wheat, was organized by the fledgling Equal Rights Party (dubbed the Locofocos by opponents), which blamed greedy merchants and the proliferation of paper money for the rising prices that were creating hardships for working people. Although the riot was short-lived and easily suppressed, the Locofocos, whose antibank and anti-paper-money rhetoric mirrored Jackson's own, posed a more enduring problem for the Democratic organization (known as Tammany Hall) that had dominated the city's politics since Jackson's election in 1828. The split within the city's Democratic Party between the conservative Tammany regulars and the radical Locofocos—the leadership of which was largely anti-Tammany Democrats—opened the way for the Whig nominee, Aaron Clark, to capitalize on the economic discontent with both high prices and tight credit to become the city's first Whig mayor. In addition, the Whigs won twelve of the seventeen seats on New York City's Board of Aldermen, giving them a majority on the board for the first time.[54]

Although only a municipal election, the results in New York City attracted the attention and stirred the hopes of despondent Whigs across the country.[55] Henry Clay praised New Yorkers for having "broken loose from the chains of party," while in Connecticut, where disappointed Whigs were still licking their wounds, the result was hailed by the Whig organ in Hartford as "one of the most important political events which has occurred in the country for many years past." The Courant's editors felt sure that the result had delivered a "rebuff which Mr. Van Buren must feel in the most sensitive part of his system" and that the voters' message "speaks in a language that cannot be mistaken . . . that the warfare against the currency, credit, and business concerns of the country must cease."[56]

In truth, the New York result probably said more about the need for party unity among Democrats than it did about the voters' verdict about an uncertain economy or the wisdom of Democratic policies. New York City's mayoral election, however, took place a good month before New York City's banks suspended payments. The real test for Van Buren and the Democratic Party would come in the elections held after the banks suspended payments and the economy crashed. As the economic conditions worsened, Democrats' electoral fortunes rapidly eroded. Congressional and state elections across the country in the late summer offered abundant opportunities for voters to express their discontent with the state of the economy and the incumbent administration.

SUMMER AND FALL 1837

A revealing indicator of the effects of the economic panic on voter choice was Maine's seventh congressional district, which had voted overwhelmingly for Van Buren in 1836. Maine had a curious electoral system that required successive runoff elections until one candidate emerged with a majority but it had no requirement that candidates outside the top two drop out. The result was that it could take months—in this case almost a year—to decide an election. In the initial election, held in September 1836, the Democratic candidate, Timothy Pillsbury, received 40 percent of the vote, more than the other candidates but not enough to avoid a second election. In the second election, held on the same day as the 1836 presidential election, and in the third election in early February 1837, Pillsbury again received more votes than any other candidate but still fell short of a majority. The fourth election was held on May 9, 1837, the day before the New York City banks suspended payment, and Pillsbury's support dropped to 25 percent, leaving the Whig candidate with a plurality of 35 percent. In the fifth and final election, held on July 17, 1837, at the height of the panic, Pillsbury's support plunged to under 10 percent, and the Whig candidate secured a majority, giving the Whig Party its second member of Maine's eight-member congressional delegation—and its first-ever representative in the district.[57]

Another bellwether was a special election in Pennsylvania's third district held on June 29, 1837. The Philadelphia seat became open after the Democrat Francis Harper died a few months after he had narrowly defeated the

Whig candidate Charles Naylor. In hopes of holding the seat, the Democrats recruited one of the state's most distinguished men, Charles Jared Ingersoll, a former member of Congress, longtime district attorney for Pennsylvania, and son of a signer of the Constitution. The Whigs again nominated the relatively obscure thirty-year old Naylor, who was six years old when Ingersoll was first elected to Congress. Ingersoll's famous name and distinguished record of service were not enough, however, as Naylor prevailed in a contest that saw substantially more people turn out than had done so in the regular election the previous fall.

Nowhere were the political repercussions of the economic downturn more dramatic than in the state of Indiana, which held congressional elections on August 7. Whigs won six of the seven congressional seats, a stunning setback for Democrats, who had carried all seven seats only two years earlier. The only Indiana House Democrat to survive the Whig wave was veteran incumbent Ratliff Boon, who barely squeaked through, defeating his Whig challenger by a mere 67 votes. In Indiana's seventh district, Democrats lost by a 3–1 margin in a district they had carried two years earlier by a 2–1 margin, and in the sixth district, the Democratic share of the vote plummeted from 62 percent to 38 percent. In the state house, the Whigs increased their share of seats from 56 percent to 68 percent. The Whigs also won the governorship by a comfortable 11-point margin.

Voters in Kentucky also went to the polls on the first Monday of August to choose their members of Congress, and here, too, the Democrats took a drubbing. Admittedly, Clay's home state leaned toward the Whigs, but in 1835 the Democrats had still managed to secure four of the state's thirteen congressional districts. In 1837, however, the Democrats triumphed in only a single congressional district—and even in that district, the incumbent Democrat, Linn Boyd, a prominent Jackson supporter, was unseated, albeit by another Democrat. The Whigs, in contrast, returned seven of their eight incumbents who ran for reelection—and the sole loss was at the hands of a prominent Kentucky politician (John Pope) who ran as an Independent but soon gravitated toward the Whig Party. Support for the Democratic Party also eroded at the state level, as "Van Buren men" won only 29 percent of the seats in the state house (down from 41 percent the year before and 39 percent the year before that).[58]

In Tennessee, which also voted in the first week of August, the Whigs consolidated their control over the House delegation that they had established toward the end of Jackson's presidency. In 1835, Tennessee Whigs had won eight of the thirteen House seats, and in 1837, they increased that number to ten seats. Only one Tennessee House Democrat garnered a majority: the unopposed (and future president) James Knox Polk. In the governor's race, the Whig incumbent, Newton Cannon, turned a comfortable 10-point margin of victory in 1835 into a more than 20-point drubbing of his Democratic opponent in 1837. The Whigs also won almost two-thirds of the seats in the state assembly.

The Whigs also made gains in August in North Carolina, where they secured control of the state assembly and picked up an additional congressional seat.[59] In Rhode Island, where voters elected members of Congress (but not state legislators) at the end of August, the Whigs reversed the outcome from two years earlier, when the Democrats had carried the state's two at-large House seats (not until 1842 did Congress require all states to use single-member rather than at-large districts). Nor was the outcome close, as both Whig candidates won by roughly 13 points, a victory fueled by their overwhelming advantage in the state's largest towns, Providence (where the Whigs won by a nearly 5–1 margin) and Newport (where the Whigs won by a better than 2–1 margin).[60]

Voters in the new state of Michigan also went to the polls in the final days of August, and while the Democratic House incumbent (who had taken his seat on January 28, 1837, the day after Michigan was admitted as a state) narrowly prevailed, his 52.5 percent of the vote far below the 96 percent of the vote he had won two years before. The same dynamic of Whig resurgence was evident a few months later in Michigan's gubernatorial race, in which the incumbent Democrat saw his 91 percent share of the vote in 1835 shrink to less than 51 percent. Michigan's Whigs were ecstatic at their newfound success. An excited Daniel Fletcher Webster—who had recently started a law practice in Detroit—reported to his father that the party had "done grandly" and that the two days of elections in August were "the most exciting ones" he had ever seen, featuring "Bands of music, Stage Coaches, Flags—a ship on wheels, the *Constitution*, filled with Sailors & covered with ensigns, one of them bearing in noble capitals 'Daniel Webster & the Constitution,' together with all sorts of placards & handbills & plenty of rows & fights."[61]

All told, in the summer of 1837, the Whigs contested sixty-eight House seats and picked up a net of fifteen.[62] It was the Democrats' great good fortune that those seats represented less than 30 percent of the 242 seats in the Twenty-Fifth Congress, which convened for a special session in September and then for the regular session in December. If the remaining seats—which had been largely filled in elections held between August and

November the year before—had been up for grabs during the summer of 1837, and had the Democrats lost seats at the same rate as they did in those summer months, the party would have lost another thirty-eight seats to the Whigs, more than enough for the Democrats to lose their House majority. Indeed, even the loss of half that number of seats would have made the Democrats the minority party.

While the Democrats could lose a host of House seats in the summer without endangering their majority status, they did not have the same luxury in the gubernatorial and state legislative elections, which (unlike with House elections) continued into the fall of 1837.[63] Three states in New England held fall gubernatorial elections, and again the news was not encouraging for the Democrats.[64] At least the Democrats did not lose ground in Vermont, where the incumbent Whig governor, Silas Jennison, faced off for a rematch against Democrat William Bradley and triumphed by virtually the same 11-point margin as the year before. In Massachusetts, though, the incumbent Whig, Edward Everett, in a rematch against Democrat Marcus Morton, turned an 8-point margin of victory in 1836 into a 21-point victory. The Whigs also tightened their grip on the lower house, winning nearly 90 percent of the seats, up from about 70 percent the year before. However, it was the Democrats' defeat in Maine, a state that Van Buren had carried by 20 points in 1836, that stunned the political establishment. In the gubernatorial contest, the Whigs defeated the Democrats for the first time, and while the margin was narrow (less than 1 point), the swing was large (the Democrats had won by 17 points the year before). Moreover, the Whigs gained a majority in the state lower house, giving them control of that body for the first time.[65]

None of the North's three most populous states—New York, Pennsylvania, and Ohio—held gubernatorial or congressional contests in 1837, but they did hold state legislative elections in the fall. In each case, the Whigs picked up seats. The party's largest gains by far were in New York, where it won nearly four of every five seats in the state assembly, compared to only about one of four the preceding year. Whereas the Whigs had carried only twelve of the state's fifty-seven counties in 1836, in 1837 they prevailed in forty-one counties. They gained ground in every county but two (Erie and Genesee, both of which already leaned strongly toward the Whigs) and swept all thirteen seats that represented New York City.[66] In neighboring New Jersey, the Whigs also made dramatic gains in state legislative races, gaining control of the lower house by boosting their seat share from 38 percent to 68 percent. In Ohio, the gains were more modest (7 percentage

Table 2.2 Percentage of Seats in Lower State Houses Won by Whig Candidates in 1837 Compared to 1836

State	Date of Election in 1837	1836	1837	Percentage Swing to Whigs	Flipped Control
Alabama	August 7	51	51	0	
Indiana	August 7	56	68	12	
Kentucky	August 7	59	71	12	
North Carolina	**August 11**	49	55	6	Yes
Vermont	September 5	73	57	(-16)	
Maine	**September 12**	35	50.5	15.5	Yes
Arkansas	**October 2**	25	44	19	
Maryland	October 4	76	60	(-16)	
New Jersey	**October 10**	38	68	30	Yes
Ohio	**October 10**	49	56	7	Yes
Pennsylvania	**October 10**	28	44	16	
Mississippi	**November 6–7**	37.5	50	12.5	Yes
New York	**November 6–7**	26	78	52	Yes
Massachusetts	November 13	69	87	18	

The seat-share data are based on Table 6 in Michael F. Holt, *The Rise and Fall of the American Whig Party* (New York: Oxford University Press, 1999), 75. States in bold are those in which state assemblies had Democratic majorities in the lower house prior to the state's 1837 election.

points), but even that relatively small increase was enough to give them control over the lower house. In Pennsylvania, Democrats retained control of the lower house but with a greatly reduced majority, as the opposition increased its share of seats from 28 percent to 44 percent.

In total, as detailed in Table 2.2, of the fourteen states that held state legislative elections between August and November in both 1836 and 1837, the Whigs on average saw a net gain of about 11 percentage points in the number of lower house seats.[67] If one separates the eight states in which the Democrats held a majority after the 1836 elections from the six states that had Whig majorities, the pattern becomes even more dramatic. The Democrats lost seats in each of the eight states in which they had won a legislative majority in 1836—and in six of those states (New York, New Jersey, Ohio, Maine, North Carolina, and Mississippi) the losses were sufficient to catapult the Whigs into the majority.[68] In the other two states, Pennsylvania and Arkansas, the Democratic majorities were greatly diminished. The mean seat loss in these eight states was about 20 percentage points. In contrast, the Whigs' gains were more uneven in the six states in which they were already in the majority: they picked up a substantial number of seats in three states (Indiana, Kentucky, and Massachusetts), broke even in one (Alabama[69]), and lost seats in two (Vermont and Maryland). But even in the two states where the Whigs lost ground, they easily retained their legislative majority.

Vermont and Maryland had several things in common that help to explain why they were anomalous. First, the Whigs had huge legislative majorities after the 1836 elections. In both states, the anti-Jackson forces controlled about three-quarters of the seats.[70] Second, both states not only had Whig governors but had either never had a Democratic governor (Vermont) or had not had one since Jackson's first term (Maryland). In both states, the Whigs controlled the levers of state government—and had done so for an extended time—so it is not surprising that economic discontent would be directed, in part at least, at Whig legislators, particularly in state elections.[71]

The state legislative results in Vermont and Maryland, though, remained the exception in the summer and fall of 1837. In the great majority of states, voters' growing unhappiness with a dismal economy translated into defeat for Van Buren's Democratic Party. Whigs who at the outset of the year had been despondent about the future of the party ended the year exultant. As one Democratic editor grumbled, the Whigs "are so flushed with victory that they expect everything."[72]

SPRING 1838

Things didn't get any better for the Democrats in the first part of 1838. In New Hampshire, the moribund Whig Party was raised from the dead by the economic discontent. The incumbent Democratic governor, Isaac Hill, who had won 92 percent of the vote in March 1837 (and 81 percent the year before that) scraped by with a narrow 6-point victory over his Whig challenger. The Whigs also won 46 percent of the seats in the lower house, doubling their total from two years before. The competitive election spurred a huge surge in turnout. The more than fifty-four thousand adult males who voted in the gubernatorial contest were more than twice the number who had voted in either the 1837 gubernatorial contest or the 1836 presidential election and nearly nine thousand more than had voted in any previous election in the state.[73]

The Whigs' resurgence in New Hampshire was bad enough for Democrats, but their misery was compounded by the results the following month of Rhode Island's gubernatorial elections. In the spring of 1837, Rhode Island's Whigs had been so dispirited that they had not even fielded a candidate to run against the entrenched Democratic incumbent, John Brown Francis. A year later, encouraged by their victories in August's congressional elections, the Whigs regrouped, nominating as their standard-bearer the former member of Congress William Sprague, who had recently defected from the Democratic Party. This time, the Democrats' familiar attacks on the moneyed "Whig-Biddle gentry" failed to resonate as Sprague snapped Francis's string of five consecutive gubernatorial victories, defeating the popular incumbent by more than 5 points. This was not a personal or idiosyncratic triumph; it was instead a comprehensive party victory in which the Democratic lieutenant governor, state treasurer, and all ten Democratic state senators (each state senator was elected on a statewide at-large basis) went down to defeat. Indeed, Sprague's vote totals lagged well behind those of each of the ten senators whose names appeared on the winning Whig ticket. The Whigs also seized control of the lower house.[74]

The results were just as bad for Democrats in Connecticut. The Democrats had won three successive gubernatorial elections, with margins of between 5 and 8 points. This time, though, buoyed by intense voter interest and Whig mobilization, the Whig nominee rolled to an easy victory. In all, a record fifty thousand men in Connecticut turned out to vote in the governor's race, a 10-percentage-point increase from the contest the previous spring. The increase in turnout also helped the Whigs more than double their number of seats in the lower house, from 35 percent to 73 percent.

In Virginia, too, Democrats suffered huge losses in the state legislative elections that spring, losing control of the state assembly. Having secured a nearly two-thirds majority in 1836, they dropped to only 45 percent of the seats in 1838.[75] Van Buren had built the Democratic Party upon the New York–Virginia axis, and now the Whigs had seized control of the lower house in both states. Indeed, by the end of the spring of 1838, the Democratic Party had been reduced to a minority in the state assemblies of all but five states, three of which (Michigan, Arkansas, and Missouri) were sparsely populated and had only 10 electoral votes between them. Of the five, only New Hampshire and especially Pennsylvania could be counted as crucial parts of the Van Buren coalition.[76]

More bad news for the Democrats came out of a special election in Maine held on April 2 to fill the congressional seat formerly held by a young Democrat, Jonathan Cilley, who had been killed a few weeks before in a duel with fellow member of Congress William Graves, a Kentucky Whig who had taken umbrage at Cilley's rebuke of a prominent Whig newspaper editor in a speech on the floor of the House. The duel, which was fought with rifles at eighty yards and took three rounds before the fatal shot was delivered, ultimately led Congress to ban the giving or accepting of a challenge to a duel within the District of Columbia (dueling was already illegal in the district, but that ban was easily evaded by crossing into Maryland).[77] The duel's more immediate political consequence, however, was to require the Democrats to defend a seat they had won the year before (at the third trial on February 7, 1837). The special election elicited huge interest—with turnout over 60 percent higher than it had been the previous February— but whatever sympathy voters might have had for Cilley counted for little in these hard times, and the Whig candidate won by a comfortable 8 points.

A special election in Maryland's fourth congressional district at the end of April spread more gloom within the Democratic ranks. The death of Democrat Isaac McKim, a staunch Jackson supporter who had served in the House of Representatives since 1833, gave the Whigs a second shot at a seat they had narrowly lost the previous year. The Whigs renominated the cultured author and politician John P. Kennedy, and this time they won, with Kennedy beating his Whig opponent by 6 points. Kennedy's victory restored the Whigs' 5–3 advantage in Maryland's congressional delegation.

The Whigs picked up two more House seats at the end of April in a special election for Mississippi's two at-large districts. The circumstances of the election were extraordinary, but the results were part of a pattern of increased turnout and Whig gains. Unlike every other state, Mississippi normally held its congressional elections in November of odd-numbered years, the month before Congress convened. But when Van Buren called a special session for the beginning of September 1837, Mississippi's governor called for a special election in July 1837 so that the state would be represented—with the stipulation that the state would elect two new representatives, as usual, in November for the regularly scheduled congressional session that would open in December. The Whigs had little time to mount an effective campaign (one of their candidates was not even in the state, and the other was largely unknown), and the Democratic incumbents from the previous Congress prevailed easily at the special election. A few months later, however, at the regularly scheduled election in November, the Whigs reversed the result in stunning fashion, winning by a better than 2–1 majority over the Democratic incumbents. The Whig victory, and especially the fact that the Whig candidates doubled their vote count while the Democratic vote count was sliced in half, may say less about the poor economy (although the Mississippi economy was in a particularly distressed state) than about the popular outrage at House Democrats' decision in October to seat the Democrats for the duration of the Twenty-Fifth Congress. In February 1838, House Democrats reversed course, declared the two seats empty, and called for another special election to be held on April 24 and 25, 1838. In July 1837, about 17,500 Mississippians had cast a ballot in the congressional election, and in November 1837, about 19,500 turned out to vote, but in April 1838, with the two parties squaring off on banking and economics, the number of voters surged to 24,000. Interest was intense and the race close, but the two Whigs prevailed, further shrinking the Democrats' increasingly tenuous majority in the House.[78]

THE VERDICT ON VAN BUREN'S FIRST YEAR

Among the best-known adages in politics is "All politics is local." Yet often it's not. Certainly it would be foolish to ignore the importance of local context: the candidates, campaigns, interests, and issues specific to a place and time. Candidates' reputations, rivalries, and rhetoric all matter. Intrigue and scandal have decided many an election. And, of course, the interests and issues that drive people are different in different places. In the mid-1830s, Nullification animated politics in Alabama, Anti-Masons thrived in Vermont, tariffs were pivotal in Pennsylvania, and the price of cotton and protection of slavery preoccupied much of the South. Voters' political identities in 1837 were complex amalgams of region, religion, ethnicity, race, class, occupation, and family upbringing. Yet amidst the kaleidoscope of political identities and interests, the powerful sway of localism, and the large cast of colorful characters in hundreds of elections across the United States, there is an unmistakable pattern in voting behavior during Van Buren's first year. From the time of the banks' suspension of specie in May 1837 through the end of April 1838, voters consistently expressed their unhappiness with the nation's economic mess by punishing what the Whigs called the "Van Buren ticket,"[79] not only in federal elections but also in state elections.[80]

There is no denying, as one historian writes, that "few Americans really understood how the financial system worked."[81] Voters are not experts in monetary policy, and even the best-informed citizen would have struggled to assess accurately how much of the economic crisis was due, for instance, to President Jackson's Specie Circular and how much to international events beyond the president's control. Historians, after all, still strenuously debate this question. But voters did not need to understand the global financial system or the complex transfer of specie among banks to render a judgment at the ballot box. Instead, voters in the 1830s, like American voters in virtually every major economic downturn since, were inclined to blame the party in power.

SPECIE CLAWS.

Specie Claws. *An 1838 lithograph dramatizing the country's economic distress,
which the artist blames on the failed hard-money policies of Presidents Jackson
and Van Buren, particularly the Specie Circular. Seated at the bare table is
a tradesman who complains, "I have no money, and cannot get any work."
His unused carpentry tools are scattered on the floor, and his toolbox contains
only empty "Loco Foco Pledges." On his lap is a copy of the "New Era," a
newspaper edited by Levi Slamm, a prominent leader of New York City's radical
Democrats (often called Locofocos). Behind him on the otherwise empty wall
are affixed portraits of Jackson and Van Buren. Next to him is his wife, who
selflessly pleads, "My dear, cannot you contrive to get some food for the children?
I don't care for myself." One of his four hungry children asks for a piece of
bread, another for some "Specie Claws." At the door are agents of the landlord
who brandish a warrant authorizing them to seize the man's goods to recover
unpaid rent. Surveying the barren room, one of the agents says, "I say Sam, I
wonder where we are to get our Costs." (Courtesy of the Library of Congress)*

To be sure, most voters used a partisan heuristic in deciding whom or
what to blame. Democratic voters largely absolved Jackson and Van Buren
of blame for the economic mess. Instead, they followed their party leaders—politicians and newspaper editors—in affixing blame squarely on
the banks. Similarly, Whig voters followed the cue of their party elites in
faulting Jackson's ruinous policies and Van Buren's stubborn adherence to

those policies.[82] But not all voters were strongly moored to a partisan identity, and those less tightly tethered to a party were particularly susceptible to blaming the incumbent. The greater the increase in turnout, moreover, the greater the number of votes cast by those with weaker partisan identities. The two parties structured politics and made policies, but the economy powerfully shaped the election results in Van Buren's first year.

Although the Democrats' electoral fortunes were buffeted by an economic gale beyond their control, two decisions by President Van Buren in his first year in office significantly reshaped elite politics. The first was his retention of the Specie Circular, and the other was his call for legislation to separate the federal government's monies from private banks and require that the government trade only in specie. Introduced by Van Buren in the September special session, the plan to establish an Independent Treasury was also known as the "sub-treasury" scheme because it mandated that the federal government deposit its gold and silver coins in federal subtreasury offices throughout the nation rather than in the many "pet banks" in which government deposits had been housed since Jackson withdrew all federal monies from the national bank in 1833. The Independent Treasury was attractive to Democrats because it was a way to blame the hundreds of banks that had sprung up in Jackson's second term while heading off the Whigs' calls for a return to a national bank. Van Buren's embrace of hard money led some self-styled Conservative Democrats, such as Virginia's William Rives and New York's Nathaniel Tallmadge, to defect to the Whig Party while bringing Nullifiers such as South Carolina's John Calhoun—who left the Democratic Party after Jackson's Nullification Proclamation—back into the Democratic ranks. Van Buren made the Independent Treasury the "touchstone of the parties," just as Jackson had done with the national bank five years before.[83]

Although the Independent Treasury proposal—which would finally be enacted into law in the final year of Van Buren's presidency—sharpened and reshaped partisan lines, there is scant evidence that it boosted or hurt Democrats at the ballot box. The Democrats lost seats and votes to the Whigs in the August 1837 elections at essentially the same rate that they did in the fall and following spring. The Democrats' heavy losses in the fall of 1837 and spring of 1838 were not a judgment on the wisdom of the Independent Treasury or hard-money policy. Nor did those losses necessarily signal a popular desire to bring back the national bank or even an acceptance of paper money. The swing to the Whigs was instead principally about punishing the incumbent party. Swing voters, in short, were asking for a change more than they were endorsing or rejecting specific policies.[84]

Like most "out" parties, however, the Whigs preferred to see their victories as a sign that voters were coming around to their political philosophy, or at least their policies. Certainly, as Michael Holt rightly points out, the Whigs "campaigned on a record, not just on economic conditions."[85] It is equally true that the Panic of 1837 was crucial in forging a Whig ideology and identity that increasingly highlighted the role of government in promoting economic development and prosperity.[86] Whereas during the Bank War, the fledgling Whig Party had united around opposition to King Andrew's "executive usurpation," the Panic of 1837 pushed the Whigs to focus less on the dangers of arbitrary executive power than on the Democrats' ruinous attachment to a radical hard-money agenda and the heartlessness of Democrats' laissez-faire ideology that told economically struggling citizens to "take care of themselves."[87]

Whatever the views of ordinary voters about specific Whig Party policies and principles, the Whigs in the spring of 1838 had every reason to be confident about the coming midterm elections in the late summer and fall—and about their chances of securing a majority in the next House of Representatives. Fourteen states would go to the polls over a period of four months to elect members of the Twenty-Sixth Congress, starting with Louisiana in early July, followed by Missouri in August; Maine and Vermont in September; Arkansas, Georgia, New Jersey, Ohio, Pennsylvania, and South Carolina in October; and Delaware, Massachusetts, Michigan, and New York in November. The largest prize of all would be the forty House seats of New York, which was one-sixth of the total number of seats in Congress—and where Democrats controlled thirty of the forty seats. The Whigs of the Empire State were confident that here especially, at the epicenter of the financial crisis, there were huge gains to be made, particularly after the impressive Whig gains in the state legislative elections the previous November. That it was Van Buren's home state would make the victory all the sweeter.

The Whigs' gaze was fixed not only on the coming congressional and state elections but also, as we shall see in the next chapter, on the next presidential election. As the economy worsened and Democratic losses piled up in the fall of 1837 and spring of 1838, visions of a Whig in the White House began to fill the heads of ambitious Whig politicians, including Henry Clay, who had lost to Jackson in 1832, and William Henry Harrison and Daniel Webster, who had been on the losing end to Van Buren in 1836.

THE TWO SENATORS
DANIEL WEBSTER AND HENRY CLAY

Every modern presidential election seems to trigger the same lament: campaigns are too long. No sooner is one election finished than the jockeying for the next begins. This is no recent affliction, however.[1] The so-called "permanent campaign" long predates television and radio. Indeed, the nineteenth century arguably had it worse given the relentless cycle of party conventions at the town, county, state, and national levels as well as congressional, gubernatorial, and local elections scattered across nearly every month of the calendar. Certainly, the leading Whig candidates waged a continuous campaign for the 1840 election beginning almost from the moment Martin Van Buren took the oath of office.[2]

DANIEL WEBSTER'S "FIRST MOVEMENT"

Only ten days after Van Buren's inaugural address, Daniel Webster traveled to New York City to address six thousand enthusiastic Whigs at a fashionable downtown venue. The speech, which lasted two and a half hours,[3] made no mention of a presidential campaign, but it was widely understood to signal the start of Webster's campaign to become the next president of the United States. The invitation to speak at Niblo's Saloon emanated from a February 21 meeting of the "political friends" of Webster, but the meeting, like the invitation to speak, had been at Webster's direct instigation.

At the end of January 1837, Webster had written to Hiram Ketchum, a well-connected New York City attorney and devoted friend, and confided that he would resign from the

Senate at the close of the legislative session on March 3, giving him the freedom to tour the country and make the case against the Van Buren administration. In the letter, Webster mapped out his strategy for securing the nomination. The "keystones" to success were New York and Pennsylvania. The candidate who won those two states would secure the Whig nomination. William Henry Harrison's strength in Pennsylvania meant that it was up to the Whigs of New York, "beginning in the City, & beginning immediately," to make "a first, decisive, & *determined* step." Once New York City's Whigs brought his "name before the public," then "assuredly" other Eastern cities and states would follow. Philadelphia "would do the same, with promptness; & the rest of Pa. would not likely to keep long aloof." Delaware and Maryland would soon follow. After the backing of most of New England and the mid-Atlantic states (in Webster's parlance, the "Central States") was secured, Webster's nomination would become irresistible. Or so Webster thought.[4]

Webster was anxious that Ketchum act quickly to rally his political allies in New York City. Holding back was not an option, he told Ketchum, because he was already hearing of plans to line up support for Harrison.[5] Two weeks later, an anxious Webster again fired off a directive to Ketchum, reiterating how important it was for the Whigs of New York City to take the lead in backing Webster. New York City, he underscored, was "the only source, to which we are to look for any effectual & vigorous first movement to establish a better state of things in the Country." Then Webster made a "suggestion": might Ketchum find "some occasion" for inviting Webster to make a speech in New York City? He hoped, he added helpfully, to be in New York City by March 12.[6] Ketchum promptly set to work to carry out the great man's wishes. A week after receiving Webster's second letter, Ketchum had assembled a glittering array of the city's commercial elite who dutifully extended Webster the invitation he sought.

In 1837, the fifty-five-year old Webster was among the most famous politicians in America and certainly its most celebrated orator. Ever since his acclaimed eulogy for John Adams and Thomas Jefferson a decade earlier, he had been hailed by admirers as the "Godlike Daniel."[7] While still in his thirties, he had established a reputation as one of the great constitutional advocates of the age, having successfully argued countless cases before the Supreme Court, including several landmark cases in which the Marshall Court closely followed his reasoning. His speeches in the Senate, where he had been ensconced since 1827, were legendary, none more so than his 1830 "Reply to Hayne," which schoolboys all across the North were tasked with memorizing.[8] Among Whigs, at least, Webster was recognized as the nation's leading expositor of the Constitution; many called him "the Great Expounder of the Constitution."[9]

Webster could transfix an audience for hours on end. Contemporaries and biographers struggled to put his mesmerizing effect into words. Some reported being riveted by his "great, staring black eyes" that were, as Thomas Carlyle expressed it, set beneath "a precipice of brows like dull anthracite furnaces needing only to be blown." Others located the power in his voice, "deep, dark, with a roll of thunder in it, tempered by a richness of tone and powered by a massive chest that sent it hurtling great distances, even in the open air." Still others attributed his command over others to the masterful marshaling of logic and facts that made him, in Emerson's formulation, "a great cannon loaded to the lips." For others, the key to his captivating presence was the "majestic calm" he projected.[10] One thing was sure: Webster was accustomed to adulation. Crowds cheered him wherever he spoke, and his legions of admirers, male and female, fawned and fussed over and fêted him. Few dared tell him no.

The 1836 election had been a major embarrassment for the Godlike Daniel, but Webster was determined that 1840 would be different. It galled Webster and his supporters that Whigs in the Northern states had lacked the courage of their convictions in 1836 and thrown over the statesman who had led the party's fight against Jackson's usurpations in favor of a non-political general of scant experience and minor accomplishments whose fame, eloquence, and intellect could not compare with Webster's. Webster blamed his defeat not only on timid politicians, such as Thurlow Weed, who feared the party could not win with a leader associated with the fight to save the national bank, but also on his Senate colleague Henry Clay, who Webster believed had sabotaged his chances by refusing to back Webster over Harrison.[11] Webster believed that the closeness of the 1836 election demonstrated that a Whig—and not merely a Whig in name only—could win the presidency, and he was convinced that he was the man to unite the Whig Party and unseat Van Buren. His speech at Niblo's was designed to show precisely how he planned to achieve that feat.

Whereas the Whig candidates had disguised their principles in 1836, Webster promised to "conceal nothing," for there was "nothing to conceal." Of his political sentiments and purposes, there was "nothing in [his] heart [to be] ashamed of," and so he vowed to "throw it all open . . . to all men." In pledging to speak his opinions "freely and frankly, . . . without non-

An 1838 etching that captures the reverence many in New England felt for
Daniel Webster. Diogenes no longer needs his lantern. His storied search is over,
for he has finally found an honest man. (Courtesy of the Yale University Art
Gallery)

committal or evasion, without barren generalities or empty phrase," he signaled his intention to be a candidate unlike the ill-defined Harrison and a
president unlike the prevaricating Van Buren.[12]

Much of what Webster spelled out that evening was the usual Whig orthodoxy on tariffs, banking, and executive aggrandizement. But the speech
was not only about rallying the Whig faithful and appealing to the commercial classes. Instead, as historian Sydney Nathans notes, it was deliberately
and boldly sectional. Webster declared himself unambiguously opposed to
the annexation of Texas, which was "likely to be a slave-holding country."
Slavery, Webster avowed, was "a great moral, social, and political evil," and
under no circumstances was he willing "to do anything which shall extend
the slavery of the African race on this Continent, or add other slave-holding
States to the Union." The nation must instead "be content with our present
boundaries." Slavery must be contained and the influence of the slaveholding states curtailed. Webster positioned himself as the champion of Northern interests and ideals.[13]

Writing off the South, a region that had given the country five of its first
eight presidents, might seem a self-defeating general election strategy.[14] But
a sectional strategy was not as crazy as it might at first appear. A candidate
who could carry the six states of New England plus the big three of New
York, Pennsylvania, and Ohio would, under winner-take-all conditions,
have 142 electoral votes in his pocket. Add New Jersey, a state the Whigs
carried in 1836, and the candidate would reach 151 electoral votes, three
more than the 148 needed to win. There was also enough Whig strength
in Delaware and Maryland, states that neither Jackson nor Van Buren had
won, to provide some cushion in the event of the defection of a New England state such as New Hampshire, where the Democratic Party was well
organized. Whereas Van Buren's political strategy had been to forge a party
and candidacy that would appeal to both Northern and Southern interests,
Webster appeared ready to gamble that he and his party could win the presidency by appealing almost exclusively to Northern voters. Given Webster's
unpopularity in the South, there was probably no other route open to him.

Webster was not writing off the Western states, however. On the contrary, only six weeks after speaking at Niblo's, Webster embarked on an
ambitious three-month speaking tour of "the Western Country"[15] that took
him to Clay's home state of Kentucky and Harrison's home state of Indiana
as well as Missouri, Illinois, Michigan, and Ohio. The aim of the tour was
to show the nation that Webster's popularity and renown extended well

beyond his native Northeast and to demonstrate that he could unite the Whigs of the North and the West.[16] Throughout his tour, he was met with adoring crowds, grand public feasts, musical bands, and the booming salute of gunfire; it was enough, noted Webster's traveling companion (and future secretary of the treasury in the Lincoln administration) William Pitt Fessenden, to keep one "continually excited." Webster spoke in numerous Western cities—including Louisville, St. Louis, Cincinnati, Springfield, Chicago, Toledo, and Detroit—and was invariably greeted with "loud and long-continued thunder-peals of applause."[17] In St. Louis, the "Webster Barbecue" attracted a crowd estimated at between four and five thousand people, "the young and the old, the professional man and the mechanic, the studious and the hard-working" alike, all dressed "in their gayest costume" and "all anxious to see and hear" the great Daniel Webster. "The Western Shores of the Mississippi," gushed one observer, had "never before witnessed such a concourse of citizens as collected" that day to "honor the talents and fame" of Webster.[18]

As news of Webster's rapturous reception made its way back to New York City—and following a string of endorsements of Webster in three influential Whig papers in the city, the *Commercial Advertiser, New-York American,* and *Journal of Commerce*[19]—Ketchum decided that the time was ripe to execute Webster's plan to place his "name before the public" as a candidate for the presidency.[20] On June 22, with Webster still in the midst of his speaking tour, Ketchum and a committee of ten other Webster partisans announced a public meeting to be held the following week "of all those Whigs and other citizens of New York" who were in favor of making Webster president.[21]

The meeting took place as planned on June 28 at the Masonic Hall, but heated opposition from Clay's supporters compelled Ketchum to settle for a compromise that called for recommending Webster's nomination rather than formally placing his name in nomination—a distinction without a difference in the eyes of Clay and others.[22] To avoid an acrimonious split between the Webster and Clay forces, Ketchum also publicly pledged that the assembled citizens would "abide the result of a National Convention, or any other course which a majority of the Whigs in Congress may recommend their fellow Whigs to adopt, in order to produce a fair expression of the sentiments of the Whig party, and ensure concert in action among the opponents of the present corrupt administration." Webster was their guy, but the "friends of Webster" would back whomever the party nominated.[23]

Webster's strategy of building early momentum in key Northern states had faltered at the first gate. Rather than make his candidacy appear irresistible, his early entry highlighted the divisions within the party and galvanized his opponents. In New York City, Webster's bid spurred Clay partisans to begin furiously organizing a network of ward committees, with "ten for each ward," as well as a seventeen-person general executive committee, a nine-person finance committee, another nine-person committee of correspondence, and a general committee of 170 that would be made up of "electioneering men, taken from the mass of the Clay party." Webster's "premature and indiscreet movements," boasted one of Clay's political operatives in New York City, have "awakened men who were slumbering at their posts." Clay's political friends also successfully lobbied political operatives elsewhere in the state to block any further efforts to hold public meetings to "recommend" Webster.[24]

Webster returned home at the end of July to plenty of praise for his "brilliant tour"[25] but with no evidence of a groundswell of support for his nomination. Indeed, the savvy Weed was confident that the "folly" of trying to secure an early nomination had "ruined" Webster's chances for the nomination.[26] Certainly, after the June 28 meeting was announced, Whig papers across the country took aim at the "premature and impolitic" effort to advance Webster's nomination.[27] Even organs generally sympathetic to Webster disavowed the effort as damaging to the party's need for a united front against the ruinous policies of the Van Buren administration. The principal effect of Webster's "first movement" was not to create the hoped-for bandwagon for his candidacy but instead to solidify the emerging conviction among many Whigs, particularly in the North, that the choice of the party's nominee must be settled at a national convention. As the generally pro-Webster *Boston Atlas* chided, "It is the CAUSE, not the MAN, for whom we labor; and it is but of secondary moment in whose person GOOD PRINCIPLES, shall triumph."[28]

Ketchum was disappointed at the response but hardly willing to admit defeat or even to concede that the early effort to secure Webster's nomination had been ill-timed, let alone a mistake.[29] He remained convinced that Webster was "the most popular man in this nation," at least in the North and West, and believed that this would have become clear had the people been "permitted to speak for themselves" at public meetings. The problem, as Ketchum saw it, was that a small but "powerful band of selfish politicians," threatened by Webster's "intellectual preeminence," used their control of the party machinery to "keep his name from the people."[30] While the effort to build early momentum for Webster had not worked as planned, Ketchum remained confident that Webster could still triumph at a national convention. "Nothing is now wanted to make Mr. Webster the candidate of the Whig convention," he declared, "but activity, perseverance, and boldness on the part of his friends."[31]

Determined not to let the machinations of politicians stand in the way of a Webster presidency, Ketchum redoubled his efforts to cultivate well-placed allies who could make the case for a Webster presidency and defend the great man against his critics. He arranged for Massachusetts Rep. Caleb Cushing to write for the *Journal of Commerce*, a paper that Ketchum placed at the forefront of "the uncompromising Webster party."[32] Ketchum suggested various lines of attack and defense aimed at advancing Webster's candidacy and undermining support for his chief rivals, Clay and Harrison, including by focusing on the need to keep slavery out of the territories and to oppose the annexation of Texas.[33]

Throughout the summer of 1837, the New York papers that had pressed for Webster's nomination—notably the *Commercial Advertiser*, the *New-York American*, and the *Journal of Commerce*—continued to make the case for Webster. Their argument for a Webster candidacy boiled down to two main points. First, the Whig Party should stand on its principles. It had tried expediency in 1836, in the person of Harrison, and failed. As the *Commercial Advertiser* thundered, "We are wearied of the miserable, trifling, temporizing policy, which abandons the truly great, and runs sneaking about after the available" (that is, those deemed electable).[34] Now, with the economy cratering and the administration growing more unpopular by the day, the Whigs should seize the opportunity to nominate one of their true leaders, particularly one who had long warned against the ruinous consequences of Democratic economic policies.[35] Second, while Henry Clay had an equal claim as great Whig statesman, he was a two-time loser (1824 and 1832) who was forever tarred in the public mind by the Corrupt Bargain charge and as a result lacked the "general popularity" to triumph, particularly in key Northern states.[36]

By the end of the summer, Webster's supporters could point to a few scattered successes in the effort to forward the great man's candidacy. On August 4, for instance, the Whigs of Hancock and Washington Counties held a "spirited convention" in Penobscot, Maine, and unanimously adopted a resolution hailing Webster as their "first choice" for the presidency.[37] But Webster's allies were mostly frustrated in their efforts to get other public meetings to come out in favor of the great man. Although

Webster remained hopeful that he could secure the party's nomination, by the end of the summer of 1837 his bold opening gambit appeared to have been checked.[38] Certainly that was the judgment of Henry Clay, Webster's most prominent rival for the nomination.

HENRY CLAY'S "POSITION OF PERFECT PASSIVENESS"

Clay believed a Webster nomination was a nonstarter. In his view, the 1836 election had established beyond a reasonable doubt that Webster's support did not extend much beyond the merchant class and the borders of his home state of Massachusetts. At the end of May, Clay privately expressed his surprise at Webster's "defective judgment in what concerns himself and his prospects." Surely, "most men," having been decisively rejected by their party and country only six months prior, "would have recoiled instinctively from [placing themselves in] a similar predicament."[39] Ambition, Clay lamented to another confidant, "has a powerful blinding effect. And I think Mr. Webster's case is a shocking proof of it."[40] Clay insisted that Webster was wrong to interpret the "cordial and distinguished reception" that he had received in the West (which included a week in Lexington as Clay's guest) as evidence of the region's disposition to support him as a presidential candidate.[41]

Even if Webster could somehow prevail in the West, the antipathy toward him in the South would doom his candidacy. On his Western tour, Webster had insisted that the country had "reached a new era" in which old "party names" no longer had the same hold on the great mass of people.[42] But while Van Buren's Independent Treasury plan reshuffled party loyalties in important ways—propelling Calhoun and his allies toward the Democratic Party and self-described Conservative Democrats toward the Whig Party—the economic downturn did not alter the South's preeminent interest in securing slavery. "If there ever was a point in which there is perfect unanimity in the South," warned a Southern Whig newspaper, "it is the resolve to vote for no man who is tinged with abolitionism." In the eyes of most Southern Whigs, Webster was far too closely identified with antislavery politics and opposition to states' rights to be an acceptable nominee. Nominate Webster, warned the *Carolina Watchman*, and "all hope of cooperation is gone."[43]

From his large Ashland estate outside Lexington, Clay carefully monitored the reactions to Webster's attempt to gain the inside track to the nomination. Criticisms of Webster's electioneering reinforced Clay's instinct to take it slow. When Alexander Hamilton's son wrote to him in the latter

Henry Clay. An 1837 lithograph by the Swiss-born artist Charles Fenderich. (Courtesy of the Library of Congress)

part of May suggesting that Clay issue a public statement on the economic crisis and consent to have his name put forward for the presidency, Clay demurred: "I have seen no indications of any general desire that [my name] should be so used; and . . . to allow myself to be forced upon the public attention is the last thing I should be willing to do." As for stating his views on the current crisis, he would wait until Congress was in session and he was back in the nation's capital. He would speak as a US senator, not as a presidential candidate.[44]

Clay shared the prevalent view that the movement in favor of Webster's candidacy had been "premature," but his fundamental complaint was that the process of holding public meetings to nominate or merely recommend a favored candidate would divide the party and doom its otherwise promising electoral prospects. In the wake of Webster's June 28 meeting, Clay urged his friends in New York to resist the temptation to follow the same ill-advised path. The party needed to focus on what united it—"the absolute failure of the measures of the Administration"—and not what divided it. A bewildering array of rival meetings and recommendations would not only accent the divisions within the party but could harden positions, generate ill feeling, and make it more difficult to unite behind a candidate. Moreover, jockeying for political advantage so early in Van Buren's term might alienate possible supporters and "drive back those of the other party who were coming out from it to oppose it or join our standard." The "public mind," he cautioned, was "absorbed with the pecuniary embarrassments of the Country; and all thoughts are now directed more to the means of the preservation than the future command of the Vessel of State. The Whigs, by stirring the Presidential subject, at this time, expose themselves to the danger of bringing the sincerity and disinterestedness of their patriotism into doubt."[45]

Clay's counsel of patience and forbearance was also rooted in his calculation that it would be better for his candidacy (and the party) to have the Whigs in Congress first unite around a candidate. As he confided to South Carolina congressman Waddy Thompson in early July, although Webster's "movements" were "to be regretted as premature," it was nonetheless important "at some time or other during the next Session [that is, before July 1838] . . . to unite on some one Candidate, if possible. We shall otherwise repeat the error of delay and postponement, committed in the former canvass, and experience again defeat and discomfiture."[46] In a letter to Hamilton ten days later, he was more explicit still: "Prior to the presentation of the name of any Candidate, whether in the form of recommendation, or a positive nomination, . . . a strenuous exertion should be made *at Washington* to bring about union and concert in behalf of some particular person. Without that every thing will be hazarded, if not lost." In other words, Clay wanted the first movement in the "presidential question" to be by congressional caucus, where the Kentucky senator knew he would have the upper hand.[47]

Webster may have been the more famous orator—though the spellbinding "silver-tongued Kentuckian" was no slouch in the rhetorical department—but Clay was the recognized leader of the congressional Whigs. Whereas Webster was aloof—even his godson William Pitt Fessenden conceded that Webster "would never gain popularity by personal intercourse"[48]—Clay was gregarious and cajoling. His legislative talents had been widely admired for decades. When first elected to the House of Representatives in 1810, at the age of thirty-three, he was immediately made

Speaker of the House, a post he held for more than a decade, transforming it into a position of substantial power.[49] As Speaker, Clay played a vital role in engineering the Missouri Compromise of 1820 that admitted Missouri as a slave state while prohibiting slavery north of the 36°30' parallel, and he was indispensable in securing the less famous but no less important Second Missouri Compromise, which defused the crisis created by Missouri's passage of a constitution that excluded "free negroes and mulattoes" from the state. Clay's solution made Missouri's admission to the Union conditional on its pledge to never enact legislation that would deprive US citizens of rights and privileges guaranteed by the US Constitution. His relentless efforts ("he begs, entreats, adjures, suplicates, & beseaches us," marveled one New Hampshire representative[50]) to secure the support of both Southern proslavery and Northern antislavery representatives earned him renown as the Great Pacificator or the Great Compromiser,[51] a reputation he burnished in the Senate by his leading role in the passage of the so-called Compromise Tariff of 1833, which helped to overcome the Nullification Crisis by gradually reducing the tariffs that many Southerners found so objectionable. There was, in short, no Whig politician who could match Clay's legislative prowess or the breadth of support among his fellow legislators from every region of the country.

However, Clay's congressional caucus plan was a nonstarter. First, it was transparently self-serving. His two principal rivals knew that they would stand no chance in a congressional caucus—Harrison was not well known by members of Congress, and Webster was not well liked—so there was no chance either would consent to such a scheme. Second, this horse had already left the barn. While Clay was pitching the idea of a congressional caucus to Thompson, Ohio's Whigs were holding a state convention in Columbus on July 4, nominating Harrison for president—and calling for a national party convention to be held the following June in Pittsburgh. Nor was Clay effective in reining in his supporters, who were actively promoting the Great Compromiser in newspapers all across the country as the only Whig candidate who could unite the party.[52] Third, and perhaps most important, the idea of Congress choosing nominees had been thoroughly discredited in 1824, and the chance that a congressional caucus could be revived, even in an advisory function, seemed far-fetched. Even if a caucus was held, there was no reason to think that it would promote party unity, any more than it had in the multicandidate contest of 1824.

That Clay believed that a congressional caucus provided a realistic path to party unity and his own nomination suggests that Webster was hardly the only great politician whose political judgment was impaired by a driving ambition to become president of the United States. Clay would later famously claim that he "would rather be right than president," but his behavior in 1837 and 1838 shows that there were few things he wanted more than to be the next president of the United States. Like Webster, Clay judged Harrison to be a political lightweight and thought that now was the time for the party to look to its true leaders. And with far greater cause than Webster, Clay believed that he could best bridge the party's regional and ideological divisions, carry it to victory in 1840, and chart a desperately needed new direction in American politics.

Political scientists have sometimes portrayed most nineteenth-century presidents as little more than glorified clerks.[53] The real policy-making power, it is suggested, lay in the legislative branch. But that both Webster and Clay, two of the country's most powerful and famed legislators, relentlessly pursued their ambition to become president is reason enough to doubt this portrayal of a weak presidency. Even in the nineteenth century, presidential power was the power to "command the Vessel of State." Clay knew it, and he desperately wanted to wield that power to steer the country away from the disastrous course that he believed had been set by Jackson and Van Buren.

Although in private Clay was beginning to map out a strategy to secure his nomination, in public he continued to feign disinterest in becoming president. In an August 8, 1837, letter to a committee of New York City Whigs, which he knew would likely find its way into publication (and indeed was made public before the end of the year),[54] he gratefully acknowledged the citizens' "desire to place me in the highest station of the government" but insisted that he "desired and sought retirement from the cares of public life" (never mind that he had been reelected to the US Senate only the year before) and that he would be "extremely unwilling, without the strongest reasons, to hazard this tranquility, and be thrown into the turmoil of a Presidential canvass." Of course, if "a majority of [his] fellow-citizens wished to assign [him] to their highest executive office," then he would be duty-bound to show "obedience to their will."[55] Until then, though, Clay resolved "to occupy a position of perfect passiveness." It was up to the people to show that they were resolved to have Clay.[56]

Over the next year, Clay would repeatedly reaffirm his vow to remain "perfectly passive."[57] He would accept no speaking invitations or engage in anything that could be construed as electioneering—a clear contrast with and implicit rebuke of Webster's behavior. "The office of president of the

United States," Clay explained to another committee of pro-Clay New York Whigs, "is of a nature so exhalted, and its functions so momentous, that it ought not to be, and, happily, never can be, reached by individual efforts to acquire it. It should only be bestowed by the free, spontaneous, and deliberate judgment of the people."[58]

Behind the scenes, though, Clay was anything but passive, orchestrating his presidential campaign actively and adroitly. A week after penning his letter to New York City Whigs, he wrote a "strictly confidential" letter to George Prentice, editor of the *Louisville Journal* and one of the party's most effective propagandists. Originally a New Englander, Prentice had come to Kentucky to write a campaign biography of Clay for use in the 1832 presidential election—which had sold twenty thousand copies[59]—and Clay now hoped to utilize his talents by sending him to the nation's capital to start a Whig paper that would rival the Democrats' *Washington Globe*. While reiterating his oft-stated position that it was "premature to hold public meetings now and publicly to discuss at large the P[residential] question," Clay suggested to Prentice that "perhaps some occasional notice of me . . . may serve to counteract the efforts to put me aside or to put me down by the zealous partizans of other Candidates." Although it was important that his rivals for the nomination were treated "with the utmost delicacy, and in a spirit of true conciliation," Clay made it clear that he did "not like to be run down by other Candidates or would be Candidates on our own side"—and that he expected his allies in the press, such as Prentice, to make sure that criticisms did not go unanswered. Clay outlined to Prentice several lines of defense and attack that he wanted to see used. He was especially eager to combat "talk of prejudices against [him] in the Jackson or V. Buren party, as if that party were to elect a *Whig* Presid[en]t!" And as "if there were not prejudices against Mr. Calhoun more recent"—that is, his support for Nullification and secession—and "against Mr. Webster of more strength and of longer standing!"—namely, Webster's past affiliation with the Federalist Party. Clay pointed Prentice to a host of prominent Democrats who had rejected Van Burenism and, far from harboring antipathy to Clay, were "anxious to atone for former injuries." While he would not want Prentice and other friends to make "invidious comparisons" between himself and his rivals, he did expect them to highlight "my services [and] my sacrifices" to the Whig cause, "my early prediction of the fatal effects of electing Genl Jackson, . . . the uniformity of my opposition to him, and . . . my denunciation of those measures which have spread bankruptcy and ruin throughout the Land." While Clay insisted that he would "cheerfully acquiesce" in any decision reached by a national convention, he made it clear to Prentice that he had "no wish . . . to be run without a high degree of probability of success."[60]

That Clay was keenly attentive to his "probability of success" was evident from the detailed sketch he gave to Prentice of the political terrain as it had been reported to him by his legion of visitors and correspondents—and they were rosy reports indeed. From James Watson Webb, editor of the *New York Courier and Enquirer*, he learned that he would "be certainly elected," that Webster's prospects were "utterly ruined," and that "in no event will the North go for . . . Harrison." Peter Buell Porter, Clay's New York confidant and de facto state campaign manager, reported that Clay was "greatly preferred" to all other candidates in the western part of New York. Correspondents from New England also assured Clay that he was "preferred to any other Candidate" and that even in Massachusetts he would outpoll Webster. His South Carolina informants reported not only an "utter repugnance" to Webster but a "decided aversion" to Harrison as well. Calhoun would be their first choice, but Clay was a highly acceptable second. In Louisiana, he was told, "they speak with great confidence" that he was the preferred candidate. He heard, too, from Georgia and Tennessee that "feelings and sentiments" were increasingly tending in his favor. For a man who claimed not to care about becoming president, Clay paid exactingly close attention to his chances of success. And Clay clearly liked his chances—and incessantly talked them up even while maintaining "the ground of entire passiveness."[61]

Six months earlier, Clay had been despondent about his own political future as well as the future of the country and the Whig Party. At the outset of the year, he had told friends that his beloved Senate was "no longer a place for any decent men" and was "rapidly filling with blackguards" and vowed that he would "escape from it as soon as I decently can, with the same pleasure that one would fly from a charnel-house."[62] Voters seemed incapable of intelligent choice, and a fractured Whig Party seemed to be slipping into irrelevance. By the middle of August 1837, though, Clay was brimming with confidence. The election results of early August in Kentucky, Tennessee, and Indiana filled him with hope that "the People have at last awakened."[63] Indeed, it now seemed to him that "the downfall of the present administration [was] inevitable" and that "some Whig must be elected" so long as "we can unite in favor of any one."[64]

Toward the end of September, Clay received a particularly encouraging report from James Watson Webb, who said he had spoken to Webster about the presidential question. According to Webb, Webster told him that the "success of the party was the main concern" and specifically instructed Webb to inform Clay that "if [Clay] should receive the nomination . . . I will commence a tour [around] the United States and mount the stump in [every] Hamlet advocating his selection, & not cease . . . until the contest is over." Webb added that such was Webster's "good feeling" toward Clay that it was even possible that Webster would consent to run on a dream Whig ticket with Clay as president and Webster as vice president.[65]

During the fall, Clay received "almost daily, gratifying proofs of attachment and confidence from all quarters."[66] But the most dramatic news of all came from New York, where Whig victories in the state legislative races had seemingly "revolutionized" the state. An excited Porter wrote to Clay that there now could be no doubt that "the next President will be a Whig," and the only remaining question was whether that president would be Webster, Harrison, or Clay. Porter conceded that Webster had many "powerful friends" in New York, especially in the mercantile community, but Clay's strength, he reported, was "decidedly greater." As for Harrison, Porter believed his star was fading: "We anticipated much more annoyance from his name some time ago, than we feel at present," in large part because Pennsylvania no longer seemed to be the keystone state of the Whig coalition. Pennsylvania's Democrats had retained control of the lower house in the fall elections, and the Anti-Masonic movement's influence—which had been a key part of Harrison's support in 1836—seemed to be waning. As Porter explained, "We supposed that Pennsylvania instead of New York was the most likely to become the leading State in the Whig confederacy—and, if so, she would have had great influence in naming the candidate, and that candidate would probably have been General H[arrison]."[67] Instead, Pennsylvania's politicians had become consumed by political infighting, particularly in a bitterly contested constitutional convention (convening in May 1837, it did not finish its work until February 1838) that strained relationships within the state's coalition of Whigs and Anti-Masons.[68] With New York seemingly now a "Whig State"—and Pennsylvania apparently anything but—Porter judged that New York had taken "a commanding position in the Whig ranks," which in turn put Clay in the driver's seat, particularly if Webster stepped aside.[69]

During the summer of 1837, Clay had labored to restrain his supporters from prematurely advancing his candidacy and refused to consent to having his name placed in nomination as a presidential candidate. But the results in New York helped to change the political calculus. Porter told Clay that the triumphant Whig legislators in New York "will be disposed to move in this business pretty early" and that they would "be doubtless glad" to know Clay's views on the subject.[70] Now back in the nation's capital for the regular congressional session that opened in December, Clay signaled his readiness to back such efforts. He was still, as ever, attentive to how the nomination would affect the Whig Party's fortunes. "The first care," he told Porter, was to do nothing that would jeopardize the Whig gains in New York. "If a nomination of any one for the Presidency should hazard that, it ought not to be made," he wrote. However, "if it would not; if it would benefit you; or if it would be merely neutral," then his nomination "ought to be made."[71] If he were to be nominated by New York, Clay was sure that "the question would be settled . . . beyond all doubt, *even if N. York were subsequently lost.*"[72]

Porter exuded confidence that the deed could be done. He informed Clay that he had met the previous day with Noah Cook, a "sensible and efficient politician" from New York City who had recently returned from a trip out West, an area with which he was "extensively acquainted." Cook's command of "the political statisticks of the day," Porter marveled, was "more ample than that of anyone." And Cook "*demonstrates* that not only New York, but a large majority of the States, will be for you, provided we can effect . . . an expression of a majority of the Whigs in [New York] in your favor." Porter assured Clay that there was "no doubt we can, in some unexceptionable way," receive such an expression of Whig support in New York. Indeed, Porter was assured by Cook that three-quarters of the assemblymen representing New York City would support a Clay endorsement. Porter also expressed confidence that they would be able to secure "the cooperation of the Webster men in the city."[73]

Reports that New York seemed ready to support his nomination helped Clay set aside his initial scheme of securing a prenomination of sorts from congressional Whigs. Instead, it seemed that he could do what Webster had set out to do at the beginning of the year: leverage a dramatic show of support in New York into a cascade of nominations across the county, which could then be capped by a unifying, drama-free national convention that would anoint the chosen one. The purpose of a congressional caucus, as Clay had envisioned it in July, was to unify the party around a single standard-bearer, but by the end of December, Clay expressed great confidence that the daily "exhibitions of public feeling . . . from almost every corner of the Union" showed that "a rapid and enthusiastic concentration [was already] taking place" around his candidacy. Clay thought even "the friends of Mr. Webster are not unaware of this state of things and of the progress of events" and that they were "*almost* ready to withdraw his name, and to yield to what they feel to be a resistless current."[74]

Porter seemed an unending fount of good news—perhaps too good to be entirely trusted. In early January 1838, Porter reported from Albany that not only did he find a substantial majority of Whig legislators in favor of Clay, but he had spoken with Thurlow Weed, who agreed that Clay was "decidedly the favorite of the Whig party and nothing can prevent [his] being their candidate." Weed also divulged to Porter that he had had a "very full and frank" conversation with Webster at the beginning of December and told the Massachusetts senator that he had been "mislead by his own friends" and that, while Webster was "greatly respected" by New York Whigs, Clay was "unquestionably their favorite, and would be their candidate." Weed reported that Webster had been "evidently somewhat surprised" by this news but promised that "as soon as he should become satisfied of this fact . . . he would immediately withdraw and give [Clay] a hearty support."[75]

The trouble was that as much as Porter and Clay might wish it to be so, Webster showed no signs of stepping aside. And despite Porter's encouraging reports about the pro-Clay proclivities of the Whig legislators in New York, no endorsement seemed to be forthcoming. While Clay waited for New York to take the initiative, his supporters in other states were seizing the initiative. In early January, the lower house in Clay's home state of Kentucky introduced a resolution recommending Clay for president. Still hoping for New York to go first, Clay initially thought the Kentucky legislature's act perhaps "displays more zeal than discretion," but he soon changed his tune.[76] He expressed no misgivings the following week when he learned that the Whig legislative caucus in Kentucky had taken the further step of calling for a national convention and endorsing Clay. Nor was there any hint of rebuke when Clay learned that the Whigs in the Maryland legislature were set to "quickly follow" Kentucky's lead in nominating him[77] or when he was informed that Whig legislators in Rhode Island had met on February 1 to nominate him.[78]

Clay was fast persuading himself that the sequence of endorsements was less consequential than he had initially thought because "popular feeling" was organically "concentrating" on him.[79] As he confidently told his son, "If I am to judge from information which daily, almost hourly, reaches me, there is *every where* an irresistible current setting in towards me."[80] Others in Washington, including on the Democratic side, shared the view that Clay would likely be the Whig nominee. Writing from the nation's capital on January 13, 1838, Tennessee congressman James Polk opined, "You may put it down as certain that Clay is to be, or rather is now the Federal candidate for the Presidency. His party will go through the forms of a National convention for the purpose of ruling Webster & Harrison off the field."[81]

The problem with being the front-runner, though, was that it gave his two rivals a shared interest in joining forces to slow the Clay bandwagon—which they did by furiously waving the flag of party unity. In a letter dated March 8, 1838, Porter reported to Clay that Harrison's partisans, although a minority, were working diligently "to prevent any action by the present Legislature on the Presidential question" on the grounds that there should be no "agitation" on the presidential issue until after the upcoming state and congressional elections in November. Their real aim, of course, was "to prevent any movement in the States favorable to" Clay, but the counsel of delay resonated not only with Webster's followers, who held out hope that "something might turn up favorable to their candidate," but also with Clay's "unsuspecting friends, who were bent on peace and conciliation."[82]

Although Clay often insisted that party unity, particularly in New York, was paramount—and that he must defer to the judgment of those "friends of the cause" closer to the action[83]—his vexation at what he characterized as the "repressing game" being played in Albany and Trenton make it clear that he desperately desired New York and other state legislative caucuses to publicly register their preference for him.[84] He later vented, "From what has been communicated to me directly and indirectly, there were majorities of 4 or 5 to one for me" in the New York, New Jersey, Connecticut, and Maine legislatures, but by "appealing to the timid," Webster's "friends succeeded at each of those points to prevent the expression of the preference which was entertained for me."[85] Clay's grousing was aimed as much or more at his fainthearted followers as his devious rivals.

After Harrison's and Webster's forces succeeded in blocking Clay's bid to have the New York legislature endorse him, Clay consented to a public meeting of his supporters in New York City with the purpose of recommending him for the presidency. The meeting took place at the end of May in the Masonic Hall, the same building in which the friends of Webster had held their meeting the year before. Clay had derided the Webster meeting the previous June as a fatal tactical mistake and a grievous threat to party unity, but when Porter asked Clay's view of the "expediency" of the May meeting, Clay gave his unequivocal approval, "There can be no doubt that the more there may be spontaneous demonstrations of popular feeling and opinion on this subject, the greater will be the probability of ultimate union and cooperation."[86]

Webster and Clay had now completely switched positions. In the summer of 1837, Clay had been the one counseling delay and chiding "premature" movements that would cause "unpleasant collisions" among the candidates' followers and thereby undermine party unity.[87] By 1838, it was Webster who was angling for delay and warning against "breaking up the Whig party" through premature efforts to secure the nomination through "com[mitt]ees, & Meeting, & Caucuses, & Commitments."[88] Upon learning that Rhode Island's Whigs had endorsed Clay, Webster fired off a searing letter to a trusted ally: "It appears to me high time for our friends to *awake*. . . . If we do not look out, & move immediately, the Convention will be no deliberating assembly, but a mere meeting to ratify previous nominations."[89] Whereas in 1837, Webster had judged that an early knockout blow was his best route to the nomination, he now calculated that his chances for the presidency depended on holding a national convention as late as possible and ensuring that the convention was a genuinely deliberative body, untrammeled by delegate commitments or pledges. Clay's strategy, meanwhile, had pivoted to winning the nomination (and unifying the party) by securing "manifestations of the public preference"—and preconvention commitments—from as many states as possible. As Clay told John Clayton in June, after being informed that Delaware's Whig legislators had endorsed him, "Whatever others may think, I am fully convinced that all demonstrations of the public feeling and opinion, spontaneously made, in regard to the next Presidency, which tend to produce concentration, are wise and judicious."[90]

By the middle of 1838, Clay had largely been stymied by the combined forces of Webster and Harrison. Clay had secured legislative endorsements in only four states—Kentucky, Rhode Island, Maryland, and Delaware—all states that he had carried in his 1832 contest against Jackson (the only other two he won that year were Massachusetts—which had nominated Webster in March—and Connecticut). Yet despite the setbacks in the spring, Clay continued to exude confidence about his chances. "I do not know," he told Porter in the middle of April, "that we have occasion to entertain any regrets about these delays. Our cause is daily gaining strength every where, whilst that of [Harrison and Webster] is certainly declining." Indeed, even in Indiana, "the strongest supposed State for Harrison," Clay felt "satisfied from various sources of information that I am stronger there than he." As evidence, he noted that "some of their papers have hauled down his flag and hoisted mine."[91]

Clay's confidence in his position stemmed in part from a steady diet of positive reports that he continued to receive while he was in Washington. But it was also rooted in his inability to imagine that the Whig Party would nominate either Webster or Harrison. Webster was too regional and would doom the party to defeat in the general election. Harrison was too insubstantial and would never be chosen by the party's best men at a national convention so long as Clay was a candidate. As he assured Porter in the middle of March, "A real want of confidence in [Harrison's] ability common with all intelligent men of the Whig Party, will ruin his prospects. He will give us no trouble six months hence."[92]

As Clay saw it, the only real obstacle to uniting the party around his nomination was Webster. If Webster would retire from the field, he told Harrison Gray Otis, "the feelings at the North, now stifled, would burst forth, and General H's friends would perceive the utter hopelessness of his remaining in the field. In six months from Mr. W's retirement, the whole matter would be finally settled." In "a long & friendly interview" with Webster on June 13, 1838, Clay gently tried to suggest to his Senate colleague that withdrawing would be "best for *him* and best for the common cause," but Webster appeared unmoved. Clay held out hope that Webster's friends— people such as Otis who shared Clay's view that it was "perfectly manifest that [Webster] cannot be elected"—would eventually persuade Webster to drop out of the race for the good of the party, but he also emerged from the meeting aware that if persuaded to step aside, Webster "will embrace [that course] slowly and sullenly."[93] Webster seemed every bit as unwilling as Clay to give up his presidential dream.

WEBSTER'S FINAL MOVEMENT

Clay thought Webster's dream of becoming president was a fantasy, brought on by a mix of ambition, adulation, and sycophants who refused to tell him bad news. He hoped that Webster's true friends might still save him from himself. In truth, though, it was Webster who played Clay for a fool. By the time Clay had his long interview with Webster on June 13, the Godlike Daniel had already decided to withdraw from the race, which probably explains why the meeting was "conducted throughout and terminated amicably."[94] Webster could afford to be gracious because he was toying with his Senate colleague.

The week before Clay met with Webster, Massachusetts governor Edward Everett, a leading Webster ally, wrote to inform another prominent Webster Whig, Robert C. Winthrop—who was then the speaker of the Massachusetts state house—that Webster had informed him that he had decided to drop out of the race. His "only anxiety," Everett reported, "was that Mass. should keep herself in a position to support Gen'l Harrison."[95] Webster was holding on, then, not because he held out hope he could become the next president but because he was determined to block Clay. He feared that if he dropped out too soon, his supporters, particularly in Massachusetts but also in Connecticut and Maine as well as New York City, might rush into Clay's welcoming arms. Delaying any announcement until the opportune time, he calculated, would better ensure that his supporters would go to Harrison.[96]

Webster's realization that he could not win the presidency owed in part to some straight talk from a few of his closest Massachusetts allies. Many of Webster's associates were initially reluctant to upset or "alienate" Webster. In February 1838, for instance, Winthrop confided to a friend that while Webster had no chance to be president, it was important to avoid any "appearance of disaffection or abandonment among his natural defenders" so as to keep "the great man in good heart and in firm co-operation with the party here and elsewhere."[97] The businessman and former (and future) Massachusetts congressman Abbott Lawrence, though, was having none of this coddling of "the great man." He met with Webster in May and conveyed to him in blunt language that the senator could not win the nomination, let alone the presidency, and that he needed to get out of the race for the good of the state and national party.[98] Webster had brushed aside Thurlow Weed's frank assessment back in December—Weed, after all, had backed Harrison in 1836. But Lawrence, whose political organizing skills and influence among Boston's Whigs rivaled Weed's in Albany, was quite another matter. The wealthy Lawrence had been a loyal "pillar of . . . support, both pecuniary and political" during Webster's past political campaigns, including his run for the presidency in 1836.[99] If Webster did not have Lawrence's support, then the game was well and truly up.

Lawrence planned to back Clay—and he told Webster so in May.[100] Other prominent Webster allies, including Otis and Massachusetts junior senator John Davis, followed suit. So why was Webster so intent on blocking Clay, particularly given the obvious affinity between their candidacies? After all, their policy positions on the most important financial issues of the day regarding banking and currency were similar, and they shared core Whig constituencies of businessmen and urban dwellers in places such as Philadelphia and New York City. One explanation is political payback and personal pique. In 1836, Clay had ultimately supported Harrison for the presidency, and for this, it is suggested, Webster never forgave him.[101] If so, Webster was being unfair to Clay, who held off publicly backing Harrison until the month before the election at a rally in Lexington, Kentucky—"a great barbecue . . . gotten up in sight of [Clay's] house"[102]—by which point Harrison was the only viable alternative to Van Buren, not only in Kentucky but in every other Northern state except Massachusetts.[103] Even then, Clay had said that Webster was his preferred candidate,[104] telling correspondents that while Harrison was honest and well-intentioned, he was also "weak, vain, and far inferior to Webster." The trouble, as Clay saw it, was that Webster, while in merit "far ahead of all his competitors," had not "the remotest prospect" of winning, and so, "as incompetent as" Harrison was, he nonetheless "deserves to be preferred" to Van Buren.[105]

Personal jealousy and spite undoubtedly played a role in Webster's desire to block Clay's candidacy. But an explanation rooted in personal pique slights Webster's own understanding of his actions, not to mention the strategic advantages of backing Harrison—after all, when Harrison won the presidency in 1840, Webster would be offered (and accept) the most prestigious cabinet position: secretary of state.[106] Nor does it explain why Webster's feelings of resentment were not directed at the upstart general who had most directly thwarted his quest for the presidency in 1836. After all, Clay's impact on Webster's 1836 campaign had been virtually zero; Harrison, in contrast, had ensured Webster's humiliating defeat across the North.

Ultimately, Webster sought to prevent Clay's nomination for much the same reason that Clay had not endorsed Webster in 1836: a conviction that the Senate giant could not win a national election. In Webster's view, Clay's unpopularity in the North—and the Whig Party's weakness in the South—would doom his candidacy. Of special concern was Clay's weakness in Pennsylvania. Webster well knew that Pennsylvania's Anti-Masons loathed Clay, a prominent Mason.[107] Making matters worse, Clay's association with the tariff-lowering Compromise Tariff of 1833—which Webster boasted of opposing "at every stage"[108]—did not play well in a state whose economy was highly dependent on high iron tariffs. Webster calculated that no Whig could win the presidency without Pennsylvania, and he adjudged Clay's chances of carrying that state to be slim to nil, whereas he knew that Harrison would be a formidable candidate there. After all, Harrison had lost

Pennsylvania in 1836 by only 2 percentage points; Clay, in contrast, in 1824, had fared worse in Pennsylvania than any of the other three candidates (Jackson, John Quincy Adams, and William Crawford), gaining less than 4 percent of the vote. In 1832, Clay wasn't even on the Pennsylvania ballot, as the state's vote was split between Jackson and the Anti-Masonic candidate William Wirt (Jackson won by 16 points).[109]

Even more important, in Webster's mind, was Clay's stance on slavery and his status as a slaveholder. Webster was convinced, as he wrote in January 1838, that "Anti Slavery feeling is growing stronger & stronger every day"[110] and that those antislavery sentiments would doom a Clay candidacy—and the Whig Party—throughout the North. "I do not believe," he confided to the editor of the Boston *Atlas* in February 1838, "that in Novr. 1840, the vote of Massachusetts *can be given* for Mr. Clay; nor the vote of any other State, north of Maryland."[111] Indeed, Webster's own candidacy had been premised in large part on capitalizing on these growing antislavery feelings in the North, and while Webster's campaign had fizzled, the strength of antislavery feeling and the anxiety about Southern slaveholders' control of federal policy certainly had not.[112] If anything, the congressional session that opened in December 1837 only underscored in Webster's mind the growing salience and divisiveness of slavery.

By the time Webster took his seat at the end of December, the Senate was engulfed in a fight not over the failing economy but over six resolutions introduced by John Calhoun that called on the federal government to give "increased stability and security" to slavery, condemned interference with slavery in the District of Columbia or the territories as "a direct and dangerous attack on the institutions of all the slaveholding States," and declared any resistance to annexing new slave territory—read Texas—to be a violation of the South's constitutional rights and a threat to the Union. Calhoun's demand that the Senate take a "holy pledge" to combat all "further aggression" against slavery had come in response to Vermont senator Benjamin Swift's introduction of resolutions passed by the Vermont legislature, which called for abolition of slavery in the District of Columbia, opposed the annexation of Texas, and instructed Vermont's senators to vote accordingly on these issues. On the theory that the best defense was a good offense, Calhoun, now aligned with the Democrats, was intent on combating abolitionist and antislavery demands by "carrying the war into the non-slaveholding states."[113]

Calhoun's resolutions placed Clay, as the Senate Whig leader, in a difficult spot. Rejecting the resolutions would alienate his Southern base—

the one region of the country where he was inarguably stronger than his two Whig rivals for the nomination—but accepting them would drive away antislavery voters in crucial Northern states such as Massachusetts, Ohio, and New York. Aware of the "traps" that Calhoun had laid for him,[114] Clay tried to thread the needle by proposing alternative resolutions that occupied what he saw as a reasonable middle ground. Clay's resolutions recognized that Congress had authority over slavery in the District of Columbia and the federal territories and that antislavery advocates had every right to petition Congress to do away with slavery where Congress had jurisdiction over slavery. But Clay's resolutions also maintained that Congress should not use that undoubted power to abolish slavery in the District of Columbia or the federal territories. Moreover, the resolutions posited that Congress had no authority over slavery within the states—a position that was broadly accepted in the North, including by Webster—or over the interstate slave trade, and that Congress should not accept petitions where it had no jurisdiction, thereby essentially endorsing a partial gag rule. Finally, Clay denounced Calhoun for agitating Texas's annexation, a position that he said only increased abolitionist agitation and endangered the Union.[115]

Clay was confident that he had escaped Calhoun's abolition "trap" by positioning himself as the voice of moderation and conciliation who refused to cater to the divisive and inflammatory language of extremists and agitators on both sides. What Calhoun derided as "expediency, concession, compromise," and "weakness,"[116] Clay held up as true statesmanship. "I have borne myself," he bragged to Porter, "in such manner as to lose nothing neither at the South nor at the North."[117] Clay was likely right that his well-publicized sparring with Calhoun on the Senate floor did him little harm in the South, especially among Southern Whigs, who had no time for Calhoun's nullification doctrines and even less sympathy for the Arch Nullifier after his defection to the Democrats.[118]

Although few in the South may have bought the "ridiculous charge" that Clay was an abolitionist,[119] there were many in the North, Webster very much included, who believed that Clay had shown himself to be overly solicitous of Southern slaveholders' interests. Webster believed that Clay had betrayed the party's principles and done his presidential prospects harm in limiting the hallowed constitutional right to petition the government, denying federal power over the slave trade in the District of Columbia, and committing the Senate to opposing the abolition of slavery in the nation's capital. From Webster's perspective, Clay was once again—as in 1833 with the Compromise Tariff—joining forces with Calhoun in an effort *"to make a new Constitution*" that would do the bidding of slaveowners.[120] Clay had gone too far in conciliating Calhoun and the other Southern extremists. Whig policy, Webster wrote to a young New York assemblyman, should be "not to yield the substantial truth, for the sake of conciliating those whom we never can conciliate, at the expense of the loss of the friendship & support of those great masses of good men, who are interested in the Anti Slavery cause."[121] In Webster's view, Clay was doing exactly that: abandoning Whig principles, forfeiting the support of antislavery supporters, and undercutting the party's electoral prospects across the North.[122]

Whatever the precise mix of motives that induced Webster to oppose Clay, by the end of the summer of 1838, with Congress now out of session, he signaled a readiness to swing his support to Harrison. Formally, Webster remained in the race, and he made no public declarations in favor of or opposition to his rivals. But behind the scenes, Webster had set the wheels in motion. On September 14, the Boston *Atlas*, which had been acquired in 1834 by two of Webster's closest confidants—Caleb Cushing and Rufus Choate—to support Webster's 1836 presidential run and was widely considered "Webster's mouthpiece," dropped Webster's name from the masthead and came out in favor of Harrison.[123] The pretext for the change was the Maine election a few days before, in which the incumbent Whig governor, Edward Kent, had gone down to defeat and the Whigs had lost their narrow majority in the lower house, essentially wiping out the gains the party had made the year before. The *Atlas* charged that the results in Maine showed that Clay, "the darling of the aristocratic Whigs," would drag down Whig candidates and hopes across the country. Sadly, though, Webster was "not an *available candidate*" either. Both men had amassed too many enemies in their long careers. Neither Clay nor Webster, although both were distinguished statesmen, possessed what Harrison had in abundance: "the favor and good will of the mass of the people, in other words *popularity*." For too long, the *Atlas* preached, "we in New England have been . . . calling upon the mountain to come to us." Now it was time for New England to come to the mountain of popular democracy.[124]

Clay was livid upon reading the editorial: "mortified—shocked—disgusted," he told Otis. He felt wronged and betrayed. How could the Maine defeat be laid at his door—a state that "on every trial, my friends have shewn greater strength than those in favor of any other Whig candidate"? Moreover, if state elections were to be linked to his presidential candidacy, then how could the *Atlas* ignore the string of Whig victories since the spring in Northern states, including Connecticut and Rhode Island in April, Indiana in August, and Vermont in September? In addition, the Whigs had done well in the South, most notably in Virginia in May but also in August in Kentucky, where they won nearly 70 percent of the seats in the lower house, and North Carolina, where the incumbent governor boosted his share of the vote from 53 percent in 1836 to 63 percent. Making the *Atlas* editorial even more inexplicable was that Clay had in his possession a confidential letter from *Atlas* publisher Richard Haughton, written in early March, in which Haughton expressed his view that there was not a single person in the Massachusetts legislature who favored Harrison as a presidential candidate. Indeed, Haughton boasted in the letter that "were Mr. Webster withdrawn and Genl. Harrison put in nomination by the Whig party, I could carry a ticket [in Massachusetts] with the name of Henry Clay at the head of it against *both* the Harrison and V. Buren tickets, by an overwhelming majority."[125] Clay had steeled himself for the stubbornness of Webster and his friends but was blindsided by what he regarded as their "treachery."[126]

During the fall, the coalescence between Webster and Harrison gained momentum. On November 13, 1838, the Anti-Masons held their national party convention in Philadelphia and nominated Harrison for president and Webster for vice president. Clay learned that Webster was "apprized beforehand and approved of that nomination."[127] Although Webster never had any intention of accepting the vice presidency, he was more than happy to participate in the joining of Webster and Harrison forces. Indeed, that had become his principal objective.

Clay dismissed the Anti-Masonic "pretended Convention" as inconsequential. Not only did he believe their "mock" nomination of a Harrison-Webster ticket had "fallen still born," but he thought it would boomerang by exciting "indignation" among Whigs who were tired of a small band of self-appointed zealots and office seekers trying to dictate the presidential choice to the Whig Party.[128] But while Clay could write off the Anti-Masons' antics, he could not shrug off the escalating criticism of his candidacy amid a run of bad election results during the fall of 1838. "From September of last year to September of this," Clay wrote in early November, "the current ran deep and strong in our favor and swept over every State." But "all at once, and without any apparent cause, the current reverses its direction." In New Jersey, which elected its members at large, the Whigs held on to only one of the six congressional seats they had won in 1836, although the swing in votes was tiny.[129] Most dispiriting of all were the October election results in Ohio, where Whigs lost control of the governorship and the state house—and lost three House seats to boot.[130]

Critics were quick to blame the setback in Ohio on Clay, just as the *Atlas* had done after the Whig defeat in Maine. Clay's baggage was dragging the party down, charged the Cincinnati *Republican*. Had Harrison had the field to himself, the *Republican* insisted, the Whigs' path to victory would have been clear.[131] These fresh attacks left Clay bewildered and aggrieved. "Why should I be held responsible for the issue of elections in States other than K[entucky] more than" his rivals? It was particularly ridiculous, he complained, that he was "assailed for losing Genl. Harrison's *own* State." If anything, surely the Ohio result showed Harrison's vulnerability.[132]

Clay fumed but seemed at a loss to explain the sudden change in the political tide. His first impulse was to blame the Whigs' fall losses on election fraud, specifically a "profuse and corrupt use . . . of the public money" by agents of the Van Buren administration. He noted that the wily Amos Kendall, the postmaster general under Jackson and now Van Buren, had been in Columbus only a week before the election. "How easy was it for him to give orders throughout the State . . . to carry the election at any cost."[133]

Clay also blamed the abolitionists, who had "gone against us."[134] The confidence Clay once felt about abolitionist support had drained away. He pointed with alarm to a letter he had received from the secretary of the American Anti-Slavery Society, Kentucky-born James Birney, that affirmed that the "election of *any* slaveholder to the Presidency [would be] a great calamity to the country." The danger, Clay told Francis Brooke, Virginia's chief justice and a trusted Clay confidant, is that "the contagion may spread until it reaches all the free States." If the proscribing of slaveholders became a rule in the North, he warned darkly, "they have the numbers to enforce it." Then would ensue a parade of horribles: "prohibiting the slave trade, as it is called, among the slave States, and . . . abolishing it in the District of Columbia, and the end will be——"[135]

Attacked from all sides—"Abolitionists . . . denouncing me as a slaveholder, and slaveholders as an Abolitionist"[136]—and blamed for all the party's defeats—but credited with none of its successes—Clay despaired of his prospects and his party. Writing to Otis on a "gloomy Nov[embe]r day," he admitted to feeling tempted, "in some suitable public way," to withdraw his name not only from the presidential contest but from any future "high office." "One can bear the taunts and reproaches and calumnies of open foes," Clay moped, "but it is too much to be picked at by friends from Boston to Cincinnati." Sometimes, he said, "the best service which can be rendered one's Country is not to serve it at all."[137]

Clay was right that it was unfair to blame him for losses the party had suffered in the fall. But nor was it enough to point the finger at voter fraud or abolitionism. The underlying cause of the change in the political tides—and in Clay's political fortunes—was the economy, which had begun to recover in the summer following the New York banks' resumption of specie payments in May, owing in no small part to the Bank of England pumping "one million pounds in gold to New York in the spring of 1838."[138] As the economy recovered, Democrats drifted back to their party. The fall 1838 elections did not wipe out all the gains the Whigs had made between the spring of 1837 and the spring of 1838. Overall, the Whigs ended 1838 in substantially stronger shape than they had been in at the end of 1836.[139] Indeed, in several states, the fall elections went well for the Whigs, most notably in New York, where they won the governorship, retained a nearly two-thirds majority in the state assembly, and picked up eleven congressional seats. Whereas 75 percent of the forty-member New York congressional delegation elected in 1836 had been Democrats, a slight majority of the state's delegation in the new Twenty-Sixth Congress would be Whigs.[140] However, the economy was no longer exerting an inexorable downward force on the Democratic Party. In his second annual address in December 1838, President Van Buren "treated the panic as though it were history," reporting that "the general business of the community [was] reviving with additional vigor" and that "confidence has been restored both at home and abroad, and ease and facility secured to all the operations of trade."[141] As the state of the economy became more open to interpretation and contestation, candidates and their campaigns mattered more. State and local issues came to the fore, leading to more disparate results.

If it made little sense to blame Clay for the Whigs' fall defeats, it made a great deal of sense for the party to be concerned about the prospect of Clay as its presidential candidate. With a tanking economy and an unpopular incumbent, almost any Whig candidate could win the presidency—so why not choose the party's best man and most authentic leader? But if a powerful economic tide was not going to carry the party into power, then it needed a candidate who could win over wayward Democratic voters. Clay, a veteran of countless partisan battles with Democratic leaders, was not that candidate. Harrison, a military hero, could very well be.

Although Webster could not help but take satisfaction in helping to derail Clay's drive for the nomination, the Whigs' electoral losses left him as dejected as Clay. Writing to a banker friend in March 1839, Webster confided, "Our Whig prospects are none of the best, owing to our irreconcilable differences, as to men. My opinion, at present, is that our only chance is with Genl Harrison, & that is not a very good one."[142] Webster had no intention, however, of waiting around to see how the contest turned out. He was finished with presidential politics. By January 1839, he had formed a plan to travel to England, where he would see the sights and try to mend his personal finances—he had massive debts, thanks to a number of ill-advised investments—by trying to find buyers in London for the many acres of Western lands that he had bought (with borrowed money) before the crash.[143] In May, he set sail for Liverpool, and ten days after arriving he penned a letter to the people of Massachusetts, formally withdrawing his name as a candidate for president and freeing the Bay State to support the candidate of its choice. The state's choice at the national convention, as Webster wished, would be William Henry Harrison.[144]

4

THE TWO GENERALS
WILLIAM HENRY HARRISON
AND WINFIELD SCOTT

In the immediate wake of the 1836 election, Daniel Webster and Henry Clay, along with almost every other Whig,
were plunged into despair about the future of the Whig
Party and American democracy. But not New York's William Henry Seward, who had been an Anti-Masonic state
senator before joining the Whig Party. Shortly after learning that Martin Van Buren had won New York—and likely
the presidency—Seward wrote to reassure his despondent
friend and close ally Thurlow Weed that "brighter prospects
are now before us."[1] Ironically, at the outset of the 1836
campaign, few had sounded the tocsin of despair more
emphatically than Seward. A year and a half before the
election, in the spring of 1835, Seward had prophesied Van
Buren's victory. Van Buren would win, Seward told Weed,
because the Democrats were aligned in the popular mind
with the working people and the Whigs with the rich. Absent "some great modification of the elements of parties all
is hopeless." For the Whig Party to win, it had to get right
with the "principle [of] Democracy."[2]

But during the 1836 campaign, Seward became impressed with the popular appeal of William Henry Harrison's candidacy. Although the party had fallen short of
victory, at least Harrison never had to defend himself—as
Webster did—against (unfounded) opposition charges that
he had once said, "Let Congress take care of the Rich, and
the Rich will take care of the Poor."[3] As "great," "wise," and
"pure" as Webster was, Seward understood that for too
many Americans, the Godlike Daniel embodied an elitist,

East Coast Whiggery that could never win presidential elections in a popular democracy.[4] Despite his patrician upbringing and elite connections, Harrison the military hero and Indian fighter was able to project an image as a man of the people, a leader in sync with the vital principle of democracy. To win in 1840, Seward told Weed, they needed to show "new zeal for the 'hero of Tippecanoe,' as a candidate by continuation."[5]

"THIS CLERK AND CLODHOPPER"

At the time of his defeat to Van Buren, Harrison was already sixty-three years old—a decade older than Van Buren and Webster. Were Harrison to win in 1840, he would be sixty-eight years old when he took the oath of office—every previous president had been between the ages of fifty-seven and sixty-one (George Washington was the youngest and Andrew Jackson the oldest) on the day of their first inauguration. That a rerun of General Harrison's candidacy could excite zeal among younger Whig politicians such as Seward—who was not yet a teenager when the War of 1812 began—is perhaps a measure of the desperation the opposition felt after a third defeat in a row but also a testament to how surprisingly well Harrison had fared in 1836. Whereas Jackson had won Pennsylvania by 25,000 votes in 1832, for instance, Harrison had come within 4,000 votes of beating Van Buren.

That Harrison was made a presidential candidate at all in 1836 came as a surprise to many, including Harrison himself.[6] The names being seriously bandied about by most people in 1833 and 1834 were almost all prominent Washington politicians, such as Senators Henry Clay, Daniel Webster, John Calhoun, and Hugh White, and Supreme Court Justice and Ohio's favorite son John McLean. Not long after learning that an opposition newspaper in Pennsylvania's capital city of Harrisburg had urged his candidacy in December 1834, Harrison wrote to an old soldier friend to relate the "strange . . . news" that "some folks are silly enough to have formed a plan to make a President of the United States out of this Clerk and Clodhopper!" While Harrison worked to make light of this news, declaiming that an "old soldier" and mere county clerk could hardly measure up to the party's "more able and experienced Warriors,"[7] he took the news of his candidacy with the utmost seriousness. Two weeks before writing the self-deprecating letter to his military pal, Harrison wrote to a friendly Pennsylvania state legislator, William Ayres, about criticism of his candidacy that had appeared in a Democratic newspaper in Harrisburg. He regarded this as a "favorable omen," he told Ayres, because "the well-trained Mercenaries . . . who serve

William Henry Harrison. An 1839 lithograph by William Sharp from a painting by the New England artist Albert Gallatin Holt. (Courtesy of the Library of Congress)

under the Van Buren Banner, fire no useless shots. They select for their victims those only whom they fear."[8]

Harrison had been largely out of the public eye during Jackson's presidency. He last held public office in 1829 (apart from his new post as clerk of the Court of Common Pleas of Hamilton County, which his friends engineered in the fall of 1834 "as a sort of retiring pension"[9]), when he finished a little-noticed sixteen-month stint as US minister to Colombia. Thus, when Harrison was first announced at Harrisburg as a "suitable candidate for the Presidency," his supporters not surprisingly felt it necessary to narrate the biography of this "long neglected but meritorious officer" to remind Americans, especially younger ones, of his distinguished record of service to the nation.[10] They stressed Harrison's links to the heroic revolutionary generation: his father, Benjamin Harrison V, signed the Declaration of Independence and served as Virginia's fifth governor. Harrison, they said, was "one of the very few . . . remaining among us, to connect the present with the departed generation" of revolutionary heroes. Moreover, he was a "pioneer of the West" who at the age of eighteen had enlisted in the American army and left the comfort of his Virginia home to brave the "privations of a frontier warfare . . . in the swamps and impenetrable wilderness of the North West." They reminded their readers that while "the subdued and humbled red man" had now "retired beyond the Mississippi," and "the great valleys of the Ohio and Mississippi" were "filled with millions of civilized men," at the time that the young ensign went west in 1791 to fight in the Northwest Indian War (he was posted to Fort Washington, the site of what would become Cincinnati), the land "was roamed over by countless nations of hostile Indians" who "stood in power" upon the banks of every river in the region. His bravery and talents were quickly recognized, and at the age of twenty Harrison was appointed an aide-de-camp and was at General Anthony Wayne's side in the momentous Battle of Fallen Timbers in 1794, "which resulted in the decisive victory over the savages."[11]

However, as with Andrew Jackson, it was the War of 1812 that cemented Harrison's reputation as a war hero and Indian fighter. As commander of the Western Army, Harrison orchestrated the "glorious and memorable" Battle of the Thames, which took place in October 1813 in present-day Ontario and resulted in the killing of the great Shawnee chief Tecumseh, the breakup of Tecumseh's tribal confederacy, and the defeat of the British force under the command of General Henry Proctor. By driving "the enemy from the North Western Territory and [giving] security to the inhabitants of the western frontiers," Harrison had "the honor and glory of closing the long and bloody British and Indian war, which had lasted for more than fifty years."[12]

While promoters of Harrison's candidacy highlighted his military exploits in a bygone age of heroic battles against the British and Indians—in which, it was said, he showed "the true bravery of the school of Washington"[13]—there was far more to Harrison's résumé and ambitions than a career as a military man. After leaving the military in 1798, he was elected the Northwest Territory's (first) delegate to Congress, where he lobbied successfully on behalf of Western settlers and secured passage of the Harrison

Land Act, which made it easier for settlers to buy land. For more than a decade, between 1801 and 1812, he was (the first) governor of the Indiana Territory, during which time he negotiated and signed many treaties with Indian tribes, including the Delaware, Shawnee, Miami, Potawatomi, and Kickapoo, which netted the United States somewhere in the order of fifty million acres, including huge swaths of land in what are now Indiana, Illinois, and Wisconsin. Harrison estimated the cost of acquiring this land to be about two cents an acre. Few if any Americans can match Harrison's record of having taken so much from Native Americans for so little.[14] Harrison was less successful, though, in his effort to persuade Congress to reverse its ban on slavery in the Northwest Territory—a ban that he feared was "driving many valuable citizens possessing slaves to the Spanish side of the Mississippi."[15]

After the War of 1812, Harrison quit the military for a second time and returned to his three-thousand-acre home on the banks of the Ohio River—mostly land bequeathed him by his well-to-do father-in-law, John Cleves Symes—where, "like Cincinnatus, he cultivated his farm for his support."[16] The legendary Roman Cincinnatus had relinquished his plow to rescue the nation—and then, once the republic's safety had been secured, relinquished power and retired to his farm. The politically ambitious Harrison, though, was no Cincinnatus. Upon returning to Ohio, he lost little time in capitalizing on his military fame to run for Congress, motivated in large part by a desire to combat unfounded rumors swirling in Washington that he had profited from kickbacks during the war.[17] His two and a half years in Congress were followed by two years representing Hamilton County in the Ohio state senate. After these two successes, however, his political career sputtered, a casualty in large part of growing populist resentment—fueled by the economic downturn following the Panic of 1819—toward Cincinnati's tight-knit local elite, of which Harrison—a director of the local branch of the national bank—was an integral part. Harrison was also not helped by some of his votes as a member of Congress and state senator—such as his vote against a resolution asking Congress not to allow Missouri to enter the Union as a slave state—which were out of step with the antislavery feelings of many of his Hamilton County constituents.[18]

Harrison, who had been an elector for Monroe in 1820, hoped for a seat in the US Senate, but the state legislature, "largely made up of men from New England," opted instead for the Connecticut man, incumbent senator Benjamin Ruggles, who believed the Constitution obligated Congress to oppose the expansion of slavery in any new territory or state. The

Virginian-born Harrison finished second on each of the four ballots.[19] The following January, in 1822, after the other Ohio Senate seat became vacant, Harrison was again considered but this time was snubbed in favor of another Connecticut man, Governor Ethan Allen Brown, a severe critic of the national bank.[20] Undaunted, Harrison ran for a House seat later that same year but lost yet again, this time to James Gazlay, whom he had defeated in his successful run for the Ohio state senate three years earlier. Gazlay's populist campaign flayed Harrison as an "aristocratic speculator" and a tool of the "old Bank and Court party" that had lined its own pockets while fleecing the people of Cincinnati. A defeated Harrison complained that "the people would listen to nothing" against the "Great Radical Reform" preached by Gazlay.[21]

Harrison's frustration was understandable since, despite his many acres that stretched for five miles along the Ohio River, his proverbial pockets were anything but well-lined. He was deeply in debt and struggling to support his large family, which at the outset of 1822 numbered five sons and four daughters between the ages of eight and twenty-five. Desperate to secure public employment to help alleviate his financial woes, Harrison begged President James Monroe in the summer of 1823 to appoint him minister to Mexico, but to no avail. Finding the post still empty the following summer, Harrison renewed his appeal to the president, citing his financial difficulties and the "interest of a very large family," but again without success.[22]

When a Senate seat opened in Ohio, Harrison organized a full-court press in the state legislature to ensure his selection. He traveled to the state capital in December 1824 to talk with legislators and to line up their support. During the just-completed presidential election, Harrison had shrewdly committed himself to Henry Clay—Harrison had been a leading Clay elector in 1824, while Clay had strongly backed Harrison's case for the Mexico appointment—and the Clay and John Quincy Adams forces, which controlled the state legislature, now returned the favor, selecting Harrison over the incumbent, Ethan Brown, who had refused to commit himself in the presidential election and whose sympathies lay with Jackson rather than the new Adams administration. After four years of pleading, campaigning, and maneuvering, Harrison had finally clawed his way back into public office.[23]

In the Senate, Harrison was a reliable supporter of the Adams administration and a particularly enthusiastic advocate of federally funded "internal improvements"—the roads, canals, turnpikes, and other transportation projects that helped facilitate the movement of goods and people across the United States. But being a US senator was not particularly lucrative work—eight dollars a day when the legislature was in session—and the hard-up Harrison soon began casting around for other, better-paying positions. He lobbied for the vice-presidential nomination but was passed over in favor of Secretary of the Treasury Richard Rush.[24] He also made an unsuccessful pitch to be appointed a major general of the army. He then set his sights on the $9,000-a-year position as minister to Simón Bolívar's Colombia, a post that paid almost five times as much as a US senator made. President Adams, who considered Harrison a "political adventurer" possessed of a "lively and active, but shallow mind," was disgusted by Harrison's "absolutely rabid . . . thirst for lucrative office." Adams wrote in his diary that Harrison wanted "the mission to Colombia much more than it wants him, or than it is wanted by the public interest." But Harrison had influential advocates in the Cabinet, particularly Secretary of State Clay, and so Adams relented and granted Harrison's wish. Unfortunately for Harrison, Adams was defeated in 1828, and Andrew Jackson made replacing Harrison one of his first acts as president—perhaps payback for Harrison's vote as a member of Congress in 1819 to censure General Jackson for having executed two British men in the Seminole War in Florida.[25]

After losing his diplomatic sinecure, Harrison again returned to his farm, not like Cincinnatus or George Washington but as an office seeker who no longer had the ear of those in power. Harrison spent most of the next five years struggling to pay off mounting debts—his and those of several of his unfortunate sons. No wonder Harrison, who had not had a sniff of political office during Jackson's presidency, was genuinely surprised—and delighted—to find his name bandied about as a possible presidential candidate at the close of 1834. The general needed no persuasion to quit his farm at North Bend and resume the rigors of public office.

Given his decidedly mixed and unremarkable record in politics over the preceding two decades, Harrison might seem an unlikely candidate for the nation's highest office. Despite his military fame, he had been defeated in a run for Congress by a rabble-rousing lawyer, losing his adopted home town of Cincinnati by a 2–1 margin.[26] If he couldn't carry his own district, what made people think he could win nationwide?[27] Many within his own party who had had the opportunity to observe him up close during his few years in the US Senate viewed him as a lightweight. Even Clay, who had championed Harrison's cause a decade before, had by 1835 come to regard him as "vain," "weak," and even "incompetent." Moreover, it had been two decades since Harrison had donned a military uniform, and many of his exploits were by now ancient history, barely remembered by many Americans. In marked contrast, when Washington and Jackson first ran for the presidency they had only recently quit the military, and their heroic deeds were still seared in the public consciousness.

But if Harrison was no Washington or even Jackson, he was the closest the Whigs could find. Tippecanoe still retained the aura of a brave frontier fighter and victorious general. Admittedly, embracing Harrison was awkward for some Whigs who, ever since Jackson first ran for the presidency in 1824, had railed against the Democrats for hiding behind a popular war hero and exciting a "military spirit." Embracing Harrison as a candidate meant admitting defeat—or at least, as Clay acknowledged, adopting the weapons of their enemy. "In politics as in War," Clay wrote in the summer of 1835, "a knowledge is acquired of the use of the instruments by which victory is achieved; and the losing party resorts to them." Clay still worried that in embracing Harrison, and emulating what they had so recently excoriated, they were inviting "a succession of Military Presidents," but that was a cost that the Whigs, Clay included, seemed ready to bear in 1836 if it might mean beating Jackson's handpicked successor.[28]

In 1835, Harrison was the party's Hail Mary candidate. The party's prospects for victory looked bleak, and it seemed to many that Harrison's impressive military résumé offered the party its best and maybe only hope of victory—and failing that, a way to minimize the party's losses—in 1836. Like Jackson in 1824 and 1828, General Harrison could run as an outsider, a "favorite citizen and not the candidate of officeholders."[29] Party insiders also hoped that Harrison's relative obscurity—at least relative to the leading Northern candidate at the time, Daniel Webster—and his lack of a clearly defined ideology and issue positions might help unite a party often deeply divided over particular policies, especially banking. To some Whigs, the appeal of Harrison's candidacy was that it enabled the Whigs to sidestep the challenge of articulating a positive vision for the future. Writing to a fellow banker in the summer of 1835, Nicholas Biddle minced no words:

If Gen. Harrison is taken up as a candidate, it will be on account of the past, not the future. Let him then rely entirely on the past. Let him say not one single word about his principles, or his creed—let him say nothing—promise nothing. Let no Committee, no convention—no town meeting ever extract from him a single word, about what he thinks now, or what he will do hereafter. Let the use of pen and ink be wholly forbidden as if he were a mad poet in Bedlam.

Not that Biddle thought Harrison a fool. Indeed, Biddle acknowledged that Harrison "can speak well & write well," but if he wanted to be president, Biddle insisted, "he should neither speak nor write—but be silent—absolutely and inflexibly silent."[30]

Harrison, though, had his own ideas about campaigning. He could not—and did not wish to—pretend to be a blank slate. Ever since entering Congress in 1816, Harrison had written countless public letters and delivered speeches by the score—as the son of a signer of the Declaration of Independence, he was a perennial speaker at Fourth of July celebrations—that staked out positions on issues of the day. Only the previous year, he had delivered a July Fourth oration at Cheviot, Ohio, extolling tariffs and internal improvements and criticizing abolitionists for their "insulting interference with the domestic concerns of the South," warning that it could lead to "indiscriminate slaughter."[31] Granted, he did not have to cast a vote during the whole of Jackson's presidency, which gave Harrison a degree of ideological freedom and flexibility that he took full advantage of.[32] Yet Harrison did have a political record as a senator, member of Congress, and territorial governor to defend and explain. Remaining "absolutely silent" therefore was not an option, nor was it in Harrison's gregarious nature.

From the moment Harrison was presented as a presidential candidate, he promoted his candidacy through carefully crafted public as well as private letters, often designed to reassure Whigs that he was one of them and to woo crucial constituencies. When Kentucky congressman Sherrod Williams asked each candidate in the spring of 1836 to respond publicly with a "frank, plain and full answer" to five specific queries, Harrison expounded at length on his views in ways that largely aligned him with Whig orthodoxy. He expressed strong support for federally subsidized internal improvements, a position consistent with his voting record as a US senator; committed to supporting Clay's bill for distributing the proceeds of public lands to the states; and strongly condemned the Senate's expunging of Jackson's censure. He also elaborated, unprompted, on the Whig philosophy of executive restraint, particularly regarding the veto power. He waffled only—and expertly—on the need for a national bank, saying he would support one if it was proved necessary but that first, "the experiment [of doing without a national bank] should be fairly tried."[33]

More surprisingly, Harrison also paid little heed to Biddle's counsel to avoid speaking. Most presidential candidates at the time, particularly once they had been nominated, avoided touring and speaking for fear of being accused of unseemly electioneering. But Harrison decided it was worth the risk to counteract the idea, which he felt was being "industriously circulated" by Democrats, that he was "an old broken down feeble man."[34] He spent the fall of 1836 on an Eastern tour, attending scores of splendid receptions and public dinners in cities and towns across Virginia, Maryland, Pennsylvania, New York, and New Jersey. In Philadelphia, an estimated thirty thousand came out to celebrate Tippecanoe and to hear Harrison speak briefly opposite Independence Hall, where his father had signed the Declaration of Independence. Reactions to the tour predictably divided along partisan lines, with Democrats assailing Harrison as an "openmouthed electioneerer" unfit for the "high and dignified station" of the presidency and Whigs celebrating the tour as a grand "movement of the People."[35] Harrison had achieved what Seward most wanted for the Whig Party—getting right with the "principle of Democracy"—and at the same time had ingeniously made Democrats sound like nothing so much as disapproving Federalists clucking over an unseemly mingling of the people and their leaders.

Although unable to defeat Van Buren, Harrison waged a campaign that impressed many a Whig. He not only radiated vitality and vigor—"as if he could go a-campaigning for twenty years more,"[36] marveled one observer— but had a knack for connecting with ordinary voters, a skill that Webster would never possess. The campaign also showed the political value of Harrison's immense popularity among veterans—and the sons of veterans, who organized "Tippecanoe Clubs"[37]—a popularity earned not only through his military career as a soldier but by a political career as an advocate of veterans' interests, including during his time in Congress. Harrison had also, again unlike Webster, demonstrated an appeal that cut across a wide swath of Northern and Western states—and although Hugh White had been the Whig candidate throughout the South, Harrison's Virginia roots and evident sympathy for Southern slaveholders gave him an untapped potential there as well. Harrison had also shown an ability to attract Anti-Mason support, a key attribute for any Whig candidate hoping to carry Pennsylvania. Finally, his victory in Ohio showed that Harrison's standing in his home state was sufficiently strong that with Harrison atop the ticket the Whigs could count on carrying a pivotal state that had twice gone for Jackson. Little wonder that Seward urged running Harrison as "a candidate by continuation."

"CANDIDATE BY CONTINUATION"

After Van Buren's victory, Harrison's supporters lost little time in reviving up enthusiasm for a second Harrison campaign. Only a few weeks after the election, Seward persuaded the *Auburn Journal* to come out in support of Harrison again.[38] In the second week of January, seizing on news that a "large number" of citizens in Somerset County in southwestern Pennsylvania had gathered to press Harrison's claim for renomination, a North Carolina paper announced that "Gen. Harrison [was] already in the field."[39] The *New Orleans American* cleverly invoked the trajectory of Jackson's political career in justifying its early call for "nailing the Harrison banner to the mast for a second campaign." Like Jackson, Harrison had "won his country's confidence as a soldier and commander, in war's dread hour, and like him he [had] been defeated in [his] first attempt . . . and like him," the New Orleans paper confidently predicted, "he will succeed in the second." Jackson was bested in 1824 by John Quincy Adams only to get his just reward in a rematch with Adams in 1828, so in 1840, "the people's choice" would prevail over Van Buren at the second trial.[40]

Shortly after Van Buren's inauguration, Colonel Charles Stewart Todd, one of Harrison's biggest boosters in the 1836 campaign, wrote to Harrison from his Kentucky home to counsel that "we must prepare for the next campaign and profit by the errors of the last." In Todd's view, their defeat had been due in large part to the "apathy in our Countrymen," but he was confident that with greater "zeal" and better organization, Harrison could prevail in 1840. Todd, who had served as an aide-de-camp to Harrison during the War of 1812 (a position he owed in no small part to the influence of his father, US Supreme Court Justice Thomas Todd), even offered Harrison advice about who would be the optimal running mate: Kentucky's John Crittenden.[41]

During the 1836 campaign, Todd had worked tirelessly on Harrison's behalf, frequently taking up his pen in the pages of newspapers such as the *Frankfort Commonwealth* and *Louisville Daily Journal* to advance Harrison's candidacy.[42] He had helped Harrison carry Kentucky in 1836 (although, not surprisingly, with far fewer votes than Clay had secured in 1832), but so long as Clay remained in the race as a candidate in the 1840 contest there were severe limits on what the zealous Todd could do to help Harrison.[43] Crittenden, the man Todd hoped to corral as a vice-presidential nominee, was laboring tirelessly for Clay's candidacy,[44] as were most of Kentucky's other leading politicians. If a Harrison candidacy was going to be successfully renewed, it would have to be launched not in Kentucky but in Harrison's adopted home state of Ohio, a state that Clay had lost in 1832 by 5,000 votes and that Harrison had carried in 1836 by 8,000 votes.

Harrison and his supporters in Ohio were only too aware that it was incumbent on the Buckeye State to take the first step in putting Harrison's name forward as a presidential candidate. They would have felt even more urgency after Webster rolled onto Harrison's home turf of Cincinnati in the first week of June as part of his grand tour of the West. Harrison was tasked with introducing the great Webster, who used his speech to delight the partisan crowd by excoriating the Van Buren administration's ruinous policies.[45] The campaign was well and truly underway—the time had arrived for Ohio to act.

On July 4, 1837, as many as a thousand Ohio Whigs descended on the capital city of Columbus for a party convention. Although largely focused on state issues, the convention issued a formal call for a national nominating convention, the first Whig state party convention to do so. The convention disagreed, though, on how far it should go in declaring support for the state's favorite son. The convention's committee on national affairs proposed a resolution that generously praised Harrison but fell well short of nominating him. The resolution read,

> That this Convention, though believing that their fellow-citizens of the State would prefer to select William Henry Harrison, whose public services and qualifications, of talents, experience, magnanimity, justice, and patriotism, they know and appreciate; yet they feel confidence, in giving the assurance that, should another person be selected, be he of the South, or of the Middle, or of the North, he will be sustained, in Ohio, with all the power, zeal, and energy, that would be employed in support of their own favorite fellow-citizen.

The resolution's wording spurred "an animated and eloquent discussion" as well as several amendments, but ultimately the convention settled on the original resolution, which passed with only a single dissenting voice. The emphasis at the convention—and in the press coverage of the campaign—was more on the importance of securing party unity than on ensuring Harrison's candidacy.[46]

Many of Harrison's supporters were underwhelmed by the actions of the Ohio convention. Some of them distrusted the idea of a national convention, which they thought would likely be controlled by the political insiders, who they believed were more likely to back Clay or Webster than a party outsider such as Harrison.[47] But there was also growing concern that the preoccupation with preserving party unity was playing into Clay's hands and blunting the momentum of Harrison's campaign by continuation. Even Weed, who in the early days of the Van Buren presidency had insisted that Harrison was "our only man,"[48] was now pressing rival candidates to keep their powder dry in the name of party unity. With the 1836 election results fading into the distance and the economy worsening, Harrison's star, which had shone so brilliantly at the outset of the year, seemed by the end of the year to dim behind Clay's rising fortunes. An anxious Harrison supporter in Virginia wrote to Harrison in the final days of 1837, "What in the name of heavens are your frends [sic] waiting for in Cincinnati? . . . The whole United States are waiting anxiously for Ohio to take the lead."[49]

Harrison immediately set about ensuring that his friends acted. On January 16, 1838, Harrison's supporters convened in Cincinnati's courthouse to nominate "the FARMER OF NORTH BEND" for president. They declared themselves opposed to a national convention and to any attempt by "the politicians of our party" to pass over Harrison in favor of another candidate. The party, they insisted, was "bound in honor to redeem the pledge" made at the close of the 1836 election that Harrison, having proven himself "the favorite of the people" and "taken us to the very verge of victory," should be given the "opportunity of measuring strength" once more against Van Buren. Nefarious efforts by politicians in Eastern states to push the choice of the nominee off into the future only weakened the party by exciting ambition among various rivals. "The delay which has already taken place," they warned darkly, "begins to threaten the disunion of our party."[50]

These sentiments mirrored Harrison's own suspicions and frustrations, which he had expressed only the day before in a letter to Noah Noble, who had recently finished two terms as governor of Indiana. Harrison vented about a Whig establishment determined to block his candidacy and elevate Clay instead. "All the Members of Congress are in favor of Mr. Clay," he complained, and "the leaders of both parties are playing into each other's hands to effect a common object." Even the newspapers were in on the conspiracy, as they refused to publish his speeches. He was particularly unhappy at the efforts of New York City's editors to "dictate to the people of the state." All were examples, he grumbled, of the concerted effort and "unworthy means which have been taken to force me out of the list of candidates."[51]

Despite the distrust of the Whig Party establishment harbored by Harrison and many of his backers, most Whigs, even those who supported

Harrison, continued to think a national convention both necessary and desirable, as was evident at the Indiana state nominating convention that convened in the capital city of Indianapolis the week following the Cincinnati gathering. Unlike the Cincinnati meeting, which had consisted of a band of Harrison's most devoted supporters, the Indiana convention included a more diverse group of 230 delegates from counties across the state, each with a different set of instructions. Some, such as the delegates from Wayne County, were instructed to insist on the paramount importance of party unity; others were commanded to press General Harrison's claim to the presidency. In the end, they compromised. They passed one resolution naming Harrison as "the choice of the people of Indiana for the next presidency" and another that pledged to support Clay, that "patriotic statesman," "should he be the choice of a national convention." They agreed that a national convention was essential to avoid a fragmented vote that risked having the selection of the president thrown into the House of Representatives.[52]

The meetings in Indiana and Cincinnati helped to give Harrison's candidacy a renewed sense of momentum that many of his supporters feared had been in danger of petering out. Harrison's cause in the North was also given an unexpected boost by the duel at the end of February that resulted in the death of Maine congressman Jonathan Cilley. Not only was Cilley killed by a friend of Clay's, Kentucky House member William Graves, but rumors swirled that Kentucky's senior senator—who had fought a duel in 1826 with fellow senator John Randolph of Roanoke—had written the challenge that Graves issued to Cilley.[53] Cilley's death not only helped to derail the efforts by Clay's allies to have the Maine legislature endorse Clay that spring but also provided Harrison with an opportunity to pen a public letter condemning dueling—and to draw an implicit but sharp contrast with his Kentucky rival. Written in early April, in response to an inquiry from a New Jersey Whig, the movingly personal letter detailed the profound aversion to dueling that Harrison had acquired as a young military officer who had witnessed not only the senseless slaughter of honorable men but the "agony" suffered by the successful duelist, who was consigned to a haunted "life of bitter regret and sorrow." Harrison boasted that under his command of the Army of the Northwest, "there was not a single duel, nor, as far as I know, a challenge given."[54]

Although Harrison's antidueling letter attracted favorable attention, many newspaper editors aligned with Clay declined to publish it, much to the frustration of Harrison and his supporters. Taking Harrison's side on this matter was Charles Hammond, the influential editor of the *Cincinnati Gazette*.[55] After publishing the letter in May, Hammond scolded the Clay press for refusing to do the same. Hammond professed that although he favored Clay's candidacy, "fair play" required that the Whig press publish a letter that was "worthy of a high-souled patriot and Christian philosopher."[56]

At the end of May, two weeks after the *Cincinnati Gazette*'s publication of Harrison's antidueling letter, two thousand Ohio Whigs, representing 90 percent of the state's seventy-three counties, convened once more to nominate candidates for statewide office. The delegates endorsed the congressional Whigs' call for a national convention to be held in Harrisburg in December 1839 and adopted a resolution expressing "undiminished confidence in Harrison" and presenting the general's "name to the National convention as a candidate for the Presidency." But the Ohio delegates also pledged their "cordial support" to Clay or Webster should they be selected by the national convention. Ohio's Whigs were still privileging party unity over their preference for their native son. Clay privately judged the "proceedings of the Ohio convention . . . perfectly satisfactory."[57]

After the Ohio convention, Harrison felt he had little choice but to pledge support for a Whig national nominating convention—and to the nominee selected by the convention. At a huge July Fourth celebration in the northeastern Ohio town of Massillon, Harrison generously sang the praises of Clay and Webster and, for the first time, vowed "to submit his claims for the Presidency to the decision of a national convention."[58] Privately, though, Harrison fumed about having been backed into a corner that he saw as a plot by party insiders to nominate the less popular Clay. To his trusted Pennsylvania ally William Ayres, Harrison complained that the idea of a Whig national convention had been "proposed for the purpose of procuring the nomination of Mr. Clay with or without the consent of the body of the people," and he chastised his naive allies for having "incautiously consented to the measure."[59] Harrison believed that Clay stood "no chance of success but by means of a packed convention, one which will represent the politicians and not the people."[60]

Harrison also continued to feel aggrieved by the Whig press, which he still believed was doing Clay's bidding. Toward the end of the summer, he complained bitterly to Ayres that the pro-Clay press "never publish any speech of mine . . . nor even any proceedings of the people which have the least tendency to show my favorable standing. By this base conduct and by publishing every thing which is favorable to Mr. C. the people in different sections of the Country are deceived as to our respective strength." Because so much of the Whig press was under the control of the Clay forces, Harrison carped, "the people in the Southern States and many of the Eastern are under the impression that Mr. Clay is all powerful in Missouri, Illinois, Indiana and Ohio," whereas "the truth" was that in a general election Clay would lose the first three and carry Ohio only with the "greatest . . . difficulty."[61]

Harrison burned with ambition for the presidency—and simmered with distrust of Clay and his partisans—yet publicly continued to cultivate the pose of the humble "old soldier" reluctant to leave his beloved farm for the vagaries of politics. Introduced at Massillon "as the Cincinnatus who may . . . be again called from the plough to hold the reins of state," Harrison declaimed any ambition to give up the "delightful occupation of the husbandmen" for the "troubles and mortifications" of office. This humble soldier, he said, had "never sought the means of placing himself in the situation of competitor to the distinguished men who have from time to time been brought forward as candidates for the highest office in the gift of the people." He stood before them as a candidate for the presidency only because he had been summoned by "the voice of the people."[62]

While Harrison disavowed politics and politicians as usual, he did not shrink from the political topics of the day. In Massillon, he spoke "at length"—and in orthodox Whig tones—on the most important and divisive issue of the day: the currency and banking. He deplored the "senseless cry" against banks, which, while certainly making the rich richer, did not, contrary to the belief of the hard-money radicals, make the poor poorer. Instead, banks were the essential means by which the poor became rich. Banks were what enabled "men of wealth to embark in enterprises useful to the country," such as internal improvements and manufacturing, which "vastly benefitted . . . the laboring, the industrious part of the community." There was no class conflict because the "credit system" made everybody better off. Harrison professed that he was a "bank man . . . because he was a democrat."[63] The old military hero sounded just like Clay or Webster.[64]

Harrison's July Fourth address at Massillon was carefully designed not only to demonstrate his Whig bona fides but also to introduce him to a northeastern area of Ohio that he had never before visited and where his principal rivals for the nomination were relatively strong—Harrison's power base was in the southwest portion of the state.[65] A report from a Whig correspondent covering the festivities for a Cleveland paper suggests that Harrison's speech had the desired effect. "With all my preference for Mr. Clay for the Presidency," the correspondent told his readers, "I must say I was agreeably disappointed in General Harrison, [whose] open, frank, off-hand manner of speaking was highly interesting, and won golden opinions from all."[66]

After speaking at Massillon, Harrison journeyed farther east (and south), visiting, among other towns, Carrollton, Steubenville (which bordered what was then Virginia and is today West Virginia), and Cadiz, where he was honored with large public dinners and copious toasts.[67] The peripatetic Harrison was on the move again in the latter part of September, this time to attend a convention of the Whig Young Men of the State of Ohio in Mount Vernon, about 170 miles northeast of his North Bend home. At the convention, Harrison was introduced to "deafening cheers" and "replied at some length" in a speech setting out his "political doctrines" as well as defending himself against "the aspersions" cast upon his character by his "political enemies." The convention, which defined the division between the parties as "those who are for, and those who are against the concentration of all power in the Executive branch of the Government," unanimously resolved to recommend Harrison "to the people of the United States as a candidate for the President," although adding that it had "equal confidence in the qualifications of Clay and Webster."[68]

By the end of September, Harrison's star appeared to be on the rise again. Robert Charles Winthrop of Massachusetts was not alone in judging—in a letter dated September 22, 1838, the week after the Boston *Atlas* had dropped its bombshell endorsing Harrison for president—that "the idea that Harrison is to be the man . . . is gaining ground rapidly."[69] Harrison, acutely conscious of the upswing in his political fortunes, was desperate to preserve his newfound advantage. On October 1, he wrote anxiously to Ayres about the upcoming Anti-Masonic national convention that had been called for the middle of November. He had learned that he would soon be contacted to find out whether he would accept the Anti-Masonic nomination, but while he of course wanted the Anti-Masons' support, particularly in Pennsylvania, he worried that it would bring him into "immediate collision" with the Whig Party's plan for a national convention. Although Harrison still grumbled about the Whig convention plan, he and his allies were now pledged to abide by its decision, and, he told Ayres, "my prospects are now so fair that nothing ought to be done to risk . . . giving disquiet to any of those who wish to support me."[70] Harrison did not want to alienate his Anti-Masonic friends in Pennsylvania, whose support had been pivotal in making him rather than Webster the Whig candidate across the North in 1836,[71] but he also knew that Anti-Masons were a fast-receding political force and that only a candidate backed by a unified Whig Party could hope to defeat Van Buren in 1840.

With the help of Ayres, Harrison negotiated an acceptance letter that made his acceptance of the Anti-Masonic nomination conditional on his nomination by the Whig Party. Harrison's acceptance letter also side-stepped the subject of Masonry altogether and instead articulated the principles that would guide his conduct in the presidency—principles that lay at the core of Whig Party identity. Chief among these were a restrained use of the veto power and removal power as well as deference to the secretary of the treasury. He also repeated the pledge that he had made earlier in the year to serve only one term and vowed to "leave the whole business of making the laws" to Congress, "the department to which the Constitution has exclusively assigned" the law-making power. He would, in short, be the anti-Jackson—and the kind of executive that Clay, Webster, and the rest of the Whig Party had been clamoring for ever since Old Hickory's 1832 bank veto.[72]

By the fall of 1838, however, the party of Jackson and Van Buren was showing, as one Whig paper put it, "an alarming capacity of renovation and revival." No Democratic victory that fall was more alarming to Whigs than the Democrats' triumph in Harrison's own state of Ohio, an election that saw the Whig Party "capsized in all quarters." Upon learning of the party's comprehensive defeat in Ohio, a despairing Millard Fillmore—originally a Webster supporter who had since come around to Harrison—wrote to Weed that he was "heart-sick of our Whig Party" and "now regard[ed] all as lost, irrevocably gone." If only, Fillmore lamented, "that Harrison flag [had been] nailed to our mast. It would have saved Ohio."[73] Ironically, as Fillmore's response suggests, the Whig Party's defeat in Ohio strengthened Harrison's cause because party leaders realized that they could no longer count on Ohio as safely in the Whig column without Harrison at the top of the ticket—and no Whig was going to the White House without Ohio. Harrison, as the Chicago American expressed it, was the "tower of strength, around which the broken fragments of that branch of our army may rally with safety."[74]

With the economy seemingly recovering and the Democratic Party recouping many of the seats it had lost in 1837 and the spring of 1838, Harrison's candidacy picked up steam. Among the Whigs lining up behind Harrison in the fall of 1838 was a young Illinois lawyer and politician, Abraham Lincoln. Lincoln would famously eulogize Clay as his "beau ideal of a statesman," but in 1838, in the pages of the Sangamo Journal, he endorsed

Harrison, whom he hailed as the "father of the North Western Territory." Nowhere in Lincoln's endorsement, revealingly, was there any mention of Democratic or Whig policies, banking or currency, or even executive power. Lincoln's case rested entirely on Harrison's "arduous and valuable" services—and, bizarrely, on the need to reward such services lest the youth of the county learn not to emulate these "noble examples."[75]

Harrison leaned into the notion that he was, as one Ohio paper put it, the "veteran Father of the West."[76] Writing in December to Ohio's recently elected antislavery congressman, Joshua Giddings, Harrison pitched himself as "the oldest and most extensively known of the Veteran Pioneers." Jackson had won the support of "almost all of the pioneers and old soldiers of the west," but with Jackson now "out of the way," Harrison predicted, their support would come to him.[77] With Democrats on the rebound, the Whig nominee needed to be able to win over Jackson voters—and Harrison's military record offered the prospect of a cross-party appeal that Clay, the mere party politician, could not match.

While the Whig Party's devastating losses in Harrison's home state of Ohio—as well as the Anti-Masons' loss of the governorship in Pennsylvania—ironically helped to bolster Harrison's candidacy, the morale-boosting gubernatorial triumph in New York of one of Harrison's earliest supporters, William Henry Seward, would, equally ironically, end up dealing a nearly fatal blow to Harrison's presidential prospects. Seward's defeat of the Democratic incumbent, William Marcy—who as a US senator had defended Jackson's removal policy by arguing that "to the victor belong the spoils"—lifted the spirits of Whigs across the country, but the jockeying for the Whig gubernatorial nomination had badly damaged Seward's and Weed's relationship with Harrison's supporters in New York. Francis Granger, who had been Harrison's vice-presidential candidate in 1836, had desperately wanted to be the Whig choice for governor, but "the Dictator"—as many had taken to calling Weed—was determined to secure the post for Seward. Weed found the allies he needed in Clay's New York City friends, who opposed Granger in large part because he was too closely identified with Harrison. The consequences of the jostling for position, writes historian Robert Gray Gunderson, was that "Seward lost Granger's friendship and gained the spirited animosity of the Harrison forces" and that "Weed lost much of his enthusiasm for Old Tippecanoe." Weed still had no intention of settling on Clay, who he was convinced would sink the Whigs in New York and the nation, but he was prepared to consider other "available" candidates should the right one come along. Eventually he found one—another general, no less.[78]

GENERAL SCOTT: THE DARK HORSE CANDIDATE

This new challenge to Harrison's nomination emerged from an unlikely source: a rebellion against British rule in "Upper Canada" (essentially Ontario) that broke out toward the end of 1837. Americans who lived near the Canadian border—especially in the northwestern part of New York—generally sympathized with the rebels, many of whom came from the US and dreamed of making Canada into an independent republic. The small rebellion was easily quashed, but some of the rebels fled across the border to raise arms and recruit men, with some success. Several hundred "would-be liberators" turned Navy Island on the Niagara River—in Canadian waters—into a military outpost, which was supplied and reinforced by an American steamship, the *Caroline*. On the night of December 29, 1837, a band of Canadian militiamen seized the boat, which was moored at a fort on the American side of the river, drove off the crew, and set it ablaze and hurtling over Niagara Falls. The raid, which resulted in one American death, provoked outrage among Americans, and many in western New York clamored for revenge and even war.[79]

President Van Buren, who had served as minister to Great Britain during Jackson's presidency, had no interest in allowing this international incident to escalate into a war between the US and Britain. What little army the United States possessed already had its hands full in the Southeast, where it was attempting to drive the Seminole Indians out of Florida. To keep the peace on the northern border, Van Buren dispatched General Winfield Scott.

General Scott was an inspired choice for this mission. He was a legend on the Niagara Frontier for his heroic exploits in one of the bloodiest battles in the War of 1812: the Battle of Lundy's Lane, also known as the Battle of Niagara Falls, which took place on July 25, 1814. Three weeks before that, the twenty-eight-year-old brigadier general had inflicted heavy damage on the British in the Battle of Chippawa, only about a mile upstream from Niagara Falls. It was in Buffalo that General Scott had rigorously drilled his troops for up to ten hours a day to prepare them for battle against the well-armed and well-trained British army. Both these famous battles, moreover, involved American forces crossing the Niagara River to invade Canada. Now fifty-one years old, Scott arrived in Buffalo with a moral authority that no living American could match. He would need all that authority in facing down the region's hotheads and warmongers, particularly since he arrived in Buffalo without an army, apart from a smattering of garrisoned soldiers that he picked up along the way.

When Scott arrived in Buffalo, he found the "whole town . . . a blaze . . . with threats of vengeance."[80] Some feared that Canada would invade Buffalo; more demanded that the US government invade Canada. All seemed to think war likely. Scott's first task was to persuade the rebels (known on the American side as the patriots) to evacuate their position on Navy Island. He immediately met with the rebel leader—a young Van Rensselaer possessed of "more ambition than brains"[81]—and tried to impress upon him that from a military point of view his situation was hopeless. Sensing that a logistical lesson alone was not enough, Scott upbraided the young belligerent for violating American neutrality and warned him that he would seize the island outpost as soon as he was authorized to do so. After a night of bombardment from the Canadian shore, Van Rensselaer and the rebels evacuated the island's fort the next day, and Scott had Van Rensselaer arrested.[82]

Having defused the Navy Island crisis, Scott, in full-dress uniform, "laden with medals and trimmed with gold epaulets," took his case to the people of Buffalo. Speaking before a large crowd, the towering six-foot-five general acknowledged that he appeared "without troops and without arms, save the blade by my side" and was therefore "in your power." But "all of you," he continued with his back to the Niagara River, "know that I am ready to do what my country and what my duty demands. I tell you then, except it be over my body, you shall *not* pass this line—you shall *not* embark." Scott's display of bravado, which met with "the applause of listening multitudes," seemed to have its desired effect on the citizenry. By the end of January, Scott reported that the border had been pacified. He headed back to New York City, receiving a hero's welcome en route in the state capital of Albany.[83]

Upon arriving in New York City, however, he received word of new troubles on the frontier, this time in Ohio. The indefatigable general immediately returned to the frontier and spent the remainder of the winter "hurrying back and forth along the northern frontier," trying to extinguish trouble and "exert his influence for peace." As Scott later recalled, that winter he "posted himself nowhere, but was by turns rapidly everywhere, and always in the midst of the greater difficulties." All across the frontier, from Michi-

Many of the most famous images of Winfield Scott are from his days as a corpulent Civil War general unable even to ride a horse. This image, though, which is from two decades earlier, captures the imposing general that a young Ulysses Grant remembered as "the finest specimen of manhood my eyes had ever beheld." (Courtesy of Collections of Maine Historical Society)

gan to Vermont, he addressed crowds, large and small, rallying "the friends of law and order." By the middle of March, the rebellion seemed to have "petered out," and an exhausted Scott returned to New York City with a newfound reputation as the "Great Pacificator"—an appellation heretofore reserved for Henry Clay. The nation's most famous active military general was fast becoming its most famous peacemaker.[84]

When the troubles on the northern frontier recurred in the fall, President Van Buren again summoned Scott to work his magic. Scott arrived in Cleveland in December to find the border again "in a state of high agitation" after Canadian forces had captured and shot without trial four rebels who had crossed the St. Clair River from Detroit and attacked the town of Windsor. In Cleveland, Sandusky, and Detroit, he pacified angry crowds both by promising to stand "shoulder to shoulder" with them should it come to war and insisting that law-abiding American citizens were duty bound to reject vigilante violence. In ten days, he traveled 350 miles along the frontier, from Michigan to Vermont, everywhere "preaching his message of restraint."[85]

While the "excitement" along the northwest frontier subsided, a potentially more ominous border conflict with the British sprang up in Maine after the governor sent a posse to arrest Canadian "timber poachers" in the forests of Aroostook, lands that both the United States and Britain claimed. Events rapidly escalated in February, with both sides mobilizing militias and demanding that the other side vacate the disputed territory. This time there seemed a genuine danger of being drawn into an unwanted war with the British.[86] Once again, Scott was the man Van Buren tasked with achieving "peace with honor."[87]

Scott understood that the situation in Maine required a vastly different approach than the one he had taken with the patriot rebels along the northern frontier.[88] Speeches and bravado would accomplish nothing. Instead, he played the peacemaker by schmoozing with Maine's most influential legislators and the governor. "A feast is a great peacemaker," Scott later remarked, "worth more than all the arts of diplomacy." Both Whigs and Democrats were persuaded to entrust the border question to Scott, who then leveraged his close personal friendship with his fellow general, the lieutenant governor of New Brunswick, Sir John Harvey, to negotiate a peaceful settlement to the standoff. The Aroostook War ended without a single casualty.[89]

By the time Scott left Maine in early April 1839, he seemed the most celebrated man in America. Newspapers across the country sang his praises for keeping the United States out of war. Public dinners were given in his honor in cities across the Northeast, and he was the guest of honor at a White House dinner hosted by the president. His arduous peacemaking tour of duty—which his friend Philip Hone estimated at 4,700 miles—had made him "the observed of all observers."[90] It also made him much talked about as a presidential candidate.

Even before he embarked on his peacemaking role in Maine, Scott had cause to think about his presidential prospects. In early February 1839, he felt the need to write a "disclaimer" to Clay from Utica, New York, informing his Kentucky friend that during his extensive travels through the Northern states, he had been "approached by persons . . . almost every where, who have tendered me assurances of eventual support for the office of President at the next election." Those assurances, he told Clay, "have come from friends of yourself, of General Harrison, Mr. Webster & Mr. Van Buren" who doubted the success of their "own favorite candidate [and] looked to me as [their] *second* choice." Scott assured Clay that he had told everybody that he was not a politician or even a statesman but merely a military man who was "absolutely indifferent whether I ever reached the office of President." Clay could not have been reassured by these professions of indifference, particularly when Scott added that he had told "some leading Whigs" who urged his candidacy "more strongly" that he might consider entering the field should the convention fail to nominate a candidate.[91]

As General Scott labored to secure peace in Maine, chatter was fast picking up about the possibility of a President Scott. In the middle of March, with Maine still teetering on the verge of war, around eighty Democrats in Rochester, New York, called for a public meeting later that month to determine "such measures as may be deemed advisable" to secure Scott's election as the next president of the United States.[92] The Boston *Atlas* reported that it had "heard on good authority" that while Scott was in Augusta he had been approached by a delegation of Whig legislators about the presidential nomination, but they had been rebuffed by the general, who said that any "movement of that sort" must wait until after he had concluded his negotiations.[93] On the penultimate day of March, the war now averted, the *New-York American,* which two years before had been among the first newspapers to endorse Daniel Webster, became the first to call for General Scott to be made the next president of the United States.[94]

That both Democrats and Whigs could dream of a Scott candidacy speaks to the general's appeal as a military man above, if not indifferent to, party politics.[95] But if General Scott played his partisanship close to the vest, his political sympathies were entirely with the Whigs. As Scott told Clay, "In my bosom, I . . . condemn almost every leading measure of the late & present administrations, & at least seven in every ten appointments which the two had made."[96] If Scott was going to be a presidential candidate, it would be as a Whig.

When Weed first received word of the Scott nomination by the meeting of Rochester Democrats—whom he knew well from a decade of doing political battle with them as the youthful editor of the *Rochester Telegraph*—he used the occasion to skewer Van Buren in the pages of the *Albany Evening Journal*. Deprived of the "'bone and muscle' of the old Jackson party" in Rochester, Weed taunted, Van Burenism "will sink into nothingness." All he would say about Scott at the time, however, was "There are worse men than Gen. Scott for President."[97]

Weed could not but be impressed by the surging enthusiasm for Scott, especially in western New York, which had hitherto been Harrison country. From Buffalo's Whig congressman Millard Fillmore, Weed received a report at the beginning of May of the "strong feeling pervading all the Western part of the State for Scott"—and a diminished interest in Harrison. By keeping the nation out of war, Fillmore noted, Scott had "gained infinitely upon the affections and confidence of the thinking portion of the community."[98] James Gordon Bennett's New York *Herald* marveled that Scott's name "runs like fire upon the mountains." Everywhere, it seemed, there was a "general and spontaneous movement burning to bring [Scott] out as a candidate for the Presidency."[99]

The independent-minded Bennett was among Scott's strongest early backers. Bennett rhapsodized that Scott was "the most extraordinary and the most perfect man," whose "character more resembles the exquisite checks and balances of Washington, than any man living."[100] Bennett saw in Scott a fresh alternative to "all the rotten politicians now before the public" and the only candidate who could regenerate a country that had become corrupted by "the politicians of both parties."[101]

Weed shared none of Bennett's disdain for politicians. Indeed, the Whig Party boss epitomized the kind of wire puller that Bennett disparaged.[102] But the two newspaper editors—one proudly independent, the other fiercely partisan—were in full agreement that Van Buren had to be defeated. Unlike Bennett, Weed was not convinced that Scott was the only opposition man who could beat Van Buren,[103] although he fully endorsed Bennett's view that Clay atop the ticket would doom the Whigs, most especially in New York. For Weed, Scott's emergence as a candidate posed both opportunity and danger. The danger was that a rising Scott would eclipse Harrison and, by dividing the anti-Clay forces, pave the way for Clay's nomination and a calamitous defeat for the Whig Party in New York. The opportunity was that with the immensely popular Scott at the head of the ticket, the Whigs would sweep New York and ride into the White House in 1840.

As a fourteen-year-old boy in the Onondaga Valley in the spring of 1812, Weed had watched in wonder as Scott, and "with him an entrancing array of plumes and epaulettes, [and] companies of soldiers with fife and drum," marched to war with the British on the Niagara Frontier.[104] He had tried then to join Scott's ranks but had been thwarted by his age and foul-tempered employer. Now the state's most influential Whig editor and political operative, Weed had to decide whether he would enlist his formidable forces in a Scott presidential campaign.

5

THE ROAD TO THE
WHIG CONVENTION

Winfield Scott had the Whigs in Congress to thank for his emergence as a possible presidential candidate, specifically their decision in April 1838 to call for a national nominating convention in December 1839 rather than earlier in the year, as both Henry Clay and William Henry Harrison had hoped. The later date was pressed by Daniel Webster's allies—who thought delay would harm Clay's chances and might help Webster's—as well as by state party leaders in key Northern states, including Pennsylvania, New York, and Ohio, who preferred to wage the fall state elections focused on the failures of Van Burenism rather than defending their own party's choice for president.[1]

Although congressional Whigs had hoped that putting off a decision about a nominee would help unify the party, the party seemed to be growing ever more divided into two warring camps, neither willing to make way for the other. "This question of Clay or Harrison," the *Cincinnati Gazette* lamented in May 1839, "is fast festering into an incurable ulcer."[2] Harrison's allies assumed the populist position, accusing Clay's well-connected supporters of rigging the game to shut out the people's favorite. Clay's friends charged Harrison's with splitting the party and plotting to disregard the will of the convention if their man was not selected.[3] Scott's candidacy found fertile ground in the spring of 1839 because it seemed to offer a way out of the logjam in which the Whig Party found itself, particularly in New York, where the two rivals had seemingly checkmated each other.

Back in the fall of 1838, after several demoralizing defeats for the Whig Party, a glum Clay had flirted with the idea of withdrawing from the race.[4] Had the Whigs lost New York, he might well have done so—certainly he would have come under strong pressure to quit the race for the good of the party. Even with the victory in New York (which saw the Whigs pick up eleven congressional seats), when the Twenty-Fifth Congress convened for its final, lame-duck session in December, there prevailed, according to Millard Fillmore, "a very general notion" that Clay would withdraw, leaving Harrison to "receive the nomination without opposition."[5] However, the "glad and glorious tidings" of the New York elections in November banished any thoughts Clay had of quitting the contest.[6] By January 1839, he was reporting that his friends in Congress, who had initially been "discouraged" by the fall results, had "recovered" and were now "nearly as confident" as they had been when Congress adjourned in the summer of 1838.[7] By the close of the Twenty-Fifth Congress's final session in March 1839, Clay was triumphant, reporting that the pessimism had "entirely dissipated" and that "the general conviction was that my cause was constantly gaining strength, and that I should *certainly* receive the nomination of the Nat[ional] Convention."[8] Clay's revived confidence in his presidential prospects, in Van Buren's defeat ("If we do not beat him, we deserve to be gibbetted," he told one correspondent[9]), and in electing anti–Van Buren majorities in the Twenty-Sixth Congress[10] meant there was no chance Clay would step aside for Harrison so long as a road to the presidency remained open. Clay was increasingly convinced that there was such a route—one that went through the South.

CLAY'S SOUTHERN STRATEGY

Whereas Webster initially embarked on a nomination strategy aimed at mobilizing the North, Clay hit upon the opposite strategy of securing the slaveholding South. Clay believed that he was the only candidate who could win over the disaffected Jackson voters in the South who had voted for Hugh White in 1836 rather than support the New Yorker Van Buren.[11] The lynchpin of Clay's Southern strategy—as it had been for Van Buren's party-building efforts in the 1820s—was Virginia. And the key to winning Virginia (as well as New York), Clay concluded, was securing the cooperation of Whigs and self-described Conservative Democrats, who opposed the administration's "hard-money" policies.[12]

Shortly after arriving back in the nation's capital in December 1838, Clay wrote to Francis Brooke to press his case. Given the "unfortunate divisions" within the party, Clay thought it "highly expedient" that the Whigs in the Virginia legislature endorse him as soon as possible. Once the Whig legislators in Richmond acted, then their endorsement would "probably be followed by & seconded [by the Whig legislators] at Albany," and "the question would be settled." In this opinion, he assured Brooke, "the most intelligent of our party, with whom I have conversed, fully concur."[13] A month later, he renewed his appeal to Brooke, emphasizing that it was "of very great importance" that Virginia should express its support for Clay. Such an expression would be a rallying point that would have "great, if not decisive . . . influence elsewhere."[14] Virginia's endorsement, Clay predicted the following week, would enable the "current," hitherto impeded, to "burst forward with accumulated strength" and wash away the "seeds of discontent" that had been sown within the party.[15]

This was the strategic backdrop for Clay's celebrated "abolition speech" in the US Senate on February 7, 1839.[16] In the speech, Clay hammered the "ultra Abolitionists" for ignoring the limits on federal power, disregarding property rights, holding the South up to "scorn and contempt," and favoring the "unnatural amalgamation" of the races. They were fanatics who allowed "a single idea" to drive out all thought of consequences and who depicted "the alleged horrors of slavery . . . in the most glowing and exaggerated colors." Their purpose in pursuing their "wild and ruinous" scheme of immediate abolition, he warned, was not only to set white and black laborers in ruinous competition with each other but to "contaminate the industrious and laborious classes . . . at the North by a revolting admixture of the black element." In the slave states, their "mad and fatal course" could result only in a race war that would "end in the extermination or subjugation of the one race or the other." Abolition could mean one of only two things: "the extermination of the blacks, or their ascendancy over the whites." Clay said that while he was "no friend of slavery," he preferred "the liberty of my own race to that of any other race." The abolitionists, he condescended, should find other "objects of humanity and benevolence" that were "more harmless" and did "not threaten to deluge our country in blood." The country should instead entrust the slavery problem to time. It was likely, he speculated hopefully, that in a couple of hundred years the higher birth rate of whites would mean that "but few vestiges of the black race will remain among our posterity." For nearly two hours, the supposed Great Pacificator went on in this vein.[17]

This was the speech about which Clay was supposed to have famously said, "I had rather be right than be president."[18] In fact, the speech was a

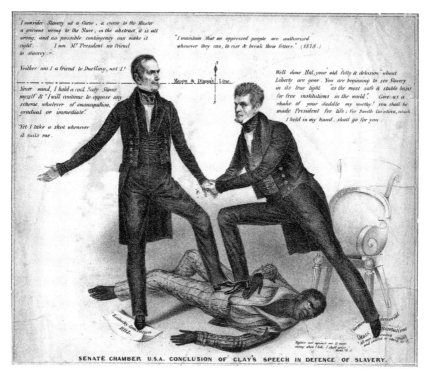

Following his antiabolition speech on the Senate floor on February 7, 1839, Clay was sharply criticized by many antislavery advocates. This cartoon takes aim at Clay's hypocrisy and duplicity on slavery. At the top (above the Mason-Dixon Line) is a quotation from Clay's previous declaration (from an 1836 speech to the Kentucky Colonization Society in Lexington) that he considered "slavery as a curse, a curse to the Master, a grievous wrong to the Slave" and that "no possible contingency can make it right." Below the line, the cartoon notes Clay's ownership of a "cool Sixty Slaves" and quotes his opposition to "any scheme . . . of emancipation gradual or immediate." With one foot, he treads on a Kentucky antislavery resolution, and with the other, with the help of John Calhoun, he pins down a defenseless slave, who quotes from the Bible ("Rejoice not against me, O mine enemy; when I fall, I shall arise."). Calhoun shakes Clay by the hand, congratulating him on finally "beginning to see Slavery in its true light" and giving up "your old folly & delusion about Liberty." Calhoun suggests, "you shall be made President for life; for South Carolina, which I hold in my hand, shall go for you." (Courtesy of the Library Company of Philadelphia)

carefully calibrated plank in his Southern strategy, which was premised on getting Virginia's Whigs to endorse him. Nothing could be better calculated to obtain that endorsement than a frontal attack on fanatical abolitionists. It was a risky play, to be sure, because it would alienate antislavery elements in New York, a state that Clay would likely need to win the nomination and the election. However, Clay calculated that he had already lost antislavery support. His strategy for securing New York was not to appease the state's antislavery elements but to ally himself with the state's Conservative Democrats led by Nathaniel Tallmadge, just as in Virginia, he was attempting to construct a coalition with the Conservative Democrats led by William Rives. Clay believed, moreover, that the Van Buren administration's strategy was to sink the Whig Party in the South by tying it to abolitionism—thus, the speech was a way to extricate himself and the Whig Party from what one correspondent called "the coils of the black Snake" of abolitionism.[19]

Clay did not believe the speech jeopardized his presidential prospects. Quite the opposite. He was convinced that it had strengthened his prospects of becoming president. His close friends all told him the same thing. Peter Porter, as ever, was effusive in his praise for Clay's "great abolition speech," which by assailing "the doctrines of those crazy men . . . will on the whole add to your personal popularity." Without "essentially" injuring Clay in the North, he judged that it "cannot fail to place you on high ground [in] the South and Southwest."[20] Ten days after the speech, Clay reported to Harrison Gray Otis that "from all quarters, the most gratifying intelligence is received as to my future prospects." The whole of the South and Southwest was now rallying behind him.[21] Indeed, the only ones criticizing the speech, he told Porter, were "the Ultra-abolitionists."[22] If the speech ultimately harmed Clay's presidential prospects, it was not because he would have rather been right than president; it was because he miscalculated how best to become president.

Clay's speech did win plaudits throughout the South and Southwest for its role in helping to "expose and check the fell demon of abolition."[23] Even John Calhoun sang its praises.[24] But the thing that Clay most wanted from the speech—an endorsement from the Virginia state legislature—was not forthcoming, although in March he did earn the imprimatur of the Louisiana state legislature, which not only endorsed Clay but chose delegates to the national convention who were instructed to vote for Clay. Clay was banking on Virginia and the South to secure him the presidency, but he fretted increasingly about the Whigs' relatively disorganized state below the Mason-Dixon Line—and their aversion to party conventions.

At the beginning of April 1839, Clay wrote to Brooke to call attention to the "prodigious effort" being made by the administration's allies in Virginia and the absence of "evidence of corresponding or counteracting exertions" by the opposition forces. Clay was particularly concerned about the effect that the Democrats' recent state convention in Richmond would have in energizing the party and healing the rift between regular and Conservative Democrats before the upcoming state elections in May. The convention, he instructed Brooke, "will strengthen them, because it is an organization of their party, and the members will return to their respective homes animated by the confidence and hopes inspired by their interchange of opinion and feeling." Where the parties are "nearly balanced," Clay continued, "that which is disciplined and in a state of complete organization is almost sure to prevail over its adversary." He warned Brooke that the Whig Party in Virginia was "too sanguine" and recommended a convention of young men to be held at either Charlottesville or Staunton, complete with "stirring and eloquent Speeches," to excite the faithful and carry them to the polls.[25]

As it turned out, Virginia's elections were a mixed bag for the Whigs. Clay judged them "neither so good as we hoped nor as bad as feared." The Van Buren opposition won nine of the state's twenty-one congressional seats, a gain of three seats with twice the turnout from two years before.[26] The Whigs lost a little ground in the state assembly races but retained their majority and gained some ground in the state senate races while remaining in the minority.[27] Disappointed that the result had not been "more decisive," Clay again urged his Virginia allies to ensure that the Whigs were "completely organized" in future elections. He queried his former Senate colleague Benjamin Watkins Leigh,

> Can you succeed without Conventions, Committees of Correspondence, Vigilance &c.? . . . These Conventions collect information, create acquaintance, produce excitement and beget zeal. . . . They enable a party to disseminate genuine information and to ascertain its actual strength. . . . They affect also the pride and vanity of men. To be a member of one of these bodies is a distinction, of which, perhaps unfortunately for poor human nature, too many of us are disposed to be flattered with.[28]

In other words, the well-bred gentlemen of Virginia needed to roll up their sleeves and do democratic politics if they wanted to defeat Van Burenism and the Democratic Party. Nothing less than the "fate of our institutions" depended on it. And Clay's fate too.

Clay felt sure that the Southern states would back him at a national convention, provided that they participated—and after his abolition speech, he brimmed with confidence that "the whole of the Southern and S.W. States" would send delegates to the national nominating convention in Harrisburg.[29] But the inability to wrangle an endorsement from the Whig legislators in Richmond together with the state party's failure to win a "more decisive" victory in the May elections had stymied Clay's efforts to make Virginia "a rallying point" that would start a stampede in his direction.[30] If Richmond would not unlock Albany, then Clay was going to need another strategy to ensure New York's support, particularly with the steep rise in General Scott's stock.

In the latter part of February 1839, Clay had received an invitation from Alexander Hamilton Jr. to speak in New York City to bolster his presidential chances in the state, but he turned it down because it would violate the "open and repeated pledges" he had made not to "enter upon electioneering tours." Even if he could be sure that such a tour would "secure the prize of the Presidency" he would not do it. If, as Hamilton warned, "the cause of another is gaining, and rapidly gaining, be it so." Clay at this point was still intent on playing the inside game, confident that the "current" was running in his favor and still hoping for an endorsement in Albany.[31]

Clay's confidence in his position in New York owed much to the frequent reports of Peter B. Porter. Indeed, at the time he was writing to Hamilton, Clay had just received a lengthy letter from Porter assuring him that he remained the preferred candidate of the Whigs in the New York legislature as well as the people of the state. Porter also informed Clay that both Thurlow Weed and Governor William Seward were "not only friendly to your election, but warmly & zealously so," although they deemed it "inexpedient" to make any "public declarations of their preference at this time." Porter also reported on a meeting he had with Weed on February 16 in which the two men had sketched a plan by which a caucus of the state's Whig legislators would pledge to support the national convention nominee, appoint two senatorial delegates (one of whom could be Porter and the other David Ogden, a friend of Webster's who Porter believed would support Clay as his second choice), and provide for the remaining delegates to be selected by each of the state's forty congressional districts. Porter confidently predicted that such a scheme would produce maybe half-a-dozen delegates for Harrison and the rest for Clay.[32]

Once again Porter was far too optimistic. The New York legislature adjourned in May "without doing anything on the presidential question" apart from approving of a national convention. The "timid" legislators, a disappointed Porter reported to Clay, had instead left the matter of delegate selection to the party's six-member state central committee.[33] Clay's confidence had already been rattled by elections held in New York City in the second week of April in which the Whigs had won only 30 percent of the seats and lost the mayoral contest. Clay was quick to attribute defeat to voter fraud—"the tricks and practices of our opponents"—something he was confident the Whig-controlled state legislature would shortly remedy with a new voter registration law aimed at combating voter fraud. But given that Clay's strength was concentrated in the city, he was understandably worried that the result could have a "discouraging effect" on his supporters elsewhere in the state.[34] Indeed, there were (unfounded) rumors afoot in western New York that Clay had written to a prominent Whig—New York's secretary of state John C. Spencer—to say that he was prepared to make way for Scott if his friends thought he could not carry New York.[35]

The Whigs' defeat in the New York City elections, Scott's meteoric rise in popularity in western New York, and the failure to secure an endorsement in Albany forced Clay to rethink his pledge to avoid electioneering. In mid-May, he informed Porter that he had decided to visit him in Niagara Falls and travel to Canada, although he added that he was "anxious . . . to proceed on the excursion as quietly, and with as little noise and parade as possible."[36] Clay was well aware that such a tour opened him up to charges of not only electioneering but hypocrisy, since he had repeatedly declared that, unlike his rivals Harrison and Webster, he would not accept any public dinners or invitations to speak that could be construed as betraying a desire to be made president.

Porter was delighted at Clay's change of heart. Although sensitive to Clay's desire not to expose himself "to the charge of making electioneering journeys," Porter told Clay that he would have to accept a public dinner in his honor at Buffalo and that he would also be expected to make a speech there. Buffalo was a particularly important site in the battle for New York.[37] Of the city's two major papers, one (the *Commercial Advertiser*) had endorsed Harrison and the other (the *Buffalo Journal*) inclined toward Clay, while Buffalo's congressman Millard Fillmore had been a Webster man.[38] Now it had become a center of the Scott fever sweeping through western New York. Not only would Clay's visit enable him to win over many in

Buffalo, Porter assured him, but "the impulse occasioned by your presence" in the surrounding Anti-Mason districts of western New York "would influence many more" to support him.[39]

Clay continued to play coy, insisting that Porter had "almost frighten[ed] me from my purpose." If he agreed to speak in Buffalo, Clay reasoned, how could he resist his friends at Rochester "and a hundred other towns in the West of your State?" He insisted that he merely wished to "pass along quietly, without noise, and without any personal public demonstrations" and urged Porter to do his best "rather to repress than to stimulate public manifestations towards me." Clay again reiterated his determination "to avoid, in appearance and in fact, all electioneering."[40] He told various correspondents that all he intended was "a Summer excursion to the Lakes, the Falls of Niagara, and the Canadas."[41] But notwithstanding the protestations, Clay embarked on an almost two-month-long tour of the US (with only a brief detour into Canada to see Montreal and Quebec City[42]); delivered a strongly political speech in Buffalo on July 17 that slammed the "radical maladministration" of the government—and sent a printed copy of the speech to editors of the *National Intelligencer* to ensure its broad circulation; and by the end of the month, having visited Lockport, Rochester, Canandaigua, Auburn, Syracuse, and Oswego, pronounced himself "worn down and prostrated" by the "enthusiastic demonstrations, . . . quasi public dinners, suppers, vast concourses of people, Committees & Speeches."[43]

The tour, which received glowing coverage in the pro-Clay press, had become exactly the sort of electioneering tour that Clay insisted he did not want but must have known all along it would become.[44] In early August, as Clay plotted his return to Lexington, he eagerly accepted an invitation to visit New York City from the avowedly partisan Committee of Whig Young Men of New York City—it was, after all, he said, "directly in the route" of his return home. So were countless other New York towns—including Troy, Albany, Kingston, Poughkeepsie, Fishkill, and Newburgh—where he was celebrated, toasted, and fêted. In Saratoga Springs, a mecca in August for the well-connected and well-to-do, Clay was paraded into town on August 9 in a procession that stretched for a mile and a half, a cavalcade the likes of which had "never [been] seen before in the county of Saratoga." In New York City, the reception was even more grandiose. Philip Hone, the fifty-eight-year-old former mayor of the city, said the "spontaneous expression of public opinion . . . exceeded anything of the kind we have ever witnessed, excepting the reception of [the Marquis de] Lafayette" fifteen years earlier. He was convinced the effusive crowds showed that Clay "must be the favorite candidate for the presidency of the Whigs hereabouts," which was exactly what Clay hoped people would think.[45]

Clay did more than bask in the adulation. At multiple stops along the way, he delivered speeches that went well beyond perfunctory acknowledgments of praise. Instead, as at Buffalo, he energized the sympathetic crowds with sharp indictments of the "misdeeds" of the Van Buren administration. At Saratoga, Clay spoke on the theme for more than an hour—an address that even the sympathetic Hone thought too long and entering "too much into political detail."[46] In New York City, he addressed a "vast multitude" and urged them to vote ("with you are the means of relief"), attacked the Van Buren administration, and defended himself: "I may be charged with improper motives; with being actuated by ambition; I may be assailed by the public press; but while I have the strength to raise my voice I will send forth the words of warning" and work to "produce a change in the management of our public affairs" and "a change of our public men."[47] On the day Clay was to leave New York City, Hone called on Clay and found him "hoarse and fatigued," "nearly annihilated . . . by the civilities of the New Yorkers."[48] Hoarse or not, he continued to speak, punctuating the tour at month's end with a rousing speech in Baltimore that again ripped into the so-called "reforms" of the Jackson and Van Buren administrations that had made the country worse off rather than better—most notably, he said, by ridding the country of the so-called "monster" bank and thereby ceding control over the nation's financial affairs to the far more dangerous and alien "foreign 'monster,'" the Bank of England.[49]

Even those most skeptical of Clay's chances of winning the state came away impressed by the frenzied attention that Clay excited as he made his way through New York. Governor Seward, who was touring the state at the same time as Clay, witnessed the senator's entrance into Burlington, Vermont, which he found as "enthusiastic as it was magnificent." The governor, who was able to travel around New York with a minimum of fanfare, admitted that he was "unaccustomed to such demonstrations." Seward traveled through several of the same counties that Clay visited and in mid-August reported to Weed, "Of the presidential question I know less than when I left Albany." Seward had clearly been wowed by the enthusiasm of the crowds, which he believed "was chiefly or altogether felt to be made toward Mr. Clay as a candidate" for president. He found "the same thing and the same feeling" in Essex and Clinton Counties in the northeast corner of New York. On the other hand, a bit to the west, in St. Lawrence and Jefferson Counties, Seward reported that Harrison seemed strong and that he had been told that Clay's reception, though of "equal ardor," was an "homage" to Clay "as a, not the, representative of Whig principles." Meanwhile, Seward found that Cayuga County—the farthest west he went on the tour—was for Scott, but he told Weed that "I did not hear anything elsewhere to that effect" in any of the other six counties he visited.[50]

Because their paths crossed on their respective tours, Seward had a chance to meet briefly with the presidential aspirant on August 5.[51] Seward recounted to Weed that Clay believed "the demonstrations were of such a kind everywhere as to convince him he was well with the people." Seward told Clay that he agreed that "all was right toward him, except the feelings of the abolitionists" and the concerns harbored by others that the "hostility of that class" could make him unelectable. Seward said that Clay brushed aside all such worries, telling Seward that "many abolitionists had come to him" during his tour of western New York, "confessing their abolitionism, but declaring their preference and devotion to him."[52] Whatever the effect of the tour on New Yorkers, it clearly swelled Clay's own sense of his popularity with Whig voters. Porter only bolstered his feelings of confidence, writing to Clay that his tour of western New York had been a spectacular success, impressing "many who were vacillating and undecided." It had even "drawn over to you from the Van Buren ranks . . . a number of his most respectable and influential supporters."[53]

Porter was also busy trying to arrest the spreading Scott fever. He had even invited Scott to his home in Niagara Falls in hopes of heading off the general's candidacy. Based on that conversation, Porter assured Clay that the general "openly and on all occasions avows his determination not to become a candidate for the Presidency, but to give you his best support."[54] Porter had traveled with Clay as far as Rochester, and almost immediately after the two men separated, he fired off a letter to state senator Gulian D. Verplanck, a leading Clay supporter in New York City: "What can . . . professed Whigs in your city mean by pushing forward Gen Scott at this time? . . . The attempt . . . to create an impression that Gen Scott is the most popular candidate in the western part of our state is altogether deceptive." Porter told Verplanck that "Mr. Clay will command 10 votes to Gen Scott's one."[55]

Clay received a more sobering assessment of his chances from Weed, who journeyed to Saratoga in hopes of persuading Clay to withdraw. Weed talked with Clay at length about the presidential question and—assuming that Weed's recollection in his autobiography is accurate[56]—in much franker terms than Seward had been willing or able to do in his brief encounter with Clay. Weed conveyed that while "warmly attached" to Clay and "preferring him over all others for president," he "did not believe that he could be elected."[57] Clay apparently took it well. According to Weed, "Nothing could be more courteous and kind than Mr. Clay's bearings throughout the conversations," which Weed characterized as "earnest and calm." Clay was still not persuaded, though. He thought, Weed recounted, "that we attached too much importance to the United States Bank controversy." To Clay, that issue was over and done with. He also thought Weed's concerns about party unity were overblown: Once the national convention had made its choice, the party would rally around the nominee. Clay told Weed he would not withdraw but that he would "cheerfully and heartily acquiesce" in the convention's choice.[58]

Clay had come too far to withdraw now. The adoring crowds that followed his every step had exceeded his expectations. Surely they were a more reliable barometer of popular feeling than the calculations of even a savvy party boss such as Weed. Moreover, his private conversations with politicians in the western part of the state, particularly Albert Tracy and Francis Granger, persuaded him that Anti-Mason opposition to his candidacy was no longer the factor it had once been.[59] Indeed, many Anti-Masons seemed receptive to his critique of abolitionism. Clay was aware that Scott was coming to be seen (in Philip Hone's words) as "the rising sun,"[60] but given Clay's strength in New York City, Scott was arguably a greater threat to Harrison's chances than Clay's. Scott's rise scrambled the state of play more than settled it and made it less likely that Clay would take Weed's advice to withdraw since doing so now would not clear the way for a single candidate around whom the party in New York would unify but instead would invite two evenly matched generals to slug it out. It was becoming a three-horse race, and Clay thought that he could win that race at the convention. He also believed even more deeply—and neither Weed nor any other Whig seemed to disagree—that he would make the nation's best president.

"THE SEASONS OF PANIC ARE OVER"

Clay had paraded triumphantly into Saratoga on August 9 to a hero's welcome, but by the time he left on the 17th, Whig spirits had been sobered by preliminary election results trickling in from the West and Southwest.[61] By the time Clay left New York City on the 24th, there was no mistaking the devastating defeats the Whigs had suffered in Tennessee, Indiana, and North Carolina, each of which held elections in early August.[62]

Clay was particularly worried by the Whig defeat in Tennessee, which he described as "a most disastrous event" that was "likely to exercise great, if not fatal, influence far beyond the limits of Tennessee."[63] The Whigs lost three congressional seats, their 10–3 advantage having shrunk to 7–6, and they lost their majority in the lower state house, slipping from a commanding 64 percent of the seats to only 44 percent. Making matters worse, the incumbent Whig governor, Newton Cannon, lost after having won by 20 points two years before. His Democratic opponent, James Polk, received almost 20,000 more votes than the Democratic gubernatorial candidate had received in 1837, whereas there was no increase in the number polled by Cannon. Turnout was way up—about nine in ten adult white males went to the polls—but the Democrats seemed to be the only ones who benefited from the heightened voter enthusiasm. [64] Basking in the party's good fortune, former president Andrew Jackson exulted, "Tennessee is again safe in the republican fold."[65]

What made Tennessee particularly devastating for Clay was not only that the loss was unexpected but that Tennessee's Whigs had cast the contest as a proxy for the coming presidential battle: "The Governor's office is but the die," the *Tennessee Whig* proclaimed. "The Presidency is the Stake."[66] In May, John Bell, who was running for reelection to Congress, had told Clay that he had appeared before the voters with his opponent on nearly a dozen occasions during the campaign, and "the debate was always chiefly and directly upon the question of preference between you & Van Buren." The "real question now before the people of this state," Bell wrote, "is will they take Henry Clay 'to rule over them.'" "As the vote shall be in August next," Bell predicted, "so will it be in 1840."[67] If Bell was right, then the voters of Tennessee were signaling their desire not only to sweep away the state's Whigs but to back Van Buren over Clay or any Whig in 1840.

Clay was desperate to divine the meaning of Tennessee's election for his presidential prospects, and as soon as he arrived back in Lexington he wrote to Allen Hall, editor of a leading Whig newspaper in Tennessee. In a letter dated September 14, 1839, he asked Hall to provide him with straight answers to several queries: was the election result "owing to the use of [his] name in connection with the Presidential Office," would he beat Van Buren, and was there another Whig who would be more likely to beat Van Buren? Hall gave Clay a mixed report. He informed Clay that the Democrats had exploited public prejudices against Clay, especially with respect to Clay's past support for a national bank. The Democrats, he noted, "were long and actively engaged in exciting [those prejudices] in every county and neighborhood in the State," further evidence that the election had been nationalized by both sides. But Hall attributed their defeat to the failure of some Whig candidates, "either from timidity or want of the proper information," to mount an adequate defense of Clay's public character and conduct. The real problem, as Hall saw it, stemmed from the Whigs' "over confidence"—with the result that they had been badly outspent and outworked. He assured Clay that the Whigs would have won had they exerted "even ordinary efforts." He also assured Clay that with improved organization and "reasonable exertions," the Whigs would win the presidency in 1840 and that, moreover, none of the other Whig candidates would do as well as Clay. Indeed, he thought that none of the other current candidates, including Harrison, could beat Van Buren. In Hall's view, Clay was the Tennessee Whigs' only hope in 1840.[68]

If Hall's information about Clay's prospects in 1840 was reassuring, his response to Clay's final query—whether Tennessee would send delegates to the national nominating convention in December—was deflating. Hall informed Clay that there was no chance that Tennessee's Whigs would be represented at the national convention absent "a general and spontaneous rising up of the people." The prejudice against such a convention among the state's Whigs was still too strong. The central rationale for Hugh White's presidential candidacy in 1836 had been the objection to Van Buren's "unrepublican" nomination at the Democrats' Baltimore convention, and the party's leaders could not now reverse their stance on the desirability of such a system without doing irreparable harm to the state party's cause. "If attempted," Hall told Clay," the project would probably fail, and we should reap all the odium, without any corresponding benefit."[69] If Tennessee's Whigs preferred Clay—as seemed clearly to be the case—then the state's failure to send delegates would seriously impair Clay's effort to win the nomination. If other Southern states followed Tennessee's lead, Clay's Southern strategy would be undone.

Hall's responses to Clay interrogatories generally focused on the failures of the Whig campaign—the timid candidates, the overconfident voters, the huge sums spent by the opposition—but they elided the change in the economic conditions between 1837 and 1839. In August 1837, when Tennessee's voters had last gone to the polls, panic about the economy was widespread. But by the summer of 1839, as one Democratic paper put it shortly before the election, it seemed that "the seasons of panic are over, the crops are coming in plentiful, [and] the husbandman is glad."[70] Tennessee's banks had resumed specie payments, and confidence in the economic outlook was returning, which bolstered Democratic arguments that neither a national bank nor federal intervention were necessary for an economic recovery.[71] The election result was much less about prejudices against Clay than it was a referendum on the Van Buren administration and the state of the economy. If so, that was bad news for the Whigs, who had been counting on a failing economy to carry them to the White House.

On the same day that Clay wrote to Hall, he sent an almost identical set of interrogatories to Indiana's Whig senator Oliver Smith.[72] The scale of the Whig defeat in Indiana—a state Harrison had carried comfortably in 1836 (Harrison's share of the vote in 1836 had been greater in Indiana than in any other state but Vermont)—caught everyone by surprise. The Whigs lost control of the state senate and the state assembly—dropping from 62 percent of the seats in the lower house to less than 40 percent—and won only two of the state's seven congressional seats after having won six the year before. If the Democrats could win handily in Indiana, the Whigs' chances of winning the presidency in 1840 were all but doomed.

At one level, Smith's response about the state of play in Indiana was more encouraging than Hall's report on Tennessee. Smith assured Clay that Indiana's election "did not turn mainly upon general politics." The election had not been nationalized. Instead, the Whigs had been defeated because of the unpopularity of the high taxes that had been instituted by the Whig governor and legislature to pay for an ambitious system of internal improvements.[73] Neither Clay's name nor the name of any other presidential candidate affected the outcome. But that was all the encouragement Smith was able to offer. In the rest of his letter, he administered hard truths.

Smith candidly told Clay that he was not the strongest candidate in Indiana. While "no name under heaven would be so well calculated as yours, to stimulate your original supporters of our party," Smith explained that with "the current that has set and is still running against us," the party could not rely only on those original Whigs. Instead, the party desperately needed "that class who joined us under the Harrison flag," and unfortunately they could not be relied on to vote for Clay because they "have not forgotten the old contest when their idol Gen. Jackson and yourself were in the field"; as a result, they "still retain a deep-rooted prejudice against you, repeating the oft-refuted charge of bargain, intrigue and management, between you and Mr. Adams." These people, Smith lamented, "are beyond the reach of reason or arguments." Were it a contest between Clay and Van Buren, Smith surmised, it would require "desperate exertions to insure our success." In contrast, Harrison would have no difficulty defeating Van Buren. Smith went one step further, offering Clay some unsolicited advice about the upcoming convention. He had conferred with Clay's leading friends in

Indiana—and "no man ever had more ardent ones"—and found that they were of the opinion that the best strategy would be for Clay to indicate his "willingness or desire" to see Harrison become the nominee. That magnanimous act would earn the goodwill of Harrison's supporters, and since General Harrison had pledged to serve only one term, Clay would be poised to be the unanimous choice of the party in 1844.[74]

Rumors that Clay was planning to withdraw from the contest were by now rampant. Only two days before Smith sat down to answer Clay's queries, Clay felt compelled to write to Seward to disavow the notion—which he had recently learned was circulating freely in New York City—that he was about to quit the race. He told Seward that instead he planned to avail himself "of Mr. V. Buren's habit of non commitalism" and asked the governor for his help in scotching the unfounded speculation.[75] In his reply to Oliver Smith, dated October 5, 1839, Clay not only tried to quash the "unfounded" rumors of his withdrawal but vented his frustrations at the entire process. The Whigs found themselves beset by "unfortunate divisions," he lamented, because they had put off for too long the choice of a nominee. He also issued a veiled threat. The delay in picking a nominee increased the chance that the supporters of the person not nominated would refuse to back the convention's choice. "This is declared to be the case with some of the friends of Gen. Harrison, without their seeming to anticipate, that it may also be the case with some of the friends of other persons who have been spoken of"—namely, Clay's supporters. The problem, in Clay's view, was a lack of leadership by the Whigs in Congress and state legislatures across the country. The party's divisions could have been averted if Whig legislators, especially in Virginia and New York, had not shunned their responsibilities to lead. If a party's "leaders will not act," Clay raged, "the members of the party will act for themselves; when the officers will not steer the ship, the crew will assume the command." In view of the failure of leadership, it was hardly surprising that the party had "broken off into fragments." In a final dig at Harrison, Clay noted that "not content with one General in the field, our friends have brought out another, and I assure you from all the information which I have, I am inclined to think that the last [Scott] is the stronger of the two."[76]

Clay's peevishness toward Harrison was perhaps heightened by a letter that he had recently received from Old Tippecanoe. At the start of Clay's tour, which took him through Ohio, Clay had graciously written to Harrison to tell him he had no intention of "poaching" votes in Harrison's home state but rather would pass through it as unobtrusively as possible en route to his summer excursion—a pledge that he honored. Harrison's reply was written "in the most friendly spirit"[77] but must nonetheless have underscored for Clay the cosmic injustice of being asked to take a backseat to an aging general. It is difficult to imagine that Clay found comfort in Harrison's expressions of regret that he found himself in this "distressing and embarissing . . . position of apparent rivalry to you, [p]articularly in relation to the Presidency, [a]n office which I never dreamed of attaining and which I had ardently desired to see you occupy." Harrison put it all down to "fate": it was "my destiny," he told Clay, "rather than my will [that] has placed me" in this position.[78]

While Clay was fending off rumors of his imminent departure from the race, the stock of the second general in the race was indeed soaring, as Clay suggested. The party's heavy losses in August, including in Harrison's own backyard of Indiana, boosted the appeal of a fresh face who might help to overcome the "unfortunate divisions" and growing enmity between the supporters of Harrison and Clay. Those divisions were particularly acute in New York, where a Scott nomination increasingly seemed to be the only way out of the party's impasse and the best way to broaden the party's appeal, particularly with the economy seemingly on the upswing. At the end of August, John Bradley, one of Weed's political lieutenants in upstate New York, confidently reported that "Scott's name . . . will bring out the Hurra boys" and would enable the Whigs to rally "all the fragments of the Conservative, Anti Masonic, and abolition parties, and all the malcontents of our opponents," whereas Clay would only "command a pure Whig vote." Recruiting from the Democrats' "ranks in mass" would be a fitting turnabout since the "Whig party were broken down by the popularity and non-committal character of old Jackson." It was "but fair to turn upon, and prostrate our opponents with the . . . weapons, with which they beat us." To properly emulate the Democrats' successful strategy, Bradley concluded, "the General's lips must be hermetically sealed, and our shouts and Hurras must be long & loud."[79]

The worse the election results, the greater the party's incentive to find a candidate who was "available"—that is, electable—rather than a candidate who would champion Whig principles. From the outset, Harrison's appeal had been that relative to Clay and Webster he was the more electable candidate. The indefatigable Charles S. Todd got the jump on Clay by journeying to New York in June to press Harrison's case in person. He carried with him a letter signed by a number of prominent Whigs in Clay's home state of Kentucky, including former governor James Morehead, attesting that in their view Harrison was "the most available candidate as he alone can secure Pennsylvania, Ohio, Illinois, and probably Indiana."[80] The unexpected setbacks in the August elections only strengthened the case for choosing the most electable candidate.

Adding to Clay's troubles—and strengthening the case for the two generals—was that the election results in the fall seemed to go from bad to worse. In the August congressional elections, the Whigs had lost eleven congressional seats to the Democrats (four in both North Carolina and Indiana and three in Tennessee), and in the only two congressional elections held in the fall they lost an additional seat in Maryland's eight-seat delegation in October and both seats in Mississippi in November. In all, seven states held congressional elections between August and November 1839, and the Whigs lost seats in all but two; in those two, Kentucky and Alabama, there was no change in the partisan balance. In total, sixty-one congressional seats were contested between August and November, leading to a net gain for the Democrats of fourteen seats. At the beginning of the year, Clay had been confident that there would be a Whig Speaker of the House, but now it looked as if the Democrats might retain control of the chamber when the new Twenty-Sixth Congress was sworn in at the end of the year.

State elections that fall were equally discouraging for the Whigs. In Maine, which held elections in the second week of September and where Clay had relatively strong support, the Whigs failed to make up for the losses in the assembly that they had incurred the preceding year. Not only did the Democrats retain a considerable majority in the lower house, but they also retained control of the governorship. In 1837, the Whig nominee for governor, Edward Kent, had squeaked by his Democratic opponent by less than 1 percentage point, and in 1838 he had lost narrowly by 3.5 points. But in 1839, in a rematch with his 1838 opponent, Kent lost by more than 8 points. The Whigs seemed to be going backward.[81]

The October state elections brought even grimmer news. The voters in six states (Arkansas, Georgia, Maryland, New Jersey, Ohio, and Pennsylvania) went to the polls in the opening week of October, and only in New Jersey, where the Whigs retained but did not increase their healthy majority in the state legislature, did the Whigs not lose ground.[82] In the other five states, the Whigs saw their share of the seats drop by an average of 11 percentage points from the previous election. In Maryland, they slipped into the minority for the first time during the Van Buren administration. In Ohio, the Whigs' share of seats plunged to less than one-third, a drop of 15 percentage points from 1838 and 24 points from their high point in

1837, when they had a majority in the assembly. The Whig Party in Ohio had never looked so weak; some thought it portended the end of the party.[83] In Pennsylvania, too, the Whig Party seemed to be fast losing ground. As in Ohio, the Whigs' share of seats in the state house dropped to less than one-third, numbers the party had not seen since before the economic Panic of 1837.

Clay was at a loss to explain why the tide was running so strongly against the Whigs. He could not believe that the people had suddenly become supportive of Van Buren's Independent Treasury scheme. The only explanation he could come up with, yet again, was "the corrupt use of money" on the part of the administration. "In every State," Clay reasoned, although "the mass is sound, there is a sufficient number of corruptible voters which, if all thrown on one side, will turn the scale." The Democratic Party victories, he concluded, were due to the Van Buren administration having "taken out hundreds of thousands of dollars" from the public treasury and then "purchased up these votes."[84]

Whatever the cause of the Whig defeats, even the habitually sanguine Clay was compelled to admit that "every where the Administration party has gained upon us." Writing to William Tompkins on October 12, a demoralized Clay remarked that if the results continued at the same rate, "it will be very questionable whether the nomination of the Whig Convention will be worth accepting by any one, to whom it may be offered."[85] Only six months before, Clay had felt certain that absent an "immense change in the tide of Mr. Van Buren's fortunes," the president would be "beaten tremendously."[86] Now that the tide had apparently changed, a befuddled Clay seemed almost resigned to defeat. The national convention was less than two months away, and the timing for Clay could not have been worse.

Support for Clay appeared to be softening, even in areas of the country where he had hitherto been strong. The day before Clay wrote to Tompkins, William A. Graham, a rising star in North Carolina politics, had written to Willie Mangum, one of the state's leading Whigs and a Clay confidant, to explain that while "Mr. Clay, of course, is preferred by us all, very much," if it should be found that Harrison was much more popular in the nation, and his election was "nearly sure," then "I would say let him be nominated . . . for the sake of success."[87] After losing four congressional seats to the Democrats, even Clay's stalwart friends in North Carolina seemed willing to set him aside if it meant winning the presidency.

The adverse election results in August, September, and October spurred panic among the Whigs in New York, which was set to hold legislative elections on November 4. New York's Whigs had done spectacularly well in the state elections of 1837 and 1838 and as a result not only controlled the governorship but had large majorities in the state legislature. Weed and his allies feared that those legislative gains could now be wiped out by a resurgent Democratic Party. Those close to Weed had been warning for some time of the danger (in Fillmore's words) that the Whigs' "political vessel" would "drift on to the *Clay Banks* where she will founder forever,"[88] and they now redoubled their efforts to secure the state for Scott. One of Weed's closest associates, Frederick Whittlesey, told Weed that he could "see no way through except with Scott as a candidate."[89] Indeed, so desperate was Whittlesey to sink Clay's candidacy that he thought it worth losing the assembly if it would force Clay's withdrawal from the presidential race.

There is no evidence that Weed attempted to throw the election in hopes of getting Clay out of the race, but the Whigs certainly lost ground in the New York City districts—which were generally pro-Clay—just as they had in the New York City elections in April. The Whigs did well enough in upstate and western New York to retain control of the state assembly despite their losses in the city, but the shifting of the tide was evident here too, as the 55 percent of the assembly seats that the Whigs won was well down from the 64 percent they secured the year before and the 78 percent the year before that. Edward Curtis, another of Weed's trusted allies, felt sure that the losses in New York City, coupled with victories in the western part of the state, would send a clear message to Clay that he should give way to Scott.[90]

Much to Curtis's dismay, however, the New York results seemed to have the opposite effect on Clay and his allies. Clay told one New York supporter that the "the glorious issue" of the New York election had filled him "with astonishment and inexpressible pleasure." To another, he wrote that the result was "very reviving" and "will reanimate the hopes, and I trust, redouble the exertions of our friends everywhere."[91] Willis Hall, New York's attorney general and a Clay backer, put the same positive spin on the "gratifying result." Hall told Clay that the party's losses in New York City were entirely attributable to the "immense foreign vote," but with their majorities in both the state assembly and state senate secured, the Whigs would be able to enact "one or two wholesome laws" that would fix that problem. In Hall's judgment, the election results showed that there was "a clear whig majority of at least 10,000" in New York, which meant that "a strict party vote" would be enough to carry the state in the presidential election the following year. And since all conceded that Clay would get Whig votes, Hall believed that the election demonstrated that Clay could carry New York. Consequently, Hall felt there was no reason for the state's Whigs to jump to Scott, particularly since nobody knew what policies Scott preferred.[92]

However, as Hall was aware, the Weed machine did not share this rosy assessment of Clay's prospects in the state, nor did it care much about what Scott's policies might be. Weed and his fellow politicos cared only about winning the presidency—and the governorship—and were pulling out all the stops to mobilize support for Scott at the convention. Hall told Clay that Weed "now declares openly for Scott as do all the heads of Departments" at Albany. "A sort of panic has been got up," Hall admitted, although he thought it "thus far confined pretty much to the politicians." In New York City, at least, where he had spent the past week, "the masses are totally unaffected." But it wasn't the masses who would decide the Whig nominee. It was the politicians who were preparing to gather in Harrisburg.

When Clay arrived in the nation's capital on the eve of the Harrisburg convention, he was taken aback by how strong the "project . . . to run Genl. Scott" had become. He admitted to Otis that it "had risen to an importance that I had never supposed it would reach." He was disappointed to find that a majority of both the New York congressional delegation and the state's delegates heading to Harrisburg had been "induced to concur in the project." Making this particularly galling for Clay was that he had been informed that both delegations conceded that as many as "nine tenths of their Constituents" preferred him. "Nevertheless," Clay groused, "they prefer to make a nomination in conformity to the wishes of the one or two tenths." Although Clay thought Weed was "playing a rash game," he admitted that he was "prepared to hear, without surprise, that [Scott] is nominated."[93] Clay was obviously disappointed about being bested by a political neophyte such as Scott, but he seemed almost resigned to it and expressed a readiness to lend his full support to Scott if he were nominated.

The same could not be said for William Henry Harrison and his allies. Willis Hall reported to Clay on November 20 that Harrison's friends were "exceedingly bitter against Gen Scott—so much so that many of them openly declare that they will not vote for him under any circumstances."[94] The bitterness against Scott was very much shared by Harrison himself. The day before Hall had written to Clay, Harrison had expressed those grievances in a long letter to Solomon Van Rensselaer, who was headed to the Harrisburg convention as a New York delegate. He told Van Rensselaer that he would feel "more than mortified" if the neophyte Scott was preferred to him at the convention. After all, Scott had "never served in any

Civil Capacity," so "his Selection could be placed on no other ground than that of his military services, and it would be at once a declaration that those services were far more important than mine." Harrison would regard such a declaration as a personal affront. It was one thing for the convention to pick an experienced statesman such as Clay, but it would be unacceptable for the convention to pick Scott, who had "never commanded in chief except for a short time in Florida" and whose "talents to lead Armies under the difficult circumstances in which I was placed has never been tested." Whipping himself up into a lather of indignation, Harrison asked whether "those who urge Genl. Scott recollect that I was at the head of an Army, and at the same time at the head of a Government vested in both capacities with the most extraordinary powers whilst he was yet a subaltern?" How, he wondered, "would they justify to the people my being pushed aside to make room for Genl. Scott?" Selecting Scott would be "an insult . . . to the 20,000 men who served under me" and to "the sons and grandsons of my soldiers." Harrison's venting halted only when he ran out of paper.[95]

During the previous few years, Harrison had kept exactingly close tabs on the relative support for Clay and himself. He knew that Clay's strength was in the South and his in Ohio and Pennsylvania as well as Indiana. He kept in touch with correspondents in the border states of Missouri, Kentucky, and Maryland and monitored his and Clay's relative levels of support in those states. Believing it was a two-man race, Harrison banked on the pragmatic politicos at the convention opting for the more available candidate with the least political baggage. But Scott's sudden emergence as a viable candidate threatened to subvert Harrison's well-laid plans. In a race with Scott, he could no longer play his trump card of electability, and if New York held out for Scott there was no viable route for Harrison to win the nomination. All roads to the Whig nomination led through New York, and as the delegates descended on Harrisburg, the upstart Scott seemed to have the inside track.[96]

6

COME TOGETHER

When it comes to the development of democracy, the Democrats are often portrayed as the leaders and the Whigs as reluctant followers. The coming of democracy is associated with the rise of Andrew Jackson, and the emergence of popular parties is credited to Martin Van Buren. The conventional tale of the 1840 election is one in which, at long last, Jackson's opponents jettisoned their ingrained elitism, embraced the common man, and became small-*d* democrats. In 1840, the Whigs borrowed and thieved from "the Democratic playbook."[1]

Yet in at least one crucial respect, the Whigs were democratic pioneers, for they were the first major political party to hold a genuinely national nominating convention to select their presidential nominee. To be sure, the Anti-Masons (almost all of whom became Whigs) had held several national nominating conventions—in September 1831, May 1836, and November 1838—but each had been dominated by a handful of states. In 1831, for instance, two-thirds of the delegates came from only two states: New York and Pennsylvania. In none of the conventions did a viable presidential candidate emerge from the deliberations. In 1838, the decision was made by a small number of people before the convention convened—which was why William Henry Harrison was approached months before to ensure that he would accept the party's nomination—and in 1836 the convention made no nomination at all. The 1831 convention was forced to make a "genuine selection" only because the "tacit understanding" before the convention that Ohio's John McLean would be the choice was undone by

McLean's unexpected refusal.[2] Moreover, the Anti-Masons' ultimate choice, William Wirt, had no effect on the 1832 election, as he carried only one state (Vermont) and received less than 1 percent of the vote in all but a couple of states. The Democratic Party held a national nominating convention in 1835, but its purpose was to nominate a vice-presidential candidate, as there was no opposition to Andrew Jackson's handpicked successor, Martin Van Buren. Similarly, at the National Republican convention in 1831, the nomination of Henry Clay merely ratified a decision that had been agreed upon beforehand. The Whigs who gathered in Harrisburg, then, embarked on something historic: a presidential national nominating convention in which nobody knew beforehand who would become the nominee and in which everybody knew that the nominee could end up becoming the next president of the United States.

SELECTING DELEGATES

The decision to hold a national nominating convention in Harrisburg, Pennsylvania, on the first Wednesday of December 1839 had been made by the Whig members of Congress in the spring of 1838. The caucus's call for a national convention proposed that each state should be represented "in proportion to their representation in the two Houses of Congress."[3] The number of delegates a state received would thus follow the same allocation mechanism as the electoral college. But the call for a convention was silent about how or when states should choose their delegates and said nothing about whether delegates should be pledged to presidential candidates, let alone vice-presidential candidates. These crucial questions were left to the state parties to decide.

Most states followed the guideline to select the number of delegates equal to the state's representation in both houses of Congress, but not all did. Delaware, to take the most egregious instance of noncompliance, selected five delegates from each of the state's three counties, giving it fifteen delegates, twelve more than prescribed by the caucus formula.[4] As it turned out, only ten of the fifteen made it to Harrisburg, but that still gave Delaware more than three times the number of delegates at the convention than it deserved under the agreed-upon formula. Indiana, which selected its delegates before congressional Whigs agreed on a time and place for a national convention, chose two delegates from each of its nine judicial circuits, giving it eighteen delegates, twice the number it was allotted under the congressional formula given its seven congressional districts. But since only ten delegates made it to the convention, the state ended up with only one more delegate than its allotted nine.[5] To take another example, Alabama selected two delegates rather than one for each of its five congressional districts, but because only four of the twelve named delegates participated at the convention, the state ended up underrepresented rather than overrepresented.[6] Louisiana also selected two delegates for each congressional district, but only one of the twelve delegates chosen, a self-professed "Adams and Clay Whig," made it to Harrisburg.[7]

The problem of delegates who were selected but did not participate was the biggest obstacle to fair representation between the states. Only one state—Delaware—sent more delegates to Harrisburg than it was entitled to, but at least thirteen states had fewer delegates at the convention than they should have based on the caucus formula. In several cases, states had dramatically fewer delegates than the number they had been allocated and had selected. Only nine of the fifteen Kentucky delegates, for instance, made the more than five-hundred-mile trek to Harrisburg. Virginia's delegation was also missing six of its members, and Ohio was four members short. New Hampshire was represented by only four of its allotted seven delegates and Maine by seven of its ten. None of Arkansas's three delegates made it to Harrisburg—a journey of one thousand miles—in time to participate, although one did arrive a few days after the convention had finished its work.

States from the South and the West were more likely to be underrepresented than mid-Atlantic and Northeastern states; indeed, only one Western state, Michigan, was lucky enough to have all of its apportioned delegates—all three of them—attend the convention. The more serious regional representational issue was posed by the three Southern states that chose to send no delegates at all: Tennessee, Georgia, and South Carolina. Together, those three states had a claim to thirty-seven delegates, and they would have been far more likely to vote for Clay than either Harrison or Scott, especially Tennessee and Georgia.

In the great majority of states, the delegate selection process was handled by a state nominating convention. A notable exception was Louisiana, where Whig state legislators, meeting in March 1839, decided early to take matters into their own hands.[8] In Maryland, too, the Whig members of the legislature selected delegates, although, in contrast to Louisiana, they selected only the two senatorial delegates, leaving it to each congressional district to select its own delegates.[9] Most state legislatures, however, felt that the selection of state delegates to a presidential nominating convention was more appropriately left to a state convention. This was not surprising since over the previous few decades, most states had gradually become accustomed to the idea of nominating candidates for statewide office through nominating conventions rather than legislative caucuses or informal meetings.[10]

Although there was general agreement that state delegates to a presidential nominating convention should be selected by a state nominating convention rather than a legislative caucus—just as delegates to state nominating conventions were typically selected at county conventions—there was less agreement on whether the convention should nominate each of the allocated delegates or only the two statewide, or senatorial, delegates. Several states decided it was better to leave the choice of district delegates to individual congressional districts, as would generally be the case for the nomination of candidates for Congress. At the Massachusetts state convention in Worcester, for instance, attended by nearly one thousand people from almost every town in the state, only the two at-large delegates were selected, leaving the district choices to local conventions.[11] Most state conventions, though, selected the entire slate of delegates, in some cases differentiating between senatorial and district delegates and in other cases not.

Connecticut, for instance, selected all eight of its delegates at a state nominating convention in Hartford on May 15, 1839. No attempt was made to differentiate between senatorial and district delegates, although the delegation included two of the state's prominent Whig politicians, former governor and member of Congress John Samuel Peters and the state's current lieutenant governor, Charles Hawley, who were de facto senatorial delegates. The Connecticut delegation also included the youngest member of the convention (at twenty-eight years of age), who had the additional distinction of possessing the convention's most memorable name: Epaphroditus Champion Bacon.[12]

In one case, it took two state conventions to pick the delegates. As many as a thousand people representing all but one Vermont county gathered for a "meeting of the people" in Woodstock in June 1839, and while they settled amicably on two at-large delegates (neither of whom ended up attending the Harrisburg convention), after "a long and animated debate" the assembled agreed to postpone the choice of the remaining delegates.[13] Whigs in towns all across the state then met again to pick delegates to the second convention, which was held in October in Montpelier. Delegates from each congressional district who were at the Montpelier convention then caucused to select one delegate for their district—and a substitute for each in case the chosen delegate could not attend.[14]

There was no statewide convention at all in the largest and most important state, New York.[15] The same divisions within the state party that had frustrated Clay's effort to persuade the state legislature to endorse him also stymied efforts to have the legislature issue a call for a state convention to select delegates. Instead, the Whig legislators punted to the six-person Whig Party state central committee, charging it to designate the proper mode and time for the selection of delegates. Plagued by the same divisions as the legislature, the committee issued its edict toward the end of June: there would be no statewide convention to pick delegates. Instead, it suggested that on November 11, in towns and wards across the state, Whigs should select delegates for district conventions. The following week, on November 19, those delegates, meeting in separate district conventions, would pick the state's forty district delegates. When the forty district delegates reached Harrisburg, they would then appoint two additional citizens to fill the at-large seats, and that delegation was also empowered to fill any vacancies that might occur from nonattendance.[16] This enabled the Whigs to put off the decision about delegates to the Harrisburg convention until after the New York elections (on November 4) and allowed the party to decentralize conflict over candidates.[17]

In Pennsylvania, where the divisions between the Clay and Harrison forces were even more contentious, the effort to hold a state nominating convention in Chambersburg resulted in a walkout by many of the Harrison supporters, who then called a convention of their own. Unlike the well-attended conventions in Massachusetts and Vermont, only about seventy-five Whigs attended the Chambersburg convention, representing about half of the state's counties. The Chambersburg convention offered resolutions endorsing Clay as "the preferred candidate" of the Whigs, and the counterconvention—christened by its supporters the "Union and Harmony Convention"—held in Harrisburg two months later offered resolutions in support of Harrison as the "only candidate" who could beat Van Buren. The Union and Harmony Convention, which included close to 120 delegates from about three-quarters of the state's counties, named the same two senatorial delegates as the Chambersburg convention—former governor John Andrew Shulze and former congressman Joseph Lawrence—but unlike the Chambersburg convention it also selected the state's allotted twenty-eight district delegates.[18]

Historian Robert Gray Gunderson suggests that the question of seating Pennsylvania's delegates at the national convention was the "first skirmish" at the national convention and that it was "adroitly won" by the Harrison forces because in agreeing to seat the delegates selected by both state conventions, they cleverly secured control of the state delegation.[19] But this account is misleading because a great majority of the Pennsylvania delegates who attended the national convention had been selected as delegates at the pro-Harrison Union and Harmony Convention or had attended that convention and were then subsequently named as substitutes by a committee designated for that purpose.[20] There were only three districts in which a seat was contested at the national convention, and that disagreement was "amicably adjusted" at the outset precisely because the decision had no effect on the balance of power within the state delegation.[21] It also may have helped the cause of conciliation that the Pennsylvania delegation was short three delegates, so adding three more delegates conveniently brought the delegation up to its allotted thirty seats.[22] Harrison's forces controlled the Pennsylvania delegation because they appointed district delegates at their state convention and the Clay forces at the Chambersburg convention did not.

The representativeness of state conventions was a problem in other states as well. In North Carolina, for instance, which had never before held a state nominating convention,[23] the convention attracted about ninety delegates from roughly three-fifths of the state's counties, but few delegates hailed from counties in the western, eastern, and southernmost parts of the state, a problem no doubt made worse by the "unceasing torrents" that had deterred some from enduring "the discomforts of a soaking ride." But neither the weather nor proximity to Raleigh, where the convention was held, could explain why so "few young men were present" and why the delegates were disproportionately "from the ranks of the venerable in years."[24] However, that North Carolina's Whigs held a state nominating convention at all showed that the party had, as Henry Clay had urged North Carolina's Willie Mangum the previous year, "overcome [its] repugnance" to conventions.[25]

In Illinois, too, the Whigs overcame—at least temporarily—their oft-expressed antipathy to nominating conventions and held their first-ever statewide convention in the fall of 1839. The state's Whigs justified their change of heart by arguing that their convention, unlike the Democratic Party's, was "not a packed convention of officeholders and expectants."[26] The Whigs of Illinois took a very different tack, however, from those of North Carolina in endorsing a candidate. Whereas North Carolina's convention recommended that the state's chosen delegates "adopt all honorable means which may serve to secure the nomination of Mr. Clay,"[27] the convention in Springfield expressed "full and entire confidence" in "both favorite 'Harries of the west,'" Henry Clay and William Henry Harrison.[28]

Refusing to take sides between the Whig candidates was particularly common in the conventions in New England. The state conventions in Massachusetts, New Hampshire, Vermont, and Connecticut all scrupulously avoided any statements favoring one candidate over another. The Southern conventions, in contrast, more freely expressed their candidate preference—for Henry Clay—which likely reflected the greater unanimity of candidate preferences in the Southern states and perhaps also the greater distrust or discomfort with the idea of a national convention.[29] Although Clay had struggled unsuccessfully to get the Virginia state legislature to endorse him in the early part of 1839, he had no difficulty receiving the unanimous endorsement of the Virginia state convention in Staunton held at the end of September. Moreover, the slate of twenty-three convention delegates chosen at Staunton was strongly committed to Clay's cause, none more so than the senatorial delegate Benjamin Watkins Leigh, who had served with Clay in the US Senate and kept in close communication with Clay in the months leading up to the national convention.[30]

Southern state conventions also often weighed in on the vice-presidential choice—something that no Northern state convention did. For instance, Mississippi's convention, held in Jackson in early February, instructed its delegates to vote for a ticket of Clay for president and Virginia's John Tyler for vice president.[31] Virginia and North Carolina also entered the vice-presidential sweepstakes, in both cases recommending the New York Conservative Democrat Nathaniel Tallmadge as Clay's running mate—a ticket that Clay had spent much of the past year trying to talk up as a way to build a winning coalition out of orthodox Whigs and disaffected probank Conservative Democrats. Getting Virginia to endorse the Clay-Tallmadge ticket was central to Clay's plan to forge an alliance between Virginia and New York, both states where Conservative Democrats were strong.[32]

It is striking that none of the resolutions drawn up by the many state conventions mentioned Winfield Scott. Some state conventions, including those in Virginia, North Carolina, and Mississippi, endorsed Clay. Others, such as those in Indiana and Ohio, as well as Pennsylvania's Union and Harmony Convention, backed Harrison. Still others, notably in Illinois, sang the praises of both Harrison and Clay. The omission of Scott was due in part to his late arrival as a serious candidate. Some states had already held conventions and selected delegates by the time it became clear that

Scott was a viable contender. But it also suggested that outside New York—which did not hold a state convention and selected its district and senatorial delegates in the two weeks prior to the Harrisburg convention—Scott might not have as many supporters as Weed and Seward hoped or Clay and Harrison feared. Scott's steep path to the nomination would depend on whether the evenly balanced Clay and Harrison forces deadlocked the convention. The longer the convention went on, the stronger Scott's chances would become. That was Weed's wager.

"FLITTING ROUND AND ROUND THE LOBBY"

Two weeks before the delegates were scheduled to descend on Harrisburg, Weed received a report from John Bradley, who had been selected as a convention delegate representing New York's eighteenth congressional district, which was coterminous with Jefferson County in upstate New York. Bradley informed Weed that "the Clay and Harrison men are at loggerheads" and conveyed his conviction that "by a judicious course [they] may be united upon Genl. Scott."[33] Weed received a far more alarming assessment, however, from New York congressman Edward Curtis, who represented New York City and had spent several weeks scurrying between New York City and the nation's capital in an effort to drum up support for Scott and head off any movement for Clay. Writing on November 18, only two days after Bradley wrote his hopeful missive, Curtis, an early backer of Daniel Webster who was now all in for Scott, warned Weed that "we shall be swamped without the most energetic efforts." He reported that the state's convention delegates were arriving in New York City with the purpose of selecting the state's two senatorial delegates and seemed to "think the City is the world." Moreover, Clay's allies, such as Dudley Selden—one of the four convention delegates selected to represent New York City, all of whom were firm friends of Clay—were "raising hell with them." "I believe we are ruined and damned," Curtis told Weed, imploring the Albany boss that before going to Harrisburg, he "come down and stand here" to quell the pro-Clay talk.[34]

Weed embarked for New York City the following week, as Curtis had urged. Whether through Weed's influence or because the excitable Curtis had exaggerated the problem—or some combination thereof—the New York delegation lined up solidly behind Scott. A first test of Scott's strength occurred when the state's district delegates gathered at the City Hotel on November 30 to select the two senatorial delegates. As the men arrived, the New York *Herald* reported, "there was a great deal of lobbying and scheming, and ear-wigging going on in the ante-rooms and in the hall and bar-room. . . . After about half an hour spent in whispering, and listening, and occasionally running up to the bar to get a drink, and gathering together in cliques and corners, the doors were closed," and the meeting commenced. Speaking "for the best part of an hour," Selden made an impassioned case for choosing Clay supporters as the senatorial delegates, and Lewis Farley Allen, a New York state legislator from Buffalo, countered by making the case for choosing those who supported Scott. Several other delegates rose to make their views known before six candidates were nominated: three who backed Scott, two who favored Clay, and one who supported Harrison. Chandler Starr, a Scott man and a former state legislator, was easily elected.[35] There was more heated discussion—and "not a little demonstration of angry feeling by the Clay men"—before the balloting for the second delegate. Clay's forces believed that their candidate deserved at least one of the two positions, but neither side was able to secure a majority for its favored candidate—the Scott forces backed New York's secretary of state, John Canfield Spencer, a Weed ally who had been among the state's prominent Anti-Masons, while the Clay partisans backed Pierre Van Cortlandt, Jr. Ultimately both candidates were dropped and the delegates settled on John Woodworth, a Harrison man, but one who preferred Scott to Clay. When it turned out that Woodworth would not be able to attend the convention, he was replaced by the third Scott man who had been nominated: State Senator Robert Nicholas, another former Anti-Mason who, like Spencer, hailed from western New York. The selection of senatorial delegates clearly revealed, as the *Herald*'s observer put it, "the position and weakness of the Clay party" in the New York delegation.[36] By Weed's estimate, conveyed to Seward on the day the Harrisburg convention opened, nearly three-quarters of the New York delegation would go for Scott.[37]

While the delegates wrangled about the selection of senatorial delegates inside the meeting room, in the adjoining lobby, "discussion and debating carried on for four hours, without ceasing, in a manner much more violent than that within the room." Clay's supporters were particularly bitter that their man was going be "throw[n] overboard merely to please the abolitionists." In the middle of all the "bawling and ranting and raving" was Thurlow Weed, "flitting round and round the lobby like a troubled spirit, running in and out, looking listening whispering and caucusing with all the energy and cunning of Satan when he tempted Eve to sin." Or so it seemed to James Gordon Bennett, who, while he heartily approved of Weed's choice of candidate, could not bring himself to approve of his motives or methods, however effective they might be.[38]

One of the principal arguments employed by Weed and his allies to build support for Scott was that Clay had so alienated abolitionists that the Kentuckian could not carry the state. But while this argument was freely expressed in the New York City Hotel—and no argument angered the Clay forces more—it was an argument that would be trickier to make in Harrisburg. As Curtis warned Weed, there was a risk that the abolitionist argument against Clay, so effective in moving New York's delegates from Clay to Scott, might undermine support for Scott in the South. "I pray you," Curtis told Weed, "to remember this in the counsels you give to our friends who are to perform *inside* of the Convention."[39]

While Weed was in New York City, he was not only marshaling the Scott forces in the New York delegation but also meeting with several New England delegates who were on their way to Harrisburg. In his autobiography, Weed reported that he met with James Wilson, a New Hampshire senatorial delegate, and George Ashmun, a Massachusetts delegate, both of whom had been "devoted friends" of Webster.[40] According to Weed, they "agreed to act together" at the convention, although the precise content of that agreement is unclear. It could have meant that Wilson and Ashmun agreed to join in supporting Scott, in which case their agreement "to act together" was effectively nullified by the convention's adoption of the unit rule since a majority of the Massachusetts and New Hampshire delegations backed Harrison. Alternatively, or in addition, the agreement to act together may have been a pledge that if their preferred general could not win, they would swing their support to the other general rather than see Clay win.[41]

The key to a Scott victory in Harrisburg was to avoid alienating Harrison and Clay supporters. Two days before the convention opened, Curtis was feeling much more optimistic about Scott's chances. Writing from Washington, he reported to Weed that there was "a general feeling among gentlemen from North South West and East . . . that if Genl Scott can be presented to the country without an open rupture with the friends of Mr. Clay, . . . he will prove the savior of the Whig & opposition party everywhere."[42] Weed also received an encouraging report from Buffalo congressman Millard Fillmore, who wrote to Weed from the nation's capital on the same day as Curtis. Fillmore told Weed that all except three members of the New York congressional delegation agreed that Clay could not beat Van Buren in New York and that when the results of this informal poll were communicated to Clay, he took the news "in kindness" and pledged "a cordial and hearty support" to the convention's choice. Fillmore judged Clay's spirit of conciliation to be "magnanimous, and worthy of Henry Clay. If the convention now does its duty and nominates Scott, all will be well."[43]

One man's duty was another's perfidy, and Harrison's supporters, who were also doing their share of planning and plotting on the eve of the convention, judged the delegates' mood differently than did Weed's friends. A diary kept by Ohio's Ephraim Cutler, among the convention's oldest delegates at age seventy-one, records small knots of conversation that occurred on steamboats, stagecoaches, and hotels in the days leading up to the convention. On the five-day journey to Harrisburg from his home in southeastern Ohio, he met and conversed with delegates from Ohio, Pennsylvania, Indiana, and Michigan. On December 2, the day after arriving in Harrisburg, he was among a group of fifteen delegates from three states—Ohio, Indiana, and Michigan—who huddled to exchange notes about candidate preferences in their various districts. "The prevailing opinion," Cutler concluded, "was that Harrison has the preference." The following day, Cutler spoke with several New York delegates and surmised that "opinions appear to be settling on Harrison, though some New York men favor Scott."[44] Even Weed had to concede that hosting the convention in Harrisburg—a bastion of Harrison support—had created an unmistakable "Harrison atmosphere."[45]

THE CURTAIN GOES UP: DAYS 1 AND 2

Two hundred Whig delegates from twenty-two states took their seats at noon on Wednesday, December 4, 1839, in Harrisburg's largest building, a new Lutheran church that had been built to replace the one that had burned down two years before.[46] By the convention's close on Saturday, December 7, the number of delegates would be closer to 225.[47] Only Arkansas, South Carolina, Tennessee, and Georgia were unrepresented at the convention, although Louisiana had to make do with a single delegate. The convention's sole task on the opening day was to select a committee made up of one representative from each state that would be charged with naming the convention's officers. The convention would get down to business the following day, with Virginia's James Barbour anointed as its presiding officer.

In a convention full of politicians, Barbour was perhaps the most distinguished. He had been secretary of war in the John Quincy Adams administration and a US senator for a decade before that as well as the governor of Virginia and speaker of the Virginia House of Delegates. Most symbolically, exactly eight years before, he had been elected the presiding offer at the National Republican Party convention that had nominated Clay for president. He was also a friend of Clay's, with whom he shared a passion for horses. Barbour's selection was a tribute to his stature within the party and a nod to the importance of Virginia but perhaps also a reflection that a majority of the states—at least twelve of the twenty-two—backed Clay.

The sixty-four-year-old Barbour treated the delegates to an opening pep talk that not only criticized the "disastrous effects of the mal-administration" of national affairs by the Van Buren administration but also underscored the high stakes of this election. In Barbour's view—which mirrored Clay's—the country was "in the midst of a revolution" as a consequence of Jackson and Van Buren's "Executive aggression," which had "broken down" the "walls of separation which our Fathers constructed between the different departments of the government." "The forms of the Constitution are retained," Barbour said, "but its spirit gone—your President is a monarch almost absolute." Barbour also underscored, not surprisingly, the paramount importance of party unity, noting that "personal predilections" were "instantly to be surrendered" once the convention made its choice. He concluded, "Present me a man that promises success, and whose character guarantees this result, and I care not what letters of the alphabet make his name, I will sing hosannas to it as loud as anyone."[48]

After Barbour concluded his speech, it was on to the important business of deciding how the convention would proceed. Some matters were easily decided. Newspaper reporters were to be admitted to the floor of the convention. Clergy of different faiths would be invited to officiate. But the big question was how the convention would vote. Would it be one person, one vote, as with a legislative body? Or would states vote as a bloc (the so-called unit rule), as they generally did in casting votes in the electoral college? After all, representation at the convention (one delegate for each House district and two extra senatorial delegates per state) precisely mirrored representation in the electoral college. But the convention had already agreed to follow the rules of order of the House of Representatives "so far as the same may be applicable," which would suggest that one person, one vote would be the more natural option. A glaring problem, however, with one person, one vote was that although delegates had been allocated on the basis of their state's representation in Congress, almost three-quarters of the states—including every Southern and Western state—had fewer delegates in attendance than they were allocated, and one state, Delaware, had more than three times the number it was allocated.[49] One person, one vote would give the ten delegates from Delaware more influence than the nine delegates from Kentucky, even though the formula gave Kentucky the right to five times the number of delegates as Delaware. One person, one vote would disproportionately harm those states whose delegates were compelled to travel the longest distances to get to Harrisburg. Using the unit rule would remove this problem.

But the unit rule had problems of its own, the most important of which was that it would effectively disenfranchise those delegates who harbored a candidate preference different from the preference of the majority of the state's delegates. For instance, according to Weed's count, ten of New York's delegates supported Clay and two supported Harrison, so the unit rule would prevent those twelve delegates from having their vote counted.[50] In addition, if delegate preferences were evenly split between candidates, it could result in a state's delegation being unable to cast its allotted votes.

No record was preserved of the debate at the convention over the unit rule, but we know that Charles Penrose of Pennsylvania, an ardent proponent of Harrison's candidacy who had led the walkout at the Chambersburg convention, was the one to move to adopt the unit rule. His proposal came as an amendment to one made by the Massachusetts delegate Peleg Sprague, a former US senator from Maine who was among a group of Webster allies at the convention working to nominate Harrison. Sprague's proposal—which had been circulated the day before the convention opened[51]—was essentially that each state should meet and vote as a group in private and that a committee composed of no more than three delegates from each state would then communicate the results of the state's balloting to a general committee of conference, which would be made up of the twenty-two state committees. If a candidate had a majority, the conference committee would announce the winner to the convention. If no candidate had a majority, the states' delegates would meet and ballot again, and the process would be repeated. Under this proposal, there would be no voting for candidates on the convention floor—and deliberations would take place away from the gaze of the newspaper reporters who had been generously invited in to observe the convention.[52]

Many efforts were made to defeat Sprague's resolution and Penrose's amendment. Willoughby Newton, a Virginia lawyer and former state legislator (and future member of Congress), moved to refer the matter to a committee composed of one delegate from each state, on which Clay's forces would have a majority. The motion was rejected, as were several similar efforts to refer the Sprague-Penrose plan to a committee. Another tack was tried by Maryland's Richard Bowie, a young state senator and whip-smart lawyer (he would go on to become not only a future member of Congress but the chief judge of Maryland's high court), who proposed replacing the Sprague-Penrose voting procedure with the simpler method of one person, one vote on the floor of the convention. He also proposed remedying the inequity issue by giving a majority of each state's delegation the right to cast the votes of any absent members "as they think proper"—which, in practice, would likely have meant using the unit rule for absent members. Louisiana's one delegate, for instance, would thus have been empowered to cast 5 votes, and a majority of Kentucky's nine-man delegation would have decided how best to cast the votes of its six absent delegates. This proposal, too, was defeated, and after a lengthy and "animated debate," the Sprague-Penrose proposal was adopted.[53]

Most commentators see the adoption of the unit rule as the crucial procedural move that killed Clay's nomination since, as David and Jeanne Heidler write, "the procedure instantly made Clay's numerous votes in New York, Pennsylvania, and Ohio immaterial."[54] The unit rule certainly served Weed's interests because it enabled New York to remain united for Scott; as Weed wrote to Seward on the convention's first day, so long as New York "were united and strong, the ground would be given to us."[55] Indeed, pro-Clay delegates from New York, with Dudley Selden predictably the most vocal, were so livid about the unit rule that Massachusetts delegate Henry Shaw chastised them for their "rabid zeal"—although Shaw quickly withdrew his "objectionable language" and, evidently to much laughter, offered to substitute "patriotic fury" instead.[56]

One should be careful not to overstate Clay's strength at the convention, however. In Ohio especially, it is doubtful Clay would have gained many or any votes; according to Ephraim Cutler's contemporaneous notes, the entire seventeen-person delegation was unanimous in its conviction that only Harrison could carry the state.[57] In New York, if we accept Weed's estimate, Clay would likely have picked up 10 votes, but Harrison would also have gained a couple. Pennsylvania is a more difficult case, but because the vast majority of the delegates were selected at the pro-Harrison Harrisburg convention, it seems unlikely that Clay would have had the support of more than about one-quarter of the state's thirty delegates.[58] Assuming the remaining nineteen states were a wash—which seems unlikely since Clay's opportunity for additional votes would have been limited to seven majority-Harrison or majority-Scott states totaling 58 votes, whereas Harrison would have been fishing in a much larger pool of fourteen majority-Clay or majority-Scott states totaling 118 votes—Clay would have picked up perhaps an additional 16 votes, which would have left him still well shy of a majority. It is by no means certain, then, that Clay would have secured a majority using Bowie's modified one person, one vote rule, although his chances would unquestionably have been improved given the much greater unanimity of opinion in Clay's Southern stronghold.[59]

Some historians have seen the adoption of the unit rule as "an egregious lapse" on the part of Clay's forces, a sign that Harrison's and Scott's partisans were shrewder and more farsighted than Clay's duller partisans.[60] This interpretation seems to assume that Clay's supporters, many of whom were experienced legislators, did not realize the effect that the voting method would have on their candidate's chances. Militating against this interpretation is the fact that delegates who supported Clay and hailed from Clay-friendly states twice tried strenuously to defeat the Sprague-Penrose proposal—and then tried again the following morning, when Cassius Clay, a Kentucky state legislator and cousin of Henry Clay, proposed without success the same plan that Bowie had offered the previous day. It seems more accurate, then, to say that Henry Clay's forces lost their bid to defeat the unit rule not so much because they were less savvy than the Harrison-Scott forces as because they lacked the votes. The essential problem was that Clay's supporters controlled only a plurality of the delegates, whereas Scott's and Harrison's forces, when acting together, commanded a majority.[61] Clay's forces lost on the procedural question, in short, because they never possessed a majority for their candidate.

After the Sprague-Penrose plan was approved, the convention adjourned for the day, leaving the delegations of each state to spend the evening, "separate and apart," deliberating about their choice. Reporting from the convention that evening, one correspondent thought it "extremely doubtful" that any candidate had the necessary votes, though he also reported that Harrison's supporters had "become very sanguine" about their candidate's chances, largely because it was "understood that the friends of Scott will generally rally upon Harrison."[62] That prediction would be tested the following day, when the convention—or more precisely the state delegations and the conference committee—would be devoted almost entirely to the main event of choosing the Whig nominee for president of the United States.

The convention's first ballot validated Bradley's surmise that the Harrison and Clay forces were "at loggerheads"; both had strength enough to check the other but no more than that. Clay received 103 votes from twelve states: from Alabama 7, Connecticut 8, Delaware 3, Illinois 5, Kentucky 15, Louisiana 5, Maryland 10, Mississippi 4, Missouri 4, North Carolina 15, Rhode Island 4, and Virginia 23. Harrison had nearly the same level of support, with 94 votes from only seven states: from Indiana 9, Maine 10, Massachusetts 14, Michigan 3,[63] New Hampshire 7, Ohio 21, and Pennsylvania 30. Scott held the balance of power with 57 votes garnered from three states: New Jersey (8), New York (42), and Vermont (7). Each candidate was well shy of the 128 votes needed to secure the nomination. So long as New York stayed with Scott, neither Clay nor Harrison had a viable path to the nomination.

Since no candidate had a majority, the convention adjourned, sent the state delegations back to work, and gave the conference committee—composed of forty-three delegates from the twenty-two states[64]—until 3 p.m. to report again to the convention. At the appointed time, the bell rang, the delegates reassembled, the gallery filled "with anxious spectators" (it was, by all accounts, a strongly pro-Harrison crowd on account of the location), and "the ladies . . . swarm[ed] into the seats gallantly provided for them."[65] Then came the announcement: the committee had nothing to report because still no candidate had a majority. The voting on the second ballot, though not publicly announced at the convention, appears to have been identical to the first. The state delegations were sent back to work, and the committee was told to report to the convention at 7 p.m. The expectant crowds again filled the gallery at the appointed hour, and again they dispersed after learning that the committee had nothing to report, although this time Scott picked up 11 votes, taking Connecticut from Clay and Michigan from Harrison. With Scott now up to 68 votes, Harrison down to 91, and Clay down to 95, it seemed that perhaps the logjam was breaking, and there might be a late movement to Scott, exactly as Weed and his allies had hoped. Any such hopes, however, were dashed when the delegates reconvened at 9 p.m. Once more, the committee, which had been negotiating feverishly in the church basement, was unable to announce a nominee. Maryland's Reverdy Johnson seized on the apparent stalemate to suggest that it was time to disband the conference committee and instead allow the convention to "take the subject into their own hands" on a one person, one vote basis. A representative of the committee pleaded for a bit more time, and the convention, while rejecting an adjournment, agreed to take a short recess to enable the committee to continue its work.[66]

At 10 o'clock, the convention reconvened, and the chair of the conference committee, John Owen, a former governor of North Carolina who had presided over the state nominating convention a few weeks earlier, reported that at last the convention had a candidate who commanded a majority. New York, Vermont, and Michigan had switched from Scott to Harrison, while Illinois had deserted Clay, giving Harrison 148 votes. The only state that mattered, though, was New York. Its switch was both necessary and sufficient to give Harrison the requisite 128 votes for the nomination.

The story that historians typically tell to explain Harrison's selection is that Pennsylvania's Thaddeus Stevens got his hands on a letter that Scott had written to Francis Granger "in a clumsy attempt to win antislavery support." Sometime shortly before the final balloting, Stevens wandered casually—or, according to one account, "limped frowning"—amid the Virginia delegation and "surreptitiously dropped" the letter on the floor, where it was discovered by the Virginians, who were so horrified that they immediately abandoned Scott as their second choice in favor of Harrison. Weed then realized that he could not get the South to go for Scott and so swung his support to Harrison. The Whig nomination, on this telling, was secured by the devious hand of the "Worshipful Master of Anti-Masonry," who executed "the decisive maneuver of the convention."[67]

Should we believe this story? There are strong reasons not to. First, the letter in question has never been found. Second, there is no mention of this event in any of the contemporary sources, whether letters, newspapers, or diaries. The claim first surfaced in 1900, more than sixty years after the event allegedly took place, in a book by veteran journalist Alexander McClure called *Our Presidents and How We Make Them*, which devoted brief chapters to every presidential election from 1789 to 1896. The chapters on the late nineteenth century are grounded in McClure's firsthand participation as a reporter and a Republican politician, but obviously he did not have that same advantage in recounting the elections of the first half of the nineteenth century—he was eleven at the time of the Harrisburg convention. But as a well-known reporter and political figure in Pennsylvania in the late 1850s and 1860s, McClure knew Stevens, and it was "Mr. Stevens himself," McClure said, who told him of this event.[68] In other words, assuming that McClure correctly recollected what Stevens had told him (and apparently nobody else) somewhere between thirty and forty years earlier (Stevens died in 1868), the account of Stevens's pivotal importance in deciding the nominee is based solely on the boast of Stevens himself.[69]

Not only is there no contemporary or subsequent corroboration for this story, but the tale also suffers from several glaring inconsistencies. First, and most important, Virginia stuck with Clay until the bitter end. In the words of Horace Greeley, whose hotel room served as the "anti-Clay head-quarters" during the convention,[70] virtually every Virginia delegate "was for Clay first, last, and all the time, for him whether he could be elected or not."[71] Virginia's second choice remained immaterial because the delegation never showed a willingness to abandon Clay. Certainly, Virginia's pro-Clay delegation had no incentive to assume a position that would trigger a move away from Clay. What seems to have changed Weed's position was not a change of heart on the part of Virginia's delegates but instead their unwillingness—and that of other Clay delegations—to throw over their favorite. As a correspondent from the Boston *Atlas* reported from the convention at 11:30 p.m., little more than an hour after Harrison's nomination was announced, "At last it became evident somebody must give way. The Scott men said to the Clay men, Make a candidate or we will. The Clay men said, We have no second choice. The Scott men then made theirs—not the choice of their feelings, but their judgment."[72]

An additional reason to be skeptical of Stevens's account is that the leader of the Virginia delegation, and Virginia's sole representative on the conference committee charged with communicating the state's vote and views to the rest of that committee, was Benjamin Watkins Leigh, who was one of Scott's oldest and dearest friends.[73] When Scott was twenty-five years old, he lived with Leigh, who was five years his senior, and the two men "spent many evenings together reading choice passages of English literature aloud and discussing what they had read."[74] Leigh had steered his young friend to give up his legal ambitions and to concentrate on his military career, and the two men had remained in intimate communication ever since. Had the Virginia delegation come into possession of a letter from Scott that "evidently sought to conciliate antislavery sentiment" in New York (McClure's words), Leigh was better positioned than any American to explain Scott's views to his fellow Virginians, and it seems unlikely that Leigh would have allowed a letter of this sort to be used to shoot down his friend's chances. In any event, Leigh's primary political loyalties (like those of the rest of the Virginia delegation) were to Clay, and that alone would have given him (and the delegation he represented) cause enough not to communicate to the conference committee misgivings they might suddenly have had about Scott.[75]

Even the logistics of this theory feel dubious. Virginia's seventeen delegates caucused privately, so how was it that they did not notice the notorious Thaddeus Stevens lurking in their midst, particularly in the latter stages of the state's deliberations? McClure's story intimates that Stevens was able to saunter in without drawing attention to himself because "the headquarters of the Virginia delegation" was "always crowded," but that is at odds with other descriptions of states caucusing in relative secrecy behind closed doors. One might also ask how likely it is that a group that included so many savvy and experienced politicians would not have wondered how such a letter miraculously appeared on the floor and whose interests this missive was put there to serve. And if they did allow themselves to walk into such a transparent trap designed to defeat both their first and second choices, it "strains credulity," as Alan Peskin rightly points out, "to imagine that, in the gossip-living world of politics, not one of the many people who would have known of the alleged incident would have tattled to Scott," not to mention to Clay or indeed any other living soul.[76]

In sum, it's clear why Stevens should have wanted us to believe that he outsmarted the dim-witted Virginians, but it's less clear why we should believe this tale, particularly when there is a far more straightforward explanation for why Weed switched from Scott to Harrison at the end of a long day that ended with Weed no closer to nominating Scott than he had been at the outset of the day.[77] The fundamental problem was that Scott's support outside New York and a few other small states was tepid at best, while the support for Clay in the South and Harrison in Ohio and Pennsylvania remained steadfast and intense. Harrison's supporters in Ohio and Pennsylvania continued to insist that only Harrison could carry their state, and Clay's supporters in Virginia and North Carolina remained similarly committed to Clay. By the end of the convention's third day, it was evident that Weed's Scott gambit had failed, and his only viable option was to resort to plan B, which had always been Harrison. While Weed still believed that Scott was the strongest candidate in New York, he also believed, as did many others in the state, that Harrison could beat Van Buren in New York.[78]

Thaddeus Stevens had less to do with Clay's defeat than did Webster's allies in Massachusetts, Maine, and New Hampshire, who helped to keep those three states and their 28 votes in Harrison's column on each ballot, even though—unlike in the cases of Ohio, Pennsylvania, and Indiana—nobody believed that Harrison was essential to carrying any of these three states. Massachusetts was a reliably Whig state, and New Hampshire seemed a lock for the Democrats. Only Maine would have been viewed as a potentially competitive state—albeit with a Democratic lean—but Scott was the only candidate who might give the party a special edge there; certainly, anti-Clay sentiment in Maine, as historian Sydney Nathans observes, was "slight."[79]

Clay was also done in by the underrepresentation of the Southern states at the convention. Had delegates from Arkansas, Tennessee, Georgia, and South Carolina shown up, Clay could have received another 40 votes on the first ballot, leaving him only 5 votes shy of the 148 he would have needed had all 24 states been present. As important, Clay's forces might then have had the votes to defeat the unit rule.[80] The case of Arkansas was simply bad luck, as its delegate failed to reach Harrisburg in time, but its 3 votes would not have changed the dynamic or outcome of the convention.[81] None of the other three states, however, came close to calling a state nominating convention or sending delegates. In Georgia, the anti–Van Buren party called itself the State Rights Party and "recognized no connection between themselves and national Whigs."[82] South Carolina marched to the beat set by Calhoun, who was now a staunch ally of Van Buren and a fierce opponent of Clay, so Clay could expect no help there. Tennessee was the only one of these three states for which Clay had a realistic hope that delegates might be sent to the convention, but that hope had been dashed in September (as we saw in the previous chapter) when he learned that the state's Whigs had no intention of sending delegates for fear it would open them up to the charge of hypocrisy and cost them dearly at the polls. Clearly, Clay's reliance on a region of the country in which the Whig Party was less well organized and developed must be counted as more than merely an unfortunate accident but instead as a fatal flaw in his Southern strategy.

Ultimately, Clay failed to secure the nomination because his supporters could not overcome deep concerns in crucial Northern states about his electability. That had been the big question mark over Clay's candidacy from the outset, but it was his great misfortune to have the convention punctuate a year in which the economy had shown signs of recovery and the Whigs had suffered a string of demoralizing electoral defeats and setbacks across the North as well as in the South. If the Whigs had held their national nominating convention six months later, as the Democrats did, the politicos' calculations would likely have looked much different. By then the economy would again be mired in recession, and it would be much easier to imagine that Clay, or any Whig, could defeat Van Buren.[83]

Having selected Harrison, the convention now had the task of molli-fying Clay's disappointed supporters. The unit rule and the caucusing of states in secret made many Clay allies feel that their candidate had been cheated out of the nomination. Delegates from the Southern states, many of whom had long distrusted conventions, now felt even more aggrieved and found that the result confirmed their early suspicions that a national convention would be used to "sacrifice the south to the north."[84] Not one Southern state had voted in favor of Harrison. All of them voted for Clay on every ballot. If the Whigs left Harrisburg with the party still divided by candidate and region, they would embark on the 1840 campaign even more divided than they had been in 1836.

The vice presidency was the obvious place to start to win back the South and heal the divisions. There are sharply divergent accounts of precisely what transpired and who was offered the vice-presidential nomination. The problem in large part is that much of what we know about John Tyler's se-lection as the vice-presidential nominee comes from accounts written after President Harrison died, by which time it was clear that the selection of Ty-ler had been a catastrophic mistake. Eager to distance themselves from the selection of a president who ended up frustrating Whig ambitions at every turn—including twice vetoing Whig bills to create a national bank—those who had a hand in the disastrous choice emphasized that the selection of Tyler had been forced upon the convention. As Weed later insisted, Tyler was offered the position only out of desperation because "we could get no-body else to accept it."[85]

It appears that the conference committee spent little or no time discuss-ing the vice presidency, although Leigh reports that there was a "unanimous sentiment" on the committee that if Clay was selected for the presidency the vice presidency would go to a nonslaveholding state, and if Harrison or Scott were nominated for the presidency the vice presidency would go to a person from a slaveholding state.[86] Harrison's nomination immediately set off a scramble to find a running mate from a slaveholding state who would accept the nomination. Weed claimed that "several delegates" spent the "whole night" coming up with an acceptable candidate, preferably "some prominent friend" of Clay,"[87] but that they were frustrated at every turn by Clay supporters still angry about the convention's presidential selection. Certainly many names would have been bandied about in informal con-versation—the likes of Kentucky's John Crittenden, Tennessee's John Bell, North Carolina's Willie Mangum and John Owen, South Carolina's Willie

John Tyler. An 1841 lithograph by Charles Fenderich completed shortly after Tyler's elevation to the presidency following Harrison's death. (Courtesy of the Library of Congress)

Preston, Virginia's Benjamin Watkins Leigh and James Barbour, and Delaware's John Clayton—but whatever "whisperings in dark corners" there may have been that night, the record suggests that Tyler was a popular choice who was selected on the first ballot.[88]

The process for selecting the vice president was the same as the process for selecting the president, although complicated by the awkward fact that the convention could not know for sure whether a nominee would accept the position if it were offered unless he was at the convention or, failing that, somebody could vouch for his intention to accept. Each state delegation was commanded to nominate a vice-presidential candidate and communicate their state's vote to the conference committee. Maine, the first state to be called, nominated Tyler. Although there was a "scattering" of votes for different individuals—including Leigh, who was nominated by Massachusetts but declined to be considered—"a majority of the whole number of votes, and a large majority too," Leigh reported, was given for Tyler, which rendered Leigh's refusal superfluous.[89]

Tyler was an appealing choice for many reasons. First, he hailed from the electorally most important Southern state, Virginia, where he had served with distinction as a state legislator, member of Congress, US senator, and governor. Second, he had been selected as Harrison's vice-presidential nominee in Maryland in 1836—a ticket that carried the state by more than 7 points—and had also been the vice-presidential choice of South Carolina (with Willie Mangum the choice for president) and Georgia and Tennessee (with Hugh Lawson White at the top of the ticket). Third, he was widely admired by Whigs for having resigned his US Senate seat in 1836 rather than follow instructions from the Democratic-controlled Virginia state legislature to expunge Jackson's censure. Finally, Tyler was a friend and admirer of Clay's and had fought to the last for his candidacy—it was even said that he shed tears at the announcement of Clay's defeat, which, although likely not true, bolstered his bona fides as a Clay loyalist.[90]

Clay greatly aided the cause of unity by having prepared a letter to be read to the convention in case the presidential nomination went to one of his rivals as well as by his prompt and unqualified embrace of the Harrison-Tyler ticket after the convention. Kentucky's senatorial delegate Leslie Combs, declaring the "heart of Kentucky" to be "bruised . . . not broken" by the convention's decision, read aloud Clay's letter, which beseeched the delegates to "discard all attachment or partiality to me" and to "heartily unite" on the convention's choice.[91] Following Combs's reading of the letter, delegates flooded onto the floor to express their deep admiration for Clay and to pledge their support for Harrison.[92]

Among the most revealing of the many speeches on that final day was that of Kentucky's other senatorial delegate, Thomas Metcalfe, who along with Combs had represented Kentucky on the conference committee. Metcalfe paid tribute to the deliberative process by which Harrison had been selected. He told his fellow delegates that he had come to the convention believing Clay to be the candidate most likely to win in November, but having "interchanged sentiments with the delegates" from other states—particularly those on the committee—he had been convinced that "he was mistaken" and that Harrison was the "strongest man" to enable the party to "overturn the powerful despotism" of the Van Buren administration.[93] Electability had carried the day for Harrison—and it was the Sprague-Penrose voting procedures, by promoting deliberation within the conference committee and backed by the unit rule, that had ensured that concerns about electability in the most populous Northern states were not pushed aside.

After the delegates had exhausted themselves in fulsome praise of Clay's character and the convention's harmonious spirit, the delegates voted to make Harrison's nomination unanimous—a resolution offered by Maryland's Reverdy Johnson, who had fought harder than almost any delegate to protect Clay's interests at the convention. With "the voice of congratulation sounding all around" them,[94] Kentucky's young William Preston, who had earned his law degree from Harvard only the year before, eagerly proposed that the convention cap its fine work by adopting "an address to the people of the United States" that would lay out the party's principles and positions. Some of the older and wiser Whigs must have groaned at the suggestion, and Leigh was quick out of his seat to shoot down the idea—and Preston almost as quick to defer.[95] Coming to an agreement on a nominee had been difficult enough for the delegates without trying to pull together a last-minute agreement on policy and principles.[96] The convention had achieved what had eluded the Whigs four years before, and there was no appetite in Harrisburg for allowing the party's hard-earned harmony to unravel acrimoniously at the eleventh hour.

"WE GO FOR PRINCIPLES, NOT MEN"
THE DEMOCRATIC CONVENTION

Word of William Henry Harrison's nomination reached the nation's capital on Sunday, December 8. Upon learning of the choice, South Carolina senator John Calhoun was quick to predict that Harrison's nomination would "throw off the Southern division of the [Whig] party."[1] Although Calhoun always set his own course, he was hardly alone in thinking that the nomination could split the Whig Party along sectional lines—indeed, the fear of such a sectional split was what had led the Whigs to spurn a national nominating convention in the 1836 presidential election. And the final vote at the Harrisburg convention could hardly have been more sectional: not one slave state voted for Harrison (or Scott), and Rhode Island was the only free state to cast its votes for Henry Clay.

Harrison's fate and that of the Whig Party rested in Clay's hands. Without the Kentuckian's support, the party might rupture, rendering Tippecanoe an unabashedly sectional candidate who would have to run against an incumbent president who could marshal support in both the North and the South. All eyes in the capital and nation were thus fixed on the Kentucky senator, watching to see how he would respond to the disappointment of being passed over for a man whom almost all of Washington recognized as Clay's intellectual and political inferior.

Legend has it that Clay reacted badly. The most commonly repeated tale is that when Clay received the news of Harrison's nomination at his Washington boardinghouse on Sunday night—where he was supposedly "drinking freely in anticipation of his success"—he erupted in a drunken "storm of desperation and curses." Stamping his feet and shaking his fists, he denounced "the diabolical intrigue" that had defeated him and damned his feckless friends for not being "worth the powder and shot it would take to kill them." Wallowing in self-pity, he supposedly declared himself "the most unfortunate man in the history of parties: always run by my friends when sure to be defeated, and now betrayed for a nomination when I or anyone, would be sure of an election."[2] Never mind that at the time of the convention, after a string of embarrassing Whig defeats in the fall, it was not at all clear to Clay and most of the rest of the party that any Whig would win, which was exactly why Harrison rather than Clay had been nominated at Harrisburg.[3]

The other oft-told story is even less flattering to Clay—and even more implausible. In this version, Clay learned of his defeat while at the Astor Hotel in New York City, where Winfield Scott and several prominent Whigs, including Kentucky's other senator, John Crittenden, were "playing a quiet game of whist to beguile the tediousness of waiting" for news from Harrisburg. Upset that "Scott's friends had not supported him," Clay proceeded to give the seated Scott "a heavy blow on the left shoulder, denouncing him at the same time in unseemly language." The angry Clay had to be led out of the room by Crittenden, talk ensued of a possible duel, Scott demanded only an apology, and by the morning Clay had cooled off enough to apologize "very courteously."[4]

Although both stories are offered as historical fact—and the "most unfortunate man" and "powder and shot" quotations especially are endlessly recycled—they warrant greater skepticism than they have received. Both accounts have the problem that they were told long after the fact and lack any corroborating contemporaneous evidence. The Astor Hotel story was relayed to a Scott biographer—and former Confederate general—more than a half century after the events by Schuyler Hamilton—Alexander Hamilton's grandson and a former aide-de-camp to General Scott—who said that Scott had told him the story in December 1851. But while Scott was in New York when he received the news of Harrison's nomination, Clay was not—he was in Washington.[5] The Washington boardinghouse story—and the colorful quotations—first surfaced in 1872 in Henry Wise's score-settling memoir, *Seven Decades of the Union*. Wise's memoir has the advantage of purporting to be a firsthand account of Clay's reaction—Wise claimed he was the one who brought Clay the news—but Wise, who "tended to personalize issues and tilt at windmills of his own paranoid construction,"[6] is neither a reliable nor an impartial observer. He and Clay fell out almost immediately after Harrison's death, with Wise—later one of Virginia's most ardent secessionists—becoming one of the few members of Congress to support his fellow Virginian Tyler and Clay becoming Tyler's most exacting congressional critic.

That Clay was disappointed to learn of his defeat is beyond question—although it is not true that Clay was confident he would be the convention's choice; his correspondence in the days leading up to the convention shows that he was bracing himself for defeat, although to Scott, not Harrison. That he would have felt a sense of betrayal is hardly surprising since disappointed allies at the convention, like Kentucky's Leslie Combs, rushed to tell Clay that he had been "deceived betrayed & beaten by Northern abolition, Antimasonry and the Dutch."[7] The feeling that Clay's forces had been cheated and outmaneuvered at the convention was widely shared in Washington. Upon learning of Harrison's nomination, Joseph Gales of the pro-Clay *National Intelligencer* privately harrumphed that it was a "triumph of Anti-Masonry" and surmised that it was "entirely the work" of the calculating New York governor William Henry Seward.[8] Clay had been grousing well before the convention about the machinations of the Anti-Masons, the scheming of Webster and Weed, and the implacable intransigence of the abolitionists. But the drunken tirades and Rumpelstiltskin-like tantrums, let alone the smacking of Scott, seem embellished if not entirely made up for the sake of a few colorful anti-Clay yarns.

These dramatic stories and manufactured quotations distract from the far more important fact about Clay's reaction to Harrisburg, namely, that whatever personal disappointment he felt, he did everything in his power to counteract the feelings of anger and betrayal among his supporters. In both private letters and public speeches,[9] Clay responded to Harrison's nomination with a steadfast and often rousing insistence on the importance of party unity and supporting the Harrison-Tyler ticket. He made his position clear in a speech given at a dinner in honor of the Harrisburg delegates at the nation's capital on Wednesday, December 11:

> If the friends or favorites are disappointed, they are bound to forget their disappointment—they are bound by every consideration of patriotism—by their hopes of changing and destroying this corrupt Administration . . . to follow my example, and vote heartily as I shall, for the nomination which has been made. . . . Look not then to Harrisburg but to the White House—not to the nomination, but to the mountain of corruption which it is designed to overthrow—not to the man who has been nominated

but to the Goths and Vandals at the Capitol. . . . Tell your constituents . . . to put forth all the energies they possess to relieve the land from the curse which rests upon it; and if they can then be indifferent, from that moment, they cease to be patriotic. . . . We have not been contending for Henry Clay, for Daniel Webster, or for Winfield Scott. . . . *We have been contending for principles. Not men, but principles, are our rules of action.*[10]

What mattered, Clay told every Whig who would listen, was not the candidates but the party, not the men but the principles.

"THE INTEGRITY OF THE PARTY"

While Clay strove to unite the party behind the Harrison-Tyler ticket, Democrats did what they could to stoke the fires of discontent. William Cullen Bryant's New York *Evening Post*, for instance, pronounced Clay "one of the fairest, and at the same time one of the most favorable impersonations of that party which can be found." That the Whigs had passed over Clay for a man "of feeble intellect and undecided character" was not only an injustice to Clay, who so clearly "deserved the nomination," but also a marker of a party that lacked the conviction of its principles and was "unwilling to leave the next presidential election to be decided by the popularity of" those principles. Unlike the sturdy Clay, Harrison was "a mere nose-of-wax to be pulled and moulded into any shape by the plastic fingers of those who stand about him."[11]

John O'Sullivan's *United States Magazine and Democratic Review* expounded on this theme at great length in a feature article ("Alas, Poor Henry Clay!") that affected great "regret and mortification" at the convention's "unworthy treatment" of the party's "master spirit" and "ablest champion." What sort of party, O'Sullivan asked, would throw over its "true and rightful candidate" for a "poor, feeble old gentleman" like Harrison? "The strength of a popular party," O'Sullivan continued, "consists in its fidelity to its principles," and those principles must be most clearly manifest in its presidential candidate, who "should always be . . . the most complete representative of its political faith." In "sacrificing the man who is the one real and rightful representative of itself, to such shallow calculations of 'availability,'" the Whig Party had inflicted "a more fatal stab on its own vitals than any of the assaults of its opponents." In a vain effort to reach the White House, the party had lopped off its head and lost its soul. The Whigs' problem was that "poor old" Harrison was too weak to carry the party, and the party's principles were too unpopular to carry Clay.[12]

Democrats in the South also worked tirelessly to drive a wedge into the Whig Party by giving Harrison's nomination a sinister sectional spin. The *North Carolina Standard*, for instance, declared that the selection of Harrison over Clay signaled "the success of the Abolitionists and . . . a triumph of the North over the South." The coming contest between Harrison and Van Buren would thus be "between the Abolitionists at the North and the Slaveholders at the South"—and at stake was "whether the negroes are to be turned loose among us or remain in their present happy and prosperous condition."[13]

Democratic efforts to stoke the grievances of Clay's supporters and to cast the Whigs as a party captured by Northern abolitionism were largely ineffectual. Despite the sectional cast of the Harrisburg balloting and the deep disappointment of Clay's supporters, Southern Whig leaders largely set aside their misgivings in favor of party unity.[14] Clay's embrace of the Harrisburg ticket was crucial to cementing party unity, but so was the underappreciated work of the Harrisburg delegates, who helped to sell Harrison and to communicate the convention's message of unity to fellow partisans back home. A prime example is a letter that North Carolina delegate Henry Miller wrote to North Carolina state legislator (and future US senator) William Alexander Graham on December 10 on his way home from the convention.

Miller began by acknowledging that "our friends in North Carolina will feel much disappointment at not getting the man of their choice," and he expressed concern that those feelings would "induce them to denounce the nomination before they give it proper reflection." He stressed to Graham that Harrison's nomination had been "received with great enthusiasm at the Convention," even by those delegations, such as North Carolina's, that had been "the last to yield." The delegates of every state had united around Harrison because "it was the best that could be done—*all* that could be done" without breaking up the party and handing "unmolested possession of the Country" to Van Buren. "Our friends," he implored, must "remember that the object of the Whig party is to break down the corrupt powers that rule." Moreover, Miller revealed that the convention's deliberations had taught him that he had been "mistaken in [Harrison's] character" and that he "is with us on the great questions of the day—Against abolition. Voted against the Missouri restriction, is for Mr. Clay's land bill, and opposes the Sub Treasury." He appealed, too, to the authority of John Tyler, Benjamin Watkins Leigh, "and in fact the whole Southern Delegation," which had "declared that the Whigs of the South would be perfectly satisfied with his political principles." It was incumbent, then, on "the *true* friends of the Whig cause" to "exert themselves to the utmost to counteract, or forestall, any precipitate opposition to the Nomination" and to elect the Whig ticket of Harrison and Tyler.[15]

Miller's letter is testament to Francis Granger's observation—offered to Weed the day before Miller wrote to Graham—that Southern Whigs had become "more disposed to stick to the integrity of the party" and "more willing to give up their peculiar, individual whims."[16] Partisan identities based on national issues and candidates had been slow to form in much of the South,[17] and Southern Whigs, although united in their loathing of Martin Van Buren, had refused to support a Northern Whig for president in 1836. That Southern Whigs rallied to the defense of the national convention's nominee—despite the selection having been made by Northern states in the face of the united opposition of Southern states—was a tribute to the new power of party loyalty and party organization in the now fully developed second party system. Try as they might, Democrats could do little to divide a galvanized Whig Party intent on defeating an unpopular incumbent.

"PASSION AND PREJUDICE, PROPERLY AROUSED"

Even in the face of a united opposition and hampered by a sputtering economy, the Democrats did not lack for confidence. The Democrats had run and won against Harrison before, and after his nomination at Harrisburg they dusted off the same attack lines they used against the general with apparently great effect in 1836. Repetition is the first law of propaganda—and the Democrats were past masters. "Granny Harrison" was the Democrats' favorite belittling nickname for the Whig nominee—an epithet they used over and over in newspapers and speeches as well as private correspondence.[18] "Granny Harrison" rolled off Jacksonian tongues almost as freely as "Crooked Hillary" did Republican tongues in 2016. Better than any other epithets the Democrats used in 1836 and 1840—"Petticoat Hero" and "old woman" were others—Granny Harrison evoked the image of feebleness, weakness, and emasculation that Jacksonians sought to instill in the public mind.

The image of Harrison as an aging dotard was a familiar refrain in Democratic campaign rhetoric, but a few days after the convention a Democratic editor in Baltimore experimented with a new riff on an old theme. "Give him a barrel of hard cider and settle a pension of two thousand a year on him," opined the *Baltimore Republican*, "and take my word for it, he will sit for the remainder of his days in his log cabin."[19] It was a sentence the Democrats would soon wish they could take back. The *Baltimore Chronicle* was quick to sense the possibilities for turning this attack back upon the Democrats. "Gen. Harrison is sneered at for being a poor man. Give him 'a barrel of hard cider' and a 'log cabin,' say the pampered officials of the government." For years, Democrats had accused the Whigs of being latter-day Federalists, elitists fearful of the multitude, yet now it was the Democrats who seemed to belittle all the hard-cider-drinking, log-cabin-owning poor men across the country. "The owners of the 'log cabins,'" warned the *Chronicle*, "possess the power and they intend to use it. Huzza for Old Tippecanoe!" Thus was born the "Hard Cider and Log Cabin Candidate."[20]

When the Democrats attacked Granny Harrison in 1836, the Whigs had tried to make light of the epithet, even trying to turn it into a term of endearment, though without much success.[21] People might like their granny, but they didn't think she should be president. Log cabins and hard cider, though, gave the Whig propagandists something they could work with. Thomas Elder, a wealthy seventy-two-year-old Harrisburg bank president who lived in a historic mansion overlooking the Susquehanna River, summoned a young Whig newspaper editor, Richard Smith Elliott, to discuss how to capitalize on the "righteous indignation" spurred by the Baltimore *Republican's* slur upon poor log-cabin dwellers everywhere. His proposal was to "build a cabin or something of that kind, which would appeal to the eye of the multitude." As Elliott later summarized Elder's thinking, "passion and prejudice, properly aroused and directed, would do about as well as principle and reason in a party contest."[22]

Sipping the old man's "excellent Madeira," Elliott proceeded to sketch "an imaginary log cabin, with a coon-skin tacked on it, an outside chimney of sticks and mud, [and] a wood-pile consisting of a log with an ax stuck in it." With some help from others, Elliott transformed his rudimentary sketch into a glowing transparency, which was unveiled at a mass meeting held in the city on January 20 for the ostensible purpose of ratifying the nominations of Harrison and Tyler. According to Elliott, the log-cabin transparency whipped up the crowd into a "frenzy of enthusiasm."

Soon thereafter, log cabins became an ever-present feature of the campaign. In February, "log cabins on wheels" were rolled out as part of a "monster gathering" of Whigs in Columbus, Ohio, which featured a grand procession the likes of which "had never been seen in the hundred years of Ohio's history or in all the nation's existence." One log cabin was drawn by six bay horses and hoisted a "large picture of General Harrison drawing a gourd full of hard cider from a barrel and handing it to an old soldier."[23] The Clark County delegation sang "The 'Log Cabin' Song" (to the tune of "Highland Laddie") from inside and atop their rolling log cabin—the first of many such "Log Cabin" ditties to be introduced in the 1840 campaign. Among the verses of another song ("The Hero of Tippecanoe") that debuted at the Ohio convention was

> They say that he lived in a cabin
> And lived on old hard cider too
> Well, what if he did, I'm certain,
> He's the hero of Tippecanoe
> He's the hero of Tippecanoe[24]

The enormous procession in Columbus showcased the pageantry and popular enthusiasm so often associated with the 1840 "log-cabin campaign." Among those transfixed by the spectacle of popular politics was a young Yale-educated New Englander, Aaron Fyfe Perry, who had only recently moved to Columbus (and who would go on to have a distinguished legal and political career, including as an Ohio congressman). In an eyewitness account for the Boston *Atlas*, Perry marveled at a scene unlike anything he had seen before. Despite steady rain and roads "all mud, deep mud, nothing but interminable unmitigated mud," Whigs from all over the state poured in, "from two to three and even up to eight hundred persons at a time," until something like twenty thousand drenched and mud-spattered Whigs had assembled in the state capital. There were log cabins aplenty—even some log canoes on wheels—but the adoration of Harrison took multitudinous forms. It seemed to Perry that "every neighborhood of farmers, every village of mechanics [had] racked their ingenuity to invent rare and expressive devices" with which to celebrate their party's nominee. Some kept it simple: one delegation was "armed with brooms" to signify the cleaning operation to come, another bore aloft a live eagle atop a long pole, while a third carried "full-length pictures of General Harrison following his plow." Other delegations put together hugely elaborate displays. For instance, "a steamboat, complete in all its parts, fixed upon wheels, loaded with people," drawn by horses, with paddles "made to revolve with a crank," steam rising "in puffs from the pipe," and each wheelhouse bearing the name of "Harrison and Tyler." All the way from Cleveland, nearly 150 miles, came a brig—called the *William Henry Harrison*—mounted on wheels and drawn by six horses, "manned with delegates in sailor caps," its "sails all set and steamers flying, followed by half a mile of carriages and curricles of all descriptions." Still another delegation had built a model of Fort Meigs—the outpost Harrison had heroically defended in the Battle of Fallen Timbers—"mounted with small brass cannon, drawn by six horses, and large enough for twenty or thirty men to ride in." There were also military companies "marching and parading every way," musical bands everywhere, and hundreds upon hundreds of banners bedecked with mottos ("The People are Coming" and "The People Must Do Their Own Voting" were favorites) could be seen "floating over the multitude." While the streets were choked with "one dense, enthusiastic mass of human bodies," the windows along the streets were "all thrown up and filled with ladies, who join in the excitement and wave their white handkerchiefs to the crowd," while "the roofs of the public buildings" were "filled with spectators, who swing their hats and shout." Perry concluded that "if anything can be judged from the appearance of the convention and the universal opinion of delegates, Harrison and Tyler will carry the state by acclamation."[25]

Democrats were of two minds about how to respond to these impressive displays of popular enthusiasm. One tack was taken by Samuel Medary's *Ohio Statesman*, which criticized the "Baboon Convention" for its "drunkenness [and] low and filthy songs" and lamented that "songs and drinking and carousing and appeals to men's worst passions are introduced into the political meeting instead of argument and appeals to their senses."[26] An alternative course was adopted by Francis Blair's Washington *Globe*, which saw nothing in these sorts of popular demonstrations but a "servile, yet clumsy imitation of the Democracy, so awkwardly put on, as to be perpetually reminding us of the ass in the lion's skin."[27] From this perspective, the problem was not so much the drinking and doggerel, neither of which were novel, as the hypocrisy. Either way, the Democrats were certain that the Whigs were committing a great fraud on the American people, concealing their true principles and policies beneath a populist veneer of log cabins and hard cider.

However loudly the Democrats might decry the fraudulence of the Whigs' log-cabin campaign, there was no denying that the raucous post-Harrisburg "ratification" meetings held in cities all across the country—including in Albany, Boston, Cleveland, Nashville, New Orleans, New York City, and Philadelphia—were energizing the party's rank and file in unprecedented ways.[28] Immediately after Harrisburg, the Democrats had held out hope that since the Whigs' "leaders were heart & soul for Clay," they would "kick up against the Nomination . . . or at least be lukewarm," but the

FEDERAL-ABOLITION-WHIG TRAP,

TO CATCH VOTERS IN.

PEOPLE OF LOUISIANA, above you have an accurate representation of the federal *"Log-Cabin"* Trap, invented by the *bank-parlor, ruffle-shirt, silk-stocking* GENTRY, for catching the *votes* of the industrious and laboring classes, of our citizens, of both town and country. The federal party has always looked upon the poor, laboring people as an ignorant class, destitute of reason and common sense. Hence they always, as in the present contest for the presidency, appeal to their passions, with mockeries, humbugs, shows, and parades, with the view of blinding and leading them away from the true principles of the constitution of their country.

In the above cut, you have a typical illustration of the means they resort to, to get your votes. The "log cabin" is raised to blind you with the belief, that they are your friends; and they have invented what they say is a poor man's drink, called 'Hard Cider,' generally made of 'bald-face' whiskey and water, with a little *sour vinegar* added. They place this drink in a barrel, inside of the 'cabin,' for the purpose of enticing you in, thinking that if they can once get you to take a *suck*, you are safe. Do you not see the man above, creeping in? Just let him get a taste, and they come down at once upon him, hard and heavy, *swig after swig*, until they get him in a *ranting way*, shouting and bawling for *Tip. and Ty.* as though they had caught the devil himself.

These *vote traps* are generally *set* and *baited* in cities and towns, and are usually infested by a considerable swarm of *loafers*. Do you see that fellow up there now? How slily he creeps under, on *all-fours*, with his lips poked out, to steal a *suck*. He is a loafer—not much to be made by him, if they catch him. And they think that the industrious, hard-working people of the country, have no better sense than to be caught just that way.

They have one of these traps setting here in New Orleans; just like the above, for all the world—only the *logs* are not so close. They have, however, made a bad business of it. No one has been caught but loafers, and they creep out between the logs, as fast as they catch them—unless it is occasionally a fellow who gets his belly popped out so full with 'hard cider,' that he has to remain awhile and go through the *roll and tumble* system, before he can squeeze through. We believe it is now nearly deserted. No one goes *to bait* it, and of course no one goes to *nibble* and *suck*. People of Louisiana, what think you of the invention? Are you willing to swallow the *bait?*

We have just understood that one at each of the towns of Monroe and Franklin, in this state, has been *set, triggered*, and *baited*; but we have not learned whether they have yet been able *to catch* many *suckers.*

Federal-Abolition-Whig Trap. An illustrated broadside published in New Orleans in 1840 that illustrates the Democrats' view that the log-cabin and hard-cider campaign was designed by wealthy Whigs ("the bank-parlor, ruffle-shirt, silk-stocking GENTRY") to ensnare the votes of the unsuspecting "industrious and laboring classes." (Courtesy of the Library of Congress) mass meetings buried those vain hopes.[29] The Democrats would not have the luxury this time of running against a divided opposition.

"TO BUCKLE ON THEIR ARMOR"

Among Democrats, there was no question about who would become their standard-bearer. Despite Van Buren's unpopularity, there were no credible challengers to his nomination. South Carolina senator John Calhoun had certainly been eyeing his chances from the outset of Van Buren's presidency—and part of Calhoun's motivation in moving back into the Democratic fold in 1837 may have been a calculation that Van Buren's weakness would open up an opportunity for him to take his place at the head of the ticket.[30] But despite the economic troubles, Van Buren never gave Calhoun that opportunity, in part because he moved the party in a states' rights direction, handing Calhoun an ideological victory even while denying him a path to the presidency.

If nominating a presidential nominee was the only purpose of a national convention, the Democrats seemed to have little need of one. In fact, as the Whigs assembled in Harrisburg for four days in December, the Democratic Party had yet to draw up any plans to hold a national nominating convention. (In 1836, in contrast, the Democrats held their national nominating convention eighteen months before the November election.) Having seen at close hand the excitement generated at Harrisburg, the *Pennsylvania Keystone*, a Democratic paper in Harrisburg, felt it necessary to remind fellow Democrats that there were other considerations that made holding a national convention "at an early date, not only politic, but imperative," namely, "The enemy [was now] in the field!" Although expressing great confidence in the Democratic Party's prospects, the *Keystone* cautioned,

It behooves the Democracy . . . to be up and doing—to buckle on their armor for the contest. Samson was shorn of his strength when balmy sleep had encroached upon his eyelids; and even the Democracy, though irresistible in power, when aroused to action, may be led captive by the puny arm of Federalism, if death-like torpor seize upon it in the day of conflict. A National Convention . . . will inspire a fresh and vigorous enthusiasm into the ranks of the Democracy and send its tocsin notes from the centre to the extremes of our Confederacy. It will, in a word, prove the beginning of a new salutary ORGANIZATION, which is as necessary to a party in civil conflict, as to an army on the gory field.[31]

Richard Mentor Johnson. A drawing of the vice president by Charles Fenderich done on July 21, 1840. (Courtesy of the Library of Congress)

Complacency was indeed a problem for a party that had been in power for almost twelve years and which believed that Whiggery was, at bottom, the political reincarnation of a discredited Federalism. But it was not complacency that led the Democrats to delay the calling of a national convention. It was instead division within their ranks over the vice presidency, a division that was particularly fraught because it ran along sectional lines.

Kentucky's Richard Mentor Johnson was the sitting vice president. From the Democrats' point of view, he had much to recommend him, particularly with Harrison as the opponent. Like Harrison, Johnson was a military hero and Indian fighter, and he had the scars and shattered hand to prove his courageous exploits. Indeed, his fame was tied to the same battle—the Battle of the Thames—that made Harrison's reputation. Moreover, Johnson was reputed to be the man who had killed Tecumseh in that battle: "Rumpsey Dumpsey, Rumpsey Dumpsey, Colonel Johnson killed Tecumseh" was a favorite Democratic slogan in the 1836 campaign. No man seemed better suited to "confront Gen Harrison's pretensions."[32] Johnson also benefited from his reputation as a champion of the common man, which he burnished, both as a US senator and member of Congress, by spearheading the fight to end debt imprisonment.

But while Johnson was immensely popular in the West and among the working class in Eastern cities, Southerners were not at all happy about his personal life, specifically that he had lived openly in a long-term relationship—a marriage in all but name—with his octoroon slave (one-eighth African by descent) Julia Chinn, with whom he had two daughters and whom he brazenly tried to "force . . . into society" as equals to whites.[33] In 1836, twenty-three Virginia electors who were pledged to vote for the Van Buren–Johnson ticket had refused to cast their ballots for the "odious" Johnson, leaving him one vote shy of the requisite majority and forcing the Senate to choose the vice president. Although Chinn had died in 1833, rumor had it that Johnson had since taken up with another mulatto, "a young Delilah of about the complexion of Shakespears swarthy Othello,"[34] which only increased Southern resistance to keeping Johnson on the ticket. Virtually every Southern Democrat seemed to agree that "there must be a new selection" and that the new vice-presidential nominee must be from a slaveholding state.[35]

One way to deal with the division was to leave the nominations up to the states, as the Whigs had done four years earlier. The other was to trust a convention to do the necessary work of "reconciling conflicting opinions" and uniting the party behind a single ticket. The *Keystone* urged the latter course, arguing that the convention could "safely be entrusted" to arbitrate "sectional predilections and conflicting notions of expediency." The editors were happy "conceding the Vice Presidency to the South" and helpfully offered up several possible names that the convention might consider in addition to Johnson's, including Alabama's William King, Tennessee's James Polk, and Georgia's John Forsyth.[36]

In 1836, the Democrats had indicted the Whigs as a disparate and disorganized collection of discontents, and the Whigs' failure to call a national convention and unite behind a single ticket was Exhibit A in that indictment. Few Democrats wanted to open themselves up to that same criticism, and their leaders well understood the power of a national convention

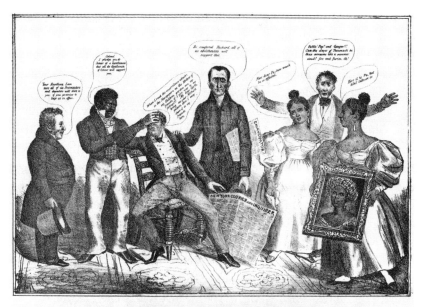

AN AFFECTING SCENE IN KENTUCKY.

An Affecting Scene in Kentucky. *An 1836 campaign cartoon depicting Van Buren's running mate, Richard M. Johnson. Seated in the center of the "affecting scene," Johnson is overcome by the "scurrilous attacks in the Newspapers on the Mother of my Children" and beckons his two elegantly dressed daughters, Adaline and Imogene, to bring him their dead mother's picture. The daughter holding the portrait says, "Here it is Pa, but don't take on so." Standing beside Johnson on his left is a white abolitionist—with William Lloyd Garrison's* Emancipator *under his arm—who reassures Johnson that "all abolitionists will support thee," and on his right is a black man who pledges with "de honor of a Gentlemen dat all de Gentlemen of Color will support you." Also pledging his support is a postmaster who promises that "all of us Postmasters and deputies will stick to you; if you promise to keep us in office." Standing behind the daughters is a man aghast that the dread "slayer of Tecumseh" can "be thus overcome like a summer cloud." (Courtesy of the Library of Congress)*

to rally the faithful, not only at the convention but in the associated state and local nominating conventions that would precede it. Indeed, shortly before the *Keystone* lifted its voice in favor of a convention—and a week after the close of the Whig convention in Harrisburg—the Democratic central committee of New Hampshire, chaired by the state's governor and party leader, Isaac Hill, took the initiative to formally call for the Democrats to hold a national nominating convention on May 5 in Baltimore, the same city and same month that the party had used in 1832 and 1835.[37] At almost the same time, an Alabama state convention, meeting in Tuscaloosa, issued the same call, and the delegates resolved to back their native son, Senator King, for vice president.[38]

Democrats across the nation were quick to respond to New Hampshire's call. Ohio, Indiana, Illinois, Kentucky, and North Carolina all called state conventions for Wednesday, January 8. Most other states held theirs in February and March. All approved of Van Buren's nomination and the May 5 date for a national nominating convention in Baltimore,[39] but there was a clear divergence when it came to the vice presidency. State conventions in at least ten states—Arkansas, Illinois, Indiana, Kentucky, Maryland, Missouri, New Hampshire, New York, Ohio, and Pennsylvania—expressed a desire to see Johnson remain on the ticket. Other states, including Mississippi, Tennessee, and Virginia, backed Governor Polk for vice president, while Georgia endorsed its native son Secretary of State Forsyth.[40] Some state conventions, including in North Carolina, made no endorsement, even though some county conventions had urged the nomination of either Polk or King.[41]

Not all Democrats were sure that the national nominating convention was a good idea. Tennessee senator Felix Grundy and the state's five Democratic House members wrote to Governor Polk at the beginning of February—a week before the state convention was to be held in Nashville—to express their trepidation about the Baltimore convention: "We anticipate no certain good of any kind from that assemblage. We fear its dissensions will weaken the Democratic cause, and produce heart-burnings, which may be injurious." Among the problems they foresaw was that if the national convention retained the rule that the party had used at the last two national conventions—which would remain in place until 1936—that a nominee must receive a two-thirds majority of the delegates, then it was unlikely that any vice-presidential candidate could secure the nomination. Nonetheless, Grundy and his colleagues were clear that since a national convention "seems now to be certain," it was crucial that Tennessee "should be fully represented" at the Baltimore convention.[42]

Meanwhile, Van Buren and his closest advisers came under escalating pressure from former president Andrew Jackson to drop Johnson. Jackson, who attended the Tennessee state convention, was convinced that Johnson would be a "dead weight upon us" and would jeopardize Democratic prospects not only in Tennessee but throughout the South. With Polk on the ticket, in contrast, Jackson thought that the Democrats would sweep every state in the Old South and Southwest. Even King or Forsyth, he thought, would be stronger than Johnson because of the entrenched Southern prejudices against the vice president. Jackson allowed that he personally had only "kind feelings" for Johnson but asked, "Why . . . should we hazard anything for men, when so much is at stake? Take the strongest say I, regardless of men." Jackson abhorred the idea being bandied about in Washington of running different vice-presidential candidates in different states. "We must be united in all things," he lectured Francis Blair, "or our cause goes down." The party and the convention must subordinate personal feelings, unify behind a single candidate, and adhere strictly to "the Motto, Everything for principle and nothing for men."[43]

Despite the party's deep divisions over the vice-presidential nomination, Democrats remained remarkably buoyant about their political prospects in the early months of 1840. In the same February 15 letter in which Jackson warned Blair of the urgent need to dump Johnson and of the dangers of disunity, he congratulated the *Globe*'s editor on his reelection as public printer to the House of Representatives, which he thought gave "evidence that Whiggery and Federalism is on the wane" and that the Independent Treasury would at last be enacted into law.[44] Blair more than reciprocated Jackson's optimism. Writing to Jackson on March 17, Blair expressed his opinion that "we have got the opposition fairly down at last. . . . All looks bright around at present." Blair predicted that "The Magician by his firmness, ability and honesty . . . will entirely succeed in stamping your principles upon the administration for years to come."[45] Tennessee congressman Julius Blackwell, who worried that the Democrats were underestimating Harrison's support, reported to Governor Polk at the end of January that the "Democrats of Congress seem to be very sanguine of Mr. Van Buren's reelection, by a triumphant majority."[46]

There were good reasons for Democrats to feel optimistic at the outset of 1840, despite the stumbling economy. State elections had gone their way in the fall. Surprising victories in Ohio, New Jersey, Georgia, Maryland, and Mississippi had boosted Democratic morale. In addition, there was their stunning victory in November's gubernatorial race in the Whig stronghold of Massachusetts. Perennial Jacksonian candidate Marcus Morton, who had run and lost in every gubernatorial election in the state since 1828—a string of eleven consecutive losses in which he had never received more than 46 percent of the vote—had upset the incumbent, Edward Everett. If Morton could win in Massachusetts, then the Democrats' future appeared bright.[47]

The Democrats' surprisingly strong showing in the fall elections had shattered Whig assumptions that they would control a majority in the House of Representatives in the Twenty-Sixth Congress. Instead, when the new Congress convened on December 2, 1839, Democrats and Whigs were evenly balanced, but, as the early House vote to give the printing contract to Blair's *Globe* rather than to the *National Intelligencer* suggested, the Democrats retained a de facto working majority. The balance of power in the new House rested with Calhoun's states' rights faction, but its members were "now Democratic in name as well as in practice."[48] Certainly, they could be counted on to back the issue Van Buren cared about most, passage at long last of the Independent Treasury plan that he had pushed without success since introducing it at the special legislative session in September 1837. And while neither the Democrats nor the Whigs had enough votes to elect their first choice as Speaker, the House ultimately settled on a relatively inexperienced Calhoun supporter, the Virginian R. M. T. Hunter. Although ostensibly a Whig, Hunter had twice supported Van Buren's Independent Treasury plan, and he proceeded to install a majority of pro–Independent Treasury Democrats on the crucial House Ways and Means Committee, selecting as its chairman John Winston Jones, who had been the administration's first choice as Speaker. The balance of power swung even further in the Democratic direction when the House decided to seat six New Jersey Democrats rather than the six New Jersey Whigs whose election had been certified by the state's Whig governor.[49] On top of that, the Democrats remained securely in control of the Senate. Little wonder that Van Buren and many other Democrats surveying the political landscape after the Whigs' Harrisburg convention felt confident about their chances in November.

Notwithstanding the sectional discord over Johnson, Van Buren's standing in the South at the beginning of 1840 seemed stronger than at any other time in his presidency.[50] Many Southerners had long eyed the New Yorker with suspicion, as the 1836 campaign dramatized, but his policies had gradually won over many doubters in the South. Van Buren was touted by many in the South as "a Northern man with Southern principles," which was how Democrats from Wake and Orange Counties expressed it when they gathered on December 7, 1839, to select delegates for North Carolina's coming state convention to recommend Van Buren for president and Polk for vice president.[51] At a minimum, Van Buren seemed the lesser of two evils. As Franklin Elmore, one of Calhoun's "most devoted proselytes," put it in September 1839, "give me a weak northern President who we can control, who professes our principles and can be made to act upon them," over a "strong Southern President, all of whose principles and policy are against us."[52]

While Van Buren had shored up support in the South, he had also managed to heal divisions within the party in crucial Northern states, particularly New York, where the Democratic Party had been riven by factionalism. His third annual message to Congress, which made a compelling case for why the country needed an Independent Treasury now more than ever in these troubled economic times, earned "unqualified praise" from across the Democratic spectrum in New York.[53] And in April 1840, a galvanized Democratic Party scored what Van Buren hailed as a "signal triumph" in the New York City elections, winning the mayor's race by more than 1,600 votes. Van Buren took particular satisfaction that the victory, which saw the Democratic mayoral candidate win a majority in 12 of the city's 17 wards, came despite the Whig Party having "never made greater effort." That the "working men" of the city had triumphed over an energized opposition seemed to augur well for Van Buren's chances in November.[54]

"HARD MONEY AGAINST HARD CIDER"

Among the final acts of the Whig convention in Harrisburg had been to vote on a motion to recommend that the "Whig young men" of the nation appoint delegates from their respective states and assemble at a convention with the purpose of taking "such measures as will most effectually aid the advancement of the Whig cause and sound principles." The resolution, which had been initially brought forward at the New Jersey state nominating convention in September, proposed that the young men's convention be held in the nation's capital on Monday, May 4, 1840, but the Harrisburg delegates amended the resolution on the floor so that the meeting would take place in Baltimore, which meant they would meet in the same place and at the same time that the Democrats would hold their national nominating convention.[55]

Historians have generally followed William Nisbet Chambers's account in suggesting that this was a prescient Whig strategy to steal the Democrats' thunder by scheduling a massive rally of enthusiastic Whig youth at the same moment that Democrat politicians huddled indoors to choose their nominee. A key premise of this thesis is that the Whigs adopted this plan after "the Democrats had already scheduled their national convention for the same time and place."[56] But the Democrats had *not* settled on a time or place for the national convention—nor even agreed to hold such a convention—when the Harrisburg convention passed its resolution. Indeed, the first call to hold a Democratic national convention in Baltimore on May 5—a call made by the Democratic central committee of New Hampshire—was not issued until December 13, six days after the Whig convention had adjourned.[57] If the many thousands of Whigs who descended on Baltimore in early May overshadowed the Democratic convention, the fault appears to lie with the Democrats' lack of concern or awareness that the Whigs had already scheduled a partisan meeting for the same time and place.

Because the Whigs held a mass meeting of thousands in Baltimore's streets the day before a relatively small conclave of Democratic politicians receded behind closed doors, it is tempting to shoehorn these two events into a narrative that pits the Democrats' supposed "defeatism" and "indifference" against the exuberant youthful energy of the Whig cause, the "melancholy business" of nominating a doomed candidate against the triumphant demonstrations of a new style of popular politics.[58] There is no gainsaying the "great commotion" of the Whigs' gathering in Baltimore. As in Columbus in February, the pageantry stretched for miles, song and banners filled the air, hard cider flowed freely, musical bands marched through the streets, and log-cabin floats were drawn by horses. There was also a huge ball made of buckskin, covered in slogans and rhyming couplets, that had been rolled all the way from western Maryland—"the ball a rolling on" that was fast becoming a fixture at Whig rallies and would later be memorialized in song for causing "this great commotion, motion, motion." Helped by its proximity to Washington, the Baltimore convention was also energized by the presence and speeches of the party's leading figures, including Clay and Webster.[59]

Without question, the "great commotion" in Baltimore confirmed what had been evident for months, namely, that the Whigs were well organized and enthusiastic about "Old Tip" and their prospects in November. But, contrary to the conventional storyline, there was nothing peculiarly "melancholy" about the Democratic outlook or the convention's proceedings.[60] Instead the two-day convention was replete with stirring partisan speeches from the floor, withering attacks on a fraudulent opposition, and combative vows of victory in November. There was no defeatism, for instance, in the pugnacious speech of Ohio delegate and newspaperman Samuel Medary, who mocked the log-cabin pretensions of the "bank aristocracy." While conceding that the contest in Harrison's home state "might be a bitter and a close one," he affirmed that he "never knew the Democrats of [Ohio] to be in better spirits than they were at present and felt sure that victory would crown their efforts."[61]

One of the best indications that Democrats were neither beset by gloom nor resigned to defeat was how much prominent Democrats, including Van Buren's secretary of state, John Forsyth, "coveted the second spot on the ticket."[62] Governor Polk, whose political antennae had been finely tuned during his tenure as Speaker of the House and chairman of the powerful House Ways and Means Committee, never made any move to discourage allies from pressing his case to be nominated as vice president. Ditto for Alabama's William King, president pro tem of the Senate, who was happy to have several of his Senate colleagues, most notably Pennsylvania's James Buchanan, aggressively push for him to be added to the ticket. None of these leading Democrats behaved as if they thought they were fighting a lost cause.

A nominating convention of several hundred delegates obviously could not rival the carnival atmosphere of a campaign rally of thousands of citizens, but the more apt comparison is with the Whig nominating convention five months earlier. The two nominating conventions mirrored each other in many respects. Both were gaveled to order exactly at noon. Both featured roughly the same number of delegates.[63] Both were populated largely by lawyers and politicians who had held local, state, or national office[64]—and both featured a great many "fusty old gentlemen" with "heads whitened by age."[65] Both began by appointing a committee made up of one person from each state to select the convention's officers. Both were preceded by state and local conventions that had selected delegates, expressed candidate preferences, and rallied the faithful. Both had some states unrepresented: Connecticut, Delaware, Illinois, Virginia, and South Carolina in the case of the Baltimore convention; Arkansas, Georgia, Tennessee, and again South Carolina at the Harrisburg convention.[66] (The Whigs' young men's convention, despite its many thousands, was also lacking representation from five states.) Both the Whig and Democratic conventions also suffered from the problem that many states that sent delegates were nonetheless underrepresented at the convention.

The problem of severely underrepresented states was admittedly greater at the Democratic than at the Whig convention, but this appears to be a sign less of what Robert Gray Gunderson sees as the Democratic Party's "apathy" than of its more haphazard delegate selection process—which resulted in several calls at the outset of the convention for "strict scrutiny" into whether all delegates were "entitled to their seats."[67] The Whig convention had been called by the party's congressional caucus eighteen months prior to the convention and had prescribed that each state select senatorial and district delegates equal to its electoral college allocation. The Democratic call, in contrast, had come from a state central committee four months prior to the convention and included no recommendation as to how delegates should be selected. If the Democratic convention had more states that were massively underrepresented—only one delegate attended from Massachusetts, two from Georgia, and three from Kentucky (states that had 14, 11, and 15 electoral votes, respectively)—it also had a greater problem with states that were hugely overrepresented, most notably New Jersey, which sent a whopping 59 delegates, 51 more than its 8 electoral votes warranted, and Rhode Island, which sent 12 delegates, three times the number of its electoral votes.[68]

In both conventions, the problem of underrepresented and overrepresented states was dealt with by apportioning a state's votes based on its representation in the electoral college. Both conventions also kept the key deliberations and voting over nominations off the convention floor, although the Democrats adopted a much simpler system than the labyrinthine procedure used by the Whigs. In Baltimore, the matter of nominations was referred to a twenty-one-person committee on nominations, which consisted of one person from each state, with each committee member casting the number of votes equal to the state's allocation of electoral votes (a de facto unit rule).[69]

On the convention's second day, the chair of the nominating committee, Alabama senator Clement Clay, reported the result of the committee's deliberations, which he said reflected the committee's devotion to "harmony, concession, and self-denial, carrying out the Democratic principle of every thing for measures, and nothing for men." Those words were a prelude to the announcement that the committee had been unable to reach an agreement "as to the person best entitled" to the vice-presidential nomination and had resolved instead that it was "expedient at the present time not to choose between the individuals in nomination, but to leave the decision to their republican fellow-citizens in the several states."[70]

Those who had hoped to replace Johnson were stymied by the vice president's broad support among the convention delegates. Although no votes were recorded, at least nine states represented at the convention—including the three electorally largest, New York, Pennsylvania, and Ohio—had endorsed Johnson at their state nominating conventions, and these nine states would have wielded 60 percent of the votes on the nominating committee. That Johnson was not nominated despite the breadth of his support was a measure of the intensity of opposition to his candidacy among Southerners. That intensity of preference among the minority, aided by the convention's adherence to the two-thirds rule and the "self-denial" of the majority, dictated the compromise to leave the question to the states.

In truth, the decision to leave the selection of the vice president to the states had all but been settled even before the convention began. Ten days before the convention opened, Missouri Senator Thomas Hart Benton wrote to Jackson to prepare him for the likelihood that the convention would "leave the second office open." Like Jackson, Benton believed Polk to be the strongest candidate the party could nominate, but Johnson's political strength together with Van Buren's "rigid neutrality" among the candidates seemed to have foreclosed any prospect of persuading a majority at the convention to back Polk or any other challenger. The best they could do under the circumstances, Benton informed Jackson, was to go for "no nomination" and instead use "the names of the most popular candidate in different states." He informed Jackson that he expected there to be a meeting of "all our friends" in the next day or so in which "this view will be sanctioned."[71] Assuming that meeting took place as planned, it seems likely that Senator Clement Clay—as well as the two other US senators on the nominating committee in Baltimore, Tennessee's Felix Grundy and Mississippi's Robert Walker—were at that meeting at which this plan was agreed upon.[72]

Herein lies the fundamental difference between the Democratic and Whig conventions. The latter was a historic event in which a major party convention, for the first time in the nation's history, made rather than ratified a decision about a party's presidential and vice-presidential nominees. The former, in contrast, like the party's two previous conventions, was largely a means to legitimate a decision that national Democratic elites had already hammered out. The difference was that in 1840, unlike in 1832 and 1835, the Democratic Party's elites were too divided to agree on a nominee for the vice presidency. In 1836, it had been a divided Whig Party that had been forced to run different tickets in different parts of the country to preserve party unity. Now it was the Democrats who, in the name of party unity, felt compelled to sanction different tickets in different states.

To help make up for its failure to unite on men, the Democratic convention agreed to a series of resolutions "expressive of the sentiments of the Democratic Party"—what was essentially the first national party platform in the history of the United States (see Appendix B). Unlike the Whigs in

Harrisburg, who had turned aside a suggestion that the party lay out its principles in an address to the people, the Democrats in Baltimore also approved and published a lengthy address to the people "in support of the principles and measures" of the Van Buren administration.[73] The Democrats might not always be able to agree on people, but unlike the Whigs they agreed on what they believed mattered most: principles and policies. "We go for principles, not men," boasted Grundy; "they go for men, and have no declared principles."[74]

If the celebrations on the streets of Baltimore had any effect on the Democratic convention, it was to whip up the delegates' indignation at the fraud the Whigs were perpetrating on the American people by hiding their elitist principles behind log cabins and to embolden the delegates to lay out a platform that would draw a clear contrast between their own party of principle and the Whigs' party of opportunism. From almost the first moment of the convention, the Democrats hammered upon this contrast between the parties. As soon as the preliminary housekeeping was out of the way, Senator Grundy rose to urge the convention "to come out with a clear, candid and true declaration of the sentiments of the . . . party as here represented. . . . Let us tell the people what we think, and not beguile or deceive them by acting contrary to our sincere belief." At this implicit swipe at the Whigs, the convention erupted with "loud cheering."[75] Soon thereafter, amid more "loud and enthusiastic cheering," Grundy was back on his feet to make the point still more explicit: "We want no pageantry and show. . . . We wish no deceptive parade of log cabins and empty cider barrels." Instead "we desire to address ourselves to the intelligence of the people," for it is "with their reason we wish to deal." Grundy implored his fellow delegates not to "follow the bad example of our adversaries, set by the Harrisburg Convention," which "dispersed without proclaiming a single principle upon which they would administer the Government." Instead, he urged them, "come out with an open, frank, and candid avowal of our opinions. We have nothing to fear. Those only shun the light whose deeds are evil." No American, Grundy concluded, should ever vote for a party or president "whose principles and policy are not openly and fearlessly avowed to them." At the close of this impassioned appeal, which lasted for the better part of an hour, the "deafening and overwhelming plaudits of the whole assembly continued for several minutes."[76] This was no sad and melancholy gathering.

After adjourning for a short while, the convention appointed a committee—with one representative from each state—to draft resolutions "declaratory of the principles of the Republican Party," a label that Jacksonian

Democrats often still used to describe their party. By the next morning, the committee had come up with nine resolutions that laid out the party's creed, including strict construction of federal power, which meant, among other things, that Congress had no power to fund internal improvement projects, establish a national bank, or interfere with slavery. A national bank was not only unconstitutional but "dangerous" because it placed "the business of the country within the control of a concentrated money power, and above the laws and the will of the people." Abolitionists were equally dangerous to "the stability and permanency of the Union," and their efforts to end slavery "ought not to be countenanced by any friend to our political institutions." The party also declared itself opposed to any efforts that would restrict immigrants' ability to become American citizens and expressed its opposition to tariffs, which unfairly favored one industry over another. The party committed itself, too, to "rigid economy," which meant that "no more revenue ought to be raised than is required to defray the necessary expenses of the government," and to the separation of government funds from private banking institutions—that is, to Van Buren's Independent Treasury.[77]

After adopting the de facto platform—and having to sit through an excruciatingly long and tedious reading of an address to the people that had been written by New Hampshire Democrat Isaac Hill—the convention got back to the business of condemning the Whig's frothy hard-cider campaign and prognosticating Democratic victory in November. To "continued cheering," Pennsylvania's Robert Fisher promised that his state would give Van Buren a 20,000-vote majority in Pennsylvania and "raise such a shout as would reach General Harrison's two story, one hundred and fifty feet wide, log cabin." Another Pennsylvania delegate declared, again to "loud and reiterated cheers," that Van Buren's margin of victory would be closer to 25,000, as the state "will be for hard money against hard cider." In the same exuberant spirit, Ohio's representative on the platform-writing committee, Peter Kauffman, forecast "a glorious victory over the hard cider party" in his state.[78] And so it went, each delegate vying to outdo the next in confident predictions and pithy put-downs of the fraudulent Whigs.

However, no amount of triumphalist rhetoric, or even the passage of a party platform, could paper over the cracks in the Democratic Party that had opened over the vice presidency. The Harrisburg convention, too, had closed with the cracks in the party still visible—cracks possessing an ominously sectional cast. The Harrisburg convention's success had depended on the way in which the convention's losers chose to respond—and the way in which voters and activists responded to the convention's choice. The decisions reached in Baltimore, like those in Harrisburg, left some delegates feeling disappointed, even aggrieved. But most left the Baltimore convention believing that they had produced what one Van Buren ally judged to be a most "satisfactory result" in view of the "many embarrassments and difficulties" the party had faced.[79]

Not everyone took the compromise well, least of all Jackson, who groused that the convention's decision on the vice presidency would lose the party the "whole religious portion" of both Tennessee and Kentucky.[80] But for Van Buren, whose gaze was fixed on more than just a handful of Southern states, the convention had done precisely the work he hoped it would. Van Buren adjudged that pushing Johnson off the ticket would be too costly in key Northern states, and he banked on the orthodox Jeffersonian states' rights platform and his own proven commitment to those same principles to keep the Southern states on board. Winning in the South would gain him nothing if he thereby lost Ohio, Pennsylvania, and New York.

As Van Buren may have anticipated, the decision not to make a choice at the convention was in effect a plan to retain Johnson on the ticket. Soon after the convention, the various rivals signaled their withdrawal from the field, leaving Johnson as Van Buren's de facto running mate in every state. As Van Buren hoped, Southern Democrats rallied around him and either set aside their misgivings about Johnson or eagerly embraced the "gallant" colonel as *the real hero of the Thames.*"[81] The truth is that the vice presidency mattered little to voters—certainly nothing like as much as Jackson imagined. Polk certainly would have boosted the Democratic vote in Tennessee, but Van Buren had good reason for thinking that Tennessee, a state he lost by 16 points in 1836, was out of reach for him even with Polk on the ticket (Van Buren would lose the state by 11 points in 1840). Certainly, no reasonable path to the 148 electoral votes he would need to win included Tennessee. What mattered was the man at the top of the ticket—and on that score, the party and convention had never had any doubts or disagreements. With the simmering vice presidential conflict largely defused, Van Buren and the Democrats now confronted a much more important and intractable problem: how to craft a message and run a campaign to reelect an incumbent presiding over an economy that seemed to be getting worse. This would be the Little Magician's most difficult trick yet.

SEE HOW THEY RUN
CAMPAIGNING FOR PRESIDENT

Nothing seems less remarkable today than a presidential candidate delivering a speech before an immense crowd. Those who wish to be president must show that they want it—that they have the requisite "fire in the belly." They must be willing to ask people to vote for them. Would-be presidents, in short, don't stand for office; they run for it. Every presidential candidate is expected to crisscross the country in pursuit of votes, just as they are expected to stake out their positions on the issues of the day so that voters know where they stand and what they will do when they get into office.

It was not always this way. In the beginning, it was widely believed that the office was "neither to be sought nor declined."[1] As Martin Van Buren wrote in accepting the Democratic nomination in 1835—the first acceptance letter by a presidential nominee of a major party in American history—"I have never solicited the aid nor sought the support of any man in reference to the high office for which I have been nominated."[2] The norm against campaigning was even stricter for incumbents. "A sense of decorum universally prevailing," according to John Quincy Adams, forbade a president "from active or even indirect canvassing of votes for himself."[3] As president, Jackson paid homage to this republican norm in 1831 when he insisted: "I meddle not with elections, I leave the people to make their own Presidents."[4]

The republican proscription against a nominee campaigning for president was woven into the founders' conception of a president above party and immune to the popular passions that infect legislatures. But the expectation that presidents should stand rather than stump for office, which had been forged in a deferential age of patrician politics, came under scrutiny in the more populist politics and competitive party system that emerged during the 1820s and 1830s. Decorum could easily be mistaken for undemocratic. Presidents weren't kings, after all. They were the people's servants. Democratic accountability would seem, at a minimum, to dictate that the people had the right to hear from their leaders and to know what their leaders believed and what they would do in office.

Jackson had played a part in dislodging some of the patrician assumptions that enveloped the presidential role. When asked in 1824 to give his views on tariffs, Jackson obliged, arguing that since his name had "been brought before the nation for the first office in the gift of the people, it is incumbent on me, when asked, frankly to declare my opinion upon any political or national question, pending before, and about which the country feels an interest." He was careful to preface his pledge, however, by stressing that his name had been brought before the country "without any agency of mine" and that he had "never solicited office." Nor, indeed, had he "ever declined" when called upon to serve the people. He could be a virtuous Old Republican and a good democrat.[5]

The old norms, though, had impressive staying power, even in a more democratic age. When Jackson ran again for the presidency in 1828, his advisers badgered him to stay mum. The then New York senator Martin Van Buren chided Jackson, "Our people do not like to see publications from candidates."[6] The strategic need for republican restraint was underscored by James Polk, who bluntly told Jackson that "the ground taken for you by your friends . . . that you live in retirement on your farm, calm and unmoved by the excitement around you, taking no part in the pending canvass for the Presidency, but committing yourself into the hands of your country, would seem to superficial observers to be inconsistent with any appeal to the public made by you at this juncture."[7] This time, Jackson largely heeded his advisers' counsel to leave the "electioneering" to his surrogates.[8]

By 1840, candidates for the presidency were awkwardly suspended between these two norms, both powerful and neither easily set aside. The president was still, ideally, supposed to be called from the plow by the people, not leave the plow to run for office. Those who publicly sought the office with too much vigor opened themselves to charges of base electioneering and of being unworthy of the high office that they sought. But this was no longer George Washington's America. Fifty years had passed since

Washington had taken the first oath of office, and stump speeches and political rallies had become commonplace. People increasingly hungered to hear from their presidential candidates. Those who avoided answering and addressing the people opened themselves up to the charge that they were hiding from the people, concealing their true views—that they were, in a word, undemocratic. So, what was a presidential candidate to do?

GENERAL MUM

When William Henry Harrison wrote a letter accepting the Whig nomination in December 1839, he acknowledged that "it may, perhaps, be expected that I should embrace this occasion to declare the principles upon which the administration will be conducted, if the efforts of my friends to place me in the presidential chair should prove successful." He then explained why such a declaration was unnecessary because he had already communicated his views "at some length" in two previous letters, the first written the year before in response to his nomination by the Anti-Mason Party and the other in 1836 in response to Kentucky congressman Sherrod Williams's five interrogatories (see chapter 4). He reiterated his pledge to serve only one term, but that was all he was prepared to reveal in his brief acceptance letter.[9]

Although Harrison felt that he had already fully communicated his views, many Americans wanted to know more about where he stood—much more. After his nomination, he was deluged with letters asking about his stance on all manner of issues, none of which was more awkward than the matter of slavery, a topic that Harrison had not had occasion to address in either his 1838 letter accepting the Anti-Mason nomination or his 1836 letter to Williams. The letters pouring in to North Bend after Harrison's nomination prompted Charles Hammond, the sixty-one-year-old Whig editor of the *Cincinnati Gazette*, to console Henry Clay that he had

great reason to be thankful that the burden of being a candidate for the Presidency was not put upon you. In my view the canvass was always full of degradation, and I think that now-a-days its humiliation is greatly increased. Since the categories of Sherrod Williams set the precedent, every one claims to question the candidate of his life, opinions and general conduct. An indecent impudence marks the movements of his friends; the foulest and often most painful imputations characterize the assaults of opponents. A man has to give up his own self-respect, or every hour give offense to some pedagogue that stands over him with uplifted rod.[10]

In 1836, the underdog Harrison had responded promptly and amply to Williams's request that he and each of the other candidates "frankly and fully avow" their political principles and opinions,[11] but in 1840 Harrison and his advisers decided, much as Jackson's team had in 1828, that it would be wiser to adhere to a more retiring and reticent posture than he had adopted in his first run at the presidency.

Harrison would receive visitors at his farm in North Bend, but he would leave the campaigning to others. A three-person committee of correspondence in Cincinnati was charged with responding to the many letters that sought information about the candidate's views, at least nine-tenths of which, Harrison estimated, came from his political opponents.[12] The committee typically referred correspondents to Harrison's previously published views and reiterated that his views, over a long career, had already "been given to the public fully and explicitly." The campaign's policy, as the committee explained to a group of citizens from upstate New York who had requested information about the general's views on the abolition of slavery in DC as well as on a national bank, was "that the general [will] make no further declaration of his principles, for the public eye, while occupying his present position."[13]

The committee's insistence that Harrison would reveal nothing "for the public eye" proved a public relations disaster. Democrats pounced on the misstep. They charged Harrison with being "cut off from all intercourse with the people, and refusing to answer their honest inquiries."[14] They attacked the general's "conscience-keeping committee."[15] The *Globe* condemned the "monstrous and incredible" news that "the keepers of Gen. Harrison's conscience have carried their . . . caution so far as actually to shut up the old gentlemen in an iron cage."[16] The *Nashville Union* thought the behavior of Harrison and his "Thinking Committee" displayed "a shameful . . . contempt for public opinion," and the *Louisville Advertiser* gave him a label that stuck: "General Mum."[17]

In the month leading up to and the weeks immediately following the Democratic national convention, the Democratic organs pressed the attack upon General Mum and his conscience-keeping committee. This rhetorical assault resonated with long-standing Democratic efforts to paint Harrison as a feeble, dim-witted "Old Granny" who was a pliable tool of Whig Party managers with their own furtive agenda. Democrats in the South were particularly effective at exploiting Harrison's refusal to answer queries about slavery and abolitionism—including one question that came from Whigs

THE POLITICAL DANCING JACK:
A Holiday Gift for Sucking Whigs !!
Sold at No. 104 Nassau, and No. 18 Division Streets, New-York.

The Political Dancing Jack. A Democratic cartoon from 1840 portraying the Whig nominee William Henry Harrison as a puppet of Kentucky senator Henry Clay (left) and Virginia congressman Henry A. Wise. (Courtesy of the Library of Congress)

in Mobile, Alabama—to foment fears that he and his handlers were closet abolitionists.[18]

Harrison's strategy of remaining silent invited an invidious contrast with his Democratic opponent, who, it was said, "had nothing to conceal 'from the public eye,'" was "perfectly committed on all subjects," and "presents himself as he is with but one life, and one set of principles for the North and the South, the East and the West."[19] The Democrats' drumbeat that their nominee, like the convention that nominated him, had nothing to conceal and that both man and party "always publish their opinions to the people"[20] became so deafening that it began to worry Whig leaders.

Toward the end of May, Henry Clay wrote to his former Senate colleague John Clayton to express his concern that their party's cause "suffers from the imputation of the other side that the Whigs have no principles which they dare openly avow."[21] To remedy the problem, Clay drafted a "rough sketch" of the party's policies and principles and asked Clayton's counsel on whether it would be "expedient" to publish it. Clay acknowledged the danger "of supplying fresh aliment for demagogues," but he also thought "promulgating [something] like a creed" could be an effective way to blunt Democratic criticism of the Whig ticket. But even Clay, anxious as he was to trumpet Whig principles and policies, ultimately decided it was better "to remain silent and not act."[22]

Harrison, too, was becoming increasingly restive with the course of silence that he had adhered to since the Harrisburg convention. He chafed at the imputation that he was weak and did not know his own mind. He decided that the time had come for him to defend himself. On May 23, only a few days before Clay wrote to Clayton, Harrison penned a public letter to answer his critics and explain his principles—ostensibly in the form of a reply to New York's Whig legislators, who in February had sent Harrison a series of laudatory resolutions enacted at a meeting commemorating George Washington's birthday.[23]

Harrison reiterated that he had already, on several occasions, "fully and frankly avowed my sentiments," and he said that "intelligent persons" could not desire him to go further than that. After all, "the people of this country do not rely on professions, promises and pledges" to judge a candidate for the presidency, and for good reason. They knew that an "unprincipled" man would "give any pledge" to get elected and, once elected, would not "hesitate to violate it." That was why candidates must instead be judged by their character and public conduct—as they had been in Washington's day.

But Harrison's argument went deeper. He acknowledged that "innumerable applications have been made to me for my opinions relative to matters of legislation" but insisted that to give his opinion on these matters would violate the very principles that he had often declared would govern his behavior if he were elected president. Harrison was not being reticent or coy, nor was he concealing his true views. Instead, he was following his bedrock principle that the president was not a "constituent branch of the legislature." The real fault lay with the assumption made by the various letter writers that "the presidential opinion was the proper source and origin of all the legislation of the country." Such an assumption, Harrison believed, was "at war with every principle of the Constitution," and he warned that the spread of "such sentiments, more than almost anything else, would tend to consolidate the whole substantial power of the Government in the hands of a single man, a tendency which, whether in or out of office, I feel it my most solemn duty to resist." The people had a right to be informed of the political opinions of candidates for office, but insofar as those opinions related to "the subjects upon which the legislature may be called to act, the pledges and opinions should be required, if required at all, of candidates of Congress," not the chief magistrate of the country. The "habit of considering a single individual as the source from which all the measures of government should emanate," Harrison concluded, "is degrading to a republic, and of the most dangerous tendency."[24]

Historians have sometimes seen in Harrison's reply little more than casuistry and politically motivated evasion.[25] But to dismiss his rhetoric as merely a cynical ploy to avoid committing himself on contentious issues does an injustice to the political philosophy that Harrison articulated. Because the Whigs were history's losers, at least when it came to executive power, it is difficult for Americans in the twenty-first century to take seriously Harrison's views on executive power. Granted, much of Harrison's message looked nostalgically backward to a bygone age, but its warning is also prescient in our increasingly president-centric age. Whether we can learn from Harrison or not, he was expressing a sincerely held Whig principle of governance that had been honed during years of opposition to Democratic rule, albeit not yet tested against the responsibilities of power.

Harrison followed up on his letter to New York's Whigs with several other letters that soon found their way into print. The first of these was to a Whig congressman from Tennessee, Joseph Williams, who had asked Harrison to clarify the role assumed by the Hamilton County corresponding committee. In Harrison's reply, which he authorized the congressman to make public, he distanced himself from the unfortunate phrasing used by the committee in the letter to the Oswego Association. He said he had had little communication with the committee, apart from authorizing it to send to those who asked about his opinions the "documents which contained the information they sought." The committee was to be a conduit for the various addresses, letters, speeches, and orders that Harrison had written over his long career, nothing more, although he admitted that the committee was authorized, "where further opinions were asked for," to affirm that he was determined to make "no other pledges of what [he] would or would not do, if [he] should be elected to the Presidency."[26]

Harrison also wrote to a prominent Virginia Whig politician, James Lyons, who had written Harrison in April to ask that he address the two charges that are "most relied upon and deemed most potent in the south," namely, that Harrison was an old Federalist and an abolitionist. To rebut the former charge, Harrison offered a detailed account of the circumstances under which he had twice been appointed to office by President John Adams. As for the charge of being an abolitionist, he dismissed it as absurd. He referred to his own previous public statements and invoked his many Southern friends who rightly "treated with scorn and contempt, the charge of my being an abolitionist, and truly assert that I have done and suffered more to support Southern rights than any other person north of Mason & Dixon's line."[27] Lyons and other Southern Whigs immediately trumpeted Harrison's letter as putting to an end "the abolition humbug."[28]

While publication of these letters helped Whigs to defuse Democratic attacks on General Mum, Harrison felt that he needed to do more to combat accusations that he was an "old imbecile," a man "muzzled" by his "guardians."[29] Now sixty-seven years of age, Harrison was more than a little thin-skinned about charges that he was too old or frail to be president. These same charges—and the same desire to demonstrate his physical vigor—had impelled him to embark on a then unprecedented campaign swing through the Eastern seaboard during September and October of 1836 (see chapter 4). Harrison believed that the 1836 tour, while derided by critics for "electioneering and hunting the Presidency," had helped him expose the accusations of his opponents as baseless lies. So Harrison, with his advisers' blessing, decided to reprise his 1836 campaign strategy, albeit closer to home.[30]

THIS "NEW BUSINESS OF STUMPING"

Much as he had in 1838, Harrison used military commemorations in his home state as a pretext to speak to the people. Specifically, he singled out three events: the first at Fort Meigs, on June 11, commemorating the famous siege there during the War of 1812; the second at Fort Greenville, on July 28, to celebrate the anniversary of a treaty signed with the Indians in 1795 following the Battle of Fallen Timbers; and the third in Dayton, Ohio, on September 10, the anniversary of Oliver Hazard Perry's famous naval victory in the Battle of Lake Erie in 1813. En route to and from these speaking engagements, Harrison gave several dozen speeches across Ohio that enabled him to put to rest the opposition narrative about a caged General Mum.

Historians have sometimes given short shrift to Harrison's summer speech-making campaign. Some have overlooked it altogether.[31] More have noticed the speaking but dismissed the speeches as little more than a rambling collection of war stories. Robert Gray Gunderson, for instance, suggests that Harrison avoided speaking about the issues "either by equivocation or by confining himself to irrelevancies about cabins and Indian fighting." In his invaluable history of presidential campaigning, *See How They Ran*, Gil Troy classifies Harrison as "silent but active"—unlike Van Buren, who was "forthright but passive."[32] That is, Harrison spoke a lot but said little. The truth is that Harrison not only spoke a lot but said a lot and in the process articulated fundamental Whig values and advanced his political objectives.[33]

Fort Meigs was two hundred miles north of Harrison's home in North Bend, so the trip took him the length of the state, providing the general with multiple opportunities to meet and speak with citizens throughout central Ohio. His first night was spent in Columbus, and on the morning of his departure, June 6, he delivered an impromptu speech at the door of his hotel to a large crowd that was said to be "anxious to see and hear him."[34] In an unapologetically political speech—arguably "the first overt political campaign speech" by a presidential nominee[35]—Harrison defended himself for nearly an hour against the many "instances of gross misrepresentation, or absolute falsehoods" that had been "invented and propagated" by the Democratic Party press, beginning with the one that clearly nettled him most, the "ludicrous" invention that he had been caged by a "committee of conscience-keepers." He recounted and refuted a string of other campaign slanders—that he was "a black cockade Federalist," that as a young man he had confessed to being an abolitionist, and that he had committed various alleged acts of cowardice on the battlefield. They were all fabrications and lies, sentences taken out of context, history rewritten. It was all a sad commentary on the state of American politics. Harrison told the crowd that he hoped soon to see a "reformation of such abuses" and a restoration of a politics that eschewed "political warfare" based on personal destruction.[36]

Ostensibly a commemoration of a military victory, the celebration at Fort Meigs was a massive multiday Whig political extravaganza, complete with a gargantuan log cabin one hundred yards long and a waving sea of banners emblazoned with political mottos such as "Matty, we go Jackson, but we can't go you—we must vote for Harrison." An estimated thirty thousand people with delegations from close to a dozen states converged on the old fort. One steamboat carried a delegation of nearly 1,500 people from Michigan.[37] Without ever leaving the state (and thereby adhering to "the rule which he had laid down for himself [after his nomination] not to go beyond the limits of his own state to attend public meetings"[38]), Harrison was thus afforded the opportunity to speak with citizens drawn from all across the Union, including New York, Pennsylvania, and Virginia.

Harrison spoke for more than an hour under a fierce sun in "trumpet-like tones" that the Whig press reported could be "distinctly heard at the distance of three hundred yards," a projection of "physical power" that the Whigs said exposed Democratic lies about Harrison for the fabrications they were.[39] Unlike at Columbus, Harrison did not dwell on the accusations made by his political opponents. Instead, he reminisced about the battle at Fort Meigs and his early military career. But this was no rambling tale of military exploits. The reminiscing was a direct appeal to the many military veterans and their families who were in the audience.[40] Indeed, Harrison used the occasion to remind his fellow citizens that many veterans who had fought under General Anthony Wayne—as he had—had been excluded from the military pension act enacted by Congress. He promised that if he became president, he would ensure that "the debt which is due these brave but neglected men shall . . . be paid." He noted, too, that during his career in Congress, he had always been an advocate for military veterans.[41]

Military veterans were special, and Harrison made no apology for that. Indeed, he suggested that the nation's veterans were a sufficient reason for his decision to put aside his own preference to remain at home in North Bend during the campaign—in keeping with his long-held belief that the "office of President of the United States should not be sought after by any individual"—and accept the invitation to speak at this event. The special nature of military veterans explains why Harrison, without a hint of irony or contradiction, could proceed to explain why the presidential nominee should avoid making pledges—because then the office would go not to the "virtuous" but to the man "who is prepared to tell the greatest number of lies." He closed by sounding the Whig alarm against unchecked executive power. Under Jackson and Van Buren, the country had become "a monarchy in spirit if not in name," and Harrison warned especially against passage of Van Buren's subtreasury plan, which would give the president an unprecedented and dangerous level of control over public funds. Harrison's speech turned the ideological tables on the Democrats, making them the agents of consolidated power and cloaking himself in the mantle of "the strictest manner of Virginian anti-Federalism." "Our rulers . . . must be watched," he explained, because "power is insinuating." Those who wielded it were not to be trusted. "In conclusion, then, fellow citizens," he thundered, "give up the idea of watching each other, and direct your eye to the Government," a call for civic vigilance that was met by the crowd with loud chants of "We will do it."[42]

After the Fort Meigs celebration, Harrison did not immediately head back to North Bend. Instead, he went east to Cleveland, where on June 13 "old man eloquent" addressed a crowd of some four thousand people outside his hotel. He prefaced his speech by admitting that even his appearance at Fort Meigs had "not [been] in strict conformity with his own views of propriety" but that he had made an exception because the defense of the fort was such "an important event in the history of our country, in which the people of all political parties were equally interested, . . . by which the whole Northwestern frontier was saved from the murderous depredations of a savage foe." And while he did not wish to take any course that could be construed as "an attempt to electioneer in his own behalf," he had promised two years ago that if he was ever in the northern part of the state again, he would visit Cleveland. He had thus felt duty bound to honor that pledge when a committee of Cleveland citizens at the Fort Meigs celebration had reminded him of that promise. The republican pieties out of the way, he proceeded to laud the area's astonishing level of economic and social development, recalling his own role as the Northwest Territory's congressional representative in securing a public lands policy that enabled "every industrious citizen, however poor, to become an owner of the soil" while also drawing attention to the crucial role that internal improvements had played in the area's economic development. He also reprised the antipower and antiexecutive philosophy he articulated at Fort Meigs, emphasizing that he would never as president "interpose the veto power between the wishes of the people and the legitimate objects of their desires, except to preserve the sacred charter of our liberties from manifest violation." Not only was the veto to be sparingly used, but Harrison said it was wholly improper for the president to threaten a veto or even to express his views about legislation until Congress, "the Legislative Department of the Government," had performed its constitutional duty to legislate, unbiased by the views and opinions of the executive.[43]

Despite his protestations about not wanting to appear to electioneer, Harrison seemed in no hurry to end the tour. Five days later, he had only reached as far as Springfield, where he had arranged to give another speech, a plan he abandoned only after he received news that his son had died. Although brought to a premature end, the tour had done its intended work. Every "honest man who saw and heard Gen. Harrison at Fort Meigs or at Cleveland," exulted one Whig editor, could see that "the epithets so freely bestowed by a partizan press—'caged hero'—'imbecile—'superannuated'—'granny'—or 'coward'" lacked any basis in reality.[44] Shortly after arriving home, Harrison boasted to Daniel Webster that he had "silenced the calumnies as to my bodily infirmities."[45]

Harrison may have felt that he had laid to rest concerns about his vitality, yet the following month, he was back on the stump, this time journeying to Fort Greenville, eighty miles north of his North Bend farm. Over six days, there and back, he traversed more than 150 miles "amidst clouds of dust with thousands thronged around him making no less than TEN speeches in the open air, to immense multitudes."[46] As at Fort Meigs, the Fort Greenville celebration afforded Harrison the chance to remain within the state and yet speak to huge numbers of people from outside the state, in this case from Indiana (the fort was only about ten miles from the Indiana border). Before "acres of Hoosiers and Buckeyes,"[47] an estimated crowd of at least twelve thousand people drawn from seven Indiana counties and eight Ohio counties, Harrison plunged into an unashamedly political speech. He again acknowledged that his appearance might be mistaken for "electioneering" and assured his listeners that he would have preferred "to remain with my family in the peace and quiet of our log cabin at the Bend."[48] But his appearance before them, he said, had "been made an act of necessity, a step which I was compelled to take for self-defense" to vindicate himself "from the continued torrent of calumny that has poured upon me, from the slanders, abuses, and obloquy which have been promulgated and circulated . . . to asperse and blacken my character." He had come, however, not only to refute and ridicule the personal slanders—the nutty notion that he was a "very decrepid old man, obliged to hobble about on crutches," that he was a caged-up "General Mum," and that he could "not speak loud enough to be heard more than four or five feet distant." He stood before them to discuss "the political conditions of our common country," trusting that there was "no impropriety in my addressing you upon subjects concerning the public weal."

Speaking without notes as he always did, Harrison reprised many of the same themes that he had covered at Fort Meigs and Cleveland, but he added new elements as well, taking special aim at the way Democrats had corrupted American politics by adopting the odious principle that "to the victors belong the spoils." Harrison deplored that the Jackson and Van Buren administrations had unjustly removed from office many high-minded and worthy public servants. As evidence he pointed to his friend General Solomon Van Rensselaer, whom Van Buren had fired from his post as Albany postmaster general, "without cause or provocation save a difference of opinion." It was not merely the injustice done to individuals that Harrison deplored; it was the deeper, systemic harm of making party the measure of a man. The nation, he warned, was being destroyed by an "intense party spirit" that allowed any "falsehood" to be justified in the name of achieving a party's purposes.

Perhaps reflecting a growing confidence about tackling political issues on the stump, Harrison confronted the charge that he was a "bank man." He said that "if the people deem it necessary to create a National Bank," he would be the last man to stand in their way. The key issue, however, was not whether there should be a national bank but whether credit was readily available and money circulated liberally: "Destroy a poor man's credit, and you destroy his capital." One only needed to look to the despotic countries of Europe to see the ill effect of Democratic "hard-money" policies. "The peasant who toils incessantly to maintain his family household in the hard-money countries of Europe," Harrison explained, "rarely, if ever becomes the noble lord of his pastures." Democratic hard-money policies threatened to undermine the economic and social mobility upon which rested not only American prosperity but American liberty.[49]

Although Harrison continued to insist that he'd rather be tending his farm than giving political speeches, the evidence suggests that, to the contrary, he enjoyed what Democrat Silas Wright called this "new business of stumping."[50] By the end of his two summer tours, he had done more than enough to discredit the "General Mum" label and to demonstrate his vigor. Indeed, Democrats were already pivoting toward attacking the general not for his silence but for his unseemly electioneering.[51] That didn't stop Harrison from scheduling another speaking tour in September. The main event was again a military commemoration, this one in Dayton, but Harrison spent the better part of the month on the road mixing with huge crowds of people and giving speeches in dozens of towns in the southern and central parts of Ohio.[52]

Harrison's hour-long speech at Dayton on September 10 was delivered before an immense crowd, estimated to be at least seventy-five thousand people.[53] The speech was largely a pastiche of themes and arguments from his previous speeches in June and July, but this time there was no preface as to how he would rather be home on the farm, no apologies for seeming to violate the proprieties in speaking to the people. Indeed, he stood the norm entirely on its head. He was "fully aware," he told his "fellow citizens, that you expect from me some opinion upon the various questions which now agitate the country, from centre to circumference, with such fierce contention." He promised he would not disappoint them.

Harrison was no great orator, certainly no Webster or Clay. He freely acknowledged as much, telling the crowd that he was "not a professional speaker, not a studied orator, but . . . an old soldier and a farmer." But despite the protestations about his lack of artifice, he had become much more skilled at working—and working up—a crowd since his first impromptu speech outside his Columbus hotel three months earlier. Rather than simply professing his views, he often offered them in the form of questions that invited the crowd's response.

Have I not declared, over and often, that the President of this Union does not constitute any part or portion of the Legislative body? (Cries from every quarter—you have). Have I not said, over and often, that the Executive should not by any act of his forestall the action of the National Legislature?—(You have, you have!) . . . Are my views on this topic correct, or are they not? (With one voice the multitude indicated they were.)

Throughout the speech, Harrison's lines were punctuated with "loud and long cheering," "cries of assent," "great laughter," and "shouts of applause." At Columbus, Harrison had seemed angry and indignant about Democratic charges of his infirmity; now these charges were the butt of his humor and the entertaining punchline to a long speech: "I have detained you, fellow-citizens, longer than I intended, but you now see, that I am not the old man on crutches, not the imbecile, they say I am—(cheering)—not the prey to disease,—(a voice cried here,—not the bear in a cage)—not the caged animal they wittingly describe me to be. (Great laughter and cheering.)" Harrison and the crowd were clearly enjoying themselves.

Harrison particularly relished turning the tables on the hackneyed Democratic charge that he was a closet Federalist. In his public letter to Lyons, he had earnestly and painstakingly detailed the circumstances of his appointment to office during the Adams administration. In front of the crowd, he offered a far more effective riposte by embracing the anti-Federalist reading of the Constitution that the "seeds of monarchy were . . . sown in the fertile soil of our federal Constitution." For half a century, those seeds "lay dormant," Harrison explained, but under Jackson and Van Buren, they "sprouted and shot forth" into the noxious monarchy that Patrick Henry and George Mason—those "patriarchs of the Jeffersonian school"—had so presciently foreseen. He reminded the crowd that under his father's tutelage, he had been "educated in the school of anti-federalism" and that his "teachers were the Henrys and the Masons of that period." After he quoted Henry's warning that the Constitution had "an awful squinting toward a monarchy" and claimed the great Virginian as his "Mentor," the crowd erupted in such thunderous applause that "some time elapsed before order could be restored." The Jacksonians were the true ultra-Federalists, Harrison preached; indeed, Jackson and Van Buren had realized an unprecedented degree of executive power that was "far greater than that ever dreamed of by the older federal party." He pledged before the wildly cheering crowd that he would "use all the power and influence vested in the office of President . . . to abridge the power and influence of the National Executive!"[54]

Perhaps the most novel aspect of Harrison's speech was his efforts to draw a contrast between his record as a chief executive and his opponent's. As governor of Indiana, Harrison pointed out, he had been vested with powers over the Northwest Territory that were every bit as great as that now "exercised by the present president of the U. States." But, he asked the crowd, "did I discharge my duties as Governor of that vast Territory in such a way as to show that I was in love with the tremendous powers vested in me?"—at which point four thousand Indiana delegates in a corner of the crowd apparently "raised their hats in the air and rent it with shouts of no, no, no." Unlike Van Buren, Harrison had not been seduced by the siren song of executive power. In contrast, Van Buren's appetite for executive power knew no bounds. Even as a delegate at the New York constitutional convention of 1821, he had backed giving that state's chief executive the power of appointing sheriffs. In contrast, when Harrison was governor, while he had "possessed the power of appointing all officers," including sheriffs, coroners, judges, and justices of the peace, he had given that power "up to the people!!"[55] In 1835, William Henry Seward had emphasized that if the Whig Party was to win a presidential election, it needed to get right with the "principle [of] Democracy."[56] Harrison was doing precisely that.

Democrats feigned horror at Harrison's speech, "which exhibits as many of the arts of the demagogue, as there are paragraphs." Bryant's *Evening Post* now adjudged that "since the muzzle has been taken from the old gentleman's mouth, he is likely to do himself and his party more injury than was done by his previous silence." Surely some loyal friend of Harrison's, Bryant gibed, would do the poor man the favor of entreating him to revert "to the policy which he began, to make no declarations for the public eye."[57] But in fulminating about the speech's demagoguery or picking at this misstep or that contradiction in Harrison's words, the Democrats abandoned the stock character of the decrepit General Mum and with it the one sure line of attack that had seemed to throw Harrison and the Whigs onto the defensive.

Harrison had no intention of reverting to his "previous silence." On the contrary, the general seemed more convinced than ever that his speeches were a necessary and effective means of defending himself against Democratic attacks. After speaking at Dayton, rather than returning home to North Bend, he headed east to speak at Chillicothe. There was no military commemoration as a pretext for speaking there, which helps explain why he felt the need to belabor his "regret" at being "compelled" to "leave the retirement of home, and go from place to place in the capacity of a public speaker," adding that he sometimes feared that "upon me will fall the responsibility of establishing a dangerous precedent to be followed in future time" by other presidential candidates. But these were no ordinary times, he told the crowd, for "we have fallen upon evil times. . . . And what once might have been justly considered wrong, circumstances seem now to render an imperative duty."[58]

Harrison chose to speak at Chillicothe with a singular purpose, for it was at this same site the previous month that close to ten thousand Democrats had heard Vice President Richard M. Johnson relate the supposedly "unvarnished tale" of the Battle of the Thames, the 1813 battle that had brought fame to both Colonel Johnson and his commanding officer, William Henry Harrison. Johnson attested that while on the frontlines during the battle with Tecumseh, he had never seen Harrison; not "until the battle was over," when Harrison had gone to see the badly wounded Johnson, had he spied him. Johnson admitted that he was unable to say whether Harrison "was half a mile, one mile, or a mile and a half in the rear" during the battle, but he reported that his brother, Lieutenant Colonel James Johnson, who commanded a division of five hundred men, confirmed that Harrison was "about a mile from the scene of action." Johnson's account was fodder for Democrats, who offered it as definitive evidence if not of Harrison's cowardice, then of his misbegotten status as a war hero. Johnson, they said, was "the real hero of the Thames."[59]

Although Johnson always repudiated any suggestion that Harrison had shown cowardice at the Battle of the Thames, the young Ohio senator William Allen—who shared the speaker's platform with Johnson throughout the two men's speaking tour of Ohio—showed no such restraint.[60] Indeed it was Allen, a Chillicothe resident, who had injected into the 1836 campaign the scurrilous rumor that many years before, the ladies of Chillicothe had presented Colonel George Croghan with an elegant sword for his gallant

defense of Fort Stephenson during the summer of 1813 while sending a petticoat to General Harrison for his failure to send reinforcements.[61] While
Johnson generally took the high road, Allen slashed his way along the low
road, assailing the "Petticoat General" and "the mock hero" in what Whigs
complained was the "most rabid, bitter, insulting, and repulsive style and
manner."[62] Not without reason did Harrison tell his Chillicothe audience,
"I am here, because I am the most persecuted and calumniated individual
now living."[63]

At Chillicothe, Harrison spoke for more than two hours, reprising and
adapting some of the familiar elements from his stock speech, but the bulk
of the speech was devoted to vindicating his conduct at the Battle of the
Thames, refuting the suggestion that he had remained far out of harm's
way during the battle, and taking sharp exception to Johnson's further
claim that the idea for his charge of the enemy had originated with Johnson.
While careful to praise Johnson's bravery, Harrison scorned the notion that
as the commander, he would have delegated a decision of such magnitude
to Johnson, whose military career "did not exceed four months," who "had
no experience in war," and who "had not been educated to military tactics."
As courageous as Johnson was, "he was no more capable of taking command of an army for battle" than a person "who had not been instructed in
the mechanism of a watch, would be to put the wheels of that instrument
together, and set it in motion." Harrison acknowledged that unless all hope
seems lost, the commanding general of an army rarely plunges "into the
hottest of the strife" at the head of the battle since "his eye must be fixed
upon all parts of the army, and he must be ready, at a moment to provide
for any emergency." But he ridiculed the notion that because Johnson "did
not see me through a thicket of 200 yards wide, I was not there." Johnson
had been on the extreme left flank, Harrison the extreme right. Moreover,
Harrison insisted, when Johnson "fell covered with wounds, and his troops
were repulsed, I marched forthwith to the rescue, and in front of where he
had fallen. I secured the conquest myself." In case there were any lingering
doubts about the veracity of Harrison's version of events, he was followed to
the rostrum by two of his former military aides, including Charles S. Todd,
who attested to the accuracy of every word uttered by Harrison and added
more details of their own that threw into question Johnson's version. Todd
even read to the crowd several affidavits he had obtained from officers who
had been at the Battle of the Thames that confirmed Harrison's story.

Harrison also took aim at his "traducer," Chillicothe's own Senator Allen, drawing on the history of ancient Rome to drive home his rebuke. He

instructed his audience that in Rome the Senate had been the bulwark of liberty, the institution that had seemed "beyond the contaminating touch of power." "The humiliation of the people of Rome," Harrison declared, "did not arrive until those who had been honored with the office of Senators became panders to the vices of a tyrant. When they acted as the scavengers of that tyrant, picking up from the vilest places, calumnious stories to destroy the reputation of the faithful servants of the country, [only] then it was that the Roman people were humbled and degraded." Harrison did not need to mention Allen by name. "Shall I say," he asked the audience, "that this State, this city, has sustained the man, the Senator, who could stoop to meanness like this?" Harrison's analogy also made clear that the damage of such "meanness" and "calumnious stories" was to be measured not only in the harm they caused to the individual whose reputation was unjustly sullied but the harm they inflicted on the fabric of a free society.[64]

Although largely devoted to revisiting past battles and vindicating his character, Harrison's speech addressed current issues as well. Most notably, he weighed in for the first time on the growing controversy over Secretary of War Joel Poinsett's innovative but politically disastrous proposal to restructure the militia so that there would be more uniform training of the nation's citizen soldiers. Particularly unpopular in the South, Poinsett's proposed legislation would have federally mandated that every man between the ages of twenty and forty-five enroll in his state's militia and that each state would then select from its reserve pool 100,000 men for active duty who would be drilled a few times a year by regular (federal) military officers. Each year a quarter of the active unit would return to the reserves, and their places would be taken by new recruits.[65] Harrison joined in the chorus of criticism of this "outrageous" power grab by the executive. "If there was any thing calculated to make the President a complete monarch," Harrison declaimed, "it would be the passage of this bill." Although he was all for "a well organized militia . . . it should be under subjection to the State governments," not the federal government. Making matters worse, the bill was unfair to the common people, as it would have obliged "alike the poor and the rich, to submit to the same expense in procuring the same arms." Apparently, this was one bill that Harrison would have been happy to veto.[66]

After his appearance at Chillicothe, Harrison still did not head for home. Instead, he turned north, speaking at Circleville, Lancaster, and Somerset.[67] At Lancaster, he responded to charges circulating in the Democratic press that he entertained "unfriendly feelings towards foreigners." These accusations stemmed from the speech he had given at Cleveland, in which he had been widely quoted in Democratic papers as saying, "I care nothing for the opinion of those who have come hither 3,000 miles across the water."[68] Harrison vehemently denied the "cruel and unjust" charge, countering that throughout his career, he had always favored and supported making naturalization easier and had backed laws providing relief and land to those who, fleeing persecution, had come to the United States "poor and without a home." He even showed the appreciative crowd a "holy relic," a small cross made of alder and wrought with silver that had recently been given to him by an exiled Pole, as a sign of how highly the Polish émigré community esteemed Harrison.[69]

Upon his return to Cincinnati on September 24, Harrison finally called an end to the touring, having spent close to fifty days since early June on the road, traveling the state and speaking at dozens of Ohio towns. Not that he was finished with public speaking, for within a week of his return, he once again ascended the speaker's platform in Cincinnati at an all-day rally on October 1 that attracted sixty thousand enthusiastic Whigs.[70] Nor was that the only time Harrison spoke in Cincinnati and its immediate environs. On August 20, he visited Carthage (which today is part of Cincinnati) for yet another political rally in the guise of a military celebration—this one to celebrate the anniversary of the 1794 Battle of Fallen Timbers.[71] What he said to the few thousand people gathered at Carthage mattered relatively little, but an excerpt of that speech laying out his views "on the Abolition question" was widely circulated in the Whig press with the aim of reassuring antislavery men of his conviction that Americans had the right to petition "for the redress of anything," while also assuring Southerners of his belief that under the Constitution "neither the General Government nor the other States, nor the citizens of the other States [could] exercise the least control" over powers retained exclusively by the states.[72]

How ironic it is, then, that the most loquacious and peripatetic presidential candidate the nation had ever seen is remembered to this day as a foolish General Mum, the label affixed by his opponents, rather than as the precedent-shattering candidate he was. It is true that Harrison tried to avoid taking clear positions on issues on which his supporters were divided, such as the national bank and slavery. But where his party was united, such as on the foolhardiness of hard-money schemes and the importance of curtailing executive power, Harrison spoke with beacon-like clarity. He retreated to generalities when it served him, but when circumstances required, he narrated with exacting specificity, as when explaining the committee of correspondence or the Battle of the Thames. There were plenty of war stories, of course, but they were calibrated to the event—often a celebration of some military battle—and to the audience populated with military veterans and their families. His speaking sometimes flitted from topic to topic, as one might expect from a relatively inexperienced orator speaking without notes, but he articulated a consistent and cogent Whig public philosophy, particularly regarding the dangers posed by executive power and hyperpartisanship under Jackson and Van Buren.

THE PRESIDENT'S LETTER-WRITING CAMPAIGN

Harrison is not the only presidential candidate in 1840 whose record is at odds with his reputation. His Democratic rival, so often portrayed as slippery and noncommittal, perhaps had even stronger grounds for complaint over an undeserved reputation. "Van Buren non-committalism" entered the American lexicon well before Van Buren became president or even vice president.[73] During the 1836 campaign, the Whigs frequently took aim at the Sly Fox's alleged "non-committalism,"[74] and they kept up the barrage of denunciation during his presidency and the 1840 campaign.[75] But notwithstanding his reputation for being a guarded and evasive politician, Van Buren was anything but noncommittal about policies when he ran for president. Both in 1836 and 1840, he ran policy-centric campaigns and labored over public letters in which he clearly communicated the specifics of those policies to the American people.

As president, Van Buren was necessarily more constrained than Harrison in his ability to campaign actively because the norm against stump speaking applied with far greater force to an incumbent president than a challenger. Many nineteenth-century nominees for the presidency, including Winfield Scott, Stephen Douglas, Horatio Seymour, Horace Greeley, and James Blaine, followed Harrison onto the stump, but not until the twentieth century would an incumbent president actively campaign for reelection by traveling the country and giving speeches. Even President Theodore Roosevelt, who relished campaigning and public speaking, felt compelled in 1904 to heed his advisers' counsel to stay off the hustings after he was nominated.[76]

Not that Van Buren avoided public speaking—or the charge of electioneering—as president. On the contrary, in the summer of 1839, he broke a half century of presidential tradition[77] by embarking on a several-months-long tour of New York that was aimed at shoring up his support and healing party divisions in his electorally crucial home state.[78] During his tour, which coincided with Clay's tour of New York that same summer,[79] Van Buren

SETTIN' ON A RAIL .

Settin' on a Rail. *Van Buren's reputation as a noncommittal politician is lampooned in this 1837 Whig cartoon that shows Van Buren straddling the fence, being tugged to the left by former president Andrew Jackson, Senator Thomas Hart Benton, and other "hard-money" Democrats and pulled to the right by a gaggle of Conservative Democrats, one of whom holds in his hand a copy of the* Madisonian, *which began publication in August 1837 under the editorship of Thomas Allen. "Take care gentlemen, you'll have me off the fence," says Van Buren, who in the struggle is losing his hat, which is emblazoned with a crown. "Look out Matty or you'll commit yourself this time," observes the man on the far right, who is meant to be the fictional Major John Downing, a popular Forrest Gump–like character of the 1830s. (The Gump analogy is made by Aaron McLean Winter in "From Mascot to Militant: The Many Campaigns of Seba Smith's 'Major Jack Downing,'"* Readex Report, *September 2010, https://www.readex.com/readex-report/mascot-militant-many-campaigns -seba-smiths-major-jack-downing.) (Courtesy of the Library of Congress)*

delivered close to fifty speeches, some of which were austerely nonpolitical but others of which struck unmistakably partisan notes, defending his administration's policies—especially the Independent Treasury—and occasionally attacking his opponents. On a number of occasions, Whig-dominated councils—including in Hudson, the town in which Van Buren began his political career nearly thirty years earlier—refused to formally welcome the president, leaving Democrats to compose the welcoming address and to organize the town's welcome, which Whigs then pounced on as further evidence of the president's unseemly "electioneering" that was "degrading" his high office.[80]

Upon arriving in New York City on July 4, 1839, Van Buren was greeted with fulsome praise of his policy agenda from Tammany Democrat John W. Edmonds, who welcomed the president on behalf of "your Democratic Fellow Citizens." Taking his cue from Edmonds, Van Buren promoted the Independent Treasury, framing it as a question of whether government was to work "for the safety of the many or the aggrandizement of the few." The opposition, Van Buren told the largely Democratic audience, wanted the public's money to be controlled by "private corporations, irresponsible to the people," whereas the administration wanted it to be in the hands of the people and their elected representatives.[81]

Perhaps Van Buren's most partisan speech came on September 10, 1839, in Onondaga County, where he took his cue from a welcoming address that contrasted the "courtesy and tolerance" Van Buren had shown "towards his political opponents" with the "the bitterness of party asperity and malignity" evinced by his opponents, who had consistently "misinterpreted and misrepresented" the president's actions. Speaking before an overwhelmingly Democratic crowd, Van Buren acknowledged that the "inveterate malignity with which [he had] been pursued by his political opponents . . . at every step" of his political career was a matter that had been frequently brought to his attention during his tour. He had no objection, he said, to partisan attacks so long as they were motivated by a sincere "regard to the real good of the country."

> But when it is quite manifest that those by whom the conduct of a public officer is arraigned are resolved to condemn his acts in any event; when they only desire to know which side of a public question he espouses in order to take their own position against him; when all considerations of comity and right are merged in an absorbing desire to expel him from office and when nothing so much mortifies and enrages them as that he should decide or adopt measures that redound to the good of the country; in all such cases it appears to me an act of inexcusable weakness on the part of the public functionary to suffer what such opponents may say or think of him to give him a moment's care or unease.

There was no point in paying attention to what his "enemies" said since their intention was not "to get at the truth and to approve what is really right" but simply to attack whatever the administration proposed.

Van Buren further maintained that the misinformation spread by Whig newspapers demonstrated that he had not given up the people's cause. "These continual attacks . . . from the same quarter," Van Buren told the crowd, "are like beacons" of light, which allow even those living "in the remotest corner of the land" to see his fidelity to the Democratic faith. So long as the people "continue to hear the hootings of the common enemy, they know that their confidence is well placed. It is only when those attacks cease," Van Buren continued, "that their suspicions are aroused, and seldom, indeed, without ground." In short, the "unceasing assaults" upon the president were proof that he was doing the people's work and not giving in to the powerful.[82]

Despite wearing the opposition's criticism as a badge of honor, Van Buren appears to have been chastened by the barrage of Whig criticisms of his electioneering. Certainly, after finishing up his tour in the latter part of September 1839, Van Buren resisted any further entreaties to travel or speak.[83] But while Van Buren felt that he could not follow Harrison out onto the hustings in 1840, he did not shy away from defending his policies during the campaign through the now widely accepted medium of public letters.

Ironically, given the stern warning that Van Buren had issued to Jackson in 1827 against writing public letters, Van Buren as a presidential candidate, both in 1836 and 1840, wrote with "unprecedented candor."[84] Indeed, even as a vice-presidential nominee in 1832, Van Buren had shown that same candor. Only a month before the 1832 election, Van Buren responded to a letter requesting his views on nullification, the national bank, and internal improvements by affirming these North Carolinians' "right . . . to be informed" of his opinions on these subjects and unambiguously declaring his opposition to nullification and to the renewal of the national bank's charter while also detailing his views on the conditions under which the federal government could become involved in internal improvements. A less "noncommittal" public statement would be difficult to imagine.[85]

Similarly, in the 1836 campaign, Van Buren responded to Sherrod Williams's interrogatories with a public manifesto that in draft form was 109 pages long and in published form "stretched across eight-and-a-half pages of double columns."[86] In providing an exhaustive accounting of his public policy views, Van Buren not only affirmed the need for "the most liberal interchange of sentiments" between candidates and voters but also articulated a relatively new understanding of presidential elections as referendums on the public policy positions of a candidate. Van Buren promised that he was committed to follow in Jackson's footsteps by opposing a national bank and reasoned that if the voters selected him as president, it would show that the majority preferred "that there shall not be any Bank of the United States." Elections were less about choosing individuals than about conferring policy mandates. The candidate was but "the honored instrument" chosen to implement the party's principles and policies.[87]

During the 1840 campaign, particularly between the close of the congressional session on July 21 and the end of September, Van Buren spent long, painstaking hours "answering interrogatories sent to him from all quarters," including from his political foes.[88] His responses, which appeared in newspapers all across the country, were invariably thoughtful and well-reasoned, and rarely dodged even the most difficult of questions. At the end of July, for instance, Van Buren penned an eight-thousand-word response to four citizens from the southeastern part of Virginia who, "prompted, not by an impertinent curiosity, but solely by a desire of ascertaining whether your views or those of Gen. Harrison coincide more nearly with our own," had asked Van Buren to state his position on several leading policy questions. Van Buren prefaced his answer, as he often did, by strongly affirming the right of voters "to call in good faith on the candidate . . . for an unreserved avowal of his opinions in regard to all matters of public concern." Indeed, Van Buren insisted that the voters' exercise of their right to demand answers and candidates' fulfillment of their duty to respond candidly were "indispensable to the maintenance of republican government."[89]

If Van Buren felt that his views on a question had already been communicated to the public, he would direct the correspondent to the prior letter that contained those views, usually taking steps to supply the correspondent with the earlier missive so it too could be republished.[90] Other times, he would quote at length from a previous letter he had written. But where the question was new, Van Buren often expounded his views at great length. For instance, the letter he received from the Virginians—which, like most letters he (and Harrison) received from the South, began with the question of slavery—put two questions to Van Buren: "Will you, if re-elected president, veto any bill having for its object the abolition of slavery in the District of Columbia; or, would you sanction any bill granting appropriations of the public money to any state, soliciting aid for the emancipation of their slaves?" On the first question, Van Buren felt he had expressed himself frequently, including in a letter he had recently written to a committee of Louisville citizens, and so asked his questioners to be content with receiving a copy of the Louisville letter. But on the second slavery-related question, which he had not previously addressed, Van Buren "unhesitatingly" answered the question in the negative. Whether a slave state consented to have federal monies appropriated for emancipating slaves and compensating slaveholders made no difference. No state could confer on the federal government a power it did not possess. Van Buren warned that "we have seen too much of the progressive character of constitutional encroachments" in the American past to trust that such a policy would not "in course of time, lead to attempts by the federal government to accomplish the same object, without either the consent of the slaveholder or indemnity for his loss." Van Buren might reasonably be charged with ideological rigidity or perhaps sectional pandering but not with being noncommittal.

The Virginians also requested the president's views on banking, internal improvements, and tariffs, which Van Buren answered largely by liberally quoting from previous letters he had written, both in the current campaign and the previous one, particularly his letter to Sherrod Williams. However, their final question ("Do you approve of Mr. Poinsett's scheme for the organization of the militia?") afforded Van Buren an opportunity to respond publicly for the first time to the widespread criticism of the secretary of war's controversial proposal. Indeed, almost half of the letter's eight thousand words were devoted to the proposal. Van Buren labored to clarify misconceptions about the proposal by carefully laying out the rationale and specifics of the plan and blasted the demagoguery of those who charged the plan with establishing a standing army of 200,000 men. "If I had been charged with the design of establishing among you, at the public expense, a menagerie of two hundred thousand wild beasts, it would not have surprised me more, nor would it . . . have been one jot more preposterous," Van Buren retorted. At the same time, the president distanced himself from the plan, noting that his "knowledge of military affairs is very limited" and that he had played no role in its formulation. Now that his attention had been drawn to the matter, however, Van Buren was inclined to think that the plan as formulated was not constitutional, even if he was not yet ready to "pronounce definitively upon its constitutionality."[91]

On September 14, Van Buren replied to two letters. In his first response, he expended five thousand words, replying with rigor and nuance to a letter from several New Yorkers who, "in view of the approaching presidential election," had solicited Van Buren's views on various specific aspects of bankruptcy legislation relating to individuals and corporations. Desiring to get his views on bankruptcy laws into print as quickly as possible, Van Buren first published his reply and then sent copies of the published reply to his

New York interrogators.[92] The second letter was a much shorter response to a query from a group of Philadelphia residents who wished to know, among other things, whether he was in favor of "reducing the standard of wages." Unlike in his long wonkish letter on bankruptcy, Van Buren used his reply to the Philadelphians to declare his affinity with labor and to broadcast his general economic philosophy that the market ("the natural order of society") could be counted on to deliver a "just and adequate" wage only when "free from the blighting influence of partial legislation, monopolies, congregated wealth, and interested combinations." He also touted an executive order, issued in the spring of 1840, in which, at the behest of "the mechanics and laborers themselves," he had mandated a limit of a ten-hour work day for all those working on federal installations such as naval yards (at many such facilities, workers labored from sunrise to sunset).[93] His order had reduced the number of hours, he insisted, but without any reduction in wages.

No question seemed too narrow for Van Buren to address if it had political implications. In the spring, for instance, he was asked by several North Carolinians to give his views on the case of Lieutenant George Mason Hooe, a Virginian who had been court-martialed for flogging several men on a US naval vessel. The accused officer had challenged his conviction by arguing that it had been based on "illegal evidence" since "two colored seamen" had testified against the officer. In his reply, Van Buren methodically explained why he had refused to overturn the officer's conviction: no law forbade "colored" persons from testifying against white persons in court-martial proceedings, and even if such testimony was assumed to be illegal, it had not been necessary to prove the charges against Hooe. However, Van Buren admitted that this legal analysis did not dispose of the broader question of whether Congress should enact legislation that would require courts-martial to follow the same principle adhered to in federal courts, which allowed for the testimony of free blacks only in federal cases in which the state where the court sat permitted such testimony. Although Van Buren believed this was a matter for Congress to decide, he volunteered the opinion that he could see no reason why military tribunals should not follow the same principles on this question as the federal courts. Such a legislative solution, he said, "would be very simple," and even courts-martial held at sea "could easily be adjusted."[94]

Not all Van Buren's public letters during the 1840 campaign were in reply to interrogatories. On July 4, 1840, the day he signed the Independent Treasury into law, he penned a public letter that was ostensibly a response to an invitation he had received to attend a public meeting in Kentucky but was really an opportunity to broadcast "the act of deliverance . . . this day consummated" of the administration's most cherished objective. Passage of the Independent Treasury, Van Buren wrote, freed the country at long last from the money power. Depositing "the people's money" into banks had allowed powerful private interests to enrich themselves and bend the nation's politics and policy to their nefarious ends. In ending the national bank, Jackson had destroyed "the unity of this interest . . . but not its power." Only now, with the establishment of an Independent Treasury, would the nation's finances, after half a century of perversion, be restored to the original form intended by the framers of the Constitution. Its passage was thus a historic "triumph of the popular intelligence . . . over the arts, arguments, . . . and alarms of the interested few."[95]

From the perspective of the twenty-first century, a president extravagantly proclaiming his accomplishments and defending his record during a reelection campaign seem unremarkable. Indeed, it is unimaginable that a president running for reelection would fail to do so. But, as unfathomable as it might seem to us today, no sitting president before Van Buren had dared to write public letters under his own name at the height of a reelection campaign for fear of being charged with degrading his office by electioneering. Previous presidents had certainly taken an active interest in their reelection campaigns, but their activities had remained concealed behind a carefully preserved facade of disinterest. Like his rival Harrison, Van Buren was an important and underappreciated innovator in helping to transform the role of the presidential candidate away from the traditional conception of a "mute tribune."[96]

Although neither Harrison nor Van Buren stayed mute, they communicated as candidates in starkly different ways. Van Buren's written replies were far more policy centered than Harrison's speeches and were designed to show the president's greater breadth of understanding and command of public policy as well as his steadfast commitment to Old Republican principles of strict construction of the Constitution, a message that was especially important in the South. Van Buren's detailed, issue-oriented letters were consistent with the overall Democratic strategy, articulated at the Baltimore nominating convention, of making the election a referendum on the party's principles and policy positions rather than a contest of personalities—a strategy that reflected the party's and the president's confidence that the Democrats were the "natural" majority party. But the public communications of both candidates also reflected genuine philosophical differences about the roles of presidents and parties. Just as Harrison believed in a polity that was not president-centric—and so was reluctant to make the campaign about his policy preferences—Van Buren believed that the public needed to know the policy positions of the president to ensure that the will of the majority prevailed over powerful special interests and the rich and privileged. Far from being a campaign without substance—a rollicking carnival of hard cider and log cabins—this was a campaign pitting two candidates with starkly different visions of executive power and party politics.

THE THIRD WAY

There was a third candidate in 1840 with a vision even more different: James Birney, a former slaveowner turned abolitionist, who was nominated for president by a new third party dedicated to the abolition of slavery that would become known as the Liberty Party.[97] Birney was born in Danville, Kentucky, in 1792 to an aristocratic, slaveowning family. He attended college at Princeton University (then known as the College of New Jersey) and read law in Philadelphia in the chambers of one of the nation's most prominent Jeffersonian Republicans, Alexander J. Dallas. As a young lawyer and aspiring politician, Birney was an enthusiastic backer of Kentucky's favorite son and Speaker of the House of Representatives, Henry Clay. He spent the summer of his twenty-third year stumping for Clay in his 1815 reelection campaign; the following year, Birney himself was elected to the Kentucky state legislature before heading off to Alabama to try his hand as a cotton plantation owner. The plantation was not a great success, and in 1823, Birney sold up, moved to Huntsville, and resumed his law practice. Birney soon became one of Huntsville's most prominent citizens and in 1829 was elected mayor. Clay was still his political hero, and his politics were resolutely anti-Jackson. In the 1828 election, Birney was one of the state's five Adams electors (not that there was any chance he would get to cast a vote in the electoral college, as Jackson won 90 percent of the vote in Alabama in 1828), and during Jackson's first term Birney strongly opposed the president's murderous Indian removal policy, backed the temperance movement, and supported Clay's "American System" of federally financed internal improvements, tariffs, and a national bank. He channeled his growing misgivings about slavery through his work for the American Colonization Society, an organization cofounded by Clay in 1816 and dedicated to solving the problems of slavery and race by sending manumitted slaves and free blacks to Africa.[98]

When Birney returned to Kentucky in 1833, he seemed to be a Whig politician in the making. Certainly, the 250-mile journey north greatly en-

James G. Birney. This lithograph is from 1844, when Birney was again nominated as the Liberty Party presidential candidate. Unlike in 1840, when Birney was out of the country for almost the entire campaign, Birney was a far more visible candidate in 1844 and the Liberty Party far better organized. In 1844, Birney received more than 62,000 votes, about nine times more than he won in 1840. In New York, his candidacy was particularly important in the 1844 election, as his 16,000 votes were three times the 5,000-vote margin that separated the Democratic nominee, James Polk, and the Whig nominee, Henry Clay. (Courtesy of the Library of Congress)

hanced his prospects for winning elected office. But his views on slavery were evolving rapidly, and within a year of his return to Danville he had freed his remaining slaves and quit the Colonization Society. In a forty-six-page "letter" to the Kentucky Colonization Society, Birney explained why he now believed that colonization was ineffectual and morally flawed. A movement grounded in "repugnant" principles, he insisted, could not bring about the "revolution of sentiments" that would be necessary to abolish slavery. By conceding that white racial prejudice must forever make "colored people" living in the United States "degraded and unhappy" and by teaching that it was ethically permissible, at least for the present, for one human being to own another, the Colonization Society helped to bolster slavery rather than bring it closer to extinction. Moreover, in practice, colonization encouraged efforts to impose "civil disabilities [and] disfranchisement" that would induce free blacks to "consent" to emigrate. After "seventeen years of trial," the verdict was clear: colonization had done nothing to weaken slavery or to combat "uncharitable feelings, unscriptural and unreasonable prejudices, and inhuman laws."[99] The only effectual and just course, Birney insisted, was the immediate abolition of slavery.

Birney's letter made him a hero among abolitionists. His public repudiation of colonization "electrified" them less because his arguments were original than because of who he was: a lifelong slaveowner, onetime Alabama cotton planter, pillar of the legal establishment, and gentleman "connected by birth and marriage with most of the leading families" of Kentucky.[100] This was hardly the usual abolitionist profile, and abolitionists hoped their new convert could help to increase the legitimacy of the movement and spread the abolitionist message in new quarters.

Birney immediately became a leading figure in the abolitionist movement, his stature within the movement only elevated by his refusal in 1836 to let mob violence deter him from publishing his new antislavery newspaper, the *Philanthropist*, which had become the official organ of the Ohio Anti-Slavery Society. (Birney had moved his family 120 miles north to Cincinnati in 1835 because of overwhelming opposition to the idea of publishing the paper in Danville.) His refusal to quit printing despite threats of personal violence (the well-to-do mob, "with due observance of the parliamentary niceties," had formally resolved to tar and feather Birney) and having his printing press dumped into the Ohio River made Birney into a nationally recognized champion of a free press and civil liberties.[101] One of the most sought-after abolitionist speakers, Birney moved to New York in 1837 to become the corresponding secretary of the American Anti-Slavery Society.

The Birney-for-president banner was first raised in November 1839 at a large antislavery meeting in Genesee County that attracted some five hundred abolitionists from the surrounding counties of western New York, where support for a third party was particularly strong.[102] The question of whether to form "a distinct and independent political party" dedicated to the abolition of slavery remained deeply divisive among abolitionists—indeed, just the month before, the American Anti-Slavery Society had held a convention in Cleveland (made up mostly of delegates from Ohio) that refused to support a third party. Most abolitionists were not yet ready to support such a party, preferring instead to stick with "the interrogation system" of asking the major party candidates their position on slavery. Even Birney, now the movement's most well-known advocate of political action, believed that the time was not yet ripe for a third party and so declined the nomination.[103]

Third-party advocates were undeterred, however, and initiated a call for another, more broad-based convention to consider afresh the question of an independent party and independent nominations. The convention, which met in Albany on April 1, 1840, was far from representative. Eighty-six percent of the 121 abolitionists who showed up were from New York, and the other seventeen delegates were from five Eastern states. Not a single delegate was from Ohio, where opposition to a third party ran strong.[104] The final vote in favor of independent nominations was far from emphatic. One-third of the delegates abstained, and the resolution carried by an underwhelming 44–33 tally. With greater unanimity, the convention then nominated Birney for president and Thomas Earle for vice president.[105]

Some political abolitionists urged Birney to decline the nomination, among them Ohio's Gamaliel Bailey, who had assumed the editorship of the *Philanthropist* when Birney left for New York.[106] This time, though, Birney was determined to accept the nomination, and on May 11, he penned a formal letter of acceptance that explained why he believed a third party was now necessary. Although he judged Van Buren's presidency to be "the most pernicious with which the republic has been cursed," he insisted that a vote for Harrison would change nothing because both political parties were equally complicit in making the North "a conquered province." The problem was not, as Harrison and the Whigs would have it, a tyrannical executive trampling on congressional power. Instead, the problem was that both the president and Congress were "in the hands of the slave power."[107]

Birney rejected the notion that the two political parties played a valuable role in knitting together slave states and free states by compromising and accommodating their divergent interests. The problem with this idea was that it was impossible "to make a harmonious whole out of parts that are, in principle and essence, discordant." Slavery and freedom were "incapable, from their natures, of being made *one*. They can no more be welded together into one body of uniform strength and consistency, than clay and brass." Granted, they might "be pressed together" and made "to cohere by extraneous appliances; and the line of contact may be daubed over and varnished and concealed." But ultimately there could be no strength in this join, and "the first shock will make them fall asunder." In Birney's view, no political party could long remain simultaneously proslavery and proliberty; inevitably, one or the other principle must "gain the entire ascendancy." By accommodating themselves to "slaveholding despotism," both the Democrats and Whigs had forged themselves into parties that protected slavery at the expense of freedom. That meant the only way to secure the nation's freedom, short of "severing . . . connections with the South," was to create a new party of liberty that demanded an immediate end to slavery.[108]

The nation could no longer afford to wait or to bracket slavery while "other interests" and issues were addressed. The slave power had now grown so strong that the nation's most precious liberties were being systematically abridged. The slave power had instituted the gag rule so that "free speech and debate on the most important subject that now agitates the country, is rendered impossible in our national legislature," and "the right of the people to petition Congress for a redress of grievances is formally abolished by their own servants." By establishing "censorship of the mail" and sanctioning violence against those who opposed it, the slave power trampled on freedom of the press, freedom of speech, and freedom of movement. Faced with such an imminent threat to the nation's most fundamental freedoms, the two parties' debates "about the currency, about the sub-treasury or no sub-treasury, a bank or no bank" seemed hardly worth having.[109]

In Birney's view, even the nation's current economic problems were, at bottom, problems of slavery and the slave power. Those who blamed Van Buren for "the low and deranged condition of the monetary affairs of the country, for the last three years" were mistaking a consequence for the cause of the economic "derangement." Van Buren did deserve the blame, though not for his monetary policies but instead for "consenting . . . to become the instrument of the Slave Power. For what can a free, republican and commercial state look for, but confusion and ruin, when they entrust their affairs to a people without commerce, without manufacturers, without arts, without industry, whose whole system of management is one of expense, waste, credit, and procrastination?" Only by freeing the country of the curse of slavery could the economy become productive and prosperous.[110]

It was imperative, then, that voters look beyond the individual candidates to the system that sustained and generated those candidates. As bad as Van Buren was, he was but "the mercury in the thermometer, influenced solely by the surrounding atmosphere, and showing with automaton accuracy the increase degree of heat to which it has risen." He was a symptom of the slave power's "growing ascendancy," not its cause. And while abolitionists had rejoiced at Clay's defeat at Harrisburg, they were naive to expect that Harrison could be anything but "the pliant minister of the Slave Power." Indeed, a Harrison presidency would only give "fresh strength to that Power." Harrison could be counted on to be every bit "as faithful to [slaveholders'] interest and as subservient to their purpose as Mr. Van Buren" had been. Thus, the time had come for freedom-loving Americans to cast off their old partisan identities and join a new party committed to liberating the country from the slave power and acting "incessantly on the South for the abolition of slavery."[111]

Birney's five-thousand-word acceptance letter—more than ten times the length of Harrison's—made a compelling case for his candidacy and the need for a third party dedicated to the abolition of slavery.[112] The letter, though, would be Birney's only contribution to his presidential campaign. On the day that he dated his acceptance letter, he set sail for England to attend the world antislavery convention in London as a delegate representing the American Anti-Slavery Society. He did not return until after the election was over.[113]

"THE PRESIDENTIAL CONTEST ABSORBS EVERY THING ELSE"

Only a sliver of the nation's electorate saw William Henry Harrison deliver a speech during the campaign of 1840. Fewer still would have been lucky enough to catch a glimpse of President Martin Van Buren holed up in the nation's capital. Yet their images, especially Harrison's, were everywhere during the campaign. Images of a youthful Harrison could be found on women's kerchiefs and men's neckties, on snuffboxes and hairbrushes, and on writing paper and campaign posters. Men could try out a Tippecanoe cane or use Tippecanoe shaving soap. They could even buy razors inscribed with the words "Try me one term" that "showed Harrison welcoming two old comrades to his log cabin." The ubiquitous log cabin adorned all manner of consumer goods, from dinner plates and whiskey flasks to earrings and watch chains.[1] In the Whig campaign, the "selling of the president" seemed at times to be two parts campaign strategy and one part profit seeking.[2]

Most American voters who wished to hear directly from the candidates during the 1840 campaign had to rely on words on the page, primarily through the widely circulated public letters that both candidates penned. But while the candidates took great care over their words, neither could be counted a gifted or even good literary stylist. Even had their prose been livelier, their ability to reach and move voters was necessarily limited. For even though Harrison and Van Buren played more active public roles in the 1840 campaign than any previous pair of presidential candidates, they nonetheless largely "remained on the campaign's periphery." As historian Gil Troy observes, in 1840, "it was not the candidate's campaign; it was the party's campaign with the candidate at the symbolic helm."[3] If the candidates were the campaign's central symbols, their images were constructed by the cartoonists and wordsmiths in the partisan press and by the parties' veritable army of political speakers who fanned out across the country to spread the party gospel.

OF PRESIDENTIAL PALACES AND LOG CABINS

No speech during the 1840 campaign was more widely circulated than the demagogic tour de force by a Whig congressman from Somerset, Pennsylvania, Charles Ogle. Ogle was born to politics. His father, one of Somerset County's most prominent men, had been oft elected as the county's state legislator and had served a term in Congress in the same three-county district to which his son was elected in 1836. Ogle started out, like his father, a supporter of Andrew Jackson but was one of the state's earliest converts to the Anti-Masonic cause and remained a leading apostle of Anti-Masonry until gravitating to the Whig Party. The well-heeled, well-educated Ogle (he read both Latin and Greek) was Somerset County's most eminent young lawyer and at the age of only thirty-seven was named by the state's Anti-Masonic governor as the presiding judge of the judicial district encompassing Lancaster County. Ogle initially accepted the position before resigning to run for Congress so he could pursue his passion for politics and make use of his impressive oratorical talents. In running for Congress in 1836, Ogle had given plenty of "powerful and eloquent" speeches attacking the "vile hypocrisy [of] the Van Buren party,"[4] but nothing to compare with the devastating speech that he delivered in the House of Representatives on April 14, 1840, which would be memorialized as the "Golden Spoon Oration."

The occasion for Ogle's speech was an appropriations bill that included a clause setting aside $3,666 (roughly $100,000 in 2020 dollars) "for alterations and repairs of the President's house and furniture, for purchasing trees, shrubs, and compost, and for superintendence of the grounds." That was all the prompt Ogle needed to speak for hours upon hours about Van Buren's supposed life of luxury in his "Presidential palace." Ogle had done his homework, going through innumerable White House receipts and bills to mock in itemized detail, room by room, the "regal splendor" of Van Buren's lavish surroundings. Theatrically brandishing the invoices, Ogle attacked Van Buren for wasting the hard-earned money of America's "farmers, mechanics, and poor laborers" to buy satin medallions, silk tassels, cords, pillows, curtains, elegant carpets, and cushioned footstools. Money spent on this "glittery display of costly finery" was not only profligate but unbecoming the "chief servant" of a plain republican people.[5]

Van Buren's fancies were said to be as effeminate as they were regal. He "loves tassels, rosettes, and girlish finery," Ogle mocked. How else to explain the $1,000 he had spent to embellish the "Ladies' Circular Parlor"? Merely to satisfy "a womanish but costly whim," Ogle said, Van Buren had also spent $350 to replace the East Room's apparently unfashionably lemon-colored wallpaper with a "'rich, chaste, and beautiful' silver paper, with golden borders." Then there was the $100 the president had spent on artificial flowers for his dinner table. Ogle lingered over the $22 the president had expended for six dozen green finger cups "in which to wash his pretty, tapering, soft, white lily fingers, after dining on fricandeau de veau and omelette soufflé."[6]

Van Buren's transgressions against republican virtue were compounded by his alleged hankering for all things foreign, especially those made in France. Ogle reeled off an endless stream of French-made goods purchased by Van Buren: French gilt bronze lamps and mantel timepieces, French china vases, French bedsteads and bedspreads, French carpets and silks, French sterling silver services, and French plates and platters. Ogle declared it intolerable that while American workmen "almost perish for lack of bread," the president was shipping "the People's money" abroad to support foreign workmen. He questioned not only Van Buren's tastes but his patriotism. He demanded to know,

> Are there no carpets made in the United States of texture firm enough, and of colors sufficiently gaudy, to please the eye of a democratic President? Are American weavers, and dyers, and manufacturers too dull and too stupid to make a decent republican carpet? Is American wool too coarse or too fine—too long or too short . . . that American mechanics cannot form a carpet out of it genteel enough for the feet of Martin Van Buren to soil? . . . Has he no American patriotism?[7]

Ogle relished lampooning Sweet Sandy Whiskers' vanity as he enumerated the various "enormous mirrors" that Van Buren had installed throughout the White House. What would "the plain republican farmers of the country say," Ogle asked, "were they to behold a democratic peacock, in full court costume, strutting by the hour before the golden-framed mirrors, nine feet high and four feet and a half wide?" So large was the mirror that if Van Buren rode his racehorse into "the palace . . . he could gaze at and admire the hoofs of his charger and his own crown at the same instant of time." In Ogle's uproarious telling, the effete president was too busy preening himself before any of the house's many "splendid mirrors" to see the people's suffering.[8]

Ogle's brilliant polemic gave new meaning to a "gold and silver Administration." Under Van Buren, and Jackson too, Ogle said, the people's hard-earned money was used to purchase gold and silver spoons, knives, and forks so that when the president sat down to dinner, "he may dine in the style of the monarchs of Europe." Ogle acknowledged that the gold and silver service might not be shown on all occasions; "probably it is only when the elite are invited."[9]

Ogle's speech enraged Democrats as much as it entertained Whigs. The *Globe* immediately condemned the speech as an "Omnibus of Lies."[10] Even a few Whigs felt that Ogle had crossed a line. Levi Lincoln, Jr., the high-minded chairman of the House Public Buildings Committee, took to the House floor to defend Van Buren, pointing out that the president had spent less on the White House than any of his predecessors and that he had not only never requested any piece of furniture but had "invariably expressed reluctance" to countenance any such expenditure.[11] The truth, though, did not stop the Harrison campaign from distributing tens of thousands of copies of Ogle's speech in pamphlet form,[12] nor did it stop virtually every major Whig paper in the country from publishing the speech.[13]

The obvious demagoguery of Ogle's speech led some Democrats to think that it could be safely dismissed, if not ignored. But the caricature of Van Buren as an effete dandy living in a presidential palace sipping French champagne hit a populist chord—particularly when contrasted with Harrison as a simple farmer living in a log cabin, quaffing hard cider.[14] One sign that the speech was doing damage to the president's public image was that the normally thick-skinned Van Buren pressed William Noland, the commissioner of public buildings, to issue a public statement affirming that "no gold knives or forks or spoons of any description have been purchased for the President's house since Mr. Van Buren became the Chief Magistrate." Noland also requested a respected silversmith in the nation's capital "to certify that the dessert flatware was not solid gold."[15] The solicitor of the treasury as well as the register of the treasury also issued statements denying that any public money had been expended during Van Buren's presidency to purchase any "gold or gilded knives, forks, spoons, plates."[16] But official statements setting the record straight on this or that claim by Ogle were no match for the Whigs' relentless repetition of the lie.

Ogle's speech inspired the material for many a verse in the campaign songs that became a defining feature of the Whig campaign. One of the Whigs' favorite ditties was the "Log Cabin Song," which included the stanza

> Let Van from his coolers of silver drink wine,
> And lounge on his cushioned settee,
> Our man on his old buck-eye bench can recline
> Content with hard cider, is he![17]

Another Ogle-inspired campaign sing-along was titled "Tippecanoe," the opening two verses of which ran

> Tippecanoe has no chariot to ride in,
> No palace or marble has he to reside in,
> No bags of gold-eagles, no lots of fine clothes—
> But he has a wealth far better than those;
> The love of a nation, free, happy, and true,
> Are the riches and portion of Tippecanoe.

> Proud Martin rides forth in his splendor and pride,
> And broad are his lands upon Kinderhook side,
> The roof of a palace is over his head,
> And his table with plate and with dainties is spread;
> But a log cabin shelters a patriot true—
> 'Tis the home of our hero, bold Tippecanoe![18]

The image of Van Buren as an effeminate dandy was not new; it had been well worked during the 1836 campaign by the Whig opposition, which had labored to contrast the "plain, republican" Harrison with a foppish Van Buren, who rode around "in a fine coach . . . attended by English waiters, dressed in livery after the fashion of an English lord."[19] But with Van Buren now in the White House and the country in economic distress, Ogle was able to give the dandified caricature greater cultural resonance by tapping into long-standing republican fears of political elites aping monarchical fashions and succumbing to the siren of luxury and corruption.

For the Whigs, there was a certain poetic justice to Ogle's speech, however unfair or outlandish its charges. Twelve years earlier, it had been the Jacksonians who had unfairly flayed President John Quincy Adams for his alleged "dandyism" and his aping of monarchy. Indeed, the focus of one of the Democrats' most effective attacks during the 1828 campaign had been Adams's purchase of a billiards table and ivory billiard balls for $50 (close

The North Bend Farmer and His Visitors. *One of many Whig campaign cartoons juxtaposing a dandified Van Buren with the rustic farmer by the plow, William Henry Harrison. In this cartoon, Van Buren and his fancy-dress politician friends (from left to right, Francis Preston Blair, Amos Kendall, and John Calhoun) have alighted from their fine coach to find Harrison hard at work on his farm. Van Buren says, "As I live that is old Harrison himself the old fool. After the many opportunities he has had of enriching himself to live in a log cabin and plough his own ground. Now look at me who never pulled a trigger, or chased an Indian unless by proxy: I roll in riches, and live in splendour, dine with kings, make my sons princes, enrich my friends, punish my enemies, and laugh in my sleeve at the dear People whom I gull." While Van Buren sneers, Harrison greets his visitors with generous hospitality. "Gentlemen," he says, "you seem fatigued. If you will accept of the fare of a log cabin, with a Western farmer's cheer, you are welcome. I have no champagne but can give you a mug of good cider, with some ham and eggs, and good clean beds. I am a plain backwoodsman, I have cleared some land, killed some Indians, and made the Red Coats fly in my time." (Courtesy of the Library of Congress)*

to $1,500 in 2020 dollars).[20] Having seen their president brought low by a demagogic populism and vague chants of republican reform, Whigs could barely disguise their glee at the opportunity to even the score.

Some Whigs, to be sure, found it all a bit distasteful. The lurid fantasies, the hackneyed ditties, and the ubiquitous log cabins hardly seemed the stuff of serious politics. On the last day of July, with Ogle's wild charges fast becoming a "keynote of the campaign,"[21] Henry Clay wrote to a friend to lament

> the necessity, real or imaginary, which has been supposed to exist, of appealing to the feelings and passions of our Countrymen, rather than to their reasons and judgments, to secure [Harrison's] election. The best, and only, justification of this course is to be found, in the practice, which was resorted to, in the instance of the election of General Jackson. But that does not prevent my regret that either party should have ever been induced to employ such means.

Clay was willing to forgive the demagoguery for another reason. The stakes, as Clay perceived them, were so high that almost any amount of rabble-rousing nonsense, even if it meant gross distortion and fabrication, could be tolerated. "I do believe," he wrote, "that if Mr. Van Buren be reelected, the Government will be ruined. Corruption, Demagoguism, and Humbuggery will receive an accelerated movement, and the only alternative remaining will be to submit quietly to that horrible state of things, or to make open & decided resistance by force."[22] Faced with that dismal choice, it was not difficult for Clay and other Whigs to reconcile themselves to the hoopla and outright lies about log cabins and presidential palaces.

"THE WHOLE COUNTRY . . . IS IN A STATE OF AGITATION"

Americans differed sharply about what was at stake in the 1840 campaign, but almost everybody seemed to agree that the country had never experienced anything like it. Writing in his diary at the end of August, former president John Quincy Adams observed that "the whole country throughout the Union is in a state of agitation upon the approaching Presidential election such as was never before witnessed." It seemed to Adams that not a week had passed over the previous four months "without a convocation of thousands of people to hear inflammatory harangues against Martin Van Buren and his administration, by Henry Clay, Daniel Webster, and all the principal opposition orators in or out of Congress." Adams himself had been invited to speak at Whig rallies in places as distant as Nashville, Tennessee (where somewhere between 40,000 and 100,000 people gathered in the middle of August to hear Clay, John Crittenden, and a host of other Whig luminaries lambaste the administration), Chillicothe, Ohio, and Wheeling, Virginia, as well as at partisan meetings closer at hand in Baltimore, Alexandria, and Georgetown—all of which Adams declined because he thought campaigning of this sort unbecoming of a former president. The enormous mass meetings and the pervasive partisan stump speaking seemed to Adams to portend "a revolution in the habits and manners of the people," and a dangerous one at that, since they whipped up enmity between rival partisans that sometimes erupted into violence. Adams believed that these partisan "meetings cannot be multiplied in numbers and frequency without resulting in yet deeper tragedies." "Their manifest tendency," Adams concluded ominously, "is to civil war."[23]

Adams's foreboding about a partisan civil war was misplaced. If anything, the intense party bonds, as Van Buren understood, forged connections that reached across the sectional divide over slavery—a divide that did portend civil war. Indeed, one of the striking features of the campaign was that Northern Whigs were invited to speak in the South, and Southern Whigs stumped across the North. Webster campaigned south of the Potomac for the first time, delivering a major speech in Richmond in early October in which he affirmed that Congress had no power "to interfere in the slightest degree with the institutions of the South." Among the most sought-after speakers in the North was Mississippi's Sergeant Prentiss, a transplanted Yankee, who exhausted himself in an unprecedented nationwide stumping tour during the summer and fall in which he had ample opportunity to show off his unparalleled "sarcastic talents and power of ridicule." Northern Whig audiences also delighted at hearing South Carolina's William Preston's "torrents of withering invective," which included fulsome borrowing from Ogle's lurid indictment of Van Buren.[24]

Still, Adams's fretting about the consequences of the extraordinary partisan agitation should not be written off as merely an old man's fear of the new and nostalgia for the old ways. Violence did disrupt some of the celebrated monster rallies as well as smaller partisan meetings. The Whigs' huge mass meeting in Baltimore in early May was marred not only by fisticuffs but by the killing of one of the procession's marshals, who was struck in the head by a Democratic partisan.[25] At the end of May, in New York City, Democratic "rioters" tried to disrupt a meeting of the German Tippecanoe Club to prevent a recent convert to Harrison's cause, state legislator Francis W. Lasak, from speaking. After the meeting, "some dozen ruffians" followed Lasak, who "escaped personal violence" only by taking refuge in a nearby public house. That night, the "ruffians" descended on Lasak's house and, armed with "brickbats and other dangerous missiles," smashed his windows.[26]

The vitriol that spewed freely in the partisan press made newspaper editors a frequent target of aggrieved partisans. After a scurrilous attack on

Harrison's morality, the editor of the *Ohio Statesman*, Sam Medary, was physically assaulted on the streets of Columbus by a Whig partisan, although apart from a vigorous bite to the finger, Medary emerged unscathed. In Springfield, an outraged Stephen Douglas caned the editor of the *Sangamo Journal*, Abraham Lincoln's good friend Simeon Francis. Although the assault on Francis ended in a "ludicrous" show of shoving and hair pulling, Andrew Davis, proprietor of the St. Louis *Argus*, was not so lucky. A Whig who took offense at being called one of "the dung hill breed of the Federalists" exacted revenge by caning Davis so severely that "after seven days of lingering torments," he died.[27] The vitriol and caustic derision of the newspapers and stump speeches may not have changed votes, but they certainly mobilized bitterness and anger against political "enemies" and magnified feelings of solidarity with political "friends."

There was nothing new about partisan vituperation, let alone a partisan press. Name-calling and incivility had been hallmarks of the partisan war of words in the United States since the 1790s. Nobody knew that better than John Quincy Adams, whose father had been relentlessly ridiculed in the Jeffersonian press. But these earlier partisan contretemps had left much of the nation untouched. It was the mass mobilization of partisan rancor and antipathy through "itinerant speech-making," designed to inflame and arouse immense crowds "of twenty, thirty, fifty thousand souls," that felt new to Adams and that concerned him deeply.[28] It is easy to see the seventy-three-year-old Adams's anxiety as an expression of a genteel elitism, but it is also possible to discern a prescient concern about the corrosive effects of an extreme partisan enmity that casts defeat in the most ominous hue and justifies victory at almost any cost.

The unprecedented excitement of the 1840 campaign, particularly on the Whig side, was heightened by an apocalyptic framing of the stakes of the election. One Michigan Whig wrote to Thurlow Weed in July to warn that if Van Buren won, it would be the "last peaceable contest" and that the opposition would have to "either submit to the tyrant contemptible and vile as he is, or resort to a mode of redress in which implements of a very different character from the ballot box will be wanted."[29] Others drew on religious language to explain the election's significance, as did the Tennessee Whig who likened the contest between Harrison and Van Buren to "the battle of Armageddon"; "should the Philistines succeed," he added, "and the ark of Liberty be taken by them, wo—wo is unto us—wo unto Israel."[30] The editor of a Whig newspaper in Jonesborough, Tennessee, implored his fellow partisans to work for the Whig cause with the same zeal as that of the preacher who knows that his flock is "in danger of everlasting burnings."[31] Even Abraham Lincoln succumbed to this sort of apocalyptic framing of the 1840 election, warning that

> the great volcano at Washington, aroused and directed by the evil spirit that reigns there, is belching forth the lava of political corruption in a current broad and deep, which is sweeping with frightful velocity over the whole length and breadth of the land, bidding fair to leave unscathed no green spot or living thing, while on its bosom are riding like demons on the wave of Hell, the imps of that Evil Spirit, and fiendishly taunting all those who dare resist its destroying course . . . ; and knowing this, I cannot deny that all may be swept away.[32]

The Whigs mobilized voters by convincing them that a Van Buren victory would be hell, a Harrison victory heaven. The choice was damnation or deliverance. Promoting what political scientists call "negative partisanship"[33]—strongly negative feelings toward the opposing party—was crucial in creating what Adams and many others saw as the unprecedented "state of agitation" during the 1840 campaign.

Democrats never tired of complaining about the Whigs' unrelentingly negative attacks on the stump—as Virginia's Thomas Ritchie did in a letter to Van Buren lamenting the "traveling orators, who . . . traverse their districts, mount their stumps, abuse the Administration, puff the military chieftain, and gull the people."[34] But the Democrats had no shortage of traveling orators touting Van Buren's record and abusing Harrison and the Whigs, among them Tennessee senator Felix Grundy, Missouri senator Thomas Hart Benton, Pennsylvania senator James Buchanan, Ohio senator William Allen, New York senator Silas Wright, former attorney general Benjamin Butler, and Vice President Richard Johnson.[35] On the stump and in print, Democrats followed campaign manager Amos Kendall's advice to "abandon your defensive warfare, and CHARGE HOME UPON THE ENEMY!"[36] Throughout the campaign, the Democrats remained on the offensive, attacking the Whigs for their "false money, false doctrines, false speeches, false biographies, false rumors, and, last not least, false heroes."[37] Like the Whigs, the Democrats staged large and rowdy campaign meetings, although because Van Buren ultimately lost the election, the enthusiasm generated by some of these Democratic events tends to be discounted if not ignored by historians. And Democrats' nonstop moaning about the humbuggery of log cabins did not prevent them from raising hickory poles, as they had done in every election since 1824, or from organizing Hickory clubs and O.K. clubs (for "Old Kinderhook") to match the organizing work being done by the many Tippecanoe clubs across the country.[38]

Although both parties organized mass political meetings, paid for stump speakers to fan out across the country, distributed cartloads of campaign materials through the mail, and started a host of special campaign newspapers, their campaign events were not carbon copies of each other. The Whigs certainly borrowed from successful past Democratic organizing techniques—the Tippecanoe clubs, for instance, were modeled on the Hickory clubs that Jacksonians had used successfully for years[39]—but the revival-like atmosphere of what Whigs sometimes described as "political Camp-meetings" was distinctive, reflecting in part the strong influence of evangelism among Whigs. Their political gatherings, as historian Ronald Formisano writes, were "rally, picnic, and revival all rolled into one."[40]

Among the most visible differences between the parties was the greater prominence of women at Whig political meetings. Despite the campaign's ostentatious celebration of hard cider, many Whig gatherings were family-friendly affairs. Here is how one observer described a Whig meeting in Macon, Georgia:

> Last night the Tips had a great celebration here and of a kind peculiar to themselves. Their club room was illuminated at an early hour and soon after the house was filled to overflowing with men, women and children. By the bye, this way of making politicians of their women is something new under the sun. But so it is they go to the strife. A select set of singers then sing a Tip song. Their orator then edifies his audience for two hours on the rascality of Van Buren and all his friends. . . . Another song, then another speech and another song. And so they carry on.[41]

Women joined in the singing that was a hallmark of the Whig campaign, and their participation extended to giving toasts and presenting banners, even on occasion giving speeches but more often inviting speakers. Henry Clay, for instance, was invited to speak at "the great Nashville convention . . . by 350 ladies" who had penned an invitation that "of course, could not be withstood."[42] Democrats often clucked their disapproval of the "unseemly" novelty of women taking part in politics. "It is much to be lamented," wrote one Democratic editor, "that so active a part in the present political strife, has been borne by women," although he did not blame the women so much as the Whig men, who "led away by the most bitter political zeal have encouraged their appearance in the arena of political warfare." Politics was about strife, battles, warfare; it was no place for "the female graces of modesty and amiability."[43]

Democrats also carped about the Whigs' constant singing of "doggerel ballads made for the occasion."[44] There was nothing novel about the singing of political ditties in the United States,[45] but the Whigs' enthusiasm for political song outstripped anything the country had seen before, prompting Philip Hone to later quip that Harrison "was sung into the presidency." Democrats tried ridicule: "We could meet the Whigs on the field of argument and beat them without effort," opined the New York *Evening Post*. "But when they lay down the weapons of argument and attack us with musical notes, what can we do?" Even some Whig politicos, including Thurlow Weed, initially had their doubts about the effectiveness of all this frivolous singing. Weed's comrade-in-arms Horace Greeley strongly disagreed, however, and published songs on the back pages of each issue of the *Log Cabin*, the hugely popular Albany-based campaign newspaper that began publication at the beginning of May (Greeley also published the most popular of these songs in the widely distributed *Log-Cabin Song-Book*). "Our songs," he told Weed, "are doing more good than anything else." Music didn't detract from the Whig message. On the contrary, Greeley noted, "people like the swing of the music [and] after a song or two they are more ready to listen to the orators." Weed came around and even helped organize some of the many glee clubs that the Whigs established to sing what Ronald Shafer has described as "the ultimate singing commercials."[46]

Whigs made no apologies for their singing or for the presence of women at campaign rallies. Indeed, they boasted that the latter was evidence that the "better part of creation were and are, almost unanimously Whig."[47] Charles Hammond, editor of the *Cincinnati Gazette*, celebrated women as "the very life and soul of these movements of the People." That women had come out in such extraordinary numbers to support the Whig cause was evidence, in Hammond's telling, of the extraordinary conditions facing the country. Women had left the "sanctum sanctorum of domestic life" precisely because the country was experiencing "a general disorganization of conventional operations—of embarrassment, stagnation, idleness, and despondency—whose malign influences have penetrated the inner temples of man's home, and aroused to indignant speech and unusual action her who is its peace, it gentleness, its love." That throngs of men and women had left their homes to attend these "Grand Gatherings" all across the country spoke to "the empty larders in the town" and "the cheerless hearth,

Song was a central part of the Whigs' 1840 campaign. Here, the sheet music to the melody for the "Tippecanoe or Log Cabin Quick Step" composes the stripes of the American flag and the siding of a log cabin. The treble and bass clefs are represented by soldiers, bayonets, and cider barrels. In front of the house, William Henry Harrison greets a military veteran and amputee. (Courtesy of the Library of Congress)

where willing hands sit without employment." Hard times made for new politics.[48]

Democrats and Whigs, men as well as women, young and old, politicians and ordinary citizens, registered time and time again that the excitement of the campaign felt unlike anything they had experienced before. From out west in Kentucky, Senator John Crittenden wrote to Daniel Webster, "Since the world began there was never before in the West such a glorious excitement & uproar among the people."[49] A fifty-four-year-old Virginia woman, Sarah Pendleton Dandridge, felt the same sense of novelty and wonder: "I never saw any thing like the excitement here," she told her sister; "we hear of nothing but Gen. Harrison."[50] Never before had presidential politics seemed so central to the lives of so many. Writing to a friend in mid-September, a young Virginia woman, Mary Steger, confided, "I never took so much interest in politics in my life . . . the fact is you have to know something about them for nobody here thinks of any thing else." She reported that "Our Log Cabin," the Whigs' campaign headquarters in Richmond, "is open almost every few nights (the regular meetings being once a week) to some speakers from a distance. The cabin holds 1,500 and it is always full."[51] In Michigan, a young man recorded in his diary that "never was a political campaign carried on with such zeal. . . . Every nerve was strained and every means tried which a fruitful imagination could" conceive.[52] Writing to the president from Ohio in early September, Pennsylvania's Democratic senator James Buchanan, more peeved than pleased, reported that the entire population of the state seemed to have "abandoned their ordinary business for the purpose of electioneering."[53]

On June 27, in a campaign speech at Taylorsville, Virginia, about one hundred miles south of the nation's capital, Clay posed the question, "Why this rabid appetite for public discussions?" Why, he asked, "is the plough deserted, the tools of the mechanic laid aside, and all are seen rushing to gatherings of the people?" Clay likened the country to an "ocean when convulsed by some terrible storm, . . . agitated upon its whole surface, and at its lowest depths." Like Hammond, he believed the explanation for "those vast and unusual assemblages which we behold in every state and in almost every neighborhood" lay in the "awful state of our beloved country." People were participating in politics in unprecedented ways, Clay said, because they were seeking "the means of deliverance" from their "sufferings" and holding the government accountable. And Clay left his audience in no doubt that the hardship and distress they and their fellow citizens were experiencing were the fault of "the action, the encroachments, and the usurpations of the executive branch."[54]

Like Adams, Clay saw a country in a state of great agitation, but unlike Adams, he viewed the immense gatherings and partisan speechmaking as essential mechanisms of democratic accountability. Rather than bemoan the "fearful" explosion of partisan electioneering, as Adams did,[55] Clay distinguished between inflammatory harangues that stoked enmity and substantive campaign speeches that educated people and enabled them to hold accountable those in power. Clay assured his audience that he appeared before them with "no purpose of exciting prejudices or inflaming passions, but to speak to you in soberness and truth."[56] Not all rhetoric was bad rhetoric. Mass meetings could be sites of discourse rather than discord. Politics could be popular without being a portent of civil war.

Whether the popular tumult of the 1840 campaign was celebrated or censured, eyed warily or embraced unreservedly, it was clear, as Clay wrote upon his return to the nation's capital at the end of June, that "the Presidential contest absorbs every thing else."[57] Nowhere was Clay's observation more apt than in the many state and federal elections that took place in the six months prior to the presidential election. Although Van Buren and

Harrison were not on the ballot, they might as well have been. Elections were nineteenth-century America's way of polling the people, gauging their mood, and forecasting the result of the presidential election in November. What happened in these state and federal elections would tell Americans who would be their next president.

"EVERY BREEZE SAYS CHANGE"

The year 1839 had not been kind to the Whigs. After eighteen months in which the Whigs had generally outperformed the Democrats at the ballot box, the Democrats rebounded impressively.[58] In 1839, Democrats won majorities in about 60 percent of state assemblies after winning control of only about 40 percent of lower houses in 1838 and a mere 20 percent in the second half of 1837. In 1839, Democrats flipped control of six state assemblies, while Whigs failed to do the same in any state. Between October 1838 and November 1839, Whigs lost state assembly seats in Arkansas, Georgia, Maryland, Ohio, Pennsylvania, Massachusetts, Mississippi, and New York and picked up seats in only one state, Michigan.[59] Democrats also outperformed Whigs in governors' races in 1839, winning seven of eleven contests, despite most of these being in Whig-leaning New England, where annual gubernatorial elections were the norm.[60] Of the eleven states that held congressional races in 1839, Democrats picked up seats in five while losing seats in only two. Now, with the economy again worsening, would the tide again turn against the administration, as it had in 1837?

The first statewide electoral test of the administration's strength in 1840 came in March in the generally Democratic state of New Hampshire, and nothing in those results suggested a surge toward the Whigs.[61] There was no change in the partisan balance of the lower house, with Democrats retaining better than 60 percent of the seats. The incumbent Democratic governor, John Page, won by 17 percentage points, 5 points higher than his winning margin a year before and far above the narrow 6-point margin by which the then-incumbent Democratic governor, Isaac Hill, had won in 1838. Nor was there any sign of a surge in popular enthusiasm. The number of people who turned out was in fact lower in the 1840 contest than in either the 1838 or 1839 contests, with the total number of Whig votes dropping from over 25,000 in 1838 to 24,000 in 1839 to fewer than 21,000 in 1840. That is not to say that New Hampshire's citizens were apathetic; indeed, nearly three of every four age-eligible voters cast a ballot in the governor's race in 1840 (over 81 percent had cast ballots in 1838). In New

Hampshire at least, 1838 looked like the Whig high-water mark, an aberration more than a growing movement.[62]

The following month there were elections in two more Northeastern states, Connecticut and Rhode Island. Connecticut had swung sharply toward the Whigs in 1838, when they handily secured the governorship—after losing in the previous three attempts—and the party had more than doubled its number of seats in the lower house. In 1839, the Whigs' share of legislative seats and the gubernatorial vote dipped somewhat, but they had retained the governorship and still won a substantial majority of the seats in the lower house as well as flipping all six congressional seats. In 1840, the incumbent Whig governor, William Ellsworth, won by a healthy 8-point margin, a bit more than the 5 points he won by in 1839 and slightly less than his 11-point margin of victory in 1838. Similarly, the Whigs boosted their share of seats in the lower state house to two-thirds, a modest improvement over the 59 percent of seats they won in 1839, although falling well short of the 73 percent of seats they had secured in 1838. Unlike in New Hampshire, moreover, where turnout slightly decreased in 1840, turnout in Connecticut's gubernatorial election showed a marginal increase in 1840, from 51,000 in 1839 to 55,000 in 1840. Connecticut's results, in short, consolidated the gains that Whigs had made in 1838 but hardly seemed to portend an election-year Whig surge. Indeed, while Ellsworth received about 2,700 more votes in 1840 than he had in 1838, the Democratic gubernatorial nominee picked up closer to 4,000 additional votes.[63]

In Rhode Island, the Whigs' gains in 1840 were more impressive. They regained control of the lower state house, which they had lost the year before, winning two-thirds of the seats, an improvement on the three-fifths they had won in 1838. As in Connecticut, Whigs had won the governorship for the first time in 1838 by defeating a Democratic incumbent who had won successive elections; in the case of Rhode Island, the incumbent, John Francis, won five elections in a row between 1833 and 1838. Whereas the Whig gubernatorial victories in Rhode Island had been relatively narrow in 1838 (winning by 6 percentage points) and 1839 (winning by a 2-point margin), in 1840, the Whigs' gubernatorial nominee, Samuel King, trounced his Democratic opponent, winning by 17 points. But while Rhode Island's April results were an unambiguous win for the Whigs, the state's turnout rate remained anemic. In 1840, only 32 percent of the age-eligible population voted, an increase from the 25 percent who had turned out in the gubernatorial contest the year before but virtually unchanged from the percentage that turned out in the 1838 contest or in most of the gubernatorial contests in the early 1830s. A resounding Whig victory, yes. An unprecedented surge in popular participation, no.

Rhode Island's politics were sufficiently idiosyncratic and its population so small that few politicians would have looked to that state for reliable signs of the country's future direction. Many more eyes that April were on New York City's mayoral contest. In 1839, the "administration candidate," Isaac Varian, had eked out a victory over the Whig incumbent by a mere 1,000 votes out of 41,000 votes cast. In 1840, Varian increased his vote total by about 250 votes, while the Whig nominee received some 400 votes fewer, turning a razor-thin 2.5-point margin of victory in 1839 into a 5-point win in 1840. The "administration aldermen" also won in twelve of the cities' seventeen wards—the same twelve wards the Democrats had won in 1839.[64] James Gordon Bennett's *New York Herald* described the result as a "Rout of the Tippecanoes"—in an election that Bennett said was "one of the drollest, quietest, soberest, and most peaceable elections that ever took place in New York." Far from being a harbinger of change, let alone a rejection of Van Buren, it seemed a status quo election, with the same turnout and the same result as the year before.[65]

Stasis rather than change also ruled Virginia's state legislative elections at the end of April. In the spring of 1838, the Whigs had scored a huge victory, picking up 25 seats and gaining a majority in the House of Delegates for the first time since 1834. But the election of 1840, like the election of 1839, saw essentially no change in the distribution of seats or in turnout levels, which remained relatively modest. Democrats won 61 seats in 1838 and 1839 and 62 in 1840.[66] Many Democrats regarded the 1840 results as something of a moral victory, as they had worried that the Whigs' demagoguery about Poinsett's militia reorganization plan—"the humbug of the Standing Army"—would devastate the state party. Virginia's Democrats emerged from the election with renewed confidence about Van Buren's chances in the fall.[67]

In sum, there was little in the spring 1840 elections, let alone the elections of the previous fall, to suggest that November's election would sweep away Van Buren and the Democrats. Both sides could point to encouraging signs. The Whigs had done particularly well in Rhode Island, but the Democratic Party continued to demonstrate remarkable resilience in the face of Whig cries of "low prices and hard times."[68] The log-cabin exuberance on display in mass meetings in places such as Columbus in February and Baltimore in the first week of May did not seem to be translating into greater turnout, although admittedly the Whig presidential campaign was not yet in high gear; the first issue of the most important Whig campaign paper, Horace Greeley's *Log Cabin*, for instance, was not published until May 2.

Nonetheless, Whigs grew in confidence as the economy stagnated. When Henry Clay spoke at Baltimore on May 4, he declared Harrison's election "certain" and predicted that he would carry twenty states. When Daniel Webster was summoned next to speak to the same crowd, he confidently told them, "The time has come . . . when the cry is change. Every breeze says change. Every interest of the country demands it."[69] Clay's prediction would not be tested until November (he was off by only one, as Harrison ended up winning nineteen states); Webster's forecast, though, would be put to the test in every state and federal election between July and October (no state or federal elections were held in May or June in 1840).

The first test of Webster's winds-of-change thesis came in Louisiana, which held its congressional elections over a three-day period in early July, making it the first state to select members for the new Twenty-Seventh Congress that would begin work in 1841. A couple of weeks before the election, former Louisiana senator Alexander Porter fretted that the great political excitement pulsing through the country seemed to be bypassing his state: "It is only in Louisiana," he wrote, "that I fear we are not so active as we should be."[70] Porter was right to worry. In 1838, the Whigs had won all three congressional seats, but in 1840, the Democrats won back the seat that they lost in 1838 (the state's second congressional district, which included Baton Rouge), with the Whig candidate increasing his party's vote total by 200 and the Democrat increasing his party's vote total by more than 500. In the third district, representing the western half of the state, where the Democrats had not even fielded a candidate in 1838 or 1836, the Democratic nominee came within a whisker (66 votes out of over 6,700 cast) of beating his Whig opponent. The winning Whig candidate received 500 fewer votes than the party's unopposed candidate received in 1838. Only in the first district—which included New Orleans—where a popular incumbent was running, did the Whig candidate increase his vote total and vote share, trouncing his Democratic opponent by a better than 2–1 margin. Overall, the Whigs received almost the same number of congressional votes in 1840 as they had in 1838, while the Democrats nearly doubled their vote totals. The state's increased turnout was attributable largely to the Democrats—and in any case remained low (about 34 percent) relative to other states (only Virginia and Rhode Island were comparably low). Even with the Democrats' impressive gains in two of the three congressional districts, the Whigs still won about 56 percent of the congressional votes owing largely to their dominance in New Orleans. Louisiana appeared to be a Whig state, but the breeze of change seemed mild at best.[71]

A more exacting test of Harrison's and Van Buren's presidential prospects came on the first Monday of August, when voters went to the polls in five states, three of which (Illinois, Missouri, and Alabama) voted for Van Buren in 1836 and two of which (Indiana and Kentucky) voted for Harrison. Of these five states, only Illinois seemed likely to be close in November, but collectively, they could be a bellwether of change.

Missouri held both gubernatorial and congressional elections. The Democratic candidate for governor won decisively, beating his Whig opponent by more than 14 percentage points. Four years earlier, in contrast, the Democratic gubernatorial candidate had won by fewer than 5 points. In the state's two at-large congressional races, Democrats won easily, and by roughly the same 15-point margin as two years before. Although there was no detectable partisan change in Missouri, there was unmistakable evidence of increased popular participation. Turnout in the congressional and gubernatorial contests in 1840 reached about 73 percent, up substantially from the 66 percent who turned out for the congressional races in 1838, although that 6-point increase was not as impressive as the 13-point jump in turnout between 1836 and 1838. There was no question about the increased popular enthusiasm in Missouri, but substantially more new voters were flocking to the Democrats than the Whigs.

In Illinois, which held state legislative elections, the Democrats seemed to gain ground, marginally increasing their majority in the lower house from 53 percent to 56 percent and winning 65 percent of the seats in the state senate, which had previously been equally divided between the parties. However, the Democrats' increase in seats disguised the closeness of the statewide vote, owing in large part to higher levels of immigration in the northern parts of the state that tended to vote Whig. The *Alton Telegraph* estimated the total number of Whig votes cast in the state assembly races to be about 40,000, which was only a few thousand behind the Democrats' vote totals. In 1838, the Democratic gubernatorial candidate beat a popular Whig opponent by about 1,000 votes, and the Democratic lieutenant governor won by 1,700 votes (out of 60,000 votes cast in both races), so the 1840 state legislative elections confirmed that both parties were attracting many new voters and in roughly equal numbers.[72]

The news was less encouraging for Van Buren in the other three states. In Alabama, which held state legislative elections, the Whig Party fell just short of gaining a majority in the lower house after having won only one-third of the seats in 1839. Despite the slippage in support, Van Buren knew he could probably count on carrying Alabama in November. It was the results in Kentucky and Indiana, however, that shook the Democrats' confidence and seemed to confirm Webster's reading of the prevailing winds.

In Indiana in 1839, the Whigs had suffered a stunning setback, losing their seemingly secure majority in the lower house. In 1840, the Whig Party came roaring back, doubling its share of the seats, from 39 percent to a stunning 78 percent, a larger share than the Whigs had ever before controlled in the state. The state's gubernatorial contest was somewhat closer than it had been in 1837, but the Whigs still secured a comfortable 7.5-point victory. More impressive still was the turnout in the gubernatorial contest, which reached 86 percent, up from a little under 70 percent three years before. Both parties, however, played a role in the turnout increase, with the Whig and Democratic nominees in 1840 each polling 17,000 more votes than their party's nominees had received in 1837. The Whigs were certainly energized by the log-cabin campaign, but so, too, the numbers suggest, were the Democrats, even in a state that everyone assumed would vote for Harrison in 1840. However, perhaps a finer gauge of the shifting winds forecast by Webster was a special congressional election held in the state's northwest corner, where Harrison was popular. The year before, a Democrat won the seat by a 10-point margin; in the special election, a Whig won by 6 points. An additional 4,200 people turned out to vote in the special election, and nearly 90 percent of those additional votes went to the Whig candidate.

The August elections also confirmed that Kentucky, a state Van Buren lost narrowly (by 5 points) to Harrison in 1836, would be far beyond Van Buren's reach in 1840, even without Clay on the presidential ticket. The Whigs increased their share of lower house seats from an already robust 58 percent in 1839 (the same percentage that they had won in 1836) to 77 percent in 1840, a number even larger than the roughly 70 percent they had won in 1837 and 1838. The gubernatorial contest suggested the same pattern of renewed Whig dominance, with the Whig candidate winning by better than 16 percentage points, 4 points more than the Whigs' margin of victory four years earlier. Turnout, moreover, reached 77 percent, way up over the 60 percent of age-eligible voters who had turned out in 1836, with almost two-thirds of the increase coming on the Whig side of the ledger.

The only other state to hold statewide elections in August was North Carolina, where voters went to the polls on August 13 to elect their governor. Once again, turnout was sharply up, exceeding 83 percent of age-eligible voters. That was not only well above the turnout in the state's previous gubernatorial elections (70 percent in 1836, the state's first gubernatorial election, and 62 percent in 1838) but also higher than in any recent federal election in the state; in the 1839 congressional elections, for instance, turnout in the state had been 67 percent, and in 1837, it had been 57 percent. Although the Democratic gubernatorial nominee fared better in 1840 than in 1838, when the party's nominee had been swamped by a popular Whig incumbent, the Democrat still lost by almost 14 points, confirming what everyone knew: North Carolina, which Van Buren had narrowly carried in 1836, seemed safe for Harrison.

The outlook became even worse for Van Buren in September, when the states of Vermont and Maine held their state legislative, gubernatorial, and congressional elections.[73] Vermont was probably the most reliable Whig state in the country, so the Democrats were under no illusions about Van Buren's prospects in November. Even so, the extent of the party's losses in 1840 revealed the strong headwinds that had developed over the summer. In the state assembly, Democrats won only one-quarter of the seats, by far the lowest number they had secured during the Van Buren years. The incumbent Whig governor, Silas Jennison, who had won three previous times during Van Buren's term, won this time by 19 points, by far his largest margin of victory and nearly four times the narrow 5-point victory he had secured in 1839. Moreover, turnout was way up. Turnout had climbed steadily in each of Jennison's gubernatorial races dating back to 1836, but in 1840, it jumped substantially, from 69 percent in 1839 to 82 percent, and virtually all (96 percent) of the 9,200-vote increase was due to the Whigs. The surge in Whig turnout led to the defeat of both of the state's Democratic House incumbents, leaving its five-member delegation composed entirely of Whigs for the first time in Van Buren's presidency.

Even more devastating to Van Buren's hopes were the results in Maine, which had been a solid Democratic state for most of the past decade. Van Buren had carried it in 1836 by more than 20 points, and Democrats had won the governor's race each year but one dating back to 1830—the only exception being 1837, when the Whig candidate, Edward Kent, had won by fewer than 500 votes. Governor Kent had lost to Democrat John Fairfield in 1838 and then again, by a larger 8-point margin, in 1839. In 1840, the two rivals faced off for a third time, and this time Kent emerged the victor, albeit by a razor-thin margin (67 votes out of more than 91,000 cast). The Whigs not only seized the governor's mansion but also gained a majority in the lower house, boosting their share of seats from 39 percent to 54 percent, a 15-point gain that was identical to the Panic-induced swing toward the Whigs between 1836 and 1837. At the congressional level, the Whigs also made big gains, winning four of the state's eight House districts and winning pluralities in two others that would be settled in runoff elections at the end of November, a pickup of two and potentially four House seats for the Whigs.[74] Unlike in Vermont, the congressional-seat swing to the Whigs was not accompanied by a surge in turnout; indeed, turnout declined marginally from its record high of 83 percent in 1838 to 79 percent in 1840, owing to a modest decline in Democratic vote totals in six of the eight House districts.[75] Of the almost 90,000 votes cast in Maine in 1840, Whig congressional candidates won 50.4 percent, which meant that Van Buren could no longer count on winning the state that had given him his largest margin of victory over Harrison four years earlier.

The presidential campaign would grind on for another six weeks of log-cabin and hard-cider hoopla, but after the Maine results, even the most optimistic Democrats did not hold out much hope for Van Buren in November. Not coincidentally, this was also the point when the Whigs began to sing about Van, Van, the "used up man." The most famous song of the campaign first appeared, set to music, in Greeley's *Log Cabin* on September 26.[76] Its chorus gave the nation the "Tippecanoe and Tyler too" slogan that to this day is identified as the signature shorthand for the campaign.

> For Tippecanoe and Tyler too.
> And with them we'll beat little Van, Van, Van
> Van is a used up man,
> And with them we'll beat little Van

But by the time the American people were singing this most famous chorus, the election, for all intents and purposes, had already been decided. All the songs and speeches, merriment and mud-slinging, mattered little. Webster's breeze of change had become, as Clay had forecast, a gale-force wind. Democrats could do little but brace for the disaster hurtling toward them.

If there were any Democrats who harbored doubts about the outcome, these were laid to rest by the elections in the first half of October in Georgia, Maryland, Ohio, and Pennsylvania. The Whigs flipped control of the lower house in each of these states, boosting their seat share by an average of 27

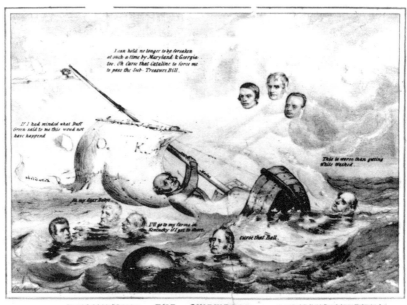

THE SHIPWRECK

The Shipwreck. *After the state and gubernatorial elections in September and October, Van Buren's defeat seemed a certainty. In this cartoon published by Henry R. Robinson in October 1840, Van Buren clings to the mast (labeled "Maine") of the distressed "O.K.", which is at the mercy of the storm emanating from the visages of William C. Rives (on the left), William Henry Harrison (in the center), and Nathaniel P. Tallmadge (on the right). Van Buren wails that he "can hold no longer," bemoans having been "forsaken at such a time by Maryland & Georgia too," and curses "that Cataline" (John Calhoun) for having forced him "to pass the Sub-Treasure Bill." Bobbing in the sea amidst the wreckage are five Van Buren supporters (from left to right): Calhoun, the* Globe *editor Francis Preston Blair, Amos Kendall, Thomas Hart Benton, and Levi Woodbury. (Courtesy of the Library of Congress)*

percentage points. In Ohio, where the Tippecanoe fever was at its height, the Whigs increased their share of seats from 32 percent to 71 percent and flipped control of the governorship. In Maryland, Whigs secured more than three-quarters of the seats in the lower house, as they also did in New Jersey. In Pennsylvania, the Democrats were relegated to the minority in the lower house for the first time in Van Buren's presidency. Congressional races in Ohio and Pennsylvania also revealed the gathering force of the winds of change. In Ohio, the Democrats lost four House seats, giving the Whigs a

12–7 advantage, although in Pennsylvania the Democrats limited their net losses to only two seats, leaving them with a narrow 15–13 advantage.[77]

In Ohio, the popular enthusiasm so evident in the many mass meetings and nonstop stump speaking translated into huge increases in turnout. Turnout reached a record 85 percent, smashing the previous state record of 71 percent set two years before in the gubernatorial election. While Democrats gained almost 27,000 more votes in 1840 than in 1838, Whigs picked up nearly 40,000 additional gubernatorial votes. In Georgia, too, turnout in the congressional races climbed from an already high 82 percent in 1838 to 92 percent, a number that the state would never reach again.

However, not every state, let alone district, was equally moved by the enthusiasm of the "log-cabin campaign." In Pennsylvania, the turnout rate in the congressional races dipped slightly, from 72 percent in 1839 to 69 percent in 1840. Stability more than change marked Pennsylvania's 1840 congressional elections. The absolute number of voters was virtually unchanged, with 254,752 having voted for a member of Congress in 1838 and 255,084 casting a congressional ballot in 1840. Democrats polled only 660 fewer votes in 1840 than in 1838, and the Whigs received fewer than 1,000 additional votes, leaving the two parties almost as evenly split in 1840 as they had been in 1838. Democratic congressional candidates had polled 51.2 percent of the vote in 1838, while in 1840, they polled 50.9 percent. Even though Van Buren had carried Pennsylvania only by the narrowest of margins (51–49) in 1836, the 1840 congressional results showed that the state remained within Van Buren's reach, a sliver of hope in a darkening fall landscape.

As bad as the results of the late summer and early fall had been for Van Buren, there remained, remarkably, a path to victory. It was a long shot but not impossible. Van Buren could count on Arkansas, Alabama, Missouri, New Hampshire, and South Carolina. Possibly those would be the only 32 electoral votes he would get, and he would suffer the biggest electoral college blowout since the days of James Monroe. But the 1840 results also suggested that the president could not be counted out in Pennsylvania (30 electoral votes), Maine (10), and Virginia (23). Wining those states would bring him to a respectable 95 electoral votes, although still well short of the 148 he would need to win. However, if he could also win his home state of New York, an outcome that could not be ruled out, that would get him to 137. There had been no state or congressional elections in New York since November 1838, when the Whigs had won about 51 percent of the vote, so even a small shift toward the Democrats could give him the state's

42 electoral votes. If that happened, he would then need 11 more electoral votes to be reelected president.

The challenge for Van Buren would be where to find those 11 additional electoral votes. One possibility would be to string together victories in three small states he had carried in 1836: Michigan (3 electoral votes), Mississippi (4), and Illinois (5). Of these three, Van Buren's best hope was likely Illinois, a state he had won by 9 points in 1836 and in which Democrats had narrowly outpolled the Whigs in both the gubernatorial election in 1838 and the state legislative elections in August 1840. Winning Michigan also seemed possible, since Van Buren had won the state by 12 points in 1836, although a more reliable measure of the two parties' relative strength was the state's 1839 gubernatorial contest, which the Whig nominee won by 3 points. The Whigs had also won 70 percent of the lower house seats in 1839, although the previous November, in a race for the state's one congressional seat, the parties were separated by only 200 votes out of over 32,000 cast. Of the three states, Mississippi was perhaps the most unlikely to go for Van Buren. Although the Democrats had won the governor's race and the congressional races in 1839 by a substantial 8-point margin, Van Buren was not popular in Mississippi and had barely eked out a victory in 1836, winning by a mere 500 votes out of 20,000 votes.

The only other viable path to victory for Van Buren involved capturing one of the above three states while also winning New Jersey's 8 electoral votes. The two parties in New Jersey had, at least until recently, remained evenly balanced. In 1836, Van Buren had lost New Jersey by only 1 percentage point, the closest margin of any state in that election. In 1838, the Democratic slate had prevailed in the state's at-large congressional elections by 100 votes out of more than 50,000 cast. Worryingly for Van Buren, though, Democrats had fared poorly in the October 1840 state legislative elections, making Van Buren a decided underdog in New Jersey. For Van Buren to be the next president, virtually every doubtful state would have to break his way.

10

TIPPECANOE AND THE
ECONOMY TOO
UNDERSTANDING THE
ELECTION OF 1840

In 1836, it was three weeks into November before Van Buren was sure of victory. In 1840, the suspense lasted less than a week. As in 1836, Ohio and Pennsylvania would go first, voting on Friday, October 30, only two weeks after voters in both these states had elected members of Congress and state legislators (and, in Ohio's case, the governor). Eighteen states would then vote in the first few days of November, with the great majority beginning on Monday, November 2, while the remaining states would hold elections in the second week of November.[1] In three-quarters of the states, including Ohio and Pennsylvania, the presidency would be the only office that voters would be deciding on. In five states (Delaware, Massachusetts, Michigan, New Jersey, and New York), voters would also select their members of Congress, votes that would help to determine whether the Whigs would take control of the House of Representatives for the first time in the party's history.[2]

Pennsylvania was Van Buren's first hurdle; fail to clear it and there was no viable path to victory. Harrison was in the catbird seat: he could afford to lose Pennsylvania and still chart innumerable routes to victory. As the *Sangamo Journal* crowed, "We can beat Van Buren and give him two Pennsylvanias."[3] Early returns from Pennsylvania seemed positive for Harrison; some Whigs hailed them as "glorious." Monday's papers reported results from about two-thirds of the state's counties, showing Harrison with a small lead. These returns indicated that Harrison was running ahead of his vote totals in 1836, when he lost by 2.4 percentage points (about 4,300 votes), and was outperforming the Whig vote totals in the congressional elections of October 13, 1840, when there had been a 1.8-point gap between the two parties' vote totals (with the Whigs again receiving about 4,400 votes fewer than the Democrats). But it was not clear that Harrison's small lead would hold up, since many of the counties yet to report had supported Van Buren in 1836. Philadelphia's *National Gazette* was not eager to "dampen the enthusiasm" of its Whig readers but felt it necessary to "check the great excitement" that many had felt on hearing the first returns. "We beg our friends," the *Gazette* wrote, "not to hazard money on the final returns. It is impossible to say which party has triumphed." The only certainty was that "the majority either way will be small." Writing on the same day (Monday, November 2), the *Adams Sentinel* agreed that the outcome remained "doubtful" and that the candidates were "running neck and neck."[4]

With Pennsylvania too close to call, Van Buren's hopes still flickered, albeit faintly. On Tuesday evening, the *Public Ledger*, Pennsylvania's first "penny paper," announced that Harrison seemed to have won the state, but the next day, following new as well as corrected returns, it walked the call back, noting that "there is as much doubt as ever in the matter. . . . A closer contest never was perhaps had in this State."[5] Democratic papers, meanwhile, were eager to call the state for Van Buren. On Wednesday, the *Republican Farmer* showed Van Buren with enough of a lead that "there is not a reasonable doubt" that he had won the state, although by a "smaller majority than was anticipated."[6] Whig papers expressed equal confidence that Harrison had narrowly won the state. On Thursday, November 5, the *National Gazette* asserted "without qualification or reservation" that Pennsylvania had voted for Harrison, although official returns had still not been received from one-third of the state's counties and two counties were missing altogether.[7] The conflicting numbers and counts in different papers led the *Daily Ledger*'s editors to suspect that "mystifying the result" was part of an intentional effort by partisan editors in distant parts of the state to affect the elections in nearby states.[8]

While the two parties argued over who had carried Pennsylvania, results from states that had voted on Monday, November 2, began to trickle in. The first states to be called in the Eastern papers were Connecticut, Rhode Island, and Maryland, each of which, as expected, voted for Harrison.[9] In Maryland, Van Buren's margin of defeat was about the same (7.5 percentage points) as in 1836, but in the other two states, both of which he had narrowly won in 1836, his support declined precipitously. He lost by 11 points in Connecticut and almost 23 points in Rhode Island. Although the steep decline in Van Buren's support in these two Northeastern states was ominous, neither was important to Van Buren's long-shot path to an upset victory. And far from taking solace from these early pickups for Harrison, some Whigs were beginning to panic that Van Buren's long-shot bid for reelection might be coming to pass.

On Thursday, November 5, at 1 p.m., James Gordon Bennett published an extra election edition of the New York *Herald* that reported "astounding" new election returns received that morning from New York, Maine, Pennsylvania, and Virginia, showing the "PROBABLE RE-ELECTION OF VAN BUREN; PROBABLE DEFEAT OF GEN. HARRISON." This news, he reiterated Friday morning, had fallen upon the Whig Party "like a huge avalanche of snow from the highest heights of heaven" while creating "a scene of extravagant joy and delirium at Tammany Hall," where "it seemed as if 'all hell was let loose.'" A despairing Bennett, who backed Harrison, opined, "These are awful times."[10]

By the end of Friday, though, Bennett's despair had turned to joy. New York, he now thought, would go for Harrison after all. On Saturday morning, Bennett hailed the "GREAT VICTORY" and called the presidential election for Harrison.[11] New York's Democratic papers, however, were not yet ready to concede the state of New York, let alone the presidency. On the Saturday that Bennett claimed victory, William Cullen Bryant, editor of the New York *Evening Post*, urged his readers against "giving too much credit to these returns" from the state's interior, since they were almost certainly exaggerated by Whigs with an eye to influencing the election in neighboring Massachusetts, where voting would begin on Monday.[12]

The trouble for Democrats, however, was that even as they held out hope that New York—as well as Virginia, Pennsylvania, and Maine—might go for Van Buren, there was no denying that Van Buren had lost New Jersey. Both New York and New Jersey finished voting on November 4, but the New Jersey results were tabulated and published far more quickly than those of the Empire State's 58 counties spread over 47,000 square miles. On Friday, November 6, the same day that Bryant crowed that "the prospect of carrying [New York] for the democratic party brightens with almost every new piece of intelligence from the interior," he reported, two columns over, the final vote totals in all eighteen New Jersey counties, showing Harrison the winner with a 2,300-vote margin. Earlier that day, with results from only about half of New Jersey's counties, the administration's principal organ, the Washington *Globe*, had already conceded that it "cannot be doubted" that Harrison had won the state.[13]

Although neither the *Globe* nor the *Evening Post* said it or maybe even recognized it, conceding New Jersey was essentially tantamount to conceding the presidency. Indeed, New Jersey, which Harrison won by 3.6 percentage points, would turn out to be the "tipping-point state" that would take him over the requisite 148 electoral votes (in 1836, the tipping-point state had been Pennsylvania, which Van Buren carried by 2.4 percentage points).[14] Without New Jersey, Van Buren not only needed to run the table by winning New York, Pennsylvania, Virginia, and Maine—each of which on Friday, November 6, was still too close to call[15]—he also needed Illinois, Michigan, and Mississippi to go his way.

By Sunday, November 8, however, it was clear to those in the nation's capital that these smaller states would not matter because Van Buren had indeed lost New York.[16] On Monday, the Washington *Globe* conceded defeat, not only in New York but also in Pennsylvania.[17] The same day, the *Evening Post* also threw in the towel, proclaiming Harrison president-elect of the United States.[18] Although several states, notably Vermont, Delaware, and North Carolina, had yet to begin voting, the presidential election was settled. When all the votes were counted, Van Buren would end up winning only seven states, less than half the number he had carried in 1836. He did manage to win narrowly in two battleground states, Illinois and Virginia, and he lost by an agonizingly small margin in Pennsylvania, where he fell short by about 300 votes out of 288,000 votes cast, and Maine, where he lost by roughly 400 votes out of nearly 93,000 votes cast. But even had his luck held in those two states, his losses in New York and New Jersey, by 3 and 3.6 percentage points, respectively, sealed his fate and made Harrison the ninth president of the United States.

THE FINAL TALLY

The 1840 election was an electoral college landslide, with Harrison winning 234 electoral votes to Van Buren's 60 (see Table 10.1). Harrison's electoral vote total was not only 64 more than Van Buren received when he won the presidency in 1836 but 15 more than Andrew Jackson won in his reelection in 1832. Indeed, Harrison's 80 percent share of the electoral college vote was higher than any candidate had won in any presidential election since 1820. Only George Washington, James Monroe, and Thomas Jefferson received a higher share of the electoral college vote than Harrison.

The electoral college, though, disguised a much closer election. Measured by the popular vote (see Table 2 in Appendix A), Van Buren's performance looked more creditable. His losing margin of 6 percentage points

NOTICE TO QUIT.

March 4ᵗʰ 1841.

Notice to Quit. *A Whig cartoon portrays Martin Van Buren, hat in hand and the Subtreasury Bill under his arm, scampering out of "The White House" on Inauguration Day, March 4, 1841. On his way out, Van Buren mutters, "Our sufferings is intolerable! D—n his hard cider how it works me!" Harrison, who has already taken up residence in the presidential mansion, watches from the window and tells Major Downing to "show the Gentleman out . . . and give him a glass of cider before he goes." From the door, Downing tells "Matty" not to "look so down in the mouth," promises that he'll get Harrison to appoint him "Collector of the port of Kinderhook," and suggests that "the New Yorkers will maybe make you Inspector of Cabbage" Although the president's residence was not formally designated the White House until Theodore Roosevelt's executive order of 1901, the doorplate in this cartoon is a reminder that the presidential residence was commonly called "The White House" long before that. (Courtesy of the Library of Congress)*

Table 10.1 Electoral Votes by State in 1840

Harrison	Electoral Votes	Van Buren	Electoral Votes
New York	42	Virginia	23
Pennsylvania	30	South Carolina	11
Ohio	21	Alabama	7
Tennessee	15	New Hampshire	7
Kentucky	15	Illinois	5
North Carolina	15	Missouri	4
Massachusetts	14	Arkansas	3
Georgia	11		
Maryland	10		
Maine	10		
Indiana	9		
New Jersey	8		
Connecticut	8		
Vermont	7		
Louisiana	5		
Rhode Island	4		
Mississippi	4		
Delaware	3		
Michigan	3		
Total	234		60

Note: States shown in italics switched from Van Buren in 1836 to Harrison in 1840.

was the best result by a losing presidential candidate since President John Adams lost to Jefferson in 1800 by 5.8 percentage points, a testament to how evenly balanced the two parties had become. As the Washington *Globe* pointed out, a shift of a little over 8,000 votes—roughly 170 in Pennsylvania, 210 in Maine, 1,150 in New Jersey, and 6,600 in New York—out of the more than 2.4 million votes would have swung the election to Van Buren.[19]

Redistributing imaginary votes is a favorite postelection parlor game, but it distracts from the magnitude of the shift away from Van Buren between 1836 and 1840. In only one state did Van Buren do better in 1840 than in 1836: Tennessee, where his vote share increased from 42 percent to 44 percent, a small boost that stemmed from no longer having to run against the state's favorite son, Hugh White. Nationally, Van Buren's share of the vote slipped 4 percentage points, from 50.8 percent to 46.8 percent. Nor was the erosion of his support limited to any one region. His share of the vote dropped more than 9 percentage points in the Southern states of North Carolina and Louisiana, the Northeastern states of New Hampshire, Rhode Island, and Maine, and the Western states of Michigan and Ken-

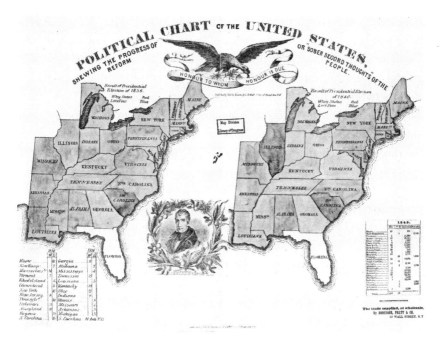

A *"Political Chart of the United States" from January 1841 depicting the presidential results in each state in the 1836 and 1840 elections, with Whig states colored red and Democratic states blue. The reference to the "'Sober Second Thoughts' of the People" is a jab at Martin Van Buren's oft-quoted maxim that "the sober, second thought of the people is never wrong and always efficient." (Courtesy of the Library of Congress)*

tucky. In his home state of New York, he slipped almost 6.5 percentage points. In Virginia, too, his vote share dropped 6 points.

Van Buren's loss of support is evident not only relative to 1836 but also compared with how Democratic gubernatorial candidates fared in the two years preceding the 1840 presidential election. In each of the nineteen states that held competitive gubernatorial elections between October 1838 and October 1840, Van Buren's 1840 vote share was lower than the share of the vote that the Democratic candidate received in that state's most recent gubernatorial election.[20] Van Buren lost six states—Georgia, Maryland, Massachusetts, Mississippi, Pennsylvania, and Tennessee—that had elected a Democratic governor in their most recent gubernatorial election.

Although Van Buren consistently fared worse than he had in 1836 and worse than Democratic gubernatorial candidates had fared in the run-up to the election, the Democratic share of the vote in recent gubernatorial elections was generally a better predictor of Van Buren's 1840 vote than was his own vote share in the 1836 presidential election, particularly in the North.[21] In eight of those nineteen states that held competitive gubernatorial elections between October 1838 and October 1840, including New York, Pennsylvania, and Ohio, the difference between Van Buren's 1840 two-party vote share and the Democratic gubernatorial candidate's two-party vote share in the most recent election was less than 1.5 percentage points.[22] This close fit speaks to the power of party in shaping voter choice in these states.

The strength of party voting—facilitated by the parties rather than the government printing and distributing the ballots (known as "party tickets")[23]—can also be seen in the close correspondence between the presidential result and the gubernatorial result in the three states—Delaware, Massachusetts, and New York—that held their gubernatorial election on the same date as the presidential contest.[24] In Massachusetts, incumbent Democratic governor Marcus Morton received 43 percent of the vote, only 2 percentage points better than Van Buren. In Delaware, Van Buren polled only about 250 fewer votes less than the Democratic gubernatorial candidate. In New York, too, Van Buren's vote share was only 1 percentage point less than that of the losing Democratic gubernatorial candidate, William Bouck. In virtually every county in New York, the difference in votes between Van Buren and Bouck was fewer than 100; in New York City, it was about 350 votes out of over 42,000 votes cast.[25] Even in Van Buren's native Columbia County, their vote totals were only 38 votes apart out of about 5,000 votes cast. Van Buren's loss in 1840 was a repudiation not only of the president but of his party.

The same pattern of repudiation of the Democratic Party was evident in November's congressional results. The Whigs flipped control of the sole congressional seat in Delaware as well as in Michigan; in both cases, Van Buren's share of the vote was less than 1 percentage point below that of the Democratic House candidate. The Whigs also picked up another seat in Massachusetts, leaving the Democrats with only one of the Bay State's twelve House members. In New Jersey, which used a single at-large district, the Democrats were shut out entirely, resulting in the loss of five seats. Here, too, Van Buren's vote share was essentially identical to that received by the Democratic congressional slate; a mere 100 votes out of more than 64,000 votes cast separated Van Buren from the top polling Democratic House candidate. In these five states, twenty House seats had been up for grabs, and the Democrats won only one. The sole good news came from

New York, where despite winning about 10,000 fewer votes than the Whigs (and 2,000 fewer votes than Bouck and 2,000 more than Van Buren), the Democrats managed to secure twenty-one of the forty congressional seats, a net pickup of two seats that was made possible by a narrow victory in New York City's four-member at-large district that flipped all four seats from the Whig to the Democratic Party.

Even with the New York City results, however, the November congressional elections produced a loss of 6 seats for the Democrats. Those losses were on top of the net loss of 7 seats that the Democrats had already suffered in the congressional elections between June and October 1840, leaving the party down 13 seats across the 15 states that held congressional elections in 1840. Although the precise composition of the new Twenty-Seventh Congress would not be known until the remaining 11 states (with their 92 House seats) held their congressional elections in 1841,[26] the narrowness of the Democratic majority in the current Twenty-Sixth Congress, where Democrats controlled 124 of the 242 seats, made it all but certain that President Harrison would have a Whig majority in the new Congress.[27] The Whigs' rout of the Democrats was complete.

THE "FRAUDS OF THE OPPOSITION"

Defeat did not come as a huge shock to Van Buren. The party's electoral setbacks in August, September, and October had prepared him for November's loss. Having resigned himself to defeat, he told James Buchanan, he "scarcely felt the catastrophe when it occurred."[28] Resigned though he may have been to defeat, he seemed at a loss to explain it. The best he could do was to put it down to voter fraud. Van Buren's postelection analysis fingering the "frauds of the opposition"[29] was a continuation of the Democratic campaign, which had tried to use allegations of electoral fraud to turn the electoral tide. A week before the polls opened in Ohio and Pennsylvania, the US attorney for the Southern District of New York, Benjamin Butler, who was in close communication with Van Buren, handed down an indictment alleging that prominent New York Whigs had engaged in the "most stupendous and atrocious fraud" to secure William Henry Seward's election as governor in 1838. According to Butler's indictment, the Whigs had paid thousands of dollars to import "pipe-layers" from Philadelphia, ostensibly to work on a public works project but in reality to vote the Whig ticket in New York City.[30] Van Buren felt confident that "the business of pipe laying"—a term that had already entered the political vocabulary as a synonym for fraudulent voters—would be found to be responsible for his defeat.[31]

Van Buren was far from the only Democrat to attribute the party's defeat to fraud. Writing to Jackson on November 7, the *Globe*'s Francis P. Blair attributed Van Buren's likely defeat to "the most enormous injustice and corruption in the canvass and fraud at the Polls ever witnessed in any country." Van Buren had been "cheated out of the election" as surely as Jackson had been in 1824. Jackson needed no convincing on this score. Writing to Van Buren on November 12, the former president lamented that "the Federal Whigg pipe layers are rejoicing" as "corruption, bribery and fraud has been extended over the whole Union." Unless the country ended election fraud, it would have to submit forever to be "ruled by the combined mony power in England and The Federalists of the Union."[32]

Invoking fraud to explain the Democrats' loss had the advantage of letting the party and the populace off the hook.[33] The problem was not with the Democratic Party's policies or ideology, nor with the people's judgment. Instead, blame lay squarely, as it always did for the Jacksonian true believer, with a nefarious, moneyed elite who would stop at nothing to thwart the progress of democracy. Those who controlled the money bought votes with the same facility with which they had long perverted the course of legislation by buying influence. Voter fraud confirmed the righteousness of the Jacksonian crusade against the money power. That the Whigs "have been enabled to practice *frauds* of the most infernal and damning character" proved yet again, a Connecticut Democrat told Van Buren, that "money is the root of all evil."[34]

The Whig Party undoubtedly did have more money than the Democrats.[35] Wealthy businessmen were disproportionately Whigs, particularly in the nation's most populous cities. There were no campaign finance laws or reporting requirements,[36] so money sloshed around with no regulation or oversight. All campaign money was dark money. But as an explanation for the Whigs' victory, money was hardly compelling. The party's immense financial advantage was long-standing. The Federalist Party had the same financial advantage over the Jeffersonian Party, but it done the party little good. Until 1840, it hadn't done the Whigs much good in presidential elections either. So what made 1840 different?

As eager as Democrats were to pin their defeat on fraud and bribery, most recognized that this could not be the whole story. Indeed, even the zealous Jackson was willing to allow that the problem lay not only in voter fraud but also in the "vilest system of slander that ever before has existed."[37] In focusing on the lies the Whigs told, though, it was more difficult to absolve the people. It was the people, after all, who had believed the lies and fallen for the tricks. As slick and clever as the Whigs might have been, what did it say about the popular intelligence that the people could be so easily misled by such obvious mistruths and misdirection? If the Democrats had, as one despairing editor put it, been "sung down, lied down, drunk down," then that judgment seemed at least as damning of the people's capacity for democracy as of the Whigs' capacity for duplicity.[38]

In the days after the election, some Democrats admitted their doubts, at least in private. Ohio's former Democratic congressman Thomas L. Hamer confessed to Van Buren that he "never had such gloomy forebodings in my life as haunt me at present," and he felt compelled to ask the question, "Can this people govern themselves?"[39] Writing to Governor James Polk, Tennessee's Democratic congressman Hopkins L. Turney had much the same thought, admitting that the election had "shaken my confidence in the intelligence and independence of the people."[40] Disdain dripped from some of the Democrats' postelection laments about the Whigs' campaign, as when Nashville attorney Robert Reynolds complained that "the Log Cabin Cry & the Hard Cider revels have great charms for the Vulgar & it has carried them off to the support of federalism."[41]

For many Democrats, the 1840 election was profoundly disorienting. The Federalists and Whigs were the ones who supposedly looked down upon the "vulgar" masses and harbored doubts about their capacity for self-government. Yet now it was the aristocratic Whig Philip Hone who sounded the more authentic democrat as he celebrated the election as "a beautiful illustration of the operation of a popular government." Hone wrote proudly, "There is not probably a country in the world where a change of such prodigious magnitude could have been effected in the same time . . . and in so orderly and decorous a manner." Hone mused that should Alexis de Tocqueville publish a new edition of *Democracy in America*, the election would provide both "striking confirmation of his principles" and a reason to offer "a new and merited eulogium [to] our institutions."[42] Hone's celebration of the rotation of power as an essential element of a democratic two-party system was a sensibility lacking among many Democrats, ironically including the man so often celebrated as the architect of the two-party system, Martin Van Buren.

Toward the end of his long life, Van Buren wrote an autobiography in which he briefly returned to the unpleasant memory of the 1840 election. The passage of several decades, however, had not enabled him to see any more deeply into the causes of his defeat. The best he could do was attribute his loss to "the instrumentalities and debaucheries of a political Saturnalia, in which reason and justice had been derided." If the people had not been cheated, they must have, temporarily at least, lost their minds. In subscribing to a populist version of history that pitted an enduringly righteous party of the people against a mendacious party of the moneyed elite, it was difficult for Van Buren and many other Democrats of his generation to understand a Whig victory except in terms of fraud, deception, or madness.[43]

For Democrats, moreover, the mad revelry of 1840 was integrally tied to the corrupting effects of money. Take away the money, the Washington *Globe* declared on the eve of the election, "and the whole complicated machinery of British Whig electioneering would at once stop. The log cabins would not have been erected—the carousals and drunken revels would cease—the Tippecanoe songs would lose their music—the Whig agents and cohorts would lose their employment and their wages." Without what the *Globe* called "the corruption fund," there would have been no immense Whig campaign rallies. Popular enthusiasm for the Whigs was no grassroots movement but was manufactured and manipulated by elites. The Whig campaign of 1840, in the Democratic view, was history's first astroturfing campaign.[44]

Much of the *Globe*'s critique was inarguable. Money did help the Whigs "carry on their business of publishing their tracts and speeches, to an extent surpassing everything which has been witnessed in this country." Communicating with voters and mobilizing them to vote cost money, although the "cart loads of speeches and tracts" that the Whigs distributed all across the country owed more to congressmen's "scandalous abuse" of the franking privilege—a bipartisan abuse—than to the party's campaign coffers. It is not at all surprising that an election that saw a huge increase in the number of voters also saw unprecedented campaign spending.[45] Bringing almost one million more voters to the polls was not cheap, even if they weren't being paid to vote.

Other Democrats recognized that blaming the party's defeat on money, corruption, and fraud let the party off the hook too easily. James Polk did not doubt that the Whigs had "mystified every thing connected with public affairs, and made false issues about comparatively unimportant matters . . . and thus diverted the public attention from the great principles involved in the contest." He shared the Democrats' frustration that the opposition had "succeeded in getting up a hurrah, and in so confusing and exciting the public mind, that many honest men would not investigate or even listen to the truth." But, in Polk's view, the fundamental problem was that they had been "beaten by the superior organization and industry of our opponents."

Polk thought part of the problem was that the Whig campaign had got off the ground much more quickly than the sluggish Democratic campaign, which began in earnest only after Van Buren's nomination in May. The Democrats had been too complacent at the outset: "Apprehending no danger," he explained to several close allies, "we suffered our opponents to enter actively into the canvass, three months earlier than we did" and thus gave "an impulse to public sentiment which it was difficult to overcome." Adding to the Democrats' problems in November was that the "succession of disasters" they had suffered in the elections between August and October "dispirited and disheartened" them. The Whigs had won, in short, because they were more energized.[46]

For Polk, who was determined to run for reelection for governor the next August (and who would end up as the Democratic presidential nominee in 1844), blaming the party's loss on money and fraud was not constructive. Instead, the party needed to honestly reckon with its missteps and learn from the opposition's innovations. While the *Globe* bemoaned "the corruption fund" by which the Whig "maintained an Executive committee at Washington [that] directed the operations of the campaign," the lesson that Polk and his allies learned was that "the Democratic members should have organized a similar committee, . . . composed of . . . the first men in Congress of our party, and furnished it . . . with money." The problem, moreover, was less that the Whigs had lied about Van Buren's positions than that Democrats had failed to immediately hit back. "Every thing taken hold of by the whigs should have been boldly refuted and a true state of the subject made manifest and circulated extensively throughout the U. States." When the Whig-nominated presidential electors crisscrossed the state, attacking the president, the Democratic electors should have "met their opponents upon all and every occasion." The Democrats, in sum, had been too slow in responding to Whig attacks and thereby allowed the opposition to define the contest and the candidates.[47]

But was Van Buren's defeat a product of campaign missteps and the party's failure to get out its message? Polk's attention to the Whigs' "superior organization and industry" was a more compelling explanation of Van Buren's defeat than fraud and corruption, particularly in a state such as Tennessee. But Democrats hardly lacked for organization, especially in crucial states like Pennsylvania and New York. Indeed, back in June, Millard Fillmore had reported to Thurlow Weed that the Democrats in New York were "much better organized and more active" than the Whigs, and he worried that the Whigs seemed overconfident, believing "the work already accomplished." "Our foe," Fillmore cautioned, "is active, vigilant, and un-principled beyond all former example."[48]

Fillmore was particularly concerned about the extraordinary reach of the *Extra Globe*, which began publication immediately after the Democratic national convention. Amos Kendall quit his job as the postmaster general to run the government-subsidized campaign paper and then leaned on the nation's thirteen thousand postmasters to help him reach his goal of getting the paper into the hands of every "Farmer, Mechanic, and Workingman." Aided by hundreds of Democratic census takers, Fillmore fretted, the *Extra Globe*'s "noxious leaves are falling in every town and hamlet" in the country. Moreover, far from being late to the game, Democrats often got the jump on the Whigs when it came to campaign papers. Early in the spring, at Van Buren's urging, the Democrats had established the *Rough-Hewer*, an Albany-based campaign paper whose goal was to "prepare the public mind against [Whig] falsehoods." Not until two months later did the Whigs counter with the highly successful *Log Cabin*, published in Albany under the editorship of Horace Greeley.[49]

The Whigs were unquestionably far better organized and better financed than they had been four years earlier. But were the Democrats any less well organized or financed than they had been in 1836, when the Whigs had blamed their defeat on the Democrats' unrivaled organizational capacity and their "drilled" and "disciplined" partisans who were like "the foot soldiers of a marching regiment"? Having won three presidential elections in a row, had the Democrats suddenly forgotten what it took to run a successful presidential campaign and turn out voters? The increase in Democratic turnout in 1840 strongly suggests otherwise. In 1840, 366,000 more people voted for Van Buren than had voted for him in 1836. In contrast, when Jackson was reelected in 1832, he received only 60,000 more votes than when he had first been elected. And when Van Buren was elected president in 1836, he received only 60,000 more votes than Jackson had four years earlier. Something dramatic happened in 1840, but a focus on the weakness of the Democratic Party's organization and campaign seems insufficient to account for it. Indeed, the record 80 percent turnout for which the 1840 election is so famous happened only because *both* parties successfully mobilized voters.

Moreover, if the Whigs showed greater "industry" and enthusiasm than the Democrats, that is less an explanation than a restatement of the thing to be explained. To ask "Why did Harrison win?" is essentially the same question as "Why were voters more excited about voting for Harrison than

A GLOBE TO LIVE ON!

A Globe to Live On! A Whig cartoon from 1840 attacking what the Whigs saw as the corrupt relationship between Washington Globe *editor Francis Preston Blair and the former postmaster general Amos Kendall, who are conjoined at the midsection by the* Extra Globe. *(Courtesy of the Library of Congress)*

Van Buren?" The Whigs' greater "industry" is ultimately not the answer to the question of why Van Buren lost so much as the phenomenon that itself needs explaining.

A few contemporaries, most notably John Calhoun, put the blame squarely on Van Buren. According to Calhoun, Van Buren lacked the "powers of a high order intellectually and mentally and excited no enthusiasm and like most men who lack in these particulars, relied too exclusively on address and management."[50] Calhoun hoped to be the Democratic Party nominee in 1844[51] and so had every reason to belittle Van Buren, but the real problem with Calhoun's claim was not motive but logic. After all, Van Buren's intellectual powers and charisma were presumably no different than they had been four years earlier, when he had triumphed. Nor could Harrison's victory over Van Buren, let alone Jackson's triumph over Adams and Clay, be plausibly construed as evidence that voters made their choice based on a presidential candidate's intellectual or mental prowess. Granted, Van Buren lacked Harrison's "halo of military victory," but that halo had not been enough to grant Harrison or deny Van Buren the election in 1836.[52]

Among the more striking aspects of the Democrats' postelection analysis is how little blame was directed at Van Buren. Indeed, a surprising number of Democrats seemed only too eager to see Van Buren as their standard-bearer again in 1844, which rather undercuts Calhoun's claim about Van Buren's inability to excite enthusiasm, at least among party loyalists.[53] Indeed, but for the Democrats' two-thirds rule, which required the nominee to receive support from two-thirds of the delegates at the national convention, Van Buren likely would have secured the party's nomination again in 1844. Four years after that, the allegedly uninspiring Van Buren would be announced as the first presidential nominee of the fledgling Free Soil Party.

After the 1840 election, more Democrats seemed ready to blame the vice-presidential candidate, Richard Johnson, than the man at the top of the ticket. Pittsburgh postmaster David Lynch, for instance, was convinced that Van Buren had been "sunk" in the Keystone State largely because of the "dead weight of our candidate for Vice President," against whom there remained the same strong "moral feeling . . . that nearly overthrew us in 1836." For Lynch, the lesson of the election was "that a candidate for high office must be as pure as well in private as public life."[54] There is little evidence that Americans learned the moral lesson that Lynch hoped they would draw from the Democrats' loss and even less evidence that the party's vice-presidential candidate cost it Pennsylvania, let alone the presidency.[55]

Blaming defeat on the candidates' intellect, charisma, or moral character, like the explanations centered on campaign organization, clever marketing, outright lies, or fraudulent voting, enabled Democrats to explain their defeat without questioning the administration's policies and the party's principles. The party's problem could and should be resolved not by changing its policies or its principles but instead by selecting more wholesome or appealing candidates and by insisting on better organization, better messaging, greater vigilance, and maybe some new laws to clean up elections. From this perspective, there was nothing wrong with the party that a new election wouldn't solve.

"THE SPIRIT OF ABOLITION"

Not all Democrats were as sanguine about what the election meant for the party's future, particularly those who were convinced that abolitionist agitation was at the root of the party's defeat. Both antislavery and proslavery forces voiced slavery-centric interpretations of the election result. From the South, Thomas Ritchie's *Richmond Enquirer* argued that abolitionists not only had secured Harrison the Whig Party nomination but had "rushed to the support of the Harrison electoral ticket with a zeal bordering upon fury" and "furnished the efficient power which turned the scale against the Democracy of the North and West [and] filled the ballot boxes." The Whig victory was an ominous sign that the North had succumbed to "the spirit of Abolition."[56] Some antislavery Democrats also blamed slavery for Van Buren's defeat. As one told Van Buren after the election, "The unnatural alliance between Slavocrats and democrats has been the cause, *the only cause* of the Waterloo defeat which Democratic principles have received at the recent election."[57]

The argument that Van Buren's defeat hinged in large party on slavery has been endorsed by some scholars. Historian Donald Cole, for instance, argues that "Van Buren's proslavery policies . . . alienated Northerners and contributed greatly to the loss of six states that Van Buren had carried in 1836," specifically, Connecticut, Maine, Michigan, New York, Pennsylvania, and Rhode Island.[58] If true, then slavery should be put down as a key factor in Van Buren's defeat since those six states accounted for 97 electoral votes, enough to give him 157 electoral votes, nine more than he needed to be reelected.

There is no question that slavery was often discussed during the campaign. The issues of slavery in the District of Columbia and the gag rule were commonly included in interrogatories posed to the candidates, and both Van Buren and Harrison—and their many proxies—worked hard during the campaign to allay Southern concerns that they were not sufficiently supportive of slavery and to paint their opponent as an abolitionist sympathizer.[59] Antislavery advocates certainly objected strenuously to administration policies they deemed proslavery, including the administration's support of the gag rule and its attempt to ensure that illegally purchased

African slaves captured aboard the *Amistad* were returned to their owners in Cuba.[60] But while Van Buren's proslavery policies were unpopular in parts of the North, it is unlikely that these policies cost him the election.

The first problem with any argument that Van Buren's proslavery policies cost him the election is that it assumes that he could have tilted the administration's policies in a more antislavery direction without a loss of Southern support that would have spelled his certain defeat. There are two reasons for thinking that he could not have done so. First, despite the best efforts of abolitionists, slavery was still more electorally salient in the South than in the North—that is, Southerners were more likely than Northerners to vote on the basis of a party's or candidate's position on slavery. Second, Van Buren edged Harrison in Virginia by a mere 1.5 percentage points; the margin by which Van Buren lost New York, by comparison, was twice as large. Only in Maine and Pennsylvania were the contests closer than in Virginia. And without Virginia's 23 electoral votes, there was no path to a Democratic victory, as Van Buren understood better than anyone. Had Van Buren tacked in an antislavery direction in handling the *Amistad* affair or the gag rule, it seems likely that he would have lost Virginia to his Virginia-born opponents, Harrison and John Tyler.

Another problem with attributing Van Buren's loss to antislavery defections is that the erosion of his support was not confined to the North, as he also lost three Southern slaveholding states that he had carried in 1836: Louisiana, Mississippi, and North Carolina. More important, the erosion of his support was little different in slaveholding and nonslaveholding states. As Table 10.2 shows, there were eleven states in which Van Buren's share of the two-party vote dropped by substantially more than the 4 percentage points it slipped nationwide. Of these eleven states, six were nonslaveholding states and five were slaveholding states. Moreover, of the five states where Van Buren saw the greatest hemorrhaging of support relative to 1836, three were slaveholding states and two were nonslaveholding states. As Table 10.2 also shows, of the eight states in which Van Buren's loss of support was notably lower than it was nationwide, four were states with slavery and four were states without slavery. Finally, if we leave out New Hampshire (an outlier and a state that Van Buren still won easily in 1840), the average decline in Van Buren's share of the two-party vote is not significantly different in slaveholding and nonslaveholding states.[61]

The absence of marked sectional differences in Van Buren's decline in support is not surprising in view of the lack of clearly defined policy differences on slavery between Harrison and Van Buren. As the Liberty Party

Table 10.2 Change in Van Buren's Share of the State Two-Party Vote between 1836 and 1840 Relative to the Change in His Share of the Two-Party Vote Nationwide

States in which Van Buren's share of the two-party vote in 1840 declined *more* than the 4 percentage points it declined nationally		States in which Van Buren's share of the two-party vote in 1840 declined *less* than the 4 percentage points it declined nationally	
State	Percentage point decrease beyond Van Buren's 4-point decline nationwide	State	Percentage point increase relative to Van Buren's 4-point decline nationwide
New Hampshire	−15.5	Tennessee	+6.2
Rhode Island	−9.7	Maryland	+3.9
Kentucky	−7.6	Indiana	+3.7
Louisiana	−7.4	Alabama	+3.1
Maine	−6.9	Pennsylvania	+2.7
North Carolina	−6.8	New Jersey	+2.7
Arkansas	−3.7	Delaware	+2.2
Connecticut	−2.2	Ohio	+1.7
New York	−2.1		
Michigan	−2.1		
Virginia	−2.0		
Mississippi	−0.7	Massachusetts	+.1.1
Vermont	−0.4	Missouri	+0.6
Georgia	−0.1	Illinois	+0.3

Note: Slaveholding states indicated in bold.

supporters anticipated, both major parties' presidential candidates rushed to assure the South that they would protect slavery and uphold the interests of slaveholders—and accused the other side of being closet abolitionists. Admittedly, Harrison and his allies wooed prominent abolitionists behind the scenes. After his nomination, for instance, Harrison twice visited Gamaliel Bailey, the Cincinnati-based editor of Ohio's leading antislavery newspaper, the *Philanthropist*, to offer assurances of his antislavery credentials. Bailey reciprocated, at least initially, with private and public support (or at least "friendly neutrality") for Harrison, whom Bailey saw as "the candidate of the free states," unlike Van Buren, whom he viewed as "*par eminence* the slaveholders' candidate."[62] For the most part, however, Harrison was more concerned during the summer and fall of 1840 with distancing himself from abolitionists than with embracing their cause, confirming the judgment of Ohio's political abolitionist (and future Liberty Party vice-presidential nominee) Thomas Morris that "both political parties . . . courted [abolitionists] in private and denounced them in public."[63]

The fledgling Liberty Party was far too weak and disorganized for Whig Party leaders to worry much about defection from their antislavery ranks. As mentioned in chapter 8, the Liberty Party's presidential candidate, James Birney, was not even in the country during the campaign. The party's largely unknown vice-presidential candidate, Thomas Earle, remained in the country but "bestirred himself no more than Birney did." So little attention did the Birney-Earle ticket receive in the press that many antislavery supporters thought Birney "had withdrawn from the canvass."[64] Because the Whigs could be confident that antislavery Whigs would not defect, they could afford to tilt their campaign toward the South, emulating the strategy usually attributed to Van Buren of carrying "the South by concessions to slavery, and the North by party machinery."[65] Antislavery Whigs, of course, loathed Van Buren, so much so—as Henry Stanton told Birney—that they would gladly "wade to their armpits in molten lava to drive Van Buren from power."[66] But that loathing is not an explanation for Van Buren's defeat in 1840 since these antislavery Whigs had voted against Van Buren in 1836. The real question, then, is whether there were enough defections among antislavery Democrats to cause Van Buren's defeat in the six Northern states he had carried in 1836.

If we use electoral support for the Liberty Party as an admittedly imperfect measure for the strength of antislavery sentiment within a state,[67] it is striking that only two (New York and Michigan) of the six Northern states that swung from Van Buren in 1836 to Harrison in 1840 were among the handful of states in which the Liberty Party attracted more than the tiniest sliver of support in 1840.[68] In New York and Michigan, the Liberty Party won between 0.6 percent and 0.7 percent of the vote in 1840, but in the other four states that swung away from Van Buren (Connecticut, Maine, Pennsylvania, and Rhode Island), it polled no more than 0.2 percent of the vote. The Liberty Party's strongest showing by far was in Massachusetts, where it won 1.3 percent of the vote, but Van Buren lost Massachusetts by equally large margins in 1836 and 1840.[69]

Maine and Pennsylvania were admittedly so close—Harrison and Van Buren were separated by about 400 votes out of over 90,000 votes in Maine and 350 votes out of nearly 290,000 votes in Pennsylvania—that one can point to almost any factor as potentially decisive, no matter how small a role it played in the campaign and voter behavior.[70] But by the same token, in Rhode Island and Connecticut, Harrison's margin of victory was so large in 1840—more than 22 percentage points in the former and 11 percentage points in the latter—that antislavery agitation could not possibly have made the difference, particularly in two states where abolitionist sentiment was not strong enough to produce any significant support for the Liberty Party.[71] Without Connecticut and Rhode Island, Van Buren would still have fallen one electoral vote shy of the presidency even if he had won Pennsylvania, New York, Maine, and Michigan.

It seems unlikely, moreover, that antislavery resistance to Van Buren's proslavery policies cost him Michigan, a state he lost by more than 4 percentage points. An absence of party competition and incomplete returns in many of the state's counties in 1836 make it difficult to meaningfully compare Van Buren's showing at the county level in 1836 and 1840, but we can compare his vote share in 1840 with that of the Democratic gubernatorial candidate in 1839 to gauge where Democratic support slipped most, at least in the year leading up to the 1840 election. Two things stand out. First, statewide, Van Buren's two-party vote share in 1840 (47.9 percent) was only fractionally lower than that of the Democratic gubernatorial nominee, Elon Farnsworth (48.4 percent), in October 1839. Second, and more relevant to assessing the impact of antislavery forces, the Democratic vote share declined *less* in counties in which political abolitionism was strong (measured by Liberty Party vote share) than where it was weak.[72] In the ten Michigan counties that polled no support for the Liberty Party in 1840, Van Buren lost an average of about 4.5 points relative to Farnsworth's vote totals. In contrast, in each of the five counties in which the Liberty Party polled more than 1 percent of the vote, Van Buren fared fractionally better than Farnsworth.[73] That Van Buren tended to lose less support in more abolitionist counties is consistent with Ronald Formisano's conclusion that in Michigan "from 1837 to 1841 . . . most abolition votes came from the Whigs," although another contributing factor is that the Whigs' 1839 gubernatorial nominee William Woodbridge was "decidedly anti-abolition and anti-black."[74] That Woodbridge—the only Whig ever to win a governor's race in Michigan— won Michigan on an antiabolition platform should give us further pause in crediting proslavery policies or antislavery agitation for Van Buren's defeat in Michigan, a state that backed even more ardently proslavery Democrats in each of the succeeding three presidential elections (Polk in 1844, Michigan native son Lewis Cass in 1848, and Franklin Pierce in 1852)—elections in which slavery was a far more prominent issue than it was in 1840.

That leaves New York, which Van Buren lost by only 3 points, as the best fit for the thesis that proslavery policies and antislavery defections lost the president a Northern state. Van Buren's close ally Churchill Cambreleng came to the same conclusion, telling Van Buren after the election that "abolition was collateral and lost us only one state . . . New York."[75] An inspection of the county returns offers support for Cambreleng's assessment of abolitionism's impact in certain parts of upstate New York. In the three counties (Madison, Oneida, and Oswego) in which the Liberty Party won at least 2 percent of the vote—each of which had voted strongly Democratic in 1836—Van Buren's share of the two-party vote dropped an average of almost 12 percentage points, while the average drop in Van Buren's vote share in other New York counties was 7.4.[76] In Madison, the county in which the Liberty Party received the highest percentage (2.8) of the vote, Van Buren saw his two-party share of the vote plummet from 63 percent to 49 percent. As Table 10.3 shows, moreover, in the nine counties in which the Liberty Party polled more than 1 percent, Van Buren's loss of support was much steeper in the five counties that he had won in 1836 than in the four counties that had backed Harrison in 1836.

It is true that Van Buren also hemorrhaged support in some downstate Democratic counties in which abolitionism was weak, for instance, Putnam County, where the Liberty Party failed to register a single vote in either 1840 or 1844. In fact, there is a strong correlation ($r = 0.74$) between Van Buren's vote share in 1836 and the change in Van Buren's two-party vote share— that is, the more votes Van Buren won in a county in 1836, the greater the size of the drop in his vote share in 1840; in contrast, the correlation with the strength of abolitionism in a county (as measured by the Liberty Party vote in 1840) is, by comparison, quite modest ($r = -0.14$).[77] However, that does not mean that abolitionism had no effect. Quite the opposite is true. Controlling for the size of Van Buren's victory in 1836 boosts the explanatory power of the abolitionism variable. When the control variable (the size of Van Buren's victory in 1836) is included, abolitionism's effect on the variance across counties in the change in Van Buren's support between 1836 and 1840 more than doubles (from about 2 percent to 4.5 percent) and becomes statistically significant ($p = 0.018$).[78] In short, the evidence is consistent with the argument that the "spirit of abolition"—and Van Buren's proslavery policies—may have lost him New York.

There remains one important obstacle to the thesis that Van Buren's defeat in New York was due to antislavery agitation during the 1840 campaign, namely, the remarkable electoral stability between the 1838 gubernatorial and 1840 presidential contests. Van Buren's 3-point margin of defeat in New York in 1840 almost exactly mirrored Democratic governor William Marcy's 2.8-point defeat in November 1838. Moreover, as Table 10.3 also shows, Van Buren's support in counties where the Liberty Party polled best

Table 10.3 Van Buren's Decline in Two-Party Vote Share in New York Counties in which the Liberty Party Won More than 1 Percent of the Vote

County (Liberty Party Vote Share in 1840 in Parentheses)	Van Buren Vote Share in 1836	Marcy Vote Share in 1838	Van Buren Two-Party Vote Share in 1840	Change in Van Buren's Two-Party Vote Share between 1836 and 1840	Change in Van Buren's Two-Party Vote Share between 1838 and 1840
Lewis (1.1)	72.7	53.1	50.5	-22.2	-2.6
Madison (2.8)	63.1	44.5	49.1	-14	+4.6
Oswego (2)	61.5	50.4	48.2	-13.3	-2.2
Oneida (2.6)	60.2	54.7	52.1	-8.1	-2.6
Cattaraugus (1.1)	55.9	49.4	45.5	-10.4	-3.9
Mean decline in Van Buren's two-party vote share in counties he won in 1836				-13.6	-1.3
Orleans (1.6)	49.5	44.7	43.8	-5.7	-0.9
Niagara (1.4)	48.6	43.8	42.8	-5.8	-1.0
Ontario (1.8)	44.2	42.1	41.7	-2.5	-0.4
Genesee (1.4)	38.2	34.4	35.0	-3.2	+0.6
Mean decline in Van Buren's two-party vote share in counties he lost in 1836				-4.3	-0.4

declined only marginally from the levels of support that Marcy had received in these counties in 1838. In Madison, in fact, Van Buren fared better than Marcy had done in 1838. Of course, antislavery agitation and Van Buren's proslavery policies existed prior to November 1838, but the similarity between the 1838 and 1840 New York election results—at both the state and the county level[79]—should at least make us wary of placing too much explanatory weight on the controversies of the 1840 campaign, including the infamous case of the *Amistad*, which did not reach US shores until the end of August 1839.[80]

Even if we grant that Van Buren's proslavery policies and antislavery agitation cost him New York, they cannot explain his loss of the presidency, since New York's 42 electoral votes would have been no more than a morale-boosting consolation prize, unlike in 1844, when a strong case can be made that antislavery sentiment, specifically votes for the Liberty Party, decided the outcome of the presidential election. Ironically, in 1844, the beneficiary was the Democrat nominee, James Polk, and the loser the Whig nominee, Henry Clay, who lost New York by a mere 5,000 votes, while the now much stronger Liberty Party, drawing disproportionately from antislavery Whigs, polled three times that number.[81] Antislavery sentiment did profoundly affect the 1840 election, but by far its greatest effect was on the Whigs' choice of their nominee, not the outcome of the general election.

"THE TIMES WERE AT FAULT"

If it wasn't slavery that cost Van Buren a second term, what was it? A few heretical Democrats and most mainstream Whigs thought the answer to that question was clear: the voters had thrown Van Buren out because they rejected the administration's economic policies, especially the Independent Treasury.

This was the position of A. O. P. Nicholson, a prominent Tennessee Democrat, who told Polk that the party had been "beaten partly because our Ind. Treas. System promised nothing to the people in the way of aiding them in their difficulties." The root problem, as Nicholson saw it, was that "our people have become so habituated to look for help and relief from Legislation, that they were not prepared to sanction the negative doctrines of the Sub-Treasury. Whilst we could only point them to their workshops & cotton-fields with the aid of economy for relief, our opponents presented them the more alluring prospect of abounding cash from a National Bank." Nicholson hastened to add that he believed "our doctrines were certainly correct" and "would have become popular" had the administration had "four years longer" to prove their success. But alas, the option had been foreclosed by defeat: "So far . . . as the result of a Presidential election is any evidence, the people have decided against the Ind. Treas. System." As a result, the party needed to rethink its position on banking and currency. He recognized that opposition to a national bank was among the party's "cardinal doctrines," and so it could not simply abandon that long-held position. Perhaps, though, it could push to amend the Constitution and thereby remove the strict constructionist constitutional argument against chartering a national bank. Nicholson recognized that this idea might not be possible but thought it nonetheless imperative that the party come up with some alternative that promised to deliver a "positive benefit in the way of a currency."[82]

Not surprisingly, Whigs often latched on to a similar interpretation of the election as a popular rebuke of Van Buren's Independent Treasury. In a speech in the Senate on December 15, 1840, Clay explained why he had introduced a resolution calling for the repeal of the legislation that established the Independent Treasury. "Whatever else" the election had decided, Clay claimed, it had "decided against this Sub-Treasury measure." Indeed, so emphatic was the Whig triumph that Clay felt that there was no need to refer the repeal resolution to committee. There was nothing for the Senate to deliberate upon because the Whig victory had made it evident that the nation "decrees the repeal of the measure." "What Senator," Clay asked, "would stand there in his place and say he opposed himself to the will of the nation?"[83]

That Clay used the 1840 election result to justify repealing the Independent Treasury was both ironic and hypocritical given that Clay had been among the first and most eloquent to criticize Andrew Jackson's claim that the 1832 election had given him a popular mandate to remove government deposits from the national bank. In December 1833, during a Senate oration spread over three days, Clay emphatically rang the alarm at Jackson's dangerous effort to invoke a "new source of executive power which is found in the result of a presidential election." Clay argued that Jackson's mandate claim was a radical departure from the founders' understanding that "the issue of a presidential election was merely to place the Chief Magistrate in the post assigned to him," not to arm him with authority beyond what the Constitution provided. Presidential elections, according to Clay in 1833, were judgments on a candidate's character and reputation, not verdicts on public policy. The people had reelected Jackson because of "his presumed merits"; they "had no idea," Clay said, "of expressing their approbation of all the opinions which the President held." As evidence, Clay pointed to Pennsylvania, which had voted overwhelmingly for Jackson in 1832 but which by all accounts was strongly supportive of the national bank.[84]

Clay and other Whigs were right that Jackson's reelection had little or nothing to do with his veto of Congress's plan to recharter the national bank; indeed, Jackson arguably might have won by more had he not issued his controversial bank veto.[85] They were even more right that in removing government deposits from the national bank, Jackson was following his own policy judgment, not some mythical mandate from the people. They were also right to point to the inherent fallacies in the mandate concept. As political scientists have repeatedly found, the idea that elections impart a policy mandate from the people is implausible because it assumes that voters (a) have opinions on issues, (b) know the candidates' and parties' stances on those issues, and (3) vote on the basis of those issue positions. Yet one or more of these conditions is frequently not met in the real world of voting behavior. Moreover, even if voters were perfectly informed about the issues and the candidates' positions and voted entirely based on those positions, the claim of a mandate would still be implausible because there are many issues but only one vote. Election results, in short, are an unreliable way of gauging public opinion on specific issues.[86]

There is little reason to think that in electing Harrison, voters were expressing an adverse judgment about the Independent Treasury that Van Buren had signed into law in July 1840. Indeed, few voters would likely have been able to explain how the Independent Treasury worked. If they supported the scheme, it was because they identified with the Democratic Party of Van Buren and Jackson, not the other way around.[87] Nor did Van Buren's defeat signal that voters now supported reestablishing a national bank. Indeed, the case for a popular mandate to abolish the Independent Treasury and reestablish a national bank was even weaker than Jackson's mandate claim after the 1832 election. At least Jackson had attempted to put his July 1832 veto of the bill rechartering the national bank at the center of his reelection campaign. Harrison and the Whig Party, in contrast, waffled throughout the 1840 campaign about whether a national bank was needed, and Harrison never made repeal of the Independent Treasury a cornerstone of his campaign in the way that Jackson had done with his opposition to a national bank. Moreover, even the most conscientious, perfectly informed, issue-oriented voter would have had an impossible time rendering an informed judgment on the proposed Independent Treasury because there had been barely any time for it to be implemented, let alone affect the economy.

The fundamental problem for Van Buren in 1840 was not his economic policies but the economic results. Cambreleng was quick to put his finger on the economic forces driving the election. At the time that he left the United States in August 1839 to become the minister to Russia, he judged that "there was no doubt" of Van Buren's reelection. But upon arriving in England, he found that the Bank of England had hiked interest rates—a reaction to a precipitous decline in its gold reserves as a result in large part of a historically poor wheat harvest in Britain in 1838. From that moment, Cambreleng told Van Buren, "I feared another crisis in America at a time most unpropitious for our cause and at an admirable moment to serve the intent and purposes of the opposition."[88] The economic crisis that began to unfold in the fall of 1839—a second wave of domestic bank suspensions, albeit less extensive than in 1837, falling cotton prices, tightening credit, a decline in foreign capital investment, and an abandonment of state-funded capital projects—put the brakes on the economic recovery that had helped to lift Democratic electoral fortunes beginning in the fall of 1838.[89] It was "this second revulsion and no other cause whatsoever," Cambreleng told Van Buren, that "has elected your opponent and would have elected any other man. It depressed every description of property below its extreme point . . . even in the revulsion of 1837 and produced a spirit of general discontent which the opposition easily and readily availed themselves of." Cambreleng assured Van Buren that "the people have gone . . . into the contest without regard to principles and without any object but that of change." The election's result should not "in the slightest degree shake our confidence," he assured Van Buren, since "the times were at fault."[90]

One way to test Cambreleng's argument is to compare Van Buren's vote share in 1840 with the Democratic vote share in the fifteen gubernatorial elections held during the first economic "revulsion" between the summer of 1837 and the summer of 1838.[91] As Table 10.4 documents, Van Buren's average two-party vote share in 1840 in these fifteen states was within about 1 percentage point of the average two-party vote share received by Democratic gubernatorial candidates during the first economic downturn.[92] The power exerted by the economy can also be seen by comparing Van Buren's vote share in 1836 with the Democratic vote share in the thirteen gubernatorial elections held during the economic upswing between the fall of 1838 and the fall of 1839. As Table 10.5 shows, Van Buren's average two-

Table 10.4 Van Buren's Two-Party Vote Share in 1840 Compared with Democratic Vote Share in Gubernatorial Elections between the Summer of 1837 and the Summer of 1838

State	Date of Gubernatorial Election	Van Buren Vote Share, 1836	Democratic Two-Party Vote Share in Gubernatorial Election, 1837–1838	Van Buren Two-Party Vote Share, 1840	Change in Van Buren Two-Party 1840 Vote Share Relative to Democratic Two-Party Vote Share in 1837–1838 Gubernatorial Election	Change in Van Buren Two-Party Vote Share between 1836 and 1840
Indiana	August 1837	44.5	44.5	44.2	-0.3	-0.3
Alabama	August 1837	55.3	54.8	54.4	-0.4	-0.9
Tennessee	August 1837	42.1	39.8	44.3	+4.5	+2.2
Maine	September 1837	60.7	49.6	49.8	+0.2	-10.9
Vermont	September 1837	40.1	44.3	35.7	-8.6	-4.4
Georgia	October 1837	48.2	49.4	44.2	-5.2	-4.0
Michigan	November 1837	54.0	50.9	47.9	-3.0	-6.1
Massachusetts	November 1837	44.8	39.5	41.8	+2.3	-3.0
Mississippi	November 1837	51.3	46.5	46.6	+0.1	-4.7
New Hampshire	March 1838	75.0	53.2	55.5	+2.3	-19.5
Connecticut	April 1838	50.6	44.2	44.4	+0.2	-6.2
Rhode Island	April 1838	52.2	46.8	38.5	-8.3	-13.7
Louisiana	July 1838	51.7	47.2	40.3	-6.9	-11.4
N. Carolina	August 1838	53.1	36.7	42.3	+5.6	-10.8
Illinois	August 1838	54.7	50.8	51	+0.2	-3.7
Average		51.9	46.5	45.4	-1.1	-6.5

Table 10.5 Van Buren's Two-Party Vote Share in 1836 Compared with the Democratic Two-Party Vote Share in Gubernatorial Elections between October 1838 and October 1839

State	Date of Gubernatorial Election	Van Buren Two-Party Vote Share, 1836	Democratic Two-Party Vote Share, October 1838 to October 1839
Maryland	October 1838	46.3	50.3
Ohio	October 1838	47.9	51.4
Pennsylvania	October 1838	51.2	51.1
Massachusetts	November 1838	44.8	44.7
New York	November 1838	54.6	48.6
New Hampshire	March 1839	75	56.1
Connecticut	April 1839	50.6	47.4
Rhode Island	April 1839	52.2	48.8
Tennessee	August 1839	42.1	51.3
Maine	September 1839	60.7	54.1
Vermont	September 1839	40	47.3
Michigan	October 1839	54	48.4
Georgia	October 1839	48.2	51.4
Average		51.4	50.1
Average without New Hampshire		49.4	49.6

party vote share in these thirteen states in the 1836 election was only a bit more than 1 percentage point greater than the average two-party vote share received by Democratic gubernatorial candidates during the year-long economic recovery; indeed, absent New Hampshire (where Van Buren won 75 percent of the vote in 1836), Van Buren's average two-party vote share in 1836 was nearly identical to the average Democratic two-party gubernatorial vote share between the fall of 1838 and the fall of 1839.[93]

There is considerable variation among states, of course. However, the state-level data in Table 10.4 establish two patterns: first, Democratic gubernatorial candidates during the panic of 1837–1838 tended to do worse than Van Buren had done in 1836 (Georgia and Vermont are the most notable exceptions);[94] second, Van Buren's vote share in 1840 tended to be closer to the Democratic vote share in 1837–1838 than to his own vote share in 1836 (Vermont and Georgia are again obvious exceptions, as is Tennessee). Particularly worth highlighting in view of our previous discussion of the electoral effects of antislavery is that in both Maine and Connecticut, two states Van Buren won in 1836 and lost in 1840, the president's two-party vote share in 1840 was virtually identical to the Democratic gubernatorial candidate's vote share at the height of the Panic of 1837. The parallels between Van Buren's electoral fortunes in 1840 and Democratic gubernatorial fortunes during the economic panic of 1837–1838 not only support Cambreleng's economic thesis but offer further reason to doubt that Van Buren's defeat was attributable to the Whigs' colorful log-cabin campaign.

Of course, Cambreleng's economic analysis conveniently absolved Van Buren and his party of blame. Yet he was fundamentally correct in his understanding of the election. The Van Buren administration's policies had little to do with the economic recovery that began toward the end of the summer of 1838 and extended into the early fall of 1839 or with the economic downturn that began toward the end of 1839 and continued through the presidential election (and beyond).[95] The disruption to the economy was fueled in part by a steep decline in the price of cotton, which stemmed both from a drop in demand from Britain and from a bumper domestic crop, neither of which were within Van Buren's control. Nor was Van Buren responsible for the short-lived boom in state governments' spending on infrastructure projects in the Northwest that helped lift the economy in 1838 or the constriction of credit that led states to halt or slow construction in 1839. Between the summer of 1839 and the fall of 1840, wholesale commodity prices fell by about 33 percent, yet, as Peter Temin has shown, "the role of government in the deflation . . . was minimal." The administration's deficit spending—largely due to lower revenues from tariffs, which were the federal government's major source of revenue—may have marginally boosted the economy, but the economy's fluctuations between 1837 and 1840—first down, then up, then down again—were largely independent of the Van Buren administration's policies.[96]

As Cambreleng's analysis suggests, Van Buren's challenge was not only that in the crucial year leading up to the election, the economy experienced severe and sustained economic deflation and a contraction in available credit. He also had to contend with the crucial fact that the Democrats had been in the White House for twelve years. Election forecasting models tell us that these are precisely the conditions under which an incumbent is most likely to be defeated. The longer the party has been in power, the more likely the president is to be blamed for adverse economic conditions.[97] Despite the enthusiastic campaign rallies for Tippecanoe and Tyler too, the presidential vote in 1840 was fundamentally a retrospective economic judgment against the incumbent, a vote against the "used up man" more than a vote for Harrison and an embrace of Whig policy doctrines.[98] It was time for a change.

THE TURNOUT STORY

If the 1840 election seems a classic instance of economic retrospective voting (that is, an electoral judgment about the incumbent based on the nation's economic conditions), where does that leave the storied log-cabin campaign? Were all the rallies and rhetoric really for nothing? Was the verdict already determined by the economic downturn and the electorate's appetite for change after twelve years of Jacksonian rule? Was it all a magnificent carnival, fun to watch but of little importance in selecting the nation's next president?

If the outcome of the 1840 election seems like a prime illustration of retrospective voting, the unprecedented spike in voter turnout would seem indisputable evidence that campaigns matter. Turnout nationwide jumped from roughly 57 percent in 1836 to an astounding 80 percent in 1840.[99] In only four years, the number of voters increased by nearly 60 percent, from 1.5 million to about 2.4 million. No subsequent presidential election has come close to rivaling this percentage increase in turnout. Election forecasting models might be good for understanding and even predicting ordinary elections, but clearly 1840 was no ordinary election or campaign. How could one reliably predict an election with so many apparent "first-time voters"?[100]

But as effective as the 1840 campaign was in boosting turnout, the turnout story is more complex than is sometimes portrayed. Too often, the effect of the 1840 campaign on turnout is measured solely by the massive difference in turnout between the presidential elections of 1836 and 1840. What this analysis neglects is that most of the mobilization of supposedly "new" voters took place well before the 1840 campaign in the congressional and state elections of 1838 and 1839.[101] Party organization and campaigns were, of course, crucial in getting these voters to the polls, but the lion's share of mobilization of new voters occurred *before* Tip and Ty had been chosen as the Whig Party's nominees and before the Whigs had embarked on the log-cabin campaign.

Consider, for instance, New Hampshire, which seems at first glance a textbook example of a presidential campaign expanding the electorate in unprecedented ways. Turnout in the 1840 presidential contest reached a stunning 88 percent, far beyond the paltry 38 percent who voted for president in 1836—a jump in raw numbers from roughly 25,000 to 60,000 voters. But in fact, the increase in turnout in 1840 was much less dramatic and the number of first-time voters relatively small. The steepest rise in turnout occurred not in 1840 but in 1838 and 1839. Whereas in 1837, only

37 percent of the electorate voted in the gubernatorial election, in both 1838 and 1839 turnout topped 80 percent. The same pattern is evident in the congressional elections, in which turnout went from 35 percent in 1837 to 82 percent in 1839. The 1840 presidential election saw only an incremental increase in turnout—about 5,000 more people voted in the 1840 presidential election than in the state and congressional elections of 1839.[102]

Or take the case of Tennessee, where turnout jumped from 57 percent in the presidential election of 1836 to nearly 90 percent in the presidential election of 1840—an increase from about 62,000 to 108,000 voters. Again, though, the 1840 campaign looks less wondrous when compared to the 1839 state and congressional elections, in which 90 percent of the electorate cast a ballot in the gubernatorial contest, up from the 76 percent who voted in 1837. Virtually the same number of voters turned out in the 1840 presidential contest between Harrison and Van Buren as had turned out eighteen months before to elect James Polk governor.[103]

One should not overstate the point. In most states, turnout in the 1840 presidential election was higher than it had been in the immediately preceding congressional elections. As Table 10.6 shows, of the eleven states that held congressional elections in 1839, only Kentucky and Mississippi saw turnout in the presidential race that was lower than in the 1839 congressional races, and in both cases the decline was small.[104] Turnout on average in these eleven states was about 8 percentage points higher in the 1840 presidential election than it had been in the 1839 congressional election. However, the 1839 congressional election turnout far more closely resembled the 1840 presidential turnout than it did the 1836 presidential turnout. Table 10.7 shows that the same basic pattern holds in the fourteen states that held congressional races in 1838.[105] By 1838 and 1839, states on average had already experienced two-thirds of the turnout rate increase that is usually attributed to the 1840 election and its mesmerizing log-cabin campaign.[106]

Even this calculation, however, greatly overstates the number of new voters in the 1840 presidential election. In most states, there were relatively few first-time voters in the 1840 *presidential* election. One way to show this is by comparing turnout rates in the eight states that had congressional elections between July and October 1840. As Table 10.8 shows, in these eight states, turnout on average in the congressional elections between July and October was almost the same as turnout in the November presidential election.[107] In half of these states, the presidential turnout was higher, and

Table 10.6 Voter Turnout Rates in States with Congressional Elections in Odd-Numbered Years

State	1836 Presidential Election	1837 Congressional Elections	1839 Congressional Elections	1840 Presidential Election	Percentage Turnout Increase Achieved by 1839
Kentucky	60.8	62.7	76.6	74.3	100
Mississippi	64.2	54.3	89.5	88.2	100
Tennessee	57.3	83.4	86.3	89.7	90
New Hampshire	38.2	34.9	82.1	87.7	89
Rhode Island	23.7	31.2	30.5	33.6	76
Connecticut	52.2	61.0	67.9	75.6	67
Indiana	69.4	72.2	78.0	86.1	51
North Carolina	52.7	57.3	66.9	83.7	46
Maryland	67.6	54.8	74.1	84.5	38
Alabama	64.8	72.9	68.1	89.7	32
Virginia	35.4	34.0	40.7	54.7	28
Average	53.3	56.2	69.1	77.1	66

Table 10.7 Voter Turnout Rates in States with Congressional Elections in Even-Numbered Years

State	1836 Presidential Election	1838 Congressional Elections	1840 Presidential Election	Percentage Turnout Increase Achieved by 1838
Arkansas	28.8	71.6	67.5	100
Maine	37.1	82.8	83.7	98
Michigan	34.7	74.6	85.4	79
Missouri	35.3	66.3	75.2	78
Pennsylvania	53.1	72.0	77.5	77
Georgia	61.9	81.8	92.4	65
Louisiana	19.1	30.7	39.4	57
New York	70.4	82.0	91.9	54
Vermont	52.8	63.6	73.9	51
Illinois	43.3	62.9	86.0	46
New Jersey	69.2	73.5	80.5	38
Massachusetts	42.8	48.5	66.6	24
Ohio	75.6	69.9	84.5	0
Delaware	69.5	67.8	82.8	0
Average	49.5	67.7	77.7	65

Table 10.8 Turnout Rates in States with Congressional Elections between July and October 1840

State (and month of congressional election)	1840 Congressional Elections	1840 Presidential Election	Difference
Louisiana (July)	33.7	39.4	+5.7
Missouri (August)	72.9	75.2	+2.3
Vermont (September)	78.1	73.9	−4.2
Maine (September)	78.7	83.7	+5.0
Arkansas (October)	78.1	67.5	−10.6
Georgia (October)	92.4	88.7	−3.7
Ohio (October)	84.8	84.5	−0.3
Pennsylvania (October)	68.8	77.5	+8.7
Average	73.4	73.8	+0.4

in half, it was lower, and in none of the states was the difference large.[108] Moreover, as Table 10.9 shows, in only one (New Hampshire) of the six additional states that held gubernatorial elections in 1840 prior to the November presidential election was the difference between turnout in the gubernatorial election and the presidential election more than 3 percentage points—and in that one case, as we have seen, turnout had already topped 80 percent in congressional and gubernatorial elections in 1838 and 1839.[109] In Indiana, for instance, about 117,200 people cast ballots for governor in August, while just shy of 117,000 people cast ballots for president in November, and in North Carolina, 80,387 voted for governor in August, and 80,735 voted for president in November. Voters, in short, did turn out in record numbers in 1840, but not only in November and not only to elect Tippecanoe and Tyler too.

Perhaps the most underappreciated aspect of the 1840 turnout story is what happened *after* the November election in the states that still had not selected their congressional representatives for the upcoming Twenty-Seventh Congress. Ten states selected members of Congress in the spring following the 1840 presidential election—and those states, which would send 87 House members to the new Congress, would determine the size of the Whig majority, or indeed whether the Whigs would have a majority at all. In each of those ten states, as Table 10.10 shows, turnout declined substantially after the presidential election. On average, turnout was 25 percentage points lower in the spring congressional election than in November's presidential election.[110]

Table 10.9 Turnout Rates in States with Gubernatorial Elections in 1840 before November

State (and month of gubernatorial election)	1840 Gubernatorial Elections	1840 Presidential Election	Difference
New Hampshire (March)	74.2	87.7	+13.5
Connecticut (April)	73.4	75.6	+2.2
Rhode Island (April)	32.2	33.6	+1.1
Kentucky (August)	77.4	74.3	−3.1
North Carolina (August)	83.3	83.7	+0.4
Indiana (August)	86.1	86.1	0.0
Average	71.1	73.5	+2.4

Political scientists might be tempted to see this as part of a normal pattern of surge and decline between presidential and so-called off-year elections,[111] but in fact, this development was novel. After the 1836 presidential election, as Table 10.10 also shows, the same ten states experienced an average *increase* of 4 percentage points between November's presidential election and the congressional elections the following year. In only three of the states was turnout in 1837 lower than it had been in November 1836, and in only one of these states (Maryland) was the decline anything more than marginal. Even if one removes the outlier of Tennessee, where turnout zoomed from 57.3 in the 1836 presidential election to 83.4 percent in the following congressional election, the other nine states still averaged a small 1.5 percent increase in turnout in the following year's congressional elections. The average increase in turnout in the odd-year congressional elections following the November presidential election was even greater in previous years.

The unprecedented decline in turnout in the 1841 congressional elections admittedly had a lot to do with some unusual circumstances owing to Harrison's decision to convene the first session of the new Twenty-Seventh Congress in June rather than in December, as would normally be the case. Six states (Alabama, Kentucky, Indiana, Tennessee, North Carolina, and Maryland) that normally held congressional elections in July and August (or in Maryland's case October) that coincided with their state elections were compelled to move their congressional elections forward to the spring.[112] One of the reasons that congressional elections tended to have higher turnout rates than presidential elections was precisely because congressional

Table 10.10 Turnout Rates by State in the Presidential Election Compared with Turnout in the Following Year's Congressional Elections, 1836/1837 and 1840/1841

State	1836 Presidential Election	1837 Congressional Elections	Change	1840 Presidential Election	1841 Congressional Elections	Change
New Hampshire	38.2	34.9	-4.3	87.7	73.7	-14.0
Connecticut	52.2	61.0	+8.8	75.6	62.5	-13.1
Virginia	35.4	34.0	-1.4	54.7	32.8	-21.9
Rhode Island	23.7	31.2	+7.5	33.6	10.6	-23.0
Kentucky	60.8	62.7	+1.9	74.3	51.4	-22.9
Indiana	69.4	72.2	+2.8	86.1	61.7	-24.4
North Carolina	52.7	57.3	+4.6	83.7	53.4	-30.3
Alabama	64.8	72.9	+8.1	89.7	56.3	-33.4
Maryland	67.6	54.8	-12.8	84.5	53.3	-31.2
Tennessee	57.3	83.4	+26.1	89.7	53.0	-36.7
Average	52.2	56.4	+4.2	76.0	50.9	-25.1

elections, unlike presidential elections, typically took place at the same time as state elections.

However, even if we limit our analysis of 1841 to the four states (New Hampshire, Connecticut, Virginia, and Rhode Island) that held congressional elections in the spring that coincided with their state elections, there is still a consistent pattern of decline (the average drop is reduced to 18 percentage points) after the presidential election. Moreover, three of the other six states (Alabama, Maryland, and Tennessee) held gubernatorial elections in the summer of 1841, and each of those elections also experienced a falloff in turnout, albeit much more modest, ranging from 6 percentage points in Tennessee to 14 points in Alabama. Indeed, of the thirteen states that held gubernatorial contests in 1841, not one exceeded the turnout rate achieved in the 1840 presidential election.[113] In contrast, ten of the twelve states that held gubernatorial elections in 1837 had higher turnout rates in those elections than in the 1836 presidential election.[114] Table 10.11 further illustrates the difference by isolating the six states that held gubernatorial elections in both 1837 and 1841 and held their congressional elections in even-numbered years. In these states, turnout had been much higher in the gubernatorial contests of 1837 than in the preceding presidential contest, yet turnout in the gubernatorial contests of 1841 lagged well behind turnout in the 1840 presidential election.

The steep decline in turnout in the spring 1841 congressional elections was particularly devastating to the demoralized Democrats, who lost an additional twelve House seats, an even higher rate of loss than they had suffered in the relatively high-turnout congressional elections of 1840.[115] In Indiana, where turnout declined below even the turnout levels reached in the 1836 presidential election and the 1837 congressional elections, the Whigs picked up four seats, giving the party six of the delegation's seven seats, and in Maryland, where turnout also dropped below the levels attained in 1836 and 1837, the Whigs picked up three seats, giving them six of the state's eight representatives. In Virginia, where turnout rates also dropped below 1836–1837 levels—despite congressional elections being held coincident with state elections, as always—the Democrats lost three seats to the Whigs. In North Carolina, too, where turnout plummeted by more than 30 percentage points from November, the Whigs gained three seats, leaving them with eight of the state's thirteen representatives. In Tennessee, where the Whigs already held a majority of the seats, they picked up an additional one. Only in Alabama did the Democrats gain a couple of seats. The gain of these twelve additional seats gave the Whigs control of

Table 10.11 Turnout Rates by State in the Presidential Election Compared with Turnout in the Following Year's Gubernatorial Elections, 1836/1837 and 1840/1841

State	1836 Presidential Election	1837 Gubernatorial Elections	Change	1840 Presidential Election	1841 Gubernatorial Elections	Change
Georgia	61.9	87.0	+25.1	88.7	86.8	-1.1
Maine	37.1	66.0	+28.9	83.7	76.2	-7.5
Massachusetts	43.4	47.6	+4.2	66.6	57.6	-9.0
Michigan	34.7	76.6	+41.9	85.4	66.9	-18.6
Mississippi	64.2	82.4	+18.2	88.2	80.7	-7.3
Vermont	52.8	59.6	+6.8	73.9	69.7	-4.2
Average	49	70	+21	81	73	-8

nearly 60 percent of the seats in the House of Representatives in the new Congress. The significance of these relatively low-turnout spring elections is underscored by the fact that had the Democrats picked up twelve seats in these spring elections, they would have all but erased their 1840 House losses and maintained, albeit only barely, their control of the House of Representatives.

The precipitous drop in turnout after November's presidential election is a tribute to the importance of the 1840 campaign in driving voters to the polls, both on the Democratic and on the Whig side, not only in November but throughout the summer and fall of 1840. The campaign clearly mattered, although ironically, at least judging by the 1841 results, it may have helped Van Buren at least as much if not more than Harrison because demoralized Democrats may have needed the campaign's energy and excitement even more than the already motivated Whigs.[116] What is certainly true is that Democrats were crucial to the record-breaking turnout in 1840. A Whig surge with Democrats staying home would have produced lower turnout and a more lopsided popular vote. The election's astounding 80 percent turnout rate supports Richard McCormick's contention that "Democrats campaigned as energetically as their opponents."[117] Arguably, the record-setting turnout may have helped to make the 1840 presidential vote closer than one might have expected given how much the economic fundamentals of the contest were stacked against Van Buren.

The final important chapter of the turnout story is more enduring than the ephemeral if colorful tale of log cabins and hard cider, for the campaign fundamentally reset American turnout patterns. The 80 percent turnout in the 1840 presidential election was unprecedented but rapidly became the new normal. Turnout would reach close to or exceed that number in most of the remaining presidential elections in the nineteenth century, including in 1844. In no presidential contest between 1840 and the end of the century did turnout fall below 70 percent. Moreover, the modern pattern of lower turnout in midterm congressional elections than presidential elections began with the 1840 election. Before 1840, turnout in off-year congressional elections held in the second and third years of a president's term was almost invariably higher than turnout in presidential elections—the sole exception was a marginal decline in congressional turnout in the 1830 and 1831 congressional elections following the 1828 presidential election. After 1840, in contrast, congressional turnout in midterm elections never exceeded turnout in presidential elections. This change, moreover, was not an evolutionary one but a dramatic break that began with the 1840 election.

Between 1796 and 1839, turnout in the midterm congressional elections of the second and third years of a president's term exceeded the turnout in the presidential election by an average of 12 to 13 percentage points, and the 1838 and 1839 midterms were typical in this respect, with turnout about 14 percentage points higher than in the 1836 presidential election. In contrast, turnout in the 1840 presidential election *exceeded* turnout in the midterm elections of 1842 and 1843 by 18 percentage points, and between 1840 and 1899, turnout in presidential elections exceeded by about 13 percentage points the turnout in the subsequent off-year congressional elections.[118] The drama of the 1840 election, in sum, helped to thrust the presidential election onto center stage—a stage the presidency never relinquished, even when turnout rates began to decline in the twentieth century.

This is among the great ironies of the 1840 election. The Whig Party was forged in opposition to a Jacksonian presidency that the Whigs believed had slipped its constitutional tether. Their presidential nominee, William Henry Harrison, pledged at every opportunity to get the presidency out of the law-making business and to restore Congress's rightful place of pre-eminence in the founders' constitutional structure. And yet, despite being determined to shrink the presidency to its proper size, Harrison and the Whigs orchestrated a campaign that did what Jackson, for all his populist appeals, had never been able to achieve: turn the contest for the presidency into the nation's most riveting political spectacle. If a central feature of American political development is the way in which "presidents increasingly took center stage in a national political drama," then the 1840 election should be counted as a formative act in the emergence of what political scientist Bruce Miroff terms "the presidential spectacle."[119]

A TRAGIC EPILOGUE

On March 4, 1841, Harrison was sworn in as president of the United States, whereupon he delivered what is still today the longest inaugural address in American history (see Appendix C). A month later, he was dead, becoming the nation's shortest-serving president. Many have seen the two events as causally connected. Bareheaded, without overcoat or gloves, the sixty-eight-year-old Harrison spoke for an hour and forty minutes on a cold and blustery day. That much is fact. But he spent the next three weeks after his inauguration running all around the nation's capital, visiting departments, going shopping, greeting well-wishers, writing letters, hosting dinners, issuing directives, and fending off office seekers, hardly the actions of a sick man. Not until the last week of March did Harrison begin to feel ill and call for a doctor. After ten days of what passed for medical care—frequent enemas and blistering by use of a hot cup pressed against the skin as well as a steady diet of laudanum, opium, castor oil, and brandy—the oldest man to be elected president became the first to die in office, likely from enteric fever and septic shock and not, as his doctor assumed, pneumonia.[120]

Harrison's death made John Tyler the nation's first "accidental president." During the campaign, gleeful Whigs had sung, "We will vote for Tyler therefore / without a why or wherefore," but after Harrison's demise, few were still chortling. As everyone knew, Tyler was a states' rights Democrat from way back. He distrusted all things national. In a Senate speech in 1833, he had groused, "Everything . . . is running into nationality. You cannot walk along the streets [of the nation's capital] without seeing the word on almost every sign—national hotel, national boot-black, national blacksmith, national oyster-house." Although he had abandoned the party of Jackson, he had not modified his states' rights sympathies or softened his opposition to a national bank. Nor had he altered his conviction that slavery was beneficent and should be aggressively defended and expanded. Twice in the Twenty-Seventh Congress's summer session, Tyler vetoed the Whigs' cherished national bank, prompting every member of his cabinet except Secretary of State Daniel Webster to resign at the session's close on September 13, 1841. (Webster would resign eighteen months later in protest of Tyler's plan to annex Texas.) Within six months of taking office, Tyler had been effectively read out of the party, making him a president without a party and leaving the Whigs in the all-too-familiar position of opposing the nation's chief executive.[121]

For all the attention lavished on the spectacular log-cabin campaign, the most consequential drama of the 1840 election would prove to be the one that played out at the Whigs' national nominating convention in Harrisburg in December 1839. If Van Buren's defeat was inescapable given the state of the economy and the Democratic Party's twelve years in power, Tyler's selection was very much a choice, one that by September 1841 virtually every Whig delegate who had been at Harrisburg wished they could do over. In one of history's crueler ironies, by blocking Clay's nomination for president, those most sympathetic to antislavery and most worried about not alienating antislavery voters ended up helping elevate to the presidency a man who not only would defend slavery where it was but was determined to spread it westward into Texas. In the cruelest twist of all, when the Whigs finally did nominate the antiannexationist Clay in 1844, he was beaten by an even more formidable proponent of annexation, James Polk.

We can't rerun the reel of history, but if the 1840 election was a vote for change more than it was a vote for the Whig candidate, a thumbs-down verdict on Van Buren's economic stewardship more than a thumbs-up for Tippecanoe, it compels us to ask whether the Whigs could have won in 1840 with Clay as their standard-bearer. After all, Clay came within a whisker (5,000 votes in New York) of winning the presidency in 1844, a far less propitious moment for the Whigs than 1840, when they had the benefit of running against an unpopular incumbent saddled with a tanking economy. The strength of party voting, as seen in the congruence between gubernatorial and congressional results in 1839 and 1840 and the presidential result in 1840, provides further reason to think that partisanship would have trumped any misgivings about the party's nominee. On the other hand, Harrison's victory in 1840 was no popular-vote landslide. Even if the effect of choosing Harrison over Clay was relatively small, that could easily have been enough to lose the Whigs Pennsylvania, Maine, New York, and Michigan, each of which was decided by relatively small margins in 1840 and each of which went for Polk over Clay in 1844. However, even if Clay had lost these four states in 1840, he would still have been elected president, barely, with one electoral vote to spare, so long as he held the remaining Harrison states in his column. The only other Harrison state in which the margin of victory was lower than 5 points was New Jersey, but Clay carried that state in 1844 as well as 1832, and there is scant reason to think he would have failed to carry it in 1840. After New Jersey, the next-closest race in a Harrison state was Mississippi, where the candidates were separated by 7 points, but it seems highly improbable that Clay would have fared less well than Harrison; if anything, Clay would likely have done a bit better. The only other states that Harrison won by fewer than 10 points were Maryland (7.5) and Ohio (8.5), and the substantial margin of victory combined with the fact that Clay won both these states in 1844 make it almost certain that Clay would have carried both had he been the nominee in 1840. In sum, it is likely that Clay could have been elected had he been the party's nominee, even if we assume that he would have lost every state that Harrison lost, which is by no means certain given Van Buren's razor-thin margin of victory in Virginia.

Of course, the election of 1840 was about more than the presidency, particularly in a state such as New York in which state and congressional elections were held on the same dates as the presidential election. Thurlow Weed's determination to prevent a Clay candidacy in 1840 was rooted above all in a fear that Clay would cost the party control of the state legislature and especially the governorship. The 1840 results arguably vindicate Weed's concern. Harrison beat Van Buren by 13,000 votes in New York, but Governor Seward's margin of victory was only a bit over 5,000 votes. With Clay at the top of the ticket instead of Harrison, Seward could very well have gone down to defeat, as the Whigs' gubernatorial nominee Millard Fillmore did in 1844.[122]

Historical hindsight is 20/20. Notwithstanding the election's tragic epilogue, Whig delegates at Harrisburg picked a winning ticket that not only secured them the presidency for the first time in the party's history but helped them triumph at the state and congressional levels in elections throughout 1840. Their choice unified the party—thanks in no small part to Clay—and helped set the stage for an exuberant campaign that not only spurred unprecedented participation, by men as well as women, but helped to forge the idea of the presidential campaign as a central event in the lives of Americans. It helped give birth to the idea that presidential campaigns matter, even if, ironically, it is better remembered as a case study in why economic and political fundamentals are often more important determinants of the presidential vote than even the most memorable campaign.

POPULAR VOTE FOR PRESIDENT IN 1836 AND 1840

Table 1. Popular Vote by State in 1836, Arrayed by Van Buren Vote Percentage

State (electoral votes)	Van Buren		Harrison		White		Webster	
	Votes	%	Votes	%	Votes	%	Votes	%
New Hampshire (7)	18,697	75.0	6,228	25.0				
Arkansas (3)	2,380	64.1			1,334	35.9		
Maine (10)	22,285	60.7	14,803	39.3				
Missouri (4)	10,995	60.0			7,337	40.0		
Virginia (23)	30,556	56.6			23,384	43.3		
Alabama (7)	20,638	55.3			16,658	44.7		
Illinois (5)	18,369	54.7	15,220	45.3				
New York (42)	166,795	54.6	138,548	45.4				
Michigan (3)	6,507	54.0	5,545	46.0				
North Carolina (15)	26,631	53.1			23,521	46.9		
Rhode Island (4)	5,673	52.2	2,710	47.8				
Louisiana (5)	3,842	51.7			3,583	48.3		
Mississippi (4)	10,297	51.3			9,782	48.7		
Pennsylvania (30)	91,466	51.2	87,235	48.8				
Connecticut (8)	19,294	50.6	18,799	49.4				
New Jersey (8)	25,592	49.5	26,137	50.5				
Georgia (11)	22,778	48.2			24,481	51.8		
Ohio (21)	87,122	47.9	105,809	52.1				

State								
Kentucky (15)	33,229	47.4	36,861	52.6				
Delaware (3)	4,154	46.7	4,736	53.3				
Maryland (10)	22,267	46.3	25,852	53.7				
Massachusetts (14)	33,486	44.8					41,201	55.2
Indiana (9)	33,084	44.5	41,339	55.5				
Tennessee (15)	26,170	42.1			36,027	57.9		
Vermont (7)	14,040	40.1	20,994	59.9				
Totals	764,176	50.9	550,816	36.7	146,017	9.7	41,201	2.7

Source: *Presidential Elections, 1789–2008* (CQ Press, 2010), 128. Percentages have been adjusted in a few states to account for the removal of miscellaneous "other" votes, which totaled 1,234 nationwide, 90 percent of which were in Maine. The vote totals for Michigan in Michael J. Dubin, *United States Presidential Elections, 1788–1860* (Jefferson, NC: McFarland, 2002) show Van Buren with a substantially larger popular vote advantage, with close to two-thirds of the popular vote.

Table 2. Popular Vote by State in 1840, Arrayed by Harrison Vote Percentage

State (electoral votes)	Harrison		Van Buren		Birney	
	Votes	%	Votes	%	Votes	%
Kentucky (15)	58,448	64.2	32,616	35.8		
Vermont (7)	32,440	63.9	18,006	35.5	317	0.6
Rhode Island (4)	5,213	61.4	3,263	38.4	19	0.2
Louisiana (5)	11,296	59.7	7,616	40.3		
North Carolina (15)	46,657	57.7	34,168	42.3		
Massachusetts (14)	72,852	57.4	52,355	41.3	1,618	1.3
Georgia (11)	40,339	55.8	31,983	44.2		
Indiana (9)	65,280	55.8	51,696	44.2	30	0.0
Tennessee (15)	60,194	55.7	46,951	44.3		
Connecticut (8)	31,598	55.5	25,281	44.4	57	0.1
Delaware (3)	5,967	55.0	4,872	44.9		
Ohio (21)	144,023	54.3	123,944	45.4	903	0.3
Maryland (10)	33,528	53.8	28,752	46.2		
Mississippi (4)	19,515	53.4	17,010	46.6		
Michigan (3)	22,933	51.7	21,096	47.6	321	0.7
New Jersey (8)	33,351	51.7	31,034	48.1	69	0.1
New York (42)	226,001	51.2	212,733	48.2	2,809	0.6
Maine (10)	46,612	50.1	46,190	49.9	194	0.2
Pennsylvania (30)	144,023	50.0	143,672	49.9	343	0.1
Virginia (23)	42,637	49.4	53,757	50.6		
Illinois (5)	45,574	48.9	47,441	50.9	160	0.2
Alabama (7)	28,515	45.6	33,996	54.4		
New Hampshire (7)	26,310	44.4	32,774	55.4	126	0.2
Arkansas (3)	5,160	43.6	6,679	56.4		
Missouri (4)	22,954	43.4	29,969	56.6		
Totals	1,275,390	52.9	1,128,854	46.8	6,966	0.3

Source: *Presidential Elections, 1789-2008* (CQ Press, 2010), 129. Percentages have been adjusted in a few states to account for the removal of miscellaneous "other" votes, which totaled 767 nationwide, nearly 80 percent of which were in Indiana. CQ omits all votes for Birney in Connecticut, Michigan, Maine, and Pennsylvania, and so in those cases, I have taken the vote totals from Michael J. Dubin, *United States Presidential Elections, 1788–1860* (Jefferson, NC: McFarland, 2002); and Reinhard O. Johnson, *The Liberty Party, 1840–1848: Antislavery Third-Party Politics in the United States* (Baton Rouge: Louisiana State University Press, 2009), 20. I have also followed Dubin and Johnson for Birney's vote totals in New Hampshire. Vote percentages for Harrison and Van Buren have been adjusted accordingly.

DEMOCRATIC PARTY PLATFORM, MAY 6, 1840

1. Resolved, That the federal government is one of limited powers, derived solely from the constitution, and the grants of power shown therein, ought to be strictly construed by all the departments and agents of the government, and that it is inexpedient and dangerous to exercise doubtful constitutional powers.

2. Resolved, That the constitution does not confer upon the general government the power to commence and carry on, a general system of internal improvements.

3. Resolved, That the constitution does not confer authority upon the federal government, directly or indirectly, to assume the debts of the several states, contracted for local internal improvements, or other state purposes; nor would such assumption be just or expedient.

4. Resolved, That justice and sound policy forbid the federal government to foster one branch of industry to the detriment of another, or to cherish the interests of one portion to the injury of another portion of our common country—that every citizen and every section of the country, has a right to demand and insist upon an equality of rights and privileges, and to complete and ample protection of person and property from domestic violence, or foreign aggression.

5. Resolved, That it is the duty of every branch of the government, to enforce and practice the most rigid economy, in conducting our public affairs, and that no more revenue ought to be raised, than is required to defray the necessary expenses of the government.

6. Resolved, That congress has no power to charter a national bank; that we believe such an institution one of deadly hostility to the best interests of the country, dangerous to our republican institutions and the liberties of the people, and calculated to place the business of the country within the control of a concentrated money power, and above the laws and the will of the people.

7. Resolved, That congress has no power, under the constitution, to interfere with or control the domestic institutions of the several states, and that such states are the sole and proper judges of everything appertaining to their own affairs, not prohibited by the constitution; that all efforts by

abolitionists or others, made to induce congress to interfere with questions of slavery, or to take incipient steps in relation thereto, are calculated to lead to the most alarming and dangerous consequences, and that all such efforts have an inevitable tendency to diminish the happiness of the people, and endanger the stability and permanency of the union, and ought not to be countenanced by any friend to our political institutions.

8. Resolved, That the separation of the moneys of the government from banking institutions, is indispensable for the safety of the funds of the government, and the rights of the people.

9. Resolved, That the liberal principles embodied by Jefferson in the Declaration of Independence, and sanctioned in the constitution, which makes ours the land of liberty, and the asylum of the oppressed of every nation, have ever been cardinal principles in the democratic faith; and every attempt to abridge the present privilege of becoming citizens, and the owners of soil among us, ought to be resisted with the same spirit which swept the alien and sedition laws from our statute-book.

Source: "1840 Democratic Party Platform," American Presidency Project, https://www.presidency.ucsb.edu/node/273160.

WILLIAM HENRY HARRISON INAUGURAL ADDRESS, MARCH 4, 1841

Called from a retirement which I had supposed was to continue for the residue of my life to fill the chief executive office of this great and free nation, I appear before you, fellow-citizens, to take the oaths which the Constitution prescribes as a necessary qualification for the performance of its duties; and in obedience to a custom coeval with our Government and what I believe to be your expectations I proceed to present to you a summary of the principles which will govern me in the discharge of the duties which I shall be called upon to perform.

It was the remark of a Roman consul in an early period of that celebrated Republic that a most striking contrast was observable in the conduct of candidates for offices of power and trust before and after obtaining them, they seldom carrying out in the latter case the pledges and promises made in the former. However much the world may have improved in many respects in the lapse of upward of two thousand years since the remark was made by the virtuous and indignant Roman, I fear that a strict examination of the annals of some of the modern elective governments would develop similar instances of violated confidence.

Although the fiat of the people has gone forth proclaiming me the Chief Magistrate of this glorious Union, nothing upon their part remaining to be done, it may be thought that a motive may exist to keep up the delusion under which they may be supposed to have acted in relation to my principles and opinions; and perhaps there may be some in this assembly who have come here either prepared to condemn those I shall now deliver, or, approving them, to doubt the sincerity with which they are now uttered. But the lapse of a few months will confirm or dispel their fears. The outline of principles to govern and measures to be adopted by an Administration not yet begun will soon be exchanged for immutable history, and I shall stand either exonerated by my countrymen or classed with the mass of those who promised that they might deceive and flattered with the intention to betray. However strong may be my present purpose to realize the expectations of a magnanimous and confiding people, I too well understand the dangerous temptations to which I shall be exposed from the magnitude of the power which it has been the pleasure of the people to commit to my hands not to place my chief confidence upon the aid of that Almighty Power which has hitherto protected me and enabled me to bring to favorable issues other important but still greatly inferior trusts heretofore confided to me by my country.

The broad foundation upon which our Constitution rests being the people—a breath of theirs having made, as a breath can unmake, change, or modify it—it can be assigned to none of the great divisions of government but to that of democracy. If such is its theory, those who are called upon to administer it must recognize as its leading principle the duty of shaping their measures so as to produce the greatest good to the greatest number. But with these broad admissions, if we would compare the sovereignty acknowledged to exist in the mass of our people with the power claimed by other sovereignties, even by those which have been considered most purely democratic, we shall find a most essential difference. All others lay claim to power limited only by their own will. The majority of our citizens, on the contrary, possess a sovereignty with an amount of power precisely equal to that which has been granted to them by the parties to the national compact, and nothing beyond. We admit of no government by divine right, believing that so far as power is concerned the Beneficent Creator has made no distinction amongst men; that all are upon an equality, and that the only legitimate right to govern is an express grant of power from the governed. The Constitution of the United States is the instrument containing this grant of power to the several departments composing the Government. On an examination of that instrument it will be found to contain declarations of power granted and of power withheld. The latter is also susceptible of division into power which the majority had the right to grant, but which they do not think proper to intrust to their agents, and that which they could not have granted, not being possessed by themselves. In other words, there are certain rights possessed by each individual American citizen which in his compact with the others he has never surrendered. Some of them, indeed, he is unable to surrender, being, in the language of our system, unalienable. The boasted privilege of a Roman citizen was to him a shield only against a petty provincial ruler, whilst the proud democrat of Athens would console himself under a sentence of death for a supposed violation of the national faith—which no one understood and which at times was the subject of the mockery of all—or the banishment from his home, his family, and his country with or without an alleged cause, that it was the act not of a single tyrant or hated aristocracy, but of his assembled countrymen. Far different is the power of our sovereignty. It can interfere with no one's faith, prescribe forms of worship for no one's observance, inflict no punishment but after well-ascertained guilt, the result of investigation under rules prescribed by the Constitution itself. These precious privileges, and those scarcely less important of giving expression to his thoughts and opinions, either by writing or speaking, unrestrained but by the liability for injury to others, and that of a full participation in all the advantages which flow from the Government, the acknowledged property of all, the American citizen derives from no charter granted by his fellow-man. He claims them because he is himself a man, fashioned by the same Almighty hand as the rest of his species and entitled to a full share of the blessings with which He has endowed them. Notwithstanding the limited sovereignty possessed by the people of the United States and the restricted grant of power to the Government which they have adopted, enough has been given to accomplish all the objects for which it was created. It has been found powerful in war, and hitherto justice has been administered, and intimate union effected, domestic tranquillity preserved, and personal liberty secured to the citizen. As was to be expected, however, from the defect of language and the necessarily sententious manner in which the Constitution is written, disputes have arisen as to the amount of power which it has actually granted or was intended to grant.

This is more particularly the case in relation to that part of the instrument which treats of the legislative branch, and not only as regards the exercise of powers claimed under a general clause giving that body the authority to pass all laws necessary to carry into effect the specified powers, but in relation to the latter also. It is, however, consolatory to reflect that 'most' of the instances of alleged departure from the letter or spirit of the Constitution have ultimately received the sanction of a majority of the people. And the fact that many of our statesmen most distinguished for talent and patriotism have been at one time or other of their political career on both sides of each of the most warmly disputed questions forces upon us the inference that the errors, if errors there were, are attributable to the intrinsic difficulty in many instances of ascertaining the intentions of the framers of the Constitution rather than the influence of any sinister or unpatriotic motive. But the great danger to our institutions does not appear to me to be in a usurpation by the Government of power not granted by the people, but by the accumulation in one of the departments of that which was assigned to others. Limited as are the powers which have been granted, still enough have been granted to constitute a despotism if concentrated in one of the departments. This danger is greatly heightened, as it has been always observable that men are less jealous of encroachments of one department upon another than upon their own reserved rights. When the Constitution of the United States first came from the hands of the Convention which formed it, many of the sternest republicans of the day were alarmed at the extent of the power which had been granted to the Federal Government, and more particularly of that portion which had been assigned to the executive branch. There were in it features which appeared not to be in harmony with their ideas of a simple representative democracy or republic, and knowing the tendency of power to increase itself, particularly when exercised by a single individual, predictions were made that at no very remote period the Government would terminate in virtual monarchy. It would not become me to say that the fears of these patriots have been already realized; but as I sincerely believe that the tendency of measures and of men's opinions for some years past has been in that direction, it is, I conceive, strictly proper that I should take this occasion to repeat the assurances I have heretofore given of my determination to arrest the progress of that tendency if it really exists and restore the Government to its pristine health and vigor, as far as this can be effected by any legitimate exercise of the power placed in my hands.

I proceed to state in as summary a manner as I can my opinion of the sources of the evils which have been so extensively complained of and the correctives which may be applied. Some of the former are unquestionably to be found in the defects of the Constitution; others, in my judgment, are attributable to a misconstruction of some of its provisions. Of the former is the eligibility of the same individual to a second term of the Presidency. The sagacious mind of Mr. Jefferson early saw and lamented this error, and attempts have been made, hitherto without success, to apply the amendatory power of the States to its correction. As, however, one mode of correction is in the power of every President, and consequently in mine, it would be useless, and perhaps invidious, to enumerate the evils of which, in the opinion of many of our fellow-citizens, this error of the sages who framed the Constitution may have been the source and the bitter fruits which we are still to gather from it if it continues to disfigure our system. It may be observed, however, as a general remark, that republics can commit no greater error than to adopt or continue any feature in their systems of government which may be calculated to create or increase the lover of power in the bosoms of those to whom necessity obliges them to commit the management of their affairs; and surely nothing is more likely to produce such a state of mind than the long continuance of an office of high trust. Nothing can be more corrupting, nothing more destructive of all those noble feelings which belong to the character of a devoted republican patriot. When this corrupting passion once takes possession of the human mind, like the love of gold it becomes insatiable. It is the never-dying worm in his bosom, grows with his growth and strengthens with the declining years of its victim. If this is true, it is the part of wisdom for a republic to limit the service of that officer at least to whom she has intrusted the management of her foreign relations, the execution of her laws, and the command of her armies and navies to a period so short as to prevent his forgetting that he is the accountable agent, not the principal; the servant, not the master. Until an amendment of the Constitution can be effected public opinion may secure the desired object. I give my aid to it by renewing the pledge heretofore given that under no circumstances will I consent to serve a second term.

But if there is danger to public liberty from the acknowledged defects of the Constitution in the want of limit to the continuance of the Executive power in the same hands, there is, I apprehend, not much less from a misconstruction of that instrument as it regards the powers actually given. I can not conceive that by a fair construction any or either of its provisions would be found to constitute the President a part of the legislative power. It can not be claimed from the power to recommend, since, although enjoined as a duty upon him, it is a privilege which he holds in common with every other citizen; and although there may be something more of confidence in the propriety of the measures recommended in the one case than in the other, in the obligations of ultimate decision there can be no difference. In the language of the Constitution, "all the legislative powers" which it grants "are vested in the Congress of the United States." It would be a solecism in language to say that any portion of these is not included in the whole.

It may be said, indeed, that the Constitution has given to the Executive the power to annul the acts of the legislative body by refusing to them his assent. So a similar power has necessarily resulted from that instrument to the judiciary, and yet the judiciary forms no part of the Legislature. There is, it is true, this difference between these grants of power: The Executive can put his negative upon the acts of the Legislature for other cause than that of want of conformity to the Constitution, whilst the judiciary can only declare void those which violate that instrument. But the decision of the judiciary is final in such a case, whereas in every instance where the veto of the Executive is applied it may be overcome by a vote of two-thirds of both Houses of Congress. The negative upon the acts of the legislative by the executive authority, and that in the hands of one individual, would seem to be an incongruity in our system. Like some others of a similar character, however, it appears to be highly expedient, and if used only with the forbearance and in the spirit which was intended by its authors it may be productive of great good and be found one of the best safeguards to the Union. At the period of the formation of the Constitution the principle does not appear to have enjoyed much favor in the State governments. It existed but in two, and in one of these there was a plural executive. If we would search for the motives which operated upon the purely patriotic and enlightened assembly which framed the Constitution for the adoption of a provision so apparently repugnant to the leading democratic principle that the majority should govern, we must reject the idea that they anticipated from it any benefit to the ordinary course of legislation. They knew too well the high degree of intelligence which existed among the people and the enlightened character of the State legislatures not to have the fullest confidence that the two bodies elected by them would be worthy representatives of such constituents, and, of course, that they would require no aid in conceiving and maturing the measures which the circumstances of the country might require. And it is preposterous to suppose that a thought could for a moment have been entertained that the President, placed at the capital, in the center of the country, could better understand the wants and wishes of the people than their own immediate representatives, who spend a part of every year among them, living with them, often laboring with them, and bound to them by the triple tie of interest, duty, and affection. To assist or control Congress, then, in its ordinary legislation could not, I conceive, have been the motive for conferring the veto power on the President. This argument acquires additional force from the fact of its never having been thus used by the first six Presidents—and two of them were members of the Convention, one presiding over its deliberations and the other bearing a larger share in consummating the labors of that august body than any other person. But if bills were never returned to Congress by either of the Presidents above referred to upon the ground of their being inexpedient or not as well adapted as they might be to the wants of the people, the veto was applied upon that of want of conformity to the Constitution or because errors had been committed from a too hasty enactment.

There is another ground for the adoption of the veto principle, which had probably more influence in recommending it to the Convention than any other. I refer to the security which it gives to the just and equitable action of the Legislature upon all parts of the Union. It could not but have occurred to the Convention that in a country so extensive, embracing so great a variety of soil and climate, and consequently of products, and which from the same causes must ever exhibit a great difference in the amount of the population of its various sections, calling for a great diversity in the employments of the people, that the legislation of the majority might not always justly regard the rights and interests of the minority, and that acts of this character might be passed under an express grant by the words of the Constitution, and therefore not within the competency of the judiciary to declare void; that however enlightened and patriotic they might suppose from past experience the members of Congress might be, and however largely partaking, in the general, of the liberal feelings of the people, it was impossible to expect that bodies so constituted should not sometimes be controlled by local interests and sectional feelings. It was proper, therefore, to provide some umpire from whose situation and mode of appointment more independence and freedom from such influences might be expected. Such a one was afforded by the executive department constituted by the Constitution. A person elected to that high office, having his constituents in every section, State, and subdivision of the Union, must consider himself bound by the most solemn sanctions to guard, protect, and defend the rights of all and of every portion, great or small, from the injustice and oppression of the rest. I consider the veto power, therefore, given by the Constitution to the Executive of the United States solely as a conservative power, to be used only first, to protect the Constitution from violation; secondly, the people from the effects of hasty legislation where their will has been probably disregarded or not well understood, and, thirdly, to prevent the effects of combinations violative of the rights of minorities. In reference to the second of these objects I may observe that I consider it the right and privilege of the people to decide disputed points of the Constitution arising from the general grant of power to Congress to carry into effect the powers expressly given; and I believe with Mr. Madison that "repeated recognitions under varied circumstances in acts of the legislative, executive, and judicial branches of the Government, accompanied by indications in different modes of the concurrence of the general will of the nation," as affording to the President sufficient authority for his considering such disputed points as settled.

Upward of half a century has elapsed since the adoption of the present form of government. It would be an object more highly desirable than the gratification of the curiosity of speculative statesmen if its precise situation could be ascertained, a fair exhibit made of the operations of each of its departments, of the powers which they respectively claim and exercise, of the collisions which have occurred between them or between the whole Government and those of the States or either of them. We could then compare our actual condition after fifty years' trial of our system with what it was in the commencement of its operations and ascertain whether the predictions of the patriots who opposed its adoption or the confident hopes of its advocates have been best realized. The great dread of the former seems to have been that the reserved powers of the States would be absorbed by those of the Federal Government and a consolidated power established, leaving to the States the shadow only of that independent action for which they had so zealously contended and on the preservation of which they relied as the last hope of liberty. Without denying that the result to which they looked with so much apprehension is in the way of being realized, it is obvious that they did not clearly see the mode of its accomplishment. The General Government has seized upon none of the reserved rights of the States. As far as any open warfare may have gone, the State authorities have amply maintained their rights. To a casual observer our system presents no appearance of discord between the different members which compose it. Even the addition of many new ones has produced no jarring. They move in their respective orbits in perfect harmony with the central head and with each other. But there is still an undercurrent at work by which, if not seasonably checked, the worst apprehensions of our antifederal patriots will be realized, and not only will the State authorities be overshadowed by the great increase of power in the executive department of the General Government, but the character of that Government, if not its designation, be essentially and radically changed. This state of things has been in part effected by causes inherent in the Constitution and in part by the never-failing tendency of political power to increase itself. By making the President the sole distributer of all the patronage of the Government the framers of the Constitution do not appear to have anticipated at how short a period it would become a formidable instrument to control the free operations of the State governments. Of trifling importance at first, it had early in Mr. Jefferson's Administration become so powerful as to create great alarm in the mind of that patriot from the potent influence it might exert in controlling the freedom of the elective franchise. If such could have then been the effects of its influence, how much greater must be the danger at this time, quadrupled in amount as it certainly is and more completely under the control of the

Executive will than their construction of their powers allowed or the forbearing characters of all the early Presidents permitted them to make. But it is not by the extent of its patronage alone that the executive department has become dangerous, but by the use which it appears may be made of the appointing power to bring under its control the whole revenues of the country. The Constitution has declared it to be the duty of the President to see that the laws are executed, and it makes him the Commander in Chief of the Armies and Navy of the United States. If the opinion of the most approved writers upon that species of mixed government which in modern Europe is termed 'monarchy' in contradistinction to 'despotism' is correct, there was wanting no other addition to the powers of our Chief Magistrate to stamp a monarchical character on our Government but the control of the public finances; and to me it appears strange indeed that anyone should doubt that the entire control which the President possesses over the officers who have the custody of the public money, by the power of removal with or without cause, does, for all mischievous purposes at least, virtually subject the treasure also to his disposal. The first Roman Emperor, in his attempt to seize the sacred treasure, silenced the opposition of the officer to whose charge it had been committed by a significant allusion to his sword. By a selection of political instruments for the care of the public money a reference to their commissions by a President would be quite as effectual an argument as that of Caesar to the Roman knight. I am not insensible of the great difficulty that exists in drawing a proper plan for the safe-keeping and disbursement of the public revenues, and I know the importance which has been attached by men of great abilities and patriotism to the divorce, as it is called, of the Treasury from the banking institutions. It is not the divorce which is complained of, but the unhallowed union of the Treasury with the executive department, which has created such extensive alarm. To this danger to our republican institutions and that created by the influence given to the Executive through the instrumentality of the Federal officers I propose to apply all the remedies which may be at my command. It was certainly a great error in the framers of the Constitution not to have made the officer at the head of the Treasury Department entirely independent of the Executive. He should at least have been removable only upon the demand of the popular branch of the Legislature. I have determined never to remove a Secretary of the Treasury without communicating all the circumstances attending such removal to both Houses of Congress.

The influence of the Executive in controlling the freedom of the elective franchise through the medium of the public officers can be effectually checked by renewing the prohibition published by Mr. Jefferson forbidding their interference in elections further than giving their own votes, and their own independence secured by an assurance of perfect immunity in exercising this sacred privilege of freemen under the dictates of their own unbiased judgments. Never with my consent shall an officer of the people, compensated for his services out of their pockets, become the pliant instrument of Executive will.

There is no part of the means placed in the hands of the Executive which might be used with greater effect for unhallowed purposes than the control of the public press. The maxim which our ancestors derived from the mother country that "the freedom of the press is the great bulwark of civil and religious liberty" is one of the most precious legacies which they have left us. We have learned, too, from our own as well as the experience of other countries, that golden shackles, by whomsoever or by whatever pretense imposed, are as fatal to it as the iron bonds of despotism. The presses in the necessary employment of the Government should never be used "to clear the guilty or to varnish crime." A decent and manly examination of the acts of the Government should be not only tolerated, but encouraged.

Upon another occasion I have given my opinion at some length upon the impropriety of Executive interference in the legislation of Congress— that the article in the Constitution making it the duty of the President to communicate information and authorizing him to recommend measures was not intended to make him the source in legislation, and, in particular, that he should never be looked to for schemes of finance. It would be very strange, indeed, that the Constitution should have strictly forbidden one branch of the Legislature from interfering in the origination of such bills and that it should be considered proper that an altogether different department of the Government should be permitted to do so. Some of our best political maxims and opinions have been drawn from our parent isle. There are others, however, which can not be introduced in our system without singular incongruity and the production of much mischief, and this I conceive to be one. No matter in which of the houses of Parliament a bill may originate nor by whom introduced—a minister or a member of the opposition—by the fiction of law, or rather of constitutional principle, the sovereign is supposed to have prepared it agreeably to his will and then submitted it to Parliament for their advice and consent. Now the very reverse is the case here, not only with regard to the principle, but the forms prescribed by the Constitution. The principle certainly assigns to the only body constituted by the Constitution (the legislative body) the power to make laws, and the forms even direct that the enactment should be ascribed to them. The Senate, in relation to revenue bills, have the right to propose amendments, and so has the Executive by the power given him to return them to the House of Representatives with his objections. It is in his power also to propose amendments in the existing revenue laws, suggested by his observations upon their defective or injurious operation. But the delicate duty of devising schemes of revenue should be left where the Constitution has placed it—with the immediate representatives of the people. For similar reasons the mode of keeping the public treasure should be prescribed by them, and the further removed it may be from the control of the Executive the more wholesome the arrangement and the more in accordance with republican principle.

Connected with this subject is the character of the currency. The idea of making it exclusively metallic, however well intended, appears to me to be fraught with more fatal consequences than any other scheme having no relation to the personal rights of the citizens that has ever been devised. If any single scheme could produce the effect of arresting at once that mutation of condition by which thousands of our most indigent fellow-citizens by their industry and enterprise are raised to the possession of wealth, that is the one. If there is one measure better calculated than another to produce that state of things so much deprecated by all true republicans, by which the rich are daily adding to their hoards and the poor sinking deeper into penury, it is an exclusive metallic currency. Or if there is a process by which the character of the country for generosity and nobleness of feeling may be destroyed by the great increase and neck toleration of usury, it is an exclusive metallic currency.

Amongst the other duties of a delicate character which the President is called upon to perform is the supervision of the government of the Territories of the United States. Those of them which are destined to become members of our great political family are compensated by their rapid progress from infancy to manhood for the partial and temporary deprivation of their political rights. It is in this District only where American citizens are to be found who under a settled policy are deprived of many important political privileges without any inspiring hope as to the future. Their only consolation under circumstances of such deprivation is that of the devoted exterior guards of a camp—that their sufferings secure tranquillity and safety within. Are there any of their countrymen, who would subject them to greater sacrifices, to any other humiliations than those essentially necessary to the security of the object for which they were thus separated from their fellow-citizens? Are their rights alone not to be guaranteed by the application of those great principles upon which all our constitutions are founded? We are told by the greatest of British orators and statesmen that at the commencement of the War of the Revolution the most stupid men in England spoke of "their American subjects." Are there, indeed, citizens of any of our States who have dreamed 'of their subjects' in the District of Columbia? Such dreams can never be realized by any agency of mine. The people of the District of Columbia are not the subjects of the people of the States, but free American citizens. Being in the latter condition when the Constitution was formed, no words used in that instrument could have been intended to deprive them of that character. If there is anything in the great principle of unalienable rights so emphatically insisted upon in our Declaration of Independence, they could neither make nor the United States accept a surrender of their liberties and become the 'subjects'—in other words, the slaves—of their former fellow-citizens. If this be true—and it will scarcely be denied by anyone who has a correct idea of his own rights as an American citizen—the grant to Congress of exclusive jurisdiction in the District of Columbia can be interpreted, so far as respects the aggregate people of the United States, as meaning nothing more than to allow to Congress the controlling power necessary to afford a free and safe exercise of the functions assigned to the General Government by the Constitution. In all other respects the legislation of Congress should be adapted to their peculiar position and wants and be conformable with their deliberate opinions of their own interests.

I have spoken of the necessity of keeping the respective departments of the Government, as well as all the other authorities of our country, within their appropriate orbits. This is a matter of difficulty in some cases, as the powers which they respectively claim are often not defined by any distinct lines. Mischievous, however, in their tendencies as collisions of this kind may be, those which arise between the respective communities which for certain purposes compose one nation are much more so, for no such nation can long exist without the careful culture of those feelings of confidence and affection which are the effective bonds to union between free and confederated states. Strong as is the tie of interest, it has been often found ineffectual. Men blinded by their passions have been known to adopt measures for their country in direct opposition to all the suggestions of policy. The alternative, then, is to destroy or keep down a bad passion by creating and fostering a good one, and this seems to be the corner stone upon which our American political architects have reared the fabric of our Government.

The cement which was to bind it and perpetuate its existence was the affectionate attachment between all its members. To insure the continuance of this feeling, produced at first by a community of dangers, of sufferings, and of interests, the advantages of each were made accessible to all. No participation in any good possessed by any member of our extensive Confederacy, except in domestic government, was withheld from the citizen of any other member. By a process attended with no difficulty, no delay, no expense but that of removal, the citizen of one might become the citizen of any other, and successively of the whole. The lines, too, separating powers to be exercised by the citizens of one State from those of another seem to be so distinctly drawn as to leave no room for misunderstanding. The citizens of each State unite in their persons all the privileges which that character confers and all that they may claim as citizens of the United States, but in no case can the same persons at the same time act as the citizen of two separate States, and 'he is therefore positively precluded from any interference with the reserved powers of any State but that of which he is for the time being a citizen'. He may, indeed, offer to the citizens of other States his advice as to their management, and the form in which it is tendered is left to his own discretion and sense of propriety. It may be observed, however, that organized associations of citizens requiring compliance with their wishes too much resemble the 'recommendations' of Athens to her allies, supported by an armed and powerful fleet. It was, indeed, to the ambition of the leading States of Greece to control the domestic concerns of the others that the destruction of that celebrated Confederacy, and subsequently of all its members, is mainly to be attributed, and it is owing to the absence of that spirit that the Helvetic Confederacy has for so many years been preserved. Never has there been seen in the institutions of the separate members of any confederacy more elements of discord. In the principles and forms of government and religion, as well as in the circumstances of the several Cantons, so marked a discrepancy was observable as to promise anything but harmony in their intercourse or permanency in their alliance, and yet for ages neither has been interrupted. Content with the positive benefits which their union produced, with the independence and safety from foreign aggression which it secured, these sagacious people respected the institutions of each other, however repugnant to their own principles and prejudices.

Our Confederacy, fellow-citizens, can only be preserved by the same forbearance. Our citizens must be content with the exercise of the powers with which the Constitution clothes them. The attempt of those of one State to control the domestic institutions of another can only result in feelings of distrust and jealousy, the certain harbingers of disunion, violence, and civil war, and the ultimate destruction of our free institutions. Our Confederacy is perfectly illustrated by the terms and principles governing a common co-partnership. There is a fund of power to be exercised under the direction of the joint councils of the allied members, but that which has been reserved by the individual members is intangible by the common Government or the individual members composing it. To attempt it finds no support in the principles of our Constitution.

It should be our constant and earnest endeavor mutually to cultivate a spirit of concord and harmony among the various parts of our Confederacy. Experience has abundantly taught us that the agitation by citizens of one part of the Union of a subject not confided to the General Government, but exclusively under the guardianship of the local authorities, is productive of no other consequences than bitterness, alienation, discord, and injury to the very cause which is intended to be advanced. Of all the great interests which appertain to our country, that of union—cordial, confiding, fraternal union—is by far the most important, since it is the only true and sure guaranty of all others.

In consequence of the embarrassed state of business and the currency, some of the States may meet with difficulty in their financial concerns. However deeply we may regret anything imprudent or excessive in the engagements into which States have entered for purposes of their own, it does not become us to disparage the States governments, nor to discourage them from making proper efforts for their own relief. On the contrary, it is our duty to encourage them to the extent of our constitutional authority to apply their best means and cheerfully to make all necessary sacrifices and submit to all necessary burdens to fulfill their engagements and maintain their credit, for the character and credit of the several States form a part of the character and credit of the whole country. The resources of the country are abundant, the enterprise and activity of our people proverbial, and we may well hope that wise legislation and prudent administration by the respective governments, each acting within its own sphere, will restore former prosperity.

Unpleasant and even dangerous as collisions may sometimes be between the constituted authorities of the citizens of our country in relation to the lines which separate their respective jurisdictions, the results can be of no vital injury to our institutions if that ardent patriotism, that devoted attachment to liberty, that spirit of moderation and forbearance for which our countrymen were once distinguished, continue to be cherished. If this continues to be the ruling passion of our souls, the weaker feeling of the mistaken enthusiast will be corrected, the Utopian dreams of the scheming politician dissipated, and the complicated intrigues of the demagogue rendered harmless. The spirit of liberty is the sovereign balm for every injury which our institutions may receive. On the contrary, no care that can be used in the construction of our Government, no division of powers, no distribution of checks in its several departments, will prove effectual to keep us a free people if this spirit is suffered to decay; and decay it will without constant nurture. To the neglect of this duty the best historians agree in attributing the ruin of all the republics with whose existence and fall their writings have made us acquainted. The same causes will ever produce the same effects, and as long as the love of power is a dominant passion of the human bosom, and as long as the understandings of men can be warped and their affections changed by operations upon their passions and prejudices, so long will the liberties of a people depend on their own constant attention to its preservation. The danger to all well-established free governments arises from the unwillingness of the people to believe in its existence or from the influence of designing men diverting their attention from the quarter whence it approaches to a source from which it can never come. This is the old trick of those who would usurp the government of their country. In the name of democracy they speak, warning the people against the influence of wealth and the danger of aristocracy. History, ancient and modern, is full of such examples. Caesar became the master of the Roman people and the senate under the pretense of supporting the democratic claims of the former against the aristocracy of the latter; Cromwell, in the character of protector of the liberties of the people, became the dictator of England, and Bolivar possessed himself of unlimited power with the title of his country's liberator. There is, on the contrary, no instance on record of an extensive and well-established republic being changed into an aristocracy. The tendencies of all such governments in their decline is to monarchy, and the antagonist principle to liberty there is the spirit of faction—a spirit which assumes the character and in times of great excitement imposes itself upon the people as the genuine spirit of freedom, and, like the false Christs whose coming was foretold by the Savior, seeks to, and were it possible would, impose upon the true and most faithful disciples of liberty. It is in periods like this that it behooves the people to be most watchful of those to whom they have intrusted power. And although there is at times much difficulty in distinguishing the false from the true spirit, a calm and dispassionate investigation will detect the counterfeit, as well by the character of its operations as the results that are produced. The true spirit of liberty, although devoted, persevering, bold, and uncompromising in principle, that secured is mild and tolerant and scrupulous as to the means it employs, whilst the spirit of party, assuming to be that of liberty, is harsh, vindictive, and intolerant, and totally reckless as to the character of the allies which it brings to the aid of its cause. When the genuine spirit of liberty animates the body of a people to a thorough examination of their affairs, it leads to the excision of every excrescence which may have fastened itself upon any of the departments of the government, and restores the system to its pristine health and beauty. But the reign of an intolerant spirit of party amongst a free people seldom fails to result in a dangerous accession to the executive power introduced and established amidst unusual professions of devotion to democracy.

The foregoing remarks relate almost exclusively to matters connected with our domestic concerns. It may be proper, however, that I should give some indications to my fellow-citizens of my proposed course of conduct in the management of our foreign relations. I assure them, therefore, that it is my intention to use every means in my power to preserve the friendly intercourse which now so happily subsists with every foreign nation, and that although, of course, not well informed as to the state of pending negotiations with any of them, I see in the personal characters of the sovereigns, as well as in the mutual interests of our own and of the governments with which our relations are most intimate, a pleasing guaranty that the harmony so important to the interests of their subjects as well as of our citizens will not be interrupted by the advancement of any claim or pretension upon their part to which our honor would not permit us to yield. Long the defender of my country's rights in the field, I trust that my fellow-citizens will not see in my earnest desire to preserve peace with foreign powers any indication that their rights will ever be sacrificed or the honor of the nation tarnished by any admission on the part of their Chief Magistrate unworthy of their former glory. In our intercourse with our aboriginal neighbors the same liberality and justice which marked the course prescribed to me by two of my illustrious predecessors when acting under their direction in the discharge of the duties of superintendent and commissioner shall be strictly observed. I can conceive of no more sublime spectacle, none more likely to propitiate an impartial and common Creator, than a rigid adherence to the principles of justice on the part of a powerful nation in its transactions with a weaker and uncivilized people whom circumstances have placed at its disposal.

Before concluding, fellow-citizens, I must say something to you on the subject of the parties at this time existing in our country. To me it appears perfectly clear that the interest of that country requires that the violence of the spirit by which those parties are at this time governed must be greatly mitigated, if not entirely extinguished, or consequences will ensue which are appalling to be thought of.

If parties in a republic are necessary to secure a degree of vigilance sufficient to keep the public functionaries within the bounds of law and duty, at that point their usefulness ends. Beyond that they become destructive of public virtue, the parent of a spirit antagonist to that of liberty, and eventually its inevitable conqueror. We have examples of republics where the love of country and of liberty at one time were the dominant passions of the whole mass of citizens, and yet, with the continuance of the name and forms of free government, not a vestige of these qualities remaining in the bosoms of any one of its citizens. It was the beautiful remark of a distinguished English writer that "in the Roman senate Octavius had a party and Anthony a party, but the Commonwealth had none." Yet the senate continued to meet in the temple of liberty to talk of the sacredness and beauty of the Commonwealth and gaze at the statues of the elder Brutus and of the Curtii and Decii, and the people assembled in the forum, not, as in the days of Camillus and the Scipios, to cast their free votes for annual magistrates or pass upon the acts of the senate, but to receive from the hands of the leaders of the respective parties their share of the spoils and to shout for one or the other, as those collected in Gaul or Egypt and the lesser Asia would furnish the larger dividend. The spirit of liberty had fled, and, avoiding the abodes of civilized man, had sought protection in the wilds of Scythia or Scandinavia; and so under the operation of the same causes and influences it will fly from our Capitol and our forums. A calamity so awful, not only to our country, but to the world, must be deprecated by every patriot and every tendency to a state of things likely to produce it immediately checked. Such a tendency has existed—does exist. Always the friend of my countrymen, never their flatterer, it becomes my duty to say to them from this high place to which their partiality has exalted me that there exists in the land a spirit hostile to their best interests—hostile to liberty itself. It is a spirit contracted in its views, selfish in its objects. It looks to the aggrandizement of a few even to the destruction of the interests of the whole. The entire remedy is with the people. Something, however, may be effected by the means which they have placed in my hands. It is union that we want, not of a party for the sake of that party, but a union of the whole country for the sake of the whole country, for the defense of its interests and its honor against foreign aggression, for the defense of those principles for which our ancestors so gloriously contended. As far as it depends upon me it shall be accomplished. All the influence that I possess shall be exerted to prevent the formation at least of an Executive party in the halls of the legislative body. I wish for the support of no member of that body to any measure of mine that does not satisfy his judgment and his sense of duty to those from whom he holds his appointment, nor any confidence in advance from the people but that asked for by Mr. Jefferson, "to give firmness and effect to the legal administration of their affairs."

I deem the present occasion sufficiently important and solemn to justify me in expressing to my fellow-citizens a profound reverence for the Christian religion and a thorough conviction that sound morals, religious liberty, and a just sense of religious responsibility are essentially connected with all true and lasting happiness; and to that good Being who has blessed us by the gifts of civil and religious freedom, who watched over and prospered the labors of our fathers and has hitherto preserved to us institutions far exceeding in excellence those of any other people, let us unite in fervently commending every interest of our beloved country in all future time.

Fellow-citizens, being fully invested with that high office to which the partiality of my countrymen has called me, I now take an affectionate leave of you. You will bear with you to your homes the remembrance of the pledge I have this day given to discharge all the high duties of my exalted station according to the best of my ability, and I shall enter upon their performance with entire confidence in the support of a just and generous people.

Source: "William Henry Harrison, Inaugural Address," American Presidency Project https://www.presidency.ucsb.edu/node/200391.

NOTES

PREFACE

1   Admittedly, one must wonder how "rational" it is for voters to blame presidents
    for economic conditions over which they may have scant control. Even if voters
    are not fooled by marketing or rhetoric, a decision rule that reflexively blames
    or credits the incumbent for economic conditions falls well short of most peo-
    ple's understanding of rational behavior.

2   The phrase "It's the economy, stupid" was coined by Clinton's campaign strat-
    egist James Carville. The best book on the 1992 election is Michael Nelson's
    Clinton's Elections: 1992, 1996, and the Birth of a New Era of Governance (Law-
    rence: University Press of Kansas, 2020). Useful in thinking about the parallels
    between Van Buren's fate in 1840 and George Herbert Walker Bush's in 1992—
    both incumbents saddled with a weak economy, the head of a party twelve years
    in power, and committed to continuing their path-setting predecessor's political
    agenda—is Stephen Skowronek, *The Politics Presidents Make: Leadership from
    John Adams to George Bush* (Cambridge, MA: Belknap Press, 1993).

3   In his classic 1960 essay "New Perspectives on Jacksonian Politics," Rich-
    ard P. McCormick calculates that the average differential between the candi-
    dates at the state level was the same in both 1836 and 1840 (11 percentage
    points), with eleven states more competitive and twelve less competitive in
    1840 than in 1836. *American Historical* Review (January 1960), 300 (Table III).
    Using the median rather than the mean, however, shows the 1836 election to
    be slightly more competitive. At the national level, too, 1836 was a somewhat
    closer contest than 1840; Van Buren won with 51 percent of the vote in 1836,
    whereas Harrison won with 53 percent of the vote in 1840. Also see William N.
    Chambers and Philip C. Davis, "Party, Competition, and Mass Participation:
    The Case of the Democratizing Party System, 1841–1852," in *The History of
    American Electoral Behavior*, ed. Joel H. Silbey, Allan G. Bogue, and William H.
    Flanigan (Princeton, NJ: Princeton University Press, 1978), Table 5.1. This does
    not mean that there was no relationship between competitiveness and voter
    turnout. On the contrary, as McCormick is at pains to argue—and as Cham-
    bers and Davis convincingly demonstrate using statistical analysis—there is
    a correlation at the state level "between the size of the voter turnout and rela-
    tive closeness of the election." "New Perspectives on Jacksonian Politics," 299.
    McCormick's argument is that the increase in voter turnout in presidential
    elections between the mid-1820s and early 1840s is best explained by the in-
    creasing competitiveness of elections, which stimulated party organizations to
    mobilize voters. Michael F. Holt questions whether McCormick has the causal
    argument backward—whether, at least in states in which turnout increased
    the most, "competitive balance was a product not a cause of that voter surge."

"The Election of 1840, Voter Mobilization, and the Emergence of the Second American Party System: A Reappraisal of Jacksonian Voting Behavior," in *A Master's Due: Essays in Honor of David Herbert Donald*, ed. William J. Cooper, Jr., Michael F. Holt, and John McCardell (Baton Rouge: Louisiana State University Press, 1986), 23. One suspects that the causal arrows run in both directions, but the data do not enable us to specify those causal relationships more precisely. For our purposes, the point is that electoral competition is insufficient to explain the dramatic jump in turnout between 1836 and 1840.

4   This is a core argument in Holt's "The Election of 1840." Also see Michael F. Holt, *The Rise and Fall of the American Whig Party: Jacksonian Politics and the Onset of the Civil War* (New York: Oxford University Press, 1999).

5   Quoted in Corey M. Brooks, *Liberty Power: Antislavery Third Parties and the Transformation of American Politics* (Chicago: University of Chicago Press, 2016), 35–36.

6   On the "presidential spectacle," see Bruce Miroff, *Presidents on Political Ground: Leaders in Action and What They Face* (Lawrence: University Press of Kansas, 2016), chapter 1; and Bruce Miroff, "The Presidential Spectacle," in *The Presidency and the Political System*, ed. Michael Nelson, 7th ed. (Washington, DC: CQ Press, 2003), 278–304.

7   John Dickerson, *Whistlestop: My Favorite Stories from Presidential Campaign History* (New York: Twelve, 2017), 327; and Robert Gray Gunderson, *The Log-Cabin Campaign* (Lexington: University Press of Kentucky, 1957), 7.

8   Ronald G. Shafer, *The Carnival Campaign: How the Rollicking 1840 Campaign of "Tippecanoe and Tyler Too" Changed Presidential Elections Forever* (Chicago: Chicago Review Press, 2016). Also see Gunderson, *The Log-Cabin Campaign*, as well as Glenn C. Altschuler and Stuart M. Blumin, *Rude Republic: Americans and Their Politics in the Nineteenth Century* (Princeton, NJ: Princeton University Press, 2000), esp. 35–37.

9   On the populism of the Anti-Masons, see especially Ronald P. Formisano, *For the People: American Populist Movements from the Revolution to the 1850s* (Chapel Hill: University of North Carolina Press, 2008), chapters 5–7. Some Anti-Masons did gravitate to the Democratic Party, particularly in Massachusetts, where the Whigs were the establishment. See, for instance, the findings in John L. Brooke, *The Heart of the Commonwealth: Society and Political Culture in Worcester County, Massachusetts, 1713–1861* (Cambridge: Cambridge University Press, 1989), 354–355.

10 William Miles, ed., *The People's Voice: An Annotated Bibliography of American Presidential Campaign Newspapers, 1828–1984* (Westport, CT: Greenwood Press, 1987).

11 Gunderson, *Log-Cabin Campaign*, 29.

12 On the Whigs' worldview, see especially the seminal work of Daniel Walker Howe, *The Political Culture of the American Whigs* (Chicago: University of Chicago Press, 1979).

13 Henry Clay to William Browne, July 31, 1840, in *The Papers of Henry Clay*, ed. Robert Seager II (Lexington: University Press of Kentucky, 1988), 9:438.

14 Gunderson, *Log-Cabin Campaign*, 169.

15 There is literally almost no place for the Liberty Party in Shafer's *Carnival Campaign*, which mentions it only twice in passing (127, 183).

16 Brooks, *Liberty Power*, 40.

17 The term "formative acts" is taken from Stephen Skowronek and Matthew Glassman, eds., *Formative Acts: American Politics in the Making* (Philadelphia: University of Pennsylvania Press, 2007).

CHAPTER 1. THE AGE OF VAN BUREN

1 Not until 1848 would every state vote on the same day in November.

2 In 1836, the sequence was Ohio and Pennsylvania (November 4); Arkansas, Connecticut, Delaware, Georgia, Illinois, Indiana, Kentucky, Maine, Maryland, Mississippi, Missouri, New Hampshire, and Virginia (November 7); New York (November 7–9); Louisiana, Tennessee, and Vermont (November 8); Michigan (November 8–9); North Carolina (November 10); Alabama and Massachusetts (November 14); New Jersey (November 15–16); and Rhode Island (November 16). Every account of the 1836 election that I am aware of mistakenly lists Rhode Island as voting on Wednesday, November 23, 1836. See, for instance, Joel Silbey, "Election of 1836," in *History of American Presidential Elections, 1789–2008*, ed. Gil Troy, Arthur M. Schlesinger Jr., and Fred L. Israel, 4th ed. (New York: Facts on File, 2012), 271. The error is understandable, as even the contemporary press frequently got this and other dates wrong. The usually reliable *Niles' Weekly Register* (November 5, 1836), for instance, mistakenly lists Rhode Island's election on the 23rd as well as wrongly placing Vermont's election day on the 15th and Tennessee's on the 17th (both states voted on the 8th). Each of these errors is reproduced in the "Election Overview" in *History of American Presidential Elections, 1789–2008*, 252. Silbey also errs in stating that "in most states the polls were open for several days." "Election of 1836," 271. In 1836, only a few states, specifically Michigan, New Jersey, and New York, held their presidential election over several days.

3 "All Hail Pennsylvania!! The Country Saved," *Albany Evening Journal*, November 9, 1836. Weed reported that his intelligence came from a delegation that had left Philadelphia at 5 p.m. the previous afternoon and arrived by train in Albany at 2 in the morning.

4 *Albany Argus*, November 9, 1836. The following day, the *Argus* revised its estimate downward to 6,000 votes.

5 *Niles' Weekly Register*, November 12, 1836, 51:161. In 1837, the weekly was renamed *Niles' National Register*.

6 On November 14, 1836, the *Albany Evening Journal* conceded Pennsylvania to Van Buren: "The public mind has been held long enough in suspension about the result of the election in Pennsylvania. Under a conviction that it is the duty of the Press to deal frankly with its readers, we are constrained to say that Pennsylvania has gone for Van Buren." That same morning, however, the *Argus* still found it necessary to combat fresh rumors that the Whigs had carried several western counties in the state by unexpectedly large majorities—a rumor the

paper denounced as a "hoax . . . designed perhaps for the Massachusetts or New Jersey elections." In some parts of the country, it would be weeks before Whigs accepted defeat in Pennsylvania. See, for instance, the *Alton Telegraph* in Illinois, which on November 30 reported that the result in the Keystone State was still "doubtful." Also see John Catron to James Polk, November 24, 1836, reporting that only with the news from Pennsylvania in "last night's mail" had the state's Whigs abandoned their belief that Harrison had won Pennsylvania, leaving them all in "flat despair." *Correspondence of James K. Polk*, ed. Herbert Weaver and Kermit L. Hall (Nashville, TN: Vanderbilt University Press, 1975), 3:786.

7 On November 14, the *Albany Argus* published the returns from "nearly all the counties" in New York and declared a certain victory of at least 24,000 votes. Van Buren ended up winning by 28,000 when all the votes were counted.

8 See *Albany Argus*, November 11–12, 1836.

9 *Albany Argus*, November 14, 1836. Before leaving Albany, Van Buren received a letter from a Virginia ally, William Cabell Rives, assuring him that he had carried the state, although Rives acknowledged it would take as much as two weeks before returns would be received from all the state's counties. William Cabell Rives to Van Buren, November 9, 1836, Martin Van Buren Papers, 1787–1910: Series 2, General Correspondence, September 5–December 31, 1836, Library of Congress, https://www.loc.gov/item/mss438280063/.

10 This estimate does not include Michigan, which became a state on January 26, 1837. If its 3 electoral votes are included, the winner needed 148 electoral votes.

11 *Albany Evening Journal*, November 19 and 21, 1836.

12 Encouraging returns from a few counties in North Carolina were first reported in the Washington *Globe*, the Jackson administration's mouthpiece, on November 16. By the following day, the *Globe* had received intelligence from additional counties enabling it to forecast a Van Buren victory in North Carolina "unless some unknown cause has arrested [the Democratic gains] in the remote counties." By Monday, November 21, the *Globe* was prepared unequivocally to "announce the triumph of the good cause in North Carolina."

13 Martin Van Buren to John Van Buren, November 22, 1836, Papers of Martin Van Buren (digital edition), ed. Mark R. Cheathem et al., http://vanburenpapers .org/document-mvb02024. On the 25th, Van Buren was still awaiting "definitive accounts" of the final results, but by this time he knew he had won the presidency. The only doubtful state that Van Buren had not yet heard from was Mississippi, but victory there was no longer essential. Martin Van Buren to John Van Buren, November 25, 1836, Papers of Martin Van Buren (digital edition), http://vanburenpapers.org/document-mvb02025.

14 *Albany Evening Journal*, November 23, 1836. Also see "The Final Issue," *Raleigh Register*, November 22, 1836. Cf. Silbey, "Election of 1836," 596.

15 The dispute about whether to count Michigan's electoral votes was sidestepped by Congress, which tallied the final electoral votes twice, once with Michigan included and once with Michigan excluded.

16   Joseph Conan Thompson, "Willie Person Mangum: Politics and Pragmatism in the Age of Jackson" (PhD diss., University of Florida, 1995), 250.

17   Forcing the election into the House would not, however, have guaranteed Van Buren's defeat since thirteen (Alabama, Arkansas, Connecticut, Georgia, Illinois, Indiana, Maine, Mississippi, New Hampshire, New Jersey, New York, Pennsylvania, and Virginia) of the twenty-five states had ostensibly pro-Jackson majorities. If Van Buren had secured a majority of each of these delegations (under the unit rule, each House delegation receives one vote), he would have been elected president. The question of whether this was a conscious Whig strategy is addressed in Richard P. McCormick, "Was There a 'Whig Strategy' in 1836?," *Journal of the Early Republic* (Spring 1984): 47–70. Also see Sean Wilentz, *The Rise of American Democracy: Jefferson to Lincoln* (New York: W. W. Norton, 2005), 448; and Michael F. Holt, *The Rise and Fall of the American Whig Party: Jacksonian Politics and the Onset of the Civil War* (New York: Oxford University Press, 1999), 39–40.

18   Holt, 42.

19   The North Carolina Whigs' successful gubernatorial nominee Edward Dudley expressed and exploited Southern distrust of Van Buren in warning that "Mr. Van Buren is not one of us. He is a Northern man . . . in soul, in principle, and in action." *Raleigh Register*, February 23, 1836, quoted in William J. Cooper, Jr., *The South and the Politics of Slavery, 1828–1856* (Baton Rouge: Louisiana State University Press, 1978), 82. Dudley won in 1836, becoming the state's first popularly elected governor.

20   *Connecticut Courant*, November 26, 1836.

21   Holt, *Rise and Fall of the American Whig Party*, 38.

22   Donald B. Cole, *Martin Van Buren and the American Political System* (Princeton, NJ: Princeton University Press, 1984), 264.

23   *Connecticut Courant*, November 26, 1836.

24   Wilentz, *Rise of American Democracy*, 449. An 1836 campaign cartoon portraying Van Buren as a snake "slithering out of a 'pool of corruption'" can be found in Bernard F. Reilly, Jr., *American Political Prints, 1776–1876* (Boston, MA: G. K. Hall, 1991), 84.

25   Cole, *Van Buren and the American Political System*, 264.

26   David Crockett, *The Life of Martin Van Buren* (Philadelphia, PA: Robert Wright, 1835), 80–81; and Cole, *Van Buren and the American Political System*, 265. The *Charlotte Journal*, which supported Hugh White, quoted a "noted Van Buren man" who supposedly said, "I wish that my candidate was less of a dandy." August 26, 1836.

27   Stephen Douglas to the Democratic Republicans of Illinois, December 31, 1835, quoted in Cole, *Van Buren and the American Political System*, 266.

28   Cole, 264.

29   Thurlow Weed to Francis Granger, November 23, 1834, quoted in Holt, *Rise and Fall of the American Whig Party*, 40.

30   Holt, 40, 49.

31 Missouri switched from odd to even years in 1836 and thus held congressional elections in both 1835 and 1836. Democrats won 62 of 98 House seats in 1835 and 85 of 145 House seats in 1836 (there were 146 seats, but one of those, in Tennessee, was won by a candidate nominated by both the Whigs and Democrats). The 1835 count includes Michigan, although it had not yet been admitted as a state at the time it held its election. The 1836 count includes four elections in Maine that were decided in runoff elections the following year (and three of which were won by Democrats). This count is derived from election results given in Michael J. Dubin, *United States Congressional Elections, 1788–1997: The Official Results of the Elections of the 1st through 105th Congresses* (Jefferson, NC: McFarland, 1998), 111–112 (for 1835), 115–117 (for 1836). The Democratic share of House seats in the elections of 1836 was essentially the same as it has been in 1834 (83 of 143 seats, or 58 percent).

32 The state legislative numbers are based on data compiled in Holt, *Rise and Fall of the American Whig Party*, 51 (Table 3). The anti-Jackson coalition did somewhat better at the gubernatorial level in 1835–1836, winning 11 of 25 contests (44 percent), but this was well below its performance in 1834, when it had won six of ten gubernatorial contests. The gubernatorial data compiled by Holt are incomplete, as his table leaves out the gubernatorial contests in Maine and New Hampshire (they occurred annually in both states), the gubernatorial contests in Delaware and Missouri in 1836, and the contests in Michigan and Tennessee in 1835.

33 The particulars of the Pennsylvania case are explained in Holt, 54.

34 Holt, 39.

35 Silbey, "Election of 1836," 263. In contrast, the Jacksonian congressman Ratliffe Boon from Indiana described himself on the floor of the House as "a party man, and one of the true collar dogs (so called by the modern 'whigs')" and insisted he was "proud to wear the collar of such a man as Andrew Jackson, whose collar is the collar of democracy." *Register of Debates in Congress of the First Session of the Twenty-Fourth Congress* (Washington, DC: Gales and Seaton, 1836), 3552 (May 9, 1836).

36 John Quincy Adams to Alexander Everett, December 1, 1835, "Letters of John Quincy Adams to Alexander H. Everett, 1811–1837," *American Historical Review* (October 1905), 349.

37 *Chicago American*, August 1, 1835, quoted in Gerald L. Leonard, *The Invention of Party Politics: Federalism, Popular Sovereignty, and Constitutional Development in Jacksonian Illinois* (Chapel Hill: University of North Carolina Press, 2002), 133. Jackson received over two-thirds of the vote in Illinois in 1828 and 1832, making it a natural home for antiparty appeals by the opposition.

38 *National Intelligencer*, quoted in the *Extra Globe* (Washington, DC), May 27, 1835, 13. The phrase "shrine of party idolatry" is also used by John Quincy Adams in a letter dated October 27, 1838, published in *Niles' National Register*, November 17, 1838, 55:186.

39 New York Whig State Convention, February 1836, quoted in Holt, *Rise and Fall of the American Whig Party*, 31.

40 *Chicago Democrat*, July 22, 1835; *Chicago American*, August 1, 1835, quoted in Leonard, *The Invention of Party Politics*, 133–134. Also see the *Tennessean* (November 8, 1836), which called on the state's citizenry to "disregard the tyranny of party" and instead act like "freemen." The *Tennessean* (September 27, 1836) also quoted from a campaign speech by the Whig congressman Balie Peyton, who called on the people of Tennessee to vote for White rather than Van Buren and thereby rekindle the revolutionary "spirit of liberty" and destroy the "degrading slavery of party." In similar language, Michigan Whigs asked the electorate "to choose between Whig 'liberty of Freemen' versus Democratic 'slavery of party.'" Ann Arbor (MI) *State Journal*, October 26, 1837 quoted in Ronald P. Formisano, *The Birth of Mass Political Parties, 1827–1861* (Princeton, NJ: Princeton University Press, 1971), 72.

41 The Whigs also captured all six US House seats in New Jersey, which elected representatives in statewide at-large elections.

42 *Connecticut Courant*, November 18, 1836.

43 *Louisville Daily Journal*, November 24, 1836.

44 *Baltimore Chronicle*, quoted in the *Louisville Daily Journal*, November 28, 1836. Similarly, the *New Bedford Mercury* charged Whig nonvoters with "criminal neglect of the highest duty of an American citizen" (November 25, 1836), a charge that was echoed in the *Richmond Whig*, which blamed the loss in Virginia on the Whigs' "criminal apathy." Reprinted in the *Pittsburgh Gazette*, November 29, 1836. Zachariah Poulson, the longtime editor of Philadelphia's *American Daily Advertiser*, also faulted the "criminal apathy" of the Whigs and Anti-Masons for Harrison's defeat in Pennsylvania. See Poulson to William Henry Harrison, December 10, 1836, William Henry Harrison Papers: Series 1, General Correspondence, 1734–1939, Library of Congress, https://www.loc.gov/resource/mss25148.002_0011_1115/?sp=652.

45 Marc W. Kruman, *Parties and Politics in North Carolina, 1836–1865* (Baton Rouge: Louisiana State University Press, 1983), 27; and Michael J. Dubin, *United States Gubernatorial Elections, 1776–1860: The Official Results by State and County* (Jefferson, NC: McFarland, 2003), 182. The same basic calculation, though with somewhat different numbers, was made by the editors of the *Raleigh Register*, November 29, 1836.

46 *Raleigh Register*, November 22, 1836.

47 *Raleigh Register*, November 29, 1836.

48 *Raleigh Register*, November 22, 1836.

49 William Henry Harrison to Indiana governor Noah Noble, December 3, 1836, in *Indiana Magazine of History* (June 1926), https://scholarworks.iu.edu/journals/index.php/imh/article/view/6391/6501. The same "want of confidence" theory was expressed by the Whig editor Zachariah Poulson in a letter to Harrison, dated December 10, 1836: "The want of [confidence] among so many of our political friends has, in part, produced the disaster we have so much cause to lament. The want of Confidence really paralyzes the power necessary to produce Success." Poulson to Harrison, December 10, 1836, William Henry

Harrison Papers, Library of Congress, https://www.loc.gov/resource/mss2514 8.002_0011_1115/?sp=653.

50 Formisano, *Birth of Mass Political Parties*, 72.

51 *Greensboro Patriot*, quoted in *Raleigh Register*, November 22, 1836.

52 *Raleigh Register*, November 22, 1836.

53 At a public dinner in his honor in Nashville in late August 1836, Jackson hailed the "motto, 'principles not men'" as the defining belief of the "good old Jeffersonian Democratic Republican" party. Charles Grier Sellers, Jr., *James K. Polk: Jacksonian, 1795–1843* (Princeton, NJ: Princeton University Press, 1957), 300. Also see Clement C. Clay to James Polk, November 2, 1835, *Correspondence of James K. Polk*, 3:352–353, and Silbey, "Election of 1836," 265 (quoting the *Globe*'s declaration 'Principles are everything; men, nothing"). The origins of the slogan "Principles, not men" in the US dated to the early 1790s, when it became a "rallying cry and article of faith" for those expressing solidarity with the new French Republic. See Marcus Daniel, *Scandal & Civility: Journalism and the Birth of American Democracy* (New York: Oxford University Press, 2009), 126.

54 Andrew Jackson, "Farewell Address," March 4, 1837, American Presidency Project, https://www.presidency.ucsb.edu/node/20177.

55 John Catron to Andrew Jackson, March 21, 1835, in *Correspondence of Andrew Jackson*, ed. John Spencer Bassett (Washington, DC: Carnegie Institution, 1926), 5:332. Silbey ("Election of 1836," 264–265) mistakenly attributes this quotation to Richard M. Johnson. It is instead from a letter written by Tennessee chief justice John Catron imploring Jackson to use his influence to block Johnson from becoming the Democratic nominee for vice president. Catron wrote, "My dear Sir we must not in this great and I trust final battle against thirty-five millions of money, against uncompromising nullification, against a scheme of protection, and of its correlative, waste by internal improvements, think of humouring third rate politicians [i.e., Johnson] from a state flatly against us." Silbey omits the last clause from the quotation.

56 Holt, *Rise and Fall of the American Whig Party*, 29.

57 Holt, 45.

58 Jackson, "Farewell Address." Also see Jackson to Van Buren, November 1, 1830, *Correspondence of Andrew Jackson*, 4:198.

59 General Jackson was no political innocent, however. As a young man, in 1796, Jackson was selected as a delegate to the Tennessee constitutional convention and then became Tennessee's first member of the US House of Representatives, albeit only briefly because after nine months the Tennessee state legislature selected him to serve in the US Senate. Jackson, who had only just turned thirty, resigned his place in the Senate after only six months, but shortly thereafter was named to the Tennessee Supreme Court, where he served for six years. Jackson also returned to the US Senate for two and a half years between 1823 and 1825.

60 Cole, *Van Buren and the American Political System*, 34.

61 Cole, 14n15.

62 Cole, 14.

63 *The Autobiography of Martin Van Buren*, ed. John C. Fitzpatrick, Annual Report of the American Historical Association for the Year 1918, vol. 2 (Washington, DC: Government Printing Office, 1920), 11; Cole, *Van Buren and the American Political System*, 14; and Joel H. Silbey, *Martin Van Buren and the Emergence of American Popular Politics* (Lanham, MD: Rowman & Littlefield, 2002), 2.

64 Benjamin L. Huggins, *Willie Mangum and the North Carolina Whigs in the Age of Jackson* (Jefferson, NC: McFarland, 2016), 9.

65 Silbey, *Martin Van Buren and the Emergence of American Popular Politics*, 2; Cole, *Van Buren and the American Political System*, 13; and Ted Widmer, *Martin Van Buren* (New York: Times Books, 2005), 27.

66 Widmer, *Martin Van Buren*, 27–28; Silbey, *Martin Van Buren and the Emergence of American Popular Politics*, 4, 6, 9; and Cole, *Van Buren and the American Political System*, 14–15. Also see John L. Brooke, *Columbia Rising: Civil Life on the Upper Hudson from the Revolution to the Age of Jackson* (Chapel Hill: University of North Carolina Press, 2010), a masterful ethnography of the social relations and political institutions of the Upper Hudson Valley, where Van Buren grew up. Also valuable are the opening chapters of Reeve Huston, *Land and Freedom: Rural Society, Popular Protest, and Party Politics in Antebellum New York* (New York: Oxford University Press, 2000).

67 *Autobiography of Martin Van Buren*, 14; Widmer, *Martin Van Buren*, 22; and Silbey, *Martin Van Buren and the Emergence of American Popular Politics*, 9.

68 *Autobiography of Martin Van Buren*, 7. This narrative is belied, too, by the fact that Van Buren's half-brother (and later law partner) James I. Van Alen was a prominent Kinderhook political figure: a town clerk from 1797 to 1801, a candidate for Congress in 1800, a delegate at the state's 1801 constitutional convention, a justice of the peace from 1801–1804, and elected to the New York state assembly in 1804. In 1806, Van Alen ran for Congress a second time, this time successfully (he won by ten votes), owing in large part to the precocious organizing talents of Van Buren, who though not yet twenty-four was already judged by one political opponent (Federalist attorney Charles Foote) to be "the life of democracy" in Columbia County "and its acknowledged head"—and, less flatteringly, "that little imp of jacobinism." James Bradley, "James Van Alen Goes to Congress," Papers of Martin Van Buren (digital edition), http://vanburenpapers.org/content/james-van-alen-goes-congress.

69 Richard P. McCormick, *The Second American Party System: Party Formation in the Jacksonian Era* (Chapel Hill: University of North Carolina Press, 1966), 105.

70 *Autobiography of Martin Van Buren*, 7, 15–16. New York's constitution, written in 1777, established a two-tiered system. To vote for governor or state senator required freeholds valued at 100 pounds; to vote for the state house, in contrast, needed only a freehold worth one-fifth that amount (McCormick, *Second American Party System*, 106). However, as McCormick notes, "many who were not properly qualified must have voted" (108), a point affirmed by Donald Ratcliffe in "The Right to Vote and the Rise of Democracy, 1787–1828," *Journal of the Early Republic* (Summer 2013): 219–254. The property qualifications were not removed from the New York Constitution until 1821.

71 *Autobiography of Martin Van Buren*, 28.

72 Silbey, *Martin Van Buren and the Emergence of American Popular Politics*, 17; and Cole, *Van Buren and the American Political System*, 33.

73 It was also a choice, as Van Buren himself emphasized, between the state Republican caucus, which had nominated Clinton, and the Republican legislative caucus in the nation's capital, which backed Madison. Cole, *Van Buren and the American Political System*, 33, 37n.

74 Cole, 35. Also see Silbey, *Martin Van Buren and the Emergence of American Popular Politics*, 18–19; and Widmer, *Martin Van Buren*, 42.

75 Silbey, *Martin Van Buren and the Emergence of American Popular Politics*, 18.

76 Cole, *Van Buren and the American Political System*, 37.

77 Cole, 35.

78 Silbey, *Martin Van Buren and the Emergence of American Popular Politics*, 19

79 Cole, *Van Buren and the American Political System*, 86–87.

80 Martin Van Buren, *Inquiry into the Origin and Course of Political Parties in the United States* (New York: Hurd and Houghton, 1867), 3–4.

81 *Albany Argus*, quoted in Cole, *Van Buren and the American Political System*, 96. Also see Martin Van Buren to Thomas Ritchie, January 13, 1827, Papers of Martin Van Buren (digital edition), http://vanburenpapers.org/document-mvb00528.

82 Van Buren to Charles Dudley, January 10, 1822, quoted in Donald Ratcliffe, *The One-Party Presidential Contest: Adams, Jackson, and 1824's Five-Horse Race* (Lawrence: University Press of Kansas, 2015), 80; and Cole, *Van Buren and the American Political System*, 96.

83 Van Buren to Ritchie, January 13, 1827.

84 Van Buren, *Inquiry into the Origin and Course of Political Parties*, 3.

85 Van Buren to Ritchie, January 13, 1827; Robert V. Remini, *Martin Van Buren and the Making of the Democratic Party* (New York: W. W. Norton, 1970), 24, 37; and Cole, *Van Buren and the American Political System*, 122.

86 Cole, 112, 115, 138; and Silbey, *Martin Van Buren and the Emergence of American Popular Politics*, 48.

87 *Autobiography of Martin Van Buren*, 149, 198; and Van Buren to Ritchie, January 13, 1827.

88 Cole, *Van Buren and the American Political System*, 128, 133; and Silbey, *Martin Van Buren and the Emergence of American Popular Politics*, 43.

89 In *The One-Party Presidential Contest*, Donald Ratcliffe shows that the conventional view that Jackson was the clear choice of the people is misleading because the popular vote totals did not include six states—most importantly New York—in which the electors were selected by state legislatures. Ratcliffe makes the case that if those six states had chosen electors by popular vote, then Adams would have ended up with more popular votes than Jackson. The Corrupt Bargain charge also ignores that Clay and Adams had far more in common ideologically than did Clay and Jackson.

90 Van Buren to Philip Norborne Nicholas, November 1, 1826, Papers of Martin Van Buren (digital edition), http://vanburenpapers.org/document-mvb00508.

Also see Lynn Hudson Parsons, *The Birth of Modern Politics: Andrew Jackson, and the Election of 1828* (New York: Oxford University Press, 2009), 126.

91 Van Buren to Ritchie, January 13, 1827. Also see Cole, *Van Buren and the American Political System*, 150–151. The phrase "noble conflict" is from a speech in Congress on March 7, 1836, by one of Van Buren's Regency allies, Churchill Cambreleng. Cambreleng's speech, like Van Buren's 1827 letter to Ritchie, is a sustained defense of parties as a positive good. Cambreleng maintained that parties are "indispensable to every Administration" and "essential to the existence of our institutions." He rejected "talk of the violence of party spirit," arguing instead that "the conflict of parties is a noble conflict" and that it was to these great conflicts "that we are almost indebted for all that is great and valuable in political science." See *Abridgment of the Debates of Congress, from 1789 to 1856*, ed. Thomas Hart Benton (New York: Appleton, 1861), 8:704.

92 John Quincy Adams, "First Annual Message," December 6, 1825, American Presidency Project, https://www.presidency.ucsb.edu/node/206789.

93 Donald P. Cole, *Vindicating Andrew Jackson: The 1828 Election and the Rise of the Two-Party System* (Lawrence: University Press of Kansas, 2009), 75–77.

94 Cole, *Van Buren and the American Political System*, 158; Ratcliffe, *The One-Party Presidential Contest*, 219; and Remini, *Martin Van Buren and the Making of the Democratic Party*, 161.

95 Cole, *Van Buren and the American Political System*, 174.

96 Cole, 171.

97 Remini, *Martin Van Buren and the Making of the Democratic Party*, 194; and Cole, *Van Buren and the American Political System*, 174–175.

98 Remini, *Martin Van Buren and the Making of the Democratic Party*, 194.

99 Donald Ratcliffe, "Popular Preferences in the Election of 1824," *Journal of the Early Republic* (Spring 2014): 71–73; and Ratcliffe, *The One-Party Presidential Contest*, 224, 234, 265.

100 Ratcliffe, "Popular Preferences in the Election of 1824," 73.

101 Cole, *Vindicating Andrew Jackson*, 90.

102 Quoted in Ratcliffe, *The One-Party Presidential Contest*, 219.

103 Cole, *Vindicating Andrew Jackson*, 193; and Cole, *Van Buren and the American Political System*, 175. Jackson's 140,000 votes were marginally more than Van Buren's 137,000 votes, but the opposition to Van Buren was split between two candidates, which helped Van Buren win comfortably (by about 20,000 votes), while Jackson's margin of victory was much narrower (roughly 5,000 votes).

104 Cole, *Van Buren and the American Political System*, 179.

105 Major L. Wilson, *The Presidency of Martin Van Buren* (Lawrence: University Press of Kansas, 1984), 36–37.

106 Van Buren, for instance, had serious reservations about Jackson's decision in 1833 to remove federal monies from the national bank and deposit them in state banks. But after failing to persuade Jackson to delay the decision, Van Buren did not hesitate to ensure that the state party in New York backed Jackson's decision with "immovable constancy" and that Jackson's bank policy was made

a core tenet of the party's appeal in the elections of 1834. Wilson, *Presidency of Martin Van Buren*, 34–36.

107 Walter Dean Burnham, "Party Systems and the Political Process," in *The American Party Systems: Stages of Political Development*, ed. William Nisbet Chambers and Walter Dean Burnham, 2nd ed. (New York: Oxford University Press, 1975), 289, 292. Also see Ronald P. Formisano, "Deferential-Participant Politics: The Early Republic's Political Culture, 1789–1840," *American Political Science Review* (June 1974): 473–487; and Ronald P. Formisano, "Federalists and Republicans: Parties, Yes—System, No," in Paul Kleppner et al., *The Evolution of American Electoral Systems* (Westport, CT: Greenwood Press, 1981), 33–76.

108 Ratcliffe, "The Right to Vote and the Rise of Democracy." Also see Richard P. McCormick, "New Perspectives on Jacksonian Politics," *American Historical Review* (January 1960): 290–293; Formisano, "Deferential-Participant Politics," 482; and Jeffrey L. Pasley, "The Cheese and the Words: Popular Political Culture and Participatory Democracy in the Early American Republic," in *Beyond the Founders: New Approaches to the Political History of the Early American Republic*, ed. Jeffrey L. Pasley, Andrew W. Robertson, and David Waldstreicher (Chapel Hill: University of North Carolina Press, 2004), 31–56.

109 Walter Dean Burnham, *Voting in American Elections: The Shaping of the American Political Universe since 1788* (Palo Alto, CA: Academica Press, 2010), 351, 396.

110 McCormick, "New Perspectives on Jacksonian Politics," 289. Also see Ratcliffe, "The Right to Vote and the Rise of Democracy"; John L. Brooke, "'King George Has Issued Too Many Pattents for Us': Property and Democracy in Jeffersonian New York," *Journal of the Early Republic* (Summer 2013): 187–217; Daniel Peart, *Era of Experimentation: American Political Practices in the Early Republic* (Charlottesville: University of Virginia Press, 2014); and Daniel Peart and Adam I. P. Smith, eds., *Practicing Democracy: Popular Politics in the United States from the Constitution to the Civil War* (Charlottesville: University of Virginia Press, 2015), esp. the chapters by Reeve Huston, Andrew W. Robertson, and Daniel Peart.

111 William G. Shade, "Political Pluralism and Party Development: The Creation of a Modern Party System, 1815–1852," in Paul Kleppner et al., *The Evolution of American Electoral Systems* (Westport, CT: Greenwood Press, 1981), 82 (Table 3.1). Although party politics in "the Age of Jackson" was sectional, Morton Keller is wrong in claiming that "92 percent of [Jackson's] 1828 electoral vote came from slave states." *America's Three Regimes: A New Political History* (New York: Oxford University Press, 2007), 81. The percentage was closer to 60 percent. A presidential candidate with 92 percent of his electoral votes from slave states in a two-candidate race in 1828 would have been a losing candidate.

112 McCormick, "New Perspectives on Jacksonian Politics," 300 (Table 3).

113 Burnham, *Voting in American Elections*, 403–404.

114 Richard P. McCormick, "Political Development and the Second Party System," in *The American Party Systems: Stages of Political Development*, ed. William Nisbet Chambers and Walter Dean Burnham, 2nd ed. (New York: Oxford Uni-

versity Press, 1975), 101. More than a half century after McCormick rendered this judgment, there remains no book-length study of the 1836 presidential election, though there have been several articles, including William G. Shade, "'The Most Delicate and Exciting Topics': Martin Van Buren, Slavery, and the Election of 1836," *Journal of the Early Republic* (Fall 1998): 459–484.

115 Gerald Pomper, "Classification of Presidential Elections," *Journal of Politics* (August 1967): 535–566, especially Table 1.4. The correlation was virtually zero (r = 0.05) between 1828 and 1836 and surprisingly weak (r = 0.22) between 1832 and 1836.

116 Shade, "Political Pluralism and Party Development," 82–83. Shade's measure of sectionalism in the presidential election (the coefficient of relative variation between the six regions of the country) shows a score of 57 percent in 1824, 30 percent in 1828, and 23 percent in 1832 before plummeting to 5 percent in 1836. It remains in the 3 to 13 percent range for the remainder of the second party system (that is, through 1852), with an average of about 5 percent.

117 McCormick, "New Perspectives on Jacksonian Politics," 292. Also see McCormick, "Political Development and the Second Party System," 101.

118 Burnham, *Voting in American Elections*, 403–404.

119 Joel H. Silbey, *The American Political Nation, 1838–1893* (Palo Alto, CA: Stanford University Press, 1991), 1. Also see Formisano, "Deferential-Participant Politics," 486 ("The universal empire of party was to come only after 1835"); Richard L. McCormick, "The Party Period and Public Policy: An Exploratory Hypothesis," *Journal of American History* (September 1979): 279–298; Stephen Skowronek, *The Politics Presidents Make: Leadership from John Adams to George Bush* (Cambridge, MA: Belknap Press, 1993), 53 (Table 2); and Keller, *America's Three Regimes*. For reflections on the limits of the "party period" construct, see Michael F. Holt, "Change and Continuity in the Party Period: The Substance and Structure of American Politics, 1835–1885," in *Contesting Democracy: Substance and Structure in American Political History, 1775–2000*, ed. Byron E. Shafer and Anthony J. Badger (Lawrence: University Press of Kansas, 2001), 93–115; and Ronald P. Formisano, "The Party Period Revisited," *Journal of American History* (June 1999): 93–120.

120 The phrase is used in Jeffrey L. Pasley, "Minnows, Spies, and Aristocrats: The Social Crisis of Congress in the Age of Martin Van Buren," *Journal of the Early Republic* (Winter 2007): 599–653.

CHAPTER 2. THE POLITICS OF BOOM AND BUST

1 Martin Van Buren, "Inaugural Address," March 4, 1837, American Presidency Project, https://www.presidency.ucsb.edu/node/201813.

2 Jessica M. Lepler, *The Many Panics of 1837: People, Politics, and the Creation of a Transatlantic Financial Crisis* (Cambridge: Cambridge University Press, 2013), 94; chapter 4 is titled "Mysterious Whispers."

3 GDP in 1996 dollars is estimated by Richard Sutch to be $17,547,000 in 1829 and $26,329,000 in 1836. See Richard Sutch, "Gross Domestic Product: 1790–2002 [Continuous annual series]," Table Ca9–19, in *Historical Sta-*

tistics of the United States: Millennial Edition Online, ed. Susan B. Carter et al. (New York, NY: Cambridge University Press, 2006), https://hsus.cambridge .org/HSUSWeb/index.do. Growth in GDP per capita during Jackson's term was close to 3 percent a year, which is about on par with the robust economic growth of the 1960s and well above that of the 1970s (2.1 percent), 1980s (2.4 percent), 1990s (2.1 percent), and 2000–2017 (less than 1 percent). GDP estimates for the 1830s are, of course, far more speculative and less precise than modern GDP numbers. GDP estimates prior to 1929, when the Bureau of Economic Analysis began gathering official estimates of national income and product, are, as Paul W. Rhode and Richard Sutch remind us, "based on fragmentary data that were not originally collected for the purpose of making national product estimates." Moreover, the further back in time one goes, the "the more degraded the quality of existing data." Paul W. Rhode and Richard Sutch discuss the pitfalls of estimating economic growth in the nineteenth century in "Estimates of National Product before 1929," *Historical Statistics of the United States*.

4   Michael F. Holt, *The Rise and Fall of the American Whig Party* (New York: Oxford University Press, 1999), 62.

5   Alasdair Roberts, *America's First Great Depression: Economic Crisis and Political Disorder after the Panic of 1837* (Ithaca, NY: Cornell University Press, 2012), 25, 20.

6   In April 1836, for instance, the Jacksonian editor William Cullen Bryant asked, "When will the bubble burst? When will the great catastrophe which the banks have been preparing for us actually come about?" Roberts, 38.

7   The order was made effective August 15, 1836, but a temporary exception was made for those purchasing fewer than 320 acres who could prove they were "actual settlers," as opposed to land speculators. After December 15, 1836, though, the circular applied to all purchases of federal land. Peter L. Rousseau, "Jacksonian Monetary Policy, Specie Flows, and the Panic of 1837," National Bureau of Economic Research, Working Paper 7528, February 2000, p. 22, http://www.nber.org/papers/w7528; Rousseau's paper was published in the *Journal of Economic History* 62 (June 2002): 457–488.

8   Andrew Jackson, "Farewell Address," March 4, 1837, American Presidency Project, https://www.presidency.ucsb.edu/node/201770.

9   Roberts, *America's First Great Depression*, 36.

10 *Extra Globe* (Washington, DC), February 10, 1838,1:6; Rousseau, "Jacksonian Monetary Policy, Specie Flows, and the Panic of 1837," 5, 36; and Roberts, *America's First Great Depression*, 38. The transatlantic sources of the Panic of 1837 are articulated most forcefully in Peter Temin's classic *The Jacksonian Economy* (New York: W. W. Norton, 1969).

11 Lepler, *The Many Panics of 1837*, 12; and Roberts, *America's First Great Depression*, 28.

12 Rousseau, "Jacksonian Monetary Policy, Specie Flows, and the Panic of 1837," 31n31.

13 Lewis C. Gray, *History of Agriculture in the Southern United States to 1860* (Clifton, NJ: Augustus M. Kelley Publishers, 1933), 1027; and Lepler, *The Many Panics of 1837*, 285n.

14 Lepler, 108–109; and Holt, *Rise and Fall of the American Whig Party*, 63.

15 Lepler, *The Many Panics of 1837*, 13, 15.

16 Lepler, 109–115, quotations at 109, 112, 115.

17 Andrew Jackson to Martin Van Buren, March 30, 1837, Andrew Jackson Papers, Library of Congress, https://www.loc.gov/resource/maj.01098_0254_0259/?st=text; and Lepler, *The Many Panics of 1837*, 117, 121. Jackson was far from alone in his anxieties about the incompatibility of rampant speculation and sober republican virtue. In January 1836, the New York bank commissioners' report to the state legislature warned that "the minds of the young particularly who are just entering upon business are perverted by this sudden though hazardous means of obtaining wealth from the more sure and steady pursuits of industry and economy, which administer so largely to the comfort, quiet and order of society." *Documents of the Assembly of the State of New York*, Fifty-Ninth Session, No. 80 (Albany, NY: E. Croswell, 1836), p. 11.

18 Rousseau, "Jacksonian Monetary Policy," 29, 25, also see 5, 15, 22, 27; and Jackson to Van Buren, March 30, 1837.

19 Rousseau, "Jacksonian Monetary Policy," 8–9, 15, quotation at 9; and Roberts, *America's First Great Depression*, 31.

20 Rousseau, "Jacksonian Monetary Policy," 28. Among those sounding the early alarm to President Van Buren was Gorham A. Worth, an old friend from his Hudson days; Van Buren had been a bank director and attorney for the short-lived Bank of Hudson (chartered in 1808, it failed in the Panic of 1819) and Worth its cashier. Now a successful New York City banker, Worth privately warned Van Buren that the nation's "monied affairs" were "in a deplorable state" and "fast tending to a fearful crisis." The "whole banking system," he told the new president, was "in danger." Gorham A. Worth to Van Buren, March 12, 1837, Martin Van Buren Papers, 1787–1910: Series 2, General Correspondence, February 7–April 7, 1837, Library of Congress, https://www.loc.gov/item/mss438280065/.

21 Jackson to Van Buren, March 30, 1837.

22 Rousseau, "Jacksonian Monetary Policy," 30; and Lepler, *The Many Panics of 1837*, 184. Also see Donald B. Cole, *Martin Van Buren and the American Political System* (Princeton, NJ: Princeton University Press, 1984), 293.

23 Lepler, *The Many Panics of 1837*, 194. Also see Rousseau, "Jacksonian Monetary Policy," 34.

24 Lepler, *The Many Panics of 1837*, 197 (quoting from Enos Throop to Van Buren, May 10, 1837).

25 Rousseau, "Jacksonian Monetary Policy," 34; and Lepler, *The Many Panics of 1837*, 198.

26 Rousseau, "Jacksonian Monetary Policy," 34–35; and Lepler, *The Many Panics of 1837*, 209–210.

27 Quoted in Roberts, *America's First Great Depression*, 43; and Lepler, *The Many Panics of 1837*, 209.

28 Holt, *Rise and Fall of the American Whig Party*, 63; and Roberts, *America's First Great Depression*, 44, 53.

29 Ronald P. Formisano, *The Birth of Mass Political Parties: Michigan, 1827–1861* (Princeton, NJ: Princeton University Press, 1971), 129.

30 Roberts, *America's First Great Depression*, 20. Writing in June 1837, Henry Clay observed, "Six months ago no Nation ever enjoyed more apparent prosperity; now none ever experienced a more sudden and sad reverse." Clay to Christopher Hughes, June 18, 1837, *The Papers of Henry Clay*, ed. Robert Seager II (Lexington: University Press of Kentucky, 1988), 9:49.

31 Henry Clay to Richard Graham, June 1, 1837, *Papers of Henry Clay*, 9:48.

32 Lepler, *The Many Panics of 1837*, 211.

33 Henry Clay to Matthew L. Davis, July 3, 1837, *Papers of Henry Clay*, 9:55. Also see Holt, *Rise and Fall of the American Whig Party*, 62.

34 *Washington Globe*, June 12, 1835, quoted in Major L. Wilson, *The Presidency of Martin Van Buren* (Lawrence: University Press of Kansas, 1984), 37.

35 Jon Meacham, *American Lion: Andrew Jackson in the White House* (New York: Random House, 2009), 278.

36 In 1834, for instance, Jackson began his annual address to Congress by claiming credit for the "prosperous condition of our beloved country." "Sixth Annual Message," December 1, 1834, American Presidency Project, https://www.presidency.ucsb.edu/node/200854. Similarly, in his final annual address to Congress, Jackson began by boasting of "the high state of prosperity which our beloved country has attained." "Eighth Annual Message," December 5, 1836, American Presidency Project, https://www.presidency.ucsb.edu/node/200873. Also see Roberts, *America's First Great Depression*, 37.

37 C. C. Trowbridge to Lewis Cass, May 29, 1837, quoted in Formisano, *Birth of Mass Political Parties*, 129n.

38 Lepler, *The Many Panics of 1837*, 194.

39 Alexander W. Stow to Henry Clay, April 22, 1837, *Papers of Henry Clay*, 9:41.

40 Lepler, *The Many Panics of 1837*, 214–215.

41 Martin Van Buren, "Special Session Message," September 4, 1837, American Presidency Project, https://www.presidency.ucsb.edu/node/201305.

42 Andrew Jackson to Francis Preston Blair, July 9, 1837, Andrew Jackson Papers, Library of Congress, https://www.loc.gov/resource/maj.01099_0045_0053/?st=text.

43 Andrew Jackson to Francis Preston Blair, July 23, 1837, Andrew Jackson Papers, Library of Congress https://www.loc.gov/item/maj015689/. Excerpts of Jackson's two letters to Blair were circulated widely in the press. See, e.g., *Niles' Weekly Register*, August 12, 1837.

44 The law was passed in 1872 but did not go into effect until the congressional elections of 1874. See Michael F. Holt, "Change and Continuity in the Party Period: The Substance and Structure of American Politics, 1835–1885," in *Contesting Democracy: Substance and Structure in American Political History, 1775–2000*,

ed. Byron E. Shafer and Anthony J. Badger (Lawrence: University Press of Kansas, 2001), 102.

45 All congressional results reported in this chapter, unless otherwise indicated, are from Michael J. Dubin, *United States Congressional Elections, 1788–1997: The Official Results of the Elections of the 1st through 105th Congresses* (Jefferson, NC: McFarland, 1998), 111–119. All gubernatorial results reported in this chapter, unless otherwise indicated, are from Michael J. Dubin, *United States Gubernatorial Elections, 1776–1860: The Official Results by State and County* (Jefferson, NC: McFarland, 2003). All state house results from 1836 and 1837 reported in this chapter, unless otherwise indicated, are from Holt, *Rise and Fall of the American Whig Party*, 75 (Table 6).

46 *Connecticut Courant*, April 15, 1837. The Whigs also failed to pick up seats in the lower house, remaining stuck at the same 35 percent that they had garnered in 1836.

47 While the Whigs also failed to win any of the six House seats in 1835, part of what made the 1837 result so disappointing for Whigs was that the state had switched away from the at-large districts used in 1835, which should have enabled them to pick up seats.

48 *Rhode-Island Republican*, April 12, 1837, and April 19, 1837. In the lower house, Rhode Island's Whigs dropped to 42 percent of the seats from 44 percent the year before.

49 William G. Shade, *Democratizing the Old Dominion: Virginia and the Second Party System, 1824–1861* (Charlottesville: University Press of Virginia, 1996), 169.

50 Had incumbent Democrat Henry Wise not switched parties and run for his eighth district seat in 1837 as a Whig, the Democrats' number of seats won would have remained the same as it had been in 1835.

51 In 1835, ten of the sixteen elected Democrats had won against their Whig opponents with less than 60 percent of the vote, whereas in 1837, only one of fifteen elected Democrats secured less than 60 percent of the vote.

52 Turnout in the House elections is calculated from the vote count in Dubin, *United States Congressional Elections, 1788–1997*, 112, 118. Also see Shade, *Democratizing the Old Dominion*, 93. Turnout declines tended to be steepest in the southeastern portion of the state and less dramatic in western Virginia.

53 Henry Clay to Alexander W. Stow, April 26, 1837, *Papers of Henry Clay*, 9:43.

54 Lepler, *The Many Panics of 1837*, 67–68; *Papers of Henry Clay*, 9:43n3.

55 Also adding to the Whigs' glee were the common council results in the state capital of Albany, where the Whigs carried four of the five wards, reversing the results of the previous year, when the Democrats had won four of the five wards. See *New-York American*, May 4, 1837.

56 Henry Clay to Alexander W. Stow, April 22, 1837, *Papers of Henry Clay*, 9:43; and *Connecticut Courant*, April 22, 1837.

57 Maine's seventh district encompassed Washington and Hancock Counties in the easternmost part of the state. Prior to the 1830 census, those two counties had made up the sixth district, which Democrats had carried in each election

dating back to statehood in 1820. The changing contours of Maine's (and every other states') districts can be traced in the invaluable volume compiled by Stanley B. Parsons, William W. Beach, and Dan Hermann, *United States Congressional Districts, 1788–1841* (Westport, CT: Greenwood Press, 1978).

58 Lewis Collins and Richard H. Collins, *History of Kentucky* (Covington, KY: Collins & Co., 1882), 1:41–42. The 1835 Kentucky state legislative results are reported in the *Arkansas Times and Advocate* (Little Rock, Arkansas), September 11, 1835.

59 Dubin's 1837 count of House seats (*United States Congressional Elections, 1788–1997*, 117) is off by one, as he mistakenly counts the winner in North Carolina's first district as a Democrat. In Table 6 in *Rise and Fall of the Whig Party* (75), Holt erroneously lists Missouri and Illinois as two other states holding August elections in which Whigs made significant gains in the lower state house. In the case of Illinois, Holt's table shows the Whig share of seats in the lower house jumping from 31 percent in 1836 to 52 percent in 1837. In fact, there were no state legislative elections in 1837 in Illinois since its state legislative elections were held in even-numbered years. See Charles Manfred Thompson, *The Illinois Whigs before 1846* (1915; repr., Urbana: University of Illinois Press, 1967), 132. According to Thompson's calculations, the Whigs increased their share of seats in the lower house from 31 percent in 1836 (56n36) to 47 percent in 1838 (60n44). Missouri, too, held its state legislative elections only in even-numbered years.

60 "Official Return of Votes for Representatives to the 25th Congress," *Rhode-Island Republican* (Newport, RI), September 6, 1837.

61 Daniel Fletcher Webster to Daniel Webster, August 28, 1837, *The Papers of Daniel Webster: Correspondence*, ed. Charles M. Wiltse and Harold D. Moser (Hanover, NH: University Press of New England, 1980), 4:234.

62 My count includes Whig pickups in the special election in Pennsylvania (+1); the runoff election in Maine (+1); and the regular congressional elections in North Carolina (+1), Rhode Island (+2), Tennessee (+2), Kentucky (+3), and Indiana (+6) as well as a loss of one seat in Maryland. There was no change in the partisan balance in the two other states that held regular congressional elections in the summer of 1837, Alabama (August 7) and Michigan (August 21–22), nor in the two other states that held special elections that summer, Arkansas (July 10) and Mississippi (July 17–18).

63 Two states held congressional elections in the fall of 1837. The first, Arkansas, which voted on October 2 (after voting in a special election several months before), returned a Democrat as its lone representative. The second was Mississippi, a complex case discussed in more depth below.

64 Georgia also held a gubernatorial contest in the fall, and for the first time the pro–Van Buren Union Democratic Party went down to defeat to the opposition, which called itself the State Rights Party. Democrats were more fortunate in Mississippi, where the anti–Van Buren opposition failed to agree on a candidate, allowing the Democrats to win the governorship despite winning only about 46 percent of the vote.

65 The Whig victory in Maine took partisans on both sides by complete surprise. On the eve of the election, for instance, the *New-York American*, a Whig organ that championed Daniel Webster's cause, conceded that the Maine election would "result, we presume, as usual, in a Van Buren success," albeit "by a diminished margin" (September 11, 1837). The Democrats meanwhile had confidently anticipated—in the words of the pro–Van Buren *Albany Argus*—"a rout more signal and overwhelming than ever before overtook federal whiggery in Maine" (September 9, 1837).

66 Holt, *Rise and Fall of the American Whig Party*, 75, 77. Vote totals by county are from the New York *Evening Post*, November 15 and 16, 1837. New York City results are reported in *Papers of Henry Clay*, 9:88.

67 This count leaves out Michigan, which was not yet a state in 1836; Delaware, Illinois, Louisiana, and Missouri, which held state legislative races in even-numbered years only; Tennessee, which held state legislative races in odd-numbered years only; and Georgia, for which 1837 data are unavailable. Four states (New Hampshire, Connecticut, Rhode Island, and Virginia) held state legislative elections in the spring. Data in this paragraph are calculated from seat percentages in Table 6 in Holt, *Rise and Fall of the American Whig Party* (75), although Holt does not distinguish between states in which the Whigs held a majority after the 1836 elections and states in which Democrats held the majority after the 1836 elections. Holt's Table 6 mistakenly lists Delaware, Illinois, and Missouri as having state elections in both 1836 and 1837 and in odd-numbered years thereafter.

68 By Holt's count, which relies on data in Melvin Lucas, *The Period of Political Alchemy: Party in the Mississippi Legislature, 1835–1846* (master's thesis, Cornell University, 1981), the Whigs had 50 percent of the seats in the Mississippi state house after the 1837 elections, an increase from 37.5 percent the year before. But while the seats were evenly split, the speakership and most of the committees were controlled by Whigs. See Lucas, 125, 133. As Lucas makes clear, accurately assessing party affiliation in Mississippi during the mid-1830s is extraordinarily difficult, if not impossible. Before the Panic, as historian James Rogers Sharp writes, "Party lines [in Mississippi] were extremely fluid. Not altogether atypical was one politician who called himself a Democrat in 1834, a Whig in 1835, a Democrat in 1836, a Whig in 1837, and a Democrat again in 1840. . . . Parties were loosely organized, often representing no more than loose coalitions of public men representing various sectional interests." *The Jacksonians versus the Banks: Politics in the States after the Panic of 1837* (New York: Columbia University Press, 1970), 56. Lucas uses roll-call votes for the election of US senator as his primary method of assigning party affiliation, and he explains why party designations in the newspapers are unreliable during this period (190–196). Cf. Edwin Arthur Miles, *Jacksonian Democracy in Mississippi* (Chapel Hill: University of North Carolina Press, 1960), 140.

69 Holt's count—or any count—of Whig Party strength in Alabama must be treated with caution, as party labels in Alabama in the mid-1830s, as in Mississippi, were often ill-fitting designations that induced fierce disagreement from

the rival sides. For instance, a Democratic paper's count of the partisan distribution in the upcoming state legislative session prompted strenuous objections from an anti-Jackson paper, which insisted that "many [legislators] placed in the Van Buren party are true White men"—that is, supporters of Hugh White (*Selma* [AL] *Daily Reporter*, October 10, 1835; for the same complaint from the opposite side with respect to the state's congressional delegation, see *Flag of the Union* [Tuscaloosa, AL], October 13, 1835). Adding to the difficulties of an accurate count is that the contingent of "White men" included Nullifiers, who were (until the summer of 1838, when they defected to the Democratic Party) vociferously opposed to Jackson and Van Buren. Historian J. Mills Thornton III estimates that in 1835, about 20 percent of the representatives "*seem to have been* Nullifier White men and 30 percent Unionist White men." *Politics and Power in a Slave Society, Alabama, 1800–1860* (Baton Rouge: Louisiana State University Press, 1978), 34n; emphasis added. That the results of Alabama's state legislative and congressional races tended to show little connection to the vicissitudes of the economy underscores not only the fluidity of party but the centrality of slavery and states' rights in Alabama politics.

70 The extent of the decline in Whig seats in Vermont (which decreased from 73 percent in 1836 to 57 percent in 1837) is misleading because, as Michael Holt observes, the 1836 number "represents the combined total of Antimasonic and Whig seats." *Rise and Fall of the American Whig Party*, 75. In 1837, unlike in 1836, Whigs and Anti-Masons no longer ran separate candidates in Vermont.

71 The Whigs' strong grip on the state government may also help to explain why Maryland was the only state holding congressional elections in the summer of 1837 (the state voted on July 26) in which the Whigs suffered a net loss of House seats. But while Maryland Whigs in 1837 had to settle for a 4–4 split in House seats (they had a 5–3 advantage after the 1835 elections), the Whigs' share of the vote increased from 52 percent in 1835 to 56 percent in 1837.

72 New York *Evening Post*, November 16, 1837.

73 Cole, *Jacksonian Democracy in New Hampshire*, 195. Cole estimates that 87 percent of those eligible voted (195; also see Tables 2 and 3 at 79, 139), whereas Walter Dean Burnham puts the turnout number at 82 percent (*Voting in American Elections: The Shaping of the American Political Universe since 1788* [Palo Alto, CA: Academica Press, 2010], 329). According to Cole, the "great interest in politics [in New Hampshire] began with the depression of 1837 and the state election of 1838" (195).

74 Sprague won by 381 votes, whereas the ten senators elected on the Whig slate won by between 776 and 935 votes. *Rhode-Island Republican*, May 9, 1938. The quotation is from the *Rhode-Island Republican*, April 18, 1838. Also see Edward Field, ed., *History of the State of Rhode Island and Providence Plantations* (Boston: Mason Publishing, 1902), 330–331.

75 Shade, *Democratizing the Old Dominion*, 169.

76 This count is based on Holt's Table 6 (*Rise and Fall of the American Whig Party*, 75) and so does not include Louisiana and Georgia, for which the data for 1837 were not available.

77 Margaret Wood, "A Duel with Rifles," July 17, 2013, https://blogs.loc.gov/law /2013/07/a-duel-with-rifles/.

78 The extraordinary saga is detailed in Miles, *Jacksonian Democracy in Mississippi*, 134–135, although Miles misleadingly suggests that the Whig candidates "easily defeated" the Democrats in the April contest (135). The two Whig candidates received 12,722 and 12,077 votes, while the two Democratic candidates polled 11,776 and 11,346 votes. The gap between the highest-polling Democrat and the lowest-polling Whig was thus only 300 votes.

79 Throughout 1837, Whigs frequently referred to the Democratic slate of candidates in local and state races as "the Van Buren ticket." See, for instance, the *Connecticut Courant* (November 13, 1837), referencing town elections in Hartford County; the *Commercial Advertiser* (March 9, 1837), referencing ward elections in Rochester; the *Wilkes-Barre Advocate* (November 1, 1837), referencing Pennsylvania's state legislative elections; and the *Baltimore Sun* (October 4, 1837), referencing Maryland's state legislative elections.

80 These election results cast doubt on Formisano's suggestion that "there is little evidence . . . that voters held political parties responsible for the vicissitudes of socioeconomic conditions . . . in the early nineteenth century." *Birth of Mass Political Parties*, 129.

81 Roberts, *America's First Great Depression*, 31.

82 Writing to Van Buren in the summer of 1837, Democratic Senator John Niles summed up the rival positions this way: "Our opponents charge the difficulties (which both parties admit to be vicious) to the government; we charge them to the banks. This is the issue between us." John Niles to Martin Van Buren, July 1, 1837, quoted in Wilson, *Presidency of Martin Van Buren*, 63.

83 Wilson, 61–63 (quotation at 62); and Holt, *Rise and Fall of the American Whig Party*, 68.

84 Holt, 64.

85 Holt, 77.

86 This is a theme rightly emphasized by Holt, 60–61, 68–70.

87 The Whigs' talking point that the Democrats were leaving the people to "take care of themselves" stemmed from a comment by Van Buren's close ally, New York senator Silas Wright, who, in introducing the Independent Treasury legislation in January 1838, said, "Let the government attend to its own affairs and let the people attend to theirs. Let the government take care that it secures a sound currency for its own use, and let it leave all the rest to the states and to the people." The next day, on the Senate floor, Daniel Webster seized on Wright's words and rendered them as "Let the government take care of itself, and the people take care of themselves." That idea, Webster said, was "the whole principle and policy of the administration." "Speech of Mr. Webster," January 31, 1838, *Niles' National Register*, March 3, 1838, 54:7. For the next three years—and into the 1840s—the Whigs recycled Webster's (not Wright's) words. See, for instance, Calvin Colton's *The Junius Tracts*, no. 2 (The Currency), first published in May 1843, which rendered "the maxim of Mr. Van Buren" as "Let the people take care of themselves, and the government take care of themselves" (3). Holt

mistakenly attributes this quotation to Colton's 1840 campaign pamphlet, *Crisis of the Country*. See *Rise and Fall of the American Whig Party*, 69.

CHAPTER 3. THE TWO SENATORS

1   Here, for instance, is a lament from the *U.S. Telegraph* in January 1837: "Editors are already breaking ground on the next Presidential election. It seems to have become a common opinion that the people have nothing to do but to elect Presidents—and the press no other employment than to designate whom they are to elect." "Views in Advance," extract printed in the *Democrat and Herald* (Wilmington, OH), January 20, 1837.

2   In truth, public jockeying for the next presidential election began even before Van Buren took office. See, for instance, the complaint of the *Vicksburg Register* (January 12, 1837) that several Northern papers were "already urging the claims of their candidates for the next presidential term." Ronald P. Formisano draws attention to the Whigs' "continuous campaign until 1840" in *The Birth of Mass Political Parties: Michigan, 1827–1861* (Princeton, NJ: Princeton University Press, 1971), 133; also see 128.

3   The *Connecticut Courant* reported that Webster held "the audience in breathless silence for two hours and a half" (March 25, 1837).

4   Daniel Webster to Hiram Ketchum, January 28, 1837, *The Papers of Daniel Webster: Correspondence*, ed. Charles M. Wiltse and Harold D. Moser (Hanover, NH: University Press of New England, 1980), 4:183–184.

5   Webster to Ketchum, January 28, 1837, 4:183.

6   Daniel Webster to Hiram Ketchum, February 11, 1837, *Papers of Daniel Webster*, 4:188–189.

7   Merrill D. Peterson, *The Great Triumvirate: Webster, Clay, and Calhoun* (New York: Oxford University Press, 1987), 111.

8   Michael F. Holt, *The Rise and Fall of the American Whig Party: Jacksonian Politics and the Onset of the Civil War* (New York: Oxford University Press, 1999), 22.

9   Robert V. Remini, *Daniel Webster: The Man and His Time* (New York: W. W. Norton, 1997), 162, 208.

10 Remini, 27–28; Robert D. Richardson, Jr., *Emerson: The Mind on Fire* (Berkeley: University of California Press, 1995), 387; and Irving H. Bartlett, *Daniel Webster* (New York: W. W. Norton, 1978), 10. Also see Holt, *Rise and Fall of the American Whig Party*, 22; and Peterson, *Great Triumvirate*, 38.

11 Holt, *Rise and Fall of the American Whig Party*, 40–41; Sydney Nathans, *Daniel Webster and Jacksonian Democracy* (Baltimore, MD: Johns Hopkins University Press, 1973), 105; and Daniel Webster to Jeremiah Mason, February 1, 1835, *Papers of Daniel Webster*, 4:25.

12 *Speech Delivered by Daniel Webster at Niblo's Saloon, in New-York on the 15th March, 1837* (New York: Harper & Brothers, 1837), 6. Also see Webster to Ketchum, March 4, 1837, 4:205.

13 *Speech Delivered by Daniel Webster at Niblo's Saloon*, 14–15; Nathans, *Webster and Jacksonian Democracy*, 108–109; and Holt, *Rise and Fall of the American Whig Party*, 91–92.

14 In 1835, Webster noted to a friend that "neither you nor I have ever believed that it would be easy to get Southern votes for *any* Northern man." Webster to Mason, February 1, 1835, 4:25.

15 Daniel Webster to Caleb Cushing, April 29, 1837, *Papers of Daniel Webster*, 4:223.

16 Holt, *Rise and Fall of the American Whig Party*, 91.

17 Remini, *Daniel Webster*, 467.

18 *New-York American*, June 30, 1837 (the account is reprinted from the *St. Louis Bulletin*).

19 Merrill Peterson mistakenly states that it was "six weeks after Webster went West" (that is, the middle of June) that the *New-York American* "hoisted [Webster's] banner." *Great Triumvirate*, 268. In fact, the New York *Commercial Advertiser* was the first to inscribe Webster's name on its banner; it did so on May 17, 1837, about two weeks into Webster's tour. The *New-York American* endorsed Webster on May 21, 1837. The *Long-Island Star* followed suit on May 22, and the *Journal of Commerce* reprinted the *Star*'s endorsement on May 29. The *Commercial Advertiser* was immediately taken to task by other Whig organs for pressing Webster's candidacy; see, for instance, the pro-Harrison *National Gazette* (Philadelphia, PA), May 18, 1837, and the pro-Clay *Morning Courier and New-York Enquirer* (edited by James Watson Webb) of the same date. The *Commercial Advertiser* defended its decision to affix Webster's name to its mast by pointing to the proposed nomination of Clay the previous day in the New York *Evening Star* (May 16, 1837), edited by Mordecai Manuel Noah.

20 Webster to Ketchum, January 28, 1837, 4:183. In the *New-York American*, the call for the public meeting was immediately followed by an account of the enthusiastic reception that Webster had received in St. Louis (June 23, 1837).

21 *New-York American*, June 23, 1837.

22 Henry Clay to Matthew L. Davis, July 3, 1837, *The Papers of Henry Clay*, ed. Robert Seager II (Lexington: University Press of Kentucky, 1988), 9:54. The distinction seems to have largely been ignored by Webster's friends as well. See, for instance, the *New-York American*, which prefaced its publication of the public call to recommend Webster by rejoicing in the "call upon the friends of Mr. Webster, to meet and put him in nomination for the Presidency" (June 23, 1837).

23 *New-York American*, June 23, 1837; and Nathans, *Webster and Jacksonian Democracy*, 114–115. Although the June 28 public meeting in New York City was the first important effort to nominate a Whig candidate for the 1840 election, it was not the first. Two months earlier, on April 22, 1837, citizens of New London, Virginia, had held a public meeting in which they nominated Jackson's old nemesis, Nicholas Biddle, to be the Whig candidate for president. The New London nomination and resolutions adopted can be found in the Natchez (MS) *Weekly Courier and Journal*, May 19, 1837. The following week, the seventy-seven-year-old Nullifier Thomas Cooper, once described by John Adams as a "talented Madcap," urged Biddle to "look to the Presidency" while dismissing Harrison as an "imbecile." Thomas Cooper to Nicholas Biddle, April 29, 1837,

in *The Correspondence of Nicholas Biddle*, ed. Reginald McGrane (Boston, MA: J. S. Canner, 1966), 272. After Biddle politely sidestepped the South Carolinian's suggestion that he run for president, Cooper renewed his suggestion a few months later—and lambasted Webster as lacking in judgment, energy, boldness, character, and courage. Thomas Cooper to Nicholas Biddle, July 1, 1837, *Correspondence of Nicholas Biddle*, 282. Also see Cooper's letters to Biddle, dated December 16, 1837, and October 1, 1838, *Correspondence of Nicholas Biddle*, 297, 333–334. To his credit, Biddle appears never to have taken Cooper's notion of a Biddle presidency seriously.

24 Matthew L. Davis to Henry Clay, July 12, 1837, and July 15, 1837, *Papers of Henry Clay*, 9:61, 9:62. Also see Nathans, *Webster and Jacksonian Democracy*, 115–116.

25 Caleb Cushing to Daniel Webster, July 28, 1837, *Papers of Daniel Webster*, 4:228. Even Thurlow Weed, who was adamantly opposed to a Webster nomination, conceded that Webster had done "nobly in the West." Thurlow Weed to William Henry Seward, July 8, 1837, quoted in Nathans, *Webster and Jacksonian Democracy*, 116. Remini writes, "As far as [Webster] was concerned, the trip had been a smashing success. Showered with gifts, praised to the heavens before thousands of people, kissed, embraced, wined, dined, and entertained with parades, regattas, and barbecues, he reckoned that this tour would place him up front among Whig candidates for the presidential nomination in 1840." Remini, *Daniel Webster*, 469–470. Contrast with Nathans's judgment that "Webster returned from the West in 1837 a defeated man." Nathans, *Webster and Jacksonian Democracy*, 114. My reading of Webster's behavior is closer to Remini's—namely, that Webster returned from his trip with "great hopes" for his presidential prospects but that he "deluded himself totally." Remini, *Daniel Webster*, 470.

26 Weed to Seward, July 8, 1837, and Thurlow Weed to Willis Hall, July 28, 1837, quoted in Nathans, *Webster and Jacksonian Democracy*, 117.

27 *Daily Commercial Advertiser* (Buffalo, NY), July 1, 1837.

28 *Boston Atlas*, quoted in *Huron Reflector* (Norwalk, OH), June 27, 1837.

29 Hiram Ketchum to Caleb Cushing, August 5, 1837, Caleb Cushing Papers, Library of Congress. Indeed, Ketchum insisted that not to have acted as they had would have been a "fatal mistake."

30 Hiram Ketchum to Caleb Cushing, July 1, 1837 and August 5, 1837, Caleb Cushing Papers, Library of Congress. In a public letter responding to a speaking invitation that fall, Webster sounded a similar theme: "However it may be with that of others, our cause is, emphatically, in the hands of the people; and let it be one of our fixed principles that the people shall be heard; that they shall in all things, *speak for themselves*, and that opinions, in regard either to men or measures, shall not be manufactured for the many, by the few." Daniel Webster to Henry Edwards et al., November 16, 1837, *Papers of Daniel Webster*, 4:250; emphasis added.

31 Hiram Ketchum to Caleb Cushing, September 15, 1837, Caleb Cushing Papers, Library of Congress.

32 Ketchum to Cushing, July 1, 1837. Upon his arrival back in Boston, Webster was met with a letter from Cushing informing Webster that he had "engaged to take charge of a department" at the New York–based *Journal of Commerce*, specifically "in reference to the Presidential canvass," with the purpose of being a conduit for Webster's views and "the channel of useful suggestions & arguments" in the coming presidential contest. Caleb Cushing to Daniel Webster, July 28, 1837, *Papers of Daniel Webster*, 4:228. Webster embraced the plan, telling Cushing that his "proposed aid" to the journal "will be of great importance." Daniel Webster to Caleb Cushing, July 29, 1837, *Papers of Daniel Webster*, 4:229.

33 Nathans, *Webster and Jacksonian Democracy*, 116. In the coming months, the *Journal of Commerce* would echo much of what Ketchum had communicated to Cushing. For instance, an article titled "The Presidential Question" claimed that "We have not the least doubt that Mr. Webster is the most popular man in the country" (reprinted in *New-York American*, November 287, 1837), language that directly echoed Ketchum's letter to Cushing.

34 *Commercial Advertiser*, May 17, 1837.

35 Webster had indeed predicted that Jackson's Bank War would lead to ruin, but hardly in the way that it happened. Webster had predicted economic stagnation, whereas the reality was the opposite: inflation and rampant speculation. And far from predicting the speculative bubble, Webster was one of many Americans caught up in the speculative mania. He had invested heavily in Western land in Michigan and Illinois, which was a large part of the reason why he wanted to travel to the West. The economic panic felt by Americans was shared by Webster, who would never entirely escape from the debt he incurred during the economic downturn of the late 1830s. Nathans, *Webster and Jacksonian Democracy*, 110. For praise of Webster as the "gifted prophet, who would have averted from [the nation's] lips the bitter cup which she is now forced to drain to the dregs," see the *Intelligencer and State Democrat* (Harrisburg, PA), reprinted in *New-York American*, May 15, 1837.

36 "The Presidential Question," Also see "A Candidate for the Presidency," *Long-Island Star*, May 22, 1837.

37 *New-York American*, August 14, 1837; also see August 17, 1837. The resolution also expressed approval of a national convention and promised to "cheerfully give our best exertions" on behalf of whichever candidate was nominated by the convention.

38 Nathans, *Webster and Jacksonian Democracy*, 116.

39 Henry Clay to Robert P. Letcher, May 30, 1837, *Papers of Henry Clay*, 9:48.

40 Henry Clay to Waddy Thompson, Jr., July 8, 1837, *Papers of Henry Clay*, 9:58.

41 Clay to Davis, July 3, 1837, 9:55. This theme was echoed repeatedly in papers friendly to Clay and Harrison. A correspondent of the *New York Express*, for instance, noted that merely because people "turned out by thousands to do honor to the man, it must not be thought that they think Mr. Webster can obtain the votes of the western states for the Presidency. They honored him as the great

northern statesman, as Daniel Webster, without intending in the least to say that he was the man for the whig candidate for the next Presidency." Reprinted in *Buffalo Patriot and Commercial Advertiser*, July 5, 1837.

42 Nathans, *Webster and Jacksonian Democracy*, 112.

43 "The Webster Nomination," *Carolina Watchman* (Salisbury, NC), July 15, 1837. How little the South regarded it as a "new era" is clear from a missive to Clay by George Bryan, who wrote from South Carolina to relay that the "Whigs in this quarter of the Country have been surprized and pained at the nomination of Mr. Webster in N.Y. . . . They cannot have regarded his relationship to the South, in this unfortunate proceeding. He has never acted with the South: from the war [of 1812] down to the compromise [tariff of 1833], on every question of interest or feeling, he has been uniformly opposed to it. If he is to be the candidate of the Party, the South will be thrown by irresistible necessity into the arms of the President. . . . Should the West take him up, the growing connection between the South and west will be rudely severed." July 14, 1837, *Papers of Henry Clay*, 9:61–62. Also see the letter from another South Carolinian, Oliver Dangerfield, August 3, 1837, *Papers of Henry Clay*, 9:65.

44 Henry Clay to Alexander Hamilton, May 26, 1837, *Papers of Henry Clay*, 9:46. Hamilton is described as an "intimate friend" of Clay in William M. Macbean, *Biographical Register of Saint Andrew's Society of the State of New York*, vol. 2 (1925), 775.

45 Clay to Davis, July 3, 1837, 9:54–55; Henry Clay to Alexander Hamilton, July 18, 1837, *Papers of Henry Clay*, 9:63. Also see Clay to Thompson, July 8, 1837, 9:58. The views Clay communicated to Davis were duly parroted back to Clay in a public letter composed by a committee made up of Clay's New York City allies (including Davis) who had convened on July 6 in response to the June 28 meeting of the friends of Webster. "Any attempt, this early, to designate a presidential Candidate," they wrote to Clay, "would expose us to the charge, however unfounded, of wanting patriotism, acting as mercenaries, and scrambling for the 'spoils of victory.'" Instead "our undivided efforts should be devoted against the men who by misrule have brought unparalleled sufferings upon our common country." *Papers of Henry Clay*, 9:68n1.

46 Clay to Thompson, July 8, 1837, 9:58.

47 Clay to Hamilton, July 18, 1837, 9:63; emphasis added. Also see Clay's "strictly confidential" letter to George D. Prentice, August 14, 1837, in which he wrote that "every exertion ought to be made during the approaching Session of Congress to produce concentration. With it, all will go well. Without it, it is to be feared that we shall, in the collisions to elect delegates to the N[ational] Convention, have all the consequences and heartburnings without the fruits of an election." *Papers of Henry Clay*, 9:70. In his response to a committee of New York City Whigs on August 8, which was written with an eye to its being released to the public, Clay was intentionally vague about how this unity prior to a national convention would be achieved. While agreeing with the committee that a national convention was necessary, he added, "This will not supersede the previous employment of all proper means to produce union, harmony and

concentration. A resort to such means is recommended by their tendency to prevent those unpleasant collisions in the choice of Delegates to the Convention, which might leave among the friends of the respective persons thought of as candidates a state of irritated feeling, unfavorable to that hearty co-operation in the final struggle, so essential to success." Henry Clay to Committee of New York City Whigs, August 8, 1837, *Papers of Henry Clay*, 9:67.

48   Remini, *Daniel Webster*, 469.

49   On Clay's role in the development of the Speakership, see Elaine K. Swift, "The Start of Something New: Clay, Stevenson, Polk, and the Development of the Speakership, 1789–1869," in *Masters of the House: Congressional Leadership over Two Centuries*, ed. Roger H. Davidson, Susan Webb Hammond, and Raymond W. Smock (Boulder, CO: Westview Press, 1998), 9–32; and Randall Strahan, Vincent G. Moscardelli, Moshe Haspel, and Richard S. Wike, "The Clay Speakership Revisited," *Polity* 32 (Summer 2000): 561–593.

50   William Plumer, Jr., quoted in Robert V. Remini, *Henry Clay: Statesman for the Union* (New York: W. W. Norton, 1991), 186.

51   Remini, *Henry Clay*, 192.

52   In a letter dated July 14, 1837, George Bryan informed Clay that the *Charlestown Mercury* "has put you in nomination." *Papers of Henry Clay*, 9:62. The paper's endorsement, on July 8, identified Clay as "the only man" around whom both North and South could unite "a conquering party," a judgment that Bryan fully shared. South Carolina's William Preston held the same view, telling Willie Mangum in a letter dated October 4, 1837, that "the only opposition man who has the slightest chance for the next Presidency is Mr. Clay." Benjamin L. Huggins, *Willie Mangum and the North Carolina Whigs in the Age of Jackson* (Jefferson, NC: McFarland, 2016), 114.

53   See, for instance, Samuel Kernell, Gary C. Jacobson, Thad Kousser, and Lynn Vavreck, *The Logic of American Politics*, 9th ed. (Washington, DC: CQ Press, 2020), chapter 7.

54   See Clay's letter to Prentice, August 14, 1837, in which he acknowledged that his letter to the New York committee "may be published" (9:69). Also see Peterson, *Great Triumvirate*, 269.

55   Clay to Committee of New York City Whigs, August 8, 1837, 9:67–68. Also see Clay's letter, dated February 27, 1837, to Edwin Harriman, editor of the *Mercantile Advertiser* (Mobile, AL), which was published in that paper and reprinted in *Niles' Weekly Register*, April 22, 1837. In it, he wrote that the presidency "never possessed any charms in my sight which could induce me to seek it by unworthy means, or to desire it but as the spontaneous grant of those who alone had the right to bestow it." *Papers of Henry Clay*, 9:33.

56   Clay to Committee of New York City Whigs, August 8, 1837, 9:68. Also see the letter, dated July 14, 1837, in which George Bryan advised Clay to "continue a passive position and hold yourself at the disposal of the Nation." *Papers of Henry Clay*, 9:62.

57   Henry Clay to Gulian C. Verplanck et al., June 8, 1838, *Papers of Henry Clay*, 9:201. Also see Henry Clay to Epes Sargent, January 13, 1838, *Papers of Henry*

Clay, 9:130; and Henry Clay to John Leeds Kerr, May 22, 1838, *Papers of Henry Clay*, 9:188.

58 Clay to Verplanck, June 8, 1838, 9:202. Also see Clay's letter to Peter B. Porter, June 3, 1838, in which he explained why his course of action was not only proper but strategically advantageous since overt electioneering "would excite jealousy and perhaps lead to alienation among the friends of the others." Moreover, since "every thing every where is going on well . . . I ought to be the last to make any efforts. . . . We have every reason to be satisfied with the present condition of affairs; and there is more danger of my impairing than improving it, by the display of eagerness." *Papers of Henry Clay*, 9:197–198.

59 Lawrence M. Crutcher, *George Keats of Kentucky: A Life* (Lexington: University Press of Kentucky, 2012), 232.

60 Clay to Prentice, August 14, 1837, 9:70–71. On Prentice, see Betty Carolyn Congleton, "The Whig Campaign of 1840: The Editorial Policy of George D. Prentice," *Indiana Magazine of History* (September 1967), 233–246.

61 Clay to Prentice, August 14, 1837, 9:69–70.

62 Henry Clay to Robert P. Letcher, January 17, 1837, *Papers of Henry Clay*, 9:14; and Henry Clay to Francis T. Brooke, February 10, 1837, *Papers of Henry Clay*, 9:27. Also see Henry Clay to Benjamin Watkins Leigh, February 4, 1837, *The Papers of Henry Clay: Supplement, 1793–1852*, ed. Melba Porter Hay (Lexington: University Press of Kentucky, 1992), 267–268; and Henry Clay to Francis T. Brooke, March 7, 1837, *Papers of Henry Clay*, 9:39. Webster had similar doubts about the party's future at the beginning of 1837. See Webster to Ketchum, January 28, 1837, 4:183.

63 Henry Clay to Seth Wheatley, August 18, 1837, *Papers of Henry Clay*, 9:72.

64 Clay to Prentice, August 14, 1837, 9:70.

65 James Watson Webb to Henry Clay, September 29, 1837, *Papers of Henry Clay*, 9:81–82. Also see James Watson Webb to Henry Clay, December 15 and 19, 1837, *Papers of Henry Clay*, 9:106–107.

66 Henry Clay to Willie P. Mangum, November 17, 1837, *Papers of Henry Clay*, 9:92.

67 Peter B. Porter to Henry Clay, November 12, 1837, *Papers of Henry Clay*, 9:91. Holt points out that a key reason that Northern Whigs opted for Harrison over Webster in 1836 was that New York seemed solidly in the Democratic column, and so Whigs needed the nation's second-largest state if they were to have any chance of winning (*Rise and Fall of the American Whig Party*, 41–42).

68 Thaddeus Stevens, a leader of the state's Anti-Masons, for instance, enraged his Whig coalition partners at the convention by proposing to reduce the number of representatives from Philadelphia. See Hans L. Trefousse, *Thaddeus Stevens: Nineteenth-Century Egalitarian* (Chapel Hill: University of North Carolina Press, 1997), 51. On Pennsylvania's constitutional convention, see Charles McCool Snyder, *The Jacksonian Heritage: Pennsylvania Politics, 1833–1848* (Harrisburg: Pennsylvania Historical and Museum Commission, 1958), 96–111.

69 Porter to Clay, November 12, 1837, 9:91; and Peter B. Porter to Henry Clay, November 14, 1837, *Papers of Henry Clay*, 9:92.

70 Porter to Clay, November 14, 1837, 9:92.

71 Henry Clay to Peter B. Porter, December 5, 1837, *Papers of Henry Clay*, 9:96. Also see Henry Clay to Peter B. Porter, December 24, 1837, *Papers of Henry Clay*, 9:114; Henry Clay to Peter B. Porter, January 5, 1838, *Papers of Henry Clay*, 9:120–121; Henry Clay to Peter B. Porter, February 10, 1838, *Papers of Henry Clay*, 9:142; and Henry Clay to Robert Swartwout, April 2, 1838, *Papers of Henry Clay*, 9:168.

72 Clay to Porter, December 5, 1837, 9:96; emphasis in original. Also see Clay to Porter, January 5, 1838, in which he wrote: "I attach paramount importance to an expression of the preference of the Whig members at Albany. I believe that it would be *decisive.*" 9:120, emphasis in original.

73 Peter B. Porter to Henry Clay, December 15, 1837, *Papers of Henry Clay*, 9:105; emphasis in original.

74 Clay to Porter, December 24, 1837, 9:114; emphasis in original. Also see Henry Clay to George Getz, December 18, 1837, *Papers of Henry Clay*, 9:110.

75 Peter B. Porter to Henry Clay, January 7, 1838, *Papers of Henry Clay*, 9:123. Porter's account of what Weed told Webster is dramatically different from what Weed reported to Francis Granger (Harrison's vice-presidential candidate in 1836) in a letter of December 24, 1837, that summarized two "long, frank talks" he had had with Webster about the presidential race. Weed told Granger that he had informed Webster that "unless it should appear quite certain that Van Buren could not be re-elected, we should go for H[arrison] with the conviction that he was the *strongest* candidate." Thurlow Weed to Francis Granger, December 24, 1837, Francis and Gideon Granger Papers, Library of Congress.

76 Henry Clay to Francis T. Brooke, January 13, 1838, *Papers of Henry Clay*, 9:130.

77 Henry Clay to Peter B. Porter, January 26, 1838, *Papers of Henry Clay*, 9:135; and Henry Clay to Peter B. Porter, January 21, 1838, *Papers of Henry Clay*, 9:132. Clay was nominated by a caucus of Maryland's Whig legislators on February 19, 1838. See *Baltimore Sun*, February 24, 1838.

78 Henry Clay to Joseph Childs, February 15, 1838, *Papers of Henry Clay*, 9:143–144. Similarly, when informed at the beginning of the year about the possibility that New Jersey might nominate him (Charles Kinsey to Henry Clay, January 3, 1838, *Papers of Henry Clay*, 9:119), Clay had apparently thought the "pushing-forward" effort premature, but in March, he complained bitterly about "the pulling-back policy" that was preventing New Jersey's Whigs from expressing their "undoubted" preference for Clay. See Henry Clay to Peter B. Porter, March 4, 1838, *Papers of Henry Clay*, 9:153.

79 Henry Clay to Peter B. Porter, January 10, 1838, *Papers of Henry Clay*, 9:127. Also see Clay's letter to Epes Sargent in which he claimed that the "same concentration which you describe as taking place, in Massachusetts in regard to the next P. Election, is going on, and perhaps more rapidly, elsewhere." Moreover, he insisted, this "concentration" was occurring "without any personal exertion on my part to direct the current of public feeling towards me." Clay to Sargent, January 13, 1838, 9:130.

80 Clay to Henry Clay, Jr., March 2, 1838, *Papers of Henry Clay*, 9:152; emphasis in original.

81 Polk to A. O. P. Nicholson, January 13, 1838, *Correspondence of James K. Polk*, ed. Herbert Weaver (Nashville, TN: Vanderbilt University Press, 1977), 4:330. Also see the judgment made by the *Richmond Whig*: "As matters now stand at this moment, there can be no question that Mr. Clay has the largest share of the whig favor." Quoted in *Boston Post*, December 30, 1837.

82 Peter B. Porter to Henry Clay, March 8, 1838, *Papers of Henry Clay*, 9:156–157. In a later letter, Porter assigned more blame to Webster's friends, who had been "systematically engaged in efforts to defer any expression of public opinion to the latest possible period—trusting to management or accident for a change more favourable to their views." Peter B. Porter to Henry Clay, May 25, 1838, *Papers of Henry Clay*, 9:189. Also see Peter B. Porter to Henry Clay, April 17, 1838, and April 22, 1838, *Papers of Henry Clay*, 9:175, 176.

83 Clay to Swartwout, April 2, 1838, 9:168.

84 Clay to Porter, March 4, 1838, 9:154.

85 Henry Clay to John M. Clayton, June 14, 1838, *Papers of Henry Clay*, 9:204. Clay added, with his typical optimism at the time, that "I do not think it of much consequence; for it only retards; and the spontaneous bursts in other quarters will supply the place of those testimonies which might have been rendered" in these four states.

86 Henry Clay to Peter B. Porter, May 25, 1838, *Papers of Henry Clay*, 9:190; and Peter B. Porter to Henry Clay, May 28, 1838, *Papers of Henry Clay*, 9:192. Clay added the proviso "that these meetings are conducted in a spirit not exclusive or intolerant," which meant not denigrating rival candidates and promising to support the nominee selected at the national convention. Also see Clay to Porter, June 3, 1838, 9:197.

87 Clay to Committee of New York City Whigs, August 8, 1837, 9:66–67.

88 Daniel Webster to Richard Haughton, February 23, 1838, *Papers of Daniel Webster*, 4:275; and Daniel Webster to Robert Charles Winthrop, May 10, 1838, *Papers of Daniel Webster*, 4:295; the latter letter was in response to a large public meeting of Clay supporters in Philadelphia on May 9, 1838.

89 Daniel Webster to Robert Charles Winthrop, February 7, 1838, *Papers of Daniel Webster*, 4:268. Also see Daniel Webster to Hiram Ketchum, February 10, 1838, *Papers of Daniel Webster*, 4:269.

90 Clay to Porter, January 5, 1838, 9:120; and Henry Clay to John M. Clayton, June 15, 1838, *Papers of Henry Clay*, 9:205. By "spontaneously made," he hastened to add, he meant "such manifestations as are voluntarily made by the People themselves, without any interested or artificial agency on the part of those who are spoken of as Candidates." In a letter at the end of the summer to Harrison Gray Otis, Clay ridiculed the idea that the party should wait for the convention to express their preference for candidates: "If it were possible for 15 millions of people to hold their breath, and suppress all expression of their wishes, until December 1839 when they shall be finally promulgated through the organ of a Nat. Convention, the explosion, and the bitterness of disappointment, would then be only the greater." September 1, 1838, *Papers of Henry Clay*, 9:226. By the end of the year, Clay was even more insistent that "the best way to ensure

success to our cause is by such a manifestation of the public choice as to leave no other duty to the Convention than to ratify & promulgate it. The Convention ought to express not to make public sentiment; but to express it, it must know it; and it cannot know it unless the public demonstrate it." Henry Clay to Harrison G. Otis, December 13, 1838, *Papers of Henry Clay*, 9:252.

91 Henry Clay to Peter B. Porter, April 15, 1838, *Papers of Henry Clay*, 9:173. Also see Henry Clay to Francis T. Brooke, April 14, 1838, *Papers of Henry Clay*, 9:172; and Henry Clay to Peter B. Porter, March 13, 1838, *Papers of Henry Clay*, 163–164. In February 1838, a convention of Indiana Whigs had endorsed Harrison but also praised Clay and promised to support him if nominated.

92 Clay to Porter, March 13, 1838, 9:163. Also see Clay to Swartwout, April 2, 1838, 9:167–168.

93 Henry Clay to Harrison G. Otis, July 7, 1838, *Papers of Henry Clay*, 9:212–213; Clay to Clayton, June 14, 1838, 9:204. Also see Henry Clay to Harrison G. Otis, June 26, 1838, *Papers of Henry Clay*, 9:209.

94 Clay to Clayton, June 14, 1838, 9:204.

95 Edward Everett to Robert C. Winthrop, June 8, 1838, quoted in Robert F. Dalzell, Jr., *Daniel Webster and the Trial of American Nationalism, 1843–1852* (Boston: Houghton Mifflin, 1973), 67.

96 In a letter to Clay written on Christmas Eve, Harrison Gray Otis explained that until Webster formally withdrew, Clay could not hope to secure a nomination from the Massachusetts legislature—a course Clay had urged upon Otis in an earlier missive (December 13, 1838, 9:252). Although rumors that Webster would quit the race were circulating in Boston, Otis said that "until [Webster] unequivocally withdraws from the canvass you can easily see that [Webster's supporters in Massachusetts] must feel under restraint. The most to be hoped prior to that event, is a declaration by the Legislature adhering to him, as their first choice & announcing yourself as the second." Harrison G. Otis to Henry Clay, December 24, 1838, *Papers of Henry Clay*, 9:260–261. Also see Henry Clay to Harrison G. Otis, January 1, 1839, *Papers of Henry Clay*, 9:264.

97 Robert C. Winthrop to John Clifford, February 12, 1838, quoted in Dalzell, *Webster and the Trial of American Nationalism*, 65. By February, Webster himself was already entertaining the possibility that it might be "found necessary to fall back on" Harrison. Webster to Ketchum, February 10, 1838, 4:269. Also see Nathans, *Webster and Jacksonian Democracy*, 124.

98 Dalzell, *Webster and the Trial of American Nationalism*, 65–66. Nathans reports that Supreme Court Justice Joseph Story also privately pressed Webster to withdraw in May. Nathans, *Webster and Jacksonian Democracy*, 122.

99 John Quincy Adams, quoted in Dalzell, *Webster and the Trial of American Nationalism*, 64; also see 66. The Adams quotation is from a diary entry dated November 16, 1838.

100 Dalzell, 65.

101 Holt, for instance, writes that Webster's "jealous determination to stop Clay" was rooted in having "never forgiven Clay for supporting Harrison rather than himself in 1836." Holt, *Rise and Fall of the American Whig Party*, 93. Also

see Peterson, *Great Triumvirate*, 249. In September 1836, William Plumer, a longtime opponent of Webster's, claimed that Webster was envious of Clay's position as head of the Whig Party and "attributed some part of his apparent unpopularity to Clay." Norman D. Brown, *Daniel Webster and the Politics of Availability* (Athens: University of Georgia Press, 1969), 163. In a letter dated January 11, 1839, Harrison Gray Otis told Clay that he had the impression that Webster thinks "you did him ill offices by favoring H[arrison] at his expense in 1836." *Papers of Henry Clay*, 9:269.

102 Henry Clay to Hugh L. White, August 27, 1838, *Papers of Henry Clay*, 9:221.

103 The *Lexington Observer and Kentucky Reporter*, a paper that, according to historian Merrill Peterson, was "generally supposed to speak for" Clay (Peterson, *Great Triumvirate*, 249), did endorse Harrison in August 1835. However, there is no evidence tying Clay to the endorsement, although, like every other sentient Kentucky Whig, Clay by this time had come to the realization that Harrison had a far better chance than Webster of beating Van Buren in Kentucky as well as in other Western states. Clay took note of the Harrison endorsement (and Harrison's fast-developing political strength in the West) in the *Lexington Observer and Kentucky Reporter*—as well as in the Frankfort *Commonwealth*—in a letter to Francis Brooke dated August 19, 1835, *Papers of Henry Clay*, 8:796.

104 In a letter to Hugh L. White, Clay insisted that at the October 5, 1836, event at which he endorsed Harrison, he had made clear that he did so because Harrison had "the greatest prospects of defeating Mr. Van Buren." "Most certainly," he told White, "the General was not my first choice. I should have preferred Mr. Webster to him, *and so stated.*" August 27, 1838, 221; emphasis added.

105 Henry Clay to Samuel Southard, July 31, 1835, *Papers of Henry Clay*, 8:795; Henry Clay to Christopher Hughes, August 25, 1835, *Papers of Henry Clay*, 8:799. Also see Clay to [John M. Bailhache], July 14, 1835, *Papers of Henry Clay*, 8:782–784.

106 Webster's supporters were aware that a Harrison victory would mean the "great man" would be invited into the Cabinet. Harrison Gray Otis, for instance, reported that "a very confidential personal friend" of Webster who approved of the *Atlas*'s support of Harrison told him that "if Harrison should be elected, W and C would be members of his Cabinet." Harrison G. Otis to Henry Clay, January 23, 1839, Harrison Gray Otis Papers, Reel 10, Massachusetts Historical Society, Boston, MA. Warren Lovering, an important Massachusetts Whig who was selected as a delegate to the 1839 Whig national convention, received assurances from a prominent Ohio Whig close to Harrison that "if the General be elected to the Presidency he would not only prefer, but rely upon it, that Mr. Webster should hold the first place in his cabinet relations." William Greene to [Warren] Lovering, May 28, 1839, quoted in Edgar Allan Holt, *Party Politics in Ohio, 1840–1850* (Columbus, OH: F. J. Heer, 1930), 13.

107 Webster, in contrast, went to great lengths to play up his sympathy for the Anti-Masonic movement and his distrust of Masonry in the 1836 campaign. He told John Quincy Adams, for instance, that "his own impression upon Masonry . . . had always been unfavorable" and that "his father had always dis-

liked the institution, and had brought him up in the dislike of it." Diary entry of January 7, 1834, *Memoirs of John Quincy Adams, Comprising Portions of His Diary from 1795 to 1848*, ed. Charles Francis Adams (Philadelphia, PA: J. B. Lippincott, 1876), 9:71.

108 Daniel Webster to Hiram Ketchum, January 20, 1838, *Papers of Daniel Webster*, 4: 263.

109 "I do not think Mr. C[lay] can get NH or PA nor that he has any chance of the South," Webster wrote to Ketchum, February 10, 1838, 4:269.

110 Daniel Webster to Benjamin Douglass Silliman, January 29, 1838, *Papers of Daniel Webster*, 4:265.

111 Webster to Haughton, February 23, 1838, 4:276.

112 Webster closed a letter to Hiram Ketchum by noting, "Will it not be felt, as a striking fact, that we have had a slave-holder for President, *forty years out of forty eight?*" January 20, 1838, 4:264.

113 Holt, *Rise and Fall of the American Whig Party*, 95; and Peterson, *Great Triumvirate*, 275.

114 In a letter to Porter, Clay identified "two traps . . . set for me here by Mr. Calhoun to affect me at the South—one relating to Abolition, and the other to Texas." Clay told Porter that Calhoun "has totally failed as to Abolition" and was equally confident that he would soon "disappoint him as to Texas." January 10, 1838, 9:127; also see Clay to Brooke, January 13, 1838, 9:129; and Clay to Porter, January 26, 1838, 9:136. In a letter to Clay, New Jersey's Charles Kinsey saw the traps as being laid by antislavery forces: "Is not this violent opposition to the annexation of Texas and this unholy excitement of abolition got up purposely to keep you from the Presidency?" January 3, 1838, 9:119.

115 Holt, *Rise and Fall of the American Whig Party*, 95–96.

116 Peterson, *Great Triumvirate*, 275.

117 Clay to Porter, January 10, 1838, 9:127.

118 Holt, *Rise and Fall of the American Whig Party*, 96. See, for instance, the supportive letter from Virginia's John Tyler, who praised Clay for "rallying the sound-headed and sound-hearted to the North" and avoiding the "snare" that abolitionists had set for the South. January 28, 1838, *Papers of Henry Clay*, 9:137.

119 Henry Clay to Willie P. Mangum, May 31, 1838, *Papers of Henry Clay*, 9:194. Also see Henry Clay to Rufus W. Griswold, July 28, 1838, *Papers of Henry Clay*, 9:215, in which Clay noted having received "several letters from the South, stating that I am charged there with being an Abolitionist." Also see William C. Preston to John Tyler, December 30, 1837, in *Letters and Times of the Tylers*, ed. Lyon G. Tyler (Richmond, VA: Whittet and Shepperson, 1884), 1:586.

120 Daniel Webster to Hiram Ketchum, January 15, 1838, *Papers of Daniel Webster*, 4:262; emphasis in original. Webster laid out his own position in a letter to Luther Christopher Peck, January 11, 1838, *Papers of Daniel Webster*, 4:261.

121 Webster to Silliman, January 29, 1838, 4:265. Silliman, who went on to have a long and illustrious career as a New York lawyer, attended the Whig national convention in December 1839 as a Harrison supporter.

122 By the spring of 1838, Clay himself was becoming more apprehensive about whether abolitionists might damage him in the North. After meeting with Francis Granger, who had been on the ticket with Harrison (and Webster in Massachusetts) in 1836 as the vice-presidential candidate, Clay wrote to Peter B. Porter, "Granger expresses great apprehensions from the Abolitionists. Do you think there is any foundation for them? From those in New England, I had much reason to believe that they preferred me to any person spoke of." April 16, 1838, *Papers of Henry Clay*, 9:173. Granger's views on abolitionism's effects on Clay's viability can be gleaned from a letter he wrote to Weed the month before in which he had highlighted "the fire that the Abolition batteries are making upon Clay." Granger told Weed that "they are gaining converts by the regiment [and] will have one fourth of the votes of the states before the grand contest of 1840." Francis Granger to Thurlow Weed, March 14, 1838, in Thurlow Weed Barnes, *Memoir of Thurlow Weed* (Boston: Houghton Mifflin, 1884), 57. Clay heard something similar from Lewis Tappan, an antislavery leader in New York, who cautioned Clay that "abolitionists can now decide the elections in every county in this State West of Albany, & that the editors of the political papers know it. In Rhode Island the abolitionists recently decided the election. They can decide the next election in this city." Lewis Tappan to Henry Clay, May 1, 1838, *Papers of Henry Clay*, 9:181. Also see Clay to Griswold, July 28, 1838, 9:215; and especially Henry Clay to Peter B. Porter, December 27, 1838, *Papers of Henry Clay*, 9: 262.

123 Remini, *Webster*, 425. Harrison Gray Otis told Clay that he could not imagine that the *Atlas* would change course without Webster's "privity and assent." September 14, 1838, *Papers of Henry Clay*, 9:229. Edward Everett, too, "suspected that Webster approved the piece." Nathans, *Webster and Jacksonian Democracy*, 123. Historian Robert Dalzell comes to the same conclusion that "in all probability," the *Atlas* articles supporting Harrison were "written with Webster's knowledge and approval." *Webster and the Trial of American Nationalism*, 310. Also see Henry Clay to Francis T. Brooke, November 3, 1838, *Papers of Henry Clay*, 9:245.

124 Nathans, *Webster and Jacksonian Democracy*, 123–124; Holt, *Rise and Fall*, 97; *Papers of Henry Clay*, 229–230.

125 Henry Clay to Harrison G. Otis, September 24, 1838, *Papers of Henry Clay*, 9:232–233.

126 Clay to Otis, December 13, 1838, 9:251.

127 Clay to Otis, 9:252.

128 Clay to Francis T. Brooke, December 20, 1838, *Papers of Henry Clay*, 9:258; and Clay to Otis, December 13, 1838, 9:252. Also see Clay to Porter, December 27, 1838, 9:262. What made the convention "a mere mockery," in Clay's view, was that "from no one of the States pretended to be represented were there any delegates chosen by the Anti M[ason]s; that they were self made delegates; that one self made delegate from Massactts cast the whole vote of that State; another from N. York did the same &c; and that Anti Masonry does not exist *in organization* in any State in the Union but Pennsa. & perhaps Vermont." Henry

Clay to Henry Clay, Jr., January 18, 1839, *Papers of Henry Clay*, 9:273; and Henry Clay to Josiah Randall, February 8, 1839, *Papers of Henry Clay*, 9:283.

129 In 1836, the Whigs had won all six congressional seats in New Jersey despite no Whig candidate getting more than 50.7 percent of the vote, whereas in 1838, they lost five of six seats even though no Whig candidate received less than 49.8 percent of the vote.

130 Pennsylvania's elections on October 9—the same day as Ohio's—were also disappointing, although the Whigs did not lose ground in the vote share despite the defeat of the incumbent Anti-Masonic governor, Joseph Ritner. Ritner had been elected in 1835 with 47 percent of the vote because of a split in the Democratic Party, and in 1838, he lost with 49 percent of the vote because the Democratic Party had united behind a single candidate. Democrats in 1838 retained their majority in the lower house but picked up no additional seats (they won 56 percent of the seats in both 1837 and 1838—as compared to 72 percent in 1836). The congressional delegation remained heavily Democratic (seventeen of the state's twenty-eight congressional seats were won by Democrats), although Democrats won one fewer seat in 1838 than in 1836.

131 Nathans, *Webster and Jacksonian Democracy*, 124; Henry Clay to Alexander R. Wyckoff, November 18, 1838, *Papers of Henry Clay*, 9:250.

132 Clay to Wyckoff, 9:250; and Clay to Otis, December 13, 1838, 9:252.

133 Clay to Brooke, November 3, 1838, 9:245.

134 Clay to Brooke. Also see Henry Clay to Harrison G. Otis, November 14, 1838, *Papers of Henry Clay*, 9:247 ("We have lost the State by abolition"). Among the factors that appear to have hurt the party in Ohio among antislavery voters was the Whig governor's extradition of an abolitionist whom Kentucky authorities had indicted for helping a runaway slave. In addition, the organ of the Ohio Anti-Slavery Society—*The Philanthropist*, edited by Gamaliel Bailey—urged voters to cast their ballot for Democratic state legislators in the hope (vain, as it turned out) that the legislature would return the state's ardently antislavery senator, Democrat Thomas Morris, to the US Senate. See Richard H. Sewell, *Ballots for Freedom: Antislavery Politics in the United States, 1837–1860* (New York: W. W. Norton, 1976), 18–19; and Corey M. Brooks, *Liberty Power: Antislavery Third Parties and the Transformation of American Politics* (University of Chicago Press, 2016), 30.

135 Clay to Brooke, November 3, 1838, 9:246. The letter from Birney is dated October 22, 1838. For Clay's reply, see Henry Clay to James G. Birney, November 3, 1838, *Papers of Henry Clay*, 9:244–245. On Clay's past association with Birney, see Betty Fladeland, *James Gillespie Birney: Slaveholder to Abolitionist* (Ithaca, NY: Cornell University Press, 1955), 5, 15, 19, 29, 44, 59, 93–95. Clay was hardly the only Whig leader shaken by the Ohio results. The day after Clay sat down to write to Brooke—and the day before voters would go to the polls in New York—Thurlow Weed dashed off an anxious note to his comrade-in-arms William Henry Seward, who was the Whig nominee for governor. Weed's worry was not so much that antislavery forces in western New York would vote Democratic as that they would abandon the Whig Party for an explicitly antislavery

party. "They hope," he told Seward, "to build an Abolition party on the ruins of the Whig party." Weed to Seward, November 4, 1838, quoted in Robert Gray Gunderson, *The Log-Cabin Campaign* (Lexington: University Press of Kentucky, 1957), 39. As Weed foresaw, the Liberty Party was formed the following year and nominated none other than Birney as its presidential candidate in 1840. Although Birney received only a tiny fraction of the presidential vote in 1840, in 1844, the Liberty Party, with Birney again as its presidential nominee, garnered almost ten times as many votes as it had in 1840. Fifteen thousand of those votes for Birney were in New York, which Weed, along with almost every other Whig, believed tipped the state and the presidency from the Whig nominee Henry Clay to the Democratic nominee James Polk (Polk won New York—without which he would not have won the presidency—by only 5,000 votes).

136 Clay to Brooke, November 3, 1838, 9:246.

137 Clay to Otis, November 14, 1838, 9:248.

138 Peter Temin, *The Jacksonian Economy* (New York: W. W. Norton, 1969), 149; and Alasdair Roberts, *America's First Great Depression: Economic Crisis and Political Disorder after the Panic of 1837* (Ithaca, NY: Cornell University Press, 2012), 44. The economic recovery of 1838–1939 was spurred, too, by state borrowing for a host of transportation infrastructure projects, particularly canals and railroads. See Temin, *Jacksonian Economy*, 151; and Namsuk Kim and John Joseph Wallis, "The Market for American State Government Bonds in Britain and the United States, 1930–1843," *Economic History Review* (November 2005): 742–743.

139 Holt, *Rise and Fall of the American Whig Party*, 98, 75.

140 In Georgia, too, the Whigs scored a spectacular success, winning all nine congressional seats owing to the state's at-large election system. Although the vote swing between 1836 and 1838 was small, with the median vote share for the Whig candidate increasing only from 49.4 percent to 51 percent, Georgia's at-large election system turned that into a seven- or eight-seat pickup for the Whigs. Georgia's election was held on October 1, 1838.

141 Roberts, *America's First Great Depression*, 45; Martin Van Buren, "Second Annual Message," December 3, 1838, American Presidency Project, https://www.presidency.ucsb.edu/node/201825.

142 Daniel Webster to Samuel Jaudon, March 29, 1839, *Papers of Daniel Webster*, 4:355. Also see Henry Clay to Harrison G. Otis, March 22, 1839, *Papers of Henry Clay*, 9:298, in which Clay said that he "was told that [Webster's] tone was discouraging of the success of the Whig cause, under the banner either of Genl. Harrison or myself." In the same letter, Clay reported that he had definitively ascertained that "Mr. Webster was endeavoring to turn the tide toward Genl. Harrison. He was not working very openly but very earnestly." For his earlier suspicions that Webster had "entered into the plan of electing Genl. Harrison," see Clay's letter to his son Henry Clay, Jr., dated January 18, 1839, 9:272. By March 1839, as we will see in chapter 5, Clay was far more optimistic than Webster about the Whigs' chances, and his own, in 1840.

143 Daniel Webster to Samuel Jaudon, January 12, 1839, *Papers of Daniel Webster*, 4:338.

144 Daniel Webster, Enclosure: To the People of Massachusetts, June 12, 1839, *Papers of Daniel Webster*, 4:370; and Nathans, *Webster and Jacksonian Democracy*, 125. At the Whig national nominating convention in December 1839, the Massachusetts delegates who were friendly to Webster were "most anxious to exclude Clay," as Supreme Court Justice John Catron found out, quite by accident, when he crossed paths with the Bay State delegation in Philadelphia. John Catron to James K. Polk, January 3, 1840, in *Correspondence of James K. Polk*, ed. Wayne Cutler (Nashville, TN: Vanderbilt University Press, 1979), 5:367.

CHAPTER 4. THE TWO GENERALS

1 William H. Seward to Thurlow Weed, November 17, 1836, *Autobiography of William H. Seward from 1801–1834, with a Memoir of His Life, and Selections from His Letters from 1831 to 1846* (New York: Appleton, 1877), 319.

2 William H. Seward to Thurlow Weed, April 12, 1835, *Autobiography of William H. Seward*, 257–258.

3 Richard N. Current, *Daniel Webster and the Rise of National Conservatism* (Boston: Little, Brown, 1955), 88.

4 Glyndon G. Van Deusen, *William Henry Seward* (New York: Oxford University Press, 1967), 44. Also see Michael F. Holt, *The Rise and Fall of the American Whig Party: Jacksonian Politics and the Onset of the Civil War* (New York: Oxford University Press, 1999), 41.

5 Seward to Weed, November 17, 1836, 319.

6 In a speech in 1838 in Massillon, Ohio, Harrison admitted that at the time of his nomination in January 1835, "he had supposed that his political career was forever ended." *Niles' National Register*, August 18, 1838, 54:398.

7 William Henry Harrison to Solomon Van Rensselaer, January 15, 1835, in *A Legacy of Historical Gleanings*, ed. Catharina V. R. Bonney (Albany, NY: J. Munsell, 1875), 2:55–56. Also see Dorothy Burne Goebel, *William Henry Harrison: A Political Biography* (Indianapolis: Historical Bureau of the Indiana Library and Historical Department, 1926), 306–307. Although county clerk was not a salaried position, its holder could earn through fees "as much as ten thousand dollars a year." Gail Collins, *William Henry Harrison* (New York: Times Books, 2012), 71. In his letter to Van Rensselaer, Harrison described it as "an office humble . . . but still honorable and lucrative."

8 William Henry Harrison to William Ayres, January 2, 1834, quoted in Freeman Cleaves, *Old Tippecanoe: William Henry Harrison and His Time* (Newtown, CT: American Political Biography Press, 1939), 291–292. Harrison also used the letter to assure Ayres, a leading Anti-Mason, that "neither myself or any member of my family . . . have ever been" Masons. The following week, a Dauphin County convention of Whigs and Anti-Masons met in Harrisburg to endorse Harrison for president.

9   Michael Chevalier, quoted in Cleaves, *Old Tippecanoe*, 291. The Frenchman Chevalier, who encountered Harrison by chance at a Cincinnati hotel during his travels through America in the fall of 1834, described Harrison as of "medium height, stout and muscular, and of about the age of sixty years, yet with the active step and lively air of youth." Chevalier was "struck with his open and cheerful expression, the amenity of his manners, and a certain air of command which appeared thru his plain dress." Michael Chevalier, *Society, Manners, and Politics in the United States* (Boston: Weeks, Jordan, and Company, 1836), 196.

10   *Carlisle (PA) Herald and General Advertiser*, January 7, 1835.

11   *Carlisle Herald and General Advertiser*, December 24, 1835; January 7, 1835. Also see Robert M. Owens, *Mr. Jefferson's Hammer: William Henry Harrison and the Origins of American Indian Policy* (Norman: University of Oklahoma Press, 2007), 16–27.

12   *Carlisle Herald and General Advertiser*, December 24, 1835; and Donald J. Ratcliffe, *The Politics of Long Division: The Birth of the Second Party System in Ohio, 1818–1828* (Columbus: Ohio State University Press, 2000), 43. The last quotation is from an autobiography, published in Cincinnati in 1853, by the Methodist clergyman James B. Finley; the others are from the *Carlisle Herald and General Advertiser*.

13   *Carlisle Herald and General Advertiser*, December 24, 1835.

14   Collins, *William Henry Harrison*, 25, 29; and Owens, *Mr. Jefferson's Hammer*.

15   Collins, *William Henry Harrison*, 33.

16   *Carlisle Herald and General Advertiser*, December 24, 1835.

17   Collins, *William Henry Harrison*, 62; and Cleaves, *Old Tippecanoe*, 234–235.

18   Collins, *William Henry Harrison*, 65; Goebel, *William Henry Harrison*, 237; and Ratcliffe, *Politics of Long Division*, 55. In making his case to Monroe for his appointment as minister to Mexico (and explaining his recent political defeats), Harrison stated that he was "the ONLY person of any political standing in the State" who opposed the "wild and dangerous sentiments" relating to slavery in Ohio (William Henry Harrison to James Monroe, June 16, 1823, quoted in Ratcliffe, *Politics of Long Division*, 55).

19   Cleaves, *Old Tippecanoe*, 252; John Craig Hammond, *Slavery, Freedom, and Expansion in the Early American West* (Charlottesville: University of Virginia Press, 2007), 160; and Goebel, *William Henry Harrison*, 235.

20   Ratcliffe, *Politics of Long Division*, 45–46; Goebel, *William Henry Harrison*, 235; and Cleaves, *Old Tippecanoe*, 253.

21   Charles Hammond to the Secretary of State [John Quincy Adams], July 12, 1823, in Clarence E. Carter, "William Henry Harrison and the Mexican Appointment, 1823–1824," *Mississippi Valley Historical Review* (September 1938): 254; and Ratcliffe, *Politics of Long Division*, 47. Also see Cleaves, *Old Tippecanoe*, 254–255.

22   Goebel, *William Henry Harrison*, 238–239. The impressive scope of the letter-writing campaign unleashed on Harrison's behalf—and at his behest—is documented in Carter, "William Henry Harrison and the Mexican Appointment,

1823–1824," 251–262. Ultimately the post went to Joel Poinsett, who was infinitely better suited and more qualified for the post.

23 Goebel, *William Henry Harrison*, 240, 242–243; and Ratcliffe, *Politics of Long Division*, 125–126.

24 See, for instance, Harrison's lengthy letter to Cincinnati's Bellamy Storer complaining about Pennsylvania's nomination of Rush and Ohio's failure to bring forward Harrison's name—and urging Bellamy that it was not too late to remedy the situation. January 17, 1828, printed in *Quarterly Publication of the Historical and Philosophical Society of Ohio* 2 (July–September 1907): 117–119.

25 Collins, *William Henry Harrison*, 65–68, Adams quotation at 66. Most House members voted to exonerate Jackson, and a minority voted to censure him. But as Collins points out, "only Harrison tried to split the difference and exonerate Jackson for one death while censuring him for the other" (68).

26 Ratcliffe, *Politics of Long Division*, 46–47.

27 Indeed, in 1834, Harrison was passed over for the Whig nomination for Ohio's first congressional district in favor of the much younger New Englander Bellamy Storer. Cleaves, *Old Tippecanoe*, 89; also see 90 ("the General was not considered particularly good political timber in his own district").

28 Henry Clay to Christopher Hughes, August 22, 1835, *The Papers of Henry Clay*, ed. Robert Seager II (Lexington: University Press of Kentucky, 1988), 8:799. While Clay would minimize Harrison's chances in 1837 and 1838, when Clay was himself a candidate for the presidency, in 1835, when Clay was not a presidential candidate, he freely admitted that Harrison would be "the most formidable candidate" on the Whig side. Indeed, he told Hughes, "I really shall not be surprised at his election" (8:798–799).

29 *Ohio State Journal*, October 15, 1836, quoted in Holt, *Rise and Fall of the Whig Party*, 41.

30 Nicholas Biddle to Herman Cope, August 11, 1835, *The Correspondence of Nicholas Biddle*, ed. Reginald McGrane (Boston, MA: J. S. Canner, 1966), 256.

31 Harrison's speech at Cheviot, Ohio, July 4, 1833, quoted in Cleaves, *Old Tippecanoe*, 284. Also see James A. Green, *William Henry Harrison, His Life and Times* (Richmond, VA: Garrett and Massie 1941), 290. Harrison renewed his attack on the dangerous and unconstitutional "mischief" of abolitionism at a public dinner in his honor in Vincennes on May 25, 1835. See Cleaves, *Old Tippecanoe*, 296.

32 In a letter to a group of New York Whigs early in 1836, for instance, Harrison stated that he would bring to the presidency "a mind uninfluenced by the passions and prejudices which the heat and violence of the late contests have unfortunately produced." William Henry Harrison to John W. Taylor, February 20, 1836, quoted in Cleaves, *Old Tippecanoe*, 302.

33 "General William Henry Harrison's Reply [to Sherrod Williams]," May 1, 1836, in Joel Silbey, "Election of 1836," in *History of American Presidential Elections, 1789–1968*, ed. Arthur M. Schlesinger Jr. (New York: Chelsea House, 1985), 608–613, quotations at 608, 610.

34 William Henry Harrison to Solomon Van Rensselaer, August 25, 1836, in Bonney, *Legacy of Historical Gleanings*, 2:56–57.

35 Mark R. Cheathem, *The Coming of Democracy: Presidential Campaigning in the Age of Jackson* (Baltimore, MD: Johns Hopkins University Press, 2018), 102–103; M. J. Heale, T*he Presidential Quest: Candidates and Images in American Political Culture, 1787–1852* (London: Longman, 1982), 115–116; and Cleaves, *Old Tippecanoe*, 305–309.

36 Cleaves, 307.

37 Cleaves, 293.

38 Van Deusen, *Seward*, 46.

39 *The Star and North Carolina Gazette* (Raleigh, NC), January 12, 1837.

40 "The Harrison Flag," *Huron Reflector* (Norwalk, OH), January 10, 1837.

41 C. S. Todd to William Henry Harrison, April 8, 1837, Harrison Papers: Series 1, General Correspondence, 1734–1939, Library of Congress, https://www.loc.gov/resource/mss25148.002_0011_1115/?sp=667. Todd told Harrison that the Anti-Mason Francis Granger, Harrison's running mate in 1836, had "brought us no strength in the quarter where it was needed."

42 Sherry Keith Jelsma, *Political Quickstep: The Life of Kentucky's Colonel Charles S. Todd* (Louisville, KY: Butler Books, 2017), 160–162.

43 Todd is sometimes described as Harrison's "de facto campaign manager" (Collins, *William Henry Harrison*, 79; also see Goebel, *William Henry Harrison*, 325), but neither Todd nor anybody else functioned as a national campaign manager in the modern sense of that term.

44 Goebel, *William Henry Harrison*, 328. Although Crittenden did not become vice president, Harrison did pick him as attorney general after he won the presidency.

45 Webster arrived first at Harrison's home in North Bend, where they breakfasted together before traveling together to Cincinnati. According to one press account, when Webster's boat reached North Bend, "the old General was seen running down to the landing to meet his old associate in the Senate. The plain farmer appeared delighted to greet his brother patriot with a hearty shake of the hand." *Louisville Daily Journal*, June 6, 1837.

46 *Huron Reflector*, July 11, 1837. Contrast the careful wording of the resolution adopted by the state convention with the emphatic resolution adopted at a meeting of Whig citizens in Wilmington that selected ten delegates from Clinton County to attend the state convention in Columbus. The Clinton County convention resolved "that having under the banner of Gen. Harrison marched to a victory in Ohio, that had only to be more closely contested to have been glorious, we will not abandon the standard of that great Statesman and Chief, unless the decision of a National Convention, or of the people in their primary capacity, should render such a step necessary in order to carry out the task of reform." *Democrat and Herald* (Wilmington, OH), July 7, 1837.

47 For instance, William Harrison Sheets, who had been Indiana secretary of state from 1833 to 1837, wrote to Harrison on January 8, 1838, "I must confess that I deprecate the idea of a National Convention exceedingly. . . . Conventions are mostly composed, and allways controuled by politicians; and I fear it would be

a difficult matter to convince such a body that Mr. Clay could not be elected." Quoted in Robert Gray Gunderson, *The Log-Cabin Campaign* (Lexington: University Press of Kentucky, 1957), 49–50.

48 Thurlow Weed to William H. Seward, April 8, 1837, quoted in Holt, *Rise and Fall of the Whig Party*, 91

49 E. Hulse to William Henry Harrison, December 29, 1837, quoted in Gunderson, *Log-Cabin Campaign*, 50.

50 *National Gazette* (Philadelphia, PA), January 22, 1838. Also see *Papers of Henry Clay*, 9:164. The Cincinnati meeting of "the friends of General Harrison" drew Weed's immediate attention and concern, although he tended to absolve Harrison's supporters of blame, an indication that he was still inclined toward a Harrison candidacy at this time. Although "from the beginning, we have deprecated these premature movements. . . . it is but an act of justice . . . to the friends of General Harrison to admit that they have been forced into this position. They were willing [at the Ohio convention of July 4, 1837] to submit the whole question to a national convention, where everything should be decided. But with that too many impatient gentlemen were dissatisfied. Demonstrations in favor of other candidates were made, and the friends of General Harrison must either see him jostled off the course or do as others had done. Thus we are hurried into a scuffle about men, when the entire energies of our party should be exerted to arrest and defeat the destructive measures of the administration." Weed closed, though, by stressing that "we are utterly opposed to the infatuated project of jarring among ourselves about a candidate for President three years before the election, and when our single and united efforts are required to save the country from the miseries inflicted by the present executive." Thurlow Weed Barnes, *Memoir of Thurlow Weed* (Boston: Houghton Mifflin, 1884), 57. Weed had the peculiar habit of using the royal "we" when referring to himself. On Clay's response to the "abortive attempt" at Cincinnati, see Henry Clay letter to Peter B. Porter, March 13, 1838, *Papers of Henry Clay*, 9:163. Also see Porter's letter to Clay, March 8, 1838, which warns that the Harrison men "seem to have in contemplation, of running him whether nominated or not by a convention." *Papers of Henry Clay*, 9:157.

51 William Henry Harrison to Noah Noble, January 15, 1838, William Henry Harrison Papers and Documents, 1791–1864, Indiana Historical Society, https://digital.library.in.gov/Record/IHS_dc050–1657. Harrison's grievances against the press were a frequent refrain in his correspondence. Ten days before unburdening himself to Noble, Harrison had moaned to his son's father-in-law Archibald Irwin (who, like William Henry, was future president Benjamin Harrison's grandfather) that "there are many articles of great importance constantly published in the Country papers which never reach the distant States from the neglect of the leading City prints." January 5, 1838 (photocopy), VFM 2708, William Henry Harrison Papers, Ohio History Connection.

52 *Richmond Weekly Palladium* (Richmond, OH), February 3, 1838. The week after publishing the convention's resolutions, the *Richmond Weekly Palladium* nailed Harrison's name to its masthead, "subject to the decision of the National

Convention." The instructions to the Wayne County delegates, enacted at a meeting of Wayne County Whigs on January 1, are in the *Richmond Weekly Palladium*, January 6, 1838. The state convention in Indianapolis also endorsed a constitutional amendment restricting the president to a single term as a means to check "the abuse of executive patronage."

53 Robert V. Remini, *Henry Clay: Statesman for the Union* (New York: W. W. Norton, 1991), 519–520. Also see Samuel Wood to Henry Clay, March 8, 1838, *Papers of Henry Clay*, 9:157.

54 William Henry Harrison to Aaron B. Howell, April 7, 1838, *Niles' National Register*, September 8, 1838, 55:28. *Niles' National Register* reprinted the letter from the *New Jersey State Gazette*, where it was first published.

55 Hammond earned Andrew Jackson's lifelong enmity for the *Gazette*'s attacks on his wife as "an adulterous paramour and seducer"—attacks that Jackson blamed for his wife's death. See Ratcliffe, *Politics of Long Division*, 192. Ratcliffe's book is a rich source of information about Hammond's early career in Ohio politics.

56 Cleaves, *Old Tippecanoe*, 311. Over the summer, the letter found its way into an increasing number of Whig newspapers across the country. The letter was published in full on July 23, 1838, on the front page of Philadelphia's *National Gazette*, a paper sympathetic to Harrison. The letter was also circulated in Southern newspapers—for example, the *Southern Argus* (Columbus, MS), July 3, 1838, and Nashville's *Daily Republican Banner*, July 11, 1838.

57 *Pittsburgh Gazette*, June 8, 1838; Henry Clay to Peter B. Porter, June 9, 1838, *Papers of Henry Clay*, 203. Some Jacksonian papers went further, interpreting the Ohio convention as "a virtual withdrawal of Harrison from the field" and concluding that it was now "certain [that] Clay is to be the man of the combined opposition" (*Blairsville Record*, reprinted in the *Republican Compiler* [Gettysburg, PA], July 10, 1838), although this judgment probably reveals more about Democrats' feeling that Clay would be an easier opponent to defeat than Harrison than about their assessment of the effects of the convention.

58 The quoted words are those of the *Raleigh Register*, August 13, 1838. Also see Henry Clay to Robert Swartwout, August 10, 1828, *Papers of Henry Clay*, 9:216. A fuller account of the speech's praise for Clay and Webster can be found in *Niles' National Register*, August 18, 1838, 54:397–398. Clay and Webster were also invited to the July Fourth celebration but instead sent letters that were read at the festivities.

59 William Henry Harrison to William Ayres, October 1, 1838, in Goebel, *William Henry Harrison*, 331.

60 William Henry Harrison to William Ayres, August 22, 1838, William Henry Harrison Papers and Documents, https://digital.library.in.gov/Record/IHS_dc050–1667.

61 Harrison to Ayres, August 22, 1838.

62 *Niles' National Register*, August 18, 1838, 54:398. The same account of Harrison's speech was published in perhaps the nation's most influential Whig newspaper, the *National Intelligencer* (Washington, DC), August 15, 1838.

63 *Niles' National Register*, August 18, 1838, 54:398.

64 Robert Gray Gunderson's claim that Harrison presented himself to the public as "simply one of 'the Veteran Pioneers' who had protected log cabins from Indians and redcoats while Martin Van Buren was opposing the war" (*Log-Cabin Campaign*, 51), is demonstrably wrong.

65 The preceding Fourth of July, Harrison had traveled almost one hundred miles to speak at Piqua, Ohio.

66 *Buffalo Commercial Advertiser*, July 11, 1838 (from the *Cleveland Herald and Gazette*). Also see Cleaves, *Old Tippecanoe*, 311.

67 Green, *William Henry Harrison*, 321.

68 *Huron Reflector*, September 25, 1838 (the convention was held on September 20). In his July Fourth speech at Massillon, Harrison also dwelled upon "'the thousand and one' calumnies which had been for twenty-five years so industriously circulated against him" (*Niles' National Register*, August 18, 1838, 54:398). In his sensitivity to criticism of his character, particularly his military record, Harrison was much like Jackson. A case can be made that both Jackson and Harrison were driven by what James C. Curtis called "the search for vindication." James C. Curtis, *Andrew Jackson and the Search for Vindication* (Boston: Little, Brown, 1976).

69 Robert C. Winthrop to John Clifford, September 22, 1838, quoted in Robert F. Dalzell, Jr., *Daniel Webster and the Trial of American Nationalism, 1843–1852* (Boston: Houghton Mifflin, 1973), 68.

70 Harrison to Ayres, October 1, 1838. Also see William Henry Harrison to Thomas H. Burrowes, November 6, 1838, William Henry Harrison Papers and Documents, http://images.indianahistory.org/cdm/ref/collection/dc050/id/1652.

71 Holt, *Rise and Fall of the Whig Party*, 41–42.

72 "Letter from General Harry Harrison to Representative Harmar Denny, December 2, 1838," in William Nisbet Chambers, "Election of 1840," in *History of American Presidential Elections, 1789–2008*, ed. Gil Troy, Arthur M. Schlesinger Jr., and Fred L. Israel, 4th ed. (New York: Facts on File, 2012), 695–699. The one-term pledge came in a public letter Harrison wrote in response to an inquiry in February 1838 from the editor of the *Missourian*, James H. Birch. Green, *William Henry Harrison*, 314.

73 *Chicago American*, reprinted in *Indiana Journal* (Indianapolis), December 8, 1838; *Steubenville Herald*, reprinted in *Carlisle (PA) Herald and Expositor*, October 20, 1838; and Millard Fillmore to Thurlow Weed, October 15, 1838, in *Millard Fillmore Papers*, ed. Frank. H. Severance (Buffalo, NY: Buffalo Historical Society, 1907), 2:173. On Fillmore's initial support for Webster, see Millard Fillmore to G. W. Patterson, February 6, 1839, *Millard Fillmore Papers*, 2:185.

74 *Chicago American*, in *Indiana Journal* (Indianapolis), December 8, 1838.

75 Editorial by Abraham Lincoln from the *Sangamo Journal*, November 3, 1838, in Chambers, "Election of 1840," 693–694.

76 Circleville *Herald*, quoted in Cleaves, *Old Tippecanoe*, 311.

77 Harrison to Joshua Giddings, December 15, 1838, quoted in Gunderson, *Log-Cabin Campaign*, 49.

78 Gunderson, *Log-Cabin Campaign*, 44. Van Deusen, *Seward*, 48–49. Millard Fillmore to Thurlow Weed, June 4, 1838, in *Millard Fillmore* Papers, 2:170.

79 Daniel Walker Howe, *What Hath God Wrought: The Transformation of America, 1815–1848* (New York: Oxford University Press, 2007), 518; and Holt, *Rise and Fall of the Whig Party*, 97.

80 Winfield Scott to Colonel William Worth, January 11, 1838, quoted in Timothy D. Johnson, *Winfield Scott: The Quest for Military Glory* (Lawrence: University Press of Kansas, 1998), 131.

81 Johnson, 131. The island's rebel leader was Rensselaer Van Rensselaer, whose father, Solomon Van Rensselaer, had been severely wounded in the disastrous Battle of Queenston Heights (about six miles above Niagara Falls), in which the American forces had tried, and failed, in October 1812 to get a foothold on the Canadian side of the Niagara River. That ill-fated battle was also Winfield Scott's—who was then a lieutenant colonel—introduction to military combat. John S. D. Eisenhower, *Agent of Destiny: The Life and Times of General Winfield Scott* (New York: Free Press, 1997), 36–41.

82 Eisenhower, 180; and Johnson, *Winfield Scott*, 131.

83 Holt, *Rise and Fall of the Whig Party*, 97; and Eisenhower, *Agent of Destiny*, 181–182. Holt describes Scott at the time as a "6-foot-5-inch, 300 pound soldier," but in 1838, he was not yet the corpulent three-hundred-pound general that he would become by the time of the Civil War, when he could not even get on a horse. In 1838, he still resembled the imposing 230-pound figure whom Ulysses Grant had encountered as a young cadet and recalled as "the finest specimen of manhood my eyes had ever beheld." Edward G. Longacre, *General Ulysses S. Grant: The Soldier and the Man* (Cambridge, MA: Da Capo, 2006), 21.

84 Johnson, *Winfield Scott*, 131; Allan Peskin, *Winfield Scott and the Profession of Arms* (Kent State University Press, 2003), 105; and Eisenhower, *Agent of Destiny*, 183.

85 Eisenhower, 196; and Johnson, *Winfield Scott*, 134. An account of Scott's speech as set down by a correspondent from the *Cleveland Gazette* can be found in the *Detroit Free Press*, December 11, 1838.

86 In his memoirs, Scott recalled telling Van Buren that if he wanted war, "the Maine people will make it for you fast and hot enough. But if peace be your wish, I can give no assurance of success" (quoted in Eisenhower, *Agent of Destiny*, 197). Also see Clay's letter to Alexander Hamilton, dated February 24, 1839, in which he reported on the "state of great anxiety [in DC] about affairs in Maine" and expressed his "hope we shall not be precipitated into War unprepared and unexpected; but there is reason to apprehend it." *Papers of Henry Clay*, 9:291.

87 Eisenhower, *Agent of Destiny*, 197. On Scott as "the Great Pacificator," see the *National Intelligencer*, February 24, 1839; also see the *Adams Sentinel* (Gettysburg, PA), April 1, 1839.

88 In Philadelphia, on his way to the nation's capital to confer with Van Buren, Scott "was heard to state that the feeling once confined to a few lawless individuals on both sides, is now pervading the whole population, and that if 20,000

men more were wanted for a Canadian invasion, they could be collected in one hour." *Baltimore Sun*, February 26, 1839.

89 Eisenhower, *Agent of Destiny*, 200; and Johnson, *Winfield Scott*, 134.

90 Peskin, *Winfield Scott and the Profession of Arms*, 112; and Eisenhower, *Agent of Destiny*, 202. The quotation is from the entry of April 26, 1839, *The Diary of Philip Hone, 1828–1851*, ed. Allan Nevins (New York: Dodd, Mead, 1927), 1:391.

91 Winfield Scott to Henry Clay, February 5, 1839, *Papers of Henry Clay*, 9:277. The day before writing to Clay, Scott had written to Secretary of War Joel Poinsett to emphasize that in his three decades in the army, he had never attended a party meeting or voted. See Charles Winslow Elliott, *Winfield Scott: The Soldier and the Man* (New York: Macmillan, 1937), 369.

92 *Madisonian* (Washington, DC), April 3, 1839. The call first appeared in a Democratic paper, the *Rochester Daily Advertiser*.

93 *Freeman and Messenger* (Lodi, NY), April 18, 1839.

94 Elliott, *Winfield Scott, 368*.

95 Eisenhower, *Agent of Destiny*, 200. Indeed, in his dealings with the Maine legislature, according to Eisenhower, Scott initially faced greater skepticism from Whigs since he was an emissary carrying out the policies and commands of a Democratic president.

96 Scott to Clay, February 5, 1839, 9:277.

97 *Madisonian*, April 3, 1839 (quoting the *Albany Evening Journal*). Weed lived in Rochester from 1821 to 1829 and was twice elected to the state legislature as a representative from Rochester.

98 Millard Fillmore to Thurlow Weed, May 1, 1839, *Millard Fillmore Papers*, 2:191.

99 New York *Herald*, April 29, 1839; April 17, 1839. Also see May 3, 1838: "The nomination of General Scott for the Presidency seems to spread far and wide. All the politicians are busy mustering their troops to choke the voice of the people."

100 New York *Herald*, May 17, 1839. Bennett even worked out a formula of sorts with which to compare the characters of the rival candidates. "Estimating character at 100 parts, and analyzed by a chemical process," Bennett judged Webster's flawed character to be 52 parts intellectual, 42 parts physical, and only 6 parts moral. Clay was similarly out of balance: half intellectual, 40 parts physical, and 8 parts moral, with 2 parts residual. Van Buren was by far the worst: 20 parts intellectual, 15 parts physical, and 1 part moral, with 64 parts residual. Scott's character, in contrast, was exquisitely balanced between the intellectual, physical, and moral (one third for each). Bennett made no mention of Harrison or his character.

101 New York *Herald*, May 27, 1839; May 11, 1839.

102 In August, for instance, Bennett listed Weed prominently among the "long catalogue of other blockheads" who were ruining the state and the Whig Party. Bennett called for "the present set of corrupt rascals in New York and Albany, who pull the wires [to] be bled and beheaded." New York *Herald*, August 20, 1839.

103 New York *Herald*, May 27, 1839.

104 Glyndon G. Van Deusen, *Thurlow Weed: Wizard of the Lobby* (Boston: Little, Brown, 1947), 10.

CHAPTER 5. THE ROAD TO THE WHIG CONVENTION

1   Henry Clay to Francis T. Brooke, April 14, 1838, *The Papers of Henry Clay*, ed. Robert Seager II (Lexington: University Press of Kentucky, 1988), 9:172; Daniel Webster to William Pitt Fessenden, April 21, 1838, *The Papers of Daniel Webster: Correspondence*, ed. Charles M. Wiltse and Harold D. Moser (Hanover, NH: University Press of New England, 1980), 4:290; and Michael F. Holt, *The Rise and Fall of the American Whig Party: Jacksonian Politics and the Onset of the Civil War* (New York: Oxford University Press, 1999), 93. When the Twenty-Fifth Congress came back into session in December 1838, some of Harrison's Ohio supporters lobbied to move the convention earlier, a move that met with Clay's approval. Henry Clay to Harrison G. Otis, January 24, 1839, *Papers of Henry Clay*, 9:275. In a letter to Peter Porter at the beginning of February, Clay judged it probable that the Whigs in Congress would move the convention to September if not earlier. Henry Clay to Peter B. Porter, February 5, 1839, *Papers of Henry Clay*, 9:276. Also see Millard Fillmore to G. W. Patterson, February 6, 1839, *Millard Fillmore Papers*, ed. Frank. H. Severance (Buffalo, NY: Buffalo Historical Society, 1907), 2:187, in which Fillmore reported being informed "that the time for holding the convention will probably be changed." Ultimately, Congress did not change the date. On December 14, 1838, Willis Hall had written to Clay suggesting that the convention be moved up to June 1839. *Papers of Henry Clay*, 9:255.

2   James A. Green, *William Henry Harrison, His Life and Times* (Richmond, VA: Garrett and Massie 1941), 327.

3   Dorothy Burne Goebel, *William Henry Harrison: A Political Biography* (Indianapolis: Historical Bureau of the Indiana Library and Historical Department, 1926), 335–336. The *Cincinnati Republican*'s retort that Harrison and his friends would abide by the convention's decision so long as it was "fairly constituted" (335) could hardly have reassured Clay's supporters. .

4   Henry Clay to Harrison G. Otis, November 14, 1838, *Papers of Henry Clay*, 9:248.

5   Fillmore to Patterson, February 6, 1839, 2:184.

6   Henry Clay to Robert Swartwout, November 15, 1838, *Papers of Henry Clay*, 9:249. This triumphant letter was written only one day after a depressed Clay had written to Otis about possibly withdrawing from the presidential contest. In the letter to Swartwout, Clay wrote, remarkably, that if New York had been lost, it would have necessitated "long, strenuous and persevering exertions, possibly terminating in a Revolution, the last resource of an oppressed People." For evidence of Clay's exultation about the New York results, also see Henry Clay to Elias Leavenworth, November 18, 1838, *Papers of Henry Clay*, 9:250 ("The Nation Posterity and Mankind owe the State a debt of eternal Gratitude"); Henry Clay to Edward Greene, November 18, 1838, *Papers of Henry Clay*, 9:249; and Henry Clay to Jonathan Thompson, November 19, 1838, *The*

Papers of Henry Clay: Supplement, 1793–1852, ed. Melba Porter Hay (Lexington: University Press of Kentucky, 1992), 272.

7   Clay to Otis, January 24, 1839, 9:274. Also see Henry Clay to Francis T. Brooke, December 20, 1838, *Papers of Henry Clay*, 9:258; and Henry Clay to Peter B. Porter, December 27, 1838, *Papers of Henry Clay*, 9:262.

8   Henry Clay to James Caldwell, March 18, 1839, *Papers of Henry Clay*, 9:296. Also see Clay's assertion in a letter to Richard H. Wilde dated June 24, 1839, that "judging from present appearances, the Whig Convention . . . will unite by a very large majority upon me." *Papers of Henry Clay*, 9:328.

9   Clay to Wilde, 9:329.

10   In June, Clay estimated that the anti–Van Buren forces would likely have a majority of about thirty in the new House of Representatives. Clay to Wilde, June 24, 1839, 9:329.

11   Clay to Porter, December 27, 1838, 9:263.

12   Henry Clay to Francis T. Brooke, December 26, 1838, *Papers of Henry Clay*, 9:261–262.

13   Clay to Brooke, December 20, 1838, 9:258. Also see Clay to Porter, December 27, 1838, 9:262–263.

14   Henry Clay to Francis T. Brooke, January 18, 1838, *Papers of Henry Clay*, 9:272. Also see Henry Clay to Peter B. Porter, February 5, 1838, *Papers of Henry Clay*, 9:276–77.

15   Henry Clay to Francis T. Brooke, January 24, 1838, *Papers of Henry Clay*, 9:275; and Clay to Porter, December 27, 1838, 9:263.

16   Two days before delivering the speech, Clay wrote to Porter to say that he "anticipated" an endorsement by the Whig legislators in Richmond. Clay to Porter, February 5, 1839, 9:277. Clay often referred to it as "My Abolition Speech." See, for example, Clay to Caldwell, March 18, 1839, 9:296.

17   Henry Clay, Speech in Senate, February 7, 1839, *Papers of Henry Clay*, 9:278–283. Clay's speech triggered Ohio's antislavery Democrat Thomas Morris's February 9 speech in reply—circulated in pamphlet form by the American Anti-Slavery Society—in which Morris coined and popularized the notion of a "slave power" that had "the whole power of the country in its hands." See Corey M. Brooks, *Liberty Power: Antislavery Third Parties and the Transformation of American Politics* (Chicago: University of Chicago Press, 2016), 25–26; and Jonathan H. Earle, *Jacksonian Antislavery and the Politics of Free Soil, 1824–1854* (Chapel Hill: University of North Carolina Press, 2004), 18.

18   The source for these words is a campaign speech on March 11 in Philadelphia by Clay's South Carolina colleague William Preston. Preston urged the enthusiastic "throng" of Clay supporters to entrust the Whig banner to the "noble" Clay and "to no other man." As evidence of Clay's high-mindedness, Preston related that Clay had shared the speech with him before its delivery and that when Preston had noted that it might "injure" Clay's presidential prospects, Clay had responded, "I did not send for you to ask what might be the effect of the proposed movement on my prospects, but whether it was right. I had rather be right than be president." *Niles' National Register*, March 23, 1839, 56:55. Also

see Preston's March 28 letter to Joseph Gales and William Seaton, the editors of the *National Intelligencer*, which was published on March 30, 1839.

19 Harrison G. Otis to Henry Clay, January 11, 1839, *Papers of Henry Clay*, 9:269.

20 Peter B. Porter to Henry Clay, February 16, 1839, *Papers of Henry Clay*, 9:286.

21 Henry Clay to Harrison G. Otis, February 18, 1839, *Papers of Henry Clay*, 9:290.

22 Henry Clay to Peter B. Porter, February 24, 1839, *Papers of Henry Clay*, 9:291–292. New York's Gerrit Smith was among the abolitionists who wrote to Clay to protest the speech. Smith warned Clay that in sacrificing justice at the altar of political gain, he invited "the contempt of a slavery-loathing posterity" from whom he could not redeem his reputation as a statesman, orator, or even president of the United States. Gerrit Smith to Henry Clay, March 21, 1839, *Papers of Henry Clay*, 9:298. New York's recently elected governor, William Henry Seward, thought the speech hurt Clay's prospects, although he admired its sentiments. Shortly after the speech, Seward confided to a friend, "I dare say to you what I would not breathe elsewhere that I regret that Mr. Clay made that excellent glorious manly speech. It is before the time for it, and is unfortunate for him." William H. Seward to Christopher Morgan, February 15, 1839, quoted in Ernest G. Muntz, "The First Whig Governor of New York, William Henry Seward, 1838–1842" (PhD diss., University of Rochester, NY, 1960), 177.

23 John C. Crump et al. to Henry Clay, April 10, 1839, *Papers of Henry Clay*, 9:302. Also see Henry Clay to John C. Crump et al., May 25, 1839, *Papers of Henry Clay*, 9:318–319.

24 Calhoun's embrace of Clay's speech excited fears in some quarters that it signaled that "a political understanding" had been reached between Calhoun and Clay and that "the South is to be consolidated in favor of the latter as a Presidential Candidate." Edward Everett to Daniel Webster, February 14, 1839, *Papers of Daniel Webster*, 4:343. But Clay harbored no illusions of luring Calhoun or South Carolina to his cause. It was the rest of the South that he aimed to consolidate.

25 Henry Clay to Francis T. Brooke, April 2, 1839, *Papers of Henry Clay*, 9:298–299.

26 About 35,000 Virginians cast a ballot in the congressional elections of 1837, whereas nearly 64,000 voted in 1839.

27 Henry Clay to Peter B. Porter, June 6, 1839, *Papers of Henry Clay*, 9:324; *Papers of Henry Clay*, 9:296; and Holt, *Rise and Fall of the Whig Party*, 75. Virginia's elections were held on May 23, 1839.

28 Henry Clay to Benjamin Watkins Leigh, June 12, 1839, *Papers of Henry Clay: Supplement*, 275.

29 Clay to Otis, February 18, 1839, 9:290.

30 Clay to Porter, December 27, 1838, 9:263.

31 Henry Clay to Alexander Hamilton, February 24, 1839, *Papers of Henry Clay*, 9:291.

32 Porter to Clay, February 16, 1839, 9:287. In his response to Porter, Clay expressed his displeasure that no endorsement was included in the agreed-upon plan. He also instructed Porter that it would be better to appoint someone

other than Ogden as a delegate since he had evidently been "influenced by Mr. Webster in the Harrison direction." Clay to Porter, February 24, 1839, 9:292.

33 Peter B. Porter to Henry Clay, May 26, 1839, *Papers of Henry Clay*, 9:320.

34 Henry Clay to Matthew L. Davis, April 20, 1839, *Papers of Henry Clay*, 9:307–308. On Clay's greater support in the city and Harrison's in more rural areas, see Robert Gray Gunderson, *The Log-Cabin Campaign* (Lexington: University Press of Kentucky, 1957), 44, 56. Also see Henry Clay to John P. Kennedy, May 16, 1839, *Papers of Henry Clay*, 9:314.

35 Millard Fillmore to Thurlow Weed, June 5, 1839, *Millard Fillmore Papers*, 2:192.

36 Henry Clay to Peter B. Porter, May 14, 1839, *Papers of Henry Clay*, 9:313.

37 Porter to Clay, May 26, 1839, 9:320. Also see Peter B. Porter to Henry Clay, May 31, 1838, *Papers of Henry Clay*, 9:197.

38 Peter B. Porter to Henry Clay, January 20, 1839, *Papers of Henry Clay*, 9:273; and Fillmore to Patterson, February 6, 1839, 2:185.

39 Porter to Clay, May 26, 1839, 9:320.

40 Clay to Porter, June 6, 1839, 9:324. Also see Henry Clay to Nathaniel P. Tallmadge, June 18, 1839, *Papers of Henry Clay*, 9:326–327; Henry Clay to Joseph Ingersoll, June 24, 1839, *Papers of Henry Clay*, 9:328; and Henry Clay to Joshua Giddings, July 13, 1839, *Papers of Henry Clay*, 9:330.

41 Clay to Wilde, June 24, 1839, 9:328.

42 Clay admitted to Nathaniel Tallmadge that he did "not intend stopping at either Montreal or Quebec longer than two or three days." July 14, 1839, *Papers of Henry Clay*, 9:331.

43 Henry Clay, Speech in Buffalo, July 17, 1839, *Papers of Henry Clay*, 9:331–332; and Henry Clay to Peter B. Porter, July 31, 1839, *Papers of Henry Clay*, 9:332–33. Clay's tour is covered in Robert V. Remini, *Henry Clay: Statesman for the Union* (New York: W. W. Norton, 1991), chap. 30 ("The Triumphal Tour"). Also see the itinerary in *Papers of Henry Clay*, 9:330n1.

44 See, for instance, "Progress of Mr. Clay," New York *Commercial Advertiser*, reprinted in *Niles' National Register*, August 31, 1839, 57:8–10. Clay's supporters excused the campaigning since the magnificent demonstrations of popular support were "done spontaneously . . . without the slightest effort on the part of the whigs to cause a gathering of the people" (8). Clay, it should be noted, was no stranger to such tours. In October 1833, he embarked on a lengthy tour that took him to Boston, which he entered "in a procession, and was paraded round the streets." A disapproving John Quincy Adams grumbled in his diary at the time that "this fashion of peddling for popularity by travelling round the country gathering crowds together, hawking for public dinners, and spouting empty speeches, is growing into high fashion. . . . Mr. Clay has mounted that hobby often, and rides him very hard." Diary entry of October 22, 1833, *Memoirs of John Quincy Adams, Comprising Portions of His Diary from 1795 to 1848*, ed. Charles Francis Adams (Philadelphia, PA: J. B. Lippincott, 1876), 9:25–26.

45 Diary entries of August 9 and 21, 1839, *The Diary of Philip Hone, 1828–1851*, ed. Allan Nevins (New York: Dodd, Mead, 1927), 1:413, 417. For a starkly different assessment of the tour's effects on Clay's presidential prospects, see the letter

written by John Cramer, a Democratic politician from Waterford, New York, who reported to James Polk that Clay's appearances had "not had a tendency to strengthen his personal influence," nor had they dimmed the burgeoning interest in Scott's candidacy. Indeed, Cramer was "fully satisfied that the leading Whigs of this State, including the Governor & his cabinet will go strongly and in good faith for the nomination of Genl. Scott." Cramer admitted that the prospect of a Scott candidacy made him "apprehensive," as Scott "would be the more formidable candidate of the two, having no decided political character and few enemies personally." John Cramer to James K. Polk, August 18, 1839, *Correspondence of James K. Polk*, ed. Wayne Cutler (Nashville, TN: Vanderbilt University Press, 1979), 5:193.

46 Diary entry of August 9, 1839, *Diary of Philip Hone*, 1:414. Weed agreed that Clay's speech was "too long and not in all respects what it should have been," though he did think the conclusion "glorious." Thurlow Weed to William H. Seward, August 10, 1839, William Henry Seward Papers, Department of Rare Books, Special Collections and Preservation, University of Rochester, NY.

47 Henry Clay, Speech in New York City, August 21, 1839, *Papers of Henry Clay*, 9:336.

48 Diary entry of August 24, 1839, *Diary of Philip Hone*, 1:419.

49 Henry Clay, Speech in Baltimore, August 26, 1839, *Papers of Henry Clay*, 9:339.

50 William H. Seward to Thurlow Weed, August 15, 1839, *Autobiography of William H. Seward from 1801–1834, with a Memoir of His Life, and Selections from His Letters from 1831 to 1846* (New York: Appleton, 1877), 431–432.

51 Some historians have suggested that Seward "tried mightily" to avoid Clay because he had already committed to Scott. See, e.g., *Papers of Henry Clay*, 9:335; David S. Heidler and Jeanne T. Heidler, *Henry Clay: The Essential American* (New York: Random House, 2010), 302; and James C. Klotter, *Henry Clay: The Man Who Would Be President* (New York: Oxford University Press, 2018), quotation at 254. But there are reasons to be skeptical of this interpretation. For starters, Seward went out of his way to meet with Clay when he discovered they were on the same lake; on August 4, Seward wrote home to say he now planned to stay where he was "till [Clay] comes, and give him my greeting to-morrow evening." *Autobiography of William H. Seward*, 432. Second, Seward wrote to Porter expressing his hope that he could meet with Clay at Auburn or Syracuse. Peter B. Porter to Henry Clay, August 9, 1839, *Papers of Henry Clay*, 9:334. Third, although it is true that Seward was not at his home in Auburn when Clay arrived, there is no evidence that Seward embarked on his tour to avoid meeting Clay. Finally, as Seward's August 15 letter to Weed indicates, he was far from convinced at this point that Scott was the most electable candidate, and for Seward, it was always, as he told one correspondent in the spring, "not a question of who we would prefer, but whom we can elect." Quoted in Glyndon G. Van Deusen, *William Henry Seward* (New York: Oxford University Press, 1967), 61. Also see Walter Stahr, *Seward: Lincoln's Indispensable Man* (New York: Simon & Schuster, 2012), 565n15.

52 Seward to Weed, August 15, 1839, 432.

53 Porter to Clay, August 9, 1839, 9:334.

54 Porter to Clay, August 9, 1839, 9:334.

55 Peter B. Porter to Gulian C. VerPlanck, July 24, 1839, quoted in Freeman Cleaves, *Old Tippecanoe: William Henry Harrison and His Time* (Newtown, CT: American Political Biography Press, 1939), 315.

56 Weed's autobiography, which was edited by his daughter, is generally reliable, unlike his "memoir," which was written by his grandson Thurlow Weed Barnes and is often not to be trusted. In his memoir, for instance, Barnes recounts a conversation that Weed allegedly had with Webster in the nation's capital in the spring of 1839. According to the memoir, Weed summoned Webster to the Capitol cloakroom, where Webster declared to Weed, "I think I shall be the Whig candidate." Weed greeted the claim with skepticism, prompting Webster to ask, "Who, then, will be?" Weed responded, "It looks to me like Harrison." Webster allegedly then told Weed that he was "misinformed," that "Harrison stood no chance," and that "the party will choose a man with longer civic experience who is better adapted to the place." Weed replied that the question was not who was better suited for the position but "who will poll the most votes," which Webster understood to mean that Weed planned "to choose a Scott delegation in New York." Weed did not deny the charge, but explained that it was just "to keep New York away from Mr. Clay." The conversation ends with Weed telling Webster that he had not come to argue about that but instead to ask whether Webster was "willing to accept the support of New York for the vice-presidency" in the event that Harrison received the presidential nomination. Webster, though, "would not listen to this." The point of this story, in Barnes's telling, is that had Webster not rejected Weed's sage suggestion, "he would, without a doubt, have reached the summit of his political ambition" because he, rather than John Tyler, would have become president when Harrison died. Thurlow Weed Barnes, *Memoir of Thurlow Weed* (Boston: Houghton Mifflin, 1884), 76. This account is riddled with errors and inconsistencies that make it difficult to credit. For starters, by the spring of 1839, Webster did not think he would be the Whig nominee—it had been at least a year since he had harbored any such illusions. Not only had he already decided to withdraw from the race, but he and most of his supporters in New York were actively working to aid Harrison and block Clay. Moreover, the idea that Weed was using the Scott candidacy only as a stalking horse "to keep New York away from Clay" is belied by Weed's own correspondence of the time (see, e.g., Thurlow Weed to William H. Seward, December 4, 1839, William Henry Seward Papers; also see Gunderson, *Log-Cabin Campaign*, 61n9). Finally, Webster left Washington when Congress adjourned on March 3, and prior to that date, neither Webster nor anybody else would have believed that the New York delegation at the national convention would go for Scott. Unfortunately, historians have sometimes relied on this "memoir" uncritically, as if it accurately described Weed's and Webster's thinking at the time. See, for instance, Robert V. Remini, *Daniel Webster: The Man and His Time* (New York: W. W. Norton, 1997), 480; and Glyndon G. Van Deusen, *The Life of Henry Clay* (Boston: Little, Brown, 1937),

327. In December 1837, Weed did hold several "long, frank talks" with Webster about the presidential contest, and some of what is related in this account about the relative prospects of Harrison and Webster probably took place then. See Thurlow Weed to Francis Granger, December 24, 1837, Francis and Gideon Granger Papers, Library of Congress.

57 *Autobiography of Thurlow Weed*, ed. Harriet A. Weed (Boston: Houghton Mifflin, 1884), 480. Weed's calculation that Clay could not be elected president was widely shared by those close to Weed. In February 1839, Millard Fillmore took "some pains" to calculate the relative chances of Clay and Harrison to win the presidency. Fillmore showed that if the election went into the House of Representatives, the Democrats would likely win, which made it incumbent for the Whigs to unite around a candidate who could win a majority in the electoral college. By Fillmore's calculation, the Whigs could count on 69 electoral votes whether they nominated Clay or Harrison, and Van Buren could count on 76 electoral votes that were securely in the Democratic column. That left 149 electoral votes up for grabs. Of these 149 "doubtful" votes, Clay had the advantage over Harrison in states with a total of 62 electoral votes, and Harrison had the advantage in states with a total of 87 electoral votes, including New York. If Clay won each of the doubtful states in which he was the stronger candidate, he would end up 17 votes shy of the requisite 148 votes needed to win, whereas if Harrison won each of his doubtful electoral votes, he would end up with 8 votes to spare. This calculation presupposed that Harrison but not Clay could carry New York—a view that Weed emphatically shared. The bottom line of Fillmore's calculation was that without New York, "neither can be elected." Fillmore concluded, "On that must turn this great question. Therefore in selecting the candidate most likely to carry our State, we are not acting for the more selfish purpose of saving ourselves, but with a more magnanimous object of saving the Union." Fillmore to Patterson, February 6, 1839, 2:186. George Washington Patterson was a New York state legislator and soon to be speaker of the state house.

58 *Autobiography of Thurlow Weed*, 480–481. Weed recounts an essentially similar version of events in his "Recollections of Horace Greeley," *Galaxy* (1873): 373.

59 Van Deusen, *Life of Henry Clay*, 328.

60 Diary entry of August 8, 1839, *Diary of Philip Hone*, 1:412. Scott, too, was at Saratoga at the same time as Clay and even stayed on the same floor in the same hotel (Remini, *Henry Clay*, 539).

61 The day after Clay left Saratoga Springs, James Gordon Bennett—a fervent Scott supporter since the spring—wrote a dispatch from Saratoga noting, "The returns from the west have depressed the spirits of the friends of Clay, while they have equally raised those of Van Buren. . . . It is now acknowledged on every hand that the whig party have met with a signal repulse—an entire overthrow, in the elections of Tennessee and Indiana." Bennett continued, "Among the whigs the most discreet men are now consulting on the absolute necessity of bringing out immediately the name of General Scott, as the only opponent

that can shake the present dynasty in power." "Mr. Bennett's Letters—No. 14," Saratoga Springs, August 18, 1839, New York *Herald*, August 20, 1839.

62 The elections in Tennessee were held on August 1, in Indiana on August 5, and in North Carolina on August 8.

63 Henry Clay to Thomas Washington, October 12, 1839, *Papers of Henry Clay*, 9:352.

64 The 89 percent turnout figure is from Jonathan M. Atkins, *Parties, Politics, and the Sectional Conflict in Tennessee, 1832–1861* (Knoxville: University of Tennessee Press, 1997), 78. All congressional results reported in this chapter, unless otherwise indicated, are from Michael J. Dubin, *United States Congressional Elections, 1788–1997: The Official Results of the Elections of the 1st through 105th Congresses* (Jefferson, NC: McFarland, 1998). The gubernatorial results reported in this chapter are from Michael J. Dubin, *United States Gubernatorial Elections, 1776–1860: The Official Results by State and County* (Jefferson, NC: McFarland, 2003). All state house results reported in this chapter, unless otherwise indicated, are from Holt, *Rise and Fall of the American Whig Party*, 75 (Table 6).

65 Atkins, *Parties, Politics, and the Sectional Conflict*, 78. Jackson's extravagant claim was belied by Polk's narrow margin of victory, which was fewer than 3 percentage points.

66 Atkins, 76.

67 John Bell to Henry Clay, May 21, 1839, *Papers of Henry Clay*, 9:316. Clay had written to Bell on April 22, furnishing him with what Bell described as "an excellent summary of the arguments which may be successfully urged against our opponents." Bell assured Clay that "we do not fail to urge them with spirit."

68 Allen A. Hall to Henry Clay, September 23, 1839, *Papers of Henry Clay*, 9:344. Also see Atkins, *Parties, Politics, and the Sectional Conflict*, 71–75.

69 Hall to Clay, September 23, 1839, 9:345. Also see Atkins, *Parties, Politics, and the Sectional Conflict*, 70.

70 Atkins, 78.

71 Atkins, 77.

72 Henry Clay to Oliver H. Smith, September 14, 1839, *Papers of Henry Clay*, 9:340.

73 Oliver H. Smith to Henry Clay, September 28, 1839, *Papers of Henry Clay*, 9:348. Also see Holt, *Rise and Fall of the American Whig Party*, 81.

74 Smith to Clay, September 28, 1839, 9:348–349.

75 Henry Clay to William H. Seward, September 26, 1839, *Papers of Henry Clay*, 9:347.

76 Henry Clay to Oliver H. Smith, October 5, 1839, *Papers of Henry Clay*, 9:350.

77 Henry Clay to William Tompkins, October 12, 1839, *Papers of Henry Clay: Supplement*, 277.

78 William Henry Harrison to Henry Clay, September 20 and 21, 1839, *Papers of Henry Clay*, 9:343.

79 John Bradley to Thurlow Weed, August 29, 1839, Thurlow Weed Papers, Department of Rare Books, Special Collections and Preservation, University of

Rochester, NY. Gunderson quotes from this letter but misidentifies the letter writer as "M. Bradley." *Log-Cabin Campaign*, 52. Bradley's letter opened by referencing "the results of the recent elections," which "ought to convince Mr. Clay of his utter hopelessness . . . of success." Even "in his strong holds he has been voted down," Bradley noted.

80 Charles S. Todd to William H. Seward, June 17, 1839, quoted in Cleaves, *Old Tippecanoe*, 315. Todd had been careful to keep in touch with Seward. He met with him in Philadelphia in June 1838 and wrote him a congratulatory letter in February 1839, in which he tactfully affirmed the case for "the most available candidate whoever he may be." Todd acknowledged that Kentucky preferred Clay but noted that "she will cordially support" Harrison if he were to be selected at the convention since he was "second only to Mr. C[lay] in the affections of the State." He hastened to add that "there would be a strong feeling of regret," however, "if even Mr. Clay should be nominated without the claims of the Gen. being fairly canvassed—such, I presume, is the feeling in Ohio and Indiana, supposing these [to be] available states for Mr. C[lay]." Charles S. Todd to William H. Seward, February 8, 1839, Charles S. Todd Correspondence, letter 83, Cincinnati History Library and Archives, OH (photocopy).

81 In the only other state elections in September, in the reliably Whig state of Vermont, the Whig governor, Silas Jennison, was reelected, but by a considerably smaller margin than in the past. In 1839, he won by only 5 points, whereas in 1836, 1837, and 1838, he had never won by fewer than 11 points.

82 I follow Holt (*Rise and Fall of the American Whig Party*, 75) in counting the Georgia results as losses for the Whig Party. However, it should be noted that in Georgia, the anti–Van Buren party styled itself the State Rights Party, and not until the summer of 1840 would it clearly align itself with the national Whig Party. While Georgia's State Rights Party shunned the Whig label and rejected the notion that Southern interests—especially that of preserving slavery—could be best safeguarded through national party alliances, its adherents were united in their opposition to Van Buren and to the Democratic Party, which in Georgia called itself the Union Party or Union Democratic Party. Unlike the State Rights Party, the Union Democrats tended to align their views and take their policy cues from the national party, and so it seems justified to count these states election results as Whig losses and Democratic gains. On the "anomalous position" of Georgia's State Rights Party during the 1830s, see Anthony Gene Carey, *Parties, Slavery, and the Union in Antebellum Georgia* (Athens: University of Georgia Press, 1997), chap. 2, esp. 38, 47–49. Also see Richard P. McCormick, *The Second American Party System: Party Formation in the Jacksonian Era* (Chapel Hill: University of North Carolina Press, 1966), 236–244.

83 On the pessimism among Ohio's Whigs induced by the defeat, see Edgar Allan Holt, *Party Politics in Ohio, 1840–1850* (Columbus, OH: F. J. Heer, 1930), 16. The October 16, 1839, issue of the *Ohio State Journal*, for instance, despaired: "It seems like madness to contend against an overwhelming fate—against a force that is sure to crush us."

84 Henry Clay to Nathaniel Tallmadge, October 12, 1839, *Papers of Henry Clay*, 9:351; and Clay to Tompkins, October 12, 1839, 277. Also see Clay to Smith, September 14, 1839, 9:340, in which Clay asked, "Is there any reason to believe that the issue of your late election was influenced in any degree by the use of public money?" He directed the same inquiry to Allen Hall relating to Tennessee's election. Neither Hall nor Smith thought the corrupt use of public money explained the adverse election results. Hall did point to "the unprecedented circulation of printed documents" but did not know whether they had been funded by private or public monies. Hall to Clay, September 23, 1839, 9:345.

85 Clay to Tompkins, October 12, 1839, 277. For more evidence of Clay's reaction to the adverse results, see Clay to Tallmadge, October 12, 1839, 9:351; and Henry Clay to Nathan Sargent, October 25, 1839, *Papers of Henry Clay*, 9:352–53.

86 Henry Clay to Samuel McKean, April 16, 1839, *Papers of Henry Clay*, 9:305.

87 W. A. Graham to Willie Mangum, October 11, 1839, *The Papers of Willie Person Mangum*, ed. Henry Thomas Shanks (Raleigh, NC: State Department of Archives and History, 1953), 3:19.

88 Fillmore to Weed, June 5, 1839, 2:192. Six months before, Fillmore had also warned Weed against the danger of being "stuck in the Clay." Millard Fillmore to Thurlow Weed, December 26, 1838, *Millard Fillmore Papers*, 2:180.

89 Frederick Whittlesey to Thurlow Weed, September 30, 1839, quoted in Gunderson, *Log-Cabin Campaign*, 53.

90 Gunderson, 53–54.

91 Henry Clay to Pierre van Cortlandt, Jr., November 25, 1839, *Papers of Henry Clay: Supplement*, 279; and Henry Clay to Robert Swartwout, November 15, 1839, *Papers of Henry Clay*, 9:353–54. Clay's assessment in a letter to Virginia's Benjamin Watkins Leigh was more measured: "The state of our information here is such as to cast a little brighter prospect on public affairs than that which they wore some weeks ago." November 17, 1839, *Papers of Henry Clay: Supplement*, 278.

92 Willis Hall to Henry Clay, November 20, 1839, *Papers of Henry Clay*, 9:355–356.

93 Henry Clay to Harrison G. Otis, December 4, 1839, *Papers of Henry Clay*, 9:360; Henry Clay to Peter B. Porter, December 4, 1839, *Papers of Henry Clay*, 9:361; and Henry Clay to Leslie Combs, December 3, 1839, *Papers of Henry Clay*, 9:359.

94 Willis Hall to Henry Clay, November 20, 1839, 9:355.

95 William Henry Harrison to Solomon Van Rensselaer, November 19, 1839, in Catharina V. R. Bonney, ed., *A Legacy of Historical Gleanings* (Albany, NY: J. Munsell, 1875), 2:114–115.

96 A week before the convention opened, Horace Greeley, a Weed ally who had reluctantly given up Clay for Scott, wrote that Weed "and the other 'Scott conspirators' entertain little doubt that the nomination of S will be carried." Horace Greeley to O. A. Bowe, November 25, 1839, quoted in Gunderson, *Log-Cabin Campaign*, 56. Also see Charles Winslow Elliott, *Winfield Scott: The Soldier and the Man* (New York: Macmillan, 1937), 379.

1   John Dickerson, *Whistlestop: My Favorite Stories from Presidential Campaign History* (New York: Twelve, 2017), 327. More generally, see Arthur M. Schlesinger, Jr., *The Age of Jackson* (Boston: Little, Brown, 1945), chaps. 22–23; and Sean Wilentz, *The Rise of American Democracy: Jefferson to Lincoln* (New York: W. W. Norton, 2005), chap. 16. Also see Louis Hartz, *The Liberal Tradition in America: An Interpretation of American Political Thought since the Revolution* (New York: Harcourt Brace Jovanovich, 1955), 111 ("We think of the Whigs in the age of Harrison as stealing the egalitarian thunder of the Democrats").

2   William Preston Vaughn, *The Antimasonic Party in the United States, 1826–1843* (Lexington: University Press of Kentucky, 1983), 60.

3   *National Intelligencer*, May 15, 1839.

4   *Niles' National Register*, November 30, 1839, 57:215. Delaware's state convention was held on June 12, 1839.

5   Indianapolis *Journal*, October 12, 1839. Indiana's delegates were chosen at a state convention in Indianapolis on January 22–23, 1838. Estimating the number of Indiana delegates at the national convention is a bit difficult. At the outset of the convention, the state had only five delegates, and the proceedings make no mention of additional Indiana delegates arriving during the convention, but the proceeding's final list of delegates counts ten delegates from Indiana. Of these ten, seven were selected at the January 1838 state convention, and three were added at some point thereafter.

6   *Niles' National Register*, November 30, 1839, 57:216. Alabama's Whigs held a state convention in Tuscaloosa in January that designated a Whig central committee to devise a plan for selecting delegates, although it was evidently slow to do so. See, for instance, the complaints expressed in the *Free Selma Press*, September 5, 1839.

7   John M. Sacher, *A Perfect War of Politics: Parties, Politicians, and Democracy in Louisiana* (Baton Rouge: Louisiana State University Press, 2003), 94. The twelve Louisiana delegates selected are listed in the *National Intelligencer*, March 30, 1839. The one Louisiana delegate who attended the Harrisburg convention was George Mason Graham, the thirty-two-year-old grandson of Virginia's famous founding father George Mason, who had been a delegate at the federal constitutional convention in Philadelphia half a century before. Graham would later become a founding father of sorts himself—of Louisiana State University. Graham was born and raised in Fairfax County in Virginia, and his father was prominent in Washington politics and society, having served as acting secretary of war in 1816–1817, president of the Washington branch of the Bank of the United States from 1819 to 1823, and commissioner of the general land office of the US from 1823 to 1830. See James L. Barnidge, "George Mason Graham: The Father of Louisiana State University," *Louisiana History: The Journal of the Louisiana Historical Association* (Summer 1969): 225–240.

8   *National Intelligencer*, March 30, 1839.

9   The legislative caucus of Maryland's Whigs selected Reverdy Johnson, a prominent Baltimore lawyer and former state senator, and John N. Steele, who had

been the Whig candidate for governor in 1838, the first year Maryland held gubernatorial elections. Steele fell short by 300 votes out of more than 55,000 votes cast in the gubernatorial contest. *Adams Sentinel and General Advertiser* (Gettysburg, PA), March 23, 1839. Steele did not attend the convention, and at the Harrisburg convention his place as a senatorial delegate was taken by John Leeds Kerr, who had been selected as a district delegate at a meeting of the Whigs of Maryland's second congressional district during the summer of 1839. *Adams Sentinel and General Advertiser*, July 1, 1839. That meeting expressed "a decided preference" for Clay but also said it would "cheerfully concur" in the decision made by the national convention, a sentiment that was the same in spirit as that which had been adopted by the legislative caucus.

10 For a useful summary of the change from legislative caucus to state convention in different regions and states, see Richard P. McCormick, *The Second American Party System: Party Formation in the Jacksonian Era* (Chapel Hill: University of North Carolina Press, 1966), 93–95 (New England), 167–168 (the Middle States), 251 (the Old South), and 323–324 (the New States).

11 *Wilmington Advertiser*, September 27, 1839. The Massachusetts state convention was held on September 11, 1839, and the two delegates chosen were former member of Congress (and future US senator) Isaac Bates and former state senator and state legislator (and future member of Congress) Barker Burnell. Among Massachusetts's district delegates at the convention was the Boston lawyer—and former Maine US senator—Peleg Sprague, who was chosen at the beginning of November by the Suffolk ward and county convention (Richard Haughton, publisher of the Boston *Atlas*, was selected as his substitute). *Hartford Courant*, November 4, 1839.

12 *Niles' National Register*, May 25, 1839, 56:208; *National Intelligencer*, May 21, 1839; and *Adams Sentinel and General Advertiser*, May 27, 1839.

13 *Rutland Herald*, July 2 1839; and *Vermont Mercury*, June 28, 1839. The meeting in Woodstock was held on June 27, 1839. The two at-large delegates who were selected but did not attend the Harrisburg convention were the state's lieutenant governor, David Camp, and state legislator George Tisdale Hodges.

14 *Vermont Mercury*, October 25, 1839. As it turned out, the delegate for Vermont's third district was unable to attend, and his selected substitute went instead. The Montpelier convention was held on October 16, 1839.

15 On October 3, 1839, there was what was billed as "a conservative state convention" representing "the unchanged democracy of New York," that is, the wing of the Democratic Party (the self-described Conservative Democrats) led by Nathaniel Tallmadge, who headlined the event with a three-hour oration. *Niles' National Register*, October 26, 1839, 57:135. This convention in Syracuse, contrary to Gunderson's claim, was not a "Whig convention." Robert Gray Gunderson, *The Log-Cabin Campaign* (Lexington: University Press of Kentucky, 1957), 52–53.

16 The New York district delegates met in New York City on November 30 and selected two at-large delegates: Chandler Starr and John Woodworth. *Long-Island Star*, December 2, 1839. Only Starr could attend the national convention, and the delegates subsequently replaced Woodworth with Robert Nicholas.

17 *National Intelligencer*, July 3, 1839. The directive from the central committee is printed in full in the *Intelligencer* and is dated June 25, 1839. The generally pro-Clay *Intelligencer* approved of this scheme and hoped that "Whig papers will now leave off discussing men, and confine themselves to the great struggle for principles."

18 The Chambersburg convention recommended that delegates be selected at the district level at some convenient time prior to the national convention. *Adams Sentinel and General Advertiser*, June 24, 1839. The proceedings of the Union and Harmony Convention can be found in full in the pro-Harrison *Pittsburgh Gazette*, September 12, 1839, including a listing of all delegates who attended and the counties they represented. The resolutions adopted at the Chambersburg convention can be found in the pro-Clay *Adams Sentinel and General Advertiser*, June 17 and 24, 1839, but a list of delegates and the counties they represented was not reported. Shulze had been sounded out before the convention, and his letter accepting his selection as a senatorial delegate was read to the convention. In that letter, dated June 7, 1839, Shulze indicated that his "first choice is Mr. Clay but I am willing to go for Gen. Harrison." *National Intelligencer*, June 22, 1839. Shulze had also been named as a presidential elector at the Anti-Mason convention in Harrisburg in May. *National Intelligencer*, May 30, 1839.

19 Gunderson, *Log-Cabin Campaign*, 58; also see 56. Gunderson writes that the decision to seat "the members of both delegations . . . meant giving control to the Stevens faction" (58), but it might be more accurate to describe it as the Penrose faction, since Charles Penrose, the speaker of the state senate, orchestrated the march out of the Chambersburg convention and was the "chief engineer" of the Pennsylvania delegations at the state convention in Harrisburg in September and at the national convention in December. Nathan Sargent, *Public Men and Events* (Philadelphia, PA: J. B. Lippincott, 1874), 2:76. Stevens, in contrast, was a delegate at none of these three conventions. He was a delegate (indeed the chairman) at the state's Anti-Mason convention in May, also held in Harrisburg.

20 Of the twenty-eight district delegates named at the Union and Harmony Convention in September, nineteen showed up at the national convention in Harrisburg. At least three of the additional district delegates who attended the national convention were likely named by the September convention's committee on the address as substitutes: these three delegates had attended the Union and Harmony Convention, and two of them, John Dickey and William Clark, had been among the Harrison faction that had walked out of the Chambersburg convention in protest. In all, twenty-two of the twenty-eight district delegates at the national convention had either been selected at or attended the pro-Harrison state convention in Harrisburg.

21 *Proceedings of the Democratic Whig National Convention* (Harrisburg, PA: R. S. Elliott, 1839), 10. It appears that the conflict over seats occurred in those few cases where a county convention met to appoint a delegate to the national convention. That is what happened in the case of George Chambers, who was

selected shortly before the national convention by Whig conventions in Adams and Franklin Counties, apparently in the belief that no appointment had been made from the twelfth congressional district. *Adams Sentinel and General Advertiser*, December 2, 1839. Chambers, a resident of Chambersburg, had served as the chairman of the Chambersburg convention in June.

22 William Nisbet Chambers's influential essay on the "Election of 1840" is among the important sources that err in suggesting that as a result of the seating compromise, Pennsylvania had a "combined delegation" that violated the convention's rule that each state had delegates equal to its number of presidential electors. Arthur M. Schlesinger, Jr., ed., *History of American Presidential Elections, 1789–1968* (New York: Chelsea House, 1985), 662. Chambers's error on this point appears to be due to his reliance on Gunderson, *Log-Cabin Campaign*.

23 Marc W. Kruman, *Parties and Politics in North Carolina, 1836–1865* (Baton Rouge: Louisiana State University Press, 1983), 26. North Carolina's Democrats held their first state convention the following year, in January 1840.

24 *Raleigh Register*, November 16, 1839. The North Carolina convention was held on November 12, 1839, and selected two senatorial delegates, John Owen and James Mebane. The selection of district delegates was left to the districts, although all but one congressional district had already selected their delegates by the time the state convention met.

25 Henry Clay to Willie P. Mangum, May 31, 1838, in *The Papers of Henry Clay*, ed. Robert Seager II (Lexington: University Press of Kentucky, 1988), 9:194. Clay was responding to Mangum, who disparaged nominating conventions as bodies typically "formed by drumming up all the officeholders" and told Clay that the state's Whigs would send delegates to a national convention only if they were "perfectly sure" that Clay would be nominated at the national convention; otherwise they would "decline being there." Willie P. Mangum to Henry Clay, March 26, 1838, *Papers of Henry Clay*, 9:166. Mangum was invited to attend the Harrisburg convention as a delegate representing the state's fourth congressional district but seems to have declined, as William H. Miller was selected in his place. Stephen Birdsall et al. to Willie P. Mangum, November 7, 1839, in *The Papers of Willie Person Mangum*, ed. Henry Thomas Shanks (Raleigh, NC: State Department of Archives and History, 1953), 3:22–23. Mangum was also encouraged by William A. Graham to attend as an at-large delegate (October 11, 1839, *Papers of Willie Person Mangum*, 3:18–19), but the senatorial delegate slots went to John Owen and James Mebane instead. However, while Mangum is not listed as a delegate in the *Proceedings of the Democratic Whig National Convention*, at least one newspaper identified Mangum as having been a member of the convention—and suggested that he offered this as the reason for declining the offer of the vice presidency. See the article from the *New York Courier and Enquirer* reprinted in *Niles' National Register*, December 11, 1841, 61:232.

26 Gerald L. Leonard, *The Invention of Party Politics: Federalism, Popular Sovereignty, and Constitutional Development in Jacksonian Illinois* (Chapel Hill: University of North Carolina Press, 2012), 201. On the opposition to party nomi-

nating conventions in Illinois, see McCormick, *Second American Party System,* 282–286.

27 *Raleigh Register,* November 16, 1839. The initial draft of the resolution used the word "instruct," but that was subsequently amended to "recommend" on the grounds that "in venturing upon instructions, the Convention transcended its powers."

28 *Niles' National Register,* November 2, 1839, 57:154. The Illinois convention was held on October 7, 1839, in Springfield. The convention named all five of the state's delegates, although only three of them made it to the convention. The state convention, like a number of others that met in 1839, also chose presidential electors, one of whom was Abraham Lincoln. *Niles' National Register,* October 26 1839, 57:138.

29 Mississippi, which held its state convention on February 4, also endorsed Clay.

30 The proceedings of the Virginia convention, which convened on September 25, 1839, are documented in *Niles' National Register,* October 19, 1839, 57:125–127. The other senatorial delegate, James Barbour, was also one of Clay's good friends and former Senate colleagues. On Clay's correspondence with Leigh in the months leading up to the national convention, see *Papers of Henry Clay,* 9:346 (September 25, 1839); and *The Papers of Henry Clay: Supplement, 1793–1852,* ed. Melba Porter Hay (Lexington: University Press of Kentucky, 1992), 274–275 (June 12, 1839), 278 (November 17, 1839).

31 *Niles' National Register,* February 16, 1839, 55:385.

32 *Raleigh Register,* November 16, 1839; and *Niles' National Register,* October 19, 1839, 57:127. Clay was disappointed that Kentucky's state convention in Harrodsburg on August 26 had declined to endorse Tallmadge for vice president (Henry Clay to Nathaniel Tallmadge, October 12, 1839, *Papers of Henry Clay,* 9:351), an endorsement he had led Tallmadge to believe he would receive (Henry Clay to Nathaniel Tallmadge, April 9, 1839, *Papers of Henry Clay,* 9:301). The selection of delegates to the national convention was not part of the agenda of the Harrodsburg convention (its main purpose instead was nominating a gubernatorial candidate) because a Whig legislative caucus had met in January 1838—several months before Congress announced a date and time for the convention. The caucus determined that two at-large delegates would be selected by legislative caucus and recommended that the remaining delegates be chosen at the district level. On August 12, 1839, the Whig central committee of Kentucky urged districts that had not already selected their delegates to do so "without delay." *Louisville Daily Journal,* August 16, 1839.

33 John Bradley to Thurlow Weed, November 16, 1839, Thurlow Weed Papers, Department of Rare Books, Special Collections and Preservation, University of Rochester, NY. Bradley's selection as a convention delegate was announced in the *New-Yorker* (November 16, 1839, 8:139) on the same date that Bradley wrote to Weed. In 1844, Bradley was nominated for Congress by the Whigs of Jefferson County, but he was defeated in the general election.

34 Edward Curtis to Thurlow Weed, November 18, 1839, quoted in Glyndon G. Van Deusen, *The Life of Henry Clay* (Boston: Little, Brown, 1937), 330. Also see

Gunderson, *Log-Cabin Campaign*, 56–57. While Curtis was sounding the alarm to Weed, Willis Hall was expressing the opposite fear to Clay that many "will be sent from the country as your friends who will go secretly pledged to Scott." Willis Hall to Henry Clay, November 20, 1839, *Papers of Henry Clay*, 9:357. Hall described the four delegates from New York City, however, as Clay's "staunch friends."

35   The New York *Herald* (December 2, 1389) reported that there were 33 district delegates at the City Hotel, and the vote was 22–11. The *Long-Island Star*, December 2, 1839, reported that there were 37 delegates but did not record vote totals.

36   New York *Herald*, December 2, 1839; and *Long-Island Star*, December 2, 1839.

37   In a letter to Seward on the first day of the Harrisburg convention, Weed reported that there were 28 "staunch" Scott men in the delegation, "though 30 go with us." Thurlow Weed to William Henry Seward, December 4, 1839, William Henry Seward Papers, Department of Rare Books, Special Collections and Preservation, University of Rochester, NY. In his autobiography, Weed mistakenly said that "twenty were for Scott, ten for Clay, and two for Harrison" (*Autobiography of Thurlow Weed*, ed. Harriet A. Weed [Boston: Houghton Mifflin, 1884], 481), which is obviously wrong since New York had 42 delegates, not 32. Gunderson reproduces this error (59), but it is corrected in Michael F. Holt, *The Rise and Fall of the American Whig Party: Jacksonian Politics and the Onset of the Civil War* (New York: Oxford University Press, 1999), 999n42. At the convention, Dudley Selden, the most ardent Clay delegate in the New York delegation, estimated that Clay supporters constituted one-third of the New York delegation, although it seems that he was generously rounding up. Anthony Banning Norton, *The Great Revolution of 1840: Reminiscences of the Log Cabin and Hard Cider Campaign* (Mt. Vernon, OH: A. B. Norton & Co., 1888), 30. In a letter to Harrison shortly after the convention, Solomon Van Rensselaer claimed that he was the sole Harrison delegate in the New York delegation. January 8, 1840, in Catharina V. R. Bonney, ed., *A Legacy of Historical Gleanings* (Albany, NY: J. Munsell, 1875), 2:117.

38   New York *Herald*, December 2, 1839. The *Herald*'s account intimated that Weed preferred Scott because he knew that the general "can preserve this state to the whig party better than any other man," and Weed "wants the whig party to retain their power in this state, because as long as they do that he expects to be state printer." In contrast, Bennett's *Herald* did "a business equal to $20,000 clear per annum," and so his motives for being "red hot for Scott" were selfless, rooted in a concern for the public good of the nation rather than the interests of the state party and its grubby office holders.

39   Curtis to Weed, November 18, 1839, quoted in Van Deusen, *Life of Henry Clay*, 330.

40   *Autobiography of Thurlow Weed*, 481.

41   Gunderson asserts that the two New England delegates with whom Weed conferred were "pledged to Harrison" (*Log-Cabin Campaign*, 61n9), but Weed does not say that in his *Autobiography* (481), nor have I found evidence to confirm

this. On the contrary, in a letter to Seward dated December 4, 1839, Weed wrote that among the New England delegates, only Wilson and Ashmun and a few others "stand firm"—which, in the context of the letter, a discussion of the need for the New York delegation to stand "united and strong" for Scott—seems to mean that they were standing firm for Scott, especially because, as Weed well knew, a large majority of the Massachusetts and New Hampshire delegates, particularly those allied with Webster, were strongly committed to opposing Clay.

42 Edward Curtis to Thurlow Weed, December 2, 1839, Thurlow Weed Papers.

43 The results of the poll were conveyed to Clay by a thirty-three-year-old congressman from western New York, Charles Mitchell, whom Clay evidently trusted. Fillmore was not at the meeting with Clay, so his report to Weed on Clay's response is based on what Mitchell communicated about his meeting with Clay. Millard Fillmore to Thurlow Weed, December 2, 1839, *Millard Fillmore Papers*, ed. Frank. H. Severance (Buffalo, NY: Buffalo Historical Society, 1907), 2:194–195. On Clay's trust in Mitchell, see Henry Clay to Peter B. Porter, December 4, 1839, *Papers of Henry Clay*, 9:361. On Mitchell's friendship and business associations with Weed, see Glyndon Van Deusen, *Thurlow Weed: Wizard of the Lobby* (Boston: Little, Brown, 1947), 139.

44 Julia Perkins Cutler, ed., *Life and Times of Ephraim Cutler* (Cincinnati, OH: Robert Clark & Co, 1890), 235.

45 Weed to Seward, December 4, 1839. Concern that the site of the convention might benefit Harrison was also expressed by the *Madisonian*, a DC paper that backed Scott. "We should not be surprised," the paper's editor groused, "if the influence of the friends of Gen. Harrison in Pennsylvania, who throng so thickly around the Convention, should ultimately control its decision." December 7, 1839.

46 *Niles' National Register*, November 30, 1839, 57:210.

47 Gunderson counts 232 (*Log-Cabin Campaign*, 57) because he follows the count of names listed at the end of the *Proceedings of the Democratic Whig National Convention*, 27–33. However, this count misleads because it counts several delegates who did not attend, namely, the three Arkansas delegates as well as two Louisiana delegates who were listed as a courtesy to the sole Louisiana delegate who attended the convention, and double-counts in the case of a few substitutions that happened during the convention.

48 *Proceedings of the Democratic Whig National Convention*, 13. The depth of Barbour's despair about the state of the country and its institutions under the Jackson and Van Buren administrations is captured in his letter to Willie P. Mangum, written on November 3, 1839, a month before the convention opened. Barbour told Mangum, "We are destined to suffer long before there is relief, & that I fear is to be found by a leap down the precipice of revolution. The system, which was introduced by Jackson, was as thorough a change of the constitution, as ever was worked by Art or by Force." *Papers of Willie Mangum*, 3:21.

49 At the time that the delegates voted to approve the unit rule on December 5, sixteen of the twenty-two states had fewer than the number of delegates

that their state had been allocated. The only states that had the allocated number of delegates were Massachusetts, Rhode Island, Connecticut, New York, and Pennsylvania. Delaware was the only state that had more than its allotted number.

50 *Autobiography of Thurlow Weed*, 481. The *National Intelligencer* (December 9, 1839), in explaining the unit rule, gave the example of New York as giving 28 votes for Scott, 12 for Clay, and 2 for Harrison. Also see note 37 above.

51 *National Intelligencer*, December 9, 1839.

52 *Proceedings of the Democratic Whig National Convention*, 15–16.

53 *Proceedings of the Democratic Whig National Convention*, 16; and *National Intelligencer*, December 9, 1839.

54 David S. Heidler and Jeanne T. Heidler, *Henry Clay: The Essential American* (New York: Random House, 2010), 308. Also see Gunderson, *Log-Cabin Campaign*, 58.

55 Weed to Seward, December 4, 1839.

56 *National Intelligencer*, December 9, 1839.

57 Cutler, *Life and Times of Ephraim Cutler*, 236. Also see Weed to Seward, December 4, 1839.

58 The Pennsylvania delegates who can likely be counted as pro-Clay are the two senatorial delegates selected at Chambersburg; three of the six district delegates who were seated as part of the seating compromise announced on December 5; two of the delegates selected at the Union and Harmony Convention, John Swift and Jonathan Roberts, who announced their "original preference" for Clay on the convention floor on the convention's last day (Norton, *The Great Revolution of 1840*, 30); and Bela Badger of Philadelphia. However, at least one of the senatorial delegates, former governor John Andrew Shulze, who was a favorite of the Anti-Masons, may have been pro-Harrison; certainly, Harrison later wrote to Shulze to thank him "for the great services you rendered me at Harrisburg last December." Harrison to Shulze, May 22, 1840, quoted in John J. Reed, "Battleground: Pennsylvania Antimasons and the Emergence of the National Nominating Convention, 1835–1839," *Pennsylvania Magazine of History and Biography* (January/April 1998): 112.

59 Ephraim Cutler, a pro-Harrison delegate from Ohio, reckoned that "on the third day of the convention a per capita vote [presumably using Bowie's modified per-capita vote plan] would probably have resulted, Clay 102; Harrison 91, and Scott 61." Cutler's estimate is almost identical to the first ballot results using the unit rule. Cutler, *Life and Times of Ephraim Cutler*, 237.

60 Holt, *Rise and Fall of the American Whig Party*, 102. Also see Heidler and Heidler, who write that "Clay supporters did not realize how they had been bested until it was too late." *Henry Clay*, 308.

61 In a letter to the *Richmond Whig* in 1841, Benjamin Watkins Leigh, Virginia's representative on the general committee, explained that the committee's "first step" had been "to collect, through the agency of the particular committees of which it was composed, the sense of the individual members of the convention as to the nomination for presidency," and from these deliberations,

"it appeared that there was *a plurality of individual votes* for Mr. Clay, but not a majority of the whole. The other votes were divided between Gen. Harrison and Gen. Scott." *Niles' National Register*, December 11, 1841, 61:232.

62 *National Intelligencer*, December 9, 1839.

63 Reports differ as to whether Michigan cast its 3 votes for Harrison on the first ballot or whether it was divided and so could not vote. On December 13, the *National Intelligencer* carried a state-by-state breakdown of the first ballot (provided by the pro-Scott *New-York American*) that reported Michigan's vote as divided. This account stated that after Michigan's third delegate arrived, the state cast its 3 votes for Scott, apparently on the third ballot. A different accounting can be found in the *Vermont Phoenix*, which on December 13 carried a report from a correspondent of the pro-Harrison Boston *Atlas* that also provided a state-by-state breakdown of the first ballot and recorded Michigan's 3 votes for Harrison. It is difficult to say which account is accurate, but there is some evidence that seems to favor the account in the *Atlas*. Specifically, the third Michigan delegate took his seat on Friday morning (*Proceedings of the Democratic Whig National Convention*, 18; Norton, *Great Revolution of 1840*, 22) and thus would have been there in time to add his vote to the state's first ballot—and if not the first ballot, then certainly the second, which was reportedly unchanged from the first ballot. If the state was indeed prevented from casting its vote, then it would have been because each of the three delegates cast their ballot for a different candidate, not from having only two delegates (cf. Gunderson, *Log-Cabin Campaign*, 60). Also working in favor of the *Atlas* count is that Ohio delegate Ephraim Cutler's contemporaneous notes record a meeting that included the two early-arriving Michigan delegates (George C. Bates and Thomas J. Drake), and Cutler seems to indicate that they concurred in a "prevailing opinion" within the group that Harrison was the preferred candidate, although he does not specifically identify the Michigan delegates' views. Cutler, *Life and Times of Ephraim Cutler*, 235. Overall, though, the evidence is sufficiently contradictory that it is very possible that Michigan, as the *Intelligencer* reported, was not able to cast a vote on the first ballot.

64 Only New York, Pennsylvania, Massachusetts, and Maryland selected three delegates to the general committee. Five states relied on one delegate to represent the votes and views of their delegation, including Virginia, which selected Benjamin Watkins Leigh. The other fourteen states each selected two delegates.

65 Correspondent of the Boston *Atlas*, report delivered at 11:30 on Friday night, in the *Vermont Phoenix*, December 13, 1839.

66 *Vermont Phoenix*, December 13, 1839; Baltimore *Sun*, December 9, 1839; Norton, *Great Revolution of 1840*, 23; and *Proceedings of the Democratic Whig National Convention*, 19. Judging by Combs's confidential letter to Clay, written at 9 p.m. on December 6, it appears that the general committee—of which Combs was a member—had already reached its decision in favor of Harrison before the adjournment. Leslie Combs to Henry Clay, December 6, 1839, *Papers of Henry Clay*, 9:362.

67 Holt, *Rise and Fall of the American Whig Party*, 102 (first quotation); Heidler and Heidler, *Henry Clay*, 308 (second quotation); and Gunderson, *Log-Cabin Campaign*, 61 (third, fourth, and fifth quotations). Also see Ronald G. Shafer, *The Carnival Campaign: How the Rollicking 1840 Campaign of "Tippecanoe and Tyler Too" Changed Presidential Elections Forever* (Chicago: Chicago Review Press, 2016), 6; and Chambers, "Election of 1840," 663. Gunderson appears to be the principal source for these other accounts. One of the only historians that I am aware of who has questioned this story is Allan Peskin, *Winfield Scott and the Profession of Arms* (Kent, OH: Kent State University Press, 2003), 288n14.

68 A. K. McClure, *Our Presidents and How We Make Them* (New York: Harper & Brothers, 1900), 68.

69 That people have been so quick to accept this story on so little evidence may say something about Stevens's historical reputation as a masterful manipulator—a reputation that Stevens seemed eager to burnish.

70 Gunderson, *Log-Cabin Campaign*, 59.

71 Horace Greeley, *Recollections of a Busy Life* (New York: J. B. Ford, 1869), 131.

72 *Vermont Phoenix*, December 13, 1839.

73 At the convention, Leigh described Scott as my "intimate, old, personal friend." Norton, *Great Revolution of 1840*, 29.

74 John S. D. Eisenhower, *Agent of Destiny: The Life and Times of General Winfield Scott* (New York: Free Press, 1997), 21. Also see Timothy D. Johnson, *Winfield Scott: The Quest for Military Glory* (Lawrence: University Press of Kansas, 1998), 21, 139.

75 The significance of Leigh's friendship with Scott is also highlighted in Peskin, *Winfield Scott and the Profession of Arms*, 288n14.

76 Peskin, 288n14. Perhaps the best evidence, albeit indirect, from the time that might be seen as supporting the "Stevens did it" theory is a letter that Weed wrote on the first day of the convention in which he told Seward that "Virginia and North Carolina are willing to go for Scott in the end" (Weed to Seward, December 4, 1839), but this seems more likely to be a miscalculation on Weed's part about the difficulty of weaning the delegations of these two states away from Clay. It seems unlikely that before the convention had begun, Weed had already accurately canvassed the more than thirty delegates from these two states. Moreover, there are a host of reasons that the deliberative process may have hardened these delegations' commitment to Clay. In addition, it is worth noting that North Carolina's delegation behaved identically to Virginia's, but there is no suggestion, even from McClure/Stevens, that North Carolina was made privy to the purported letter from Scott.

77 Stevens is not the only person at the convention to claim credit for Clay's defeat and Harrison's victory. In a letter to Harrison a month after the convention, Solomon Van Rensselaer boasted that he had "single handed" been responsible for the New York delegation's shift from Scott to Harrison on the final ballot. He reported to Harrison that he had told his fellow New Yorkers, "If your votes are cast for Scott upon this last ballot, the friends of Harrison will elect Clay."

This warning, he wrote, "came like a clap of thunder upon them," and when he was asked whether he was serious, he responded, "Never more so in my life," as "there stand my two Messengers, the one for the Ohio, and the other for the Pennsylvania Delegations." Faced with the threat of Pennsylvania and Ohio bolting for Clay, according to Van Rensselaer, the Scott forces of New York abandoned Scott in favor of Harrison. Van Rensselaer also claimed that on his way to Harrisburg, he had traveled with an undecided Massachusetts delegation and was responsible for persuading them to back Harrison at the convention. Solomon Van Rensselaer to William Henry Harrison, January 8, 1840, in Bonney, *Legacy of Historical Gleanings*, 2:117–118. Gunderson rightly discounts the boasting of Van Rensselaer on the grounds that he was "an eager aspirant for Harrison's patronage" (*Log-Cabin Campaign*, 61n9)—indeed a desperate one since Van Buren had finally determined to oust him from his position as Albany postmaster general. Donald B. Cole, *Martin Van Buren and the American Political System* (Princeton, NJ: Princeton University Press, 1984), 352. Curiously, according to Alexander McClure (*Our Presidents*, 68), Thaddeus Stevens's motivation for surreptitiously delivering the Scott letter into the hands of the Virginia delegation was that Stevens had in his possession another letter—this one from Harrison—that promised him a Cabinet position in the Harrison administration (this letter too has never been found). If true, it is exceedingly odd that Stevens apparently never relayed to Harrison or those closest to Harrison the story of his convention-altering maneuver that allegedly delivered the nomination to Old Tippecanoe.

78 Immediately after the convention, the *New York Courier and Enquirer* (the state's most ardently pro-Clay paper) predicted that Harrison would carry New York by 15,000 votes. Harrison's actual margin of victory was 13,300. See *Hartford Courant*, December 12, 1839.

79 Sydney Nathans, *Daniel Webster and Jacksonian Democracy* (Baltimore, MD: Johns Hopkins University Press, 1973), 128.

80 Holt, *Rise and Fall of the American Whig Party*, 103–104.

81 On the second day of the convention, Louisiana's sole delegate, G. Mason Graham, produced a letter from the chairman of the Whig state committee of Arkansas that authorized Louisiana's former US senator Alexander Porter (who did not attend the convention despite being selected as a delegate) to cast Arkansas's 3 votes for Clay for president and Tyler for vice president (Norton, *Great Revolution of 1840*, 21; and *National Intelligencer*, December 9, 1839). There is no evidence that Arkansas's 3 votes were recorded for president or vice president, so the convention must have refused the request, either because Porter was not present at the convention or because the delegates refused to allow one state to cast votes for another state.

82 Anthony Gene Carey, *Parties, Slavery, and the Union in Antebellum Georgia* (Athens: University of Georgia Press, 1997), 47; and Holt, *Rise and Fall of the American Whig Party*, 103.

83 Holt, 103.

84 "Whig National Caucus," *Salisbury Carolinian*, printed in *Liberty Advocate* (Liberty, MS), December 19, 1837. Also see Mangum to Clay, March 26, 1838, 9:166.
85 Thurlow Weed Barnes, *Memoir of Thurlow Weed* (Boston: Houghton Mifflin, 1884), 77.
86 *Niles' National Register*, December 11, 1841, 61:232.
87 Barnes, *Memoir of Thurlow Weed*, 77; and *Autobiography of Thurlow Weed*, 482
88 The quotation is from "Mr. Leigh and the Vice Presidency," *Tyler Quarterly Historical and Genealogy Magazine* (1922): 215. For a sampling of the various names said to have been offered the vice presidency, see the *New York Courier and Enquirer* article reprinted in *Niles' National Register*, December 11, 1841, 61:232; Weed, *Memoir*, 77; *Autobiography of Thurlow Weed*, 482; Cutler, *Life and Times of Ephraim Cutler*, 238; and Sargent, *Public Men and Events*, 2:93. Daniel Walker Howe even suggests that Clay himself was offered the vice-presidential nomination but, in "a costly fit of pique," did not take up the offer, but I have found no evidence to support this claim. Daniel Walker Howe, *What God Hath Wrought: The Transformation of America, 1815–1848* (Oxford: Oxford University Press, 2007), 572. In a letter to Clay written on the night of Harrison's nomination, Kentucky's Leslie Combs speculated that the "bargain is no doubt to make Webster V.P. & thus carry out the Antimasonic nomination," a claim that well reflects the anger Combs felt but does not illuminate the thinking of Harrison's supporters. Combs to Clay, December 6, 1839, 9:362.
89 *Niles' National Register*, December 11, 1841, 61:232. It appears that Clayton—Weed's preferred candidate—was among those who were nominated—likely by New Hampshire—but Reverdy Johnson, Maryland's sole delegate on the committee, produced a letter that he said showed that Clayton would decline the nomination. While Weed (*Autobiography of Thurlow Weed*, 481) offers this as evidence that Tyler was a choice of last resort, the testimony of Leigh—who, unlike Weed, was in the room when Harrison was selected by the committee—shows that Johnson's withdrawal of Clayton's name did not matter since a large majority of the state delegations were already prepared to cast their ballots for Tyler.
90 Tyler's appeal to the delegates is highlighted in Greeley, *Recollections*, 131–132. On Tyler's hope and expectation that Clay would win the nomination, see John Tyler to Henry Clay, September 18, 1839, *Papers of Henry Clay*, 9:342. Ironically, although Tyler was selected to balance the ticket, his background was similar to Harrison's. Both were "to the manor born"—indeed, those manors in Virginia's Charles City County were no more than twenty miles apart. Edward P. Crapol, *John Tyler: The Accidental President* (Chapel Hill: University of North Carolina Press, 2006), 30. Both Tyler and Harrison were born and raised on large plantations worked by slaves, and both were from politically prominent, aristocratic families. Harrison's father was a signer of the Declaration of Independence, Tyler's father a college roommate of Thomas Jefferson, and both fathers had been three-term governors of the state. Evidently to Americans of 1839, a ticket consisting of two aristocratic Virginians could still look balanced.

91 Norton, *Great Revolution of 1840*, 27; and *Proceedings of the Democratic Whig National Convention*, 23.

92 Norton's *Great Revolution of 1840* is an invaluable source for what was said at the convention on the fourth day, December 7, 1839. For the first three days of the convention, it largely (apart from the evening of December 6) reproduces the official proceedings, but for the convention's final day, it provides far more detailed coverage of what was said (25–37).

93 Norton, 33.

94 Alabama's Henry Hilliard, quoted in Norton, 33.

95 Norton, 36. In 1831, the National Republican Party convention had adopted an address of precisely the sort that young Preston was suggesting. See Richard P. McCormick, *The Presidential Game: The Origins of American Presidential Politics* (New York: Oxford University Press, 1982), 137.

96 Apropos is Millard Fillmore's cautionary remark about the Whig Party, offered earlier in the year. "It must be recollected," he wrote, "that we have got to cement the fragments of many parties and it is therefore very important that we get a substance to which all can adhere, or at least that presents as few repellant qualities as possible. Into what crucible can we throw this heterogeneous mass of old national republicans, and revolting Jackson men; Masons and anti-Masons; Abolitionists and pro-Slavery men; Bank men & anti-Bank men with all the lesser fragments that have been, from time to time, thrown off from the great political wheel in its violent revolutions . . . ?" Fillmore to G. W. Patterson, February 6, 1839, *Millard Fillmore Papers*, 2:185.

CHAPTER 7. "WE GO FOR PRINCIPLES, NOT MEN"

1 John Calhoun to Thomas Clemson, December 8, 1839, *The Papers of John C. Calhoun*, ed. Clyde N. Wilson (Columbia: University of South Carolina Press, 1983), 15:14.

2 Henry Wise, *Seven Decades of the Union* (Philadelphia, PA: J. B. Lippincott, 1872), 171–172. The first quotation is from Robert Gray Gunderson, *The Log-Cabin Campaign* (Lexington: University Press of Kentucky, 1957), 68. This story—and especially the quotations—has been recycled in countless histories of the period. In addition to Gunderson, see, for example, Ronald G. Shafer, *The Carnival Campaign: How the Rollicking 1840 Campaign of "Tippecanoe and Tyler Too" Changed Presidential Elections Forever* (Chicago: Chicago Review Press, 2016), 9; Joseph Bucklin Bishop, *Presidential Nominations and Elections* (New York: Charles Scribner's Sons, 1916), 23; Sean Wilentz, *The Rise of American Democracy: Jefferson to Lincoln* (New York: W. W. Norton, 2005), 497; and Robert V. Remini, *Henry Clay: Statesman for the Union* (New York: W. W. Norton, 1991), 554–555. While relating the story in full, Remini does concede in a footnote that as "Clay's enemy," Wise "most likely . . . added more than the facts warranted" (555n31).

3 Even Peter B. Porter, the most ardent and tireless champion of Clay's candidacy, admitted, in a letter to Clay written shortly after the Harrisburg convention, that "the scale of party is so nearly balanced, that a small diversion from

our ranks would turn it." December 16, 1839, *The Papers of Henry Clay*, ed. Robert Seager II (Lexington: University Press of Kentucky, 1988), 9:366.

4 "Anecdotes of General Winfield Scott," *Publications of the Southern History Association* 4, no. 3 (May 1900): 193–194. This story is repeated as fact in Charles Winslow Elliott, *Winfield Scott: The Soldier and the Man* (New York: Macmillan, 1937), 381; and John S. D. Eisenhower, *Agent of Destiny: The Life and Times of General Winfield Scott* (New York: Free Press, 1997), 206. In *Winfield Scott and the Profession of Arms* (Kent, OH: Kent State University Press, 2003), Alan Peskin creatively combines both versions of the story (115-116).

5 The day Harrison was nominated, Clay was certainly in the nation's capital, as he wrote a letter that day from Washington, DC. See Henry Clay to Luther Bradish, December 6, 1839, Luther Bradish Papers, MS 71, New-York Historical Society. There is no evidence that Clay left for New York City between December 6 and December 11, when he gave a speech in Washington, DC.

6 William G. Shade, *Democratizing the Old Dominion: Virginia and the Second Party System, 1824–1861* (Charlottesville: University Press of Virginia, 1996), 217.

7 Leslie Combs to Henry Clay, December 6, 1839, *Papers of Henry Clay*, 9:362. Combs wrote this confidential letter late on the Friday night that Harrison was nominated, but it is unclear when Clay received it.

8 Diary entry of December 8, 1839, *Memoirs of John Quincy Adams, Comprising Portions of His Diary from 1795 to 1848*, ed. Charles Francis Adams (Philadelphia, PA: J. B. Lippincott, 1876), 10:181–182.

9 See, for instance, Clay's remarkable letter to William Browne, July 31, 1840, *Papers of Henry Clay*, 9:437–438. Also see Henry Clay to Thomas Hart Clay, December 12, 1839, *Papers of Henry Clay*, 9:364; and Henry Clay to Henry Clay, Jr., December 14, 1839, *Papers of Henry Clay*, 9:365.

10 Speech in Washington, DC, December 11, 1839, *Papers of Henry Clay*, 9:363–364. Also see Gunderson, *Log-Cabin Campaign*, 69.

11 New York *Evening Post*, December 9, 1839.

12 "Alas, Poor Henry Clay!," *United States Magazine and Democratic Review* (February 1840), 100–101, 104, 107.

13 "Downfall of Whiggery," *North Carolina Standard*, December 25, 1839.

14 Gunderson, *Log-Cabin Campaign*, 70–71.

15 Henry W. Miller to William A. Graham, December 10, 1839, *Papers of William A. Graham*, ed. J. G. de Roulhac Hamilton (Raleigh, NC: State Department of Archives and History, 1959), 2:69–70.

16 Francis Granger to Thurlow Weed, December 9, 1839, quoted in Gunderson, *Log-Cabin Campaign*, 71. Illustrative of Granger's observation was the reaction of former (and future) Tennessee senator Ephraim H. Foster, who admitted in a letter to Tennessee congressman William B. Campbell, "The nomination . . . struck many of us dumb. For one, I sank down to the very earth under the blow. 'I am done,' I exclaimed, 'Let them fight it out who will.' A few hours of sober reflection restored my feelings & convinced me of my own rashness. I am once again erect . . . and will do my duty faithfully, and battle to the bitter

end." Quoted in Philip M. Hamer, *Tennessee: A History, 1673–1932* (New York: American Historical Society, 1933), 1:299.

17 See Richard P. McCormick, *The Second American Party System: Party Formation in the Jacksonian Era* (Chapel Hill: University of North Carolina Press, 1966).

18 See, for instance, Julius Blackwell to James Polk, January 28, 1840, *Correspondence of James K. Polk*, ed. Wayne Cutler (Nashville, TN: Vanderbilt University Press, 1979), 5:375.

19 *Baltimore Republican*, December 11, 1839, quoted in Shafer, *Carnival Campaign*, 12. Also see Gunderson, *Log-Cabin Campaign*, 74.

20 *Baltimore Chronicle*, excerpted in *Pittsburgh Gazette*, December 17, 1839. Also see "Hard Cider and Log Cabin Candidate," *Baltimore Patriot*, excerpted in *Adams Sentinel*, December 30, 1839.

21 See, for example, "Granny Harrison," *Rutland Herald*, August 16, 1836.

22 Richard Smith Elliott, *Notes Taken in Sixty Years* (St. Louis, MO: R. P. Studley, 1883), 121. Also see Shafer, *Carnival Campaign*, chapter 2.

23 Elliott, *Notes Taken in Sixty Years*, 122; and Anthony Banning Norton, *The Great Revolution of 1840: Reminiscences of the Log Cabin and Hard Cider Campaign* (Mt. Vernon, OH: A. B. Norton & Co.,1888), 44, 51; also see 55.

24 Elliott, *Notes Taken in Sixty Years*, 123; and Anthony Banning Norton, ed., *Tippecanoe Songs of the Log Cabin Boys and Girls of 1840* (Mount Vernon, OH: A. B. Norton & Co., 1888), 52, 57. Lest there be any doubt as to how they felt about drinking hard cider, the song's final verse went:

> And if we get any ways thirsty
> I'll tell you what we can do
> We'll bring down a keg of hard cider
> And drink to old Tippecanoe
> And drink to old Tippecanoe

25 Norton, *Great Revolution*, 53–57. Perry's report is dated February 24, 1840. Also see Shafer, *Carnival Campaign*, 19–24.

26 *Ohio Statesman* (Columbus), February 22, 1840, quoted in Shafer, *Carnival Campaign*, 23; and Gunderson, *Log-Cabin Campaign*, 117.

27 Washington *Globe*, April 4, 1840.

28 Gunderson, *Log-Cabin Campaign*, 72.

29 Blackwell to Polk, January 28, 1840, 5:375.

30 Certainly, the Whigs thought Calhoun was angling for the presidency. See, for instance, Daniel Webster's letter to Thurlow Weed, dated June 23, 1838, in which he declared that "suggestions" in the newspapers "already point to Mr. Calhoun as the next Candidate." *The Papers of Daniel Webster, Correspondence*, ed. Charles M. Wiltse and Harold D. Moser, (Hanover, NH: University Press of New England, 1980), 4:311–312. Also see Thomas Cooper's letter to Nicholas Biddle from the previous year deploring Calhoun's "strange infatuation" with the presidency. May 24, 1837, *The Correspondence of Nicholas Biddle*, ed. Reginald McGrane (Boston, MA: J. S. Canner, 1966), 280. Also see Irving H.

Bartlett, *John C. Calhoun: A Biography* (New York: W. W. Norton, 1993), 239; and John Niven, *John C. Calhoun and the Price of Union* (Baton Rouge: Louisiana State University Press, 1988), 236, 238. On Calhoun's belief that "Van Buren goes in very weak and may be easily crushed with any thing like a vigorous effort," see John Calhoun to James Edward Colhoun, March 22, 1837, *The Papers of John C. Calhoun*, ed. Clyde N. Wilson (Columbia: University of South Carolina Press, 1983), 13:499.

31 *Pennsylvania Keystone*, quoted in Washington *Globe*, December 28, 1839.

32 Martin Van Buren to Andrew Jackson, [April 1840], *Correspondence of Andrew Jackson*, ed. John Spencer Bassett (Washington, DC: Carnegie Institution, 1926), 6:55.

33 John Catron to Andrew Jackson, March 21, 1835, *Correspondence of Andrew Jackson*, 5:331. Also see Thomas Brown, "The Miscegenation of Richard Mentor Johnson as an Issue for the National Election Campaign of 1835–1836," *Civil War History* (March 1993): 5–30.

34 Amos Kendall to Martin Van Buren, August 22, 1839, quoted in Gunderson, *Log-Cabin Campaign*, 81.

35 James Polk to A. O. P. Nicholson, January 13, 1838, *Correspondence of James K. Polk*, ed. Herbert Weaver (Nashville, TN: Vanderbilt University Press, 1979), 4:329.

36 *Pennsylvania Keystone*, reprinted in Washington *Globe*, December 28, 1839.

37 The New Hampshire circular is dated December 13, 1839. It was printed in the *New Hampshire Patriot* on December 16 and adjoined to the *Pennsylvania Keystone* article that was printed in the Washington *Globe*, December 28, 1839.

38 Washington *Globe*, January 31, 1840. The Tuscaloosa state convention met on December 16, 1839. Initially it called for the national convention to meet in April but then switched the date to May. There were four dissenting votes relating to the selection of King.

39 That the Democrats selected Baltimore as the site of their convention—for the third time running—while the Whigs selected a city in a free state eighty miles to the north perhaps reveals something about the different sectional centers of gravity of the two parties. Not until 1856, when they held their convention in Cincinnati, would the Democrats hold a national convention in a city other than Baltimore. In 1831, the National Republicans and Anti-Masons also held their national conventions in Baltimore, but in 1836 and 1838, the Anti-Masons held their conventions in Philadelphia. The Whigs held their 1848 convention in Philadelphia, but in 1844 and 1852, they also held their convention in Baltimore.

40 *Democratic Free Press* (Detroit), April 29, 1840.

41 Iredell County Democrats, for instance, who had gathered on Christmas Day to select delegates to the January 10 state convention in Raleigh, expressed their preference for Polk while also promising to "cheerfully join our Democratic brethren of the Union, in electing any who may be considered most likely to unite a general support." *Weekly Standard* (Raleigh, NC), January 1, 1840. On

April 7, 1840, the Democrats of Lenoir County, who had met to select a district delegate to the national convention, resolved that they "decidedly prefer[red]" King for vice president but would "cheerfully support" the nominee chosen at the national convention in Baltimore. *Weekly Standard*, April 22, 1840.

42 Felix Grundy et al. to James Polk, February 3, 1840, *Correspondence of James K. Polk*, 5:377. New York senator and Van Buren confidant Silas Wright shared Grundy's concern and "tried to convince the president that a convention would only add to the confusion existing in the Democratic ranks." Van Buren, though, thought it was too late to pull the plug on the convention and that it "might anger those states that had already chosen delegates." James C. Curtis, *The Fox at Bay: Martin Van Buren and the Presidency, 1837–1841* (Lexington: University Press of Kentucky, 1970), 194.

43 Andrew Jackson to Francis P. Blair, February 15, 1840, *Correspondence of Andrew Jackson*, 6:50–51; Andrew Jackson to Amos Kendall, April 16, 1840, *Correspondence of Andrew Jackson*, 6:58–59. Tennessee congressman Julius Blackwell expressed the same concern, in the same language, describing Johnson as "a dead weight upon us, in the south and south west." Blackwell to Polk, January 28, 1840, 5:376.

44 Jackson to Blair, February 15, 1840, 6:49–50. Jackson's view mirrored Van Buren's own judgment, conveyed to Jackson in a letter written two weeks before, that the vote to give the House printing contract to the *Globe* will "be the vote also upon the Independent Treasury." February 2, 1840, *Correspondence of Andrew Jackson*, 6:48.

45 Francis Blair to Andrew Jackson, March 17, 1840, *Correspondence of Andrew Jackson*, 6:54.

46 Blackwell to Polk, January 28, 1840, 5:376.

47 Morton's upset victory owed much to the Whigs' unpopular "fifteen-gallon law" that prohibited selling liquor in quantities smaller than fifteen gallons. Harrison Gray Otis thought it an "absurd act" and a "monstrous abomination" that he predicated could lose the Whigs the state. Harrison G. Otis to Henry Clay, January 11, 1839, *Papers of Henry Clay*, 9:269. Clay agreed entirely with Otis that the law was "indefensible," adding, "No man likes to have, or ought to have, cold water or brandy, separately or in combination, put in or kept out of his throat upon any other will than his own." Henry Clay to Harrison G. Otis, January 24, 1839, *Papers of Henry Clay*, 9:275. Also see Ronald P. Formisano, *The Transformation of Political Culture: Massachusetts Parties, 1790s–1840s* (New York: Oxford University Press, 1983), 298; and John L. Brooke, *The Heart of the Commonwealth: Society and Political Culture in Worcester County, Massachusetts, 1713–1861* (Cambridge: Cambridge University Press, 1989), 356–359.

48 John Niven, *Martin Van Buren: The Romantic Age of American Politics* (New York: Oxford University Press, 1983), 457.

49 Niven, 459.

50 Niven, 455.

51 *Weekly Standard*, January 1, 1840. The anti–Van Buren *Charlotte Journal* countered that rather than "a northern man with southern values," Van Buren was

"a northern man with no values." May 21, 1840. The same line of attack against Van Buren as "the northern man with no principles" was pursued in Weed's *Albany Evening Journal*, May 23, 1840.

52 Franklin Elmore to General A. Bailey, September 18, 1839, quoted in Niven, *Martin Van Buren*, 458.

53 Niven, 458.

54 Van Buren to Jackson, [April 1840], 6:56. Van Buren claimed that the Democrats had won the mayoral contest by 1,800 votes, but the vote tabulation in *Niles' National Register* indicated that it was closer to 1,600. May 2, 1840, 58:135.

55 Norton, *Great Revolution of 1840*, 37; *Proceedings of the Democratic Whig National Convention* (Harrisburg, PA: R. S. Elliott, 1839), 25; also see *National Niles' Register*, November 23, 1839, 57:199.

56 William Nisbet Chambers, "Election of 1840," in *History of American Presidential Elections, 1789–1968*, ed. Arthur M. Schlesinger, Jr. (1971; repr., New York: Chelsea House, 1985), 665. Also see Major L. Wilson, *The Presidency of Martin Van Buren* (Lawrence: University Press of Kansas, 1984), 202; and Mark R. Cheathem, *The Coming of Democracy: Presidential Campaigning in the Age of Jackson* (Baltimore, MD: Johns Hopkins University Press, 2018), 131.

57 Washington *Globe*, December 28, 1839. The same call was made at the Alabama Democratic state convention, which convened on December 16. Washington *Globe*, January 31, 1840. Also see Cave Johnson's letter to James Polk, dated December 12, 1839, in which he reported that Ohio's William Allen was working to have the Ohio Democratic state convention (scheduled to meet on January 8, 1840) recommend holding a national nominating convention in May in Baltimore. *Correspondence of James K. Polk*, 5:338.

58 Chambers, "Election of 1840," 667; and Gunderson, *Log-Cabin Campaign*, 79, 4.

59 The "great commotion" in Baltimore is well described in the first chapter of Gunderson, *Log-Cabin Campaign*, 1–6. The opening verse to the song "Tippecanoe and Tyler, Too" was

> What has caused this great commotion, motion, motion
> All the country through?
> It is the ball a rolling on
> For Tippecanoe and Tyler, too.

The Whigs' giant rolling ball was a riposte to Democratic senator Thomas Hart Benton's oft-quoted boast that he had put "this Ball in motion" on the Senate resolution expunging Jackson's censure in January 1837. A Whig caricature of Benton from 1837 showed the Missouri senator as a dung beetle rolling a massive dung ball (denoting the expunging resolution) up the hill toward the Capitol. The "Ball in motion" quotation from Benton's Senate speech of January 12, 1837, was "Solitary and alone and amidst the jeers and taunts of my opponents, I put this Ball in motion." Benton continued, "The people have taken it up and rolled it forward." The image can be found in Bernard F. Reilly, Jr., *American Political Prints, 1776–1876* (Boston, MA: G. K. Hall, 1991), 109.

60　See Gunderson, *Log-Cabin Campaign*, 79.

61　*Proceedings of the Democratic Whig National Convention*, 21

62　Curtis, *Fox at Bay*, 195.

63　There were about 250 delegates at the Democratic convention and 225 at the Whig convention, but that difference was attributable entirely to the gargantuan New Jersey delegation of 59. The size of the Democratic convention was way down compared with the party's national convention five years earlier, when more than six hundred delegates had attended, but nearly 60 percent of that total come from only three states: Maryland (183), Virginia (102), and New Jersey (73). Another sixty stemmed from Pennsylvania, which sent two rival 30-man delegations. A count of the delegates at the 1835 convention can be found in the *Mississippian* (Jackson), June 15, 1835.

64　The Democratic convention, perhaps because of its proximity to DC, did have more current members of Congress than the Whig convention. The Whig convention included no current US senators, for instance, whereas the twenty-one-person committee of nominations at the Democratic convention included three sitting US senators, all from the South (Tennessee's Felix Grundy, Mississippi's Robert Walker, and Alabama's Clement Clay), as well as Missouri congressman John Jameson and Kentucky congressman William O. Butler.

65　Both quotations are descriptions of the Whig national convention by those sympathetic to the Whigs. The first is from a correspondent from the pro-Harrison Boston *Atlas*, and the second is from pro-Harrison Ohio delegate Ephraim Cutler. *Vermont Phoenix*, December 13, 1839; and Julia Perkins Cutler, ed., *Life and Times of Ephraim Cutler* (Cincinnati, OH: Robert Clark & Co, 1890), 237. Also see James Barbour's presidential address at the Whig convention, in which he paid tribute to "the many grey heads" among the delegates. *Proceedings of the Democratic Whig National Convention*, 12.

66　The same number of states (twenty-one) were represented at the Democratic convention in 1840 as at the Democratic convention in 1835, although only three states were absent in 1835, since Michigan and Arkansas had not yet been admitted as states (both territories had, however, sent nonvoting delegates to the 1835 convention). Niven is mistaken in suggesting that "many more states were represented [at the Democratic convention in 1840] than four years earlier." *Martin Van Buren*, 463.

67　Gunderson, *Log-Cabin Campaign*, 79; *Proceedings of the National Democratic Convention Held in the City of Baltimore on the 5th of May 1840* (Baltimore, MD: Office of the Republican, 1840), 3. Gunderson counts six delegations that had less than half their prescribed strength, but the correct number is five (Massachusetts, Kentucky, Georgia, North Carolina, and Arkansas). Two states (Rhode Island and New Jersey) had more than twice their prescribed strength. In the Whig convention, one state (Louisiana) had less than half its prescribed strength, and one state (Delaware) had more than twice its prescribed strength. In both conventions, only eight states had the number of delegates equal to the number of their electoral votes. In the Democratic convention in 1835, several states also had delegations well below what their electoral college votes would have allowed, notably Tennessee, which was represented by only one delegate who cast all 15 of the state's allocated votes, and Georgia, which had three delegates, well short of its 11 electoral votes. Missouri and Mississippi, which both had 4 electoral votes, were each represented by only two delegates. The total number of underrepresented states in the Democrats' 1835 and 1840 conventions was essentially the same, nine in 1840 and eight in 1835. The Whig convention in 1839 had twelve underrepresented states. For the 1835 convention, see the proceedings published in *The Mississippian* (Jackson), June 15, 1835.

68   The list of delegates at the 1840 convention is in the *Proceedings of the National Democratic Convention*, 7–8.

69   For Clement Clay's affirmation that this was the voting method in the committee, see *Proceedings of the National Democratic Convention*, 22. In the case of Massachusetts, which had only one delegate, selected at the district level, only 1 vote was cast rather than the 14 votes warranted by the state's electoral vote count. *Proceedings of the National Democratic Convention*, 23. The voting method is also discussed in *Proceedings of the National Democratic Convention*, 12, 20.

70   *Proceedings of the National Democratic Convention*, 18–19.

71   Thomas H. Benton to Andrew Jackson, April 24, 1840, *Correspondence of Andrew Jackson*, 6:59. Also see diary entries of April 28 and 29, 1840, "Diaries of S. H. Laughlin, of Tennessee, 1840, 1843," *Tennessee Historical Magazine* (March 1916): 52. The "rigid neutrality" quotation is from Martin Van Buren's letter to Jackson, [April 1840], *Correspondence of Andrew Jackson*, 6:55. Benton tried to cheer up Jackson with the thought that "we shall be safe . . . if it should come to the Senate"—that is, if no vice-presidential candidate received a majority in the electoral college, as happened in 1836, Polk would surely get the nod.

72   The committee's decision did not sit well with all the delegates, particularly those who had come instructed by their district or state to vote for Johnson. Several pleaded at least for the chance to carry out their duty to cast a ballot for Johnson. Having done so, they vowed that they would be happy to accept "with all unanimity" the convention's decision.

73   In 1835, the Democratic convention appointed a committee of six, which then formulated a statement of principles that was issued several months later. The lengthy statement, dated July 31, 1835, is reprinted in the appendix of Joel H. Silbey, "Election of 1836," in *History of American Presidential Elections*, 616–638. The 1832 Democratic convention did not compose a statement of principles, but its published proceedings did include an address to the Democrats of New York by delegates at the New York state convention. For the 1832 proceedings, see *Summary of the Proceedings of a Convention of Republican Delegates . . . Held at Baltimore in the State of Maryland, May 1832, with an Address to the Republicans of the State of New-York Prepared by their Delegates in Compliance with the Recommendation of Said Convention* (Albany, NY: Packard and Van Benthuysen, 1832).

74   *Proceedings of the National Democratic Convention*, 23. Grundy was explicit in admitting "that our adversaries would attempt to make something out of" the

failure to agree on a vice president; "they would say we were disunited." The adoption of the platform, Grundy said, provided the "obvious and plain" answer to that criticism: "We have agreed upon the principles upon which the Government should be administered; we only differ in regard to one of the officers who is to assist is carrying those principles into effect."

75 "Proceedings of the Democratic National Convention, Baltimore, May 5, 6, 1840," in Chambers, "Election of 1840," 715. Also see diary entry for May 4, 1840, "Diaries of S. H. Laughlin," 54–55.

76 *Proceedings of the National Democratic Convention*, 4, 6. A speech later that same afternoon by Indiana congressman Tilghman Howard developed the same contrast between the parties: "This convention had assembled here for the purpose of sustaining those principles, which bound [the party] together, . . . not in order to drink hard cider." "Proceedings of the Democratic National Convention," 720.

77 *Proceedings of the National Democratic Convention*, 9.

78 *Proceedings of the National Democratic Convention*, 24, 22; and "Proceedings of the Democratic National Convention," 729. The second quotation is from Pennsylvania delegate John J. McCahen.

79 John A. Dix to Azariah Flagg, May 6, 1839, quoted in Gunderson, *Log-Cabin Campaign*, 82n6.

80 Andrew Jackson to Francis P. Blair, May 22, 1840, *Correspondence of Andrew Jackson*, 6:61.

81 Gunderson, *Log-Cabin Campaign*, 73. Philip Hone remarked that Forsyth retired from "the contest with a very bad grace, snarling and showing his teeth" (diary entry for May 11, 1840, *The Diary of Philip Hone, 1828–1851*, ed. Allan Nevins [New York: Dodd, Mead, 1927], 1:479), but while the remark is highly quotable (see, e.g., Donald B. Cole, *Martin Van Buren and the American Political System* [Princeton, NJ: Princeton University Press, 1984], 358), it hardly seems a fair reading of Forsyth's letter of withdrawal or a reliable barometer of Forsyth's feelings—which Hone attributed to his "Southern pride." While Forsyth coveted the vice presidency, he had no reason to anticipate that he would be the nominee at the convention. Unlike Polk, who had been nominated by at least four state conventions and many county and district meetings, Forsyth had been nominated only by his home state of Georgia. And since Georgia sent only two delegates to the convention, there was little support for a Forsyth vice presidency at the convention. Hone's remark is better read as a barometer of his own partisanship than of Forsyth's pique, as is suggested by the rest of his commentary on the "Van Buren Convention," which he characterized as "a sickly concern, a creeping plant withering under the shade of the mighty Harrison tree, which overshadows the land and keeps the sun of popular favor from shining upon its 'unwholesome neighbor.'"

CHAPTER 8. SEE HOW THEY RUN

1 "Mr. Polk's Acceptance of the Nomination," June 12, 1844, *Niles' National Register*, July 6, 1844, 66:294. Also see M. J. Heale, *The Presidential Quest: Candi-*

dates and Images in American Political Culture, 1787–1852 (London: Longman, 1982), 1 (quoting William Lowndes in 1821); and Gil Troy, See How They Ran: The Changing Role of the Presidential Candidate (New York: Free Press, 1991), chap. 1.

2 "Mr. Van Buren's Acceptance," May 23, 1835, Niles' Weekly Register, June 13, 1835, 48:257.

3 Niles' National Register, November 14, 1840, 59:175. Also see diary entry of August 29, 1840, Memoirs of John Quincy Adams, Comprising Portions of His Diary from 1795 to 1848, ed. Charles Francis Adams (Philadelphia, PA: J. B. Lippincott, 1876), 10:352.

4 Andrew Jackson to David Burford, July 28, 1831, The Papers of Andrew Jackson, ed. Daniel Feller et al. (Knoxville: University of Tennessee Press, 2013), 9:442.

5 Andrew Jackson to Littleton H. Coleman, April 26, 1824, The Papers of Andrew Jackson, ed. Harold D. Moser, David R. Hoth, and George H. Hoemann (Knoxville: University of Tennessee Press, 1996), 5:398. Also see Richard McCormick, The Presidential Game: The Origins of American Presidential Politics (New York: Oxford University Press, 1982), 145; and Heale, Presidential Quest, 49.

6 Martin Van Buren to Andrew Jackson, September 14, 1827, The Papers of Andrew Jackson, ed. Harold D. Moser and J. Clint Clifft (Knoxville: University of Tennessee Press, 2002), 6:393.

7 Quoted in McCormick, Presidential Game, 145.

8 See Jackson's letter to George W. Campbell, dated February 14, 1828, in which he wrote, "Was I now to come forth, and reiterate my political opinions on these subjects, I would be charged with electioneering views for selfish purpose." Jackson also recognized that it was his "enemies" and not his friends who were attempting to "inveigh me into a reply" to cause him political embarrassment. Papers of Andrew Jackson, 6:417.

9 The acceptance letter, dated December 19, 1839, is printed in William Ogden Niles, ed., The Tippecanoe Text-Book (Philadelphia, PA: P. G. Collins, 1840), 85–86 (quotation at 86).

10 Charles Hammond to Henry Clay, January 21, 1840, The Life, Correspondence, and Speeches of Henry Clay, ed. Calvin Colton (New York: A. S. Barnes, 1857), 4:443.

11 Sherrod Williams's interrogatories to each of the presidential candidates in 1836 began from the premise that it was "the right of every citizen of the United States to ask and demand, and to be fully informed of the political principles . . . of those who are candidates for the various offices in the gift of the people." Sherrod Williams to General William Henry Harrison, April 7, 1836, Joel Silbey, "Election of 1836," in History of American Presidential Elections, 1789–1968, ed. Arthur M. Schlesinger Jr. (New York: Chelsea House, 1985), 607.

12 William Henry Harrison to James Lyons, June 1, 1840, Niles' National Register, June 20, 1840, 58:247.

13 David Gwynne, J. C. Wright, and O. M. Spencer's reply to the Oswego Association, dated February 29, 1840, and the letter to which the corresponding committee was responding, dated January 31, 1840, from Miles Hotchkiss to

William Henry Harrison, can be found in the "Speech of Hon. A. Duncan of Ohio," April 10, 1840, *Appendix to the Congressional Globe*, 26th Cong., 1st sess., 429. The *Albany Argus* published the letter from the corresponding committee on March 31, 1840. See Troy, *See How They Ran*, 289n11. Also see Freeman Cleaves, *Old Tippecanoe: William Henry Harrison and His Time* (Newtown, CT: American Political Biography Press, 1939), 323; and the extract from Harrison's letter to Joseph Williams, dated May 28, 1840, in the *National Intelligencer* (Washington, DC), June 11, 1840.

14 *Address to the Democratic Republican Electors of the State of New York* (Washington, DC: Globe Office, 1840), 16. The address was issued on May 4, 1840, by New York's Democratic legislators and published in the *Albany Rough-Hewer*.

15 "Speech of Hon. A. Duncan of Ohio," 429.

16 "Horrid Barbarity!—The Man in the Iron Cage," Washington *Globe*, April 13, 1840.

17 "Gen. Mum," *Daily Republican Banner* (Nashville, TN), May 5, 1840. Also see "General Harrison's Thinking Committee," *Richmond Enquirer*, April 10, 1840 (from the *Pennsylvanian*).

18 "Gen. Mum"; and *Selma Daily Reporter*, April 11, 1840. Also see *Richmond Enquirer*, June 26, 1840; and Vernon L. Volpe, "The Anti-Abolitionist Campaign of 1840," *Civil War History* (December 1986): 325–339.

19 The first two quotations are from the *Richmond Enquirer*, June 26, 1840. The final quotation is from the Democratic national convention as quoted in Troy, *See How They Ran*, 28.

20 *North Carolinian* (Fayetteville), May 16, 1840.

21 Henry Clay to John Clayton, May 29, 1840, *The Papers of Henry Clay*, ed. Robert Seager II (Lexington: University Press of Kentucky, 1988), 9:416. Clay would have had in mind, among other things, the searing public repudiation of Harrison and the Whigs by the prominent Lexington newspaper editor and Whig politician Robert N. Wickliffe, who had supported Harrison in 1836. In a public letter to the *Kentucky Gazette*, Wickliffe condemned the committee's "dishonorable" letter to the Oswego Association as well as "the refusal of the Harrisburgh Convention to publish to the world the principles by which the Whigs are known." Wickliffe thundered that "no man should be placed in the Presidency save it be as the representative of some principles." If Harrison and the Whig Party were not willing to trust the people by openly avowing their principles, then the country should not put its trust in them. Wickliffe's indictment of Harrison and the Whigs was widely reprinted in the Democratic press, starting with Medary's *Ohio Statesman*. See *Detroit Free Press*, June 9, 1840. On "Greasy Bob" Wickliffe, see *Papers of Henry Clay*, 9:251.

22 Clay to Clayton, May 29, 1840, 9:416.

23 G. C. Verplanck et al. to William Henry Harrison, February 28, 1840, Anthony Banning Norton, *The Great Revolution of 1840: Reminiscences of the Log Cabin and Hard Cider Campaign* (Mt. Vernon, OH: A. B. Norton & Co., 1888), 39.

24 William Henry Harrison to G. C. Verplanck et al., May 23, 1840, Norton, 40–41.

25 The casuistry charge is made, for example, by Troy, *See How They Ran*, 25. Also see Robert Gray Gunderson, *The Log-Cabin Campaign* (Lexington: University Press of Kentucky, 1957), 169.

26 Extract from Harrison's letter to Joseph Williams, May 28, 1840. Also see *Niles' National Register*, June 20, 1840, 58:246

27 Harrison to Lyons, June 1, 1840. Lyons's letter to Harrison is dated April 14, 1840.

28 *Niles' National Register*, June 20, 1840, 58:246. In his letter to Lyons, Harrison said he did "not wish what I have said above to be published, but I have no objection that the facts should be stated, and reference made to me as having furnished them" (58:247). Certainly, the opening of the letter, which references Harrison's poor health and confesses to committing "to the flames . . . a large portion" of the letters sent to him, suggests that Harrison did not write it with an eye to having it published. Either Lyons disregarded Harrison's express wishes or, more likely, Harrison reconsidered. Harrison made the same confession to Clay that he threw "a full half of the letters I receive in the fire without replying to them." May 7, 1840, *Papers of Henry Clay*, 9:410.

29 *Richmond Enquirer*, May 1, 1840; and *Weekly Standard* (Raleigh, NC), May 27, 1840. Also see *The Democrat* (Huntsville, AL), May 30, 1840; and Boston *Morning Post*, June 3, 1840.

30 Based on a letter Harrison wrote to Daniel Webster at the end of June, Cleaves writes that "Harrison was persuaded to make a personal appearance at the Fort Meigs rally . . . somewhat against his own wishes." Cleaves, *Old Tippecanoe*, 323. But in view of Harrison's peripatetic behavior between June and September, one could be forgiven for wondering whether the reluctance he expressed to Webster was more about maintaining the requisite republican pose than about any real misgivings he felt regarding the wisdom of speaking at Fort Meigs.

31 Daniel Walker Howe, *What God Hath Wrought: The Transformation of America, 1815–1848* (Oxford: Oxford University Press, 2007), 573–574 ("Harrison himself, deferring to nineteenth-century sensibilities, stopped actively campaigning once he received the Whig nomination and relied on supporters to electioneer for him").

32 Gunderson, *Log-Cabin Campaign*, 169; and Troy, *See How They Ran*, 21. Gunderson writes, "On the few occasions when Harrison did discuss serious issues, he made oracular pronouncements even more confusing than his silence." *Log-Cabin Campaign*, 170.

33 Gunderson counts "some twenty-three speeches" delivered by Harrison during his various tours in 1840 (*Log-Cabin Campaign*, 165), a count echoed by Michael F. Holt in *The Rise and Fall of the American Whig Party: Jacksonian Politics and the Onset of the Civil War* (New York: Oxford University Press, 1999), 110, but Robert Friedenberg is closer to the mark when he states that although "Harrison delivered approximately twenty major addresses, he delivered scores of other addresses . . . as he was traveling to the site of a scheduled major

address." Robert V. Friedenberg, *Notable Speeches in Contemporary Presidential Campaigns* (Westport, CT: Praeger, 2002), 28n35.

34 "Harrison among the People, His Speech at Columbus, Ohio," Norton, *Great Revolution of 1840*, 167.

35 Friedenberg, *Notable Speeches*, 19. The accuracy of Friedenberg's description of this speech as "the first overt political campaign speech by a presidential candidate" depends on what counts as "overt" and what counts as a "presidential candidate." Certainly, Clay and Van Buren had given what can only be described as overt political campaign speeches in 1839—as Harrison had in 1838—although they had not yet been formally nominated by their national parties. In the late summer and early fall of 1836, Harrison conducted a speaking tour as the de facto Whig nominee in most of the Northern states, but these speeches were far less overtly political than his 1840 speeches.

36 "Harrison among the People," 166–177 (quotations at 169, 172–173, 176).

37 *Huron Reflector* (Norwalk, OH), June 16, 1840,

38 This quotation is from a public speech that Harrison gave in Cleveland on June 13, 1840. See *Madisonian*, June 25, 1840. The candidate had evidently broadcast this rule before his tour; see the *Cincinnati Republican* article excerpted in the *Fayetteville Observer* (NC), June 10, 1840. Harrison adhered to this rule in each of his speaking tours in 1840, contrary to Jeffrey Bourdon's suggestion that he gave one speech outside the state in Carthage, Indiana. Jeffrey Bourdon, "Symbolism, Economic Depression, and the Specter of Slavery: William Henry Harrison's Speaking Tour for the Presidency," *Ohio History* (August 2011): 6, 19. The speech in question was delivered (at a celebration commemorating the anniversary of the 1794 Battle of the Fallen Timbers) in Carthage, Ohio, which today is part of Cincinnati (see *Raleigh Star and North Carolina Gazette*, September 9, 1840). Bourdon also errs in suggesting that Harrison delivered the speech at Carthage ten days after the Dayton speech of September 10; it was delivered on August 20, three weeks before the Dayton speech. Despite this and several other small errors, Bourdon's article is an instructive guide to Harrison's speeches on tour in 1840 and a useful corrective to Gunderson's and other scholars' more dismissive treatment of Harrison's speeches. "Symbolism, Economic Depression, and the Specter of Slavery," 7–8.

39 Cleaves, *Old Tippecanoe*, 324; and *Huron Reflector*, June 16, 1840. Also see *Madisonian*, June 11, 1840.

40 Harrison's confidence in his support from military veterans in the areas where he served is evident in a letter he wrote to Nathaniel Tallmadge, shortly before leaving to speak at Fort Greenville, in which he estimated that "nineteen-twentieths of [old soldiers] have declared themselves in my favor in Kentucky and throughout the Northwestern States." William Henry Harrison to Nathaniel Tallmadge, July 22, 1840, quoted in Gunderson, *Log-Cabin Campaign*, 48.

41 "Harrison's Fort Meigs Speech," Norton, *Great Revolution of 1840*, 183.

42 "Harrison's Fort Meigs Speech," 178, 181, 183–187.

43 "Gen. Harrison at Cleveland," *Madisonian*, June 25, 1840 (reprinted from the *Cleveland Herald*).

44 "Gen. Harrison at Cleveland." Also see Friedenberg, *Notable Speeches*, 24–25.

45 William Henry Harrison to Daniel Webster, June 27, 1840, quoted in Cleaves, *Old Tippecanoe*, 326. Persistent Democratic attacks on Harrison's supposed frailties had prompted his team to have a prominent Cincinnati doctor issue a letter testifying to the state of the general's mental and physical health. His intellect, the doctor attested in a letter originally published in the *Louisville Journal* on May 30, 1840, was "unimpaired by age" and his physical constitution "as good as that of most men half of his age." Quoted in Friedenberg, *Notable Speeches*, 30n52.

46 *Harrison Democrat*, quoted in Friedenberg, *Notable Speeches*, 28n35. Among the towns at which he spoke en route were Germantown, Franklin, and Middletown.

47 "Gen. Harrison at Old Fort Greenville," *Madisonian*, August 11, 1840 (from correspondence of the *Newark Daily Advertiser*).

48 Contrast this with Harrison's more carefully hedged claim in his speech at Columbus, in which he said, "It is true that a part of my dwelling house is a log cabin." Norton, *Great Revolution of 1840*, 177.

49 "Speech of Gen. Harrison," *Madisonian*, August 25, 1840 (from the *Cincinnati Gazette*).

50 Silas Wright to Martin Van Buren, August 20, 1840, quoted in Heale, *Presidential Quest*, 97. Wright was careful to preface his description of this supposedly "new business of stumping" by saying that it was new "to me." Of course, campaign "stumping" by presidential surrogates was by no means novel in 1840— and its development varied significantly by region—but I have nonetheless used Wright's phrase because it pithily captures the novelty of Harrison's behavior as a presidential candidate. On the greater prominence of stump speaking in the South relative to a place like New York City, which relied more on flooding voters with "little bits of paper," see John L. Brooke, "To Be 'Read by the Whole People': Press, Party, and Public Sphere in the United States, 1789– 1840," *Proceedings of the American Antiquarian Society*, vol. 110, part 1 (2000), 41–118, in which he quotes a Southern novelist from 1834 observing that "New Yorkers never have what we call 'stump speeches'" (111).

51 See Troy, *See How They Ran*, 26.

52 Prior to speaking at Dayton, Harrison first traveled north of that city, speaking at Piqua (on Friday the 4th), Sidney (on Saturday the 5th), and Urbana. In Urbana, estimates put the crowd that heard him speak at twenty thousand people, at least five thousand of whom were women ("the fair daughters" of Ohio). The "whole journey" to Dayton was described as being "like a triumphant procession," which grew larger the closer the procession got to Dayton. One account says that Harrison, accompanied by former Kentucky governor Thomas Metcalfe, rode "on fine steeds throughout," another that the party traveled by carriage (and on occasion spoke from the carriage). For Harrison's movements prior to arriving at Dayton, see *Raleigh Register*, September 29, 1840; and *Detroit Free Press*, September 19, 1840. After Dayton, Harrison traveled to Lebanon, speaking to eight thousand people on Saturday the 12th; to

Wilmington, where he spoke on Monday the 14th; and to Chillicothe on the 18th, followed by speeches at Somerset, Lancaster, and Circleville. Harrison avoided delivering speeches or traveling on a Sunday, which earned him praise from evangelical Whigs; see Mark R. Cheathem, *The Coming of Democracy: Presidential Campaigning in the Age of Jackson* (Baltimore, MD: Johns Hopkins University Press, 2018), 142.

53   "The Number of Persons Present," *National Intelligencer*, September 18, 1840 (from the *Cincinnati Gazette* of September 12, 1840).

54   "Gen. Harrison at Dayton," *Daily Republican Banner*, September 21, 1840. Also see Clay's "Speech on the State of the Country under Van Buren," Taylorsville, Virginia, June 27, 1840, in which he also warned that twelve years under Jackson and Van Buren had produced in the office "an awful squinting toward monarchy." *Papers of Henry Clay*, 9:426.

55   "Gen. Harrison at Dayton."

56   William H. Seward to Thurlow Weed, April 12, 1835, in *Autobiography of William H. Seward from 1801–1834, with a Memoir of His Life, and Selections from His Letters from 1831 to 1846* (New York: Appleton, 1877), 257–258.

57   New York *Evening Post*, September 23, 1840. Similarly, the *Ohio Statesman* complained, "The other day he was General Mum, now he speaks too much. . . . If General Harrison's friends had one particle of common sense, they would take him home and keep him there." Quoted in Ronald G. Shafer, *The Carnival Campaign: How the Rollicking 1840 Campaign of "Tippecanoe and Tyler Too" Changed Presidential Elections Forever* (Chicago: Chicago Review Press, 2016), 147.

58   "Gen. Harrison at Chillicothe," *Huron Reflector*, October 13, 1840.

59   "Speech of Col. Johnson at Chillicothe," *Richmond Enquirer*, August 28, 1840; and Gunderson, *Log-Cabin Campaign*, 244.

60   Allen and Johnson were accompanied by Ohio governor Wilson Shannon throughout their August tour of Ohio. See Gunderson, *Log-Cabin Campaign*, 243–244.

61   *Madisonian*, February 25, 1840; and Reginald Charles McGrane, *William Allen: A Study in Western Democracy* (Columbus, OH: F. J. Heer, 1925), 50–51. Also see "The Harrison Petticoat Story," *Extra Globe* (Washington, DC), October 13, 1840, 6:361.

62   Gunderson, *Log-Cabin Campaign*, 243–244.

63   "Gen. Harrison at Chillicothe."

64   "Gen. Harrison at Chillicothe."

65   James C. Curtis, *The Fox at Bay: Martin Van Buren and the Presidency, 1837–1841* (Lexington: University Press of Kentucky, 1970), 199.

66   "Gen. Harrison at Chillicothe." Harrison felt the need to address the issue in part because Democrats had tried to defend Poinsett's plan by pointing to similar legislation Harrison had introduced as the House chairman of the Committee on Military Affairs. Harrison countered that his bill did "not resemble in a single principle" that which had been introduced by Poinsett. For starters, Harrison claimed, Poinsett's proposal put the burden of furnishing arms on

the poor man, whereas his proposal had called for arms to "be furnished at the cost of the government." Also see Curtis, *Fox at Bay*, 200.

67 For Harrison's movements after the Chillicothe speech, see "General Harrison's Late Tour," *Pittsburgh Gazette*, October 5, 1840 (from the *Cincinnati Republican*, September 26). Harrison returned to Cincinnati on September 24, traveling twenty-four consecutive hours by stagecoach from Columbus.

68 See, for example, Washington *Globe*, June 20, 1840.

69 *National Intelligencer*, October 13, 1840. The speech at Lancaster was delivered on September 21. The text of the speech—or at least that part of it dealing with immigration—can be found in Norton, *The Great Revolution of 1840*, 342–344, but the date is mistakenly given there as October 21, which has led other scholars to make the same mistake. For instance, Bourdon mistakenly suggests that Harrison gave this speech "right before the election." "Symbolism, Economic Depression, and the Specter of Slavery," 13. Shafer also mistakenly claims that "Harrison continued making speeches into late October." *Carnival Campaign*, 147.

70 Friedenberg, *Notable Speeches*, 30n47. In addition, on the previous day, September 30, Harrison spoke for two hours before "an immense crowd"—estimated at around thirty thousand people, including five thousand women—at Ripley, a fifty-mile steamboat journey down the Ohio River. *Commercial Advertiser & Journal*, October 10, 1840 (quoting from the *Cincinnati Republican*); and James A. Green, *William Henry Harrison: His Life and Times* (Richmond, VA: Garrett and Massie, 1941), 367–368.

71 "The Anniversary Celebration," *Raleigh Star and North Carolina Gazette*, September 9, 1840.

72 "Gen. Harrison on Abolition," *Raleigh Star and North Carolina Gazette*, September 23, 1840 (from the *Lynchburg Virginian*). "Gen. Harrison's Speech at Carthage," *Raleigh Register*, September 15, 1840 (from the *Cincinnati Republican*). In the published excerpt, which seems more of a public letter in the guise of a speech, Harrison carefully laid out answers to two written questions that had been put to him about the right of petition. Dorothy Burne Goebel explains that the questions were carefully crafted by Harrison's allies so that Harrison could reassure antislavery men of his commitment to the right to petition without alienating Southerners. *William Henry Harrison: A Political Biography* (Indianapolis: Historical Bureau of the Indiana Library and Historical Department, 1926), 358–359. The letter to which Harrison was responding was dated August 10, 1840, and is printed in full in Goebel, *William Henry Harrison*, 360-361.

73 *Advocate & Register* (Vicksburg, MS), April 26, 1832.

74 *Richmond Enquirer*, September 2, 1836.

75 See, for example, *Madisonian*, September 12, 1837; and *Detroit Free Press*, September 27, 1837. Also see Troy, *See How They Ran*, 26.

76 On the difference between the norm governing the campaign behavior of incumbent presidents and that of challengers, see Richard J. Ellis and Mark Dedrick, "The Rise of the Rhetorical Candidate," in *The Presidency, Then and Now*,

ed. Philip G. Henderson (Lanham, MD: Rowman & Littlefield, 2000), 185–200. In light of this difference, it is not surprising that President Van Buren refused to emulate Harrison's stumping in 1840. Compare with the analysis in Cheathem, *Coming of Democracy*, 143; and Shafer, *Carnival Campaign*, 63.

77 Previous presidents had toured the country, most notably Washington, Monroe, and Jackson, but none had invited charges of electioneering. While Washington and Monroe had toured the country in the year before they were up for reelection—and Monroe on occasion spoke about public policy—both presidential candidates had been essentially unopposed. Jackson's 1833 tour took place the year after his reelection. Jackson, to be sure, did make the journey to his home in Tennessee and then the return to Washington, DC, on four occasions while he was president, and one of those occurred in 1832. But both en route to Tennessee in late July and early August and then heading back to the nation's capital in the latter part of September and first part of October, Jackson avoided making speeches and declined all invitations to attend public meetings or dinners, though he did take the opportunity to shake a lot of hands and greet his fellow citizens. It was campaigning of a sort, but it was nothing like Van Buren's 1839 tour. On the tours of Washington, Monroe, and Jackson, see Richard J. Ellis, *Presidential Travel: The Journey from George Washington to George W. Bush* (Lawrence: University Press of Kansas, 2008), chapters 1 and 2.

78 Van Buren had initially planned on making a tour of the South, leaving Washington, DC, at the beginning of April for New Orleans, visiting Jackson at the Hermitage, and taking in "all the Southwestern, and Western States." Martin Van Buren to Andrew Jackson, February 17, 1839, Image 3 of Martin Van Buren Papers, 1787–1910: Series 7, Miscellany, 1814–1910; Typescripts of letters in Series 2, 1814–1845; 1839–1841, Library of Congress, https://www.loc.gov /item/mss438280158/. However, Van Buren was warned off the tour by the Democrats' Tennessee gubernatorial candidate (and outgoing Speaker of the US House of Representatives) James Polk, who bluntly advised him that his presence "in the midst of our elections" (Tennessee's gubernatorial, state legislative, and congressional elections were to be held on August 1) would invite the "hue and cry of *dictation*" and have "disastrous consequences" for Democratic hopes in the state. James Polk to Andrew Jackson, February 7, 1839, *Correspondence of James K. Polk*, ed. Wayne Cutler (Nashville, TN: Vanderbilt University Press, 1979), 5:53. Also see Martin Van Buren to Andrew Jackson, March 23, 1839, Image 9 of Martin Van Buren Papers, 1787–1910: Series 7, Miscellany, 1814–1910; Typescripts of letters in Series 2, 1814–1845; 1839–1841, Library of Congress, https://www.loc.gov/item/mss438280158.

79 Their paths crossed in August in Saratoga Springs, where they stayed at the same hotel. In his diary, Philip Hone recorded a gathering in "the grand saloon" that included Van Buren and Clay (as well as Scott): "Each had fair ladies receiving his attention, and many good-natured jokes were passed between them. 'I hope I do not obstruct your way,' said the President . . . to Mr. Clay, who was endeavoring to pass. 'Not here, certainly,'" was Clay's quick reply.

The Diary of Philip Hone, 1828–1851, ed. Allan Nevins (New York: Dodd, Mead, 1927), 1:416.

80 On Van Buren's tour (and Whig criticisms of it), see Ellis, *Presidential Travel*, 59–69. Also see Troy, *See How They Ran*, 28–29.

81 *Albany Argus*, July 6, 1839. Also see John W. Edmonds to Van Buren, June 21, 1839, and June 27, 1839, Martin Van Buren Papers, 1787–1910: Series 2, General Correspondence, April 14–September 30, 1839, Library of Congress, https://www.loc.gov/item/mss438280077/.

82 The President in Onondaga," *Albany Argus*, September 23, 1839 (from *Onondaga Standard*).

83 Troy, *See How They Ran*, 28–29. For an example of the many invitations to attend a public celebration or public meeting that Van Buren received during the 1840 campaign, see William Love et al. to Martin Van Buren, September 7, 1840, "Unpublished Letters from North Carolinians to Van Buren," *North Carolina Historical Review* (April 1938): 137–138. Van Buren declined the invitation in a letter dated September 28, 1840. Also see Van Buren's letter dated June 17, 1840, declining an invitation to attend a celebration at Milledgeville, Georgia; another letter at the end of June to Samuel S. Wandell et al., declining an invitation to attend a Fourth of July celebration in New York; and a third letter dated July 4, 1840, to the Lexington Committee, declining an invitation to a public meeting at White Sulphur Springs, Kentucky. Martin Van Buren Papers, 1787-1910: Series 2, General Correspondence, May 5–July 31, 1840, Library of Congress, https://www.loc.gov/item/mss438280081/.

84 Troy, *See How They Ran*, 27.

85 "Van Buren's letter to the Shocco Springs, N.C. Committee," October 4, 1832, in Samuel Rhea Gammon, Jr., *The Presidential Campaign of 1832* (1922; repr., Westport, CT: Greenwood Press, 1971), 163. Also see Heale, *Presidential Quest*, 92.

86 Heale, *Presidential Quest*, 93.

87 Martin Van Buren to Sherrod Williams, August 8, 1836, quoted in Heale, *Presidential Quest*, 93; "Mr. Van Buren's Acceptance." On the crucial role of Jackson, the bank war, and the 1832 election in the development of the idea of elections as conferring policy mandates, see Richard J. Ellis and Stephen Kirk, "Presidential Mandates in the Nineteenth Century: Conceptual Change and Institutional Development," *Studies in American Political Development* (Spring 1995): 117–186.

88 William Marcy to Prosper Wetmore, August 11, 1840, quoted in John Niven, *Martin Van Buren: The Romantic Age of American Politics* (New York: Oxford University Press, 1983), 470. Also see Troy, *See How They Ran*, 27.

89 "Mr. Van Buren's Reply" [to John B. Cary et al.], July 31, 1840, *Niles' National Register*, August 21, 1840, 58:393. The letter writers were from Elizabeth City County.

90 See, for example, Van Buren's reply of March 27, 1840, to the letter dated March 21, 1840, from Walter F. Leak, both of which can be found in "Unpublished

Letters from North Carolinians to Van Buren," 131–132. Van Buren's reply was reprinted in the *North Carolina Standard*, April 29, 1840.

91 "Mr. Van Buren's Reply" [to John B. Carey et al.].

92 "Mr. Van Buren's Letter of a General Bankruptcy Law," September 14, 1840 (from the *Albany Argus*), *Niles' National Register*, October 24, 1840, 59:122–124.

93 "Letter of Van Buren on Wages," *Niles' National Register*, September 14, 1840, 59:59. On Van Buren's executive order, see Richard J. Ellis, *The Development of the American Presidency*, 3rd ed. (New York: Routledge, 2018), 266–268.

94 "Letter from Mr. Van Buren to Eugene Burras, of Jamestown, Martin County, North Carolina," April 4, 1840, *Niles' National Register*, August 29, 1840, 58:408–409. On June 12, several months after Van Buren wrote his letter (and two months before it was published in *Niles' National Register*), Virginia's Whig congressman John Minor Botts—who was on the party's executive committee directing the Harrison campaign—helped to elevate the matter to greater national prominence by championing Hooe's cause in Congress. Botts faulted the president for allowing "negroes and private servants of the prosecutors as witnesses to testify against the characters of gentlemen of the navy," a practice that "ought not to be tolerated by southern men, or 'northern men with southern principles.'" *Journal of the House of Representatives*, 26th Cong., 1st sess. (Washington, DC: Blair and Rives, 1840), 1107. Also see "Amos Kendall's Letter VIII, to the Hon. J.M. Botts," *Extra Globe*, August 19, 1840, 6:157–159.

95 Martin Van Buren to John M. McCalla et al., July 4, 1840, *Niles' National Register*, August 8, 1840, 58:364–365.

96 Heale, *Presidential Quest*, chapter 1.

97 The party was not formally designated the Liberty Party until 1841. During the 1840 campaign, "it appeared under several names—occasionally the 'Liberty Ticket,' but most often the Abolitionist, or Independent Abolitionist, party." Richard H. Sewell, *Ballots for Freedom: Antislavery Politics in the United States, 1837–1860* (New York: W. W. Norton, 1976), 72.

98 This biographical profile is drawn from the opening chapters of Betty Fladeland, *James Gillespie Birney: Slaveholder to Abolitionist* (Ithaca, NY: Cornell University Press, 1955).

99 James G. Birney, *Letter on Colonization, Addressed to the Rev. Thornton J. Mills, Corresponding Secretary of the Kentucky Colonization Society* (New York: Office of the Anti-Slavery Reporter, 1834), 7–10, 43. The letter is dated July 15, 1834.

100 The "electrified" quotation is from a letter to Theodore Weld from Elizur Wight, secretary of the American Antislavery Society. Fladeland, *James Gillespie Birney*, 88. The second quotation is from a one-paragraph introduction to the Boston edition of James G. Birney, *Letter on Colonization, Addressed to the Rev. Thornton J. Mills, Corresponding Secretary of the Kentucky Colonization Society* (Boston: Garrison and Knapp, 1834), 3.

101 Fladeland, *James Gillespie Birney*, 140, 144–145.

102 The convention was called at the instigation of Myron Holley, editor of the *Rochester Freeman* and a leading advocate of a third party. The resolutions (including the call for "a distinct and independent political party") adopted at the

convention can be found in the *Rochester Freeman*, November 27, 1839; in the same issue, the paper endorsed Birney for president. On Holley, see Sewell, *Ballots for Freedom*, 54–58.

103 Fladeland, *James Gillespie Birney*, 182; and Sewell, *Ballots for Freedom*, 61–62, 57.

104 Sewell, 69, 57. The other five states represented were Maine, Vermont, Massachusetts, Connecticut, and New Jersey. In contrast, the special national abolitionist convention in Albany the previous summer (July 31–August 2, 1839) was attended by five hundred abolitionists from twelve states. This more representative convention overwhelmingly approved a resolution declaring it the duty of abolitionists to vote only for candidates who favored immediate abolition but refused to support a new, independent party dedicated to abolition or to make independent nominations for the presidency. The convention did work out a compromise that left local abolitionist groups free to make independent nominations, and there were scattered efforts in the fall of 1839—including in a number of counties in western New York—to make independent nominations for state and local office. Sewell, 51–53, 58.

105 Sewell, 71. Corey M. Brooks, *Liberty Power: Antislavery Third Parties and the Transformation of American Politics* (Chicago: University of Chicago Press, 2016), 38. A Philadelphia Quaker, Earle provided a certain partisan balance to the ticket since he was a former Democrat who had run afoul of his party for advocating African American voting rights at the state's 1837–1838 constitutional convention.

106 Gamaliel Bailey to James Birney, April 18, 1840, *Letters of James Gillespie Birney*, ed. Dwight L. Dumond (New York: D. Appleton, 1938), 1:556–558. Bailey warned Birney that his nomination would "not be sustained by abolitionists generally." To accept this "premature" nomination, Bailey advised, would be "political suicide" for Birney and injurious to the abolitionist movement because it would appear weak and divided—and thus easier for politicians to ignore in the future. By accepting the nomination, Birney would be made "merely an altar on which a few men will offer up their votes" while damaging his reputation. Much better, Birney advised, to wait until after "the storm of the present party warfare [has] blown over," when a new party, with Birney at its head, might launch "their bark in safety." "What is the use," Bailey asked his former partner, "of blowing against a whirlwind?" (1:556). Birney had hired Bailey as an assistant at the *Philanthropist* in 1836. Fladeland, *James Gillespie Birney*, 144. Also see John G. Whittier to James Birney, *Letters of James Gillespie Birney*, April 16, 1839, 1:555.

107 James Birney to Myron Holley, Joshua Leavitt, and Elizur Wright, Jr., May 11, 1840, *Letters of James Gillespie Birney*, 1:562–574; quotations at 567–568.

108 Birney to Holley, Leavitt, and Wright, 1:570–571; emphasis in original.

109 Birney to Holley, Leavitt, and Wright, 1:566–567.

110 Birney to Holley, Leavitt, and Wright, 1:572–573.

111 Birney to Holley, Leavitt, and Wright, 1:569–571, 573.

112 Harrison's letter accepting the Whig nomination in December was about four hundred words. Not until well after the Civil War would a major party presi-

dential nominee—Democrat Samuel Tilden in 1876—write an acceptance letter that matched Birney's in length. See Richard J. Ellis, "Accepting the Nomination: From Martin Van Buren to Franklin Delano Roosevelt," in *Speaking to the People: The Rhetorical Presidency in Historical Perspective*, ed. Richard J. Ellis (Amherst: University of Massachusetts Press, 1998), 114–115.

113 Fladeland, *James Gillespie Birney*, 194. Birney returned to New York on November 24, 1840 (206).

CHAPTER 9. "THE PRESIDENTIAL CONTEST ABSORBS EVERY THING ELSE"

1   Ronald G. Shafer, *The Carnival Campaign: How the Rollicking 1840 Campaign of "Tippecanoe and Tyler Too" Changed Presidential Elections Forever* (Chicago: Chicago Review Press, 2016), 115–122; and Robert Gray Gunderson, *The Log-Cabin Campaign* (Lexington: University Press of Kentucky, 1957), 128. Also see Roger Fischer, *Tippecanoe and Trinkets, Too: The Material Culture of American Presidential Campaigns, 1828–1894* (Urbana: University of Illinois Press, 1988), chapter 2.

2   "The selling of the president" is the title of Joe McGinniss's classic account of the political admen who helped Richard Nixon win the presidency in 1968. *The Selling of the President 1968* (New York: Simon & Schuster, 1969).

3   Gil Troy, *See How They Ran: The Changing Role of the Presidential Candidate* (New York: Free Press, 1991), 30. It is not true, however, as Troy claims, that in 1840, "voters were preoccupied with local candidates and offices [and] newspapers concentrated on local efforts and neglected the presidential candidates." Local candidates and issues were undoubtedly important, but newspapers were filled with coverage of the presidential race, and votes on state races were often seen as proxies for the presidential race. Although presidents were not yet the center of their campaigns, the presidential contest was certainly at the center of American party politics.

4   *Pittsburgh Gazette*, August 29, 1836.

5   "Speech of Mr. Ogle of Pennsylvania on the Regal Splendor of the President's Palace," April 14, 1840, printed in full in *White House History* (Winter 2002): 36, 47, 51; and William Seale, "About the Gold Spoon Oration," *White House History* (Winter 2002): 11. Glyndon Van Deusen suggests that the idea of focusing on Van Buren's White House expenditures may have come from Thurlow Weed. *Thurlow Weed: Wizard of the Lobby* (Boston: Little, Brown, 1947), 111–112.

6   "Speech of Mr. Ogle of Pennsylvania on the Regal Splendor of the President's Palace," 48, 60, 69.

7   "Speech of Mr. Ogle of Pennsylvania on the Regal Splendor of the President's Palace," 61, 64.

8   "Speech of Mr. Ogle of Pennsylvania on the Regal Splendor of the President's Palace," 72–73. "Sweet Sandy Whiskers" was Weed's favorite nickname for Van Buren and was used in Ogle's speech (44).

9   "Speech of Mr. Ogle of Pennsylvania on the Regal Splendor of the President's Palace," 66–67.

10 Washington *Globe*, April 17, 1840.

11 Shafer, *Carnival Campaign*, 60; and Gunderson, *Log-Cabin Campaign*, 106.

12 Seale, "About the Gold Spoon Oration," 11

13 The *Sangamo Journal*, for instance, devoted its entire front page and several columns of its back page (it was only two pages) on August 21, 1840, to printing Ogle's speech. Also see, for instance, *National Intelligencer*, June 30, 1840; *Log Cabin*, July 13, 1840; *Star & Republican Banner* (Gettysburg, PA), August 25, 1840; and *Rushville Whig* (Indiana), August 29, 1840, as well as Van Deusen, *Thurlow Weed*, 112–113.

14 Gunderson, *Log-Cabin Campaign*, 107.

15 William Noland, statement of June 12, 1840, quoted in Seale, "About the Gold Spoon Oration," 11; and William Noland to Walter Coles, June 25, 1840, quoted in William Allman, "Those Princely Objects in Charles Ogle's Speech," *White House History* (Winter 2002): 29

16 "Letter from the Register of the Treasury," July 28, 1840, and "Letter from the Solicitor of the Treasury," July 29, 1840, *Extra Globe* (Washington, DC), August 19, 1840, 6:147.

17 *Log Cabin*, October 3, 1840 (from the *Louisville Journal*).

18 *Harrison Melodies: Original and Selected* (Boston: Weeks, Jordon, 1840), 71.

19 *United States' Telegraph* (Washington, DC), September 7, 1836, quoted in Freeman Cleaves, *Old Tippecanoe: William Henry Harrison and His Time* (Newtown, CT: American Political Biography Press, 1939), 385n21. Also see David Crockett, *The Life of Martin Van Buren* (Philadelphia, PA: Robert Wright, 1835).

20 Van Deusen, *Thurlow Weed*, 111; Donald P. Cole, *Vindicating Andrew Jackson: The 1828 Election and the Rise of the Two-Party System* (Lawrence: University Press of Kansas, 2009), 149–150; and Troy, *See How They Ran*, 290n32.

21 Gunderson, *Log-Cabin Campaign*, 101

22 Henry Clay to William Browne, July 31, 1840, in *The Papers of Henry Clay*, ed. Robert Seager II (Lexington: University Press of Kentucky, 1988), 9:437–438.

23 Diary entry of August 29, 1840, *Memoirs of John Quincy Adams, Comprising Portions of His Diary from 1795 to 1848*, ed. Charles Francis Adams (Philadelphia, PA: J. B. Lippincott, 1876), 10:351–352. Also see diary entry of September 24, 1840, 10:352–353.

24 Gunderson, *Log-Cabin Campaign*, 189, 191, 194.

25 Gunderson, 144; and diary entries of May 6, 1840, and September 24, 1840, *Memoirs of John Quincy Adams*, 10:282, 10:353. For a Democratic account of the killing, see "Diaries of S.H. Laughlin, of Tennessee, 1840, 1843," *Tennessee Historical Magazine* (March 1916): 55.

26 *Pittsburgh (PA) Gazette*, June 2, 1840; *National Gazette* (Philadelphia, PA), May 30, 1840; and *Native American* (Washington, DC), April 18, 1840. Also see Gunderson, *Log-Cabin Campaign*, 144, who misidentifies the man as Henry Lasak.

27 "Whig Outrage," *Indiana Democrat* (Indianapolis), September 18, 1840; Gunderson, *Log-Cabin Campaign*, 145–146; and *Extra Globe*, June 24, 1840, 6:37. The story in the *Indiana Democrat* also enumerated three other partisan-

motivated assaults on Democratic newspaper editors. On the ubiquitous threat of violence against newspaper editors, see Francis J. Grund's account written at the close of 1840, quoted in Armin Mattes's introduction to Grund's *Aristocracy in America: From the Sketch-Book of a German Nobleman*, ed. Armin Mattes (Columbia: University of Missouri Press, 2018), 10.

28 Diary entry of September 24, 1840, *Memoirs of John Quincy Adams*, 10:352–353.

29 John Van Fossan to Thurlow Weed, July 20, 1840, quoted in Gunderson, *Log-Cabin Campaign*, 146.

30 Quoted in Mark R. Cheathem, *The Coming of Democracy: Presidential Campaigning in the Age of Jackson* (Baltimore, MD: Johns Hopkins University Press, 2018), 141.

31 Quoted in Joe L. Kinchelow, Jr., "Similarities in Crowd Control Techniques of the Camp Meeting and Political Rally: The Pioneer Role of Tennessee," *Tennessee Historical Quarterly* (Summer 1978): 164.

32 Lincoln's speech, which was delivered in December 1839 and circulated in pamphlet form during the campaign, is quoted in William Lee Miller, *Lincoln's Virtues: An Ethical Biography* (New York: Knopf, 2002), 144; Miller calls this passage of Lincoln's speech "not a little disproportionate, not to say goofy."

33 On the importance of "negative partisanship" in contemporary American politics, see Alan I. Abramowitz, *The Great Alignment: Race, Party Transformation, and the Rise of Donald Trump* (New Haven, CT: Yale University Press, 2018), esp. 5–8, 142–173.

34 Thomas Ritchie to Martin Van Buren, June 1, 1840, quoted in Cheathem, *Coming of Democracy*, 150.

35 See Gunderson, *Log-Cabin Campaign*, esp. chap 18; and Cheathem, *Coming of Democracy*, 147.

36 *Extra Globe*, June 16, 1840, 6:30.

37 *Extra Globe*, August 5, 1840, 6:118.

38 Cheathem, *Coming of Democracy*, 152; and Gunderson, *Log-Cabin Campaign*, 232. According to linguistic historian Allen Walker Read, the word "OK" was coined in the spring of 1839 as a shortening of "oll korrect," a waggish misspelling of "all correct." In 1840, New York's Democrats seized on this new expression as a way both to humorously signal that Van Buren was "all correct" and to give the president a popular nickname (Old Kinderhook) that was comparable to Jackson's famous nickname, Old Hickory. The anti-Jackson editor James Gordon Bennett strove to frustrate the Democrats' efforts by circulating an alternative (and false) account of O.K.'s origins that traced the expression to Jackson's poor spelling. See Allan L. Metcalf, *OK: The Improbable Story of America's Greatest Word* (New York: Oxford University Press, 2011).

39 Richard McCormick, *The Presidential Game: The Origins of American Presidential Politics* (New York: Oxford University Press, 1982), 199. Also see Gunderson, *Log-Cabin Campaign*, 142.

40 Cheathem, *Coming of Democracy*, 141; and Ronald P. Formisano, *The Birth of Mass Political Parties: Michigan, 1827–1861* (Princeton, NJ: Princeton University Press, 1971), 133, 135. Also see Richard Carwardine, "Evangelicals, Whigs, and

the Election of William Henry Harrison," *Journal of American Studies* (April 1983): 47–75.

41 A. P. Powers to Howell Cobb, October 1840, quoted in Arthur Charles Cole, *The Whig Party in the South* (Washington, DC: American Historical Association, 1914), 60–61.

42 *Hartford Courant*, August 18, 1840; and Shafer, *Carnival Campaign*, 150.

43 "Women and Politics," *Indiana Democrat*, September 18, 1840; and *Spirit of the Age* (Woodstock, VT), October 2, 1840. Also see Vice President Richard M. Johnson, quoted in Gunderson, *Log-Cabin Campaign*, 245 ("I am sorry to say that I have seen ladies too joining in with them [singing Tippecanoe blaggard songs] and wearing ribands across their breasts with two names printed on them"). On women's participation in the 1840 campaign in Virginia, Massachusetts, and Tennessee, see Elizabeth R. Varon, "Tippecanoe and the Ladies, Too: White Women and Party Politics in Antebellum Virginia," *Journal of American History* (September 1995): 494–521; Ronald J. Zboray and Mary Saracino Zboray, "Whig Women, Politics and Culture in the Campaign of 1840: Three Perspectives from Massachusetts," *Journal of the Early Republic* (Summer 1997): 277–315; and Jayne Crumpler DeFiore, "*COME, and Bring the Ladies*: Tennessee Women and the Politics of Opportunity during the Presidential Campaigns of 1840 and 1844," *Tennessee Historical Society* (Winter 1992): 197–212. Also see Elizabeth R. Varon, *We Mean to Be Counted: White Women and Politics in Antebellum Virginia* (Chapel Hill: University of North Carolina Press, 1998), esp. chap. 3.

44 Thomas Hart Benton, *Thirty Years' View* (New York: D. Appleton, 1856), 2:205.

45 At least one popular Harrison song from the 1840 election, "The Harrison Cause," actually debuted in the 1836 election as an "impromptu song" at a dinner given to Harrison in September 1836. Sung to the tune of "Bonnets of Blue," the song's final verse closed with

> Here's success to the man of the Plough
> Here's a Health to the man who sticks to his friend
> And lives by the sweat of his brow
> Huzza for the just and the true
> And the hero of Tippecanoe
> It's good to support the Harrison cause
> And the star spangled "Red, White & Blue."

The song was reprinted in the *Albany Evening Journal*, October 26, 1836. It was included in various 1840 Whig campaign songbooks, although without attribution to the 1836 campaign; see, for instance, *Harrison Melodies*, 33. Other examples of political song in campaigns prior to 1840 can be found in Cheathem, *Coming of Democracy*, 15–17, 55–57, 79–81, 107–109. Also see Kirsten E. Wood, "'Join with Heart and Soul and Voice': Music, Harmony, and Politics in the Early American Republic," *American Historical Review* (October 2014): 1083–1116.

46 Gunderson, *Log-Cabin* Campaign, 123–125; and Shafer, *Carnival Campaign*, 106.

47 *Richmond Whig*, October 9, 1840, quoted in Varon, "Tippecanoe and the Ladies, Too," 502.

48 *National Intelligencer*, September 21, 1840 (from the *Cincinnati Gazette*). Also see *Madisonian*, September 22, 1840.

49 John Crittenden to Daniel Webster, October 27, 1840, quoted in Gunderson, *Log-Cabin Campaign*, 118.

50 Sarah (Pendleton) Dandridge to Martha Taliaferro Hunter, April 18, 1840, quoted in Varon, "Tippecanoe and the Ladies, Too," 500.

51 Mary Pendleton (Cooke) Steger to Sarah Harriet Apphis Hunter, September 13, 1840, quoted in Varon, "Tippecanoe and the Ladies, Too," 500–501.

52 Quoted in Formisano, *Birth of Mass Political Parties*, 135.

53 James Buchanan to Martin Van Buren, September 5, 1840, quoted in Gunderson, *Log-Cabin Campaign*, 212.

54 *Niles' National Register*, July 25, 1840, 58:322.

55 Diary entry of September 24, 1840, *Memoirs of John Quincy Adams*, 10:352.

56 *Niles' National Register*, July 25, 1840, 58:322.

57 Henry Clay to Alexander Hamilton, Jr., June 30, 1840, *The Papers of Henry Clay: Supplement, 1793–1852*, ed. Melba Porter Hay (Lexington: University Press of Kentucky, 1992), 281.

58 A contemporary state-by-state estimate, "prepared with great care," calculated the popular vote totals by the two parties between 1836 and 1839 and found that while in 1837 and 1838 the Whigs had gained popular vote majorities of about 100,000, in 1839, as in 1836, a majority of votes had been cast for Democrats. *Niles' National Register*, August 22, 1840, 59:393. This estimate, which seems to have been drawn up by a Whig, was also published, among other places, in the *New York Herald*, April 15, 1840.

59 Michael F. Holt, *The Rise and Fall of the American Whig Party: Jacksonian Politics and the Onset of the Civil War* (New York: Oxford University Press, 1999), 75 (Table 6). According to Holt's calculations, the six state assemblies that flipped to the Democrats in 1839 were Rhode Island, Indiana, Georgia, Maryland, Massachusetts, and Mississippi.

60 Calculated from Michael J. Dubin, *United States Gubernatorial Elections, 1776–1860: The Official Results by State and County* (Jefferson, NC: McFarland, 2003); all gubernatorial vote totals in this chapter are drawn from this source. The Democrats flipped control of governorships in Tennessee, Georgia, and Massachusetts, while the Whigs flipped Michigan. The Whigs retained the governor's house in Connecticut, Rhode Island, and Vermont, while the Democrats won again in New Hampshire, Maine, Alabama, and Mississippi.

61 A week after the New Hampshire elections, Van Buren wrote confidently to New England Democrat George Bancroft that "the accounts we receive from every part of the Union are truly flattering, and leave us without apprehension." March 18, 1840, in "Van Buren–Bancroft Correspondence, 1830–1845," ed. Worthington C. Ford, *Proceedings of the Massachusetts Historical Society* 42 (June 1909): 385.

62 All turnout percentages in gubernatorial contests used in this chapter can be found in Walter Dean Burnham, *Voting in American Elections: The Shaping of the American Political Universe since 1788* (Palo Alto, CA: Academica Press, 2010), 251–391 (Table 7). Turnout percentages in House contests can be found in Table 8, specifically 402–403.

63 While Connecticut's turnout rate of 73 percent was only a marginal increase over the nearly 69 percent that had turned out the previous year, it was nonetheless a record for a state that had historically (prior to about 1835) generally had low turnout. Burnham, *Voting in American Elections*, 266–267.

64 *Niles' National Register*, May 2, 1840, 58:135.

65 *New York Herald*, April 15, 1840. In county supervisor elections across the state, the Whigs showed some improvement, gaining a dozen seats. But Democrats still retained majorities in 26 counties, just as they had after the 1839 elections, while Whigs won majorities in 24 counties, down one from 1839. The remainder of the state's 57 counties were evenly balanced between the parties. *Niles' National Register*, May 2, 1840, 58:135.

66 William G. Shade, *Democratizing the Old Dominion: Virginia and the Second Party System, 1824–1861* (Charlottesville: University Press of Virginia, 1996), 169 (Table 5.2). Holt's percentages are slightly different than Shade's but tell essentially the same story of very little change in the distribution of seats between 1838 and 1840. *Rise and Fall of the American Whig Party*, 75.

67 "The Virginia Elections," *Richmond Enquirer*, April 28, 1840; also see May 5, 1840, and May 12, 1840. There was one special congressional election held in Virginia in January 1840, the only special congressional election held in the first half of the year. In that election, Whigs retained control of the congressional district, but both sides polled many fewer votes than they had in the regular election the preceding May. The Whig who won the special election received about 300 fewer votes than the Whig who won the regular election, and the Democrat received about 200 fewer votes. The percentage received by both parties in the runoff election remained essentially the same as the percentage won in the regular election. Michael J. Dubin, *United States Congressional Elections, 1788–1997: The Official Results of the Elections of the 1st through 105th Congresses* (Jefferson, NC, McFarland, 1998), 124; all congressional vote totals in this chapter are calculated from this source.

68 "The Virginia Elections."

69 *National Gazette*, May 6, 1840.

70 Alexander Porter to William T. Palfrey, June 18, 1840, quoted in John M. Sacher, *A Perfect War of Politics: Parties, Politicians, and Democracy in Louisiana* (Baton Rouge: Louisiana State University Press, 2003), 99. Sacher discounts Porter's perceptions as "skewed" by his disappointment at the party's failure to nominate Clay. However, the July congressional elections, which resulted in the party losing one seat and nearly losing a second, show that the concerns Porter expressed in June were fully justified. By June, moreover, Porter and other Clay supporters had long since gotten over their disappointment at Harrison's nomination.

71 Dubin, *United States Congressional Elections*, 121, 126. Louisiana also held its state legislative elections at the same time, and while the Whigs gained ground, winning 46 percent of the lower house seats, up from 35 percent in 1838, they still fell short of a majority. Holt, *Rise and Fall of the American Whig Party*, 75.

72 "Tell Chapman to Crow," *Alton Telegraph*, August 29, 1840; and Charles Manfred Thompson, *The Illinois Whigs before 1846* (1915; repr., Urbana: University of Illinois, 1967), 76–77; on the partisan composition of the Illinois state assembly and state senate in 1838, see 60n44. On the state assembly and state senate data for 1840, see "Illinois Legislature," *Sangamo Journal*, August 21, 1840, as well as the appendix in Thompson, *The Illinois Whigs*, 132–150.

73 Vermont voted on September 4, Maine on September 14.

74 In the runoff elections held after Harrison's election, the Democrats ended up winning both seats.

75 About 1,000 fewer votes were cast for Democratic House candidates in 1840 than in 1838, whereas Whig House candidates totaled a little over 3,000 more votes in 1840 than in 1838.

76 The song had also appeared a few days earlier in some newspapers; see, for instance, the *New York Herald*, September 22, 1840; and *Auburn Journal and Advertiser*, September 23, 1840. Only after the song appeared in the *Log Cabin* did Van Buren became widely heralded in the Whig press as the "used up man."

77 The Whigs flipped three seats in Pennsylvania, the Democrats one. No seats were flipped in two other states that held congressional elections: Arkansas and Georgia. In Georgia, which selected all nine House members in one at-large district, Whigs stretched their average margin of victory from 2 to about 5 percentage points. In Arkansas, the Democratic incumbent retained his seat, although his margin of victory was reduced from 23 percentage points to 15, while turnout increased from 72 to 78 percent. South Carolina, which had a politics all its own, also held congressional elections in October, but the Whigs contested only two of the state's nine seats, winning one of them, a seat in the northeast corner of the state that they had also won in 1836 and 1838. South Carolina was the only state that did not select presidential electors by popular vote, and there was never any doubt that the state legislature would go for Van Buren over Harrison.

CHAPTER 10. TIPPECANOE AND THE ECONOMY TOO

1 The states holding their presidential election in the first week of November were Connecticut, Rhode Island, Maine, New Hampshire, Maryland, Virginia, Missouri, Illinois, Arkansas, Georgia, Indiana, and Kentucky, all on November 2; Michigan on November 2 and 3; New York on November 2, 3, and 4; Louisiana and Tennessee on November 3; and New Jersey and Mississippi on November 3 and 4. In New York City itself, the election was held on a single day, November 4. The five states holding elections in the second week of November were Massachusetts and Alabama on November 9, Vermont and Delaware on November 10, and North Carolina on November 12. South Carolina's legisla-

ture would not meet to make its choice until November 23. The dates of each state's presidential election are given, among other places, in the *Pittsburgh Gazette*, November 2, 1840; and *Adams Sentinel*, November 3, 1840. Robert Gray Gunderson mistakenly lists Rhode Island as voting on November 18. *The Log-Cabin Campaign* (Lexington: University Press of Kentucky, 1957), 253. Rhode Island was in fact among the first states to be called for Harrison.

2   Michigan also selected state legislators at the same time, while New York, Massachusetts, and Delaware selected both their governor and state legislators. One congressional district in Louisiana and another in Connecticut held special elections in November to fill House seats that had been vacated due to resignation. Mississippi selected its state legislators in November.

3   *Sangamo Journal* (Springfield, IL), November 6, 1840.

4   *National Gazette* (Philadelphia, PA), November 2, 1840; and *Adams Sentinel* (Gettysburg, PA), November 2, 1840. On the evening of Monday, November 2, Philadelphia Democrat George Plitt dashed off a note to Van Buren declaring Pennsylvania "certainly safe" and enclosing county returns that showed the president ahead by about 1,000 votes. He told Van Buren to pay no heed to the "false returns" that had been produced the night before by Thaddeus Stevens, as they had been fabricated by Stevens to influence the voting in New York. George Plitt to Martin Van Buren, November 2, 1840, Papers of Martin Van Buren (digital edition), ed. Mark R. Cheathem et al., http://vanburenpapers.org /document-mvb09558.

5   *Public Ledger* (Philadelphia, PA), November 4, 1840. On Tuesday, November 3, the day before voting was to commence in New York City, Philip Hone recorded in his diary, "The greatest excitement prevails. Men's minds are wrought up to a pitch of frenzy, and like tinder a spark of opposition sets them on fire. The vote for Presidential electors in Pennsylvania is so close that out of 280,000 votes it is probable that neither will have 500 majority. Both parties here claim the victory, and every hour the wheel turns and each is uppermost; betting is going on at enormous extent." *The Diary of Philip Hone, 1828–1851*, ed. Allan Nevins (New York: Dodd, Mead, 1927), 1:506.

6   *Republican Farmer* (Wilkes-Barre, PA), November 4, 1840. Also see the *Perry County (PA) Democrat*, November 5, 1840. Even some Whig papers, such as the *Carlisle Herald and Expositor*, which published at 3 p.m. on Wednesday the 4th, adjudged that based on the returns to that point, "the chances are slightly favorable to the success of the Van Buren Electors" ("Pennsylvania Election"). Major Democratic papers continued to report that Pennsylvania was "safe for Van Buren" for at least a week after the election. See, for instance, the New York *Evening Post*, November 7, 1840; Washington *Globe*, November 6, 1840; and *Boston Morning Post*, November 9, 1840. Also see the November 6 letter written to Van Buren from Philadelphia by William J. Leiper, which included an enclosed page from the extra edition (November 6, 9 p.m.) of the *Pennsylvanian* showing Van Buren with a 530-vote advantage with returns official in all but ten counties. The *Pennsylvanian* acknowledged that early reports "in many cases" had proved "inaccurate," which had resulted in the president's lead hav-

ing been reduced since the last count. The editors also conceded "that it may go still lower" but thought the "chances still appear in favor of Van Buren, but by a very small majority." Leiper's letter is in the Martin Van Buren Papers, 1787–1910: Series 2, General Correspondence, October 9–December 31, 1840, Library of Congress, https://www.loc.gov/item/mss438280083/.

7   *National Gazette*, November 5, 1840; also see November 6, 1840.

8   "The Result of the Election in the State of Pennsylvania," *Public Ledger* (Philadelphia, PA), November 5, 1840.

9   See, for instance, *National Gazette*, November 4, 1840.

10   New York *Herald*, November 6, 1840.

11   New York *Herald*, November 7, 1840.

12   New York *Evening Post*, November 7, 1840.

13   New York *Evening Post*, November 6, 1840; and Washington *Globe*, November 6, 1840. Also see *Sangamo Journal*, November 6, 1840, which reported that it had been furnished with the state's "complete returns" by the *Newark Advertiser*, showing that Harrison had won the state, carrying thirteen of the eighteen counties.

14   The tipping-point state is calculated by arraying all states in order of their two-party presidential vote margins so that one pole is the largest margin of victory for one party and the other pole is the largest margin of victory for the other party. The tipping-point state is the state that puts the winning candidate "over the top" in the electoral college vote.

15   See, for instance, the extra edition of the *Pennsylvanian*, published at 9 p.m. on November 6, which indicated that Maine, Virginia, New York, and Pennsylvania were still too close to call; and Leiper to Van Buren, November 6, 1840.

16   On Sunday, November 8, for instance, Miner K. Kellogg wrote to Polk from the nation's capital to report that New York, Pennsylvania, and Maine "have gone against the administration." *Correspondence of James K. Polk*, ed. Wayne Cutler (Nashville: Vanderbilt University Press, 1979), 5:579. On the same day, Democrat David Lynch, who had written to Polk from Pittsburgh on the 5th to report that Pennsylvania "was safe for Van Buren," now wrote again to tell Polk that it appeared that Van Buren had lost Pennsylvania. *Correspondence of James K. Polk*, 5:579. Also see the letter dated November 8, 1840, to Van Buren from Anthony J. Bleecker, who wrote from New York City to express his grief and "heartfelt regret at the disastrous state of affairs the recent elections have produced." Van Buren Papers, Library of Congress.

17   Washington *Globe*, November 9, 1840.

18   New York *Evening Post*, November 9, 1840.

19   Washington *Globe*, December 28, 1840.

20   The nineteen states included three that had held their most recent gubernatorial election in 1838 (Pennsylvania, New York, and Maryland) and five that had held their most recent gubernatorial election in 1839 (Massachusetts, Michigan, Mississippi, Georgia, and Tennessee). The other eleven had held their most recent gubernatorial election in 1840 (Connecticut, Indiana, Kentucky, Louisiana, Maine, Missouri, New Hampshire, North Carolina, Ohio,

Rhode Island, and Vermont). Arkansas (October 1840) and Alabama (August 1839) also held gubernatorial contests, but the Democrat ran essentially unopposed.

21 Among the nineteen states, the average difference between Van Buren's two-party vote share in 1840 and the Democratic share of the vote in the most recent gubernatorial election was almost half of the difference between Van Buren's two-party vote share in 1840 and 1836 (3.5 percentage points in the former versus 6.5 points in the latter). In six states (Massachusetts, Indiana, Maryland, Mississippi, Tennessee, and Georgia), Van Buren's 1840 vote share was substantially closer to his 1836 vote share than to the Democratic gubernatorial candidate's vote share.

22 The eight states—only two of which were slave states—where the difference between Van Buren's two-party vote share in 1840 and the Democratic share of the vote in the most recent gubernatorial election was less than 1.5 percentage points were New York (0.1), Maine (0.4), Michigan (0.5), Missouri (0.6), North Carolina (0.9), Pennsylvania (1.2), Connecticut (1.4), and Ohio (1.4). Six states, five of which were slave states, had a difference of more than 5 percentage points: Kentucky (5.9), Louisiana (6.9), Tennessee (7.0), Georgia (7.2), Mississippi (7.7), and Massachusetts (8.0).

23 On the party ticket system, see Richard Franklin Bensel, *The American Ballot Box in the Mid-Nineteenth Century* (Cambridge: Cambridge University Press, 2004), esp. 14–17; and Jill Lepore, "Rock, Paper, Scissors: How We Used to Vote," *New Yorker*, October 6, 2008.

24 The connection between the gubernatorial and presidential vote was not new to 1840. In 1836, Van Buren's share of the vote had been within 0.5 percentage point of that of the Democratic gubernatorial candidate in New York, 1 point in Delaware, and 1.3 points in Massachusetts. The only difference was that in 1836, Van Buren had done slightly better than the gubernatorial candidate in both New York and Massachusetts. In 1832, Andrew Jackson's vote share had also been less than 1 percentage point different from that of the Democratic gubernatorial nominee in both Massachusetts and New York—Jackson had done slightly better than the Democratic gubernatorial standard-bearer in New York and slightly worse in Massachusetts (Delaware did not hold a gubernatorial contest in 1832).

25 The exceptions were Schoharie County and adjacent Fulton County, where Van Buren's share of the vote lagged about 3 percentage points behind Bouck's share of the vote. A resident of Schoharie County, Bouck had represented that county in the state assembly and state senate for almost a decade. These were also two of only three counties (the other was Sullivan County) in which Van Buren received a higher share of the vote than he had in 1836, suggesting that in 1840, Van Buren benefited in these two counties from Bouck's coattails.

26 Two states, Illinois and Mississippi, would not select their House members until August and November 1841, respectively.

27 To retain their majority in the House of Representatives, Democrats would have needed to pick up eleven seats in the 1841 congressional elections. In-

stead, they lost an additional 12 seats, leaving the Whigs with nearly 60 percent of the seats (142 out of 241) in the Twenty-Seventh Congress. The Whigs also secured the same percentage of the seats in the US Senate.

28   Martin Van Buren to James Buchanan, November 24, 1840, quoted in James C. Curtis, *The Fox at Bay: Martin Van Buren and the Presidency, 1837–1841* (Lexington: University Press of Kentucky, 1970), 205.

29   Martin Van Buren to Andrew Jackson, October [November] 10, 1840, *Correspondence of Andrew Jackson*, ed. John Spencer Bassett (Washington, DC: Carnegie Institution, 1926), 6:82. Also see Martin Van Buren to George Bancroft, November 20, 1840, in "Van Buren–Bancroft Correspondence, 1830–1845," ed. Worthington C. Ford *Proceedings of the Massachusetts Historical Society* 42 (June 1909): 388, in which Van Buren attributed his defeat to the Whigs' "fraudulent practices" and accused the opposition of "defrauding the nation of its free choice." In a seventy-five-page memorandum titled "Thoughts on the Upcoming Election Contest in New York," written in March 1840, Van Buren had also attributed Whig victories in recent elections largely to "frauds at the election" in the form of both "illegal votes" and "legal votes by illegal means." See Major L. Wilson, *The Presidency of Martin Van Buren* (Lawrence: University Press of Kansas, 1984), 205; John L. Brooke, *Columbia Rising: Civil Life on the Upper Hudson from the Revolution to the Age of Jackson* (Chapel Hill: University of North Carolina Press, 2010), 449; and Gerald L. Leonard, *The Invention of Party Politics: Federalism, Popular Sovereignty, and Constitutional Development in Jacksonian Illinois* (Chapel Hill: University of North Carolina Press, 2002), 177.

30   Gunderson, *Log-Cabin Campaign*, 249–251; Curtis, *Fox at Bay*, 204–205; and Ernest G. Muntz, "The First Whig Governor of New York, William Henry Seward, 1838–1842" (PhD diss., University of Rochester, NY, 1960), 193–194.

31   Van Buren to Jackson, October [November] 10, 1840, 6:82. In his letter to Jackson, Van Buren comforted himself that "we carried all the Counties with only one exception on both sides of the River to Albany. . . . So complete was our success in the old parts of the state that I can go from the City to my House 150 miles away without touching a Whig County." But Van Buren's analysis was myopic and showed how little voter fraud had to do with his loss in New York State. Although it's true that Van Buren carried seven of the eight counties (the exception was Ulster) along the Hudson River between New York City and Albany, his share of the vote in those counties dropped an average of about 11 points between 1836 and 1840, which was almost twice the 6.5-point drop he experienced statewide. In 1836, for instance, Van Buren had handily carried Westchester, Dutchess, Orange, and Greene Counties, winning over 60 percent of the vote, whereas in 1840, he barely won each of these counties with a vote share between 50 and 52.5 percent. Far from being a success to crow about, Van Buren's performance in these counties along the Hudson River was symptomatic of his statewide decline.

32   Francis P. Blair to Andrew Jackson, November 7, 1840, *Correspondence of Andrew Jackson*, 6:81; Andrew Jackson to Martin Van Buren, November 12, 1840, November 24, 1840, in *Correspondence of Andrew Jackson*, 6:82–83. Also see

Azariah Flagg to Martin Van Buren, November 15, 1840, lamenting that "the pipe layers have cheated us out of almost every thing except our honor and our democratic principles." Another correspondent wrote to Van Buren on the same day, declaring that the defeat of the president "and the people . . . has only been effected by frauds and corruptions of every kind." P. Kaufmann to Martin Van Buren, November 15, 1840. Both the Flagg and Kaufmann letters are in the Van Buren Papers, Library of Congress.

33 Democrats were not alone in blaming fraud for their electoral defeats. Upon learning that the Whigs had lost Virginia, Clay immediately "presumed it was the result of fraud and other causes." Henry Clay to Francis T. Brooke, December 8, 1840, in *The Papers of Henry Clay*, ed. Robert Seager II (Lexington: University Press of Kentucky, 1988), 9:457. He also blamed Harrison's defeat in Illinois on election fraud, specifically the votes of "unnaturalized foreigners," a favorite target of Whig complaints. Speech in Senate, January 6, 1841, *The Papers of Henry Clay: Supplement, 1793–1852*, ed. Melba Porter Hay (Lexington: University Press of Kentucky, 1992), 282. As we saw in chapters 3 and 5, Clay was also quick to credit election fraud and the corrupt use of money for the Whig defeats in the fall of 1838 (Henry Clay to Francis T. Brooke, November 3, 1838, *Papers of Henry Clay*, 9:245) and the fall of 1839 (Henry Clay to Nathaniel Tallmadge, October 12, 1839, *Papers of Henry Clay*, 9:351) as well as the Whig losses in the New York City elections of the spring of 1839 (Henry Clay to Matthew L. Davis, April 20, 1839, *Papers of Henry Clay*, 9:307–308). Indeed, Whigs were usually more likely than Democrats to lead the charge against voter fraud, in large part because they worried that new immigrants tended to vote Democratic. In New Jersey in 1839, for instance, the Whig-dominated state legislature pushed through comprehensive changes to the election laws designed to eliminate voter fraud and make it more difficult for naturalized citizens to vote. See Richard P. McCormick, *The History of Voting New Jersey: A Study in the Development of Election Machinery, 1664–1911* (New Brunswick, NJ: Rutgers University Press, 1953), 122–129.

34 William Gear to Martin Van Buren, November 9, 1840, Van Buren Papers, Library of Congress. Gear echoed the identical charge about money being "the root of all evil" and "the life and soul of modern British Whiggery" that had been made shortly before the election in the Washington *Globe*, October 26, 1840 ("The Government for Sale").

35 John Niven, *Martin Van Buren: The Romantic Age of American Politics* (New York: Oxford University Press, 1983), 470.

36 Gunderson, *Log-Cabin Campaign*, 159.

37 Jackson to Van Buren, November 24, 1840, 6:83.

38 Wheeling (VA) *Times*, quoted in Gunderson, *Log-Cabin Campaign*, 257.

39 Thomas L. Hamer to Martin Van Buren, November 18, 1840, Van Buren Papers, Library of Congress.

40 Hopkins L. Turney to James Polk, November 12, 1840, *Correspondence of James K. Polk*, 5:581. A little more than a month before the election, Jackson told Blair that he "never for one moment doubted" that Van Buren would be reelected

because he could not believe that the American people would fall for the Whigs' show of "hard cider, coons, Log cabins and bag balls." Should "any part of the people submit to . . . this marked insult to their morals and understanding . . . such part, are fit for slaves, and must become hewers of wood and drawers of water to the combined money power of England and [A]merica." Andrew Jackson to Francis P. Blair, September 26, 1840, *Correspondence of Andrew Jackson,* 6:78.

41 Robert B. Reynolds to James Polk, November 6, 1840, *Correspondence of James K. Polk,* 5:575.

42 Diary entry of December 2, 1840, *The Diary of Philip Hone, 1828–1851* ed. Allan Nevins (New York: Dodd, Mead, 1927), 1:512.

43 *The Autobiography of Martin Van Buren,* ed. John C. Fitzpatrick, Annual Report of the American Historical Association for the Year 1918, vol. 2 (Washington, DC: Government Printing Office, 1920), 394. Also see Wilson, *Presidency of Martin Van Buren,* 205. In his *Inquiry into the Origin and Course of Political Parties in the United States* (New York: Hurd and Houghton, 1867), Van Buren explained the 1840 election more diplomatically as a "mistake in the public mind" (349).

44 "The Government for Sale," Washington *Globe,* October 26, 1840

45 "The Government for Sale."

46 James Polk to David Burford, November 7, 1840; James Polk to A. O. P. Nicholson, November 7, 1840; Polk to George W. Jones, November 7, 1840; and Polk to Robert B. Reynolds, November 18, 1840, *Correspondence of James K. Polk,* 5:576–578, 594. In his letter to Reynolds, Polk put the point about party organization most baldly: "Our opponent had organization and we had none." Similarly, Archibald Wright explained the party's defeat by suggesting, "We were over-sanguine, had little or no organization and no one believed" at the outset that Harrison could win. Archibald Wright to James Polk, November 13, 1840, *Correspondence of James K. Polk,* 5:582. In his March 1840 memorandum, "Thoughts on the Upcoming Election Contest in New York," Van Buren had also attributed Democratic defeats in the preceding elections in New York to the Whigs' "superior activity and better organization . . . all year round, both young and old, in season and out of season." Quoted in Brooke, *Columbia Rising,* 448.

47 The Government for Sale," Washington *Globe,* October 26, 1840; and David Burford to James Polk, November 14, 1840, *Correspondence of James K. Polk,* 5:584. Also see Polk to Reynolds, November 18, 1840, 5:594–595.

48 Millard Fillmore to Thurlow Weed, June 1, 1840, in Frank. H. Severance, ed., *Millard Fillmore Papers,* ed. Frank. H. Severance (Buffalo, NY: Buffalo Historical Society, 1907), 2:209.

49 Donald B. Cole, *Amos Kendall and the Rise of American Democracy* (Baton Rouge: Louisiana State University Press, 2004), 227–228; Fillmore to Weed, June 1, 1840, 2:209; and Gunderson, *Log-Cabin Campaign,* 84–87. The *Log Cabin* began publication on May 2, 1840, by which time there had already been nearly a dozen issues of the *Rough-Hewer,* the first of which was published on February

20, 1840. The first issue of the *Extra Globe* was published on May 16, 1840. The circulation of the *Log Cabin* was far greater than that of the *Rough-Hewer*. The latter never exceeded 24,000 subscribers, whereas the *Log Cabin*'s first run was 34,000; the circulation reached 56,000 by early July and ultimately reached about 80,000. Muntz, "The First Whig Governor of New York," 188–189. The *Extra Globe*'s reach appears to have been more comparable to that of the *Log Cabin*, with a circulation of about 50,000. Ronald G. Shafer, *The Carnival Campaign: How the Rollicking 1840 Campaign of "Tippecanoe and Tyler Too" Changed Presidential Elections Forever* (Chicago: Chicago Review Press, 2016), 105.

50 John C. Calhoun to Virgil Maxcy, February 19, 1841, quoted in Niven, *Martin Van Buren*, 471.

51 Calhoun's hope of becoming the Democratic nominee was not his alone. The "expectation that Calhoun may be made the most available of our party for the next race" was expressed, for instance, by A. O. P. Nicholson in a November 6, 1840, letter to Polk. *Correspondence of James K. Polk*, 5:574.

52 Jabez Hammond, quoted in Donald B. Cole, *Martin Van Buren and the American Political System* (Princeton, NJ: Princeton University Press, 1984), 374. Following Hammond, Cole argues that "Van Buren's personality played a part in his downfall" because his "bland personality gave [people] nothing to make them forget the depression." Cole also suggests that Van Buren somehow "lost his two genuinely exciting qualities—his 'adroitness and skill' during his years in the White House" (374). How and where he lost them is not at all clear. Even less satisfying is the suggestion that Van Buren lost the election because he "lost his 'vitality' while President" (374n62).

53 One of the first letters Van Buren received after the election posed the question "Who will be our next Candidate for the Presidency?" The letter writer's unhesitating answer: "Our duty as well as our policy points to you" since "your defeat was not owing to a want of personal popularity on your part nor from a want of confidence in your principles or ability, for at this moment you enjoy more of the esteem and attachment of the Democratic Party than ever before." William L. Helfenstein to Martin Van Buren, November 7, 1840, Van Buren Papers, Library of Congress. The letter writer was from Ohio, which Van Buren lost by 10 percentage points in 1840 and 4 points in 1836.

54 Lynch to Polk, November 8, 1840, 5:580.

55 In the context of the modern presidency, where individual-level voter behavior can be accurately measured, political scientists have consistently found infinitesimal effects of the vice-presidential selection on voter choice, particularly outside the vice president's home state. See, for instance, Bernard Grofman and Reuben Kline, "Evaluating the Impact of Vice Presidential Selection on Voter Choice," *Presidential Studies Quarterly* (June 2010): 303–309. On the surprisingly "paltry" home-state effect, see Nate Silver, "The Overrated Vice Presidential Home-State Effect," *FiveThirtyEight*, April 23, 2012, https://fivethirty eight.com/features/the-overrated-vice-presidential-home-state-effect/.

56 "The Abolition Ticket," *Richmond Enquirer*, November 13, 1840.

57 Anonymous letter to Martin Van Buren, December 9, 1840, Van Buren Papers, Library of Congress.

58 Cole, *Martin Van Buren and the American Political System*, 373. Sean Wilentz offers an even stronger claim that the *Amistad* affair alone may have cost Van Buren these six states. According to Wilentz,: "Both John Niven and Donald Cole argue that the *Amistad* affair may have contributed greatly to Van Buren's loss of six Northern states he had carried in 1836." *The Rise of American Democracy: Jefferson to Lincoln* (New York: W. W. Norton, 2005), 902n55. But Cole's claim is about "proslavery policies" generally, not the *Amistad* affair specifically, and Niven lists the *Amistad* affair as one of five factors—the others being Cherokee removal, the Seminole War, Poinsett's militia system, and votes for the Liberty Party—that "may have made the difference" *in New York*; Niven makes no mention of these factors having been potentially decisive in the other Northern states. Niven, *Martin Van Buren*, 471.

59 David Waldstreicher is right that "the Harrison campaign gave as good as it got on the race issue . . . , calling Van Buren a closet abolitionist and a lover of blacks." "The Nationalization and Racialization of American Politics: Before, Beneath, and Between Parties, 1790–1840," in *Contesting Democracy: Substance and Structure in American Political History, 1775–2000*, ed. Byron E. Shafer and Anthony J. Badger (Lawrence: University Press of Kansas, 2001), 55. Also see Anthony Gene Carey, *Parties, Slavery, and the Union in Antebellum Georgia* (Athens: University of Georgia Press, 1997), 51; and William J. Cooper, Jr., *Liberty and Slavery: Southern Politics to 1860* (New York: Alfred A. Knopf, 1983), 194–195.

60 The *Amistad* affair began with the illegal capture, enslavement, and transportation of a large number of Africans from West Africa to Cuba. Fifty-three of these Africans were bought by two Spaniards who at the end of June 1839 hired the *Amistad*—also owned by a Spanish national—to transport their newly acquired property from Havana to their Caribbean sugar plantation. The captives seized control of the ship, killing the ship's captain and one other crew member. The *Amistad* was intercepted by an American ship off Long Island, and the slaves were taken into the custody of the US federal government while the two slaveowners aboard were released. The Van Buren administration tried to extradite the Africans to Cuba, but abolitionists took the case to court. In January 1840, a district court ruled that the government must return the illegally enslaved Africans to their homeland (modern-day Sierra Leone), a verdict that the Van Buren administration appealed. In April 1840, the court of appeals upheld the district court's judgment, and the government once again appealed, this time to the US Supreme Court. The Court did not hear oral arguments in the case until February 1841, several months after the election. In March 1841, the Court ruled that the Africans should be freed, although it rejected the lower court's argument that the federal government must return them to Africa.

61 The two-party vote percentages in Table 10.2 are calculated from the Whig and Democratic vote totals reported in *Presidential Elections, 1789–2008* (Washing-

ton, DC: CQ Press, 2010), 128–129. Those vote totals can also be found in Appendix A of this book.

62   Richard H. Sewell, *Ballots for Freedom: Antislavery Politics in the United States, 1837–1860* (New York: W. W. Norton, 1976), 64. Bailey urged Birney to decline the third-party nomination in the spring and waited until the summer before he "grudgingly placed Birney's name above the *Philanthropist's* masthead." Jonathan Earle, *Jacksonian Antislavery and the Politics of Free Soil, 1824–1854* (Chapel Hill: University of North Carolina Press, 2004), 150. Also see Corey M. Brooks, *Liberty Power: Antislavery Third Parties and the Transformation of American Politics* (Chicago: University of Chicago Press, 2016),, 39. For a useful profile of Bailey's political abolitionism, see Earle, *Jacksonian Antislavery and the Politics of Free Soil*, 151–154. Birney talked up Harrison in two letters to Birney, dated February 21, 1840, and March 30, 1840, *Letters of James Gillespie Birney*, ed. Dwight L. Dumond (New York: D. Appleton, 1938), 1:531–532; 545–548. Also see Theodore Clark Smith, *The Liberty and Free Soil Parties in the Northwest* (1897; repr., New York: Russell & Russell, 1967), 38.

63   Brooks, *Liberty Power*, 26.

64   Sewell, *Ballots for Freedom*, 78.

65   Corey Michael Brooks, "Building an Antislavery House: Political Abolitionists and the U.S. Congress" (PhD diss., University of California, Berkeley, 2010), 44, https://escholarship.org/uc/item/1b385471.

66   Henry B. Stanton to James G. Birney, March 21, 1840, *Letters of James Gillespie Birney*, 1:542. Whether that loathing would have been sufficient to induce them to vote for Clay had he been the Whig nominee in 1840 is a fascinating counterfactual question—Clay at least thought the answer was yes.

67   It is obviously an imperfect measure because only a fraction of abolitionists voted for the Liberty Party in 1840; Sewell estimates that nine out of ten abolitionists in 1840 voted for either Harrison or Van Buren rather than the Liberty Party. *Ballots for Freedom*, 78–79. On the other hand, the Liberty Party tended to be stronger where "the spirit of abolition" was stronger—and this was especially true within New York, which I analyze in more depth below. Especially in exploring county-level variation, I have also used the Liberty Party vote in 1844—which as a percentage of the total vote was eight times higher than in 1840—as an alternative measure of the distribution of abolitionist sentiment in 1840.

68   For the Liberty Party's vote, I have followed Michael J. Dubin, *United States Presidential Elections, 1788–1860* (Jefferson, NC: McFarland, 2002), which includes votes by county, rather than CQ Press's *Presidential Elections, 1789–2008*. The latter misses Liberty Party votes in some states entirely (most notably Michigan but also Maine, Connecticut, and Pennsylvania) and massively overstates the Liberty Party vote in New Hampshire, where it counts more than seven times the number of votes listed in Dubin. As Sewell points out (*Ballots for Freedom*, 79n81), W. Dean Burnham's *Presidential Ballots, 1836–1892* (Baltimore, MD: Johns Hopkins University Press, 1955) entirely leaves out the Liberty Party vote

for New Hampshire as well as for Michigan, New Jersey, and Pennsylvania (246, 248). The Liberty Party vote count in Dubin is generally close to the count given in Reinhard O. Johnson, *The Liberty Party, 1840–1848: Antislavery Third-Party Politics in the United States* (Baton Rouge: Louisiana State University Press, 2009), 20 (Table 1), although the latter mistakenly calculates that the 194 Liberty Party votes in Maine constituted 0.6 percent of the total vote when they in fact represented 0.2 percent of the state's total vote for president. Dubin appears to have misplaced a decimal point in calculating Connecticut's Liberty Party vote at 1 percent of the vote when the 57 votes he identifies are only 0.1 percent of the total votes cast; Dubin's percent calculations by county for Connecticut are also in error.

69 In Massachusetts, Van Buren did lose more support in counties where political abolitionism was stronger (correlation coefficient = −0.36). In the six counties where the Liberty Party polled 1 percent or less of the vote, Van Buren averaged a little over a 1 percent gain in the two-party vote—and in the only county in Massachusetts where the Liberty Party received a negligible number of votes, Van Buren did almost 8 percentage points better than in 1836. In contrast, in the other eight counties where the Liberty Party polled more than 1 percent, Van Buren lost about 5 percentage points in his two-party vote share between 1836 and 1840.

70 Antislavery sentiment would grow in strength in Maine after the 1840 election (the Liberty Party would receive almost 6 percent of the vote in the 1844 presidential election), but at the time of the 1840 election it played little role in the state's politics. According to Lee D. Webb, the 1841 election was "the first time, the slavery issue entered into state politics." "Party Development and Political Conflict in Maine, 1820–1860: From Statehood to the Civil War" (PhD diss., University of Maine, May 2017), 182, https://digitalcommons.library.umaine .edu/etd/2653. It is also worth pointing out that Maine, like Michigan, voted for the Democrat presidential nominee in 1844, 1848, and 1852, when the Democratic Party nominated more strongly proslavery candidates.

71 The Liberty Party polled 19 votes in Rhode Island in 1840 and 0 votes in 1844. Indeed, "there was no organized Liberty Party in Rhode Island before 1846." Johnson, *The Liberty Party*, 135. Abolitionist sentiment was more important in Connecticut than in Rhode Island but was not nearly strong enough to be credited with being a difference maker in a contest that Van Buren lost by 11 points. In Connecticut in 1844, the Liberty Party received 3 percent of the vote (as opposed to 0.1 percent in 1840), but the state still lagged far behind Massachusetts, Vermont, New Hampshire, Michigan, and Maine in Liberty Party support. Moreover, Van Buren lost the least support in his two-party vote share between 1836 and 1840 in the two Connecticut counties (Windham and Litchfield) that in 1844 would give the Liberty Party the *most* support, and he slipped the most between 1836 and 1840 in the county (Fairfield) where the Liberty Party fared worst in 1844, which undercuts the idea that antislavery sentiment drove the erosion of Van Buren's support in Connecticut. On the weakness of

abolitionism in Connecticut throughout the 1830s, see Johnson, *The Liberty Party*, 130.

72   The correlation coefficient is 0.33. If one uses Liberty Party support in 1844 as a measure of abolitionist strength in a county, the correlation decreases but is still positive ($r = 0.19$). In making these calculations, I have had to leave out four counties for which data is missing for either 1839 (St. Clair, Livingston, or Genesee) or 1840 (Chippewa). The gubernatorial vote totals by county are taken from Michael J. Dubin, *United States Gubernatorial Elections, 1776–1860: The Official Results by State and County* (Jefferson, NC: McFarland, 2003), 121. The county-level presidential vote totals here and elsewhere in this section are from Dubin, *United States Presidential Elections*.

73   The average increase in Van Buren's vote in 1840 relative to 1839 in the five counties (Calhoun, Jackson, Kalamazoo, Washtenaw, and Ingham) in which the Liberty Party polled better than 1 percent in 1840 is 0.7 (with a low of 0.1 and a high of 1.1). The Liberty Party also polled above 1 percent in Genesee County, which is not included in this calculation because Genesee County vote totals in the 1839 gubernatorial election are missing from Dubin, *United States Gubernatorial Elections*, 121. However, in the 1836 presidential contest, Van Buren won 42.1 percent of the vote in Genesee County, and in 1840, he polled 42.6 percent, a marginal uptick in support that is consistent with the pattern reported here. Calhoun and Ingham were counties in which the two parties were evenly balanced, but the other four (Genesee, Jackson, Kalamazoo, and Washtenaw) were Whig-leaning counties. On Washtenaw County, see John W. Quist, *Restless Visionaries: The Social Roots of Antebellum Reform in Alabama and Michigan* (Baton Rouge: Louisiana State University Press, 1998).

74   Ronald P. Formisano, *The Birth of Mass Political Parties: Michigan, 1827–1861* (Princeton, NJ: Princeton University Press, 1971), 28; also see 120–122; and Johnson, *The Liberty Party*, 165.

75   Churchill C. Cambreleng to Martin Van Buren, December 15, 1840, Van Buren Papers, Library of Congress. Niven misquotes Cambreleng as saying, "Abolitionism was contained and lost us only one vote." *Martin Van Buren*, 472. Special thanks to Mark Cheathem for helping me to decipher this sentence.

76   In the 33 counties in which the Liberty Party polled less than 0.5 percent of the vote, Van Buren's share of the two-party vote declined by 6.9 points; in the 14 counties in which the Liberty Party polled between 0.5 and 1 percent of the vote, Van Buren dropped an average of 8.1 points, and in the 9 counties in which the Liberty Party polled more than 1 percent of the vote, Van Buren dropped 9.5 points.

77   If one instead uses Liberty Party support in 1844—when the party polled 3.3 percent of the statewide vote, compared to the 0.6 it polled in New York in 1840—as a measure of strength of abolitionism, the correlation with Van Buren's change in vote is marginally higher ($r = -0.16$). These correlations are based on the vote totals in Dubin, *United States Presidential Elections*. Between the elections of 1836 and 1840, Montgomery County was split into three coun-

ties (Fulton and Hamilton were the two new counties), and to facilitate comparison, I have added the 1840 vote totals in Fulton and Hamilton to Montgomery. I have also corrected for a couple of computational errors in New York, notably for Allegany County in 1836 and Putnam County in 1840.

78 Using Liberty Party support in 1844 as the measure of abolitionism's strength by county enhances the variable's explanatory power (R^2 = 6.5 percent) and its statistical significance (p = 0.003).

79 The only county in which Van Buren's two-party vote share slipped more than 5 percentage points relative to Marcy's vote share was Clinton County in the northeastern corner of New York. Van Buren's two-party vote share in 1840 was within 3 percentage points of Marcy's in 86 percent of New York's counties.

80 There is no correlation (r = −0.01) between the strength of abolitionism by county (as measured by the Liberty Party vote in 1840) and the change between Van Buren's 1840 vote share and Marcy's 1838 vote share. If we instead measure strength of abolitionism by the Liberty Party vote in 1844, however, there is a small correlation (r = −0.12) that is consistent with the argument that abolitionism may have cost Van Buren support.

81 Had Clay won New York, he would have won the presidential election in 1844, but while the conventional wisdom has long been that the Liberty Party cost Clay the state of New York, historians have questioned that conclusion. See, for instance, Vernon L. Volpe, "The Liberty Party and Polk's Election, 1844," *Historian* (Summer 1991): 691–710. If each of the 15,800 New York voters who cast their ballot for Birney in 1844 had cast a ballot for one of the two major party candidates instead, then Clay would have needed to gain roughly two out of every three of those votes to win the state, an eminently reasonable assumption. But if the Liberty Party voters had simply stayed home, Clay still would have lost—and the evidence from the state elections held between 1841 and 1843 suggests that these voters had largely been lost to the Whig Party well before Clay's nomination. If even one-third of Liberty Party voters had stayed home, then Clay would have needed to receive the support of about three-quarters of the Liberty Party voters. And had two-thirds stayed home, Clay would have needed nearly 100 percent of the remaining Liberty Party voters. While the Liberty Party generally drew heavily from Whig ranks, it also drew support from antislavery Democrats. Alan Kraut shows, for instance, that the town of Smithfield, New York (in Madison County), which had been a "Democratic stronghold" in the 1830s, became the Liberty Party's "banner town" in the 1840s. In the 1840 election, a majority of the town voted for Van Buren (10 percent voted for Birney), but in the 1844 presidential election, nearly half of the town's electorate voted for the Liberty Party and only 30 percent voted for Polk. Between the 1840 and 1844 presidential elections, the Democratic vote count dropped by 74 votes, whereas the Whig count declined by only 49 votes. Alan M. Kraut, "The Forgotten Reformers: A Profile of Third Party Abolitionists in Antebellum New York," in *Antislavery Reconsidered: New Perspectives on the Abolitionists,* ed. Lewis Perry and Michael Fellman (Baton Rouge: Louisiana State University Press, 1979), 126–127. Also see Johnson, *The Liberty Party,* 46–47.

82 A. O. P. Nicholson to James Polk, November 15, 1840, *Correspondence of James K. Polk*, 5:587–588. Nicholson was named to the US Senate at the end of December after the sudden death of Senator Felix Grundy on December 19, 1840.

83 Speech in Senate, December 15, 1840, *Papers of Henry Clay*, 9:464. Also see Clay's letter to David Campbell, in which he calls on the new administration to "fulfill all the promises and redeem all the pledges which our party made, when it was out of power." December 11, 1840, *Papers of Henry Clay*, 9:461.

84 Richard J. Ellis and Stephen Kirk, "Presidential Mandates in the Nineteenth Century: Conceptual Change and Institutional Development," *Studies in American Political Development* (Spring 1995): 152–153. Also see James W. Ceaser, *Presidential Selection: Theory and Development* (Princeton, NJ: Princeton University Press, 1979), 74.

85 Although Jackson won reelection handily, he received a slightly lower share of the popular vote (54 percent) in 1832 than he did in 1828 (55 percent). Essentially, all that decline was due to Jackson's significant loss of support in Pennsylvania, where the national bank, which was headquartered in Philadelphia, was a particularly salient concern. Whereas Jackson secured 67 percent of the popular vote in Pennsylvania in 1828, he won less than 57 percent in 1832 (Jackson received about 11,000 fewer votes in Pennsylvania in 1832 than in 1828, whereas the opposition won about 16,000 more votes in 1832). Jackson's vote share in the rest of the country—that is, not counting Pennsylvania—was 53.6 percent in both elections. These calculations are taken from vote totals in Dubin, *United States Presidential Elections, 1788–1860*.

86 See Robert A. Dahl, "Myth of the Presidential Mandate," *Political Science Quarterly* (Fall 1990): 355–372; Raymond E. Wolfinger, "Dealigment, Realignment and Presidential Mandates," in *The American Elections of 1984*, ed. Austin Ranney (Washington, DC: American Enterprise Institute, 1985), 277–296, esp. 293; V. O. Key, "Public Opinion and the Decay of Democracy," *Virginia Quarterly Review* (Autumn 1961): 487; George C. Edwards III, *At the Margins* (New Haven, CT: Yale University Press, 1989), 144–166; and Stanley Kelley, Jr., *Interpreting Elections* (Princeton, NJ: Princeton University Press, 1983).

87 See Gabriel Lenz, *Follow the Leader? How Voters Respond to Politicians' Policies and Performance* (Chicago: University of Chicago Press, 2012); and Christopher H. Achen and Larry M. Bartels, *Democracy for Realists: Why Elections Do Not Produce Responsive Government* (Princeton, NJ: Princeton University Press, 2016).

88 Cambreleng to Van Buren, December 15, 1840.

89 Peter Temin, *The Jacksonian Economy* (New York: W. W. Norton, 1969), 152–154; and Michael F. Holt, *Rise and Fall of the American Whig Party: Jacksonian Politics and the Onset of the Civil War* (New York: Oxford University Press, 1999), 71.

90 Cambreleng to Van Buren, December 15, 1840.

91 My dating of the first economic downturn in Table 10.4 follows Holt, who marks the initial economic panic as extending from June 1837 to August 1838. Holt dates the economic recovery as extending from September 1838 to October 1839 and the second economic crisis as beginning in November 1839. Holt,

Rise and Fall of the American Whig Party, 74. At least initially, as Peter Temin points out, the second economic crisis, which began at the end of 1839, was not "as severe as the earlier panic" of 1837. For instance, while Biddle's Bank of the US of Philadelphia suspended payments in October 1839, and other banks in the South and West followed suit, "banks in New York and New England did not suspend." Temin, *The Jacksonian Economy*, 154. This may explain why the electoral effects of the second economic crisis appear to have been more lagged than in the Panic of 1837, particularly in New England (where Democrats, recall, did well in New Hampshire's and Connecticut's elections in March and April 1840) and in New York City, where Democrats fared well in the elections of April 1840. But while the crisis of 1839 was a less violent shock to the nation's economy and psyche than the Panic of 1837, "no recovery followed the panic in 1839. Prices did not recover, and the signs of prosperity disappeared." Temin, 154. The gradually darkening economic mood of the country was reflected in the election results of the summer and fall of 1840.

92 The two-party vote percentages by state in 1836 and 1840 in Table 10.4 are calculated from the data reported in *Presidential Elections, 1789–2008*, 128–129. The numbers reported in Dubin's *United States Presidential Elections* yield slightly different state-level estimates for 1836 (only in Michigan is the discrepancy large) but do not change the point being made in the table; indeed, in the case of Michigan, it would only strengthen the argument since Dubin has Van Buren's vote share in Michigan in 1836 at 64 percent. Fewer Southern (6) than Northern (9) states held gubernatorial elections during this period because no Southern states held annual gubernatorial elections, which were common in New England. In addition, three Southern states—Arkansas, Delaware, and Kentucky—held their gubernatorial elections every four years in the same year as the presidential election, something no Northern state did (Illinois was the only Northern state to hold its gubernatorial election every four years but did not hold it in the same year as the presidential election). Virginia and South Carolina, like New Jersey, left the selection of the governor to the legislature.

93 Not included in Table 10.5 is Alabama, which held a gubernatorial election in August 1839, but the Democratic incumbent ran essentially unopposed. The returns reported by Dubin are fragmentary and give the Democrat over 92 percent of the vote.

94 Not coincidentally, Vermont and Georgia were atypical states in the second party system in that their state politics tended to be weakly integrated into national party politics. As noted in chapter 5 (note 82), Georgia's anti–Van Buren party (the State Rights Party) remained disassociated from the national Whig Party until the middle of 1840. Vermont's politics, too, as Richard McCormick observes, "could not be adjusted to a national norm." Vermont was a three-party state throughout Jackson's presidency, with the Anti-Mason Party the dominant party until the merger of Anti-Masons and Whigs. Vermont's only two-party gubernatorial contests between 1829 and 1855 occurred between 1836 and 1840. See Richard P. McCormick, *The Second American Party System: Party Formation in the Jacksonian Era* (Chapel Hill: University of North Caro-

lina Press, 1966) for a description of Vermont's "atypical" and "disoriented" politics (69) and Georgia's "peculiar" politics (236).

95 According to estimates by Richard Sutch, gross domestic product (measured in 1996 dollars) between 1838 and 1839 increased by almost 8 percent, from $26,726,000 to $28,768,000, and then fell by over 2 percent in 1840 to $28,113,000. The per-capita decline was even sharper, closer to 5 percent, from $1,727,000 in 1839 to $1,642,000 in 1840. See Richard Sutch, "Gross Domestic Product: 1790–2002 [Continuous annual series]," Table Ca9–19 in *Historical Statistics of the United States, Millennial Edition Online*, ed. Susan B. Carter et al. (New York, NY: Cambridge University Press, 2006), https://hsus .cambridge.org/HSUSWeb/index.do.

96 Temin, *The Jacksonian Economy*, 69, 168–170; quotation at 170; and Namsuk Kim and John Joseph Wallis, "The Market for American State Government Bonds in Britain and the United States, 1930–1843," *Economic History Review* (November 2005): 743–744. Kim and Wallis challenge Temin's thesis that the economic downturn in the United States after October 1839 was caused by a tightening of British capital markets, but while they find that the "shock" to bond markets in the fall of 1839 originated in the United States, they attribute the downturn not to Van Buren administration policies but "to the market for American state government bonds and failing efforts of American states, particularly in the west, to finance public investments in finance and transportation" (761; also see 756). It is worth noting that Temin acknowledges that "there is no single cause of the crisis in 1839" (Temin, *The Jacksonian Economy*, 152), but the main point for our purposes is that arguing that Van Buren was blamed for economic outcomes over which he had relatively little control as president does not require taking sides in the long-standing historical debate about whether the financial crises of the late 1830s originated in the United States or Great Britain. It is to acknowledge, however, the truth of political scientist V. O. Key's judgment that elections "have within themselves more than a trace of the lottery." "Public Opinion and the Decay of Democracy," 487.

97 On forecasting presidential elections, see Steven J. Rosenstone, *Forecasting Presidential Elections* (New Haven, CT: Yale University Press, 1983); Ray C. Fair, *Predicting Presidential Elections and Other Things*, 2nd ed. (Palo Alto, CA: Stanford University Press, 2012); James E. Campbell, *The American Campaign: U.S. Presidential Campaigns and the National Vote*, 2nd ed. (College Station: Texas A&M University Press, 2008); Allan J. Lichtman, *Predicting the Next President: The Keys to the White House 2016* (Lanham, MD: Rowman & Littlefield, 2016); Robert S. Erikson and Christopher Wlezien, *The Timeline of Presidential Elections: How Campaigns Do (and Do Not) Matter* (Chicago: University of Chicago Press, 2012); and Lynn Vavreck, *The Message Matters: The Economy and Presidential Campaigns* (Princeton, NJ: Princeton University Press, 2009). Vavreck shows that campaigns can matter in close contests in which "the insurgent candidate, the one predicted to lose based on the state of the economy," successfully "refocuses the election off the economy and onto something else" (xxii). Between 1952 and 2008, Vavreck finds, there were only four instances

in which the campaign message affected the outcome: 1960, 1968, 1976, and 2000. In each of these instances, unlike in 1840, there was no incumbent running and no economic recession.

98 On retrospective voting, see Morris P. Fiorina, *Retrospective Voting in American National Elections* (New Haven, CT: Yale University Press, 1981); and V. O. Key, *The Responsible Electorate: Rationality in Presidential Voting, 1936–1960* (Cambridge, MA: Harvard University Press, 1966). On voting behavior as "blindly" or "myopically retrospective," see Achen and Bartels, *Democracy for Realists.* Michael Holt's analysis of the 1840 election rightly focuses on the "crucial role" of the economy but tends to conflate "economic conditions" with "economic issues" or policies. For instance, Holt criticizes traditional interpretations of the 1840 election for ignoring that the "Whigs believed they won because of economic issues" and then quotes two Whigs, the first William Henry Harrison, who in February 1840 explained that "we have many recruits in our ranks from the pressure of the times," and the second an Indiana Whig who claimed in 1844 that the voters "cast [Van Buren] out because they were opposed to his Sub Treasury." Michael F. Holt, "The Election of 1840, Voter Mobilization, and the Emergence of the Second American Party System: A Reappraisal of Jacksonian Voting Behavior," in *A Master's Due: Essays in Honor of David Herbert Donald,* ed. William J. Cooper, Jr., Michael F. Holt, and John McCardell (Baton Rouge: Louisiana State University Press, 1986), 22. But these quotations offer two distinct claims: the first, by Harrison, posits the importance of economic conditions, not issues or policies, and is well supported by social science research; the second assumes an issue-oriented electorate and adopts a view of elections as bestowing policy mandates that is far less plausible. Holt is right to criticize so-called ethnoculturalist interpretations of nineteenth-century voting behavior for their narrow conceptualization and measures of economic influences—usually correlations between occupation or class and vote choice—but the ethnoculturalists are right to emphasize that partisan preference and voting behavior are rooted in social identities and group attachments more than policy preferences. As Achen and Bartels put it, for most people, vote choices are "based on who they are rather than on what they think." What the ethnoculturalist interpretation leaves out—and Holt helps to put back in—are the "myopic retrospections" that are also a primary source of voting behavior. Achen and Bartels, *Democracy for Realists,* 264, 267. On the "disjunction between public policy and voting behavior" (294) in mid-nineteenth-century American politics, also see Richard Franklin Bensel, *The American Ballot Box in the Mid-Nineteenth Century* (New York: Cambridge University Press, 2004).

99 Walter Dean Burnham gives the 1836 presidential turnout as 56.5 percent, whereas Michael Holt estimates it at 57.8 percent. See Walter Dean Burnham, *Voting in American Elections: The Shaping of the American Political Universe since 1788* (Palo Alto, CA: Academica Press, 2010), 68, 404; and Holt, "The Election of 1840," 16.

100 Voters in the 1840 presidential election are often described as "first-time voters" or "new voters." See, for instance, Alasdair Roberts's claim that "almost

40 percent of ballots in 1840 were cast by first-time voters." *America's First Great Depression: Economic Crisis and Political Disorder after the Panic of 1837* (Ithaca, NY: Cornell University Press, 2012), 93. Similarly, Gail Collins writes, "New voters constituted more than a third of the turnout, and the election was perhaps the last in which the parties focused on converting the newcomers rather than turning out the base and trying to tack on added support from the uncertain middle." *William Henry Harrison* (New York: Times Books, 2012), 114.

101   This same point is stressed by Holt in "The Election of 1840." Also see Holt, *Rise and Fall of the American Whig Party*, 76. It's also important to remember, as Jon Grinspan emphasizes, that even many genuinely "virgin voters"—the young who had recently turned twenty-one—were not part of what Gail Collins characterizes as "the uncertain middle" (*William Henry Harrison*, 114) but instead had been socialized by their families and communities into strongly partisan political cultures. "By the time they cast their first ballots," Grinspan writes, "many virgin voters were veterans of at least a decade of popular democracy." *The Virgin Vote: How Young Americans Made Democracy Social, Politics Personal, and Voting Popular in the Nineteenth Century* (Chapel Hill: University of North Carolina Press, 2016), 16.

102   Burnham, *Voting in American Elections*, 329, 402. Admittedly, New Hampshire is an unusual case because it was one of the few states in which the number of people who voted in the 1836 presidential election was substantially lower than in the 1832 presidential election. Whereas almost 44,000 voters went to the polls in 1832, only about 25,000 did so in 1836, so much of the increase in turnout in 1838 and 1839 relative to 1836 was due to mobilizing voters who had previously voted in 1832 and/or in the gubernatorial and congressional elections of the early 1830s, where turnout exceeded 40,000 on several occasions. Maine is another state in which many fewer people voted in the 1836 presidential election than in the 1832 presidential election, and so many of the dramatic gains in turnout in the 1838 election (see Table 10.8) were due to mobilizing voters who had previously turned out in large numbers in 1832, when two-thirds of eligible voters participated, and in even larger numbers in 1834, when about three-quarters of the electorate voted. In raw numbers, 73,000 people voted in the Maine gubernatorial election in 1834, nearly double the roughly 38,000 who voted in the 1836 presidential election. By way of comparison, nearly 90,000 voted for governor in 1838, and just shy of 93,000 voted for president in 1840. Even more reason, then, to be wary of loose talk of the many "new" or "first-time" voters in 1840, particularly since one cannot assume that even this small increment of 3,000 was all or even mostly new voters since voters for any number of reasons may skip a given election. That 3,000 figure, then, is more likely the outer limit on the number of possible new voters than an accurate count of new voters.

103   Burnham, 365, 403.

104   These and all other turnout estimates in this chapter are calculated based on turnout percentages in Tables 7 and 8 in Burnham.

105 Five of the states listed in Table 10.7 held gubernatorial elections in 1839: Vermont, Maine, Georgia, Massachusetts, and Michigan. In two of the five states, turnout in the 1839 gubernatorial election was higher than the 1838 congressional turnout: Vermont, where turnout reached 68.8 percent in 1839, and Massachusetts, where it reached 55.1 percent. Using those 1839 gubernatorial numbers instead of the 1838 congressional numbers boosts the percentage of turnout increase achieved prior to 1840 from 24 percent to 52 percent in Massachusetts and from 51 percent to 76 percent in Vermont.

106 Holt uses different numbers and calculations but comes to essentially the same conclusion. See "The Election of 1840," esp. 47.

107 The largest gain was in Pennsylvania, but, as Table 10.7 shows, two years earlier, Pennsylvania had already reached 72 percent turnout in its congressional elections.

108 Illinois is missing from Table 10.8 because while its congressional elections were normally held in even-numbered years, it delayed holding its election for the Twenty-Seventh Congress until 1841.

109 Several states not listed in Table 10.9—notably Virginia, Alabama, Illinois, and Maryland—also held state legislative elections between May and October 1840, but statewide turnout data for these state legislative elections is less readily available.

110 These ten states were New Hampshire, Connecticut, Virginia, Rhode Island, Alabama, Kentucky, Indiana, Tennessee, North Carolina, and Maryland. Although each of these states held its 1841 congressional elections between March and May, only the first three held their congressional elections in the spring in 1837 (and 1839). The other seven held their congressional elections in July and August 1837 as well as in 1839. Part of the precipitous decline in turnout in the latter seven states is likely because they were holding their congressional elections at an earlier date that was not aligned with the regular date for other state elections.

111 The classic article is Angus Campbell, "Surge and Decline: A Study of Electoral Change," *Public Opinion Quarterly* (Autumn 1960): 397–418.

112 Rhode Island also moved its congressional elections from the summer to the spring in 1841, but the elections were moved to coincide with the state's annual gubernatorial and state legislative elections in April. So, unlike the other six states that moved their congressional elections into the spring, turnout in Rhode Island's congressional elections in 1841 should have been helped rather than hurt by the move.

113 The thirteen states, in addition to the states in Table 10.11, were Alabama, Connecticut, Maryland, New Hampshire, Pennsylvania, Rhode Island, and Tennessee.

114 The twelve states, in addition to the states in Table 10.11, were Alabama, Connecticut, Indiana, New Hampshire, Rhode Island, and Tennessee. The two states in which there was a drop were New Hampshire (1 percentage point) and Rhode Island (8 percentage points).

115 Democrats lost a net of 13 seats between July and November 1840, during which period 150 House seats were contested—or 9 percent—whereas between March and May 1841, they lost 12 of the 87 House seats up for grabs, or 14 percent. This count leaves out the five seats of Illinois and Mississippi, which held elections in August and November 1841, respectively, neither of which produced a change in the partisan composition of their House delegation.

116 There is little if any correlation between how much a state's turnout increased between 1836 and 1840 and how much Van Buren's support in a state slipped between the two presidential elections. In fact, the correlation is essentially zero ($r = -0.03$) if one excludes the outlier of New Hampshire, where turnout increased almost 50 percentage points between 1836 and 1840, while Van Buren's share of the vote plummeted about 20 points, far more than in any other state. If New Hampshire is included, the correlation climbs to -0.26, suggesting some relationship, albeit a weak one, between increase in turnout and decline in support for Van Buren. The same pattern holds if one looks only at states in which both Harrison and Van Buren ran in 1836—that is, if one excludes Southern states in which Hugh White was the Whig candidate and Massachusetts, where Webster was the Whig candidate. Although this boosts the correlation to a more robust -0.38, that correlation is almost entirely owing to New Hampshire; without New Hampshire the correlation again drops, to -0.10.

117 See McCormick, *The Second American Party System*, 145. McCormick is speaking specifically about Pennsylvania, but his observation applies to other states as well.

118 These numbers are calculated from turnout data in Burnham, *Voting in American Elections*, Table 8.

119 Bruce Miroff, *Presidents on Political Ground: Leaders in Action and What They Face* (Lawrence: University Press of Kansas, 2016), 10. Miroff elaborates on his concept of "the presidential spectacle" in chapter 1.

120 For a fresh look at what likely killed Harrison, see Jane McHugh and Philip A. Mackowiak, "What Really Killed William Henry Harrison," *New York Times*, March 31, 2014. The course of Harrison's illness and the medical care he received are described in Freeman Cleaves, *Old Tippecanoe: William Henry Harrison and His Time* (Newtown, CT: American Political Biography Press, 1939), 336, 340–342; Collins, *William Henry Harrison*, 124; and James A. Green, *William Henry Harrison: His Life and Times* (Richmond, VA: Garrett and Massie, 1941), 398–399.

121 Edward P. Crapol, *John Tyler: The Accidental President* (Chapel Hill: University of North Carolina Press, 2006), 18–19; Jill Lepore, *These Truths: A History of the United States* (New York: W. W. Norton, 2018), 233–234; and *Register of Debates in Congress* (Washington, DC: Gales and Seaton, 1833), 9:63 (February 6, 1833).

122 In Clay's defense, it should be noted that in 1844, he outperformed the Whigs' gubernatorial nominee, with Fillmore's 10,000-vote loss double Clay's margin of defeat.

BIBLIOGRAPHIC ESSAY

"Tippecanoe and Tyler too" may be the most famous campaign slogan in all of American history, but for sixty years, Robert Gray Gunderson's *The Log-Cabin Campaign* (Lexington: University Press of Kentucky, 1957) remained the only book-length treatment of the 1840 election, a tribute to the book's thoroughness and deep grounding in primary materials. In 2016, Ronald G. Shafer published *The Carnival Campaign: How the Rollicking 1840 Campaign of "Tippecanoe and Tyler Too" Changed Presidential Elections Forever* (Chicago: Chicago Review Press, 2016), a lively but far less well-sourced account of the 1840 campaign that tends to reinforce the older stereotype of the 1840 election, to which Gunderson at times contributed, as all "clatter and nonsense." Not that historians have slighted the election or accepted this popular stereotype. Valuable surveys of the 1840 election include William Nisbet Chambers, "Election of 1840," in *History of American Presidential Elections, 1789–1968*, ed. Arthur M. Schlesinger, Jr., and Fred L. Israel, 4 vols. (New York: Chelsea House, 1971), 1:643–744; Ronald P. Formisano, "The New Political History and the Election of 1840," *Journal of Interdisciplinary History* (Spring 1993): 661–682; and Richard Carwardine, "Evangelicals, Whigs, and the Election of William Henry Harrison," *Journal of American Studies* (April 1983): 47–75. In my judgment, the most convincing analysis of the 1840 election is Michal F. Holt, "The Election of 1840, Voter Mobilization, and the Emergence of the Second American Party System: A Reappraisal of Jacksonian Voting Behavior," in *A Master's Due: Essays in Honor of David Herbert Donald*, ed. William J. Cooper, Jr., Michael F. Holt, and John Mc-Cardell (Baton Rouge: Louisiana State University Press, 1985). Holt elaborates and refines his analysis of the 1840 election in his magisterial *The Rise and Fall of the American Whig Party: Jacksonian Politics and the Onset of the Civil War* (New York: Oxford University Press, 1999).

The 1840 election cannot be understood apart from the 1836 election, which sadly remains one of the least studied presidential elections. Although historians have yet to write a book on the 1836 election, Joel Silbey provides an excellent overview in "Election of 1836," *History of American Presidential Elections, 1789–1968*, ed. Arthur M. Schlesinger, Jr., and Fred L. Israel, 4 vols. (New York: Chelsea House, 1971), 575–640. There are also a number of valuable articles about aspects of the 1836 election, including Richard P. McCormick, "Was There a 'Whig Strategy' in 1836?," *Journal of the Early Republic* (Spring 1984): 47–70; William G. Shade, "'The Most Delicate and Exciting Topics': Martin Van Buren, Slavery, and the Election of 1836," *Journal of the Early Republic* (Fall 1998): 459–484; Thomas Brown, "The Miscegenation of Richard Mentor Johnson as an Issue for the National Election Campaign of 1835–1836," *Civil War History* (March 1993): 5–30; and Jonathan M. Atkins, "The Presidential Candidacy of Hugh Lawson White in Tennessee, 1832–1836," *Journal of Southern History* (February 1992): 27–56.

In addition to needing a full-length book treatment of the 1836 election, there is also a need for more studies that systematically compare and contrast the 1840 campaign with preceding campaigns so that we can be more precise about what was distinctive about the 1840 campaign. A vitally important contribution in this respect is Mark R. Cheathem, *The Coming of Democracy: Presidential Campaigning in the Age of Jackson* (Baltimore, MD: Johns Hopkins University Press, 2018), which compares the evolution of print culture, political music, visual culture, and women's participation in presidential campaigning between 1824 and 1840. Essential for understanding the evolution of presidential selection, especially the selection of party nominees, in the first half century of the republic is Richard P. McCormick, *The Presidential Game: The Origins of American Presidential Politics* (New York: Oxford University Press, 1982). The change in presidential campaigns, especially the president's place in the campaign, is also explored insightfully in M. J. Heale, *The Presidential Quest: Candidates and Images in American Political Culture, 1787–1852* (London: Longman, 1982). Also see Gil Troy, *See How They Ran: The Changing Role of the Presidential Candidate* (New York: Free Press, 1991); and Richard J. Ellis and Mark Dedrick, "The Rise of the Rhetorical Candidate," in *The Presidency, Then and Now*, ed. Philip G. Henderson (Lanham, MD: Rowman & Littlefield, 2000). On Harrison's groundbreaking speech-making campaign in 1840, see the prologue to Robert V. Friedenberg, *Notable Speeches in Contemporary Presidential Campaigns* (Westport, CT: Praeger, 2002); and Jeffrey Bourdon, "Symbolism, Economic Depression, and the Specter of Slavery: William Henry Harrison's Speaking Tour for the Presidency," *Ohio History* 118 (August 2011): 5–23.

One aspect of the 1840 election that has received sustained attention is the innovative role of women in the Whig campaign. Three outstanding studies are Ronald J. Zboray and Mary Saracino Zboray, "Whig Women, Politics, and Culture in the Campaign of 1840: Three Perspectives from Massachusetts," *Journal of the Early Republic* (Summer 1997): 277–315; Jayne Crumpler DeFiore, "*COME, and Bring the Ladies*: Tennessee Women and the Politics of Opportunity during the Presidential Campaigns of 1840 and 1844," *Tennessee Historical Society* (Winter 1992): 197–212; and Elizabeth R. Varon, "Tippecanoe and the Ladies, Too: White Women and Party Politics in Antebellum Virginia," *Journal of American History* (September 1995): 494–521. Also see Elizabeth R. Varon, *We Mean to Be Counted: White Women and Politics in Antebellum Virginia* (Chapel Hill: University of North Carolina Press, 1998), chap. 3.

The most accessible introduction to William Henry Harrison's life is Gail Collins's excellent short biography, *William Henry Harrison* (New York: Times Books, 2012). There is no modern, full-length academic biography of Harrison, but some older biographies are still useful, notably Dorothy Burne Goebel, *William Henry Harrison: A Political Biography* (Indianapolis: Historical Bureau of the Indiana Library and Historical Department, 1926); Freeman Cleaves, *Old Tippecanoe: William Henry Harrison and His Time* (Newtown, CT: American Political Biography Press, 1939); and, to a lesser extent, James A. Green, *William Henry Harrison, His Life and Times* (Richmond, VA: Garrett and Massie 1941). There have, however, been a number of valuable studies of Harrison's early life and career, for which primary materials are more abundant. Among the most notable are Robert M. Owens, *Mr. Jefferson's Hammer: William Henry Harrison and the Origins of American Indian Policy* (Norman: University of Oklahoma Press, 2007); David Curtis Skaggs, *William Henry Harrison and the Conquest of the Ohio Country: Frontier Fighting in the War of 1812* (Baltimore, MD: Johns Hopkins University Press, 2014); and Hendrik Booraem, *A Child of the Revolution: William Henry Harrison and His World, 1773–1798* (Kent, OH: Kent State University Press, 2012). Norma Lois Pederson's *The Presidencies of William Henry Harrison and John Tyler* (Lawrence: University Press of Kansas, 1989) is more about Tyler than Harrison's short-lived presidency. An extensive bibliography of Harrison-related materials, secondary as well as primary, can be found in Kenneth R. Stevens, *William Henry Harrison: A Bibliography* (Westport, CT: Greenwood Press, 1998).

Harrison's chief rivals for the 1840 Whig nomination have been well served by historians. Readers have their pick of many fine biographies of Henry Clay, including Glyndon G. Van Deusen, *The Life of Henry Clay* (Boston: Little, Brown, 1937); Robert V. Remini, *Henry Clay: Statesman for the Union* (New York: W. W. Norton, 1991); David S. Heidler and Jeanne T. Heidler, *Henry Clay: The Essential American* (New York: Random House, 2010); and James C. Klotter, *Henry Clay: The Man Who Would Be President* (New York: Oxford University Press, 2018). There is no substitute, though, for immersion in *The Papers of Henry Clay*, 10 vols. (Lexington: University Press of Kentucky, 1959–2015), specifically volume 9 (*The Whig Leader*), edited by Robert Seager II, which covers the period from January 1837 through the end of the 1840 election. Some Clay correspondence from this period is also to be found in *The Papers of Henry Clay: Supplement, 1793–1852*, ed. Melba Porter Hay (Lexington: University Press of Kentucky, 1992).

There are also a number of good biographies of Daniel Webster, among them Richard N. Current, *Daniel Webster and the Rise of National Conservatism* (Boston: Little, Brown, 1955); Irving H. Bartlett, *Daniel Webster* (New York: W. W. Norton, 1978); and Robert V. Remini, *Daniel Webster: The Man and His Time* (New York: W. W. Norton, 1997). Particularly good on Webster's maneuvering in the 1840 campaign is Sydney Nathans, *Daniel Webster and Jacksonian Democracy* (Baltimore, MD: Johns Hopkins University Press, 1973). Webster's quest for the presidency in 1836 is explored in depth in Norman D. Brown, *Daniel Webster and the Politics of Availability* (Athens: University of Georgia Press, 1969). Also essential for understanding Webster's pursuit of the presidency is volume 4 of *The Papers of Daniel Webster*, ed. Charles M. Wiltse and Harold D. Moser (Hanover, NH: University Press of New England, 1980), which covers the period from 1835 through the end of 1839.

The principal modern biographies of Winfield Scott are Allan Peskin, *Winfield Scott and the Profession of Arms* (Kent, OH: Kent State University Press, 2003); Timothy D. Johnson, *Winfield Scott: The Quest for Military Glory* (Lawrence: University Press of Kansas, 1998); and John S. D. Eisenhower, *Agent of Destiny: The Life and Times of General Winfield Scott* (New York: Free Press, 1997). Also still of value is the older biography by Charles Winslow Elliott, *Winfield Scott: The Soldier and the Man* (New York: Macmillan, 1937). Unlike with Clay and Webster, there is no published collection of Scott's correspondence, though Scott did publish a memoir in 1864, which in 2015 was edited by Timothy D. Johnson and published by the University of Tennessee Press.

The Whigs' vice-presidential nominee, John Tyler, has attracted several studies in the twenty-first century, most notably Edward P. Crapol, *John Tyler: The Accidental President* (Chapel Hill: University of North Carolina Press, 2006); and Dan Monroe, *The Republican Vision of John Tyler* (College Station: Texas A&M University Press, 2003). Readers also have their choice between two readable biographies: Gary May's concisely written *John Tyler* (New York: Times Books, 2008) and the older but far more detailed account by Robert Seager II, *And Tyler Too: A Biography of John & Julia Gardiner Tyler* (New York: McGraw-Hill, 1963). Some of Tyler's letters are collected in Lyon G. Tyler, ed., *The Letters and Times of the Tylers* (Richmond, VA: Whittet and Shepperson, 1884).

Modern biographies of other Whig politicians who played significant roles in the 1840 campaign tend to be scarcer. One of Harrison's top campaign aides, Charles S. Todd, is the subject of a recent biography by Sherry Keith Jelsma, *Political Quickstep: The Life of Kentucky's Colonel Charles S. Todd* (Louisville, KY: Butler Books, 2017), but the book has little to recommend it and is largely a missed opportunity. Webster confidant and campaign helper Caleb Cushing, in contrast, is expertly served by John M. Belohlavek, *Broken Glass: Caleb Cushing and the Shattering of the Union* (Kent, OH: Kent State University Press, 2005). Also valuable is Benjamin L. Huggins, *Willie Mangum and the North Carolina Whigs in the Age of Jackson* (Jefferson, NC: McFarland, 2016). Mangum is also one of those rare second-tier nineteenth-century politicians whose correspondence has been published. See Thomas Shanks, ed., *The Papers of Willie Person Mangum* (Raleigh, NC: State Department of Archives and History, 1952).

Unfortunately, there has been no biography of Thurlow Weed since Glyndon G. Van Deusen's *Thurlow Weed: Wizard of the Lobby* (Boston: Little, Brown, 1947). Fortunately, Robert Gray Gunderson made extensive use of Weed's papers for *The Log-Cabin Campaign* as well as "Thurlow Weed's Network: Whig Party Organization in 1840," *Indiana Magazine of History* (June 1952): 107–118. Thurlow Weed's *Autobiography*, edited by his daughter, is useful, but the so-called memoir, written by his grandson Thurlow Weed Barnes, should be approached with caution. The former was published as volume 1 and the latter as volume 2 in Thurlow Weed Barnes, ed., *Life of Thurlow Weed, Including His Autobiography and a Memoir* (Boston: Houghton Mifflin, 1884). William Henry Seward has received much greater attention from biographers than Weed, although most generally focus on Seward's later career as a presidential candidate and especially as Lincoln's secretary of state. Most helpful for understanding Seward's early career in New York politics is still Glyndon G. Van Deusen, *William Henry Seward* (New York: Oxford University Press, 1967), but also good is Walter Stahr's *Lincoln's Indispensable Man* (New York: Simon & Schuster, 2012). By far the most detailed account of Seward's gubernatorial years is Ernest G. Muntz, "The First Whig Governor of New York, William Henry Seward, 1838–1842" (PhD diss., University of Rochester, NY, 1960), a dissertation that would have made a first-rate monograph. Some of Seward's early correspondence can be found in *Autobiography of William H. Seward from 1801–1834, with a Memoir of His Life, and*

Selections from His Letters from 1831 to 1846 (New York: Appleton, 1877). Another Weed ally, newspaperman Horace Greeley, has been favored with a number of biographies, largely because of his subsequent fame in the Civil War as well as his presidential candidacy in 1872. Among them are William Harlan Hale, *Horace Greeley: Voice of the People* (New York: Harper, 1950); and Robert C. Williams, *Horace Greeley: Champion of American Freedom* (New York: New York University Press, 2006). Also see Horace Greeley's autobiography, *Recollections of a Busy Life* (New York: J. B. Ford, 1869). Millard Fillmore, because he later became president, is the only other person in Weed's extensive political network who has been favored by biographers, most notably Robert Rayback, *Millard Fillmore: Biography of a President* (Buffalo, NY: Buffalo Historical Society, 1959), as well as the more recent but not more readable Robert J. Scarry, *Millard Fillmore* (Jefferson, NC: McFarland, 2001). Particularly valuable is Fillmore's correspondence collected in *Millard Fillmore Papers*, ed. Frank H. Severance (Buffalo, NY: Buffalo Historical Society, 1907).

One wily politician from the late 1830s who has not lacked for attention from biographers and historians is South Carolina senator John Calhoun. With one eye fixed on how best to defend slavery and the other on how best to become president, he aligned himself first with Jackson, then with the Whigs, and then again with the Democrats during Van Buren's presidency. The principal biographies are Charles Wiltse's three-volume *John C. Calhoun* (Indianapolis, IN: Bobbs-Merrill, 1944–1951); John Niven, *John C. Calhoun and the Price of Union* (Baton Rouge: Louisiana State University Press, 1988); and Irving H. Bartlett, *John C. Calhoun: A Biography* (New York: W. W. Norton, 1993). Calhoun has also been treated together with Clay and Webster in Merrill D. Peterson, *The Great Triumvirate: Webster, Clay, and Calhoun* (New York: Oxford University Press, 1987); and H. W. Brands, *Heirs of the Founders: The Epic Rivalry of Henry Clay, John Calhoun and Daniel Webster, the Second Generation of American Giants* (New York: Random House, 2018). Like Clay and Webster, Calhoun has also been fortunate to have his papers annotated and published by a university press. Of the twenty-eight volumes of *The Papers of John C. Calhoun*, published between 1961 and 2003 by the University of South Carolina Press, the most relevant to the late 1830s and the election of 1840 are volumes 14 (1837–1839) and 15 (1839–1841), both of which were edited by Clyde N. Wilson.

Van Buren has had a number of fine biographers. One of my favorites is Donald B. Cole, *Martin Van Buren and the American Political System* (Princeton, NJ: Princeton University Press, 1984), a book that captivated me as a graduate student and sparked a lifelong interest in Van Buren and antebellum political history. Also excellent is John Niven, *Martin Van Buren: The Romantic Age of American Politics* (New York: Oxford University Press, 1983). John L. Brooke's *Columbia Rising: Civil Life on the Upper Hudson from the Revolution to the Age of Jackson* (Chapel Hill: University of North Carolina Press, 2010) is a masterful ethnography of the social relations and political institutions of the Upper Hudson Valley, where Van Buren grew up, and is a must-read for anyone interested in Van Buren's political career. For shorter but pithy syntheses of Van Buren's life and significance, see Joel H. Silbey, *Martin Van Buren and the Emergence of American Popular Politics* (Lanham, MD: Rowman & Littlefield, 2002); and Ted Widmer, *Martin Van Buren* (New York: Times Books, 2005).

Van Buren's presidency is the focus of James C. Curtis, *The Fox at Bay: Martin Van Buren and the Presidency, 1837–1841* (Lexington: University Press of Kentucky, 1970); and Major L. Wilson, *The Presidency of Martin Van Buren* (Lawrence: University Press of Kansas, 1984). Also see James C. Curtis, "In the Shadow of Old Hickory: The Political Travail of Martin Van Buren," *Journal of the Early Republic* (Fall 1981): 249–267. On Van Buren's innovative understanding of political parties, see Michael Wallace, "Changing Concepts of Party in the United States: New York, 1815–1828," *American Historical Review* (December 1968): 453–491; Richard Hofstadter, *The Idea of a Party System: The Rise of Legitimate Opposition in the United States, 1780–1840* (Berkeley: University of California Press, 1969); James Ceaser, *Presidential Selection: Theory and Development* (Princeton, NJ: Princeton University Press, 1979); Gerald L. Leonard, "Party as a 'Political Safeguard of Federalism': Martin Van Buren and the Constitutional Theory of Party Politics," *Rutgers Law Review* (Fall 2001): 221–281; and Martin Van Buren's own *Inquiry into the Origin and Course of Political Parties in the United States* (New York: Hurd and Houghton, 1867). Also not without interest, despite its many gaps and incompleteness, is *The Autobiography of Martin Van Buren*, ed. John C. Fitzpatrick, Annual Report of the American Historical Association for the Year 1918 (Washington, DC: Government Printing Office, 1920).

It is regrettable that a political leader of Van Buren's significance has never had his papers transcribed and published. Fortunately, that injustice is in the process of being remedied by James Bradley and Mark Cheatham, who in 2014 began work on *The Papers of Martin Van Buren* (http://vanburenpapers.org/) with the heroic aim of transcribing all of Van Buren's microfilmed papers, totaling some thirteen thousand documents, and producing an annotated and freely available digital edition. They also plan to produce a four-volume letterpress edition of the most significant papers (*The Selected Papers of Martin Van Buren*) that will be published by the University of Tennessee Press. In the meantime, digital scans of the Library of Congress collection (which consists of about half of the total thirteen thousand documents available on microfilm) of Van Buren's correspondence, in all its often illegible glory, are available on the Library of Congress website.

Van Buren's immediate Democratic predecessor and successor in the White House have been much more fortunate. *The Papers of Andrew Jackson* began publication in 1980 and have now reached 10 volumes, each of which can be downloaded for free as pdfs at https://trace.tennessee.edu/utk_jackson/. As of this writing, the *Papers* have only reached the end of Jackson's first presidential term, and at the present rate of one presidential year per volume, it will be volume 15 (and the year 2031) before the project reaches Jackson's postpresidential years. Fortunately, readers can rely on the older but still useful *Correspondence of Andrew Jackson*, ed. John Spencer Bassett (Washington, DC: Carnegie Institution, 1926–1935), which includes correspondence from the postpresidential years: volume 5 covers 1833–1838, and volume 6 covers 1839–1845. Jackson has been the subject of many fine biographies, including Jon Meacham's Pulitzer Prize–winning *American Lion: Andrew Jackson in the White House* (New York: Random House, 2009), and his prepresidential and presidential years have been the subject of many penetrating studies, but no book has made the years after 1837 its main focus. For more on the primary and secondary sources relating to Andrew Jackson's life, see Robert Remini and Robert O. Rupp, eds., *Andrew Jackson: A Bibliography* (Westport, CT: Meckler, 1991) as well as the bibliographic essay in Mark R. Cheathem, *Andrew Jackson and the Rise of the Democrats: A Reference Guide* (Santa Barbara, CA: ABC-CLIO, 2015).

The first volume of the *Correspondence of James K. Polk* was published by Vanderbilt University Press in 1969 under the editorship of Herbert Weaver and Paul Bergeron, and in the spring of 2019, the James K. Polk Project celebrated the completion of the fourteen-volume project, the last seven of which were published by the University of Tennessee Press. As of this writing, the first twelve volumes are available online for free at https://trace.tennessee.edu/utk_polk/. Volume 5, edited by Wayne Cutler, covers the years 1839–1841 (Nashville, TN: Vanderbilt University Press, 1975) and is a rich source of Democratic thinking relating to the 1840 election. The most in-depth biography of Polk's career before becoming president remains Charles Grier Sellers, *James K. Polk: Jacksonian, 1795–1843* (Princeton, NJ: Princeton University Press, 1957).

Among the biographies of Democratic politicians who played an important role in the politics of the late 1830s and/or the 1840 campaign are Donald B. Cole, *Amos Kendall and the Rise of American Democracy* (Baton Rouge: Louisiana State University Press, 2004); John Arthur Garraty, *Silas Wright* (New York: Columbia University Press, 1949); Ivor Debenham Spencer, *The Victor and the Spoils: A Life of William L. Marcy* (Providence, RI: Brown University Press, 1959); Elbert B. Smith, *Francis Preston Blair* (New York: Free Press, 1980); Elbert B. Smith, *Magnificent Missourian: The Life of Thomas Hart Benton* (Philadelphia, PA: J. B. Lippincott, 1958); and Robert D. Sampson, *John L. O'Sullivan and His Times* (Kent, OH: Kent State University Press, 2003).

Two recent books discuss the economic Panic of 1837, its aftermath, and its implications in ways that are accessible to a general audience and useful to historians: Jessica M. Lepler, *The Many Panics of 1837: People, Politics, and the Creation of a Transatlantic Financial Crisis* (Cambridge: Cambridge University Press, 2013); and Alasdair Roberts, *America's First Great Depression: Economic Crisis and Political Disorder after the Panic of 1837* (Ithaca, NY: Cornell University Press, 2012). Still invaluable is Peter Temin, *The Jacksonian Economy* (New York: W. W. Norton, 1969), although an important correction is provided by Peter L. Rousseau, "Jacksonian Monetary Policy, Specie Flows, and the Panic of 1837," National Bureau of Economic Research, Working Paper 7528, February 2000, http://www.nber.org/papers/w7528; Rousseau's paper was published in the *Journal of Economic History* 62 (June 2002): 457–488. Also relevant is James Rogers Sharp, *The Jacksonians versus the Banks: Politics in the States after the Panic of 1837* (New York: Columbia University Press, 1970); and Jonathan M. Atkins, "Van Buren and the Economic Collapse of the Late 1830s," in *A Companion to the Antebellum Presidents, 1837–1861*, ed. Joel H. Silbey (New York: John Wiley & Sons, 2014).

On antiabolitionism and antislavery in the 1840 campaign and the years leading up to it, see Vernon L. Volpe, "The Anti-Abolitionist Campaign of 1840," *Civil War History* (December 1986): 325–339; William J. Cooper, Jr., *The South and the Politics of Slavery, 1828–1856* (Baton Rouge: Louisiana University Press, 1978); David

Waldstreicher, "The Nationalization and Racialization of American Politics: Before, Beneath, and Between Parties, 1790–1840," in *Contesting Democracy: Substance and Structure in American Political History, 1775–2000*, ed. Byron E. Shafer and Anthony J. Badger (Lawrence: University Press of Kansas, 2001); and Donald Ratcliffe, "The Decline of Antislavery Politics," in *Contesting Slavery: The Politics of Bondage and Freedom in the New American Nation*, ed. John Craig Hammond and Matthew Mason (Charlottesville: University of Virginia Press, 2011).

The Liberty Party has attracted many very good books and articles, including Richard H. Sewell, *Ballots for Freedom: Antislavery Politics in the United States, 1837–1860* (New York: W. W. Norton, 1976); Alan M. Kraut, "The Forgotten Reformers: A Profile of Third Party Abolitionists in Antebellum New York," in *Antislavery Reconsidered: New Perspectives on the Abolitionists*, ed. Lewis Perry and Michael Fellman (Baton Rouge: Louisiana State University Press, 1979); Reinhard O. Johnson, *The Liberty Party, 1840–1848: Antislavery Third-Party Politics in the United States* (Baton Rouge: Louisiana State University Press, 2009); and Corey Michael Brooks, *Liberty Power: Antislavery Third Parties and the Transformation of American Politics* (Chicago: University of Chicago Press, 2016). On the Liberty Party's 1840 presidential nominee, James Gillespie Birney, see Betty Fladeland, *James Gillespie Birney: Slaveholder to Abolitionist* (Ithaca, NY: Cornell University Press, 1955); and the *Letters of James Gillespie Birney*, ed. Dwight L. Dumond (New York: D. Appleton, 1938).

On the Anti-Masonic Party, the standard source is William Preston Vaughn, *The Antimasonic Party in the United States, 1826–1843* (Lexington: University Press of Kentucky, 1983). Also see Ronald P. Formisano, *For the People: American Populist Movements from the Revolution to the 1850s* (Chapel Hill: University of North Carolina Press, 2008); and Michael Holt, "The Antimasonic and Know Nothing Parties," in Holt, *Political Parties and American Political Development from the Age of Jackson to the Age of Lincoln* (Baton Rouge: Louisiana State University Press, 1992). Important for the 1840 election specifically is John J. Reed, "Battleground: Pennsylvania Antimasons and the Emergence of the National Nominating Convention, 1835–1839," *Pennsylvania Magazine of History and Biography* (January/April 1998), 77–115.

On the partisan press in the early republic, see Culver H. Smith, *The Press, Politics, and Patronage: The American Government's Use of Newspapers, 1789–1875* (Athens: University of Georgia Press, 1977); Jeffrey Pasley, *"The Tyranny of Printers": Newspaper Politics in the Early American Republic* (Charlottesville: University of Virginia Press, 2001); John L. Brooke, "To Be 'Read by the Whole People': Press, Party, and Public Sphere in the United States, 1789–1840," *Proceedings of the American Antiquarian Society*, vol. 110, part 1 (2000), 41–118; Stephen W. Campbell, *The Bank War and the Partisan Press: Newspapers, Financial Institutions, and the Post Office in Jacksonian America* (Lawrence: University Press of Kansas, 2019); Marcus Daniel, *Scandal and Civility: Journalism and the Birth of American Democracy* (New York: Oxford University Press, 2009); and William Miles, ed., *The People's Voice: An Annotated Bibliography of American Presidential Campaign Newspapers, 1828–1984* (Westport, CT: Greenwood Press, 1987). A rich source of political cartoons and caricatures in nineteenth-century campaigns is Bernard F. Reilly, Jr., *American Political Prints, 1776–1876* (Boston, MA: G. K. Hall, 1991). Many of the Whig cartoons of the late 1830s were published by Henry Robinson, whose work is the focus of Peter Welsh, "Henry R. Robinson: Printmaker to the Whig Party," *New York History* (January 1972): 25–53.

There are many monographs focused on individual states that shed important light on the parties and politics of the late 1830s as well as the 1840 election. Among those I found most stimulating or useful are Ronald P. Formisano, *The Birth of Mass Political Parties: Michigan, 1827–1861* (Princeton, NJ: Princeton University Press, 1971); Gerald L. Leonard, *The Invention of Party Politics: Federalism, Popular Sovereignty, and Constitutional Development in Jacksonian Illinois* (Chapel Hill: University of North Carolina Press, 2002); Charles Manfred Thompson, *The Illinois Whigs before 1846* (1915; repr., Urbana: University of Illinois, 1967); Ronald P. Formisano, *The Transformation of Political Culture: Massachusetts Parties, 1790s–1840s* (New York: Oxford University Press, 1983); Donald B. Cole, *Jacksonian Democracy in New Hampshire, 1800–1851* (Cambridge, MA: Harvard University Press, 1970); Lee D. Webb, "Party Development and Political Conflict in Maine, 1820–1860: From Statehood to the Civil War" (PhD diss., University of Maine, May 2017); Donald J. Ratcliffe, *The Politics of Long Division: The Birth of the Second Party System in Ohio, 1818–1828* (Columbus: Ohio State University Press, 2000); Edgar Allan Holt, *Party Politics in Ohio, 1840–1850* (Columbus, OH: F. J. Heer, 1930); Charles McCool Snyder, *The Jacksonian Heritage: Pennsylvania Politics, 1833–1848* (Harrisburg: Pennsylvania Historical and Museum Commission, 1958); Marc W. Kruman, *Parties and Politics in North Carolina, 1836–1865* (Baton Rouge: Louisiana State University Press, 1983); William G. Shade, *Democratizing the Old Dominion: Virginia and the Second Party System, 1824–1861* (Charlottesville: University Press of Virginia, 1996); Jonathan M. Atkins, *Parties, Politics, and the Sectional Conflict in Tennessee, 1832–1861* (Knoxville: University of Tennessee Press, 1997); John M. Sacher, *A Perfect War of Politics: Parties, Politicians, and Democracy in Louisiana* (Baton Rouge: Louisiana State University Press, 2003); Anthony Gene Carey, *Parties, Slavery, and the Union in Antebellum Georgia* (Athens: University of Georgia Press, 1997); Edwin Arthur Miles, *Jacksonian Democracy in Mississippi* (Chapel Hill: University of North Carolina Press, 1960); and J. Mills Thornton III, *Politics and Power in a Slave Society, Alabama, 1800–1860* (Baton Rouge: Louisiana State University Press, 1978). Also see B. G. Golden, "The Presidential Election of 1840 in Alabama," *Alabama Review* (April 1970): 128–142; and Thomas B. Alexander, "The Presidential Campaign of 1840 in Tennessee," *Tennessee Historical Quarterly* (March 1942): 21–43. The centrality of slavery in the politics of Southern states is stressed in Cooper, *The South and the Politics of Slavery* (1978). Also still useful is Arthur Charles Cole, *The Whig Party in the South* (Washington, DC: American Historical Association, 1914).

Historians and political systems have written a great deal about the development of political parties and the increase in voting rates during the Jacksonian period. The seminal work on the second party system of Democrats and Whigs is Richard P. McCormick, *The Second American Party System: Party Formation in the Jacksonian Era* (Chapel Hill: University of North Carolina Press, 1966). On the connection between party competition and increased voting rates, see Richard P. McCormick, "New Perspectives on Jacksonian Politics," *American Historical Review* (January

1960): 288–301. Also see William Nisbet Chambers and Walter Dean Burnham, eds., *The American Party Systems: Stages of Political Development* (New York: Oxford University Press, 1967); William N. Chambers and Philip C. Davis, "Party, Competition, and Mass Participation: The Case of the Democratizing Party System, 1841–1852," in *The History of American Electoral Behavior*, ed. Joel H. Silbey, Allan G. Bogue, and William H. Flanigan (Princeton, NJ: Princeton University Press, 1978); and William G. Shade, "Political Pluralism and Party Development: The Creation of a Modern Party System, 1815–1852," in Paul Kleppner, et al., *The Evolution of American Electoral Systems* (Westport, CT: Greenwood Press, 1981). On the distinction between the first and second party systems, see Ronald P. Formisano, "Federalists and Republicans: Parties, Yes—System, No," in Kleppner et al., *Evolution of American Electoral Systems*. Also see Ronald P. Formisano, "Deferential-Participant Politics: The Early Republic's Political Culture, 1789–1840," *American Political Science Review* (June 1974): 473–487.

The idea of a distinct second party system has been criticized from several different angles. The first suggests that the party system that emerged in the 1830s ushered in a new "party period" with unprecedented rates of voter mobilization that endured well beyond the life of the so-called second party system. This thesis is argued in different ways in Joel H. Silbey, *The American Political Nation, 1838–1893* (Palo Alto, CA: Stanford University Press, 1991); Richard L. McCormick, "The Party Period and Public Policy: An Exploratory Hypothesis," *Journal of American History* (September 1979): 279–298; and Morton Keller, *America's Three Regimes: A New Political History* (New York: Oxford University Press, 2007). Also see Ronald P. Formisano, "The Party Period Revisited," *Journal of American History* (June 1999): 93–120; and Michael F. Holt, "Change and Continuity in the Party Period: The Substance and Structure of American Politics, 1835–1885," in *Contesting Democracy: Substance and Structure in American Political History, 1775–2000*, ed. Byron E. Shafer and Anthony J. Badger (Lawrence: University Press of Kansas, 2001), 93–115.

The second line of critique points to the often high levels of political participation below the presidential level as well as strong partisanship in the opening decades of the nineteenth century. An essential essay is Donald Ratcliffe, "The Right to Vote and the Rise of Democracy, 1787–1828," *Journal of the Early Republic* (Summer 2013): 219–254; but also particularly valuable are Jeffrey L. Pasley, "The Cheese and the Words: Popular Political Culture and Participatory Democracy in the Early American Republic," in *Beyond the Founders: New Approaches to the Political History of the Early American Republic*, ed. Jeffrey L. Pasley, Andrew W. Robertson, and David Waldstreicher (Chapel Hill: University of North Carolina Press, 2004), 31–56; and John L. Brooke, "'King George Has Issued Too Many Patents for Us': Property and Democracy in Jeffersonian New York," *Journal of the Early Republic* (Summer 2013): 187–217; as well as the chapters by Reeve Huston, Andrew W. Robertson, and Daniel Peart in *Practicing Democracy: Popular Politics in the United States from the Constitution to the Civil War*, ed. Daniel Peart and Adam I. P. Smith (Charlottesville: University of Virginia Press, 2015); and Daniel Peart, *Era of Experimentation: American Political Practices in the Early Republic* (Charlottesville: University of Virginia Press, 2014).

The third line of critique calls into question the idea of the Jacksonian era as a "golden age of democracy" by showing that high levels of participation may have been less a sign of civic virtue or engagement with politics than a product of social coercion and the inducements of alcohol. See Richard Franklin Bensel's outstanding *The American Ballot Box in the Mid-Nineteenth Century* (Cambridge: Cambridge University Press, 2004), which also provides an invaluable account of the logistics of casting votes in the mid-nineteenth century. Equally provocative and essential is Glenn C. Altschuler and Stuart M. Blumin, *Rude Republic: Americans and Their Politics in the Nineteenth Century* (Princeton, NJ: Princeton University Press, 2000). Also see Altschuler and Blumin, "Limits of Political Engagement in Antebellum America: A New Look at the Golden Age of Participatory Democracy," *Journal of American History* (December 1997): 855–885; and the responses in "Public Engagement and Disengagement in Antebellum America: A Round Table," particularly Harry L. Watson's spirited "Humbug? Bah! Altschuler and Blumin and the Riddle of the Antebellum Electorate," *Journal of American History* (December 1997): 886–893. Also relevant to this debate is Jon Grinspan, *The Virgin Vote: How Young Americans Made Democracy Social, Politics Personal, and Voting Popular in the Nineteenth Century* (Chapel Hill: University of North Carolina Press, 2016).

The voting results for presidential elections can be found, among other places, in Michael J. Dubin, *United States Presidential Elections, 1788–1860* (Jefferson, NC: McFarland, 2002); W. Dean Burnham, *Presidential Ballots, 1836–1892* (Baltimore, MD: Johns Hopkins University Press, 1955); *Presidential Elections, 1789–2008* (Washington, DC: CQ Press, 2010); and Svend Petersen, *A Statistical History of the American Presidential Elections* (New York: Ungar, 1963). For congressional elections, see Michael J. Dubin, *United States Congressional Elections, 1787–1999: The Official Results of the Elections of the 1st through 105th Congresses* (Jefferson, NC: McFarland, 1998); and for gubernatorial elections, Michael J. Dubin, *United States Gubernatorial Elections, 1776–1860: The Official Results by State and County* (Jefferson, NC: McFarland, 2003). An invaluable source for presidential, congressional, and gubernatorial elections is Walter Dean Burnham, *Voting in American Elections: The Shaping of the American Political Universe since 1788* (Palo Alto, CA: Academica Press, 2010). Also invaluable is Stanley B. Parsons, William W. Beach, and Dan Hermann, *United States Congressional Districts, 1788–1841* (Westport, CT: Greenwood Press, 1978), which maps the changing congressional district lines through 1841.

Finally, readers looking for general histories of the period have their pick of many fine syntheses, including Daniel Walker Howe, *What Hath God Wrought: The Transformation of America, 1815–1848* (New York: Oxford University Press, 2007); Sean Wilentz, *The Rise of American Democracy: Jefferson to Lincoln* (New York: W. W. Norton, 2005); and Harry Watson, *Liberty and Power: The Politics of Jacksonian America* (New York: Farrar, Straus and Giroux, 1990). If a person is to read only one book about the politics of the 1830s and 1840s, though, it should be Holt, *The Rise and Fall of the American Whig Party*. One day, maybe somebody will write as good a book about the Democratic Party.

Clay, Henry, *continued*, caucus plan and, 63; character of, 121, 153; Clayton and, 183, 184; Corrupt Bargain and, 314n89; criticism of, 77, 79, 111, 120; defeat of, 211, 252, 369–370n77; on demagoguery of campaign, 218; electoral votes for, 356n57; on fifteen-gallon law, 376n47; Fillmore and, 140; Hall and, 121, 122, 127–128; hard-money/paper money and, 34, 109; Harrison and, 64, 70, 71, 72, 74, 87, 88, 89, 92, 93–94, 96–97, 109, 123–124, 125, 129, 134, 137, 138, 152, 156, 157, 278, 335n91, 343n28, 371n89, 373n5, 373n7, 382n21; illustration of, 111 (fig.); Independent Treasury and, 261; Jackson and, 314n89; land bill of, 158; Liberty Party and, 410n81; lithograph of, 61 (fig.); Missouri Compromise and, 63; nomination of, xiv, 74, 107, 131, 143, 333n77, 335n96, 371n88; Otis and, 79, 112, 334–335n90, 336n101, 338n123, 350n6; Panic of 1837 and, 320n30; party unity and, xvii, 71, 72, 154–157, 279; Porter and, 67, 68, 69, 72, 112, 114, 115, 116, 337n114, 338n122, 350n1, 352–353n32, 397n70; prospects for, 80, 128, 352n22, 353–354n45, 356n57, 358n79; public lands and, 90; pushing-forward/ pulling-back policy and, 333n78; Scott and, 104, 105, 106, 118, 128, 139, 349n91; Selden and, 138; Seward and, 118, 123, 352n22, 354n51; Southern base of, 75–76, 112, 114, 121, 144; Southern strategy of, 109–110, 112–113; speeches by, 11, 110, 112, 114, 222, 225, 229, 351n17, 352n24, 354n46, 384n35; support for, xvii, 68, 69–70, 71, 78, 132, 138, 142, 144, 145, 147, 148, 149, 150, 334n88, 343n34, 346n57, 346n58, 350n3, 351n18, 353n44, 361n9, 363n29,

364n30, 364n32; Tompkins and, 126; Tyler and, 156, 337n118, 371n90; Van Buren and, 19, 126, 139, 336n103, 388–389n79; vote for, xii, 93, 127–128, 145, 154, 367n50, 368n61, 370n81; Webster and, 60, 61–62, 70, 71, 72, 73, 74, 77, 78, 80–81, 82, 93, 95, 96, 172, 335n101, 340n142, 341n144; Weed and, 100, 118, 119, 128, 143, 278, 356n57; Whig Party and, 80, 82, 127, 154; Whigs and, 40, 97, 121

Clay, Henry Jr., 340n142

Clayton, John, 71, 151, 183, 184, 371n89

Cleaves, Freeman, 383n30

Cleveland Gazette, 348n85

Clinton, Bill, xii, 305n2

Clinton, DeWitt, 15, 16, 19, 20, 314n73

Clinton, George, 15–16, 21

Cole, Donald, 253, 324n73, 405n52, 406n58

Collins, Gail, 343n25, 415n100, 415n101

Colton, Calvin, 325–326n87

Combs, Leslie, 152, 156, 371n88, 373n7

Commercial Advertiser, 57, 59, 115, 327n19

Committee of Whig Young Men of New York City, 116

Compromise Tariff (1833), 63, 74, 76

congressional elections, 8, 36, 37, 41, 43, 44, 47, 51, 125, 235, 236, 245, 310n31, 320n44, 398n77, 401n27, 416n110, 416n112; gubernatorial elections and, 278; influence of, 230; moving of, 271; regularly scheduled, 37 (table); special, 397n67; turnout rates and, 25, 37, 38, 48, 232, 268, 269 (table), 270 (table), 271, 272 (table), 275, 276, 415n102. *See also specific states*

Connecticut, 70, 71, 73, 391n104; congressional and state elections in, 36, 37, 39, 46, 77, 227, 273, 321n46, 323n67, 396n60, 399n2, 400n20, 412n91, 416n110, 416n113, 416n114;

Van Buren and, xiv, xv, 6, 37, 51, 56, 74, 78, 83, 122, 177, 190, 198, 201, 202, 205, 209, 212, 216, 220, 252, 253, 254, 256, 268, 388n76, 398n77; vote for, 83, 87, 93, 122, 144, 145, 231, 238, 240, 242–245, 250–251, 256, 279, 284 (table), 308n6, 367n50, 368n61, 368n63, 370n78, 399n1, 400n13, 407n67, 417n116; Webster and, 54, 63, 66, 70, 78, 81, 93, 142, 190, 336n101, 338n123, 340n142, 344n45, 353n32, 383n30

"Harrison Cause, The" (song), 395n45

Harrison Land Act, 85–86

Harvey, Sir John, 104

Haughton, Richard, 78, 361n11

Hawley, Charles, 132

Heidler, David, 143, 367n60

Heidler, Jeanne, 143, 367n60

Henry, Patrick, 192

Hermann, Briggs & Co., 29, 30

"Hero of Tippecanoe, The" (song), 161

Hickory clubs, 221–222

Hill, Isaac, 45, 167–168, 177, 226

Hilliard, Henry, 372n94

Hodges, George Tisdale, 361n13

Holley, Myron, 390n102

Holt, Michael F., 8, 305n3, 310n32, 322n59, 323n67, 323n68, 323n69, 332n67, 358n82, 396n59; 1840 election analysis by, 414n98; on Scott, 348n83; on Webster, 335n101; on Whigs, 51; work of, xvii, 419, 429

Hone, Philip, 33, 105, 116, 117, 119, 223, 247, 380n81, 388n79, 399n5

Hooe, George Mason, 204, 390n94

Hotchkiss, Miles, 381n13

House of Hermann, 30

House Public Buildings Committee, 125

House Ways and Means Committee, 170, 173

Howard, Tilghman, 380n76

Howe, Daniel Walker, 371n88

Hunter, R. M. T., 170

identity: partisan, 9, 49, 159, 211; political, 48; social, 414n98; Whig, 51, 99

Illinois, 56, 86, 97, 125, 329n35; antiparty/anticonvention sentiment among Whigs in, 135, 310n37, 363–364n26; congressional and state elections in, 230, 322n59, 323n67, 398n72, 401n26, 412n92, 416n108, 416n109, 417n115; Democratic convention delegates from, 168, 173; election of 1836 in, 307n2, 309n17; election of 1840 in, 236, 240, 398n1, 403n33; Whig convention delegates from, 135, 136, 145, 146, 364n28

Independent Treasury, 50, 60, 126, 170, 171, 177, 199, 204, 205, 260, 261, 262–263

Indiana, 31, 56, 86; Clay's support in, 71, 97, 122–123, 335n91, 358n80; congressional and state elections in, 8, 41, 44, 66, 78, 119, 122, 124, 125, 231, 271, 322n62, 356n61, 357n62, 396n59, 400n20, 416n110; Democratic convention delegates from, 168, 380n76; election of 1836 in, 3, 230, 307n2, 309n17; election of 1840 in, 398n1, 401n21; Harrison's strength in, 125, 129, 136, 190, 193, 230, 335n91, 358n80; turnout in, 270, 273; Whig convention delegates from, 131, 140, 145, 148, 360n5; Whig state convention in, 95, 136, 346n52;

Indiana Democrat, 393–394n27

Ingersoll, Charles Jared, 41

interest rates, 29, 263

Irwin, Archibald, 345n51

Jackson, Andrew, xiv, 4, 7, 24, 26, 40, 47, 64, 75, 87, 100, 107, 109, 120, 122, 124, 130, 168, 169, 175, 178, 182, 187, 188, 192, 201, 202, 215, 240, 246, 267, 310n35, 327n23, 346n55; annual addresses of, 320n36;

Jackson, Andrew, *continued*, banks and, 36; Bank War and, 27, 51, 329n35, 389n87; cartoon of, 199 (fig.); constitutional convention and, 312n59; election of, xv, 20, 22, 27, 51, 179, 218, 252, 262, 411n85; electoral vote for, 9–10; executive power and, 141, 261; Harrison and, 84, 88, 89, 190, 343n25; land boom and, 28; lithograph of, 49 (fig.); national bank and, 34, 205, 262; Nullification Proclamation and, 50; on paper money, 28, 36; partisanship of, 198; populism and, 276; presidency of, 29, 30, 90, 276; Specie Circular and, 48; spoils system and, 10; states' rights and, 277; support for, 6, 27, 91, 372n96; Van Buren and, 6, 12, 17, 18, 19, 20, 21, 23, 31, 32, 34, 49, 56, 65, 99, 131, 180, 315n106, 366n48, 402n31; vote for, xii, 2, 83, 315n103; vote share for, 401n24, 411n85

Jacksonians, 8, 9, 23, 176–177, 193, 216, 246; Whigs' disdain/envy for, 10–11; Harrison and, 159, 193; and Hickory clubs, 222

Jameson, John, 378n64

Jefferson, Thomas, 10, 13, 15, 18, 21, 240, 242, 371n90; election of, 23–24; Webster eulogy for, 53

Jeffersonian: press, 220; principles of states' rights and strict construction, 22, 178, 192, 220

Jeffersonian Republicans, 13, 15, 18, 21, 23, 206, 246, 312n53

Jennison, Silas, 43, 232, 358n81

J. L. & Joseph, 30

Johnson, James, 194

Johnson, Reverdy, 145, 153, 360n9, 371n89

Johnson, Richard Mentor, 165–166, 167 (fig.), 168, 174, 175, 221, 252, 312n55, 379n72; drawing of, 165 (fig.); Harrison and, 194, 195;

popularity of, 166; Van Buren and, 166, 178

Journal of Commerce, Webster and, 57, 59, 327n19, 329n32, 329n33

Junius Tracts, The, 325n87

Kauffman, Peter, 177, 403n32

Kellogg, Miner K., 400n16

Kendall, Amos, 79, 221, 234, 250, 251; cartoon of, 217 (fig.)

Kennedy, John P., 47

Kent, Edward, 77, 125, 232–233

Kentucky, 65, 74, 92–93, 129, 204, 339n134; congressional and state elections in, 8, 41, 44, 66, 78, 125, 231, 271, 322n62, 364n32, 400n20, 412n92, 416n110; Democratic convention delegates from, 168, 174, 378n64, 378n67; election of 1836 in, 3, 92, 167, 230, 307n2, 336n103; election of 1840 in, 178, 269, 358n80, 384n40, 398n1, 401n22; legislative caucus backs Clay, 69, 71, 364n32; turnout in, 269, 416n110; Whig convention delegates from, 132, 142, 143, 145, 152, 153

Kentucky Colonization Society, 111, 208

Kentucky Gazette, 382n21

Kerr, John Leeds, 361n9

Ketchum, Hiram, 52, 53, 328n29, 329n33, 337n112; Webster and, 57, 58, 59

Key, V. O., 413n96

Kickapoo, treaty with, 86

Kinderhook, 216, 241, 313n68, 394n38; Van Buren and, 13, 14

King, Samuel, 227

King, William, 166, 169, 173, 375n38; support for, 168, 376n41

Kinsey, Charles, 337n114

Kraut, Alan, 410n81

Lafayette, Marquis de, 116

Lasak, Francis W., 219, 393n26

Lawrence, Abbott, 73

Shade, William G., 25, 317n116, 397n66

Shafer, Ronald, xiv, 223, 387n69

Shannon, Wilson, 386n60

Sharp, William: lithograph by, 84 (fig.)

Shaw, Henry, 143

Sheets, William Harrison, 344n47

"Shipwreck, The," 234 (fig.)

Shulze, Andrew, 134, 362n18

Silbey, Joel, 25, 307n2

Silliman, Benjamin Douglas, 337n121

silver coins, 28, 31, 50

Silvester, Francis, 13

Slamm, Levi, 49

slaveholders, 9, 26, 56, 79, 91, 158, 208, 210, 254; abolitionists and, 255; compensation for, 203

slavery, xiv, xvi, xvii, 56, 59, 60, 63, 75, 110, 166, 177, 203, 209, 219; abolition of, 76, 86, 182, 202, 206, 208, 210, 211; centrality of, 324n69; defending, 111, 255, 277; expansion of, 86; jurisdiction over, 76; as political issue, 257; protection of, 48

Smith, Gerrit, 352n22

Smith, Oliver, 122, 123

songs, campaign, xii, 161, 162, 215, 216, 223, 224, 233, 377n59, 395n45, 398n76

South Carolina: Calhoun and 149, 352n24; congressional and state elections in 51, 398n77; delegates not selected in, 132, 140, 149, 173; in election of 1840, 235, 398n77, 398n1; governor selected by legislature in, 412n92; popular presidential vote not held in 1, 23; presidential and vice-presidential choice in 1836 election in, 4, 13, 152; Webster viewed by, 66, 330n43

specie, 28, 29, 31–32, 50, 121; resumption of, payments, 80; suspension of, payments, 33, 36, 39, 48; transfer of, 48

Specie Circular, 31, 32, 34, 48, 49, 50

"Specie Claws," 49 (fig.)

Spencer, John Canfield, 115, 138

Sprague, Peleg, 142; voting plan of, 143, 144, 153

Sprague, William, 46, 324n74

Stanton, Henry, 256

Starr, Chandler, 138, 361n16

state elections, xii, xvii, 8, 9, 36–46, 48, 51, 77–78, 108, 113, 125, 127, 169, 229, 267, 271, 323n67, 358n81, 410n81, 416n110; turnout rates in, xiii, 25, 73, 273. See also specific states

State Rights Party, 149, 322n64, 358n82, 412n94

states' rights, 6, 19, 277, 324n70

Steele, John N., 360–361n9

Steger, Mary, 224

Stevens, Thaddeus, 362n19, 399n4; Anti-Masons and, 332n68, 362n19; role at Whig national convention, 146–149, 369n69, 369n76, 370n77

St. Louis Argus, 220

Storer, Bellamy, 343n24, 343n27

Story, Joseph, 335n98

stumping, 67, 180, 181, 186–198, 206, 219, 220, 221, 222, 235

sub-treasury, 50, 158, 188, 210, 260, 261

Subtreasury Bill, 241

Sutch, Richard, 318n3, 413n95

Swartwout, Robert, 350n6

Swift, Benjamin, 75

Swift, John, 367n58

Symes, John Cleves, 86

Tallmadge, Nathaniel P., 50, 112, 361n15, 364n32, 384n40; cartoon of, 234 (fig.)

Tammany Hall, 39, 239

Tappan, Lewis, 338n122

tariffs, 19, 48, 56, 63, 177, 206, 266

Tecumseh, 85, 166, 167, 194

Temin, Peter, 412n91, 413n96

Tennessee, 218, 220, 312n59, 373n16, 388n77; Clay support in, 66; congressional and state elections in, 41–42, 119–121, 125, 273, 310n31, 310n32, 322n62, 323n67, 356n61, 357n62, 359n84, 396n60, 400n20; Democratic convention delegates from, 168–169, 175, 378n64; election of 1836 in, 4, 6, 9, 11, 152, 307n2, 311n40; election of 1840 in, 178, 242, 243, 249, 265, 398n1, 401n21, 401n22; no delegates from, sent to Whig convention, 132, 140, 149, 173; Polk warns Van Buren off from visiting, 388n78; turnout in 268, 271, 273, 357n64

Tennessee Whig, 120

"Thinking Committee," criticism of, 182

Thompson, Charles Manfred, 322n59

Thompson, Waddy, 62, 63

Thornton, J. Mills, III, 324n69

Tilden, Samuel, 392n112

"Tippecanoe" (song), 216

"Tippecanoe and Tyler Too" (song), xii, 233, 377n59

Tippecanoe Clubs, 91, 219, 222

"Tippecanoe or Log Cabin Quick Step" (song), lyrics of, 224 (fig.)

Tocqueville, Alexis de, 247

Todd, Charles Stewart, 124, 195, 358n80; Harrison and, 92, 344n41, 344n43

Todd, Thomas, 92

Tompkins, Daniel, 15, 16, 21

Tompkins, William, 126

Tracy, Albert, 119

Troy, Gil, 116, 187, 213, 392n3

Turney, Hopkins L., 247

turnout rates, 11, 23, 24, 46, 113, 228, 231, 235, 397n62, 416n107, 416n109, 416n112; competitiveness and, 305n3; congressional elections and, 25, 38, 48, 232, 268, 269

(table), 270 (table), 271, 272 (table), 275, 276, 415n102; decline of, 273, 321n52; Democratic, 250; estimates of, 415n104; gubernatorial elections and, 270, 271 (table), 273, 274 (table), 415n102; increase in, xii, 25, 47, 120, 232, 233, 267–268, 275, 306n3, 416n105; midterm elections and, 276; presidential elections and, xii, 24–25, 38, 268, 270, 271, 272 (table), 273, 274 (table), 275, 276, 415n102; spring elections and, 275; state elections and, 25, 73, 273

Twenty-Fifth Congress, 8, 42, 47, 109, 350n1; elections for, 37 (table)

Twenty-Seventh Congress, 229, 271, 277, 402n27, 416n108; composition of, 245

Twenty-Sixth Congress, 51, 80, 109, 125, 170, 245

Tyler, John, xiii, 158; Clay and, 156, 337n118, 371n90; criticism of, 156; Harrison and, 152, 157, 160, 161, 162, 254, 371n90; lithograph of, 151 (fig.); national bank and, 277; nomination of, 150, 151, 152, 159, 277; rallies for, 266; vote for, 370n81

Union and Harmony Convention, 134, 136, 362n18, 362n19, 362n20, 367n58

Union Democratic Party, 322n64, 358n82

United States Magazine and Democratic Review, 157

US Constitution, 63, 86, 184, 193, 197, 205; amending, 261; anti-Federalist reading of, 192

US House of Representatives, 4, 11, 36, 38, 43, 47, 51, 62, 94, 141, 169, 170, 213, 237, 275; Adams and, 18

US Senate, 8, 17, 64, 86, 88, 110, 152, 312n59, 402n27

US Supreme Court, 53, 406n60